Preaching Bondage

The publisher gratefully acknowledges the generous support
of the Classical Literature Endowment Fund of the
University of California Press Foundation.

Preaching Bondage

*John Chrysostom and the Discourse of
Slavery in Early Christianity*

———

Chris L. de Wet

UNIVERSITY OF CALIFORNIA PRESS

University of California Press, one of the most distinguished university presses in the United States, enriches lives around the world by advancing scholarship in the humanities, social sciences, and natural sciences. Its activities are supported by the UC Press Foundation and by philanthropic contributions from individuals and institutions. For more information, visit www.ucpress.edu.

University of California Press
Oakland, California

Library of Congress Cataloging-in-Publication Data

De Wet, Chris L., author.
  Preaching bondage : John Chrysostom and the discourse of slavery in early Christianity / Chris L. de Wet.
     p.   cm.
  Includes bibliographical references and index.
  ISBN 978-0-520-28621-4 (cloth) —
  ISBN 978-0-520-96155-5 (electronic)
  1. John Chrysostom, Saint. 2. Slavery and the church—History—To 1500. 3. Slavery—Philosophy—History—To 1500. 4. Slavery—Religious aspects—History—To 1500. 5. Slaves—Family relationships—History—To 1500. 6. Slaves—Social conditions—History—To 1500.
I. Title.
  BR65.C46D4   2–15
  241′67509015—dc23   2014045939

32   30   29   28   27   26   25
10   9   8   7   6   5   4   3   2   1

GPSR Authorized Representative: Easy Access System Europe, Mustamäe tee 50, 10621 Tallinn, Estonia, gpsr.requests@easproject.com

For my beloved, Artemisa
Ἔρος δ' ἐτίναξέ μοι φρένας, ὡς ἄνεμος κὰτ ὄρος δρύσιν ἐμπέτων.
—SAPPHO, *FRAGMENTA* 47.1–2

If heaven has into being deign'd to call
Thy light, O Liberty! To shine on all;
Bright intellectual Sun! Why does thy ray
To earth distribute only partial day?
Since no resisting cause from spirit flows
Thy universal presence to oppose;
No obstacles by Nature's hand imprest,
Thy subtle and ethereal beams arrest;
Not sway'd by matter is thy course benign,
Or more direct or more oblique to shine;
Nor motion's laws can speed thy active course,
Nor strong repulsion's pow'rs obstruct thy force;
Since there is no convexity in Mind,
Why are thy genial beams to parts confin'd?

—HANNAH MORE, "SLAVERY"

CONTENTS

ACKNOWLEDGMENTS

My interest in the topic of ancient Roman slavery did not result directly from reading scholarly volumes on slavery as such; rather, my curiosity began via a different route, through cultural historical studies on embodiment, as well as through gender studies, philosophy, and critical theory—particularly my love for the work of Michel Foucault. My reading on this topic led me to a book that in fact first made me consider slavery in late antiquity as a topic for my doctoral dissertation. That book was Jennifer Glancy's *Slavery in Early Christianity*. Glancy's book approaches slavery from the perspective of the rhetoric of the body, and in this I saw an opportunity for a novel research project—a study of slavery as a corporeal discourse in the works of John Chrysostom.

Ideas and sections of this book were presented at the annual meetings of the Society of Biblical Literature and the North American Patristics Society and at the Oxford Patristics conference, the New Testament Society of Southern Africa conference, and the annual University of South Africa (UNISA) Symposium for New Testament and Early Christian Studies. I gratefully acknowledge the College of Human Sciences at UNISA for several research grants that made it possible to present my research in both local and international contexts.

I would also like to acknowledge colleagues and friends who were kind enough to read the entire, lengthy manuscript, and gave treasured input. I owe an enormous debt of gratitude to Jennifer Glancy, not only for her wonderful work on slavery in early Christianity, but also for encouraging me to pursue this project, and her involvement in its development. She read the full manuscript and made very incisive comments on its value and also how to improve it. The friendship and collegiality of Blake Leyerle continue to humble me—her meticulous suggestions as an expert scholar on Chrysostom and his sociocultural world were invaluable; she was able not only to highlight the strengths of my work, but also to point out in detail areas for improvement. Another *amica academica* is Christine Shepardson, whose creative edge made apparent to me questions and issues I had not considered before. I must also thank Susanna Elm and Ilaria Ramelli, as well as my colleague at UNISA, Pieter Craffert, all of whom read the manuscript; their feedback was a creative stimulus beyond any doubt. J. Albert Harrill's generous and insightful comments on the manuscript assisted in wider contextualization of some points in the book, for which I am very grateful.

I can truly say that I have the most admirable colleagues and friends in the Department of Biblical and Ancient Studies at UNISA, with whom I am every day honored to work. I thank my mentors and friends, Pieter Botha, Pieter Craffert (again), Gerhard van den Heever, and Johannes Vorster for their stimulating and challenging contributions to my own development as an academic. I also thank the chair of the department, Elelwani Farisani, for his support in providing me with valuable time away from the bustle of the office to complete this book.

Anyone who knows Wendy Mayer, who joined UNISA for three months as a visiting researcher during the completion of this book, knows that her encyclopedic knowledge of Chrysostom and late antiquity is matched only by her generous collegiality and warm friendship—I am privileged to share in both. I must also acknowledge two very dear friends who, while they were not directly involved in this project, added immeasurably to my own critical thinking—I thank Evan Stapelberg for those wonderful theological conversations we had almost thirteen years ago, and Leonard Maré for his friendship and support throughout the years.

Among those mentioned above, I would also like to thank the following scholars, who in one way or another, be it in conversation, collaboration, or consultation, contributed to the success of this project: Pauline Allen, Cynthia Baker, Philip Bosman, Phil Botha, Sheila Briggs, Bernadette Brooten, Kate Cooper, Jitse Dijkstra, Benjamin Dunning, Peter Lampe, Nickolas Roubekas, Hennie Stander, Annika Thiem, Ronald van der Bergh, Johannes van Oort, Julia Watts Belser, Jamie Wood, and the late Abraham Malherbe.

At the University of California Press, I would like to thank Eric Schmidt, Maeve Cornell-Taylor, and Cindy Fulton for their patience and encouragement, and for believing in this project. Marian Rogers's professional and elegant copyediting transformed the manuscript.

To all the friends and colleagues mentioned above, I express my gratitude in the eloquence of Cicero: *Amicitiae nostrae memoriam spero sempiternam fore!*

Finally, I need to thank my family and friends (outside the academy) for their love, support, and most of all, their patience, while I was completing this book. I could not have asked for a better mother in this life than my own, Sarie Jacobs. She believed in me often when others did not, when I fell she picked me up, and also inspired me to excel. Because of her, I am what I am. I thank my dearest aunt, Jackie Sanders, a second mother to me, and my cousin Len-John, the brother I never had, and Chandelle, as well as my new family, Rui and Letitia Rodrigues, Rosa and Akina Croeser, and my dear friends Justin, Samantha, and Liaan. At the time of the writing of this book, I lost three very dear family members, Len Sanders (Boetie), Tjaart van der Walt, and Jimmy Christensen, whose memory I recall here, along with my father, Chris, and grandparents Len, Joekie, Koenie, and Magriet, who would hopefully be proud of me today. Most importantly, I must thank the love of my life, my fiancée, Artemisa Rodrigues, for her love and companionship. I treasure our every moment together, the stimulating conversations, and warm embraces—thank you, Artemisa, for feeling with me, laughing with me, crying with me, thinking with me, living with me. I dedicate this book to you.

Introducing Doulology

It was an exciting time. The dawn of the fifth century was at hand, and the birth of a new era. As the fourth century drew to a close, orthodox Christianity was at its zenith in practically every sense of the word. It was a period of rapid Christianization, the golden age of patristic preaching—the age of Ambrose of Milan, Augustine of Hippo, and, in the East, a man named John of Antioch, later to be hailed as the Golden-Mouthed. Dominating the news and gossip in church halls and homes alike were the doctrinal developments of orthodoxy, the state of heterodoxy, the religio-political agenda of the emperor, and the threat of those who lived outside the borders of the great Roman Empire—the barbarians. These were the topics that gained most attention in philosophical and theological discussions and political debates. But one day, during a church service in Syrian Antioch, the presbyter John, whom we shall call Chrysostom, preached a sermon on the apostle Paul's Letter to the Ephesians and posed two frequently asked questions, with an unequivocal answer: "If someone were to ask, where does slavery come from, and why has it come to humanity?—and I know that many are asking these questions and desire to have them answered—I will tell you. Slavery is the result of greed, of degradation, of brutality, since Noah, we know, had no slave, nor Abel, nor Seth, nor those who came after them. The institution was the fruit of sin."[1]

---

1. *Hom. Eph.* 22.1 (F4.334): Εἰ δέ τις ἔροιτο πόθεν ἡ δουλεcleία, καὶ διὰ τί εἰς τὸν βίον εἰσῆλθε τὸν ἀνθρώπινον· καὶ γὰρ οἶδα πολλοὺς καὶ ἐρωτῶντας τὰ τοιαῦτα ἡδέως καὶ μαθεῖν βουλομένους, ἐγὼ πρὸς ὑμᾶς ἐρῶ· Ἡ πλεονεξία τὴν δουλείαν ἔτεκεν, ἡ βαναυσία, ἡ ἀπληστία· ἐπεὶ Νῶε δοῦλον οὐκ εἶχεν, οὐδὲ Ἄβελ, οὐδὲ Σὴθ, ἀλλ᾽ οὐδὲ οἱ μετὰ ταῦτα. Ἁμαρτία τοῦτο τὸ πρᾶγμα ἔτεκεν. Most of the translations from Chrysostom's works are my own, unless otherwise indicated. I have tried to use modern translations of Chrysostom's works in certain instances, and I compare translations of certain

To Chrysostom's audience, which consisted mainly of people who owned slaves, along with some actual slaves, these may seem banal questions. Yet they were questions that cut to the very core of their everyday life, since most of the moments that would eventually make up their life-span, including getting dressed, cooking, cleaning, dealing with money, going to the shops, and numerous other events, involved in some way or another the activity of slaves. Slavery did not directly form part of the great doctrinal controversies, nor did it visibly play any deciding role in the politics of the day. Yet it was perhaps more relevant to the ordinary person than any other issue. Slavery—the ownership and domination of one human body by another—influenced every aspect of life in the Roman world and was one of the most influential social institutions in defining one's identity. One was either a slave (or an ex-slave) or free.[2]

DOULOLOGY: THE DISCOURSE OF SLAVERY IN EARLY CHRISTIANITY

This book is primarily concerned with the dynamics of the discourse of slavery, what I term "doulology," in the homilies of John Chrysostom (347–407 C.E.), one of the most prolific personalities of fourth-century Christendom.[3] The term may

---

texts, especially those from the more archaic *NPNF* series. Regarding the primary texts of Chrysostom, I have attempted to use the latest versions available, either from Migne's Patrologia graeca (PG) or the Sources chrétiennes series (SC). In the case of Chrysostom's homilies on the Pauline epistles and Hebrews, I do not use the texts from Migne, but those edited by Frederick Field; *Ioannis Chrysostomi interpretatio omnium epistularum Paulinarum,* 7 vols. (Oxford: J. H. Parker, 1854–62). References to Field's texts are indicated with an F, followed by the volume and page number. In cases where the numbering of the Field homilies differs from that of Migne, I provide the PG number in square brackets. At times I compare the Field and Migne readings, when significant. The editions and translations I use for non-Chrysostomic texts are indicated in the notes where relevant. I do not spend too much time on the provenance of Chrysostom's homilies here unless it is directly related to the argument at hand. Slavery was widespread in the areas in which Chrysostom ministered, and its form and function would not have differed too much between Antioch and Constantinople. This makes it very difficult to use any discussion of slavery to address problems of provenance; for more details about the provenance of the homilies I cite in this book, see Wendy Mayer, *The Homilies of St John Chrysostom—Provenance: Reshaping the Foundations,* Orientalia christiana analecta 273 (Rome: Pontificio Istituto Orientale, 2005).

2. When I refer to "slaves," I am including both male and female slaves unless I specifically emphasize a certain gender. The same applies for the terms "master" and "owner."

3. Studies that specifically focus on slavery in the works of John Chrysostom are sparse. Chrysostom features as a major source in Harper's encyclopedic analysis of slavery in the late Roman world, *Slavery in the Late Roman World, AD 275–425* (New York: Cambridge University Press, 2011), although it is not a focused study of slavery in Chrysostom. The only study that is devoted solely to slavery in Chrysostom is Wulf Jaeger, "Die Sklaverei bei Johannes Chrysostomus" (PhD diss., Christian-Albrechts-Universität zu Kiel, 1974). Supplementary studies include Johann A. Möhler, "Bruchstücke aus der Geschichte der Aufhebung der Sklaverei," in *Gesammelte Schriften und Aufsätze,* vol. 2, ed. Johann J. I. von Döllinger (Regensburg: Manz, 1939), 54–140; Georg Kontoulis, *Zum Problem der Sklaverei*

seem alien to many readers. *Doulology* is a term of my own, made up from two ancient Greek words, *doulos* (slave) and *logos* (word, argument, discourse). Doulology is therefore the discourse of slavery—that is, when slavery as a constitution of knowledge, a language, and a social practice is used to produce and reproduce meanings and behaviors in various contexts. In writing this book, I was constantly challenged to develop a new analytical language for speaking about slavery, a language that would assist in laying bare the *discursivity* of slavery. I must apologize in advance if some of the neologisms in the book seems copious, overambitious, or arduous; they represent my own struggle with the problem of slavery and my desire to enunciate those pervasive and often ineffable operations at the core of the discourse, operations that are both material and symbolic, somatic and psychic. It would perhaps be more appropriate to speak of "despotology," the discourse of mastery, since all the sources I will examine in this book were written not from the viewpoint of the slave, but from the perspective of the master. But to limit my neologistic verbosity, I will consider despotology as a correlative of doulology, and assume in the use of the term *doulology* also the discourse of mastery.

Another related term that will surface in the course of this book is doulomorphism. When speaking of doulomorphism, I refer to the instance where a certain subjectivity will be provided with or assume the subjectivity of a slave. My ambition for this new linguistic and rhetorical venture in slavery studies was fuelled by that prolific scholar of early Christianity, Elizabeth Schüssler Fiorenza, who took the same approach in feminist biblical criticism. Two of her neologisms are also very prevalent in this book—namely, "kyriarchy" and "kyriarchization"—which she understands as appellations for the intersectional structures of domination, and those processes by which a dominant subjectivity exercises power over a subordinated subjectivity.[4] Kyriarchization, in essence, points to the formation of masters and attitudes of mastery.

What is meant by doulology, or a discourse of slavery? In approaching ancient slavery as a discourse, I rely particularly on the analytical concepts of Michel Foucault, although I have also found the critical theories of Michel de Certeau and

(ΔΟΥΛΕΙΑ) *bei den kappadokischen Kirchenvätern und Johannes Chrysostomus* (Bonn: Habelt, 1993), 315–79; Antonino González Blanco, *Economía y sociedad en el Bajo imperio según San Juan Crisostomo,* Publicationes de la Fundacíon universitaria española 17 (Madrid: Fundación universitaria española, 1980), 261–307; Chris L. de Wet, "John Chrysostom on Slavery," *Studia Historiae Ecclesiasticae* 34, no. 2 (2008): 1–13. For a more detailed analysis of the *status quaestionis* of slavery in Chrysostom's works, see Chris L. de Wet, "John Chrysostom and Slavery: The *Status Quaestionis,*" *Journal of Early Christian History* 4, no. 2 (2014): 31–39.

4. Elizabeth Schüssler Fiorenza, "Introduction: Exploring the Intersections of Race, Gender, Status, and Ethnicity in Early Christian Studies," in *Prejudice and Christian Beginnings: Investigating Race, Gender, and Ethnicity in Early Christian Studies,* ed. Laura Nasrallah and Elizabeth Schüssler Fiorenza (Minneapolis: Fortress Press, 2010), 1–25.

Pierre Bourdieu helpful. The discourse of slavery should be understood as a system of statements, signs, ideas, and practices discursively associated not only with a framework of labour regulation and the possession of human bodies as fungible property, but perhaps more importantly, one that shaped the very essence of late ancient subjectivity and relationships.[5] While the economic dimension of slavery cannot possibly be downplayed, the discourse of slavery is much more complex—it touches on aspects of late ancient domesticity and housecraft, education, discipline and punishment, and sexualities, in addition to views of human beings as property. The economy of slavery will be problematized in the next section.

I will argue here that the discourse of slavery directly shaped late ancient subjectivities, with a focus on Christian subjectivity in Chrysostom's homilies. The main aim of this book can be stated thus: to define, examine, and critique the doulology of one important figure, John Chrysostom, who operated within the regime of power-knowledge-domination that sustained the discourse of slavery in late ancient Christianity, and also to identify and critique its place and dynamics in the broader operation of late antique social discourses. My aim is not simply to say how bad and wrong ancient slavery was, or to assert its importance and influence or downplay its effects. Rather, the study of Chrysostom's views on slavery forms part of a crucial scholarly enterprise that aims (1) to account for how ancient slavery is "put into discourse" in the context of everyday life and is spoken about, how it is enunciated and what it says (or is made to say), (2) to determine who does the speaking (and who compels the slave body to speak), and (3) to discover which institutions prompted individuals like Chrysostom to speak about slavery, who stores, distributes, and utilizes the things that were said, and most importantly, how the pervasive technologies of power, the discursive "power tools," behind various statements in this discourse led to the formation of various Christian identities. Slavery seeped into later Roman culture and reached its very roots. Thus, I will investigate domination and what Foucault calls "those polymorphous techniques of power,"[6] and the discourses they permeated, to produce and maintain individual modes of behavior performing the discourse of slavery, and how this discourse penetrated, controlled, and reproduced enslaved bodies and bodies of domination lost in *l'invention du quotidien*. This book is a search for discursive productions, and their accompanying silences and ignorance, for productions of

---

5. Foucault developed his thoughts on discourse and discursive analysis in his early work *The Archaeology of Knowledge and the Discourse on Language,* trans. Alan M. Sheridan Smith (New York,: Pantheon, 1971), esp. 3–39. More than a decade later Foucault splendidly illustrated the dynamics between discourse and subjectivity in some of his lectures, which were later published as *The Hermeneutics of the Subject: Lectures at the Collège De France, 1981–1982,* ed. François Ewald and Alessandro Fontana and trans. Graham Burchell (New York: Picador, 2006).

6. Michel Foucault, *The History of Sexuality: An Introduction,* trans. Robert Hurley, vol. 1 of *The History of Sexuality* (New York: Vintage, 1978), 11.

power, which tend to dominate, and for propagations of knowledge that directly influence the formation of corporeal subjectivities and, especially in the case of slavery, their pathologization. The process of pathologization involves characterizing and classifying the slave body as abnormal, deviant, and socially ill or dead.

The focus on discourse is particularly appropriate for the genre of ancient sources on which this book focuses: the homilies of Chrysostom. Homilies are excellent sources for discursive analysis, since they often represent the tension between the vision of the preacher for an ideal society, and real social phenomena and problems people faced every day.[7] Hence the title of this book, *Preaching Bondage*, since preaching is in itself a manifestation and modalization of discourse. While the discourse of slavery in Chrysostom is my focus, it is my hope that this book will also serve as a conceptual bridge for approaching slavery in other late ancient Christian and non-Christian authors, and in modern discussions of the topic. I will also place Chrysostom in dialogue with the broader Christian discourse on slavery in antiquity. There is a great need for studies on slavery in individual ancient authors. Too many studies on slavery in antiquity focus instead on a vast array of ancient authors across a long time span (sometimes across centuries), with the result that the evidence and conclusions are often generalized or cursory.

Late ancient Christianity seized this discourse of slavery because it was a discourse of potential, or perhaps more appropriately stated, a power discourse; the discourse of slavery exhibits immense potential for the production and reproduction of subjectivities, but also shows potential for controlling, regulating, and disciplining these produced and reproduced subjects. Slavery contributed to the definition of personhood in Roman times. The habitus of slaveholding feeds into this discursive operation, but is also sustained by it. Moreover, ancient slavery was a highly somatic discourse—that is, a discourse preoccupied by and expressing itself in statements relating to the human body as a discursive formation and strategy in itself. Jennifer Glancy makes a crucial point in this regard: "Slaveholders in the first century characterized their slaves as bodies, and their treatment of slaves was commensurate with that characterization. This was equally the case in the fourth century, when Constantine came to power, and a century after that."[8] Building on Glancy's work, this book also approaches slaves as bodies, and aims to evaluate the discourse of slavery in Chrysostom's homilies as a corporeal discourse.

I need to stress here that any reconstruction of slavery remains an informed scholarly conjecture. It is crucial to understand that the discourse of slavery as

---

7. For more on the value of the homiletic corpus for ancient cultural historiography, see Wendy Mayer, "Homiletics," in *The Oxford Handbook of Early Christian Studies*, ed. Susan A. Harvey and David G. Hunter (New York: Oxford University Press, 2008), 565–83.

8. Jennifer A. Glancy, *Slavery in Early Christianity* (Minneapolis: Fortress Press, 2006), 10.

reconstructed from ancient sources is fragmented and fissured at best, with many lacunae. The reconstruction of doulology in antiquity involves numerous scholarly decisions and can often be problematic and inconclusive; indeed, the complexities of this task can seem overwhelming. Furthermore, the evidence for slaveholding in this period is notoriously difficult to assess and interpret.[9] Some of the main sources are Christian homilies and treatises, which are not concerned with slavery per se, but rather present the discourse of slavery interwoven with many other discourses, some theological and some socioethical. Thus one of the aims of this book is to extrapolate the discourse of slavery from other discourses, including those concerning domesticity, education, discipline, sexuality, and the economy. In addition, the majority of ancient sources are highly biased in favor of slaveholders—none of the sources from antiquity were written by slaves, and all of them exhibit a social disinvestment in the concerns of the enslaved. They display only one dimension of domination, and the voice of the slave is deafeningly silent. Despite this, one cannot ignore slavery in the understanding of ancient culture. All aspects of everyday life in antiquity were influenced by slavery—architecture, education, sexuality, wealth and poverty, household management, even something as banal as putting on one's shoes or defecation and sewerage management. Slavery was an integral part of daily life, and thus must figure in any project of writing a cultural history of late antiquity.

The phenomenon of slavery in the Roman Empire has held the fascination of scholars for more than a century, and was of particular interest during the period of the transatlantic slave trade and the abolition of slavery. In an interesting comparative study, Enrico Dal Lago and Constantina Katsari have identified some striking continuities between Roman slaveholding and slaveholding in the antebellum American South.[10] They point out that models of slave management in the South often mirrored their Roman counterparts. The well-being of slaves, punishment and reward, and dependency and reciprocity appear to be commonalities of the Roman Empire and the American South. Drawing especially from Roman agronomical sources like Cato, Varro, and Columella, Dal Lago and Katsari conclude that "the master-slave relationship as it expressed itself through reciprocity, interference, and the fiction of father-child relations highlights what in our view are the main features of the ideal model of slave management in the Roman world and the ante-bellum American South."[11] Of course, there were also some important differences between these slave systems, which Dal Lago and Katsari also

9. For more on the problems of late antique evidence for slavery, see Harper, *Slavery in the Late Roman World*, 1–32.

10. Enrico Dal Lago and Constantina Katsari, "Ideal Models of Slave Management in the Roman World and in the Ante-Bellum American South," in *Slave Systems: Ancient and Modern*, ed. Enrico Dal Lago and Constantina Katsari (New York: Cambridge University Press, 2008), 187–213.

11. Ibid., 213.

highlight: for instance, Roman slavery was not based on racial difference to the extent that transatlantic slavery was.[12] Orlando Patterson has come to similar conclusions on the continuities and discontinuities between Graeco-Roman slavery and slavery in the modern period.[13]

APPROACHING LATE ROMAN SLAVERY

Before approaching the discourse of slavery in Chrysostom's homilies, we should consider what axioms serve as foundations for reconstructing slavery more broadly in later Roman society. Three presuppositions are central to the study of slavery. The first two presuppositions have been recounted and reinforced in Kyle Harper's work *Slavery in the Late Roman World, AD 275–425*, and I will refer to them in overview.[14] The third presupposition calls for thorough qualification.

One of the major challenges in writing about slavery in the late Roman Empire is to prove that it was actually functional as a social institution during this period, and if it was, to determine what type of slave system it was and how it was sustained. These questions remain important and cannot be said to have been completely answered. However, significant progress has been made to date in arriving at some conclusions, and two presuppositions that are central to the study of

12. Dal Lago and Katsari also address issues of comparatism regarding slave systems in their introductory chapter, "The Study of Ancient and Modern Slave Systems: Setting an Agenda for Comparison," in Dal Lago and Katsari, *Slave Systems*, 3–31.

13. Orlando Patterson, *Slavery and Social Death: A Comparative Study* (Cambridge, MA: Harvard University Press, 1982); Patterson, "Slavery, Gender, and Work in the Pre-Modern World and Early Greece: A Cross-Cultural Analysis," in Dal Lago and Katsari, *Slave Systems*, 32–69.

14. Harper, *Slavery in the Late Roman World*, 1–66. There are of course numerous other studies that are crucial to understanding late Roman slavery, including Cam Grey, "Slavery in the Late Roman World," in *The Cambridge World History of Slavery*, vol. 1, *The Ancient Mediterranean World*, ed. Keith Bradley and Paul Cartledge (New York: Cambridge University Press, 2011), 482–509; Noel Lenski, "Constantine and Slavery: Libertas and the Fusion of Roman and Christian Values," *Atti dell' Accademia Romanistica Costantiniana* 19 (2011): 235–60; Lenski, "Captivity, Slavery and Cultural Exchange between Rome and the Germans from the First to the Seventh Century CE," in *Invisible Citizens: Captives and Their Consequences*, ed. Catherine M. Cameron (Salt Lake City: University of Utah Press, 2008), 80–109; Domenico Vera, "Essere 'schiavi della terra' nell'Italia tardoantica: Le razionalitá di una dipendenza," *Studia Historica* 25 (2007): 489–505; Chris Wickham, *Framing the Early Middle Ages: Europe and the Mediterranean, 400–800* (New York: Oxford University Press, 2005); Wickham, "The Other Transition: From the Ancient World to Feudalism," *Past and Present* 103, no. 1 (1984): 3–36; Michael McCormick, "New Light on the 'Dark Ages': How the Slave Trade Fuelled the Carolingian Economy," *Past and Present* 177, no. 1 (2002): 17–54; McCormick, *Origins of the European Economy: Communications and Commerce, A.D. 300–900* (New York: Cambridge University Press, 2001), 237–60, 733–77; Geoffrey S. Nathan, *The Family in Late Antiquity: The Rise of Christianity and the Endurance of Tradition* (London: Routledge, 2000), 169–84; Ramsay MacMullen, "Late Roman Slavery," *Historia* 36 (1987): 359–82.

slavery in Chrysostom can be noted—first, slavery was indeed a functional institution in the Roman Empire up to the mid-fifth century, and even into the Byzantine period in certain territories;[15] and second, the Roman institution of slavery did not slowly decline into medieval serfdom, but rather suffered a complete systemic collapse due to the lack of both supply and demand during the years of the disintegration of the later Roman Empire. I will not argue these points here again; I accept them as presuppositions. For the sake of clarity, however, I will attempt to briefly summarize the crucial points of departure. It has been argued by Chris Wickham, and more recently by Kyle Harper and Cam Grey,[16] that late Roman slavery did not slowly morph into what could be called medieval serfdom, nor did the crisis of the assumed "decline" of the slave mode of production lead to the rise of feudalism. Roman slavery was alive and well probably until the mid-fifth century. The many references to slaves and slavery in Chrysostom's homilies are a testament to this. The problem that Harper identifies is that some scholars, especially Weberian and Marxist scholars, relied on the concept of conquest to give an account of Roman slavery, and thus as conquest declined slavery declined as well since the channels of supply were becoming more limited.

But as scholarship has progressed, the view that the later Roman Empire was dependent on military conquest to sustain its slave system has become less convincing. Indeed, it appears that late Roman slavery was sustained by means of natural reproduction of slaves, and with the booming Roman economy, the demand for slaves remained high. Rather than promoting a theory of conquest, Harper bases his argument for the endurance of late Roman slavery, specifically for the period 275–425 C.E., on the concept of capital and the importance of supply and demand of slaves, which were well sustained in the Roman economy of that period.[17] It is not surprising then to find ample references to slavery in the Christian homilies of the fourth century.[18] The homilies of John Chrysostom contain numerous references to slaves, and Harper rightly identifies John Chrysostom as "an unparalleled source for the realities of Roman slavery."[19]

---

15. The development of slavery during the Byzantine period is examined in depth by Youval Rotman, *Byzantine Slavery and the Mediterranean World*, trans. Jane Marie Todd (Cambridge, MA: Harvard University Press, 2009).

16. Wickham, "The Other Transition"; Harper, *Slavery in the Late Roman World*, 1–99; Grey, "Slavery in the Late Roman World," 482–509. Grey highlights the continuities of slavery during the period of late antiquity with other periods despite various socioeconomic and juridical changes related to slavery.

17. Harper, *Slavery in the Late Roman World*, 67–99.

18. An excellent overview of slavery in late ancient Christianity is provided by Jennifer A. Glancy, "Christian Slavery in Late Antiquity," in *Human Bondage in the Cultural Contact Zone: Transdisciplinary Perspectives on Slavery and Its Discourses*, ed. Raphael Hörmann and Gesa Mackenthum (Münster: Waxmann, 2010), 63–80.

19. Harper, *Slavery in the Late Roman World*, 226.

In the homilies of John Chrysostom, the issue of slavery surfaces sporadically in the context of discussions of other socioethical issues, including household relationships, education, discipline, sexuality, and wealth renunciation.[20] Slaves were owned by individual Christians, priests, bishops, churches, and monasteries. Both slaveholders and slaves attended Chrysostom's services.[21] In fact, the diverse makeup of Chrysostom's audience suggests that many owned slaves.[22] Chrysostom's homilies provide a tinted window into the lives of slaves and slaveholders— tinted with the common ancient prejudice most elite persons had against slaves; the homilies are filters through which cultural-historical data may be sifted, and this data should be interpreted with great care. Chrysostom writes from the perspective of the slaveholders. Slaves are advised to be submissive, to serve their masters with their whole life, and to fear them. They do not own any property, for they are the property of their owners. Moreover, Chrysostom is of the opinion that masters do more for their slaves than vice versa, since masters have to care for their slaves.

Furthermore, the church not only accepted slavery as a social institution, but it used the slave model of behavior and mode of existence as a metaphor for the practice of Christian religion, the composition of Christian theology, and the formation of Christian subjectivity, and the metaphor of slavery also played an important role in Christian leadership formulations.[23] The use of scripture was central to the process of subjectivizing slavery. But along with assuming the subjectivity of the slave in its theological and ethical formulations, we find that Christianity also had a clear vision for real, institutional slaves in society. It was not a vision of the abolition of slavery. Because slaves were part of the household, they were included in the vision of pastoral power to transform the household into an institution that closely mirrored the church, a process I will call pastoralization. All these issues will be explored in greater depth in the chapters that follow.

20. I have provided an introductory discussion of Chrysostom's views on slavery in De Wet, "John Chrysostom on Slavery."

21. In *Hom. Eph.* 22.2 (F4.336–337), Chrysostom complains that churchgoers often neglect to bring their slaves to church, showing that it was a practice among some, and one that is lauded by Chrysostom.

22. On the diversity of Chrysostom's audience, see Wendy Mayer, "John Chrysostom: Extraordinary Preacher, Ordinary Audience," in *Preacher and Audience: Studies in Early Christian and Byzantine Homiletics,* ed. Mary B. Cunningham and Pauline Allen, A New History of the Sermon 1 (Leiden: Brill, 1998), 105–37; Mayer, "Who Came to Hear John Chrysostom Preach?," *Ephemerides Theologicae Lovanienses* 76, no. 1 (2000): 73–87; *contra:* Ramsay MacMullen, "The Preacher's Audience (AD 350–400)," *Journal of Theological Studies* 40, no. 2 (1989): 503–11.

23. This has been illustrated by Sessa in her work on formations of episcopal leadership, in which she demonstrates how a domestic model was used for episcopal authority; Kristina Sessa, *The Formation of Papal Authority in Late Antique Italy: Roman Bishops and the Domestic Sphere* (New York: Cambridge University Press, 2011), 1–33.

This brings me to the third presupposition of this book—namely, that late ancient Christianity accepted slavery as a necessary social institution, and that the rise of Christendom did not change or abolish the oppressive system of slaveholding.[24] Late ancient Christianity did not once utter a word supporting the formal abolition of slavery. In fact, from the earliest days of Christianity, during the time of Paul the apostle, the discourse of slavery was assimilated into the language of Christian subjectivity,[25] and the Christian legacy of slavery is present to this very day within Christian communities.[26]

If by some miracle slavery were to be erased from the pages of human history, the appearance and expression of Christian identity would be fundamentally different. As I will argue, in addition to accepting slavery as a socioeconomic phenomenon, all facets of Christian subjectivity, whether socioethical or theological, were shaped at their very core by the discourse of ancient slavery. It is clear that Christianity did not ameliorate slavery in late antiquity, but rather adopted and transformed it into something different—not better, but different.

The Christianization of doulology in late antiquity is a central concern of this book. The first question I ask is why Christianity chose to adopt both the language and the practice of slavery as legitimate means of expression and behavior. We see the Christian movement(s) seizing on slavery, and then pinning it on its very body of subjectivity as early as the New Testament and the noncanonical literature of the first few centuries.[27] In the letters of Paul, some of the earliest Christian documents, he identifies himself, first and foremost, as a "slave of Christ" and calls Christ his "Lord" (e.g., Rom. 1:1; Phil. 1:1). On a more practical level, certain other documents claiming to have been written by Paul, the Deutero-Pauline epistles of Colossians and Ephesians, provide some very basic guidelines for how to treat one's slaves (Eph. 6:5–9; Col. 3:22–4:1), and in another authentic letter by Paul, his Epistle to Philemon, he directly intervenes in a possible dispute between a Christian neophyte slave, Onesimus, and his master, Philemon. Paul does not advise manumission, but urges the slave to return to his master and the master to gracefully accept the slave "as a brother" (Philem. 16). Why did early Christian leaders like Paul, and leaders up to the fifth century, deem it so crucial to claim and transform the

---

24. Kontoulis, *Zum Problem der Sklaverei*, 325–54; Glancy, "Christian Slavery in Late Antiquity," 63–80. For an approach to the problem of slavery and Christianity focusing especially on hermeneutical issues, see Hector Avalos, *Slavery, Abolitionism, and the Ethics of Biblical Scholarship*, The Bible in the Modern World 38 (Sheffield: Sheffield Phoenix, 2011).

25. John Byron, *Slavery Metaphors in Early Judaism and Pauline Christianity: A Traditio-Historical and Exegetical Examination*, Wissenschaftliche Untersuchungen zum Neuen Testament 162 (Tübingen: Mohr Siebeck, 2003), esp. 144–257.

26. These legacies are examined extensively in an excellent collection of essays: Bernadette J. Brooten, ed., *Beyond Slavery: Overcoming Its Religious and Sexual Legacies* (New York: Palgrave Macmillan, 2010).

27. The *Acts of Thomas*, for example, has slavery as its central motif; see Jennifer A. Glancy, "Slavery in *Acts of Thomas*," *Journal of Early Christian History* 2, no. 2 (2012): 3–21.

discourse of slavery instead of rejecting it? Why do we have this discursive colonization of an institution considered to be so vile and oppressive?

Jennifer Glancy has argued that slaveholding in late ancient Christianity should
be understood as a corporeal habitus.[28] She states that "conditioning to slavery was
habitual, a dimension of a corporal vernacular rather than an area of conscious
decision-making."[29] Authors of late antiquity therefore find themselves in this symbolic social space and operate socially within its "naturalness," or rather, its banality. The potency of corporeal habitualization within the operation of social reproduction should not be underestimated. I am in agreement with Glancy that slavery
functioned as a habitus, a set of nearly inescapable social dispositions, which are
translated onto bodies, or rather, into bodily performances. But is it enough to say
that late ancient Christianity transformed slavery simply because it could not
escape it; because of habitualization and social reproduction, Christianity was
unable to think beyond the presence of slavery, and, as the argument often
goes, Christians were "children of their times," trapped within the sociocultural
confines of ancient Mediterranean society? Slavery was indeed a moral problem for
the early Christians, and we do find some criticism of slavery in early Christian
writers.

For instance, Gregory of Nyssa's fourth homily on Ecclesiastes has been described
by Harper as "in some ways anticipating the moral groundwork and poetry of the
abolitionist movement by nearly a millennium-and-a-half."[30] There is also a rather
obscure rumour about the Eustathians in the fourth-century synodical letter from
the Council of Gangra, accusing the group of allowing slaves to wear strange clothing, act insolently toward their masters, and even leave their masters.[31] Were the
Eustathians premodern abolitionists? This information is very difficult to assess,
but what we do know is that these acts led to the anathematization of the Eustathians. Furthermore, the majority of late ancient Christian authors, Chrysostom
included, linked slavery to the origins of sin, and displayed some discomfort with
the idea of slavery.[32] Thus, some Christians were at least able to comprehend the
moral turpitude of slavery. While I agree that the habitualization of slavery in
late Roman society played a significant role in the assimilation of slavery into
ancient Christian culture, I do not think this was the determining factor of its assi-
miliation, nor does this fact absolve late ancient Christianity from its moral failure

---

28. For details on the notion of habitus, see Pierre Bourdieu, *The Logic of Practice*, trans. Richard
Nice (Cambridge: Polity, 1990), 52; Bourdieu, *Distinction: A Social Critique of the Judgement of Taste*,
trans. Richard Nice (Cambridge, MA: Harvard University Press, 1984), 166–68.

29. Glancy, "Christian Slavery in Late Antiquity," 68.

30. Harper, *Slavery in the Late Roman World*, 346.

31. Glancy, *Slavery in Early Christianity*, 90–91.

32. Chris L. de Wet, "Sin as Slavery and/or Slavery as Sin? On the Relationship between Slavery and
Christian Hamartiology in Late Ancient Christianity," *Religion & Theology* 17, nos. 1–2 (2010): 26–39;
De Wet, "John Chrysostom on Slavery," 6–8.

in accepting slavery. Along with the corporeal habitualization of slavery, I am arguing that slavery as a discourse, and a power discourse at that, proved to be too valuable, irresistible, and influential to be ignored by the Christian authors of late antiquity.

Now that we know that slavery existed in the late Roman world, and have noted its importance as a discourse in early Christianity, it should be asked what the basic features of slavery in late antiquity were, and how slavery should be understood as an economic institution.

THE ECONOMY AND CARCERALITY OF SLAVERY

The economy of slavery in late Roman antiquity was quite complex. It would be incorrect to state that slaves were simply the property of slaveholders. Slaves were not only seen as assets of the owner, but they also had some inherent social value when they were displayed. On the one hand, slaves were considered subjects in their own right who still had some limited social mobility and limited means to secure their own freedom. On the other hand, the slave body was subject to a potent operation of objectification and commodification.[33] Slaves were commodified and fungible objects and possessions that had both economic and symbolic, or status-based, value. No matter what a slave was, whether a menial field worker or a court official, whatever his or her position in the *familia* or broader society, all slaves had one common denominator of identity—their deed and point of sale, or at least their vulnerability to being sold. All unfree bodies were subject to sale as an object, a commodity.

In the context of Roman law, slaves were grouped within the category of *res mancipi*.[34] In Roman private law, this category represented the acquired property of a person. The Latin term *res* implies an object or a thing, and specifically in this context, private property. Thus it seems that in terms of the legal management of slavery, it was easiest to treat slaves as property or things. This does not imply that the average free person considered all slaves simply as property or objects, but in terms of the administration of human bondage, property rights rather than human rights applied. Chrysostom himself sometimes finds it difficult to conceptualize slavery outside of its fungibility. He refers to slaves as "the master's goods" or "commodities of domination" (*ta despotika chrēmata*).[35]

Such a social disposition implies that slaves were provided with value measures, and injuring a slave was considered damage to property. The term *res mancipi* therefore functions within a very specific set of legal parameters, and Leonard Schumacher

33. Paul Veyne, *A History of Private Life*, vol. 1, *From Pagan Rome to Byzantium*, ed. Paul Veyne, trans. Arthur Goldhammer (Cambridge, MA: Belknap Press of Harvard University Press, 2000), 51.

34. For more on *res mancipi*, see Hans Ankum, "*Mancipatio* by Slaves in Classical Roman Law," *Acta Juridica* 1 (1976): 1–18; Peter M. Tiersma, "Rites of Passage: Legal Ritual in Roman Law and Anthropological Analogues," *Journal of Legal History* 9, no. 1 (1988): 3–25.

35. *Propt. fornic.* 4 (PG 51.214.18–20).

rightly notes the tension in Roman law between the slave as *res mancipi* and the slave as *ius naturale*—that is, a human being.[36] It becomes difficult, if not impossible, to separate these two dimensions in the practical sense.[37] Varro's references to the slave as *instrumentum vocale*, as well as his use of the phrase *venalium greges*, also emphasize the fungible nature of slavery.[38] As we will see, Chrysostom's numerous references to "herds" of slaves also attest to the commodification of slave bodies in the late Roman world. The exploitation of slaves for their reproductive capital is also an instance of objectification[39]—slaves who had many children were rewarded, since this implied a "profit" for the slaveholder.[40] Of course, early Christian attitudes toward the regulation of slave sexualities and the proliferation of chastity among slaves, as we will see in chapter 6, may have influenced their status as reproductive capital.

The frequent reference to slaves as simply "bodies" also highlights their objectification.[41] The body of the slave determined his or her price—beauty, age, and build were as important as education and practical skills in deciding the price of a slave.[42] The process of objectification of slaves also included a potent operation of alterization.[43] In objectifying the slave body, its alienness and otherness are stressed. The objectification of the slave body is blatantly clear in both the language and economic systems of the Romans. Slaves were *res mancipi*—property possessed, especially by the *paterfamilias* as part of the *patrimonium*.

36. Leonard Schumacher, "Einleitung," in *Corpus der römischen Rechtsquellen zur antiken Sklaverei*, pt. 6, *Stellung des Sklaven im Sakralrecht*, ed. Leonard Schumacher, Forschungen zur antiken Sklaverei—Beihefte 3.6 (Stuttgart: Franz Steiner, 2006), 3.

37. William W. Buckland, *The Roman Law of Slavery: The Condition of the Slave in Private Law from Augustus to Justinian* (Cambridge: Cambridge University Press, 1908), 10–12.

38. Varro, *Rust.* 1.2.20–21 (Hooper and Ash, 178–79); see William Fitzgerald, *Slavery and the Roman Literary Imagination*, Roman Literature and Its Contexts (Cambridge: Cambridge University Press, 1996), 6; Sandra R. Joshel, "Slavery and the Roman Literary Culture," in Bradley and Cartledge, *Cambridge World History of Slavery*, 1:214–16. It should be noted in this instance that both *instrumentum vocale* and *venalium greges* are quite ambiguous, and their traditional connotations suggesting the venality of slavery have been disputed and problematized; see Jesper Carlsen, "Varro, Marcus Terentius," in *The Historical Encyclopedia of World Slavery*, vol. 2, *L–Z*, ed. Junius P. Rodriguez (Santa Barbara, CA: ABC-CLIO, 1997), 669–70; Ulrike Roth, "No More Slave-Gangs: Varro, *De re rustica* 1.2.20–1," *Classical Quarterly* 55 (2005): 310–15; Leah Kronenberg, *Allegories of Farming from Greece and Rome: Philosophical Satire in Xenophon, Varro, and Virgil* (New York: Cambridge University Press, 2009), 118.

39. For more on reproductive capital, see Marianne B. Kartzow, "Navigating the Womb: Surrogacy, Slavery, Fertility—and Biblical Discourses," *Journal of Early Christian History* 2, no. 1 (2012): 38–54.

40. See Xenophon, *Oec.* 9.5 (Marchant 440–41); Columella, *Rust.* 1.8.16–19 (Ash 1:92–95).

41. Glancy, *Slavery in Early Christianity*, 10–12.

42. For a more detailed analysis of slave prices, see Walter Scheidel, "Real Slave Prices and the Relative Cost of Labour in the Greco-Roman World," *Ancient Society* 35 (2005): 1–17; Kyle Harper, "Slave Prices in Late Antiquity (and in the Very Long Term)," *Historia* 59 (2010): 206–38.

43. Rainer Emig and Oliver Lindner, introduction to *Commodifying (Post)Colonialism: Othering, Reification, Commodification and the New Literatures and Cultures in English*, ed. Rainer Emig and Oliver Lindner, Cross/Cultures 127: ASNEL Papers 16 (Amsterdam: Rodopi, 2010), vii–xxiv.

The economy of slavery then was an economy of both subjectified and objectified bodies. It was an economy based on supply and demand, and just before the collapse of the channels of supply and demand in the fifth century, the slave system of late antiquity was a well-oiled machine. For any economic system to be effective, it needs to be sustainable. One of the main channels by which the Roman slave supply was sustained was natural reproduction. Other channels included kidnapping and trading outside the borders of the empire, child exposure, self-sale, debt-slavery, and new slaves coming in as captives of war.[44] Many slaves therefore started out as home-born slaves—such a slave was known in Greek as an *oikogenēs* and in Latin as a *verna*.[45] Having slaves born in the very household that possessed them may have been beneficial for the owners, since it enabled them to habituate the slave from the period of infancy.[46] But slaves who were not home-born were purchased either at the slave market or from another family. Many transactions involving slaves, home-born or not, were minor, informal exchanges between slaveholders.[47]

The one figure that stands out with regard to the venality of the slave body is the slave trader. The Roman government had an "uneasy alliance" with slave traders, as with pimps, who were also often slave traders.[48] The derogatory Greek term for a slave trader is the same used for a kidnapper: *andrapodistēs*. Another term used for a slave trader is *sōmatemporos*, "trader of bodies." The equivalent Latin terms are *plagiarius, venaliciarius,* and *mango,* the latter probably a Grecism related to the verb *manganeuō,* meaning "doctor, trick, or dress artificially."[49] Slave traders were often grouped with social undesirables and criminals.[50]

44. Studies focusing in detail on the Roman slave supply are Walter Scheidel, "Quantifying the Sources of Slaves in the Early Roman Empire," *Journal of Roman Studies* 87 (1997): 156–69; Ulrike Roth, *Thinking Tools: Agricultural Slavery between Evidence and Models,* Bulletin of the Institute of Classical Studies Supplement (London: Institute of Classical Studies, School of Advanced Study, University of London, 2007); Harper, *Slavery in the Late Roman World,* 67–99; Scheidel, "The Roman Slave Supply," in Bradley and Cartledge, *Cambridge World History of Slavery,* 1:287–310.

45. Chrysostom often refers to home-born slaves; see *Hom. Gen.* 35.4 (PG 53.327.13–16); *Princ. Act.* 1.2 (PG 51.69.23–25); for a detailed discussion of home-born slaves, see Elizabeth Herrmann-Otto, *Ex ancilla natus: Untersuchungen zu den "hausgeborenen" Sklaven und Sklavinnen im Westen des römischen Kaiserreiches,* Forschungen zur antiken Sklaverei 24 (Stuttgart: Steiner, 1994); Scheidel, "Roman Slave Supply," 306–8.

46. See chapter 4 for a full discussion of the habituation and education of slaves.

47. Keith R. Bradley, "On the Roman Slave Supply and Slavebreeding," in *Classical Slavery,* ed. Moses I. Finley (London: Routledge, 1987), 53–81; Harper, *Slavery in the Late Roman World,* 72–74.

48. Harper, *Slavery in the Late Roman World,* 84.

49. For a discussion of the stereotype of the slave trader, see J. Albert Harrill, "The Vice of Slave Dealers in Greco-Roman Society: The Use of a Topos in 1 Timothy 1:10," *Journal of Biblical Literature* 118, no. 1 (1999): 97–122.

50. See, in the New Testament, 1 Tim. 1:10; Chrysostom, *Hom. 1 Tim.* 2.2 (F6.16–17); Harrill, "Vice of Slave Dealers," 97–122.

Two activities of slave traders stand out in these appellations. First is the suggestion that they kidnap free persons to sell as slaves. This was a major problem in the later Roman Empire. It was such a significant issue that Augustine sought help from the courts to intervene—he wrote a letter to Alypius pleading for imperial assistance to weed out such kidnappers.[51] One of the greatest fears of a free citizen was being kidnapped and sold into slavery, or having their children kidnapped by slave traders.[52] Chrysostom warns his audience that kidnappers often try to lure children with sweets and cakes in order to abduct them.[53] Slave traders knew how to play on the appetites of children (and probably adults). Kidnapped children were then sold in faraway countries to minimize detection.[54] Chrysostom was very aware of the problem of people with uncertain social status due to abduction by criminal slave traders; masters were being sold as if they were slaves.[55]

The other trait suggested by the terms identified above is the slave trader's capacity to deceive clients. Roman law included provisions to guard buyers from being duped, although the extent to which a deceived buyer was recompensed is difficult to determine.[56] *Caveat emptor* was the best advice for people dealing with slave traders. Slave traders had to disclose any relevant information about the slave, especially if the slave was disloyal, disobedient, prone to flee, physically disabled, or ill. However, slave traders were famous for concealing possible defects and manipulating the bodies of slaves so that they appeared fairer, sexier, and younger.[57]

Chrysostom describes in detail the anxieties a buyer might face: "Those who want to purchase a slave, show him to the physician, and request sureties for the sale, and information about him from their neighbors, and after all this they still do not confirm the venture without asking for a period of time to scrutinize the slave."[58] Purchasing a slave, especially an expensive slave, was a long process, and

51. Augustine, *Ep.* 10*.2–8 (CSEL 88.46–52); see Marie-François Berrouard, "Un tournant dans la vie de l'église d'Afrique les deux missions d'Alypius en Italie à la lumière des lettres 10*, 15*, 16*, 22* et 23*A de saint Augustin," *Revue des Études Augustiniennes* 31 (1985): 46–70; Harper, *Slavery in the Late Roman World*, 92–95. Elm has convincingly argued that the presence of people with uncertain social status was such a problem to Augustine that it even influenced his theological formulations of freedom; Susanna Elm, "Augustine, Romans, and Late Roman Slavery" (paper presented at the Society of Biblical Literature Annual Meeting, Baltimore, 2013).
52. *Hom. Act.* 6.3 (PG 60.60.59–60); for more on kidnapping and child-sale, see Harper, *Slavery in the Late Roman World*, 80–81; Scheidel, "Roman Slave Supply," 297–99.
53. *Adv. Jud.* 1.7 (PG 48.855.30–34); see *Stat.* 16.4 (PG 49.168.2–23).
54. *Mut. nom.* 1.1 (PG 51.115.44–60).
55. *Hom. Col.* 2.5 (F5.196).
56. *Dig. Just.* 21.1.37, 44; in Harrill, "Vice of Slave Dealers," 104–5.
57. In Harrill, "Vice of Slave Dealers," 108–12.
58. *Sacr.* 4.2.17–20 (SC 272.240): ἀνδράποδον μὲν πρίασθαι βουλομένους καὶ ἰατροῖς ἐπιδεικνύναι καὶ τῆς πράσεως ἐγγυητὰς ἀπαιτεῖν καὶ γειτόνων πυνθάνεσθαι καὶ μετὰ ταῦτα πάντα μηδέπω θαρρεῖν, ἀλλὰ καὶ χρόνον πολὺν πρὸς δοκιμασίαν αἰτεῖν.

we see here all the measures someone may take to secure their investment. As a commodity, the slave body was subject to inspection at any time. Physicians could examine slaves to ensure a good bill of health, and slaves were often stripped naked in the slave market to be inspected. Even the virginity of some slaves was tested. Slaves were also scrutinized for a period, in a type of probation known as *dokimasia,*[59] before some sales were finalized. This seems to have been a common practice. "A new slave is not entrusted with anything in a house," Chrysostom tells us, "till he has given proof of his character, having undergone many trials."[60] Chrysostom also says that possible buyers asked slaves if they wanted to be in their service—this may have happened in some cases, but it was perhaps more a courtesy; essentially slaves did not have any choice in the matter; they had to accept their fate after being sold.[61] However, it would be beneficial to all parties involved if the sale created no ill feelings on the part of either the slaves or their prospective owners. Once the transaction was finalized, the slave was named, while *vernae* were often named in consultation with the master.[62]

Slave nomenclature was very telling—it could give information about the character of the slave or his or her occupation (the names of prostitutes were recognizable), details about the slaveholder, and whether he or she was a freed person. Slaves were sold with a name, but the name could be changed. Most notable was the absence of any name related to ancestry; the natal alienation of slaves was most clearly visible in their names. Chrysostom refers to Adam, who gave names to the animals like a master giving names to his slaves, as a "symbol of his domination" (*to symbolon tēs despoteias*).[63] This domination-by-name was all-encompassing. While expounding the significance of God being called the "God of Abraham, Isaac, and Jacob," Chrysostom explains: "What happens in the case of human beings you can see occurring in the case of God as well; for example, with human beings, slaves are called after their masters, and it is customary for everyone to speak in these terms: 'So-and-so the custodian belonging to so-and-so.'"[64] This is

59. The term δοκιμασία was also used for the scrutiny of sinners in the late ancient church; see Kyle Harper, *From Shame to Sin: The Christian Transformation of Sexual Morality in Late Antiquity* (Cambridge, MA: Harvard University Press, 2013), 144.

60. *Hom. 1 Tim.* 11.1 (F6.85): εἰς μὲν οἰκίαν νεώνητον οἰκέτην μὴ πρότερον ἐγχειρίζεσθαί τι τῶν ἔνδον, πρὶν ἂν διὰ πολλῆς τῆς πείρας τῆς αὐτοῦ γνώμης πολλὰ τεκμήρια δῷ.

61. *Illum. catech.* 2.5 (PG 49.239.17–20).

62. For more on the naming of slaves, see Christer Bruun, "Greek or Latin? The Owner's Choice of Names for *Vernae* in Rome," in *Roman Slavery and Roman Material Culture,* ed. Michele George (Toronto: University of Toronto Press, 2013), 19–42.

63. *Hom. Gen.* 9.2 (PG 53.79.11–13); see also *Hom. Gen.* 14.5 (PG 53.116.45–46), 40.1 (53.568.8–12); *Mut. nom.* 3.3 (PG 51.137.22–46).

64. *Anna* 4 (PG 54.665.26–30): Καὶ ὅπερ ἐπ' ἀνθρώπων οὐ γίνεται, τοῦτο ἐπὶ τοῦ Θεοῦ συμβαίνον ἔστιν ἰδεῖν. Οἷόν τι λέγω· ἐπὶ τῶν ἀνθρώπων ἀπὸ τῶν δεσποτῶν οἱ δοῦλοι καλοῦνται, καὶ οὕτως ἔθος ἅπασι λέγειν, 'Ο δεῖνα ἐπίτροπος τοῦ δεῖνος. Translation: Robert C. Hill, trans., *Homilies on Hannah,*

an exceptional case, he continues, for although slaves are always named after their masters, God is named after his slaves, and slaves after God. Chrysostom compares biblical theophorisms (names that have the name of God embedded in them) with the naming of slaves—illustrating a type of kyriophorism (when the slaveholder gives a new name to a slave that signifies and affirms his domination over the slave). Kyriophorism shows that the body of the slave becomes the possession and the surrogate body of the owner in all respects.

Kyriarchy writes its name on the body of the slave, like someone marking his tools with his name. It also implies that the slave represents the master, and any shame or honor that accrues to the slave reflects on the slaveholder.[65] The slaveholder must also protect his or her property, and hence any injury to a slave was considered an injury to the slaveholder.[66] Kyriophorism binds the individual doulological body to the kyriarchal body politic.

Once slaves were in the service of their owners they could be allocated whatever service their owners deemed fit. Some slaves were allotted a *peculium*, basically the right to earn extra money via various entrepreneurial pursuits. The money in the *peculium* could be used for whatever the slave desired, of course in consultation with the master. A slave could use it to purchase freedom or to buy his or her own slaves. But the *peculium* was not always what it seemed to be, as Harper rightly notes: "The institution of the *peculium* also allowed masters to act as silent partners in unsavoury forms of commerce, such as the slave trade, tavernkeeping, and prostitution."[67] Chrysostom himself states that some slaveholders compelled their slaves to engage in fraud, theft, and other dodgy deals.[68] Slaves often had to manage some of the owner's funds and account for how the funds were used.[69] Chrysostom makes it very clear that "it is the privilege of the master to claim what belongs to the slaves."[70]

The conditions in which slaves lived were quite varied. On one hand, Chrysostom tells of slaves who eat only bread, sleep on straw, and always live in fear, and on the other, he does not hesitate to mention that the master cares for all the physical needs of slaves, including lodging and food.[71] Some slaves in the higher echelons of Roman society may have lived better lives than many free persons. Chrysostom also says that prostitutes, who were often slaves or freed persons, made far

David and Saul, St. John Chrysostom: Old Testament Homilies 1 (Brookline, MA: Holy Cross Orthodox Press, 2003), 113–14. See *Hom. Gen.* 40.1 (53.568.8–12).

65. *Hom. Eph.* 15.2 (F4.259); *Hom. Phlm.* arg. (F6.328); *Hom. 1 Tim.* 16.2 (F6.141).
66. *Stat.* 20.4 (PG 49.202.43–45).
67. Harper, *From Shame to Sin,* 127.
68. *Hom. Phlm.* 1.2 (F6.333).
69. *Stat.* 20.6 (PG 49.206.29).
70. *Hom. Phlm.* 2.2 (F6.345): τοῦτο δόξα δεσπότου, τὸ οἰκειοῦσθαι τὰ ἐκείνων.
71. *Hom. 1 Cor.* 19.6 (F2.224); *Hom. 1 Tim.* 16.2 (F6.144).

more money than the average poor person. Yet if we look at the majority of slaves in late antiquity, who were not well educated or literate, it seems probable that their lives closely mirrored the lives of the poor in society. It is also strange, then, that while Chrysostom may have been one of the most outspoken advocates of the poor, slaves receive very little sympathy from him by comparison.

But the sustainability of the slave economy of the late ancient world depended on much more than the means to supply slaves to willing buyers. It extended far beyond corporeal transactions in the slave market or the accumulation of *vernae* in the household. The internal dynamics of Roman slavery ensured its continued existence. This means that every aspect of the system of slaveholding served the function of sustaining it. Roman slavery was an institution that operated on the principle of carcerality—indeed, without carcerality there can be no system of enslavement. By carcerality I mean a state of durance, a symbolic imprisonment that manifests itself in many ways. Slaves found themselves in a constant state of carcerality. Kyriarchal power is the nexus of slave carcerality—the authority of the slaveholder, which is attributed to him or her by both society and judiciary, is the most potent prison of the slave body. Even if the slave is not physically surrounded by walls or chained, kyriarchal authority still incarcerates the slave body.

The mechanisms of carcerality were manifold. When I speak of a carceral mechanism here, I am referring to those technologies that actually intensify the enslaved state of the unfree. In its most basic sense, a carceral mechanism could be something that physically imprisoned or bound a slave. Some slaves were physically locked up, chained, wore slave collars,[72] and had their movement limited to certain spaces within the household and society.

But there are some mechanisms of carcerality that are more difficult to identify; here I am referring to such mechanisms as reward, kinship, social mobility, manumission, and freed status. These are all modalities of slave carcerality, and each has very distinct features.[73] The historian of slavery should be aware of these mechanisms especially, since at face value they may seem positive and benevolent. Yet without these "positive" carceral mechanisms, the economy of slavery would be unsustainable. The greatest danger in this case is that these positive carceral mechanisms may lead some to romanticize certain aspects of ancient slavery. Let me give some examples.

We will see in the course of this book that many ancient authors, including Chrysostom, stressed the humanity of slaves. Emphasizing the humanity of slaves may seem good, yet its carceral dynamics are extremely oppressive. In this regard,

---

72. David L. Thurmond, "Some Roman Slave Collars in CIL," *Athenaeum* 82, no. 72 (1994): 459–78.

73. For an excellent discussion of the containment and mobility of slaves in Roman society, see Sandra R. Joshel, "Geographies of Slave Containment and Movement," in George, *Roman Slavery and Roman Material Culture*, 99–128.

Saidiya Hartman states: "I argue that the barbarism of slavery did not express itself singularly in the constitution of the slave as object but also in the forms of subjectivity and circumscribed humanity imputed to the enslaved."[74] Hartman goes on to argue that notions of the humanity of slaves in fact intensified the suffering of slaves. It was this recourse to the human characteristics of the slave that opened up new avenues for oppression, such as threats to partners and children, sexual regulation, and deprivation of food. Here, humanity operates as a carceral mechanism that actually ramifies the enslaved state of a person. Humanized slave language can also be offensive and disparaging, and used to confirm slave stereotypes. Chrysostom often refers to the "race" or 'stock" (*genos*) of slaves, a derogatory term that typically exemplifies their social exclusion and pathologization (but is not to be confused with modern racism).[75] The subjectivation of the slave body was just as oppressive as its objectification—both sustained the economy of slavery.

Another problem is that humanity is often used as an argument to highlight the "equality" between slaves and slaveholders—an "equality" with very little impact on institutional slavery. It was an extremely common motif in Stoicism and early Christianity. Cyprian, for instance, uses a similar argument, advising masters not to treat their slaves harshly, based on their shared humanity. But Glancy is correct in noting: "Beyond an implicit critique of slaveholders who wielded excessive force against their slaves, Cyprian sketched no practical consequences from his strongly worded statement of equality."[76] In the same way, the fourth-century author Aphrahat, while musing on the impartiality of death, states: "He leads away to himself both slaves together with their masters; and there the masters are not honored more than their slaves. Small and great are there, and they hear not the voice of the oppressor. The slave who is freed from his master there pays no regard to him who used to oppress him."[77] Equality had a very relative and limited meaning in the context of ancient slavery.

Kinship, freedom, and social mobility are also often identified as positive features of ancient slavery. Marleen Flory notes the "social cohesion of the *familia* and how its quasi-familial bond, which persisted beyond slavery and into freedom, helped to contribute to the social stability of the slave population" and "gave slaves

74. Saidiya V. Hartman, *Scenes of Subjection: Terror, Slavery, and Self-Making in Nineteenth-Century America* (New York: Oxford University Press, 1997), 6. I am grateful to Jennifer Glancy for pointing out this source.

75. See *Hom. 1 Cor.* 40.6 (F2.515); *Hom. Eph.* 15.2 (F.4.259); *Hom. Phlm.* arg. (F6.327); *Hom. Tit.* 4.1 (F6.298); *Serm. Gen.* 5.1 (PG 54.599.26–28).

76. Jennifer A. Glancy, "Slavery and the Rise of Christianity," in Bradley and Cartledge, *Cambridge World History of Slavery*, 1:473.

77. Aphrahat, *Dem.* 22.7 (PS 1.1008; translation: revised *NPNF*); see also Job 3:18–19.

and ex-slaves a sense of social security."[78] Yet, the notions of *familia* and kinship were in themselves carceral mechanisms. These strategies were also very common in the New Testament, where, for instance, Paul tells Philemon to accept Onesimus as a "brother" (Philem. 16). Such strategies create the illusion of softening the harshness of slavery, but in actual fact, they only ramify it. The inclusion of slaves in kinship structures like the *familia* made it extremely difficult, indeed almost impossible, to escape the channels of domination.

The subjectivity of the slave was, then, perhaps one of the most complex subjectivities in ancient times. Patterson's definition of slavery as "the permanent, violent domination of natally alienated and generally dishonored persons" certainly rings true.[79] Others, like Paul Bohannan, refer to slavery as "antikinship,"[80] in line with what Moses Finley noted as exclusion from "the most elementary of social bonds, kinship."[81] Bohannan makes a distinction between antikinship and nonkinship. Slaves are not included under nonkinship because they are not like individuals in a business relationship or a contract established by rank.[82] Slaves can have no kin in the legal sense of the word; they are, as Patterson states, natally alienated. Although slaves are transplanted into the patriarchal structure of the *familia*, which appears to be a kinship structure, they are still socially and economically valuated in terms of antikinship standards. They are part of the *domus*, but they are also a threat to the *domus*[83]—they are social outsiders, Others, and objects.

Notions like Bohannan's antikinship and Patterson's natal alienation do indeed help us to understand the social exclusion slaves experienced, but we need to take care in the direct application of these theories to early Christianity. There is also a rhetoric of "natal association" in early Christian texts (e.g., calling slaves brothers and sisters), in which slaves are included in kinship structures like the *familia*; but this natal association is perhaps even more pervasively oppressive than natal alienation. Natal association, or at least the profession of including slaves in kinship

---

78. Marleen B. Flory, "Family in *Familia*: Kinship and Community in Slavery," *American Journal of Ancient History* 3 (1978): 89–90.

79. Patterson, *Slavery and Social Death*, 13.

80. Paul J. Bohannan, *Social Anthropology* (New York: Holt, Rinehart and Winston, 1963), 181. The idea of slavery as antikinship has been influential in anthropological studies on slavery; see Steven Freierman, "African Histories and the Dissolution of World History," in *Africa and the Disciplines: The Contributions of Research in Africa to the Social Sciences and Humanities,* ed. Robert H. Bates, V. Y. Mudimbe, and Jean F. O'Barr; Chicago: University of Chicago Press, 1993), 191–95; Gyan Prakash, *After Colonialism: Imperial Histories and Postcolonial Displacements* (Princeton, NJ: Princeton University Press, 1994), 56–58; Leland Donald, *Aboriginal Slavery on the Northwest Coast of North America* (Berkeley: University of California Press, 1997), 300–301.

81. Moses I. Finley, *Ancient Slavery and Modern Ideology* (New York: Viking Press, 1980), 143.

82. Bohannan, *Social Anthropology*, 180.

83. J. Albert Harrill, *Slaves in the New Testament: Literary, Social, and Moral Dimensions* (Minneapolis: Fortress Press, 2005), 145–62.

structures, gave rise to other additional technologies of regulation and domination that aided in the reproduction of kyriarchal social structures.

While slaves were included in the kinship structure of the Roman *familia,* they were still denied basic elements of kinship in the Roman world—namely, acknowledgment of legal and legitimate heirs, the ability to own property, and possession of a name that signified one's own lineage. Roman society did of course substitute weak equivalents for these missing elements, such as informal recognition of marriage and children, and the right to have a *peculium.*[84] All of these "privileges" were still subject to the owner's authority. The Roman *familia* was perhaps the most common carceral space for slaves in antiquity, a prison not made from bricks and mortar, but by free bodies and kyriarchal authority.

Dale Martin also reads the upward social mobility of slaves as a positive factor, and quotes John Myers's statement that slavery functioned as "a compulsory initiation into a higher culture." Martin explains: "As surprising as it may sound to modern ears, slavery was arguably the most important channel through which outsiders entered the mainstream of Roman power structures."[85] It is true that slaves had recourse to upward mobility, and many slaves did indeed have a great deal of authority. Yet they remained slaves, and their situation could change quite swiftly. Not all freed persons shared in the idyllic life that Martin emphasizes.[86]

Some slaves indeed preferred to stay in their carceral state and make use of opportunities within this disposition to better themselves and eventually be manumitted. Manumission was a very important element of slavery; it sustained the very system of slaveholding.[87] It was an incentive of domination; it motivated slaves to work harder.[88] Manumission was not only a reward, but also a necessity. It opened

84. For more on the dynamics of *peculium,* see Buckland, *Roman Law of Slavery,* 159–238; Boaz Cohen, "Peculium in Jewish and Roman Law," *Proceedings of the American Academy for Jewish Research* 20 (1951): 135–234; Ulrike Roth, "Food, Status, and the *Peculium* of Agricultural Slaves," *Journal of Roman Archaeology* 18 (2005): 278–92; Jane F. Gardner, "Slavery and Roman Law," in Bradley and Cartledge, *Cambridge World History of Slavery,* 1:414–37; Harper, *Slavery in the Late Roman World,* 127.

85. Dale B. Martin, *Slavery as Salvation: The Metaphor of Slavery in Pauline Christianity* (New Haven, CT: Yale University Press, 1990), 32.

86. See Henrik Mouritsen, *The Freedman in the Roman World* (New York: Cambridge University Press, 2011); Matthew J. Perry, *Gender, Manumission, and the Roman Freedwoman* (New York: Cambridge University Press, 2013).

87. For an excellent overview of manumission in early Christianity, see J. Albert Harrill, *The Manumission of Slaves in Early Christianity,* Hermeneutische Untersuchungen zur Theologie 32 (Tübingen: Mohr Siebeck, 1998). For the issue of manumission in later Roman society, see Harper, *Slavery in the Late Roman World,* 238–46, 463–93.

88. For more on manumission as a labor incentive, see Ronald Findlay, "Slavery, Incentives, and Manumission: A Theoretical Model," *Journal of Political Economy* 83, no. 5 (1975): 923–33; Thomas E. J. Wiedemann, "The Regularity of Manumission at Rome," *Classical Quarterly* 35, no. 1 (1985): 162–75; Keith R. Bradley, *Slaves and Masters in the Roman Empire: A Study in Social Control* (New York: Oxford University Press, 1987), 80–110.

up positions of exploitation for new slaves. Old, sick, and long-overworked slaves were also manumitted because of their physical condition.[89] In many cases, slaves were manumitted after the death of their master by his or her testament. Chrysostom reminds slaveholders: "At your death you would not choose to leave the slave that has served you well unhonored, but compensate him both with freedom, and with a gift of money." The good slaveholder did not have to make provisions, then, for only his or her spouse and children, but also his or her slaves. "And having passed away, you will not be able to do him good, you make arrangements for him with the future heirs of your estate," Chrysostom explains, "ensuring, exhorting, doing everything, so that he may not stay unrewarded."[90]

Slaves were also able to buy their freedom if their *peculium* was enough.[91] It should not, however, be assumed that all slaves desired freedom. Sudden manumission could be very traumatic and debilitating for a slave, who would be released into a society inherently antagonistic toward him or her. Chrysostom in fact notes that many slaves feared manumission, since some died of famine and others lived hard lives outside the care of their former owner.[92] This is also why many slaves allegedly revolted after the famous mass manumission by Melania.[93] Manumission could also break up families and marriages. The process of manumission was in itself complex.[94] Along with the usual channels of manumission by testament or in court, *manumissio in ecclesia*, "ecclesiastical manumission," also became a common occurrence in late ancient society. There was also *manumissio inter amicos*, manumission "before friends," which was a more informal way of manumitting slaves.

Chrysostom does not comment much on the method of manumission, focusing rather on the motives and purpose. Manumission had an ascetic impetus in Chrysostom's view, because it could be a form of wealth renunciation. Manumission was not good in itself, especially because it could be a display of vainglory. Manumission was at the discretion of the slaveholder, but Chrysostom also tells

89. *Hom. 1 Tim.* 16.2 (F6.144).

90. *Hom. Matt.* 13.4 (PG 57.215.48–54): οὐκ ἂν ἕλοιο τὸν οἰκέτην τὸν εὔνουν γενόμενον τελευτῶν ἀφεῖναι ἄτιμον, ἀλλὰ καὶ ἐλευθερίᾳ ἀμείβῃ, καὶ χρημάτων δωρεᾷ· καὶ ἐπειδὴ αὐτὸς λοιπὸν ἀπιὼν οὐδὲν δύνασαι εἰς αὐτὸν ἐργάσασθαι ἀγαθὸν, τοῖς μέλλουσί σου κληρονομεῖν τῆς οὐσίας ἐπισκήπτεις ὑπὲρ αὐτοῦ, δεόμενος, παρακαλῶν, πάντα ποιῶν, ὥστε μὴ μεῖναι αὐτὸν ἀγέραστον. For more on the issue of posthumous manumission, see John Bodel, "Slave Labour and Roman Society," in Bradley and Cartledge, *Cambridge World History of Slavery*, 1:259–81.

91. *Virg.* 28.1.31–33 (SC 125.184).

92. *Hom. 1 Tim.* 16.2 (F6.144).

93. Harper, *Slavery in the Late Roman World*, 39–49, 181–97.

94. For the methods of manumission, see R. G. Nisbet, "The Festuca and the Alapa of Manumission," *Journal of Roman Studies* 8 (1918): 1–14; A. J. Boudewijn Sirks, "Informal Manumission and the Lex Iunia," *Revue Internationale des Droits de l'Antiquité* 28 (1981): 247–76; Harper, *Slavery in the Late Roman World*, 465–85; Perry, *Gender, Manumission, and the Roman Freedwoman*, 43–68.

slaves not to seek freedom in principle, as we will see in chapter 2.[95] God chooses to keep slaves in bondage, according to Chrysostom, so that the nature of true freedom may be revealed. A slave may ask: "Why did He let him continue as a slave?" (1 Cor. 7:21–22). Some people may have rightly asked how God could not want freedom for slaves. "Just as keeping the bodies of the three boys unharmed with the furnace still burning was much more remarkable than extinguishing it," Chrysostom explains with an analogy from Daniel 3:27, "so demonstrating His freedom with slavery in force was much more important and more remarkable than freeing the slave from it."[96] Chrysostom believed that slaves had much more potential to exhibit spiritual freedom while being enslaved than after manumission. Freedom, then, is quite relative, and also a carceral mechanism.

Even in the New Testament, manumission does not really have much prominence. The imminent eschatology of early Christian thinking was probably the main cause for this philosophical divestiture of manumission—because Christ is coming very soon, it makes no sense to seek freedom. This being said, Chrysostom does tell slaveholders to instruct their slaves in virtue and a trade, and thereafter to manumit them.[97] This type of advice was common in the Roman world, and in fact very important in the mechanics of the slaveholding system. Educating slaves and then manumitting them could be profitable to the slaveholder, but what was more important was that even after manumission, many slaves still continued in the service of their former owners as tradesmen and tradeswomen.[98] There were many successful freed persons in the Roman world, showing how prevalent and effective the system was.[99] It provided the former slave with a means for upward social mobility and also for the acquisition of wealth.[100]

Not all were successful and secure, as Chrysostom has already noted. Freed persons still had numerous obligations to their former owners. A freed person always had to show "gratitude" to his or her former owners; thus, the kyriarchal grip even extended into so-called freedom. In legal terms, this kyriarchal hold on the freed person was called *obsequium,* a rather vague concept that implied a type

---

95. *Hom. 1 Cor.* 19.4–5 (F2.221–25).

96. *Serm. Gen.* 5 (PG 54.600.43–50): Τίνος δὲ ἕνεκεν ἀφῆκε μένειν δοῦλον; Ἵνα τῆς ἐλευθερίας μάθῃς τὴν περιουσίαν. Ὥσπερ γὰρ τοῦ σβέσαι τὴν κάμινον τὴν ἐπὶ τῶν τριῶν παίδων πολὺ θαυμαστότερον ἦν τὸ μενούσης αὐτῆς ἀσινῆ διατηρῆσαι τὰ σώματα· οὕτω τοῦ λῦσαι τὴν δουλείαν τὸ μενούσης αὐτῆς δεῖξαι τὴν ἐλευθερίαν πολλῷ μεῖζόν ἐστι καὶ θαυμαστότερον. Translation: Robert C. Hill, trans., *St. John Chrysostom: Eight Sermons on the Book of Genesis* (Brookline, MA: Holy Cross Orthodox Press, 2004), 84–85.

97. *Hom. 1 Cor.* 40.6 (F2.515).

98. For the manumission and freed status of women in the Roman world, see Perry, *Gender, Manumission, and the Roman Freedwoman.*

99. Mouritsen, *Freedman in the Roman World,* 219–20.

100. Aaron Kirschenbaum, *Sons, Slaves, and Freedmen in Roman Commerce* (Washington, DC: Catholic University of America Press, 1987), 127–30.

of debt that could never be fully repaid to the patron of the freed—*obsequium* could be money, labor, or favors, for example. It was a means of showing one's gratitude for being manumitted.[101] This is also why the metaphor of slavery to God was so effective and common in late ancient Christian discourse, deriving especially from its use in 1 Corinthians 7:21–22. Christ had freed the Christian from slavery to sin and the passions, and in this way the freed person, who was now under the kyriarchal hold of Christ, needed to constantly show gratitude, respect, and service.[102] Thus, outside of abolition, there are no aspects of slavery that are truly in the greater interest of slaves, nor are there any that do not serve the interest of slaveholders.

So the challenge to the scholar of doulology is to be aware of this pervasive yet sustaining carcerality of the slave economy, which seems at face value to be positive, but is actually highly inhuman and tyrannical. One of the further aims of this book is to identify these pervasive carceral mechanisms in Chrysostom's rhetoric, and to expose their function in sustaining slavery. This being said, I believe one of the most important and pervasive carceral mechanisms of the economy of slavery was its interiorization and metaphorization. By having people focus on moral slavery, one immediately shifts the focus away from the oppression of real-life slavery. The interiorization of slavery in the ancient social imagination is worth highlighting.

THE HETERONOMY OF THE BODY: DENATURALIZING AND INTERIORIZING SLAVERY

"But perhaps it was not in this way that the term 'slave' was originally applied— that is, to a person for whose body someone paid money, or as the majority think, to one who was sprung from persons who were called slaves, but rather to the man who lacked a free man's spirit and was of a servile nature," contemplates the first-century Stoic philosopher Dio of Prusa, also called Chrysostom. He continues: "For those who are called slaves we will, I presume, admit that many have the spirit of free men, and among free men there are many who are altogether servile."[103]

The interiorization of the principles of mastery as a practice of subjectivation was a decisive moment in the history of slavery. It was so significant that Dio

---

101. Renato Quadrato, "*Beneficium manumissionis e obsequium*," *Index* 24 (1996): 341–53.

102. *Hom. 1 Cor.* 19.4–5 (F2.221–25).

103. Dio Chrysostom, *2 Serv. lib.* 15.29.1–8 (Cohoon 170–71): ἀλλὰ μὴ οὐχ οὕτως ἢ λεγόμενος ἐξ ἀρχῆς ὁ δοῦλος, ὑπὲρ ὅτου ἀργύριόν τις τοῦ σώματος κατέβαλεν ἢ ὃς ἂν ἐκ δούλων λεγομένων ἢ γεγονώς, ὥσπερ οἱ πολλοὶ νομίζουσι, πολὺ δὲ μᾶλλον ὅσπερ ἀνελεύθερος καὶ δουλοπρεπής. τῶν μὲν γὰρ λεγομένων δούλων πολλοὺς ὁμολογήσομεν δήπου εἶναι ἐλευθερίους, τῶν δέ γε ἐλευθέρων πολλοὺς πάνυ δουλοπρεπεῖς. ἔστι δὲ ὡς περὶ τοὺς γενναίους καὶ τοὺς εὐγενεῖς; Translation: Peter Garnsey, *Ideas of Slavery from Aristotle to Augustine* (Cambridge: Cambridge University Press, 1996), 66.

Chrysostom could not decide whether metaphorical (or moral) slavery existed before institutional slavery. It seems to be a chicken-egg riddle, one that cannot be answered except by speculation. More importantly, it is very problematic to speak about slavery outside of its use as a metaphor, since metaphors and reality, as we read above in Dio's statement, often intersect, overlap, and influence each other. The metaphor of slavery had a direct impact on the economy of slavery, and with all the accompanying carceral mechanisms served to sustain the institution of slavery. We must therefore commence with an act of *désévénementialisation*, isolating this *event* in the history of doulology and using it as a point of departure for the discussions in the chapters that follow. If we want to understand slavery in late ancient Christianity, and in John Chrysostom, we must make sense of how the interiorization of slavery took place.

To trace this development, I will draw on sources predating late antiquity and Chrysostom: most notably, Aristotle, Xenophon, and the Roman agronomists; yet, at the outset I want to emphasize that these ancient sources were fundamentally and directly relevant in shaping later Roman society, and were neither discarded nor ignored during late antiquity. Their relevance will be delineated as the discussion progresses.

To begin, institutional slavery, in ancient thought, presents itself as a subset of a much larger discursive formation in Christian discourse—namely, that of the heteronomy of the body and the polymorphous levels of domination required by the subject. What is meant by this? In ancient Christian thought all bodies were heteronomous; in other words, the body, by definition, was made to be ruled by another. The mode of domination is complex—men could rule over women, but men were also expected to rule or control themselves, and God or sin also ruled over all. These modes of domination were also interconnected, and had an ancient legacy. As early as Plato, in *Alcibiades,* the control and government of others and the city were inseparable from the government of the self.[104] Therefore, in order to comprehend the discourse of slavery, the concept and development of corporeal heteronomy needs to be laid bare, since it is this form of self-governance in early Christian thought that not only defined but also justified the existence of institutional slavery, and vice versa. And, by implication, it is also on account of the heteronomy of the body that many ancient Christian authors simply accepted institutional slavery. It is thus impossible to write a history of slavery, as a discourse, without giving attention to the metaphorization and interiorization of slavery, since the metaphor, in turn, shaped and reshaped the reality of institutional slavery. The heteronomy of the body is the semantic bridge between metaphorical and institutional slavery; it is the basis and starting point of Christian doulology.

104. Foucault, *Hermeneutics of the Subject,* 25–106.

Here I am specifically concerned with how the heteronomy of the body shaped early Christian doulology, and in particular, Chrysostomic doulology. In the first instance, I will attempt to reconstruct late ancient Christian doulology by looking at developments in classical and Hellenistic thought that served as a foundation for Roman slavery, since Christian doulology was simply another expression of Roman doulology. Two important developments will be central to this examination of the formulation of corporeal heteronomy and the foundations of Christian views on slavery: first, the denaturalization (or perhaps better, the "de-Aristotelianization") of slavery in Roman thought in favor of a Xenophonian understanding of slavery based on a strategy of alterization or "othering"; and, second, the popularization of metaphorical and moral slavery by Stoicism and its transfusion into and evolution in Hellenistic Judaism, particularly in Philo of Alexandria, which gave rise to the revolutionary concept of slavery to God. These two developments lie at the core of what would become corporeal heteronomy in early Christian thought, and help illuminate the Christian understanding of slaveholding in the late Roman world.

The Denaturalization of Slavery:
Xenophon and the Agronomists

In some instances, it has become conventional when speaking about the development of slavery in the Roman world to start with Aristotle's famous theory of natural slavery. This theory uses the strategy of naturalization to make sense of the distinction between slaveholders and slaves. To Aristotle, the art of governance was something visible in nature, and nature provided a norm for people to follow.[105] The strategy of naturalization is quite potent, especially in the premodern, prescientific world—"nature" provided something stable, it functioned as a norm, something that should be imitated, and something beneficial.

The concept of nature is of course a conjecture in itself. In current science, there is no such thing as "nature"—there are "natures," and as theories of evolution have shown, nature is anything but stable—nature adapts to its surroundings and reciprocates on the basis of its need to reproduce itself. Nature is, in the same breath, both stable and unstable. In antiquity, however, the discourse of naturalization was

---

105. Studies on slavery in Aristotle's thought include William W. Fortenbaugh, "Aristotle on Slaves and Women," in *Articles on Aristotle,* ed. Jonathan Barnes, Malcolm Schofield, and Richard Sorabji (London: Duckworth, 1975), 2:135–39; Wayne Ambler, "Aristotle on Nature and Politics: The Case of Slavery," *Political Theory* 15, no. 3 (1987): 390–410; Malcolm Schofield, "Ideology and Philosophy in Aristotle's Theory of Slavery," in *Aristoteles' "Politik": Akten des XI. Symposium Aristotelicum,* ed. Günter Patzig (Göttingen: Vandenhoeck & Ruprecht, 1990), 1–27; Eugene Garver, "Aristotle's Natural Slaves: Incomplete Praxeis and Incomplete Human Beings," *Journal of the History of Philosophy* 32, no. 2 (1994): 173–95; Michael Levin, "Aristotle on Natural Subordination," *Philosophy* 72, no. 280 (1997): 241–57; Malcolm Heath, "Aristotle on Natural Slavery," *Phronesis* 53 (2008): 243–70.

a powerful rhetorical strategy for explaining and manipulating sociocultural phenomena.

Aristotle explains natural slavery thus: "For that which can foresee with the mind is the naturally ruling and naturally mastering element, while that which can do these things with the body is the naturally ruled and slave; hence the same thing is advantageous for the master and the slave."[106] Nature is presented as the architect of slavery, and marks the master with foresight (*prooraō*) to command and the slave with body (*sōma*) to labor. Again the link between slavery and corporeality in Aristotle is clear. Aristotle is one of the main sources for the theory of natural slavery. But how influential was the theory of natural slavery in the later Roman world, particularly among early Christian authors like Chrysostom? I will argue here that reliance on Aristotle to reconstruct Roman slavery is problematic, and that we have instead a denaturalization of slavery and proliferation of Xenophonian ideas of slavery.

The reason for the denaturalization is somewhat difficult to determine, but it seems that it may have occurred by chance rather than choice. The status of the Aristotelian corpus during the nascent years of Roman civilization is a highly contested matter.[107] While the legendary accounts of Strabo and Plutarch on the disappearance of the library of Theophrastus, from a broad perspective, seems to be exactly that, mostly legend, there does seem to be some truth to their stories. If we examine the extant catalogues of the Aristotelian corpus—namely, those of Diogenes Laertius, the anonymous *Vita Menagiana,* and especially the medieval Arabic translation of the catalogue of Ptolemy (probably based on the edition of Andronicus)—we see that some treatises that were known in earlier decades fell into disuse for quite some time. Ironically, for the discussion of slavery, Aristotle's *Politica* is one such document (the other being the *Poetica*).

The status and presence of the biological treatises are somewhat more complex. Carnes Lord makes the following astute observation: "Why were the *Politics, Parts of Animals,* and the *Generation of Animals* not included among the works sold to Ptolemy? The two latter works may have been too long and specialized for regular use, and the *HA* [*History of Animals*] was available as an apparent substitute. In the case of the *Politics,* changing political circumstances could readily account for its falling into disuse."[108] While the older Diogenes catalogue, in entry seventy-five,

---

106. Aristotle, *Pol.* 1252a7–1252b5 (Rackham 4): τὸ μὲν γὰρ δυνάμενον τῇ διανοίᾳ προορᾶν ἄρχον φύσει καὶ δεσπόζον φύσει, τὸ δὲ δυνάμενον [ταῦτα] τῷ σώματι πονεῖν ἀρχόμενον καὶ φύσει δοῦλον· διὸ δεσπότῃ καὶ δούλῳ ταὐτὸ συμφέρει. Translation: Carnes Lord, trans., *Aristotle's Politics* (Chicago: University of Chicago Press, 2013), 2.

107. Carnes Lord, "On the Early History of the Aristotelian Corpus," *American Journal of Philology* 107, no. 2 (1986): 137–61; Lord, *Aristotle's Politics,* vii–xli; H. Gregory Snyder, *Teachers and Texts in the Ancient World: Philosophers, Jews, and Christians* (London: Routledge, 2000), 66–92.

108. Lord, "Aristotelian Corpus," 159–60.

cites a "lecture course on politics like that of Theophrastus," it does not seem to indicate that the *Politica* was known to the cataloguer and, as Lord states, "had been supplanted by the similar treatise of Theophrastus for the purposes of the school."[109] This could explain the absence of the notion of natural slavery in later treatises on slave and household management, especially among ancient Roman philosophers and agronomists. The concept is almost completely absent in early Christian writings. While Aristotle's influence is contested (and I must state that I do not assert that it was completely absent) in discussions on domestic slaveholding, Xenophon's influence is much more apparent, especially the influence of his work the *Oeconomicus*. Xenophon is widely cited or alluded to in the agricultural treatises of Cato, Varro, and Columella, and Philodemus's entire treatise *De oeconomia* is aimed at refuting Xenophon and pseudo-Aristotle, or Theophrastus (Philodemus attributed the pseudo-Aristotelian *Oeconomica* to Theophrastus), but not Aristotle per se.[110]

While the availability of Aristotle's *Politica* was extremely limited, the *Oeconomicus* of Xenophon was translated into Latin by Cicero.[111] Xenophon does not subscribe to natural slavery, but rather views slaves as social outsiders subject to suspicion, exclusion, and domination.[112] Of course, I am not saying that Xenophon is the first to promote such a view of slaves, but he was the most influential proponent of this view in the Roman world. Xenophon also supported the notion of holistic household management (*oikonomia*)—the idea that the governance of the household represented a microcosm of state and other macrocosmic examples of government.[113] Aristotle was much more skeptical about holistic *oikonomia*.[114] In

109. Ibid., 161.

110. Philodemus's work on household management is important for its emphasis on the virtue of the householder rather than the profit of the estate; see Marcello Gigante, *Philodemus in Italy: The Books from Herculaneum*, trans. Dirk Obbink (Ann Arbor: University of Michigan Press, 2002); Elizabeth Asmis, "Epicurean Economics," in *Philodemus and the New Testament World*, ed. John T. Fitzgerald, Dirk Obbink, and Glen S. Holland (Leiden: Brill, 2004), 133–76; David L. Balch, "Philodemus, 'On Wealth' and 'On Household Management': Naturally Wealthy Epicureans against Poor Cynics," in Fitzgerald et al., *Philodemus and the New Testament World*, 177–96; Voula Tsouna, *The Ethics of Philodemus* (New York: Oxford University Press, 2007), 164–82; *Philodemus, On Property Management*, Writings from the Greco-Roman World (Atlanta: Society of Biblical Literature, 2012).

111. Jesper Carlsen, *Vilici and Roman Estate Managers until AD 284* (Rome: L'Erma di Bretschneider, 1995), 16.

112. This view has been argued convincingly by Sarah Pomeroy, *Xenophon, Oeconomicus: A Social and Historical Commentary*, trans. Sarah B. Pomeroy (Oxford: Clarendon Press, 1995), 65; Pomeroy, "Slavery in the Greek Domestic Economy in the Light of Xenophon's *Oeconomicus*," *Index* 17 (1989): 11–18.

113. Niall McKeown, "Resistance among Chattel Slaves in the Classical Greek World," in Bradley and Cartledge, *Cambridge World History of Slavery*, 1:153–75.

114. Aristotle distinguished between the rule of masters over slaves (*despoteia*) and governance among free persons (*politikē*). He concluded that one cannot govern the free as one governs slaves; see *Pol.* 1255b16–40 (Rackham 30–31).

late antiquity, however, holistic *oikonomia* became very popular, even with Chrysostom.[115]

Finally, the notion of natural slavery is almost totally absent in late ancient Christian authors. A notable exception here is Athanasius, who seems to subscribe to some theory of natural slavery, probably more influenced by his natural theology and anti-Arian theological presuppositions than Aristotelian naturalization. Influenced by Origen, Athanasius especially emphasizes the notion that all human beings are slaves to God by nature, as Peter Garnsey points out in his discussion of Athanasius's slave language: "Athanasius accepted and reinforced Origen's distinction between sonship by nature and sonship by adoption: Christ was a/the son by nature, we in contrast are slaves by nature. God is our natural master."[116] Garnsey notes that the idea that people are slaves by nature is also present in Augustine's thought.[117] Chrysostom, on the other hand, disagreed with this view, attributing this fact to sin, and the turpitude of slaves to their upbringing.[118]

Thus it was Xenophon, not Aristotle, who had a major influence on Roman slaveholding. Whereas Aristotle promoted the theory of natural slavery, Xenophon's theory of slaveholding was based on alterizing (or othering) rather than naturalizing discourses. As noted above, slave management formed part of the more expansive discourse of *oikonomia*, the art of household governance.[119] But ancient *oikonomia* was an androcentric discourse—one that sought to shape and sustain ancient masculinities.[120] *Oikonomia* was primarily concerned with how a man must master the persons in his house so as to be respectable in the eyes of his peers. The way a man treated his slaves was crucial to his self-fashioning. A man had to exhibit himself as someone who could sufficiently master his slaves.[121]

115. See, for instance, *Hom. Eph.* 22.2 (F4.334–35).

116. Garnsey, *Ideas of Slavery,* 228. Natural Christological slavery is especially prevalent in Athanasius, *Ap. contr. Ar.*

117. Garnsey, *Ideas of Slavery,* 227–28.

118. *Hom. Tit.* 4.1 (F6.298); *Serm. Gen.* 5 (PG 54.599.2–604.40); see chapter 2.

119. For an overview of *oikonomia* in ancient Hellenistic thought, see Carlo Natali, "*Oikonomia* in Hellenistic Political Thought," in *Justice and Generosity: Studies in Hellenistic Social and Political Philosophy,* ed. André Laks and Malcolm Schofield (New York: Cambridge University Press, 1995), 95–128. Household management also played a very important role in early Christian literature; see John Reumann, "The Use of Oikonomia and Related Terms in Greek Sources to about A.D. 100 as a Background for Patristic Applications" (PhD diss., University of Pennsylvania, 1957); Gerhard Richter, *Oikonomia: Der Gebrauch des Wortes Oikonomia im Neuen Testament, bei den Kirchenvätern und in der theologischen Literatur bis ins 20. Jahrhundert* (Berlin: De Gruyter, 2005).

120. Sessa, *Formation of Papal Authority,* 1–2.

121. For more on the issue of masculinity and mastery, see Jonathan Walters, "Invading the Roman Body: Manliness and Impenetrability in Roman Thought," in *Roman Sexualities,* ed. Marilyn B. Skinner and Judith P. Hallet (Princeton, NJ: Princeton University Press, 1997), 29–46; Glancy, *Slavery in Early Christianity,* 10–14.

Principles for governing the household served well as correlates for state governance.

In contrast to Aristotle, the concept of holistic *oikonomia* lay at the heart of Xenophon's work, as Niall McKeown infers: "Xenophon's aim . . . is neither reportage nor even managerial advice; nor is his primary focus slavery. He wants his audience to become better leaders of people. Both the *Memorabilia* and the *Oeconomicus* equate managing a household (an *oikos*) and other forms of power, notably military and political (*Mem.* 3.4.6; *Oec.* 5.14–17, 21.2, 21.12)."[122] Holistic *oikonomia* and its relationship to processes of social othering with regard to slavery were instrumental, in my view, to preparing the ground for Christian corporeal heteronomy. Holistic *oikonomia* suggests that dominance operates on various levels, with an ideological and conceptual congruency between macro- and microcontexts. Aristotle saw governance as something more complex. But if, as in Xenophon's view, *in principle* dominance works the same regardless of context, the implication is that bodies are, *principally,* subject to be ruled—otherwise holistic governance or *oikonomia* would not be possible.

Moreover, from a very early point in classical antiquity, there is conceptual symbiosis between doulology and polemology, or the discourse of war and warfare. Peter Hunt has shown the links between Xenophon's thoughts on slaveholding and the relational dynamics between soldiers and generals.[123] But Xenophon did not believe that slaves belonged in the army, most likely because of his highly aristocratic perception of the military—a view many in the Roman world shared. Slaves were inferior in this sense, not because of their nature, as Aristotle would argue, but because of their egotistical interests and social positioning. Slaves were outsiders, Others, who posed a considerable risk both socially and in a military sense. In her stimulating analysis of Xenophon's *Oeconomicus*, Sarah Pomeroy explains: "At first all three [wife, housekeeper, and farm foremen] are outsiders, who must be transformed into insiders so that they will be concerned as he [the male head] is about the success of the oikos."[124]

The householder therefore must hold a suspicious view of slaves, and very strict corporeal regulation is necessary. Slave bodies, according to Xenophon, must be controlled via the intermediary of the passions, with the strategic use of rewards and punishments. This corporeal control of the passions lies at the core of successful mastery. Xenophon's slaveholder is someone, then, who is quite adept at reading and manipulating the passions of his slaves. For example, Xenophon's states that sexual intercourse or cohabitation can be used successfully as a reward, or

---

122. McKeown, "Resistance among Chattel Slaves," 166.

123. Peter Hunt, *Slaves, Warfare and Ideology in the Greek Historians* (Cambridge: Cambridge University Press, 2002), 144–46.

124. Pomeroy, *Xenophon, Oeconomicus,* 65.

depriving slaves thereof as punishment. These measures of control and mastery were to be translated onto the very architecture of the house. Ischomachus describes the layout of his house so: "Then I pointed out to her the [slave-]women's apartments, separated from the men's by a bolted door, so that nothing may be taken out that shouldn't be and so that the slaves may not produce offspring without our knowledge. For the useful ones, for the most part, feel even better once they have had children, but when wicked ones are paired together, they become only more resourceful in their bad behavior."[125]

Moreover, Xenophon advised slaveholders to allow obedient slaves to have families and never to utter a word of manumission.[126] Manumission may have been very traumatic for some slaves, since it removed them from the ephemeral care of the slaveholder and also broke up families. This shows how pervasive slavery was in antiquity; by its very operation it had systems built in to ensure it remained stable. While manumission may seem positive at first glance, it was far more complex, and actually sustained slavery. Furthermore, when the passions of the slaves are mastered, Xenophon assures his readers, slaves are less likely to run away, steal, or be lazy.[127] Xenophon was in favor of treating slaves well, and taking responsibility for their health, since this boosted productivity and profits for the landowner.

The ideas of the ancient Greek philosophers, and historians of the classical period such as Xenophon, were well known in late antiquity, and having possibly studied under the rhetorician Libanius (or a teacher with similar skills),[128] Chrysostom himself would have been most likely aware of their views. It is also clear in his homilies that he was aware of ancient Athenian views on slaveholding.[129] Thus, it is important to understand the foundational social narratives that continued to shape society even centuries after the passing of their authors. While Xenophon is often referenced in the development of the novel in late antiquity, he was especially influential in the formation of Roman ideas on slaveholding, ideas that persisted into late antiquity.

---

125. Xenophon, *Oec.* 9.5 (Marchant 440–41): ἔδειξα δὲ καὶ τὴν γυναικωνῖτιν αὐτῇ, θύρᾳ βαλανωτῇ ὡρισμένην ἀπὸ τῆς ἀνδρωνίτιδος, ἵνα μήτε ἐκφέρηται ἔνδοθεν ὅ τι μὴ δεῖ μήτε τεκνοποιῶνται οἱ οἰκέται ἄνευ τῆς ἡμετέρας γνώμης. οἱ μὲν γὰρ χρηστοὶ παιδοποιησάμενοι εὐνούστεροι ὡς ἐπὶ τὸ πολύ, οἱ δὲ πονηροὶ συζυγέντες εὐπορώτεροι πρὸς τὸ κακουργεῖν γίγνονται. See Leo Strauss, *Xenophon's Socratic Discourse: An Interpretation of the "Oeconomicus"* (Ithaca, NY: Cornell University Press, 1970), 45.

126. Strauss, *Xenophon's Socratic Discourse*, 45.

127. See Xenophon, *Oec.* 3.3 (Marchant 383–83); *Mem.* 2.1.9 (Marchant 86–87); *Oec.* 21.10–11 (Marchant 524–25).

128. There is still some uncertainty about whether Chrysostom studied under Libanius; Pierre-Louis Malosse, "Jean Chrysostome a-t-il été l'élève de Libanios?," *Phoenix* 62 (2008): 273–80, is doubtful about Chrysostom's tutelage under Libanius.

129. See chapter 6.

Xenophonian ideas about slaveholding, based on alterizing practices and the mastery of slaves' passions, were transmitted to Roman thinking through agronomical literature. After the Punic Wars, the Roman Republic entered a period of vast expansion, which had profound effects on slaveholding.[130] The second century of the republic, especially in Italy, saw the rise of the villa system of landholding,[131] in which estates, mostly owned by illustrious Roman citizens, relied for their operation on very large agricultural tracts that produced cash crops like grapes and olives.[132] The main purpose of the villa estate was to generate products and profits.[133] As Keith Bradley has shown, this process was not a rapid consolidation but a gradual assimilation of smaller landholdings into large estates.[134] This phenomenon was complemented by rapid urbanization as a result of the military expansion of the republic.

Most of the large landholdings had absentee owners, who had to rely on a slave-foreman (called a *vilicus*, or an *epitropos* in Greek) to manage day-to-day operations, including the management of other slaves.[135] These estates had large contingents of slaves who performed most of the labor, and the development of the estates led to the rise of the so-called slave mode of production. Estate management was a topic of discussion for several elite authors of the period. Most notably, the writings of Cato the Elder (*De agricultura*) and Varro (*Rerum rusticarum*) illustrate the requirements of owning a large villa estate. Both are also very concerned with how slaves should be managed. Both Cato and Varro drew directly on

130. Arnold J. Toynbee, *Hannibal's Legacy: Rome and Her Neighbours after Hannibal's Exit* (Oxford: Oxford University Press, 1965), 2:167–70.

131. For more detail on the villa system of landholding, see Elizabeth Fentress, "Spinning a Model: Female Slaves in Roman Villas," *Journal of Roman Archaeology* 21 (2008): 419–22; Roger J. A. Wilson, "Vivere in Villa: Rural Residences of the Roman Rich in Italy," *Journal of Roman Archaeology* 21 (2008): 479–88; Annalisa Marazano, *Roman Villas in Central Italy: A Social and Economic History* (Leiden: Brill, 2007); Andrea Carandini, "La villa romana e la piantagione schiavistica," in *Storia di Roma,* ed. Aldo Schiavone and Andrea Giardina (Turin: Einaudi, 1990), 101–200; Mario Torelli, "La formazione della villa," in *Storia di Roma,* ed. Arnaldo Momigliano and Aldo Schiavone (Turin: Einaudi, 1990), 2:123–32.

132. Harper, *Slavery in the Late Roman World,* 178–79, 195–96.

133. Marazano, *Roman Villas in Central Italy,* 224.

134. Keith R. Bradley, "Slavery in the Roman Republic," in Bradley and Cartledge, *Cambridge World History of Slavery,* 1:241–64.

135. Carlsen, *Vilici and Roman Estate Managers,* 27–56; Egon Maróti, "The Vilicus and the Villa System in Ancient Italy," *Oikumene* 1 (1976): 109–24. The office of the *vilicus* is somewhat complex. *Vilici* were often slaves, but it also happened that *vilici* were freeborn or manumitted slaves; Walter Scheidel, "Free-Born and Manumitted Bailiffs in the Graeco-Roman World," *Classical Quarterly* 40, no. 2 (1990): 591–93. In some cases there were also *subvilici* present on estates; Jesper Carlsen, "Subvilicus: Subagent or Assistant Bailiff?," *Zeitschrift für Papyrologie und Epigraphik* 132 (2000): 312–16.

the views of Xenophon in their understanding of slave management.[136] Manipulating the needs and passions of slaves was central to their argument.[137]

Although the *vilicus* was a surrogate for the absentee owner,[138] the absenteeism of landholders did not escape criticism. The Roman agronomist Columella, writing during the early years of the empire, believed that landowners should be present and directly involved in their estates.[139] In his view, the absenteeism of landowners and the baseness of slaves were the reasons why farming had, according to him, lost its former republican luster: "I do not believe that such misfortunes [bad crops, the decline in fertile soil, and the general state of farming] come upon us as a result of the fury of the elements, but rather because of our own fault; for the matter of husbandry, which all the best of our ancestors had treated with the best of care, we have delivered over to all the worst of our slaves, as if to a hangman for punishment."[140] Although these agronomists do not fall within the period

136. Varro is famously known for his grouping of slaves under "articulate tools" (*instrumentum vocale*), although the difficulties of this Latinism have been duly noted, and there is little certainty about what Varro actually meant by this phrase; see Craige Champion, "Columella's De re rustica," in *The Historical Encyclopedia of World Slavery*, vol. 1, A–K, ed. Junius P. Rodriguez (Santa Barbara, CA: ABC-CLIO, 1997), 174–75.

137. For example, Cato's remarks on slave management are extremely interesting and do show influence from Xenophonian ideas about slaveholding. Cato is a firm believer in the manipulation of slaves' passions; see Joshel, "Slavery and the Roman Literary Culture," 223–24. Slaves who are sick have their rations limited (*Agr.* 2.4), and on rainy days slaves can perform numerous other tasks if they cannot work outside, even if it is simply mending their own clothing (*Agr.* 2.3). Cato is highly specific and detailed regarding the diet of slaves, which is a high-carbohydrate diet with very little protein, fruits, or vegetables (*Agr.* 56–59); see Sandra R. Joshel, *Slavery in the Roman World* (New York: Cambridge University Press, 2010), 131–32; Phyllis P. Bober, *Art, Culture, and Cuisine: Ancient and Medieval Gastronomy* (Chicago: University of Chicago Press, 1999), 183. Cato gives details regarding the consumption of wine, often a contested matter in debates on slave management, and he also advises about the role of slaves in feasts such as the Saturnalia and Compitalia (*Agr.* 57). Clothing and blankets are regulated (*Agr.* 59). These precise guidelines for rationing not only show the intricacy of accounting on these villa estates, but the precise regulations concerning bodily needs reinforce the authority-based hierarchical taxonomy, and also lay bare its complexity. Female and child slaves had their respective roles to fulfill on these estates; Roth, *Thinking Tools*, 15–16. Thus, in Cato we have a source from the second century Republic, one that is very traditional and sentimental. Cato writes to an emerging class of Romans who were extremely wealthy and powerful, but absent from their villa estates. To help them cope with the challenges of this type of management by proxy, Cato writes a detailed and precise guide on *oikonomia* on these villa estates, and also gives advice to men on how to be the best *oikonomos;* see Brendon Reay, "Agriculture, Writing, and Cato's Aristocratic Self-Fashioning," *Classical Antiquity* 24, no. 2 (2005): 331–61.

138. Glancy notes that slaves often served as surrogate bodies for their owners; Glancy, *Slavery in Early Christianity*, 15–16.

139. Champion, "Columella"; Neville Morley, "Slavery under the Principate," in Bradley and Cartledge, *Cambridge World History of Slavery*, 1:265–86.

140. *Rust.* 1.preface.3 (Ash 1:4–5): Nec post haec reor violentia caeli nobis ista, sed nostro potius accidere vitio, qui rem rusticam pessimo cuique servorum velut carnifici noxae dedimus, quam maiorum nostrorum optimus quisque optime tractaverat.

of late antiquity, they are important for understanding later agricultural attitudes and practices. The late ancient agronomist Palladius made use of these writings, especially those of Columella, in his own work on farming, and we should not underestimate their value for the period with which we are concerned.[141] The lack of extensive writing on agriculture from this period also supports the use of these sources.

While these agronomists differed in many ways, they agreed that slave bodies should be manipulated so that they were optimally productive, since the main purpose of an estate was to generate maximum profits; any notion of natural slavery was absent. The Epicurean philosopher Philodemus (110–40 B.C.E.), on the other hand, argued that landowners should be interested not simply in maximizing profits, but should conduct their *oikonomia* in a virtuous manner, including treating their slaves well.[142] It is not that Xenophon, Cato, Varro, and Columella were not concerned about virtue; they simply chose to emphasize economic profitability. These authors also agreed that slaves should not be treated harshly. They said this not only because they feared slave revolts, but also because treating slaves well would ensure optimum productivity. Philodemus wanted the estate manager to be a quasi virtuoso, not only helping to make a profit, but leading people toward the virtuous life—even slaves. This discourse persisted in later Christian rhetoric about slaveholding.[143]

The suspicious attitude of late ancient Christian authors toward slaves is a testament to the influence of the Xenophonian understanding of slavery, and the views of the Roman agronomists. Most late ancient Christian authors, including Chrysostom,[144] accepted the common stereotype that slaves were social outsiders, prone to laziness, theft, and other social vices, and also believed that the passions of slaves should be mastered by the slaveholder to ensure not only good and diligent work but also virtuous behavior. All these authors advised against the harsh treatment of slaves.

Moral Slavery: The Stoics and Philo

The second development in classical and Hellenistic thought that served as a foundation for Roman slavery and influenced late ancient Christian doulology was the spread of the Stoic-Philonic ideology of moral slavery. The development of moral (or, as some call it, "spiritual" or "metaphorical") slavery in ancient thought is complex and difficult to trace. It seems that it emerged from a conceptual

---

141. Carlsen, *Vilici and Roman Estate Managers,* 16–17; Harper, *Slavery in the Late Roman World,* 123.

142. Philodemus, *Oec.* 7.16–26; see Tsouna, *Ethics of Philodemus,* 173.

143. In Chrysostom's case, see *Hom. 1 Cor.* 40.6 (F2.515); *Hom. Eph.* 22.2 (F4.336–37); *Hom. Phlm.* arg. (F6.325–28); *Hom. Tit.* 4.1 (F6.298–99).

144. See *Hom. Tit.* 4.1 (F6.298).

conglomeration of power discourses both from "below," pertaining to the regulation of bodily practices and performances during the Augustan era, and from "above," within Stoic physics and psychotheological discursive formations. Moral slavery also seems to have emerged from the interiorization of the principle of mastery. This principle provided masculinity with a new impetus: it no longer simply depended on the ability to master one's wife, children, and slaves; a man also had to master his passions. It is incorrect, however, to suggest that the operation of interiorization occurred independently of the first development—namely, the denaturalization and alterization of slavery in Roman thought.

An example from the correspondence between Marcus Aurelius and Fronto helps to illustrate this.[145] The young Marcus Aurelius describes his day to his mentor Fronto in a letter. He relates his sleeping patterns, the time he spent with his father and mother, his participation in religious sacrifices, and even his gargling routine. He also says that he read Cato's De agricultura from eleven at night to about five in the morning. Why does Marcus Aurelius mention his reading of Cato? Why, in the first place, does he read Cato, especially at such strange hours while being ill? The entire correspondence is a record of Marcus Aurelius's regimen; it describes his health in terms of sleep, eating, and hygiene, and it also provides insights into his familial and religious duties—all part of his self-fashioning. Marcus Aurelius, destined to be emperor, would probably never only lead the life of a farmer. So why does he read Cato? Because the Roman agronomical writings present the vita rustica as preparing the individual not simply for farming, but for governance. Based on Xenophon's Oeconomicus, Cato's work prepares someone like Marcus Aurelius for domination—not only of others, but also of himself. Agronomical writings such as Cato's thus served a purpose in self-fashioning and subject formation and portrayed both the exterior and the interior dimensions of mastery. Marcus Aurelius reads Cato not to become a farmer, but to become an emperor—one who must govern himself and others.

This interiorization of mastery formed part of a larger socio-intellectual enterprise—the idealization of individualism in Augustan Rome, especially with the Augustan reforms pertaining to the control of sexuality,[146] as well as the rise of Stoic ethics and asceticism.[147] As we have seen above in the case of Marcus Aurelius, the political self is now essentially defined as one who governs himself, and this makes him capable of ruling over others. Unbridled indulgence in the passions was to be avoided. This was enforced juridically by Augustan legislation, and

145. Ep. 4.6 (Haines 180–82); see Foucault, Hermeneutics of the Subject, 160–61.

146. Kristina Milnor, Gender, Domesticity, and the Age of Augustus: Inventing Private Life (New York: Oxford University Press, 2005).

147. Michel Foucault, The Care of the Self, trans. Robert Hurley, vol. 3 of The History of Sexuality (New York: Vintage, 1988), 37–67.

also popularized philosophically by Stoicism (and perhaps even earlier by Cynicism). One's passions had the potential to enslave the self, and true freedom could be gained only when there was control of the passions.

The notion of the soul (*psychē*) also plays a role. While the Christian concept of the soul had hamartiological and soteriological aspects, it also had a very strong ethical background. Foucault juxtaposes the Christian invention of the soul with the formulation of the soul as a power over the body, but I am of the opinion that the distinction proposed by Foucault is not really visible. The notion of the soul as a technology of power and self-control was indeed prevalent in Christianity, especially in patristic literature, because of the strong Stoic influence on early Christian thinking. Foucault has shown how the concept of the soul became a technology of power over the body,[148] and in this formulation the soul represented those mechanisms that should exercise control over the passions. The soul virtually became a prison for the body. It should also be remembered that the soul was seen as a material entity, having a very physical effect on the body; an enslaved soul resulted in the deterioration of the health of the body.[149] In line with the Augustan reforms, Stoic ethics became increasingly concerned with the problem of enslavement to the passions, and here we have the popularization of moral slavery in the Roman world. By means of those psychic technologies of control over bodily passions, the self can truly be free and the body in good health, and this freedom became a defining trait of Roman masculinity.

But the Stoics also promoted a shift from "above" in the development of their physics. In Stoic physics, the principle of holistic *oikonomia* was elevated to a new level in the form of divine *oikonomia*. Stoic physics was very dependent on two interrelated concepts: nature (*physis*) and reason (*logos*).[150] The nature of the cosmos is rational, it is guided by the divine *Logos,* and within nature there is also a certain arrangement or order (*dioikēsis*). Naturalizing a concept therefore gives it not only authority, but also structure—there exists a predetermined order, which is good for copying.[151] Aristotle did the same in his theory of natural slavery, although the Stoics used nature in a different way, which had a direct influence on how they understood both metaphorical and institutional slavery.[152] Not one Stoic author agreed with the concept of natural slavery, although there is also no

148. Michel Foucault, *Discipline & Punish: The Birth of the Prison,* trans. Alan Sheridan (New York: Vintage, 1977), 24–31.

149. Teresa M. Shaw, *The Burden of the Flesh: Fasting and Sexuality in Early Christianity* (Minneapolis: Fortress Press, 1998), 27–74.

150. Reumann, "Oikonomia and Related Terms," 391–402.

151. For more detail on Stoic physics and ethics, see Troels Engberg-Pedersen, *The Stoic Theory of Oikeiosis: Moral Development and Social Interaction in Early Stoic Philosophy* (Aarhus: Aarhus University Press, 1990).

152. Garnsey, *Ideas of Slavery,* 128–29.

evidence of any Stoic directly opposing Aristotle's formulations of natural slavery.[153] The metaphorization of slavery by the Stoics came at the cost of not giving
much attention to the social problem of institutional slavery, often leading to indifference about the matter. The Stoics rather emphasized moral slavery.[154] Because
slavery is not a natural phenomenon, but rather a legal phenomenon and the result
of fate, it makes no difference to one's ability to live a good and virtuous life—it is
merely a social title.[155]

For the sake of brevity, I will use the first-century Stoic writer Seneca's formulation of divine *oikonomia,* moral slavery, and institutional slavery as an example to
illustrate the dynamics of the metaphorization of slavery. Seneca is well known for
his *Epistula 47,* in which he calls for the "humane" treatment of slaves. Seneca
bases this principle on the grounds of divine *oikonomia:*

> Kindly remember that he whom you call your slave sprang from the same stock,
> is smiled upon by the same skies, and on equal terms with yourself breathes, lives,
> and dies. It is just as possible for you to see in him a free-born man as for him to
> see in you a slave. . . . I do not wish to involve myself in too large a question, and
> to discuss the treatment of slaves, towards whom we Romans are excessively
> haughty, cruel, and insulting. But this is the kernel of my advice: Treat your
> inferiors as you would be treated by your betters. And as often as you reflect how
> much power you have over a slave, remember that your master has just as much
> power over you. "But I have no master," you say. You are still young; perhaps you will
> have one.[156]

Masters ought to treat their slaves humanely because they "sprang from the
same stock" or seed (*semen;* in the Greek sense we have the *logos spermatikos*); in
other words, they share the same preexistential origin.[157] In Stoic reasoning, the

153. Peter Garnsey, "The Middle Stoics and Slavery," in *Hellenistic Constructs: Essays in Culture,
History, and Historiography,* ed. Paul Cartledge, Peter Garnsey, and Erich S. Gruen (Berkeley: University of California Press, 1997), 161–62.

154. See Dio Chrysostom, *2 Serv. lib.* 15.29.1–8 (Cohoon 170–71).

155. John T. Fitzgerald, "The Stoics and the Early Christians on the Treatment of Slaves," in *Stoicism
in Early Christianity,* ed. Tuomas Rasimus, Troels Engberg-Pedersen, and Ismo Dunderberg (Grand
Rapids, MI: Baker Academic, 2010), 154–62.

156. Seneca, *Ep.* 47.10–12 (Gummere 306–8): Vis tu cogitare istum quem servum tuum vocas ex
isdem seminibus ortum eodem frui caelo, aeque spirare, aeque vivere, aeque mori! tam tu illum videre
ingenuum potes quam ille te servum. . . . Nolo in ingentem me locum immittere et de usu servorum
disputare, in quos superbissimi, crudelissimi, contumeliosissimi sumus. Haec tamen praecepti mei
summa est: sic cum inferiore vivas quemadmodum tecum superiorem velis vivere. Quotiens in mentem venerit quantum tibi in servum tuum liceat, veniat in mentem tantundem in te domino tuo licere.
"At ego" inquis "nullum habeo dominum." Bona aetas est: forsitan habebis.

157. For more details on this, see Niall McKeown, "The Sound of John Henderson Laughing:
Pliny 3.14 and Roman Slaveowners' Fear of Their Slaves," in *Fear of Slaves—Fear of Enslavement in the
Ancient Mediterranean,* ed. Anastasia Serghidou, Actes du XXIXe colloque international du groupe

spermafunction of the divine *Logos* is that it establishes an isomorphism between the slave and the master.[158] There is also an inherent cyclicality in this type of reasoning. Since nature consists of life cycles—birth, growth, and death—both slave and master are entrapped within these cycles. But there is also the cycle of enslavement, and in one breath a slave can become free, and a master can become enslaved. Similar reasoning is presented by Epictetus, who mentions the universal kinship of humanity,[159] and Cicero, who states that all human beings are the offspring of the gods.[160] There is a telling feature of divine *oikonomia* in Seneca's statement about the power of a master over a slave. Seneca is not only referring to the power of the slaveholder as conferred upon him or her by society. In Stoic thinking the universal *Logos* had a *hegemonikon*, "a soul center from which the powers go into the body,"[161] and this great *hegemonikon* governed power within the cosmos. Seneca's reasoning then entails that while the master may have power over his or her slave, there is also the *hegemonikon* of the universal *Logos* that governs the slaveholder. This view of Stoic physics fed into the previous view that the self had to master its passions. Stoic metaphysical naturalism also denaturalized slavery. These then were the two crucial moves that popularized the notion of metaphorical slavery: the enslavement and/or mastery of the passions by means of psychic technologies of control, and the view of Stoic physics that there is a divine *oikonomia* and a universal *hegemonikon* that governs all of nature.

Stoic physics and ethics were very influential in early Christian thinking, but many of the Stoic ideologies were transmitted into early Christianity through the intermediary of Hellenistic Judaism. This transmission is most clear in the works of Philo and Paul the apostle. In their writings we have the discourses of mastering the passions and divine *oikonomia* intact, although the latter would undergo some evolution. Philo in particular transformed the Stoic concept of divine *oikonomia* into the unique notion of slavery to God.[162] Slavery to the divine is implicit in Stoic writings, as seen above, although it certainly had a different character and emphasis in Philonic literature.

---

international de recherches sur l'esclavage dans l'antiquité (Besançon: Presses universitaires de Franche-Comté, 2007), 265–79; Paul Veyne, *Seneca: The Life of a Stoic*, trans. David Sullivan (New York: Routledge, 2003), 139–43; Guillaume Rocca-Serra, "Le stoicisme pré-imperial et l'esclavage," *CRDAC* 8 (1976): 205–22; Will Richter, "Seneca und die Sklaven," *Gymnasium* 65 (1958): 196–218. The notion of shared origins can be traced as far back as Zeno of Citium—in early Stoicism the idea of a shared primordial fountain was very common; Piet A. Meijer, *Stoic Theology: Proofs for the Existence of the Cosmic God and of the Traditional Gods (Including a Commentary on Cleanthes' Hymn on Zeus)* (Delft: Eburon, 2007), 3–7.

158. Meijer, *Stoic Theology*, 7–8.

159. Epictetus, *Diss.* 1.13.3–4 (Oldfather 100–101); see Jackson P. Hershbell, "Epictetus: A Freedman on Slavery," *Ancient Society* 26 (1995): 185–204.

160. Cicero, *Leg.* 1.24 (Keyes 340–43); see Fitzgerald, "Treatment of Slaves," 156.

161. Meijer, *Stoic Theology*, 5.

162. Byron, *Slavery Metaphors*, 97–116.

In the first century c.e., Philo wrote a treatise entitled *De agricultura*.[163] At this time, when the works of Cato the Elder and Varro on agriculture were well in circulation, there is already a noticeable shift in philosophical thinking toward the notion of the cultivation of the soul—the main theme of Philo's work. Although Cato, for instance, emphasized the importance of maximizing profit from agricultural holdings, it is clear from the letter of Marcus Aurelius that Cato's work on agriculture lent itself to interiorization and self-fashioning. While an author like Philodemus was concerned with how the householder and farmer could fulfill their duties in an ethical manner, rather than focusing only on profit making, with Philo there is a complete shift away from physical agriculture to the cultivation of the soul as a landscape within itself.

The leap from Cato, and implicitly Xenophon, to Philo is not as great as one may think. Agricultural language seems to have been quite useful to Philo in explaining the management of the self, and the metaphor of slavery to the passions is very common in his treatise. Every person is now a farmer, or a shepherd, and the inner workings of the self are related to the dynamics of rural occupations. In *De agricultura* the discourse operates on a very high level of abstraction. The shepherd, for instance, is one who controls bodily appetites as a shepherd controls livestock. In contrast, a cattle feeder is simply one who feeds the desires of the body, and is in fact a slave of the passions. The thinking here is that a shepherd controls the livestock, manages them, while the cattle feeder, who simply feeds the animals, is a slave of them.[164] Philo did not believe that any human being could be totally free, and psychic bondage is only one side of the metaphysical coin. Philo's thinking was firmly entrenched in the notion of corporeal heteronomy. "Since then it has been shown that no mortal can in solid reality be lord of anything, and when we give the name of master we speak in the language of mere opinion, not of real truth," Philo says, "since too, as there is subject and servant, so in the universe there must be a leader and a lord, it follows that this true prince and lord must be one, even God, who alone can rightly claim that all things are His possessions."[165] Whether one is a master over real slaves or a master over one's passions, the fact remains that every master is a slave, a slave of God. The integration of slavery to the passions and slavery to God is seamless. Philo is simply one of the testimonies to the development of what John Byron calls a "Jewish slave of God"

---

163. See Albert C. Geljon and David T. Runia, eds., *Philo of Alexandria, On Cultivation* (Leiden: Brill, 2013).

164. Ibid., 120–62.

165. Philo, *Cher.* 83 (Colson and Whitaker 60–61): ἐπειδὴ τοίνυν θνητὸς οὐδεὶς οὐδενὸς ἐπιδέδεικται παγίως καὶ βεβαίως κύριος, οἱ δὲ λεγόμενοι δεσπόται δόξῃ μόνον, οὐ πρὸς ἀλήθειαν, ὀνομάζονται, ἀνάγκη δ᾽ ὡς ὑπήκοον καὶ δοῦλον, οὕτως ἡγεμόνα ἐν τῷ παντὶ εἶναι καὶ κύριον, γένοιτ᾽ ἂν ὁ τῷ ὄντι ἄρχων καὶ ἡγεμὼν εἷς ὁ θεός, ᾧ λέγειν ἦν πρεπῶδες, ὅτι πάντα αὐτοῦ κτήματα.

tradition.[166] In his *Quod omnis probus liber,* Philo distinguishes between two forms of slavery: institutional slavery and moral/metaphorical slavery.[167] There is a hybridity in Philo's thinking here: he combines the Stoic notion of moral slavery with the view of the believer as a slave of God, the latter of which is undoubtedly an influence from his monotheistic and Jewish background.[168] Slavery to God is an acceptable form of slavery for Philo, and he cites heroes like Abraham and Joseph as exemplary slaves of God. Philo explains: "For to be the slave of God is the highest boast of man, a treasure more precious not only than freedom, but than wealth and power and all that mortals most cherish"[169]

Most importantly, this interlocking of power discourses from Stoic and Philonic philosophy gave rise to the heteronomy of the body. It basically entails that, in ancient Judeo-Christian thought, all bodies were made to be ruled, and true somatic autonomy never really existed[170]—the closest one could get to freedom was to be ruled by the most beneficial force, which also enabled the subject to rule over his or her passions, or submit to them. It is a universal doulologization of bodies.

Unfortunately, as already mentioned, the type of Stoic-Philonic thinking delineated above often leads to indifference with regard to institutional slavery. Most Stoic and Christian authors, including Chrysostom, agreed that one should not be concerned with one's social status as slave or free, but rather with one's moral and spiritual status as being enslaved to the passions or, in the case of Christian thinking, enslaved to sin and the devil. In chapter 2 we will look in detail at how the metaphor of slavery functioned in Chrysostom's homilies through the intermediary of Pauline theology and ethics.

In conclusion, I want to stress again that the border between metaphorical and institutional slavery is opaque at best. This is also why the metaphorization of slavery must be viewed as a carceral mechanism in the economy of slavery. It is not at all possible to understand institutional slavery without examining its metaphorization, since the process of making metaphors of objects entails a complexification and to some extent a universalization of the discourse at hand—it takes the process of enunciation to an extremely potent level, and its power effects become

166. Byron, *Slavery Metaphors,* 47–59. See also Catherine Hezser, *Jewish Slavery in Antiquity* (New York: Oxford University Press, 2006), 323–79.

167. See Charles Duke Yonge, trans., *The Works of Philo: Complete and Unabridged* (Peabody, MA: Hendrickson, 1993); Garnsey, *Ideas of Slavery,* 157–58.

168. For ancient Jewish views on slavery, see Hezser, *Jewish Slavery.*

169. Philo, *Cher.* 107 (Colson and Whitaker 72–73): τὸ γὰρ δουλεύειν θεῷ μέγιστον αὔχημα καὶ οὐ μόνον ἐλευθερίας ἀλλὰ καὶ πλούτου καὶ ἀρχῆς καὶ πάντων ὅσα τὸ θνητὸν ἀσπάζεται γένος τιμιώτερον. See Garnsey, *Ideas of Slavery,* 160–61.

170. Klaus Berger, *Identity and Experience in the New Testament,* trans. Charles Muenchow (Minneapolis: Fortress Press, 2003), 60–69.

distributed over a much wider symbolic expanse, and it often also transforms into other metadiscourses. The metadiscourses born from the metaphorization of slavery include the proliferation of masculinities, racism, and domination of minorities. The study of doulology is then distinctive in its mandate to investigate not only the separate operations of metaphorical and institutional slavery, but also their interactive dynamics with these metadiscourses.

. . .

Slavery studies have fostered extensive development of critical theory, as slavery as a discourse permeates a vast array of fields, from socioeconomic and political studies to archaeology and literary studies, and so on.[171] The development of critical theory is evident in Orlando Patterson's *Slavery and Social Death* (1982), for instance, in which the comparatisms and dialectics of slavery are examined within a very wide historical scope. In the field of early Christian studies, to cite another example, Jennifer Glancy's *Slavery in Early Christianity* (2002) demonstrates the utility of understanding slavery from a corporeal and a habitual perspective, as we have seen above.

This book aims to continue this tradition of utilizing critical theoretical approaches in the study of slavery by examining the discourse of slavery in Chrysostom's homilies, within the wider enterprise that is cultural historiography. More specifically, the approach to slavery here falls within the framework of new cultural history. One of the trademarks of this new paradigm in cultural historiography is its valuation of the body—that is, the history and rhetoric of the body, and its occurrence in discourse and practice. The most important theorists who will figure in my approach to slavery in this book are Michel Foucault, Michel de Certeau, and Pierre Bourdieu, all of whom have made considerable contributions to the development of new cultural theory.

In sum, then, I am interested in revealing the discourse of slavery embedded in Chrysostom's homilies by examining how the slave body is enunciated therein. The slave body does not speak itself, but is spoken for by the operations of corporeal domination. In his earlier work, Foucault showed that this process of creating discourse, the formation of discursive enunciations, occurs as a modal and positional operation. The slave body, then, is not simply enunciated within its discursive framework (that is, the economy of slavery), but is put into discourse from a position, a somatic enunciative modality and positionality—that is, a "mode" in which, and a "position" from which, the slave body is enunciated.

Doulology then enunciates itself from a network of symbolic positionalities, a conceptual and interconnected framework of discourses. It is impossible to

171. For an example of this, one need only examine the list of articles published in the journal *Slavery & Abolition: A Journal of Slave and Post-Slave Studies*.

understand ancient slavery in a discursive vacuum. It has permeated other aspects of ancient life so thoroughly that it is almost impossible to isolate it without seriously affecting its nature. The discourses I will highlight in this instance are the metaphor of slavery and its theologization, which has already been treated in some detail in this introduction, and the modalizations of domesticity—specifically the pastoralization of the household and its slaves, education, discipline and punishment, and sexuality. At the intersection of these discourses and modalizations we find the interlocking of power that epitomizes the kyriarchal hold on the slave body.

Chapter 2 investigates the metaphor of slavery in Chrysostom's theology, as well as the relevance of the heteronomy of the body. Chrysostom was very dependent on the thinking of Paul in this regard, and like Paul, he also juxtaposed slavery to God to slavery to sin and the passions. This chapter explores the role of sin in the dynamics of doulology, since Chrysostom does not attribute slavery to nature or fate, but to sin and disobedience. Central to this discussion is the dynamics of free moral agency, as well as how slavery, through the catalyst of hamartiology (the discourse of sin), functioned in other modes of Chrysostom's theology, especially his anthropology, protology, Christology, and eschatology. Thus, the chapter concerns the theologization of the slave metaphor. Chapter 2 also examines slavery to the passions. Although slavery to sin and slavery to the passions are inseparable in Chrysostom, they have different emphases and implications for behavior and status. The discussion of slavery to the passions in chapter 2 will focus on Chrysostom's reading of 1 Corinthians 7:21–23, and why Chrysostom feels that it is better to be an institutional slave than a slave of sin and the passions.

Chapter 3 examines the place of slavery within Chrysostom's program of domestic pastoralization. The chapter starts by delineating the nature and dynamics of domestic pastoralization, especially as it relates to the slaves in the household. Domestic pastoralization had implications both for the character of the slave in contrast to the wife and children, and for the number of slaves a household was supposed to have. Chapter 3 focuses on the latter to distinguish between strategic slaveholding, based on a large number of slaves, and tactical slaveholding, based on a minimal number of slaves—which Chrysostom promotes. The chapter concludes with an examination of the implications of pastoralization and tactical slaveholding for elite Roman aristocrats, including women, and how pastoralization and tactical slaveholding relate to the crisis of masculinity in the fourth century.

Chapter 4 considers the role of slaves in education and the formation of masculinity according to Chrysostom. Slaves were very involved in educational practices in the Roman world, and their involvement, chapter 4 argues, both reproduced and destabilized patriarchal and kyriarchal power. Attention is given to Chrysostom's comments on the offices of nurse and pedagogue, which were most commonly occupied by slaves or former slaves. The nurse and pedagogue were the most important and influential slave figures in the life of a Roman child. Nurses both suckled and cared for infants, and even after infancy, they helped to protect the modesty of the young Roman girl. Pedagogues were key in guiding the young *filiusfamilias* to manhood. The pedagogue not only had to school the boy in formal education, as a tutor and assistant to the teacher, but also had to teach the boy masculine virtue and what it meant to be a slaveholder. In addition to the nurse and pedagogue, the chapter highlights the role of ordinary household slaves in the education of children. It concludes by looking at how slaves themselves were educated.

Chapter 5 delineates those discursivities related to the discipline and punishment of slaves. The very essence of slave life was the slave's capacity to be disciplined, punished, or rewarded. Chapter 5 starts by looking at how Chrysostom envisions the discipline of slaves, which is directly related to the teaching of virtue, or aretagogy. What was the dynamic between virtue, essentially a discourse of masculinization, and doulology? Why should slaves be taught virtue, and what did it mean for their status and identity as slaves? A second aspect of discipline, which was also part of aretagogy, was surveillance. In ancient thought, slaves always had to be monitored to ensure good productivity and behavior. But how does Chrysostom envision slave surveillance? As will be shown, Chrysostom introduces the notion of the Christic panopticon for the surveillance of slaves. Finally, chapter 5 discusses Chrysostom's comments on the punishment of slaves, specifically the theological justification, methods, and limits of punishment.

Chapter 6 addresses the exploitation, regulation, and restructuring of slave sexualities as presented in Chrysostom. Slaves were viewed as bodies to be used and abused by their owners, especially sexually. Chrysostom opposes such exploitation of slaves, and does so by totally restructuring the concept of slave sexuality within his wide project of domestic pastoralization. Chapter 6 investigates how Chrysostom restructures slave sexuality in the context of his universal sexual ethics related to marriage, adultery, and sexual dishonor; it also explores the problem of prostitution, one of the greatest domestic threats in Chrysostom's view. Finally, the chapter takes up the question of eunuchism and castration.

The conclusion of this book not only summarizes the points raised above, but also looks at their relevance in understanding slavery as a discourse preached by Chrysostom. It is widely accepted that Christianity did not ameliorate slavery; however, Christianity did not leave slavery untouched. Thus, we must ask, what can be deduced from Chrysostom's homilies about how Christianity changed late Roman slavery, and what are the implications of these findings for the broader study of slavery in antiquity?

The purpose of this book is to discover the lost bodies of slaves in the pages of Chrysostom's homilies. The appearance of these bodies is phantasmal at best, and the voices of slaves are silent, without any possibility of being adequately and justly recovered. Slavery is a great failure of humanity, with an enduring legacy. Perhaps then, in analyzing the discourse of slavery as it manifested itself in antiquity in authors like Chrysostom, we may be able to more clearly discern the disturbing legacy of slavery in our own context. In this way, a study on slavery becomes an act of academic activism. If this book can in some way assist in identifying and critiquing the discursive tremors of slavery not only within the project of late ancient cultural historiography, but also in the broader study of slavery in human society, and in some way challenge and resist that oppressive legacy, it will have been a worthwhile endeavor.

2

Divine Bondage

Slavery between Metaphor and Theology

During his service as a priest in Antioch, sometime between 392 and 393, Chrysostom gave a sermon on chapter 7 of Paul's First Epistle to the Corinthians. At one point in the sermon, Chrysostom boldly proclaims: "It is not slavery itself, beloved, that hurts us, but the real slavery is that of sin. . . . And if you are a slave of sin, even though you are ten thousand times free, your freedom is of no advantage."[1] One can only speculate about what the slaves in the audience thought upon hearing a statement such as this. Did they nod in agreement, or feign some emotion, perhaps thinking that this supercilious preacher could not possibly know what it felt like to be a slave? Of course, we will never know. Like most other ancient writers, John Chrysostom used metaphors from his own social world to construct his vision of Christian culture and subjectivity.

Among these metaphors, slavery was often used to describe the dynamics of the Christian life and a Christian's relationship to God.[2] In this chapter I will

1. *Hom. 1 Cor.* 19.6 (F2.224): Οὐχ αὕτη βλάπτει ἡ δουλεία, ἀγαπητὲ, ἀλλ' ἡ φύσει δουλεία ἡ τῆς ἁμαρτίας. . . . ἂν δὲ ταύτης ᾖς δοῦλος, κἂν μυριάκις ἐλεύθερος ᾖς, οὐδὲν ὄφελός σοι τῆς ἐλευθερίας.

2. For a discussion of the metaphor of slavery in Greek and Jewish sources, see, respectively, Kurt A. Raaflaub, *The Discovery of Freedom in Ancient Greece,* trans. Renate Francisono (Chicago: University of Chicago Press, 2004), 203–49; Peter Hunt, "Slaves in Greek Literary Culture," in *The Cambridge World History of Slavery,* vol. 1, *The Ancient Mediterranean World,* ed. Keith Bradley and Paul Cartledge (New York: Cambridge University Press, 2011), 23–47; John Byron, *Slavery Metaphors in Early Judaism and Pauline Christianity: A Traditio-Historical and Exegetical Examination,* Wissenschaftliche Untersuchungen zum Neuen Testament 162 (Tübingen: Mohr Siebeck, 2003). Origen freely utilized the concept of spiritual slavery in his commentaries on scripture, which seemed to have influenced some later authors, such as Jerome and Chrysostom; Ronald E. Heine, *The Commentaries of Origen and Jerome on St. Paul's Epistle to the Ephesians,* Oxford Early Christian Studies (Oxford: Oxford University Press, 2002), 249–50.

examine how the metaphor of slavery, as an expression of Christian corporeal heteronomy, became theologized and was implemented in the making of Christian subjectivity. I will focus on slavery to sin and slavery to the passions, and juxtapose these to what Chrysostom understands as slavery to God. Although slavery to sin and slavery to the passions are inextricably linked in Chrysostom's thought, I will separate them here for the sake of clarity and description. In the discussion of each, I will also ask how the metaphor may have influenced institutional slavery. But first we need to understand Chrysostom's primary source for the metaphor and theology of slavery—the apostle Paul. Relying on the concept of corporeal heteronomy, Paul transformed the concept of slavery to God as it appeared in Philo's works into something distinctly Christian. It was this new Pauline theology of slavery, which integrated the moral and the institutional, that would resonate throughout the centuries of Christianity, and become especially prominent in the thinking of John Chrysostom.

THE METAPHORS WE LIVE BY:
PAUL AND SLAVERY TO GOD

The first Christians used manifold metaphors to articulate that seemingly ineffable interaction between themselves and their God. The most common metaphors were taken from everyday life, especially domestic and other social relationships. God is described as father, son, and brother; God is also seen as a king, a patron, and, of course, a master, and even as a slave. The metaphor of the church as the household of God opens up the possibility of using all of these metaphors to express Christian identity. As we will see in chapter 3, the idea of the church as a household and the priest or bishop as *paterfamilias* had profound consequences for real households and their slaves. But the metaphor of slavery was probably one of the most influential and, at the same time, pervasive forms of speech to seize early Christian discourse. It can be well argued that no other metaphor was as dominant in the formation of early Christian theology and ethics.

From the earliest sources—the epistles of Paul—divine slavery is already advanced in its function. The denaturalization and interiorization of the discourse of slavery had a significant effect on the theology of Paul the apostle, who was the primary influence on Chrysostom's thinking. Paul describes himself, first and foremost, as a slave (*doulos*) of God, and Jesus is described as his "Lord" (*kyrios*; Rom. 1:1; Phil. 1:1). At this point it is necessary to mention that the metaphor of divine bondage in biblical writings often functions within the very syntax of the text, in its vocabulary and grammar, and at other times, more broadly speaking, in its rhetoric. Syntactically, Paul calls himself *doulos* to make sense of his relationship with Christ, and also to project his authority as an emissary of Christ. The term *diakonos* (servant) of course also features in Paul's writings, but more often than not, it is used to describe service to other members of the Christian community. The term *doulos,* in Pauline literature, was not a synonym for *diakonos.* Why mention this seemingly obvious distinction? Because it may appear problematic for some, perhaps more conservative, readers to consider that one of Christ's primary appellations was that of a slaveholder. It is also true that *kyrios* does not always mean "slaveholder" in New Testament texts. However, arguing over the prevalence of the metaphor in syntactical instances in New Testament texts is not exactly helpful. The point is that the metaphor does not work if it is reduced to a form of paid servanthood (slaves also received payment and rewards)—the slave of God metaphor also needs to be seen in its extrasyntactical and rhetorical prevalence in biblical literature. The potency and radicalism of the metaphor lie in its extremity. The slave is one who has no agency outside of the volition of the master; the will of the slave is renounced and totally subservient to that of the slaveholder. Any authority the slave has is not his own; it is a transplanted and surrogate authority. This is more coherent in Paul's views of the relationship between the disciple and Christ. In one of the first letters Paul may have written, Galatians, divine bondage is ingrained in the argumentative essence of the epistle. In Galatians 4:3–9 Paul speaks of enslavement to the *stoicheia,* whether understood as the elements or idols, which implies a rejection of slavery to God. He also uses ample reference to slavery when describing the Law—one is enslaved either to the written law or to the law of Christ. Similar references are found in other authentic Pauline writings.

Paul's letter to the Romans displays the metaphor in an advanced form—here the dichotomy between enslavement to God and enslavement to sin comes to full fruition. The process of Christian subjectivation in the Pauline sense was in many respects a veiled doulologization. In Romans 6:15–23,[3] Paul clearly distinguishes between slavery to God and slavery to sin: "What then? Shall we sin because we are not under the law but under grace? By no means! Don't you know that when you offer yourselves to someone as obedient slaves, you are slaves of the one you

---

3. NA28: Τί οὖν; ἁμαρτήσωμεν, ὅτι οὐκ ἐσμὲν ὑπὸ νόμον ἀλλ' ὑπὸ χάριν; μὴ γένοιτο. οὐκ οἴδατε ὅτι ᾧ παριστάνετε ἑαυτοὺς δούλους εἰς ὑπακοήν, δοῦλοί ἐστε ᾧ ὑπακούετε, ἤτοι ἁμαρτίας εἰς θάνατον ἢ ὑπακοῆς εἰς δικαιοσύνην; χάρις δὲ τῷ θεῷ ὅτι ἦτε δοῦλοι τῆς ἁμαρτίας ὑπηκούσατε δὲ ἐκ καρδίας εἰς ὃν παρεδόθητε τύπον διδαχῆς, ἐλευθερωθέντες δὲ ἀπὸ τῆς ἁμαρτίας ἐδουλώθητε τῇ δικαιοσύνῃ. Ἀνθρώπινον λέγω διὰ τὴν ἀσθένειαν τῆς σαρκὸς ὑμῶν. ὥσπερ γὰρ παρεστήσατε τὰ μέλη ὑμῶν δοῦλα τῇ ἀκαθαρσίᾳ καὶ τῇ ἀνομίᾳ εἰς τὴν ἀνομίαν, οὕτως νῦν παραστήσατε τὰ μέλη ὑμῶν δοῦλα τῇ δικαιοσύνῃ εἰς ἁγιασμόν. ὅτε γὰρ δοῦλοι ἦτε τῆς ἁμαρτίας, ἐλεύθεροι ἦτε τῇ δικαιοσύνῃ. τίνα οὖν καρπὸν εἴχετε τότε; ἐφ' οἷς νῦν ἐπαισχύνεσθε, τὸ γὰρ τέλος ἐκείνων θάνατος. νυνὶ δὲ ἐλευθερωθέντες ἀπὸ τῆς ἁμαρτίας δουλωθέντες δὲ τῷ θεῷ ἔχετε τὸν καρπὸν ὑμῶν εἰς ἁγιασμόν, τὸ δὲ τέλος ζωὴν αἰώνιον. τὰ γὰρ ὀψώνια τῆς ἁμαρτίας θάνατος, τὸ δὲ χάρισμα τοῦ θεοῦ ζωὴ αἰώνιος ἐν Χριστῷ Ἰησοῦ τῷ κυρίῳ ἡμῶν. I have used the NIV translation in this instance because it successfully renders the terminology of slavery to God and to sin.

obey—whether you are slaves to sin, which leads to death, or to obedience, which leads to righteousness?" Paul explains here that being under grace is not a state free from corporeal heteronomy—it is simply a change in ownership. The Christian offers his or her body as a slave unto obedience to God. "But thanks be to God that, though you used to be slaves to sin, you have come to obey from your heart the pattern of teaching that has now claimed your allegiance. You have been set free from sin and have become slaves to righteousness," Paul writes; he uses similar rhetoric in 1 Corinthians 7:21–23. Slavery to God entails freedom from sin, yet the body is unable to rule itself. Paul realized the effectiveness of this metaphor, since it was something his audience was familiar with and saw daily: "I am using an example from everyday life because of your human limitations. Just as you used to offer yourselves as slaves to impurity and to ever-increasing wickedness, so now offer yourselves as slaves to righteousness leading to holiness."

This is why early Christian discourse could not let the opportunity slip to use slavery as a metaphor to illustrate how Christian theology and identity work. This early discourse drew ideological support from and was based on the traditions of Hellenistic Judaism, and it also came from the experiences of everyday life. By the time of Chrysostom the metaphor had developed and functioned on various levels, featuring different types of slaves, like eunuchs, prostitutes, nurses, and pedagogues, to persuade the audience of particular truths. Paul continues: "When you were slaves to sin, you were free from the control of righteousness. What benefit did you reap at that time from the things you are now ashamed of? Those things result in death! But now that you have been set free from sin and have become slaves of God, the benefit you reap leads to holiness, and the result is eternal life. For the wages of sin is death, but the gift of God is eternal life in Christ Jesus our Lord." One of the basic elements in the slaveholding relationship was punishment and reward, and Paul indicates that the same dynamics apply to metaphorical slavery. Obedient slaves of God are rewarded with eternal life, and slaves of sin with death and damnation. This element in the metaphor never changed—it remained intact and is frequently found in Chrysostom's discourse. Just as reward and punishment are used to manipulate the behavior of institutional slaves, so the teachings of eternal life, judgment, and hell are supposed to influence the behavior of slaves of God and slaves of sin.

Thus, in Paul's thinking, as in Philo's, no person is truly a free agent. The body is never autonomous, but always heteronomous—it is always ruled by another. There is a caveat when speaking of the heteronomy of the body, however, and that has to do with the implicit meaning of freedom. It would be anachronistic to understand freedom, as many moderns do today, as complete and independent agency or volition (whether this is even existentially possible has been a matter of debate for centuries). In Paul and Philo, as well as the Stoics, it appears as if freedom is a matter of perspective and disposition. Freedom is a transitory status—

one is "set free" from one master to be enslaved to another. This paradox will receive much attention below. Absolute freedom is absolutely foreign to Pauline thinking. Carcerality is not missing from freedom; in fact, freedom is a powerful carceral mechanism. It is striking that Paul does not use the metaphor of slaves and free persons. Rather, all are slaves, only with different masters, and one is only a freed person in the sense of being freed from sin, but under the patronage of Christ (1 Cor. 7:21–23). The only freedom one perhaps has, according to Paul, is the freedom to choose one's slavery. This observation is crucial to understanding early Christian formulations of free will.

It seems then as if slavery to God was one of the very first and most popular forms of expression in early Christian discourse. While discussing the value of humility in Philippians 2:1–13, Paul cites an early Christian hymn (Phil. 2:6–11). This hymn was probably in circulation in the earliest Christian communities, and in the hymn, Christ himself is described as a humble and obedient slave. The hymn reveals two very important signifiers in the metaphor of slavery and corporeal heteronomy. First, although this is not explicitly mentioned in the hymn, God the father functions as the slaveholder to whom Christ has been obedient, obedient unto death. Second, and perhaps more importantly, Christ becomes a slave only when he takes on human form (Phil. 2:8). The fundamental principle in the hymn is that by becoming human, Christ himself became heteronomous—corporeal heteronomy is a condition of humanity in the hymn. Christ is a slave only while he is in human form, but then the hymn muses that after his exaltation, which seems to imply a return to his divine status, only then does Christ become *kyrios* again, to whom every knee should bow, bowing here being typically an action of slaves and subordinates but also of subjects. Christ was subjected into human form, but after his exaltation, all humans are brought under his subjection. This shows the immense flexibility of the metaphor of slavery especially when used in theological formulations.

Far from falling into disuse, the metaphor of slavery to God was institutionalized and pastoralized in the next decades, and absorbed into Christian teachings on *oikonomia*. Paul's thought was very influential in early Christian theology and ethics, especially in Chrysostom, and as the movement developed, Paul's ideologies also evolved to suit the ethical and theological needs of the community.

In the Deutero-Pauline household codes,[4] metaphor meets reality, and the commands to slaves and slaveholders show a complete fusion between institutional and

4. The household codes are a technical class of literature in the New Testament and Apostolic Fathers that provide domestic instructions to Christian households, specifically on how each household member should behave toward the *paterfamilias,* and vice versa. The household codes are found in Eph. 5:22–6:5, Col. 3:18–4:1, 1 Tim. 2:1ff., Titus 2:1–10, and 1 Pet. 2:13–3:9. Similar codes pertaining specifically to slaves are also found in later documents, like *Doctrina Apostolorum* 4.10–11, *Didache* 4:10–11, and the *Epistle of Barnabas* 19.7; see J. Albert Harrill, *Slaves in the New Testament: Literary, Social, and Moral Dimensions* (Minneapolis: Fortress Press, 2005), 85–118.

metaphorical slavery. One such command is found in Ephesians 6:5–9,[5] one of several parallel passages found in the household codes, where Christians are told how the relationship between slaves, masters, and God works: "Slaves, obey your earthly masters with respect and fear, and with sincerity of heart, just as you would obey Christ." The command is not to seek freedom, even though Paul did advise slaves to do so in 1 Corinthians 7:21–23, as we will see in the course of this chapter. Although early Christianity sought to distinguish itself from various institutions of the Roman world, it did not oppose the institution of slavery. This is the main reason why few early Christian writers promoted the abolition of slavery. Slaves owe obedience to their earthly masters, as stated in Ephesians 6:6–7: "Obey them not only to win their favor when their eye is on you, but as slaves of Christ, doing the will of God from your heart. Serve wholeheartedly, as if you were serving the Lord, not people." As this passage shows, there are no clear lines between institutional and metaphorical slavery in early Christian theology. Being a slave of Christ had real and direct implications for institutional slavery. Christ is depicted as the heavenly slaveholder, so slaves in fact owe a double allegiance, to both their earthly and their heavenly slaveholder, and the work they do in their earthly sphere of domination should be influenced, for the better, by their place in the empyreal sphere. Christ's interests in fact have priority over those of the earthly master. Yet the logic of the text is simplistic, even idealistic; it assumes relationships between slaves and masters are at least moderately reciprocal, and does not make much of those common circumstances where slaves may be abused. Slaves also receive the bulk of the commands.

The element of punishment and reward is still present: "Because you know that the Lord will reward each one for whatever good they do, whether they are slave or free." And the mastership of Christ is emphasized—he is the one who ultimately rewards or punishes. Finally, slaveholders receive a brief yet striking command in Ephesians 6:9: "And masters, treat your slaves in the same way. Do not threaten them, since you know that he who is both their Master and yours is in heaven, and there is no favoritism with him."

This command to slaveholders mirrors Seneca's comments cited in chapter 1. Whereas in Stoic thought the slave and master spring from the same *semen* or *sperma*, and are subject to the same *hegemonikon*, here pseudo-Paul states that both slave and master share the same empyrean domination, they have the same heavenly slaveholder. Because of the heteronomy of all bodies, even though a mas-

---

5. NA28: Οἱ δοῦλοι, ὑπακούετε τοῖς κατὰ σάρκα κυρίοις μετὰ φόβου καὶ τρόμου ἐν ἁπλότητι τῆς καρδίας ὑμῶν ὡς τῷ Χριστῷ, μὴ κατ᾽ ὀφθαλμοδουλίαν ὡς ἀνθρωπάρεσκοι ἀλλ᾽ ὡς δοῦλοι Χριστοῦ ποιοῦντες τὸ θέλημα τοῦ θεοῦ ἐκ ψυχῆς, μετ᾽ εὐνοίας δουλεύοντες ὡς τῷ κυρίῳ καὶ οὐκ ἀνθρώποις, εἰδότες ὅτι ἕκαστος ἐάν τι ποιήσῃ ἀγαθόν, τοῦτο κομίσεται παρὰ κυρίου εἴτε δοῦλος εἴτε ἐλεύθερος. Καὶ οἱ κύριοι, τὰ αὐτὰ ποιεῖτε πρὸς αὐτούς, ἀνιέντες τὴν ἀπειλήν, εἰδότες ὅτι καὶ αὐτῶν καὶ ὑμῶν ὁ κύριός ἐστιν ἐν οὐρανοῖς καὶ προσωπολημψία οὐκ ἔστιν παρ᾽ αὐτῷ. Translation: NIV.

ter is such on earth, he or she still remains under the domination of nonearthly governing forces—in this case, Christ. This represents a perfect fusion between Stoic and Philonic ideas of slavery.

The household codes of the New Testament had a strong influence on Chrysostom's views on slaveholding. The idea of divine bondage was also adopted in other, later New Testament documents. It was a common theme in the parables of Jesus found in the Gospels, where God is often seen as an absentee slaveholder entrusting his estate to his slaves.[6] In the later centuries leading up to Chrysostom's time, Christian doulology developed extensively, but it remained founded on ideas of slavery in the New Testament, particularly those of Paul and pseudo-Paul.[7]

SLAVERY AND SIN

The slave metaphor transformed early Christian subjectivity, and filtered through Christian discourse into Christian theology and ethics. It stands to reason, then, that our discussion of the slave metaphor needs to start with *doulogenia,* or the origins of slavery. What are the origins of slavery, according to Chrysostom? Chrysostom links the birth of slavery, *doulogenia,* with *hamartigenia,* the beginnings of sin (*hamartia*). Thus, I will start by focusing on the function of slavery to God in Chrysostom's teachings on sin, or his hamartiology, and I will also demonstrate how anthropological, Christological, and eschatological elements function in these teachings. Chrysostom and numerous other Christian authors linked both the origins and the consequences of slavery with sin.[8] Slavery to sin is the

6. This is the main theme in Jesus's parable of the talents in Matt. 25:14–30; Luke 19:12–27; see Harrill, *Slaves in the New Testament,* 85–118.

7. Jennifer A. Glancy, "Christian Slavery in Late Antiquity," in *Human Bondage in the Cultural Contact Zone: Transdisciplinary Perspectives on Slavery and Its Discourses* (Münster: Waxmann, 2010), 67–70.

8. Basil, for example, linked slavery to sin and destructive human behavior; see *Spir.* 20.15 (SC 17.253); Peter Garnsey, *Ideas of Slavery from Aristotle to Augustine* (Cambridge: Cambridge University Press, 1996), 14. In one of the most scathing attacks on slavery in the ancient world, Gregory of Nyssa saw in it humankind's thirst for domination. Only God should dominate, so when one human being sought to own and dominate another, he was in fact usurping the role of God—an extreme form of pride and a most horrible sin; see *Hom. Eccl.* 4.1–2 (SC 416.224–28); Rachel Moriarty, "Human Owners, Human Slaves: Gregory of Nyssa, *Hom. Eccl.* 4," *Studia Patristica* 27 (1993): 62–69; Maria M. Bergadá, "La condemnation de l'esclavage dans l'homélie IV," in *Gregory of Nyssa, Homilies on Ecclesiastes: An English Version with Supporting Studies,* ed. Stuart G. Hall, *Proceedings of the Seventh International Colloquium on Gregory of Nyssa (St. Andrews, 5–10 September 1990)* (Berlin: De Gruyter, 1994), 185–96; Hans Boersma, *Embodiment and Virtue in Gregory of Nyssa: An Anagogical Approach* (New York: Oxford University Press, 2013), 146–62. Although from a slightly different theological trajectory, Augustine also linked slavery to sin; see *Civ.* 19.15 (CC 48.682–683); Kyle Harper, *Slavery in the Late Roman World, AD 275–425* (New York: Cambridge University Press, 2011), 213. For a general overview of the relationship between sin and slavery in late ancient Christianity, see Chris L. de Wet, "Sin as Slavery

polar opposite of divine bondage. The idea of slavery to sin represents a significant departure from Stoic thought, which considered slavery the result of fate, an idea that explains the Stoics' indifference to institutional slavery.[9] This protological link between slavery and sin is significant, since it implies recognition of the inherent immorality of slavery—unfortunately this link had little practical consequence.

Chrysostom understands slavery as the consequence of sin, and sin also becomes a form of slavery. "Where does slavery come from?" Chrysostom asks his audience, and then responds:

> Slavery is the result of greed, of degradation, of brutality, since Noah, we know, had no slave, nor Abel, nor Seth, nor those who came after them. The institution was the fruit of sin, of rebellion against parents. Let children listen carefully to this, that whenever they are disobedient to their parents, they deserve to be slaves. A child such as this discards his birthright; for he who rebels against his father is no longer a son; and if he who rebels against his father is not a son, how will he be a son who rebels against our true Father? He has turned his back on his nobility of birth, he has gone against nature. It is also the result of people taken as prisoners in wars and battles.[10]

Linking slavery to the Christian myth of origins and cosmogony is curious; origin myths and protologies describe not so much how things came into being, but why things are the way they are in the present, and they also insinuate how things ought to be. They explain, affirm, and justify current realities and also provide a rationale for various social and cultural institutions, practices, and rituals. How should this link between slavery and sin be understood? Chrysostom believed that human beings were originally created with the capacity to exercise moral freedom (*autexousia*).[11] Why then does sin cause slavery according to Chrysostom? The

---

and/or Slavery as Sin? On the Relationship between Slavery and Christian Hamartiology in Late Ancient Christianity," *Religion & Theology* 17, nos. 1–2 (2010): 26–39.

9. Garnsey, *Ideas of Slavery*, 151–52.

10. *Hom. Eph.* 22.1 (F4.334): Ἡ πλεονεξία τὴν δουλείαν ἔτεκεν, ἡ βαναυσία, ἡ ἀπληστία· ἐπεὶ Νῶε δοῦλον οὐκ εἶχεν, οὐδὲ Ἄβελ, οὐδὲ Σὴθ, ἀλλ' οὐδὲ οἱ μετὰ ταῦτα. Ἁμαρτία τοῦτο τὸ πρᾶγμα ἔτεκεν, ἡ εἰς τοὺς πατέρας ὕβρις. Ἀκουέτωσαν οἱ παῖδες, ὅτι ἄξιοί εἰσι δοῦλοι εἶναι, ὅταν εἰς τοὺς πατέρας ἀγνώμονες ὦσιν. Ἀφείλετο ἑαυτοῦ ὁ τοιοῦτος τὴν εὐγένειαν· ὁ γὰρ ὑβρίζων τὸν πατέρα, οὐκ ἔστιν ἔτι υἱός. Εἰ δὲ ὁ πατέρα ὑβρίζων, οὐκ ἔστιν υἱὸς, ὁ τὸν ὄντως ἡμῶν Πατέρα ὑβρίζων, πῶς ἔσται υἱός; Ἐξῆλθεν ἀπὸ τῆς εὐγενείας, ἐξύβρισεν εἰς τὴν φύσιν. Εἶτα καὶ πόλεμοι καὶ μάχαι αἰχμαλώτους ἔλαβον.

11. See *Hom. Gen.* 19.1 (PG 53.158.44–160.30); Pagels compares Chrysostom's reading of Gen. 1–3 with that of Augustine, with some interesting results. Chrysostom believed that human beings were created with free will, while Augustine eventually saw the corruption of the human will as a seminal event—corruption takes place within the *semen*—and so all people are conceived and born into the slavery of sin. While Chrysostom believed that people could regain their *autexousia* by means of *askēsis* and mastery of the passions, Augustine saw this as a type of neurosis—an illness caused by guilt; Elaine Pagels, "The Politics of Paradise: Augustine's Exegesis of Genesis 1–3 versus That of John Chrysostom,"

moment that sin entered human existence, it disrupted the harmony of human relationships and marred the first human couple's capacity for *autexousia;* in other words, it created the need for governance, which then took a turn for the worst and resulted in slavery, which is also a form of punishment to Chrysostom. In the discussion about slavery in Chrysostom's *Sermo in Genesim* 4, the hamartiological link renders slavery not a natural but an unnatural phenomenon. In several instances in *Adversus Judaeos* Chrysostom notes that Israel's various exiles and enslavements were the result of its sin and disobedience, and that even in the preacher's own time Israel is still enslaved.[12] The only natural form of government present before sin takes place is the hierarchy of male over female.[13] Interestingly, Chrysostom notes that humans also originally ruled over animals as they rule over slaves (note the animalization of the slave), yet sin caused this form of governance to diminish.[14] The husband's government over his wife is natural, yet a master ruling over a slave is due to sin. "From the beginning, God made only one form of government, placing man over woman," Chrysostom explains, "but after our race ran aground into much disorder, other forms of rule appeared, that of slaveholders,

Harvard Theological Review 78, no. 1–2 (1985): 83–85. For a more general discussion of free will in other Greek church fathers, see Robert L. Wilken, "Free Choice and the Divine Will in Greek Christian Commentaries on Paul," in *Paul and the Legacies of Paul,* ed. William S. Babcock (Dallas: Southern Methodist University Press, 1990), 123–40. Raymond J. Laird also makes several important points in *Mindset, Moral Choice and Sin in the Anthropology of John Chrysostom,* Early Christian Studies 15 (Strathfield: St. Paul's, 2012). Laird argues that notions of free will and sin should be understood in the wider context of mind-set (*gnōmē*).

12. *Adv. Jud.* 5.5 (PG 48.891.29–31), 6.2 (PG 48.905.20–907.19); also *Hom. Gen.* 19.1–2 (PG 53.158.44–162.3).

13. The status of man's natural governance over woman is unclear in Chrysostom. In his *Serm. Gen.* 4 (PG 54.594.3–55), which Robert Hill dates to 386, Chrysostom says that male and female were originally created equal (ὁμότιμος), but that the woman exchanged her governance for submission because of her disobedience; Robert C. Hill, trans., *St. John Chrysostom: Eight Sermons on the Book of Genesis* (Brookline, MA: Holy Cross Orthodox Press, 2004), 1–2, 63–64. In this sermon, the governance seems unnatural and postlapsarian, like slavery, a result of sin. But in his *Hom. 1 Cor.* 34.7 (F2.427), which was probably preached in 392 or 393, as well as in his *Hom. Eph.* 20.2–3 (F4.308–12) and 22.1–2 (F4.334–37), delivered even later, in 396 or 397, Chrysostom notes that from the beginning God created man to rule and woman to be submissive. Is Chrysostom being inconsistent? Did he change his mind later in his ministry? Or was he perhaps admonished for his claim regarding prelapsarian equality in *Serm. Gen.* 4 (hence the explicit and repeated emphasis against equality of male and female in the later homilies)? While the present study is not the avenue for addressing this problem in detail, since it would imply comparing more of the source material, I will assume (for now) that the governance between male and female is natural and prelapsarian in Chrysostom's thought. For the provenance of the exegetical homilies, see Wendy Mayer, *The Homilies of St John Chrysostom—Provenance: Reshaping the Foundations,* Orientalia christiana analecta 273 (Rome: Pontificio Istituto Orientale, 2005), 181–88.

14. *Serm. Gen.* 3 (PG 54.590.16–593.26).

that of secular governors."[15] Sin introduced the need for and humiliation of labor, causing humanity to earn its living "by the sweat of your brow" (Gen. 3:19).

For Chrysostom, even secular government is not natural, but a result of sin.[16] Juridical structures are necessary for controlling the consequences of sin.[17] This is also why Chrysostom never questions the legal aspects of owning slaves—slavery falls within the scope of general law and is necessary for managing the effects of sin. He also believes that ascetic piety removes the need to be governed, since righteous people do not need to be punished.[18] Chrysostom envisioned that truly pious Christians had no need for slaves or secular governance. The rise of slavery, and other forms of secular government and dominance, are the result of the decline of *autexousia*. Chrysostom does believe that freedom of will and moral choice are attainable especially by means of a correct moral mind-set (*gnōmē*),[19] and this form of freedom is equated with divine bondage. A person's free will, however, always functions within the dynamics of God's merciful aid.[20] The most striking example of an agent of free will for Chrysostom is the apostle Paul. In his encomium on Paul, Chrysostom affirms that it was Paul's freedom from the passions and his free will (*proairesis*) that led to his various victories.[21]

In addition to being based on notions of moral freedom and the need for governance, origin myths that link slavery and sin operate within the discourse of nature and naturalization—they explain, or provide a standard for, more often than not, what must be seen as natural and unnatural. Chrysostom made a distinction between natural and artificial forms of government.[22] Naturalization is also, at the same time, normalization, and denaturalization serves to abnormalize and pathologize. Thus, the discursive construction of nature also rationalizes principles of theodynamics. "Nature" often serves as a synonym for, or at least, an

---

15. *Hom. 1 Cor.* 34.7 (F2.427): Καὶ ἐξ ἀρχῆς μὲν μίαν ἐποίησεν ἀρχὴν, τὸν ἄνδρα ἐπιστήσας τῇ γυναικί· ἐπειδὴ δὲ εἰς πολλὴν ἐξώκειλεν ἀταξίαν τὸ γένος ἡμῶν, καὶ ἑτέρας κατέστησε, τὰς τῶν δεσποτῶν, τὰς τῶν ἀρχόντων·

16. *Hom. 1 Cor.* 40.6 (F2.515); *Hom. Eph.* 22.1 (F4.335–36); see Pagels, "Politics of Paradise," 70.

17. *Stat.* 6.1–2 (PG 49.81.14–84.26); Pagels, "Politics of Paradise," 72.

18. *Stat.* 6.2 (PG 49.83.15–84.26); Pagels, "Politics of Paradise," 73. This was the polar opposite of Augustine, as Pagels shows, who believed that even the most pious ascetics need ecclesiastical government, since all human beings are seminally corrupted by sin; see *Civ.* 13.14 (Levine 180–81); Pagels, "Politics of Paradise," 80–81.

19. Laird, *Mindset, Moral Choice and Sin*, 36.

20. *Hom. Heb.* 12.3 (F7.153–55); see Georg Kontoulis, *Zum Problem der Sklaverei (ΔΟΥΛΕΙΑ) bei den kappadokischen Kirchenvätern und Johannes Chrysostomus* (Bonn: Habelt, 1993), 325–329.

21. See *Laud.* 5.3 (SC 300.234–36), 6.3–7 (SC 300.264–74); Margaret M. Mitchell, *The Heavenly Trumpet: John Chrysostom and the Art of Pauline Interpretation* (Louisville, KY: Westminster John Knox Press, 2002), 169, 198, 214, 246–50.

22. *Stat.* 7.3 (PG 49.94.19–95.42); Pagels, "Politics of Paradise," 70.

inference of "God."[23] The *ordo naturalis* is congruent with the *ordo Dei*. But slavery was denaturalized in the Roman period, especially in Christian literature. The move to denaturalize slavery facilitated what we can call its hamartiologization. I stress here that Aristotelian natural slavery was not at all absent in late antiquity—it may have been rather prevalent as a popular discourse, especially since we see that Chrysostom makes some effort to refute natural slavery.

Chrysostom is vehement on this point, and insists that "it is admitted that the race of slaves is inordinate, not open to impression, stubborn, and does not show much aptitude for being taught virtue"; he warns, however, that it is "not from their nature, it cannot be, but from their bad upbringing, and the neglect of their masters."[24] Chrysostom makes it very clear that slaves are not slaves by nature, but because of their upbringing and social neglect—it is nurture, not nature, that corrupts the "race" of slaves. Thus, since sin is not part of God's natural intent, slavery is also not part of the natural course of affairs—it is an artificial form of governance born out of necessity related to sin. What is the purpose, then, of this hamartiological link with slavery in Chrysostom's thought? The slavery/sin coadunation anchors itself in four fundamental points of Christian discourse.

First, the metaphor of slavery to God is qualified by linking slavery to sin.[25] Being in a state of institutional enslavement is not a sin per se; however, being in sin means being enslaved to it. Yet, Chrysostom argues, as we just saw above, that slaves are prone to sin and vice, but not because of nature, but because of social circumstances. The slavery/sin link, then, serves as a type of conceptual scaffold that supports the bifurcation of reality and dichotomization of human subjectivity to which the slavery to God/sin metaphor lends itself. Thus, sin caused both institutional and moral slavery; they share the same root. There is no grey area in this instance; one is either a slave of sin or a slave of God. This is how reality is constructed and how human subjectivity is identified.

Second, the original unity of slavery and sin authorizes the intensive labor ethic we find in late ancient Christianity and especially in Chrysostom. What does this mean? In Chrysostom's mind, each person has been created by God to be self-sufficient, which means that slavery is not a necessity. Necessity (*anankē*) was a

23. John J. Winkler, *The Constraints of Desire: The Anthropology of Sex and Gender in Ancient Greece* (New York: Routledge, 1990), 17–18; Elizabeth A. Clark, "Ideology, History and the Construction of 'Woman' in Late Ancient Christianity," in *A Feminist Companion to Patristic Literature*, ed. Amy-Jill Levine and Maria M. Robbins (London: T&T Clark, 2008), 111.

24. *Hom. Tit.* 4.1 (F6.298): [καὶ πανταχοῦ] τοῦτο διωμολόγηται, ὅτι τὸ τῶν δούλων γένος ἰταμόν πώς ἐστι, δυσδιατύπωτον, δυστράπελον, οὐ σφόδρα ἐπιτήδειον πρὸς τὴν τῆς ἀρετῆς διδασκαλίαν, οὐ διὰ τὴν φύσιν, μὴ γένοιτο, ἀλλὰ διὰ τὴν ἀνατροφὴν καὶ τὴν ἀμέλειαν τὴν παρὰ τῶν δεσποτῶν. See *Serm. Gen.* 5 (PG 54.599.2–604.40).

25. See Wulf Jaeger, "Die Sklaverei bei Johannes Chrysostomus" (PhD diss., Christian-Albrechts-Universität zu Kiel, 1974), 157–201.

very important virtue to Chrysostom. Chrysostom's labor ethic is based on and authorized by anthropogony and Christomorphism. "The class of slaves did not originate out of necessity at all," Chrysostom observes, "otherwise a slave would have been created along with Adam; but it is the penalty of sin and the punishment of disobedience."[26] From a labor perspective, slaves are unnecessary. However, just after making this remark, Chrysostom famously adds that if there is a need, people should own no more than one or two slaves. There is a double irony here: in the very same paragraph, Chrysostom contradicts himself. Anthropogenically speaking, slaves are not necessary; human beings were created to be self-sufficient. But if someone cannot be without slaves, own only one or two at the most is Chrysostom's advice. There is also a self-renunciative Christomorphism in this labor ethic, which adds a great deal of authority to the argument. This self-renunciation is modeled on the example of Christ—since Christ, the slavemaster of all, performed service, the onus is even greater on human slaves of God to serve. Alluding to Philippians 2:5–11, Chrysostom notes that Christ took the form of a slave to free humankind from slavery to sin.[27] It stands to reason then that slaves of God are co-slaves (*syndouloi* or *homodouloi*) of each other.[28] Chrysostom explains:

> For Christ is Teacher and Lord, but you are fellow-slaves of one another.... Christ washed the feet of the traitor, the sacrilegious, the thief, and that close to the time of his betrayal, and immedicable as Judas was, he made him partake of his table. And are you pompous, and do you raise your eyebrows? "Let us then wash one another's feet," says someone, "well, then we must also wash the feet of our domestic slaves." And why is it a great thing if we wash the feet of our slaves? Here with us "slave" and "free" simply consists of a difference of words; but when Christ was washing his disciples' feet, it was truth by actions. For by nature he was Lord and we were slaves, yet even this service he did not refuse to do. But now, beloved, it is acceptable if we do not treat free persons as slaves, like menial slaves bought with money.[29]

26. *Hom. 1 Cor.* 40.6 (F2.515): Οὐδὲ γὰρ χρείας ἕνεκεν τὸ τῶν δούλων ἐπεισήχθη γένος, ἐπεὶ μετὰ τοῦ Ἀδὰμ ἐπλάσθη ἂν καὶ δοῦλος· ἀλλ' ἁμαρτίας ἐστὶ τὸ ἐπιτίμιον, καὶ τῆς παρακοῆς ἡ κόλασις.

27. *Hom. Jo.* 4.4 (PG 59.50.36–51.53).

28. The notion that Christians are *syndouloi* (Chrysostom uses the term *homodouloi* at times) to each other is a very early development. The concept is very common in Deutero-Pauline literature. Paul is Christ's slave, and hence his companions are *syndouloi* (Col. 1:7, 4:7). The concept also features in the parable of the unforgiving servant in Matt. 18:21–35. In Rev., the term is already synonymous with fellow Christians (Rev. 6:11). Ignatius also uses the term extensively (*Eph.* 2.1 [Ehrman 220–21]; *Mag.* 2 [Ehrman 242–43]; *Phld.* 4 [Ehrman 286–87]; *Smyr.* 12:2 [Ehrman 308–9]); see BAGD4). Chrysostom saw the emperor as a fellow slave to the general population; *Stat.* 7.3 (PG 49.94.54–56).

29. *Hom. Jo.* 71.1 (PG 59.385.51–52, 385.60–386.20): Αὐτὸς μὲν γὰρ διδάσκαλος καὶ Κύριος, ὑμεῖς δὲ ἀλλήλων ὁμόδουλοι.... Τοῦ προδότου τοὺς πόδας ὁ Χριστὸς ἔνιψε, τοῦ ἱεροσύλου καὶ κλέπτου, καὶ παρὰ τὸν καιρὸν τῆς προδοσίας, καὶ ἀνιάτως ἔχοντα τραπέζης κοινωνὸν ἐποίησε· καὶ σὺ μέγα φρονεῖς καὶ τὰς ὀφρῦς ἀνασπᾷς; Τοὺς πόδας οὖν ἀλλήλων νίπτωμεν, φησίν· οὐκοῦν καὶ τῶν οἰκετῶν. Καὶ τί μέγα, εἰ καὶ τῶν οἰκετῶν; Ἐνταῦθα μὲν γὰρ ὁ δοῦλος καὶ ὁ ἐλεύθερος, ὀνομάτων ἐστὶ διαφορά· ἐκεῖ δὲ, πραγμάτων

Christ provided the foundation and example for the self-renunciative Christian labor ethic. It is based on the concept that Christ is the empyreal slaveholder and all Christians are slaves of Christ. Yet because Christ set the example of service, despite his lordship, service becomes inherently a Christomorphic operation.[30] We also see something resembling the natural theology of Athanasius in this passage—Christ is Lord by nature. Chrysostom also affirms here that the lordship of Christ and divine bondage are a greater reality than institutional slavery. The argument of nature surfaces again. Christ is by nature Lord, and people ought to be, by nature, his slaves—hence the unnaturalness of slavery to sin. The Christological use of nature and slavery here should not be confused with Aristotelian natural slavery. Slavery to God is natural, according to Chrysostom, but institutional slavery is not natural. Since Christ renounced his lordship and served others, so too Christians must renounce pride and mastery over others and serve those who may appear to be of a lesser status. Chrysostom is uncomfortable with institutional slavery, but we should not lose sight of the fact that this type of slavery to Christ removed the attention from the problem of slavery and also resulted in a rhetoric that insisted slaves should remain enslaved and be content with it. The example here of free persons serving slaves also seems to be more hyperbole than an actual command, although we can speculate that it may have occurred in some instances for symbolic value, as it does even today.

Chrysostom also uses the metaphor of buying slaves to illustrate the relationship between Christ and his slaves. He takes this degrading practice and provides it with a new, religious impetus. In an address to catechumens preparing for baptism, Chrysostom states:

> And as when we buy slaves, we first ask those who are being sold if they are willing to be our slaves, so too does Christ. When he is about to receive you into his service, he first asks if you want to leave that cruel and harsh tyrant, and he receives agreements from you. For his domination is not forced on you. And behold the kindness of God. For before putting down the price, we ask those who are being sold, and when we have determined that they are willing to serve us, only then do we confirm the price. But this is not the case with Christ; he put down the price for us all—his precious blood. *For, he says, you were bought with a price* [1 Cor. 7:25]. And furthermore, he does not even force those who are unwilling to serve him. But except if you

---

ἀλήθεια. Φύσει γὰρ αὐτὸς Κύριος ἦν, καὶ ἡμεῖς δοῦλοι, καὶ οὐδὲ τοῦτο παρητήσατο νῦν ποιεῖν. Νυνὶ δὲ ἀγαπητὸν, εἰ μὴ τοῖς ἐλευθέροις ὡς δούλοις ἡμεῖς χρησαίμεθα, ὡς ἀνδραπόδοις ἀργυρωνήτοις.

30. Chrysostom uses the notion of Christ taking the form of a slave to rebuke several heretical traditions denying the humanity of Christ. Christ humbled himself by setting the example of servanthood. This of course was not subordinationism, since Christ was restored—it was rather the formation of an ethical model that followers of Christ are supposed to imitate; see *Hom. Phil.* 8[7] (F5.74–75); Pauline Allen, trans., *John Chrysostom, Homilies on Philippians*, Writings from the Greco-Roman World 16 (Atlanta: Society of Biblical Literature, 2013), 115.

have grace, he says, and by your own choice and volition decide to subjugate yourself under my rule—I do not compel you, I do not force you. And we should not have chosen to purchase wicked slaves. But if we decided to do so at some point, we buy them with a bad choice, and put down an appropriate price for them. But Christ, when buying ungrateful and lawless slaves, puts down the price of a top-quality slave, even much more, and so much greater that neither word nor thought is able to compare its magnitude.[31]

The salvific moment of repentance and baptism is likened to God's purchasing of a slave, based on the metaphor Paul uses in 1 Corinthians 7:23. We can see here the high level of abstraction on which the slavery to God metaphor functions. The metaphor is meticulously and strategically constructed. Each human being is regarded as a slave of a terrible master, a tyrant, in this case referring to the symbolic kyriarchal constellation of sin, the passions, and Satan. Christ is still a slaveholder, but he is merciful and kind. The price paid for the slave is the ultimate one—the blood of Christ. The death of Christ ransoms Christians from the bondage of sin and evil. What is most important for Chrysostom, however, is the presence of free choice—the symbolic slave has the agency to choose a better master. The metaphor is structured to highlight the free moral agency of the slave—he or she must choose Christ, Christ asks them if they want to be his slaves. The corporeal heteronomy is again visible in this instance. Finally, the price is not dependent on the quality of the slave—unlike the case in actual earthly slave deals, even the wicked slaves receive the best price (although they are then, of course, expected to renounce their wickedness). Salvation is here sketched as the perfect slave transaction, supposedly from the perspective of the slave. The two elements that provide the most value to the metaphor are the agency of the slave, and the quality of the price paid.

It is quite poignant that Chrysostom, at times, comes so very close to dismissing and even abolishing slavery, and yet, at other times, his rhetoric imprints slavery onto the very fabric of Christian society and ideology. It is also ironic that the

31. *Illum. catech.* 2.5 (PG 49.239.17–37): Καὶ καθάπερ ἡμεῖς οἰκέτας ἀγοράζοντες, αὐτοὺς τοὺς πωλουμένους πρότερον ἐρωτῶμεν, εἰ βούλονται ἡμῖν δουλεῦσαι, οὕτω καὶ ὁ Χριστὸς ποιεῖ· ἐπειδὴ μέλλει σε εἰς δουλείαν λαμβάνειν, πρότερον ἐρωτᾷ, εἰ βούλει τὸν τύραννον ἐκεῖνον ἀφεῖναι τὸν ὠμὸν καὶ ἀπηνῆ, καὶ συνθήκας δέχεται παρὰ σοῦ· οὐ γὰρ κατηναγκασμένη αὐτοῦ ἡ δεσποτεία ἐστί. Καὶ σκόπει Θεοῦ φιλανθρωπίαν. Ἡμεῖς μὲν γὰρ πρὶν ἢ τὴν τιμὴν καταβαλεῖν, ἐρωτῶμεν τοὺς πωλουμένους, καὶ ἐπειδὰν μάθωμεν, ὅτι βούλονται, τότε τὴν τιμὴν καταβάλλομεν· ὁ δὲ Χριστὸς οὐχ οὕτως, ἀλλὰ καὶ τὴν τιμὴν κατέβαλεν ὑπὲρ ἁπάντων ἡμῶν, τὸ τίμιον αὐτοῦ αἷμα. Τιμῆς γὰρ, φησὶν, ἠγοράσθητε· καὶ ὅμως οὐδὲ οὕτως ἀναγκάζει μὴ βουλομένους αὐτῷ δουλεῦσαι, ἀλλ᾽ εἰ μὴ χάριν ἔχεις, φησὶ, καὶ παρὰ σαυτοῦ καὶ ἑκὼν θέλεις ἐπιγράψασθαι τὴν δεσποτείαν, οὐκ ἀναγκάζω οὐδὲ βιάζομαι. Καὶ ἡμεῖς μὲν οὐκ ἂν ἑλοίμεθα πονηροὺς οἰκέτας πρίασθαι· εἰ δὲ καὶ ἑλοίμεθά ποτε, αἱρέσει κακῇ τούτους ἀγοράζομεν, καὶ τοιαύτην καταβάλλομεν τιμήν· ὁ δὲ Χριστὸς ἀγνώμονας οἰκέτας ἀγοράζων καὶ παρανόμους, πρωτείου δούλου τιμὴν κατέβαλε, μᾶλλον δὲ πολλῷ μείζονα, καὶ τοσούτῳ μείζονα, ὡς μηδὲ λόγον μηδὲ ἔννοιαν αὐτῆς παραστῆσαι τὸ μέγεθος.

very labor ethic that principally denies the need for slaves also contributes to keeping slaves in bondage. Chrysostom believed that masters and slaves should serve one another. So since both master and slave should be slaves to God and each other (cf. Gal. 5:13), it makes no difference whether slaves remain enslaved or are emancipated. This inconsistent Christian labor ethic both negated the necessity of slavery and, at the same time, sustained it.

Third, the conjunction of slavery and sin has an eschatological function. Slavery has always played a role in the formulation of early Christian eschatology.[32] This is especially evident in the parables of Jesus. Two parables in particular illustrate how central slavery was to early Christian eschatology—the parable of the faithful slave[33] and the parable of the talents.[34] Both of these parables compare the kingdom of God to the typical organization of a villa estate, and the followers of Jesus to slaves working on these landholdings. Both deal with the problem of Christ's second coming, the *parousia*. Christ is depicted here as the absentee landowner who has entrusted his estate to his slaves, including the *vilicus,* or slave-foreman—an image that is typical in Roman agronomical literature.[35] The slave-foreman must then manage the estate until the unexpected return of the master. The faithful slave does a good job, but the wicked one abuses his power and oppresses other slaves. When the master finally arrives, the faithful slave is rewarded, and the wicked slave punished.

The parable of the talents follows a similar logic, where the master leaves and entrusts his capital to his slaves, who need to do business and make a profit—a common arrangement in Roman society, especially on villa estates. Slaves often acted as accountants and financial managers.[36] The slaves who made a profit are rewarded, but the slave who was fearful and buried his talent is punished. The most important drama of the Christian eschatological theater—the coming of Christ—is modeled on the practice of agricultural slavery, a phenomenon that was familiar to the rural audience of Jesus.

32. See D. Bentley Hart, "The 'Whole Humanity': Gregory of Nyssa's Critique in Light of His Eschatology," *Scottish Journal of Theology* 54, no. 1 (2001): 51–69; Harrill, *Slaves in the New Testament,* 89–91, 228–33.

33. See Matt. 24:42–51; Mark 13:34–37; Luke 12:35–48.

34. See Matt. 25:14–30; Luke 19:12–28. See also J. Albert Harrill, "The Psychology of Slaves in the Gospel Parables: A Case Study in Social History," *Biblische Zeitschrift* 55 (2011): 63–74.

35. Harrill has shown how this ideology developed from sources like the Deutero-Pauline household codes and the parables of Jesus; Harrill, *Slaves in the New Testament,* 85–118. It was not uncommon for a landowner to entrust the management of the villa estate to the *vilicus;* Jesper Carlsen, *Vilici and Roman Estate Managers until AD 284* (Rome: L'Erma di Bretschneider, 1995); Harper, *Slavery in the Late Roman World,* 139–42.

36. See Cato, *Agr.* 2.7–8 (Hooper 8–9); Varro, *Rust.* 1.17.5–6 (Hooper and Ash 226–29), 1.18.6–8 (Hooper and Ash 230–31); Sandra Joshel, *Slavery in the Roman World* (New York: Cambridge University Press, 2010), 56.

Chrysostom interprets these parables with an emphasis on virtue—the estate and goods that the slaves of God ought to manage and increase are virtue.[37] The reward they receive is salvation, and the punishment is damnation. The image of eternal punishment is especially informed and justified by the punishment of institutional slaves. The punishment for sin is equal to the punishment of disobedient slaves. "If slaves should destroy the family of their masters, if they should insult them to their faces, if they should steal everything, if they should overturn everything, if they should treat them as enemies, and they would not threaten them, nor discipline them, nor punish them, nor even verbally admonish them," Chrysostom asks, "would this be any sign of goodness?" Rather, Chrysostom concludes: "Is it not a sign of goodness to punish, and of cruelty not to punish, and is it not so in the case of God? Since he is good, he has therefore prepared a hell."[38] Once again, the theodynamics of punishment are based on the logic of slavery— God punishes, as any good slaveholder ought to. The real punishment of slaves informs this metaphor, but then the metaphor of God who punishes his slaves, in turn, justifies the punishment of institutional slaves.

The use of fear is very important for Chrysostom. Eschatological judgment instills fear in both God's slaves and institutional slaves. In fact, according to Chrysostom, teaching delinquent slaves about eternal judgment is an excellent way to discipline, subjugate, and normalize them:

> When it is therefore seen that the power of religion, imposing a restraint upon the class of slaves who are naturally so self-willed, has rendered them singularly well behaved and gentle, their masters, however unreasonable they may be, will form a high opinion of our doctrines. For it is clear that having previously instilled in their souls a fear of the resurrection, of the judgment, and of all those things which we are taught by our philosophy to expect after death, they have been able to resist wickedness, having in their souls a firm principle to counterbalance the pleasures of sin.[39]

The teaching of eschatology and the consequences of sin function as a technology for disciplining and normalizing slaves. And when these Christian slave bodies are

---

37. See *Hom. Matt.* 77.3–4 (PG 58.705.12–707.53), 78 (PG 58.711.2–718.5).

38. *Hom. Phlm.* 3.2 (F6.352): Καὶ τί λέγω οἰκέτας τοὺς προχειρότερον ἐπὶ τὰ ἁμαρτήματα ταῦτα ἐρχομένους; 'Αλλ' ἐχέτω τις υἱοὺς, καὶ πάντα ἐπιτρεπέτω τολμᾶν ἐκείνοις, καὶ μὴ κολαζέτω, τίνος οὖν οὐκ ἔσονται χείρους, εἰπέ μοι; Εἶτα ἐπὶ μὲν ἀνθρώπων τὸ κολάζειν ἀγαθότητος, τὸ δὲ μὴ κολάζειν ὠμότητος, ἐπὶ δὲ Θεοῦ οὐκέτι; Ὥστε ἐπειδὴ ἀγαθός ἐστι, διὰ τοῦτο γέενναν προητοίμασε.

39. *Hom. Tit.* 4.1 (F6.298–99): Ὅταν οὖν ἴδωσιν, ὅτι τὸ γένος τὸ οὕτως αὔθαδες ἡ τοῦ κηρύγματος δύναμις χαλινὸν περιθεῖσα πάντων εἰργάσατο κοσμιώτερον καὶ ἐπιεικέστερον, κἂν σφόδρα πάντων ὦσιν ἀλογώτεροι οἱ δεσπόται, λήψονται ἔννοιαν μεγάλην περὶ τῶν δογμάτων τῶν παρ' ἡμῖν. Δῆλον γὰρ ὅτι καὶ τὸν περὶ τῆς ἀναστάσεως φόβον καὶ τὸν τῆς κρίσεως καὶ τὸν τῶν ἄλλων ἁπάντων μετὰ τὸν θάνατον φιλοσοφουμένων παρ' ἡμῖν πρότερον ἐγκαταθέντες αὐτῶν τῇ ψυχῇ, οὕτως ἴσχυσαν ἀποκρούσασθαι τὴν κακίαν, ἀντίρροπόν τινα φόβον τῆς ἀπὸ τῶν κακῶν ἡδονῆς εἰς τὴν ἑαυτῶν ἐνιδρύσαντες ψυχήν.

docile and subjugated, they become a testimonial to the power of Christianity. The effects are both personal and institutional. Thus, Christian slaves are supposed to be well behaved and harder workers—better slaves!—than non-Christian slaves. This then adds to the productivity of slaves and, more generally speaking, enhances the Christian labor ethic. Rather than rejecting the oppression of slaveholding, many Christian authors believed that when slaves and slaveholders became Christians, they should become better in those roles. Christian slaves should be "better" slaves, because they worked harder for Christ, and Christian slaveholders should be better at managing slaves, which did not exclude punishing them for disobedience. Other Christian authors had similar views. Cyprian, for instance, hardly notices the problem of owning slaves, but seems to move the issue onto a level of labor relations, also noting that Christian slaves should be better workers.[40] Ambrosiaster also admonishes Christian slaves to work more diligently than their non-Christian counterparts.[41]

More disturbingly, Christian eschatological teaching directly contributed to the physical abuse and punishment of enslaved people. Because Christ punishes the disobedience and sin of his own slaves, so too must earthly slaveholders punish unruly slaves on earth.[42] To Chrysostom this is an act of salvation. The discourse of love appears here; God punishes his slaves because he loves them, and the same is expected in earthly slave-slaveholder relationships—the just punishment of slaves is seen as an act of love. Love here is curative, an act of correction and normalization. This is an extremely important moment in the Christian understanding of punishment. True correction and punishment is an act of care and love; the paternal language of love aims to soften the blow of the whip. As we will see in the course of this book, the language of love was very common in Christian doulology; it was an effective means of habituating and normalizing slaves to accept their oppression. It is especially in Chrysostom's eschatology, then, that the implications of slavery to sin as disobedience, and its effects on institutional slaveholding, are laid bare.

Fourth, the notion of asceticism is common in the rhetoric of slavery/sin. Chrysostom's ideal was for no one to own any slaves, not because of the oppressiveness of slavery, but because the use of slaves is linked to luxury and is not a necessity.[43] This view was shared by many other Christian authors, most notably the Cappadocian

---

40. Cyprian, *Test.* 3.72 (PL 4.771); see Glancy, "Slavery and the Rise of Christianity," 473.

41. Ambrosiaster, *Comm. 1 Cor.* 7.21 (CSEL 81.2.79; see Sophie Lunn-Rockliffe, *Ambrosiaster's Political Theology,* Oxford Early Christian Studies (New York: Oxford University Press, 2007), 97–102.

42. Chrysostom also uses the comparison between having been a slave and now being a son of God. But being a son of God, and having sinned, incurs an even greater punishment, since sons who commit slavish offenses, according to Chrysostom, are punished more severely; see *Hom. Matt.* 12.4 (PG 57.206.35–207.46); *Comm. Gal.* 4 (F4.66–76). This comparison is found in Gal. 4:1–7; see Sam Tsang, *From Slaves to Sons: A New Rhetoric Analysis on Paul's Slave Metaphors in His Letter to the Galatians,* Studies in Biblical Literature 81 (New York: Peter Lang, 2005).

43. *Hom. 1 Cor.* 40.6 (F2.515); *Hom. Eph.* 13.3 (F4.241).

fathers.[44] In Chrysostom we will see how slaveholding and slave management become a spiritual exercise, an *askēsis,* not only an important tool for fashioning Christian subjectivity, but also an apparatus for displaying one's self-renunciation. Slaveholding becomes an ascetic exercise, for instance, when one has few or no slaves, or performs acts of mass manumission. It is inherently a strategy to earn Christian honor and elevate one's status. Chrysostom does, however, seem to believe that slavery is an inevitable social reality, and negotiates with this reality by having people own one or two slaves at the most. Taking his urban audience into account, Chrysostom typically avoids being rigoristic, instead advising ascetic moderation; if he had been preaching to monks living in the wilderness, his advice would probably have been different. Commanding urban Christians to own no slaves at all would be perceived as telling them to eat only dry bread and drink water—abolition would have been understood by many in the audience as extreme and unrealistic ascetic rigorism. Since the choice to have few or no slaves is a form of *askēsis* and wealth renunciation, it is also a move closer to the prelapsarian state. We have then the ideal of a society without slaves, a slaveless world, where there is no distinction between slave and free. Chrysostom's labor ethic is based on this social ideology—although there are still slaves, Christians ought to behave *as if* the distinction does not exist; ironically, this slaveless labor principle simply sustained institutional slavery.

Both the ascetic and labor-related effects of this ideal vision of society are based on the idea that Christ does not recognize social status, and, as before the Fall, the distinction between slave and free will not exist in heaven. All claims for the current earthly dispensation without slaves are then part of a realized eschatology, a manifestation of God's heavenly kingdom in the material temporality. This basically entails that some utopian and postapocalyptic principles are already partially affected in the present. The annulment of status distinctions is one of the most common examples of a realized eschatology. In this regard, Chrysostom reiterates: "In the kingdom of heaven there is no master and slave; all are slaves, all are free. And do not think the proverb is a riddle, for they are indeed slaves of each other, and masters of each other."[45] This slaveless ideal is also found in earlier Christian discourse. One of the most famous baptismal formulas of the early church, found in Galatians 3:28,[46] showcases this realized eschatology, and it is certainly one of

44. See Gregory of Nyssa, *Hom. Eccl.* 4.1–2 (SC 416.224–28); Basil, *Spir.* 20.15 (SC 17.253–55); Gregory of Nazianzus, *Paup. am.* (PG 35.857.61–909.42); see Kontoulis, *Problem der Sklaverei,* 119–301; Ilaria Ramelli, "Gregory of Nyssa's Position in Late Antique Debates on Slavery and Poverty, and the Role of Asceticism," *Journal of Late Antiquity* 5, no. 1 (2012): 87–118.

45. *Hom. Matt.* 69.4 (PG 58.653.37–40): Οὐκ ἔστιν ἐκεῖ δεσπότης καὶ δοῦλος· πάντες δοῦλοι, πάντες ἐλεύθεροι. Καὶ μὴ νομίσῃς αἴνιγμα εἶναι τὸ εἰρημένον· καὶ γὰρ δοῦλοι ἀλλήλων, καὶ δεσπόται ἀλλήλων εἰσίν.

46. The text reads: "There is neither Jew nor Greek, there is neither slave nor free, there is no male and female, for you are all one in Christ Jesus" (NA28: οὐκ ἔνι Ἰουδαῖος οὐδὲ Ἕλλην, οὐκ ἔνι δοῦλος

the more common verses quoted in Christian literature. Yet, noted above, the eschatological ideal of having no slaves did not erode the institution of slavery in late ancient society; rather, it sustained it.

There is another effect of this slaveless ideal. When status and class distinctions are ignored, slaves are subject to the same value standards as any other person. While this may seem laudable, it is likely that it made life very difficult for slaves. The universal social measure of value in late ancient Christianity was virtue, but virtue itself was a very masculine discourse. Chrysostom was very vocal about teaching slaves virtue—it was the duty of the *paterfamilias* to educate his slaves in virtue.[47] Slaves who did not meet these standards were subject to punishment. Methods of training varied from peaceful exercises like reading scripture to violent and intrusive behavior manipulation. Sometimes a slave, especially a licentious female slave, had to be chained and locked up in the house to be compelled to accept chastity.[48]

Texts such as these, which project an isomorphism of social status in the context of a realized eschatology, cannot, therefore, be taken at face value. A text like Galatians 3:28 presupposes a tripartite realized eschatology: nonethnic ("neither Jew nor Greek"), statusless ('slave nor free"), and asexual ("male nor female"). But maintaining this schema proves difficult for Chrysostom—he believes that both men and women, slave and free, are capable of attaining virtue, yet he still upholds the patriarchal hierarchy of husband and wife,[49] and never does he suggest the abolition of institutional slavery.[50] Thus, this statusless and asexual (or androgynous) idealization is not an isomorphism—everyone is not made equal—but rather a subsuming of the weaker subjectivity (female/enslaved) into the stronger

οὐδὲ ἐλεύθερος, οὐκ ἔνι ἄρσεν καὶ θῆλυ· πάντες γὰρ ὑμεῖς εἷς ἐστε ἐν Χριστῷ Ἰησοῦ). A similar but later variation on this text is found in Col. 3:11: "Here there is not Greek and Jew, circumcised and uncircumcised, barbarian, Scythian, slave, free; but Christ is all, and in all" (NA28: ὅπου οὐκ ἔνι Ἕλλην καὶ Ἰουδαῖος, περιτομὴ καὶ ἀκροβυστία, βάρβαρος, Σκύθης, δοῦλος, ἐλεύθερος, ἀλλὰ [τὰ] πάντα καὶ ἐν πᾶσιν Χριστός).

47. See *Hom. 1 Cor.* 40.6 (F2.515); *Hom. 1 Tim.* 16.2 (F6.141–43); *Hom. Tit.* 4.1 (F6.298–99); *Hab. eun. spir.* 3.7 (PG 51.287.4–8); see chapter 4 in this book.

48. *Adv. Jud.* 2.124ra; this description comes from the rediscovered text of the second discourse; see Wendy Pradels, Rudolf Brändle, and Martin Heimgartner, "Das bisher vermisste Textstück in Johannes Chrysostomus, *Adversus Judaeos*, Oratio 2," *Zeitschrift für antikes Christentum* 5 (2001): 22–49. See also Susanna Drake, *Slandering the Jew: Sexuality and Difference in Early Christian Texts*, Divinations (Philadelphia: University of Pennsylvania Press, 2013), 89.

49. Martin provides a good overview of this tension in Chrysostom; Dale B. Martin, *Sex and the Single Savior: Gender and Sexuality in Biblical Interpretation* (Louisville, KY: Westminster John Knox Press, 2006), 85–86.

50. In all fairness toward Chrysostom, he does acknowledge, with some frustration, that there is some tension in the realization of Gal. 3:28 in church and society; see *Hom. 1 Cor.* 12.6 (F2.145–46).

(masculine/free); it is a process of masculinization.[51] The consequence of this real-ized eschatology is that for females and slaves there is no social equality,[52] only a very difficult set of standards to which it is practically impossible to adhere. Despite their disadvantaged and oppressive background, and the lack of support structures that free men have access to, such as education and civic honor, slaves are now expected to conform to the same measure of virtue as free men. So once again, the theologico-ethical language of slavery serves to disadvantage institu-tional slaves.

Chrysostom's views on slavery and sin were deeply embedded in his wider theologico-ethical framework. But along with his theological use of the metaphor of slavery to sin and to God, we also have the notion of being enslaved to the pas-sions and, along with this, a very developed yet paradoxical view of "true" spiritual freedom.

THE PARADOX OF FREEDOM AND SLAVERY
TO THE PASSIONS

We know very well that one of the main influences on Chrysostom's theology was the apostle Paul.[53] The problem is that Paul's own thoughts on slaveholding are not always clearly articulated in the authentic Pauline sources, and like many interpreters,[54] Chrysostom reads Paul in such a way as to suit his own agenda for the development of Christian subjectivity. One of the most difficult Pauline per-icopes about slavery is found in 1 Corinthians 7:21–23—specifically, in verse 21. The text reads (NA28): *doulos eklēthēs, mē soi meletō; all' ei kai dynasai eleutheros genesthai, mallon chrēsai.* Initially the translation seems simple: "Were you a slave when you were called? Do not let it trouble you, but if you can become free . . . "; then the Greek text reads: *mallon chrēsai.* A very literal translation might read:

---

51. See Martin, *Sex and the Single Savior,* 83–85; Johannes N. Vorster, "Androgyny and Early Christianity," *Religion & Theology* 15, nos. 1–2 (2008): 97–132.

52. Despite some similarities, Chrysostom's views on the government of women and the govern-ment of slaves are quite different. The rule of a man over a woman was natural, but not men ruling over men, as in the case of slavery and regular secular governmentality; see chapter 3.

53. For a general overview of Chrysostom's appropriation of Paul and Paulisms, see Mitchell, *Heavenly Trumpet.* Chrysostom also envisioned the formation of Christian identity as a type of Pauli-nomorphism. For Chrysostom, Paul was much more than a mere hermeneutical key. "Rather, Paul and Paulinomorphism were the dominant language of ecclesiastical power. . . . In Chrysostom's reconstruc-tion of Paul all the necessary elements constituting a powerful political apparatus converge, a perfect discursive storm of power"; Chris L. de Wet, "Paul and Christian Identity-Formation in John Chryso-stom's Homilies *De laudibus sancti Pauli apostoli,*" *Journal of Early Christian History* 3, no. 2 (2013): 45.

54. Pervo gives an excellent overview of how Paul was constructed in the early Christian centu-ries; see Richard I. Pervo, *The Making of Paul: Constructions of the Apostle in Early Christianity* (Min-neapolis: Fortress Press, 2010).

"rather use [it]." But what is it that the Corinthian slaves should use? Is it their freedom, their enslaved status, their calling from God? The verse is littered with grammatical, syntactical, and semantic ambiguities due to the brachylogy evident in this expression. Not to mention the numerous possibilities for translating the Greek verb *chraomai*. I will refrain from discussing the various options for interpreting this verse here—they are numerous, complex, and problematic, and will not add much to the argument at hand.[55] My own view is that Paul probably meant that people ought to seek and use their freedom to serve the Christian community, but my view is beside the point. How did Chrysostom interpret this verse?

Chrysostom's commentary on 1 Corinthians 7:21–23 can be found in his *Homiliae in epistulam I ad Corinthios* 19.5–6.[56] His reading of the phrase *mallon chrēsai* is supplemented with the phrase *mallon douleue* ("rather remain a slave"), and thus supports the idea that slaves should remain enslaved and *not* seek freedom, since Paul means "that slavery is not a hindrance, but rather an advantage."[57] The same interpretation of the verse is also given in the preface of Chrysostom's homiletic series on Philemon.[58] Chrysostom does acknowledge that *mallon chrēsai* poses an exegetical problem, and he affirms that some read the term as referring to seeking freedom. Chrysostom's view, however, seems to represent that of the majority of patristic writers.[59] Early writers like Ignatius of Antioch believed that slaves should retain their bondage in service to God, and actually states that slaves should not seek to be set free at the church's expense.[60] Like Chrysostom, Ignatius also resorts to the argument of metaphorical slavery to remove the focus from institutional slavery. Authors like Ambrose[61] and Ambrosiaster[62] also prefer to focus on the problem of moral slavery when reading this verse. The exceptions

---

55. Studies dealing with this problem in 1 Cor. 7:21 are S. Scott Bartchy, ΜΑΛΛΟΝ ΧΡΗΣΑΙ: *First Century Slavery and 1 Corinthians 7:21*, SBL Dissertation Series (Missoula, MT: Society of Biblical Literature, 1973); Hans Conzelmann, and James Waterson Leitch, trans., *1 Corinthians: A Commentary on the First Epistle to the Corinthians*, Hermeneia (Philadelphia: Fortress Press, 1975), 127; Gordon D. Fee, *The First Epistle to the Corinthians*, New International Commentary on the New Testament (Grand Rapids, MI: Eerdmans, 1987), 315–20; Martin, *Slavery as Salvation*, 66–70; J. Albert Harrill, *The Manumission of Slaves in Early Christianity*, Hermeneutische Untersuchungen zur Theologie 32 (Tübingen: Mohr Siebeck, 1998), 74–75; Anthony C. Thiselton, *The First Epistle to the Corinthians*, New International Greek Testament Commentary (Grand Rapids, MI: Eerdmans, 2000), 553–59; Byron, *Slavery Metaphors*, 234–40.

56. F2.221–25.

57. *Hom. 1 Cor.* 19.5 (F2.222): Θέλων δεῖξαι, ὅτι οὐδὲν βλάπτει ἡ δουλεία, ἀλλὰ καὶ ὠφελεῖ.

58. F6.325–28.

59. Thiselton, *First Epistle to the Corinthians*, 554–55.

60. Ignatius, *Pol.* 4.3 (Ehrman 314–15).

61. Ambrose, *De virg.* 1.3 (PL 16.266.15–267.5).

62. Ambrosiaster, *Comm. 1 Cor.* 7.21 (CSEL 81.2.79); see Lunn-Rockliffe, *Ambrosiaster's Political Theology*, 103–5.

here seem to be Origen[63] and Jerome,[64] who understand that slaves should use the opportunity of freedom to serve their calling.

To support his substitution of *mallon douleue* for *mallon chrēsai*, Chrysostom proposes, first, that Paul did not attach any value to social status, alluding to Galatians 3:28, and that slavery did not by any means influence one's personhood. This was typical Stoic thinking on the status of enslavement—it was a matter of indifference (*adiaphoron*). According to Chrysostom, Paul, like the Stoics, did not take social status into consideration, and thus neither freedom nor enslavement had any benefit over one another in the eyes of God. In *De virginitate* 41.59–66,[65] where this verse is also cited, Chrysostom states that neither virgins nor slaves should shun their status, but use it to glorify God. As virgins should not seek marriage, so too slaves should not seek freedom. This is a striking example of where indifference to institutional slavery in fact sustained the oppressive practice.

Chrysostom's second premise for this reading is based on the admonitions to slaves in the Deutero-Pauline household codes.[66] Since these household codes never motivate slaves to forsake their masters and seek freedom,[67] so too this verse should be read in the light of these principles. We have, then, an entire economy of Pauline and Deutero-Pauline texts working in tandem, in which institutional and metaphorical slavery function interchangeably. These are the main threads in Chrysostom's exegetical tapestry of 1 Corinthians 7:21. But what stands out in this homily is how Chrysostom uses the metaphor of divine bondage to directly manipulate institutional slavery. Having dealt with the problem of *mallon chrēsai* in verse 21, Chrysostom continues to expand on the significance of moral slavery:

> Incredible! Where has Paul placed slavery? In the same way that circumcision has no benefit, and not being circumcised has no disadvantage—neither does slavery nor freedom bear any advantage. . . . He wants to show that slavery is no hindrance but rather an advantage. . . . *For the one that was called in the Lord while being a slave, is the Lord's freed person; in the same way, the one that was called, being free, is Christ's slave* [1 Cor. 7:22]. For Paul says, regarding the things that relate to Christ, both are equal [Gal. 3:28; Col. 3:11]; and as you are the slave of Christ, so also is your master. How then is the slave a freed person? Because Christ has freed you not only from sin, but also from outward slavery while continuing to be a slave. For he does not allow the slave to be a slave, not even if such a person is someone enslaved; and this is a great wonder. But how is the slave free while continuing to be a slave? When this

63. Origen, *1 Cor. frag.* 38.5–21 (Jenkins 9.353ff.).
64. Jerome, *Jov.* 1.11 (PL 23.234.47–237.10).
65. SC 125.240.
66. Chrysostom specifically quotes 1 Tim. 6:1–2, and refers, in passing, to the household codes in Eph. 6:5–9 and Col. 3:22–4:1.
67. Glancy, *Slavery in Early Christianity*, 132–52.

person is freed from the passions and the diseases of the soul, frowning upon riches, and anger, and all other similar passions.[68]

Having determined the fundamentals of Chrysostom's exegesis of the troublesome phrase *mallon chrēsai,* we now need to examine his interpretation more closely. The passage cited above raises several questions. First, how can institutional slavery be advantageous? Chrysostom sees slavery as an opportunity to impress non-Christian outsiders. By rendering *mallon chrēsai* as *mallon douleue,* the church shows both social and juridical continuity with ancient culture, tradition, and legislation. Most importantly, as seen in the previous passage, it is part of the control of the consequences of sin. Ironically, by conforming to these social and cultural norms, the church does not shame its reputation by promoting a "lawless" activity like abolition. Conformity also functions as a potent apologetic strategy: "But now many are reduced to the necessity of blasphemy, and to say that Christianity has come into the world for the subversion of everything, masters having their slaves taken them, and it is a deed of violence."[69] Chrysostom relates questioning the traditional slave-slaveholder social roles to subversiveness and even blasphemy, probably because of developments following the Council of Gangra, held some years earlier, where the Eustathians were accused of illegally setting slaves free.[70]

In earlier times we also hear of the Marcionites, who resisted traditional social structures; Tertullian accuses them of removing slaves from their masters. "For what is more unrighteous, more unjust, more dishonest, than so to benefit an alien slave as to take him away from his master, claim him as the property of another, and suborn him against his master's life," laments Tertullian, "and all this, to make the matter more iniquitous, still while he is yet living in his master's house and on his master's garner, and still trembling beneath his stripes?" Like Chrysostom, Tertullian sees such acts of liberation as unrighteous and illegal, and even calls his opponents kidnappers: "Such a deliverer, I had almost said kidnapper, would even meet with condemnation in the world."[71] While it is difficult to exactly determine

---

68. *Hom. 1 Cor.* 19.5 (F2.221–22): Ὁ γὰρ ἐν Κυρίῳ κληθεὶς δοῦλος, ἀπελεύθερος Κυρίου ἐστίν· ὁμοίως καὶ ὁ ἐλεύθερος κληθείς, δοῦλός ἐστι τοῦ Χριστοῦ. Ἐν γὰρ τοῖς κατὰ Χριστόν, φησίν, ἀμφότεροι ἴσοι· ὁμοίως γὰρ καὶ σὺ τοῦ Χριστοῦ δοῦλος, ὁμοίως καὶ ὁ δεσπότης ὁ σός. Πῶς οὖν ὁ δοῦλος ἀπελεύθερος; Ὅτι ἠλευθέρωσέ σε οὐ τῆς ἁμαρτίας μόνον, ἀλλὰ καὶ τῆς ἔξωθεν δουλείας μένοντα δοῦλον. Οὐ γὰρ ἀφίησιν εἶναι δοῦλον τὸν δοῦλον, οὐδὲ ἄνθρωπον μένοντα ἐν δουλείᾳ· τοῦτο γάρ ἐστι τὸ θαυμαστόν. Καὶ πῶς ἐλεύθερός ἐστιν ὁ δοῦλος, μένων δοῦλος; Ὅταν παθῶν ἀπηλλαγμένος ᾖ καὶ τῶν τῆς ψυχῆς νοσημάτων, ὅταν χρημάτων καταφρονῇ καὶ ὀργῆς καὶ τῶν ἄλλων τῶν τοιούτων παθῶν.

69. *Hom. Phlm.* arg. (F6.328): ἐπεὶ εἰς ἀνάγκην καθίστανται πολλοὶ τοῦ βλασφημεῖν καὶ λέγειν, ἐπὶ ἀνατροπῇ τῶν πάντων ὁ Χριστιανισμὸς εἰς τὸν βίον εἰσενήνεκται, τῶν δεσποτῶν ἀφαιρουμένων τοὺς οἰκέτας, καὶ βίας τὸ πρᾶγμά ἐστιν.

70. Glancy, *Slavery in Early Christianity,* 90.

71. Tertullian, *Marc.* 1.23.7 (PL 2.273): Quid enim iniustius, quid iniquius et improbius quam ita alieno benefacere servo ut domino eripiatur, ut alii vindicetur, ut adversus caput domini subornetur,

to what extent and for what reasons groups like the Marcionites and Eustathians may have resisted slaveholding, it is clear that such "heretical" groups, which advocated for the dissolution of the bond between slave and master, perhaps as an act of ascetic rigorism, were vilified for their semiabolitionist stances. The Council of Gangra also condemned extreme fasting and exclusive vegetarianism.[72] Since the New Testament does not call for slaves to be set free, but rather to remain obedient to their masters, the church cannot take a stance contrary to scripture.

This is the first advantage; Chrysostom also lists a second, which is even more important. By remaining in slavery, the Christian slave demonstrates that not even a practice as degrading and oppressive as slavery can stifle Christian virtue. This is a very common argument found in Chrysostom. Christian slaves were expected to be better slaves than non-Christian slaves. "This is the nature of Christianity," Chrysostom muses, "in slavery it bestows freedom."[73] The same doulology found in Cynicism and Stoicism[74] now also surfaces in Chrysostom's thinking. The Cynics and Stoics maintained that social status did not and should not hinder the philosophical life. "But if it is impossible for the one who is a slave to be a proper Christian," Chrysostom warns, "the Greeks will condemn the true religion of having a great weakness; but if they can be shown that slavery in no way hinders godliness, they will marvel at our message."[75] The proliferation of slavery, then, was much more than adherence to scriptural tradition. It was a powerful tool both for managing appearances in ancient Mediterranean society, and for regulating the dynamics of out-group relations. Doulology played an important part in group identification. Within Christian thinking, this carefully crafted doulology, therefore, served a fundamental function in the operations of alterity. For instance, the Eustathians were pathologized for their seemingly liberal and perhaps even abolitionary stances toward slavery, and the so-called Greeks cause anxiety for Chrysostom because of their conservative attitudes toward institutional and moral slavery. Conservative doulology was part of the cohesion of the sound Christian body politic. Tragically, slavery, to Chrysostom at least, had to be maintained so as to keep the reputation of the church sound in the eyes of ancient society.

---

et quideni, quo indignius, in ipsa adhuc domo domini, de ipsius adhuc horreis vivens, sub ipsius adhuc plagis tremens? Talis assertor etiam damnaretur in saeculo, nedum plagiator. Translation: *ANF.*

72. Teresa M. Shaw, *The Burden of the Flesh: Fasting and Sexuality in Early Christianity* (Minneapolis: Fortress Press, 1998), 231–33.

73. *Hom. 1 Cor.* 19.6 (F2.223): Τοιοῦτον ὁ Χριστιανισμός· ἐν δουλείᾳ ἐλευθερίαν χαρίζεται.

74. See Diogenes Laertius, *Vit. phil.* 7.32–33 (Marcovich 464–65), 7.121–22 (Marcovich 514–16); Athenaeus, *Deipn.* 267b (Gulick 198–201); Seneca, *Ben.* 3.22.1 (Griffin and Inwood 48–49); *Ep.* 47; Garnsey, *Ideas of Slavery,* 130.

75. *Hom. 1 Cor.* 19.6 (F2.224): Εἰ δ' οὐ δυνατὸν δοῦλον ὄντα εἶναι Χριστιανὸν, οἷον χρὴ, πολλὴν τῆς εὐσεβείας ἀσθένειαν κατηγοροῦσιν Ἕλληνες· ὥσπερ, ἂν μάθωσιν, ὅτι τὴν εὐσέβειαν οὐδὲν βλάπτει δουλεία, θαυμάσονται τὸ κήρυγμα.

The first question, concerning the advantages of institutional slavery, had several implications for the body politic of late ancient Christianity. But what of individual bodies? It is clear that the church's policy of maintaining slavery hardly took the slaves themselves into consideration; doulology, in this instance, was a corporate ecclesiastical matter. But the passage quoted above also raises a second question. What defines the slave of Christ as an individual subject? Chrysostom seems to give a simple answer to this: freedom, or rather, freed status. Slaves of Christ, whether they are slaveholders or the institutionally enslaved, are in fact also freed persons, emancipated slaves (apeleutheroi). According to Chrysostom, when someone becomes a slave of God, he or she is also, at the same time, emancipated from other forms of slavery. The primary characteristic of God's slaves is that they are freed persons, but freed persons still had an obligation to show gratitude and service to their patrons (obsequium). The body never stops being heteronomous, and freedom never sheds its carcerality. Freed status is simply a diluted type of slavery in a different social and legal garb. Yet, for the slaves of Christ, being freed means that they start moving away from the need to be governed, which sin caused, and proceed toward a prelapsarian state.

Chrysostom uses a rather controversial rhetorical technique here—a paradox (paradoxon)—juxtaposing two contrasting statements and then letting them agree. One of the advantages of this figure of speech, notwithstanding classical rhetoricians' abhorrence of it,[76] is that it adds shock value to the argument; it is thaumatic.[77] The slavery-freedom paradox was by far the most popular paradox in early Christian discourse.[78] Albeit in a totally different manner from Chrysostom, Augustine attempted to make sense of this paradox with the notion of "free slavery" (libera servitus).[79] However, as we can see in Chrysostom, the use of this paradox is hardly problematic or contradictory; it is evident in his quotation of 1 Corinthians 7:22, and in his interpretation thereof (Hom. 1 Cor. 19.5–6): "In Christ both are equal: and as you are the slave of Christ, so also is your master." There are four points that need to be considered when dealing with this paradox.

76. Both Quintilian and Tacitus link the use of paradox with the corruption of eloquence; see Peter Goodrich, "Anti-Teubner: Autopoiesis, Paradox, and the Theory of Law," Social Epistemology 13, no. 2 (1999): 197–98.

77. There are several semantic and syntactical variants of thaumazō in Hom. 1 Cor. 19.5–6 (F2.221–23).

78. See Narry F. Santos, Slave of All: The Paradox of Authority and Servanthood in the Gospel of Mark (London: Sheffield Academic Press, 2003); James Anderson, Paradox in Christian Theology: An Analysis of Its Presence, Character, and Epistemic Status, Paternoster Theological Monographs (Eugene, OR: Wipf & Stock, 2007); Laura C. Sweat, The Theological Role of Paradox in the Gospel of Mark (London: T&T Clark, 2013).

79. Augustine, Civ. 14.15 (Levine 344–53); Pagels, "Politics of Paradise," 79–80.

First, in *Hom. 1 Cor.* 19.5–6 Chrysostom implies that one needs to read this paradox in a positive rather than a negative sense; in other words, the paradox becomes a "unity of opposites," and is therefore also polarized but not necessarily, in this case at least, antinomic. This is the first point to understand about the slavery-freedom paradox. But since the convergence of these opposites is stressed, rather than their divergence, the paradox also implies that both are part of the same discursive unity.[80] This is the second point. A very important fissure of early Christian freedom is hereby exposed and confirmed—namely, that freedom in itself, as we have stated in numerous instances, is a carceral mechanism. By this I mean that freedom should not be seen as the opposite of enslavement, but as a necessary part of its operation. The paradox illustrates that this "spiritual" or "true" freedom, freedom from sin and the passions, was in fact a strategy to keep slaves in their state of bondage. Since they are spiritually freed persons, they do not require physical emancipation. This early Christian "freedom" was one of the central ideologies that kept institutional slavery alive. Thus, early Christian formulations of freedom and free will need to be read with a great deal of suspicion. The third point (I will come to the fourth point shortly) is that the slavery-freedom paradox assumes a bifurcation of reality. This bifurcation assumes that there is a higher reality, the spiritual or the godly, which has precedence over the nongodly reality. Slavery to God is the paradoxical isomorphism of freedom from sin and the passions. This is also why there is an attitude of indifference toward institutional slavery in Chrysostom's discourse.

But Chrysostom's ordering of this bifurcation is somewhat complex. Being enslaved to God means having freedom from various other despotic forces. "How then is the slave a freed person?" Chrysostom asks, and then responds: "Because Christ has freed you not only from sin, but also from outward slavery while continuing to be a slave. . . . When the slave is freed from passions and the diseases of the mind, frowning upon riches and anger and all other similar passions."[81] The retort here is exhaustive. Slavery to God means freedom both from sin and from the passions. "It is not slavery itself, beloved, that hurts us," Chrysostom says, "but the real slavery is that of sin. . . . But if you are a slave of sin, even though you are ten thousand times free, your freedom is of no advantage."[82] What becomes evident now is quite disturbing: spiritual freedom devalues social and personal freedom from oppression. Freedom from sin and the passions is obviously conceptually related to Chrysostom, but perhaps with different emphases.

80. Santos, *Slave of All*, 6–7.
81. *Hom. 1 Cor.* 19.5 (F2.222): Πῶς οὖν ὁ δοῦλος ἀπελεύθερος; "Ὅτι ἠλευθέρωσέ σε οὐ τῆς ἁμαρτίας μόνον, ἀλλὰ καὶ τῆς ἔξωθεν δουλείας μένοντα δοῦλον. . . . "Ὅταν παθῶν ἀπηλλαγμένος ᾖ καὶ τῶν τῆς ψυχῆς νοσημάτων, ὅταν χρημάτων καταφρονῇ καὶ ὀργῆς καὶ τῶν ἄλλων τῶν τοιούτων παθῶν.
82. Ibid. (F2.224): Οὐχ αὕτη βλάπτει ἡ δουλεία, ἀγαπητέ, ἀλλ' ἡ φύσει δουλεία ἡ τῆς ἁμαρτίας. . . . ἂν δὲ ταύτης ᾖς δοῦλος, κἂν μυριάκις ἐλεύθερος ᾖς, οὐδὲν ὄφελός σοι τῆς ἐλευθερίας.

Having discussed spiritual freedom from sin, I will now limn the intricate façade of slavery to the passions. Chrysostom uses an interesting term for the latter form of enslavement: "outward slavery" (tēs exōthen douleias). While freedom from sin, here, seems to imply more of a theological and existential concept, freedom from a certain condition or disposition, this "outward slavery," which I read as slavery to the passions, appears to denote more of an ethical and behavioral mode of emancipation.[83] The phrase "diseases of the soul" (tōn tēs psychēs nosēmatōn) appears to be a synonym, making the kai between the two phrases epexegetical. Moreover, Chrysostom believed that a diseased soul, infected by the passions, had very physical effects on the body—psychic slavery to the passions had highly corporeal consequences. I will return to this phrase momentarily.

As an example that highlights the dynamics of divine bondage and slavery to the passions, Chrysostom exposits the life of Joseph.[84] Joseph, although he was institutionally enslaved in Egypt, is seen as a man free from his passions, while the wife of Potiphar, according to Chrysostom, was ironically the real slave, since she was enthralled by her lust and pride. Joseph's actions, his behavior, signify the character of one who is free. The opposite is said of Joseph's brothers, who displayed a lifestyle "more servile than all slaves, both lying to their father, and trading with the merchants under false pretences."[85] But Joseph, Chrysostom eloquently tells us, "nothing was able to enslave him, neither chain nor bondage nor the love of his mistress nor his being in a strange land. . . . For this is freedom in the truest sense when even in bondage it shines through."[86] To Chrysostom then, slavery is not so much a social status as it is a behavioral habitus, a set of sociosomatic practices that distinguishes true slavery from its counterpart. This is qualified by another interesting argument from Chrysostom:

So, tell me, what use is it when, although you are not enslaved to a person, you bow in subjection to your passions? Since human masters often know how to be lenient,

83. See Kontoulis, Problem der Sklaverei, 355–68.
84. The figure of Joseph features in many Jewish and early Christian discussions of moral slavery. Joseph was one of the most common epitomes of a slave who did not let his status lead to corruption. The Testament of Joseph notes in several instances that, despite being a slave, Joseph acted like a noble and freeborn man; T. Jos. 14.3–4, 106, 248; see Byron, Slavery Metaphors, 132–39. Philo devoted an entire treatise, De Josepho, to this topic. In early Christian literature, Joseph, often used alongside the example of Daniel, was seen as someone who was morally free despite being enslaved; Tertullian, Idol. 18 (PL 1.764–66); Ambrose, Off. 2.5 (PL 16.25). Joseph is also a frequent example in several other works of Chrysostom; see Hom. Matt. 59.1 (PG 58.575.12–14); Hom. Jo. 71.3 (PG 59.387–89), 76.3 (PG 59.414.27–29); Hom. Phil. 6[5] (F5.53–54), 13[12].2 (F5.138).
85. Hom. 1 Cor. 19.5 (F2.223): οὐχὶ πάντων ἦσαν τῶν δούλων δουλικώτεροι, καὶ πρὸς τὸν πατέρα ψευδόμενοι, καὶ πρὸς τοὺς ἐμπόρους τὰ μὴ ὄντα λέγοντες.
86. Hom. 1 Cor. 19.5 (F2.223): καὶ οὐδὲν αὐτὸν δουλώσασθαι ἠδυνήθη, οὐ δεσμὸς, οὐ δουλεία, οὐ δεσποίνης ἔρως, οὐ τὸ ἐν ἀλλοτρίᾳ εἶναι· ἀλλ᾽ ἔμενεν ἐλεύθερος πανταχοῦ. Τοῦτο γὰρ μάλιστά ἐστιν ἐλευθερία, ὅταν καὶ ἐν δουλείᾳ διαλάμπῃ.

but those masters are never satisfied with your destruction. Are you enslaved to a person? Think about it: your master is also a slave to you, in providing you with food, in taking care of your health, and in looking after your shoes and all the other things. And you do not worry so much, unless you should offend your master; but the master, in the same way, worries if you do not have any of those necessities. But the master sits down, while you stand. So what? Since this may be said of you as well as of the master. Often, at least, when you are lying down and sleeping peacefully, the master is not only standing, but experiencing countless problems in his business dealings, he tosses and turns more restlessly than you.[87]

Once again the conceptual boundaries between moral and institutional slavery are blurred in yet another doulological paradox. It is also curious to note that this same argument occurs, almost verbatim, in Libanius[88] and Theodoret,[89] showing that it was probably a very common anecdote in late ancient society. We have here a figure of speech known as *dialexis,* in which opposites are equated for the sake of irony. In the anecdote Chrysostom tells us that the slaveholder is in fact shown to be a slave to his slaves since he is burdened with their care. This type of paternalism only serves to conceal the dependence of the slaveholder on the slaves.[90] But what about slaves who need to care for their masters? How can they avoid becoming "true" slaves of people? "There are limits set to slaves by God himself. . . . When your master commands nothing which is displeasing to God," Chrysostom elaborates, "it is correct to obey, but not further. For so the slave becomes free."[91] Slaves' first priority is to please God, and if the master's and God's principles are in opposition, the slave may find him- or herself in a difficult position. Here is an extreme case of double standards, obviously: the slave becomes "free" when performing the reasonable duties of a slave, as long as they are not an offense to God; but the

---

87. *Hom. 1 Cor.* 19.6 (F2.224): Τί γὰρ ὄφελος, εἰπέ μοι, ὅταν ἀνθρώπῳ μὲν μὴ δουλεύῃς, τοῖς δὲ πάθεσι σεαυτὸν ὑποκατακλίνῃς; Οἱ μὲν γὰρ ἄνθρωποι καὶ φείσασθαι ἐπίστανται πολλάκις, ἐκεῖνοι δὲ οἱ δεσπόται οὐδέποτε κορέννυνταί σου τῆς ἀπωλείας. Δουλεύεις ἀνθρώπῳ; 'Αλλὰ καὶ ὁ Δεσπότης σοι δουλεύει, διοικούμενός σοι τὰ τῆς τροφῆς, ἐπιμελούμενός σου τῆς ὑγιείας καὶ ἐνδυμάτων καὶ ὑποδημάτων, καὶ τῶν ἄλλων ἁπάντων φροντίζων. Καὶ οὐχ οὕτω σὺ δέδοικας, μὴ προσκρούσῃς τῷ Δεσπότῃ, ὡς ἐκεῖνος δέδοικε μή τί σοι τῶν ἀναγκαίων ἐπιλίπῃ. 'Αλλ' ἐκεῖνος κατάκειται, σὺ δὲ ἕστηκας. Καὶ τί τοῦτο; οὐδὲ γὰρ τοῦτο παρ' αὐτῷ μόνον, ἀλλὰ καὶ παρὰ σοί. Πολλάκις γοῦν σοῦ κατακειμένου καὶ ὑπνοῦντος ἡδέως, ἐκεῖνος οὐχ ἕστηκε μόνον, ἀλλὰ καὶ μυρίας ὑπομένει βίας ἐπὶ τῆς ἀγορᾶς, καὶ ἀγρυπνεῖ σοῦ χαλεπώτερον.

88. Libanius, *Or.* 2.5.66–67 (Foerster 1.170).

89. Theodoret, *Prov.* 7.677b-680 (PG 83.665–85).

90. Orlando Patterson, *Slavery and Social Death: A Comparative Study* (Cambridge, MA: Harvard University Press, 1982), 337.

91. *Hom. 1 Cor.* 19.5 (F2.223): Καὶ γὰρ εἰσὶν ὅροι δούλων παρὰ τοῦ Θεοῦ κείμενοι· καὶ μέχρι ποῦ δεῖ φυλάττειν αὐτούς, καὶ τοῦτο νενομοθέτηται, καὶ ὑπερβαίνειν αὐτοὺς οὐ χρή. "Οταν γὰρ μηδὲν ὁ δεσπότης ἐπιτάττῃ τῶν μὴ δοκούντων τῷ Θεῷ, ἕπεσθαι δεῖ καὶ πείθεσθαι· περαιτέρω δὲ μηκέτι· οὕτω γὰρ ὁ δοῦλος ἐλεύθερος γίνεται.

slaveholder is a "slave" because he takes care of the needs of his slaves. So simply by being a slave, the slave is in fact free—again the doulological paradox shows how this type of "freedom" actually kept slaves in a state of physical bondage. The slaveholder becomes free when he is no longer troubled by the care of slaves. The slaves enslave the slaveholder. This is obviously an anecdote spoken from the perspective of the supercilious culture of the slaveholders, and although it is shameful in its blatant denial of the real oppression of slaves in ancient society, it again shows that slavery is bifurcated and shifted to a different level, no longer of social status, but of theological condition and, especially, ethical or virtuous behavior.

There is also another dimension to this paradox. It was shown above that the proliferation of slavery to God is also a strategy in service of the broader Christian program of self-renunciation. Part of this self-renunciation is the idea that to serve is better than to command, and service is a sign of love. Chrysostom states: "And if someone is a slave, it renders slavery sweeter than freedom. For the one who loves rejoices not really in commanding, as in being commanded, although to command is surely sweet."[92] Slaves, therefore, should not only consider their slavery as a form of freedom, but their service needs to be conducted with love, because love "makes hardships light and easy, causing our virtues to be effortless, but vice even more bitter to us."[93] The Christian labor ethic we have in late antiquity, which could be described as principally labor/service intensive, also sustained institutional slavery. When all people submit to each other as slaves of Christ (alluding to Gal. 5:13), Chrysostom imagines, "then there will be no such thing as slavery. . . . It is much better to be a slave in this way [a slave of Christ] than free in any other way."[94] In all fairness, Chrysostom did envision a perfect world where masters and slaves served each other—but such rhetoric remained utopian and was never realized in mainstream society.

Love and submission to Christ mean servitude, and this love is cooperative and reciprocal—people ought to be slaves of one another. One immediately notices that this discourse of love, amorous servitude, in addition to being corrective, as we noted above, allows two more inferences: it is both a measure of productivity and a measure of security. Love makes slavery bearable, and because of love, slaves ought to perform their duties even better. Love also aims to prevent dominicide, since it serves to bond the slave to his or her master, or at least to virtue and

92. *Hom. 1 Cor.* 32.12 (F2.399): Κἂν δουλεύῃ τις, ἡδίω τῆς ἐλευθερίας ἀποφαίνει τὴν δουλείαν. Ὁ γὰρ φιλῶν οὐχ οὕτως ἐπιτάττων. ὡς ἐπιτατόμενος χαίρει, καίτοι γε τὸ ἐπιτάττειν ἡδύ.

93. *Hom. 1 Cor.* 32.12 (F2.399): καὶ τὰ ἐπίπονα κοῦφα ποιεῖ καὶ ῥᾶστα, τὴν μὲν ἀρετὴν εὔκολον, τὴν δὲ κακίαν πικροτάτην ἡμῖν ἀποφαίνουσα.

94. *Hom. Eph.* 19.3 (F4.298): οὕτω γὰρ οὐκ ἔσται δουλεία. . . . πολλῷ βέλτιον οὕτως εἶναι δοῦλον, ἢ ἑτέρως ἐλεύθερον.

God.[95] While people like Chrysostom may have been sincere in their comments about love, the reality is that the Christian doulologization of love was a measure to increase labor efficiency and productivity, and also served as a safeguard to prevent dominicide and rebellion.

Furthermore, Chrysostom also warns that the passions are much harsher than any earthly master. Potiphar's wife, again, is a perfect example of the tyranny of the passions, according to Chrysostom, along with others like Cain, who was enslaved to his envy.[96] Thus, when Paul said, "Do not become slaves of men,"[97] in 1 Corinthians 7:23b, Chrysostom opines, he meant this type of slavery. Moreover, having honor in virtue, according to Chrysostom, is better than having freedom from institutional slavery, since virtue gives true freedom, although "not emancipating [slaves] from slavery, but while they continue to be slaves, showing them to be more honorable than free persons; which is much better than giving them freedom."[98] Chrysostom uses virtue and love, like freedom, as carceral mechanisms to keep slaves in bondage. True freedom is freedom of the soul, psychic freedom, and psychic and hamartiological slaves are, in fact, the true slaves.

I now come to the fourth point about the paradox of Christian freedom in Chrysostom's thought, which concerns the strategic role of the term "freedom" in the appropriation and affirmation of the subordinated subjectivity of the slave of God. When Philo, Paul, and Chrysostom admonish people to become slaves of God, we have an instance of doulomorphism. People are told to become a certain type of slave. Doulomorphism could be negative or positive. Generally, ancient people did not want to be slaves of anything. But when it came to being slaves of God, Christians considered it a type of doulomorphism worth striving for and attaining. It was even seen as a move that had much power and authority, as the letters of Paul show. By elevating slavery to God as an essential subjectivity to a position of power, we have what Raewyn Connell refers to as the replacement of a hegemonic masculinity with a subordinated masculinity.[99] Whereas slavery was previously seen to be a deficient and degenerate state of subjectivity, it now usurps

---

95. The anxiety caused by dominicide in antiquity should not be underestimated. The Roman state implemented the most stringent legislation against dominicide—in most instances all slaves living under the same roof would be executed. The execution of slaves guilty of dominicide was public and quite brutal, with the purpose of serving as both a deterrent and a statement of the power of the slaveholding state over the body of the slave; it was a measure of social control; see Harrill, *Slaves in the New Testament*, 351–52.

96. *Hom. 1 Cor.* 19.6 (F2.224).

97. NA28: μὴ γίνεσθε δοῦλοι ἀνθρώπων.

98. *Hom. Matt.* 32.11 (PG 57.387.15–18): οὐκ ἀπαλλάττουσα τῆς δουλείας, ἀλλὰ δούλους μένοντας ἐλευθέρων ἀποφαίνουσα σεμνοτέρους, ὃ τοῦ δοῦναι ἐλευθερίαν πολλῷ πλέον ἐστίν·

99. Raewyn W. Connell, *Gender and Power: Society, the Person, and Sexual Politics* (Stanford, CA: Stanford University Press, 1987), 167–90.

the position of the dominant masculinity. This usurpation of hegemony by the discourse of slavery was extremely successful in early Christianity. The reason for its success is related to its paradoxical nature; a paradox that, as we saw above, was solidified and popularized in early Christian discourse over more than three centuries. The shift from subordination to hegemony was facile because slavery to God is in fact "true" freedom. By seizing the concept of "true" freedom, and providing it with a new paradoxical impetus, which in fact diverted the attention from the shame of institutional slavery, Christian doulology presented itself as a sensible and meaningful expression of the self with which inhabitants of the ancient Mediterranean could associate. It dressed the shame of slavery in acceptable, even authoritative, garb.

Spiritual freedom was the conceptual camouflage by which Christian doulology infiltrated late ancient institutions of power. The fact that it was based on authoritative scriptures, accompanied by a lengthy *Nachwirkung* in tradition (even from Cynic and Stoic lines), also facilitated this shift. Furthermore, since the heteronomy of the body in Christian thinking entails that all people are in any case slaves, universalizing moral slavery, it stands to reason that the wise would choose slavery to God over and against slavery to sin. I will return to this issue of subordinated and hegemonic masculinities in due course.

Thus, the Christian concept of freedom as divine bondage sustained institutional slavery, and it also created a very distinct Christian subjectivity (and masculinity), founded on a paradox. The final question that *Hom. 1 Cor.* 19.5–6 prompts us to ask is this: how did slavery to God function as a pathologizing discourse? In other words, if slaves of God are characterized by spiritual freedom, what are the characteristics of those who are free from the Christian god and enslaved to other things? We have, in Chrysostom's thought, a very potent dichotomy between slaves of God and slaves of sin and the passions. There is no golden mean in this matter; one is either enslaved to God, or, if one is not, the automatic implication is that one is enslaved to sin and the passions. The heteronomy of the body is absolute.

So how are slaves of sin and passion described by Chrysostom? The most important point to make here is the following: when slavery is elevated to a moral and metaphorical plane, it more easily becomes a universalizing and totalizing discourse. This was a categorical form of invective in the ancient world, and it was not only the Christians who used the metaphor of slavery to vilify their opponents.[100] Chrysostom was very fond of this invective strategy,[101] and it operates within three rhetorical strategies: medicalization, tyranny, and the combination of

---

100. Jennifer W. Knust, *Abandoned to Lust: Sexual Slander and Ancient Christianity* (New York: Columbia University Press, 2006), 15–50.

101. See Chris L. de Wet, "The Vilification of the Rich in John Chrysostom's Homily 40 *On First Corinthians*," *Acta Patristica et Byzantina* 21, no. 1 (2010): 82–94; Drake, *Slandering the Jew*, 88–89.

shame and feminization. One could perhaps highlight others, but these, I believe, are the most commonly used in Chrysostom's rhetoric. I will also refer here to slavery to sin and the passions interchangeably, since, although they appear to be conceptually different, they are also inseparable in Chrysostom's works. Experiencing the call of the passions is not sinful, but submitting to and indulging excessively in them lead to sin. I will treat each of these discourses using examples from the primary texts.

The first and perhaps most common strategy in pathologizing slaves of passion is medicalization.[102] We have already seen in *Hom. 1 Cor.* 19.5 that Chrysostom refers to the passions as "diseases of the soul". Such individuals are pestiferous in their innermost being. The pitiful state of pathic and hamartiological slaves is bemoaned even further in a vivid and nauseating ekphrasis:

> But we return to our former vomit, after the youth of grace, building up the old age of sins. For both the lust for money, and the slavery to disgusting desires, and whichever other sin, have the habit of making the one who works for them old. *Now that which is decaying and growing old soon disappears* [Heb. 8:13]. For there is no body, not one, to be seen so paralyzed by the passing of time as a soul that is festering and collapsing with many sins. This soul is led out further to extreme prattling, producing unintelligible sounds, like people who are very old and mad, bloating with stupidity, and much derangement, and forgetfulness, and having eyesores, and nauseating people, and an easy prey to the devil. Such then are the souls of sinners. But not those of the righteous, for they are youthful and invigorated, and are constantly in the very prime of life, always ready for any fight or struggle.[103]

Here we see how a list of passions practically forms a moral nosography, accompanied by a detailed geriatric symptomatology: Chrysostom describes slaves of sin and the passions here as old, withered, and diseased chattel. One can appreciate this image when looking at its intricate construction and multilayered nuancing. The image here is of an old, sickly slave who has been laboring hard until old age without ever being manumitted. The hard, menial labor of this soul has disabled it

---

102. For a more general discussion of medicalized pathologization in Chrysostom, see De Wet, "Paul and Christian Identity-Formation," 42–44.

103. *Hom. Rom.* 11[10].3 (F1.152): ἡμεῖς δὲ ἐπὶ τὸν πρότερον ἐπανερχόμεθα ἔμετον, μετὰ τὴν ἀπὸ τῆς χάριτος νεότητα, τὸ ἀπὸ τῶν ἁμαρτιῶν κατασκευάζοντες γῆρας. Καὶ γὰρ τὸ χρημάτων ἐρᾶν, καὶ τὸ δουλεύειν ἐπιθυμίαις ἀτόποις, καὶ πᾶσα ἁπλῶς ἁμαρτία παλαιοῦν εἴωθε τὸν ἐργαζόμενον· τὸ δὲ παλαιούμενον καὶ γηράσκον ἐγγὺς ἀφανισμοῦ. Οὐ γὰρ ἔστιν, οὐκ ἔστιν οὕτω σῶμα ὑπὸ χρόνων παραλελυμένον ἰδεῖν, ὡς ψυχὴν ὑπὸ ἁμαρτημάτων πολλῶν σαθρουμένην καὶ καταπίπτουσαν. Ἡ γὰρ εἰς ἐσχάτην ληρωδίαν ἐξάγεται λοιπόν, ἄσημα φθεγγομένη καθάπερ οἱ γεγηρακότες καὶ παραπαίοντες, καὶ κορύζης ἀναπεπλησμένη καὶ παραπληξίας πολλῆς καὶ λήθης, καὶ λήμας πρὸ τῶν ὀφθαλμῶν ἔχουσα, καὶ ἀνθρώποις βδελυρὰ, καὶ τῷ διαβόλῳ εὐχείρωτος· καὶ γὰρ τοιαῦται αἱ τῶν ἁμαρτωλῶν ψυχαί. Ἀλλ᾽ οὐχ αἱ τῶν δικαίων, ἀλλὰ νεάζουσι καὶ σφριγῶσι, καὶ ἐν αὐτῷ τῷ ἄνθει τῆς ἡλικίας εἰσὶ διαπαντός, πρὸς ἅπασαν μάχην καὶ πάλην ἀεὶ παρεσκευασμέναι·

and caused it to suffer numerous ailments, including madness and dementia. Language of disease, notably related to the unhealthy accumulation and discharge of fluids—that is, unbalanced humors[104]—and especially mental illness, abounds. The life of sin and the passions is described as vomit (*emetos*). The body of this slave is paralyzed (*paralyō*) and festered (*sathros*). It is a soul likened to a person collapsing with seizures and other neurological ailments (*katapiptō*). The soul becomes phonetically corrupt (*lērōdia*, which has heretical nuances; *asēma phthengomenē*, a phrase that suggests mantic frenzy).

Along with the metaphor of old age, which is synonymous with weakness, various psychoses are listed by Chrysostom: *parapaiō*, which I translated as "madness," but which can also mean "folly"—the term shares a semantic domain with *mainomai; koryzēs anapeplēsmenē*, a phrase translated here as "bloating with stupidity"—it is probably used here medico-metaphorically rather than literally, and denotes phlegm (the excess of phlegm being the typical mark of decrepit old age), driveling, and being "snotty" (it is based on the ancient medical belief that accumulation of bodily fluids can result in both physical and mental illness—the result of humors in disarray[105])—the runny nose and driveling also signify a return to childhood, as old age was often seen as a second infancy;[106] *paraplēxia*, "derangement"; Chrysostom also provides a neat assonance and alliteration between *lēthē* (forgetfulness) and *lēmē* (eyesores). In sum, this aged slave soul is a sight that causes other people to become sick (*anthrōpois bdelyra*). While Chrysostom's language of medicalization is metaphorical, the effects of pathic slavery were also quite physical. A diseased soul results in a diseased body, and just as a harsh master damages the physical body of the institutional slave, so too the kyriarch of the passions ruins and ravages the physical body of the psychic slave. Excessive indulgence in sin and the passions ages the body and the soul badly. Because of these serious physical consequences of bondage to the passions, it comes as no surprise that many people were less concerned with the physical maltreatment of institutional slaves.

There is also a measure of demonization here.[107] The psychically afflicted individual becomes an easy target for demonic activity, like an old, sick, wounded animal in the wild. In a different homily Chrysostom describes the devil in the manner of a slave trader, and the slave of passion as one who is "like a bad and

---

104. The notion of the balance of fluids or humors is notably present in Galen's thought, and was accepted by the fourth-century physician Oribasius; see Susan P. Mattern, *Galen and the Rhetoric of Healing* (Baltimore: Johns Hopkins University Press, 2008), 34–35. Chrysostom, here, effortlessly conjoins the medical knowledge of his day with his own theological virtue-ethics.

105. Mattern, *Galen and the Rhetoric of Healing*, 152–56.

106. Tim G. Parkin, *Old Age in the Roman World: A Cultural and Social History* (Baltimore: Johns Hopkins University Press, 2003), 83.

107. See *Hom. Matt.* 58.1 (PG 58.565.42–567.47).

captive slave, whom the devil has caught, and leading him away, fleeing, while flogging him everywhere, and surrounding him with ten thousand insults."[108] Enslavement to sin and the passions also means one is a slave of the devil. These ailing souls stand in stark contrast to the righteous souls, who are young, strong, and invigorated. Masters were, after all, in the end responsible for the health of their slaves. Slavery to God is then curative to these psychic infirmities. Greed and vainglory are common in such descriptions. Chrysostom describes these passions as "dreadful maladies," which turn people into "slaves in extreme slavery."[109] In some instances, the language of purity and defilement is also used.[110] The expression "slaves to the stomach" (*gastridouloi*), with reference to gluttony, is also very prevalent in this regard.[111]

Another strategy very common in Chrysostom is that of the tyranny of the passions. The lordship of God is often contrasted with the destructive domination of the passions. While God is described as a gentle, kind, and loving slaveholder, the passions are tyrannical:

> But the souls of those who are slaves to wealth are not noble and free, but like those that are under ten thousand pedagogues, and taskmasters, so that these people dare not even lift up their eye, and speak confidently on behalf of virtue. . . . For such a person has neither one master, nor two, nor three, but ten thousand. . . . Now then, let us see if this person is not one who is more enslaved than all; and let us compare him to, not simply a slave, but a slave's slave, for many domestics have slaves despite being slaves themselves. This slave's slave then has one master. . . . For although his master's master seems to rule over him, yet presently he obeys only one; and if things between them are well, he will abide in safety all his life. But the slave of wealth does not only have one or two, but many, and harsher masters. . . . Do you see the swarm of masters, and of harsh masters?[112]

108. *Hom. Matt.* 58.5 (PG 58:570.24–27): ὡς ἀνδράποδον κακὸν καὶ αἰχμάλωτον λαβὼν αὐτὸν ὁ διάβολος ἄπεισι, καὶ ἄγει καὶ φέρει, ῥαπίζων πάντοθεν καὶ μυρίαις περιβάλλων ὕβρεσιν.

109. *Hom. Jo.* 69.1 (PG 59.377.30, 39–40): δεινὸν τὸ νόσημα . . . δοῦλοι δουλείαν τὴν ἐσχάτην.

110. *Hom. Heb.* 31.2 (F7.345–46).

111. See *Hom. Matt.* 13.2–5 (PG 57.210.5–218.17); *Hom. Jo.* 44.1 (PG 59.247.64–65); *Hom. Rom.* 33[32].1 (F1.486–87); *Hom. Heb.* 25.8 (F7.287). For more on gluttony in Chrysostom, see Shaw, *Burden of the Flesh*, 131–39.

112. *Hom. Matt.* 58.6 (PG 58.571.16–19, 24–25, 30–34, 36–40, 61, 572.1): 'Ἀλλ' οὐχ αἱ τῶν πλούτῳ δουλευόντων ψυχαὶ τοιαῦται, ἀλλ' ὥσπερ οἱ ὑπὸ μυρίους ὄντες παιδαγωγοὺς καὶ δημίους, οὕτως οὐδὲ ἐπᾶραι τὸ ὄμμα τολμῶσι, καὶ ὑπὲρ ἀρετῆς παρρησιάσασθαι. . . . Οὐδὲ γὰρ ἕνα δεσπότην καὶ δύο καὶ τρεῖς, ἀλλὰ μυρίους ὁ τοιοῦτος ἔχει. . . . Ἴδωμεν τοίνυν εἰ μὴ οὗτός ἐστιν ὁ πάντων δουλικώτερος· καὶ ἀντιστήσωμεν αὐτῷ, μὴ δοῦλον ἁπλῶς, ἀλλὰ δοῦλον δούλου· πολλοὶ γὰρ καὶ οἰκέται δούλους ἔχουσιν. Οὗτος μὲν οὖν ὁ δοῦλος τοῦ δούλου ἕνα ἔχει δεσπότην. . . . Κἂν γὰρ ὁ τούτου δεσπότης αὐτοῦ δοκῇ κρατεῖν, ἀλλὰ τέως ἑνὶ μόνῳ πείθεται· κἂν τὰ πρὸς ἐκεῖνον αὐτῷ καλῶς ἔχῃ, ἐν ἀδείᾳ τὸν ἅπαντα καθεδεῖται βίον. Οὗτος δὲ οὐχ ἕνα καὶ δύο μόνον, ἀλλὰ πολλοὺς καὶ χαλεπωτέρους ἔχει δεσπότας. . . . Εἶδες δεσποτῶν ἐσμόν, καὶ δεσποτῶν χαλεπῶν;

The slave of the passions is described as the lowliest of all slaves; in fact, this person is more like the slave of a slave. It often happened that slaves owned other slaves. The result here is that the slave of the passions is a slave of many harsh masters, since all of the passions have an effect on the soul and the body. Each passion demands its pound of flesh. This person is like the overcommitted slave, one who is robbed of all decency, with no confidence to speak in favor of virtue. Chrysostom states that being an institutional slave, even the lowliest one who is owned by another slave, is "better" than being a slave of the passions. While the purpose of this type of hyperbolic rhetoric is to shock the audience, statements like these did nothing to ameliorate institutional slavery. Vainglory, Chrysostom warns, makes people slaves in a worse condition than those bought with money; hence people should strive to be subject only to the dominion of God.[113]

The final strategy Chrysostom utilizes is that of shaming and feminization. Here we find the invective of gynaecodouly (from the word *gynaikodouloi*), men being slaves of women. The term *gynaikodouloi* is a neologism Chrysostom himself invented, showing his utter disdain of women exercising power over men. Chrysostom slanders men in the general sense, who are slaves to their lust for women, but he also uses this argument in a very particular context, against syneisaktism (spiritual marriage). The crux of the argument, however, remains the same: all these men

> are the slaves of women, these above all do women drag around like menial slaves, and will never consider treating them like men, flogging them, spitting on them, leading them, and taking them around everywhere, and giving themselves airs, and in everything only giving them orders. . . . And he himself too, in order to guard the character of his desperation, exhibits the character of a slave of the masses, flattering them, serving them, slaving away with a servitude more grievous than that of one bought for money.[114]

The first point I want to raise here is this: in all three examples that I have cited above, it was noted by Chrysostom that the life of an institutional slave is better than the life of a slave of sin and the passions. The problem Chrysostom has with gynaecodouly is that men, driven by lust, who become slaves of women, are acting contrary to their nature. They become subordinated to women and serve them in a shameful fashion. There seems to be an ironic pun in the passage quoted above—the men are described as both *gynaikodouloi* (slaves to women) and *andrapoda* (man-footed

113. *Hom. Tit.* 2 (F6.274–83).
114. *Hom. Matt.* 62.6 (PG 58.603.3–8, 603.12–604.4): γυναικοδούλους, τούτους μάλιστα ὡς ἀνδράποδα περιφέρουσιν αἱ γυναῖκες, καὶ οὐκ ἄν ποτε καταξιώσαιεν ἐκεῖναι ὡς ἀνδράσιν αὐτοῖς κεχρῆσθαι, ῥαπίζουσαι, διαπτύουσαι, ἄγουσαι καὶ περιάγουσαι πανταχοῦ, καὶ θρυπτόμεναι, καὶ πάντα ἐπιτάττουσαι μόνον. . . . Καὶ αὐτὸς δὲ ἐκεῖνος, ὥστε διατηρῆσαι τὸ σχῆμα τῆς ἀπονοίας, τὰ τῶν ἀνδραπόδων πρὸς τοὺς πλείονας ἐπιδείκνυται, κολακεύων, θεραπεύων, παντὸς ἀργυρωνήτου δουλείαν δουλεύων χαλεπωτέραν.

animals, one of the worst terms used for slaves[115]). By being slaves of lust and of women, they only appear to be men, or man-footed animals.[116] For Chrysostom, Paul believed that being "slaves to men" was wrong, so being slaves to women was even worse.[117] It must be remembered here that Chrysostom considered the hierarchy of men over women as natural, and not related to sin. In one of Chrysostom's letters, he cites the example of David and Solomon, who were both caught by the snare of gynaecodouly; he asks: "Do you see how great an evil it is not to master pleasure, not to overturn the ruling principle in nature, and for a man to be the slave of women?"[118]

Chrysostom sees the disjunction of this natural governmentality and losing control over the passions as typically sinful. It is also a direct assault on their masculinity, and they appear to be the weaker sex. Their servile nature implies that the woman now occupies the role of the man, and the man that of the woman and slave. In this relationship, reality is overturned, and nature is inverted.[119] This manifestation of excessive chivalry revolted Chrysostom. Chrysostom also disapproved of men running after women with whom they have engaged in a "spiritual marriage." These men are also called *gynaikodouloi,* and they are compared specifically to eunuchs to highlight their unnatural and overturned gender ambiguity.[120]

A vast array of slave types are used in Chrysostom's complex formulations of divine bondage and slavery to sin and the passions, including the old, run-down, and demented slave, slaves of slaves, the *andrapodon,* the *gynaikodoulos,* and the eunuch. In this section we have seen how concepts of spiritual freedom enforced institutional slavery, and how metaphorical slavery was universalized to bifurcate reality and dichotomize society into slaves of God and slaves of sin and the passions; and it was shown that metaphorical slavery directly influenced ideas about institutional slavery.

. . .

In one of Chrysostom's sermons, he consoles the slaves who may be in his audience in a very Stoic manner: "Slavery is nothing but a name. The domination is

---

115. Tracey E. Rihll, "Classical Athens," in Bradley and Cartledge, *Cambridge World History of Slavery,* 1:48–73.

116. Blake Leyerle, *Theatrical Shows and Ascetic Lives: John Chrysostom's Attack on Spiritual Marriage* (Berkeley: University of California Press, 2001), 46–49.

117. Elizabeth A. Clark, *Reading Renunciation: Asceticism and Scripture in Early Christianity* (Princeton, NJ: Princeton University Press, 1999), 303–4.

118. *Theod. laps.* 2.2.18–20 (SC 117.54): Ὅρα πόσον κακὸν τὸ μὴ κρατεῖν ἡδονῆς, ἀλλὰ τὴν τῆς φύσεως ἀνατρέπειν ἀρχήν, καὶ ἄνδρα ὄντα γυναικῶν εἶναι δοῦλον.

119. Chrysostom uses exactly the same argument in his polemic against homoeroticism in *Hom. Rom.* 5[4] (F1.44–52); see Chris L. de Wet, "John Chrysostom on Homoeroticism," *Neotestamentica* 48, no. 1 (2014): 187–218.

120. *Subintr.* 10.38–45 (Dumortier 80); see chapter 6.

according to the flesh, brief and temporary; for whatever is of the flesh, is not permanent."[121] We have seen in this chapter that the metaphor of slavery in Chrysostom's theology was meticulously constructed. It is a complex metaphor, with various levels of meaning, that was theologized in an equally complex and elaborate way. For Chrysostom, divine bondage is what defines, paradoxically, Christian freedom. This was juxtaposed to slavery to sin and slavery to the passions, two related yet distinct concepts. The heteronomy of the body is therefore distributed over two spheres—either that of enslavement to sin, the passions, and the devil, or that of slavery to God. Most importantly, the theologization of the metaphor of slavery directly influenced institutional slavery. Sadly, the metaphor of slavery in Chrysostom's theology simply ramified and sustained institutional slavery. In very much the same way for Chrysostom as for the Stoics, and Chrysostom's views on slavery are particularly Stoic, the indifference caused by the metaphorization and interiorization of slavery suffocated any possible seeds of abolitionist thought in antiquity. Having explained the complex dynamic between the metaphor and reality of slavery, in the rest of this book I will attempt to expose the façade of institutional slavery and perform an archaeology of the slave body in the thought of Chrysostom, and develop some of the findings from this chapter. While the focus will be on institutional slavery henceforth, we will often return to this elusive metaphor of divine bondage.

121. *Hom. Eph.* 22.1 (F4.334): ὄνομα δουλείας ἐστὶ μόνον· κατὰ σάρκα ἐστὶν ἡ δεσποτεία, πρόσκαιρος καὶ βραχεῖα· ὅπερ γὰρ ἂν ᾖ σαρκικὸν, ἐπίκηρόν ἐστι.

3

Little Churches

The Pastoralization of the Household and Its Slaves

Slaves were part of the Roman household, and they often occupied the same intimate spaces shared by other occupants of the house. One of the primary signifiers of slave subjectivity was domesticity—slaves were a fundamental feature of elite households in antiquity. There was no separate term to distinguish the nonslave members of the household from the slaves. In its legal sense, the term *familia* referred to those under the authority of the *paterfamilias;* in its ordinary usage, the term often refers exclusively to the slaves of the household.[1] The Greek near equivalents for these terms, *oikos* and *oikeios* (terms related to the house, property, or household), and sometimes *oikogenēs* (house-born; referring often to house-born slaves or *vernae*), are equally ambiguous. The latter term is often used exclusively to denote slaves who were born in a household as opposed to those purchased outside it. In essence, it tells us that slaves were inseparable from the very essence of the household. There is also the very common, and specialized, term for a domestic slave: *oiketēs.*[2]

1. Richard P. Saller, "The Hierarchical Household in Roman Society: A Study of Domestic Slavery," in *Serfdom and Slavery: Studies in Legal Bondage,* ed. Michael L. Bush (London: Routledge, 1996), 114–16.

2. There are numerous other terms used for slaves that will be noted in the course of the book. I will not provide an extensive lexicographical overview of slave terminology here; it has been successfully done in numerous instances, see Wulf Jaeger, "Die Sklaverei bei Johannes Chrysostomus" (PhD diss., Christian-Albrechts-Universität zu Kiel, 1974), 9–22; Antonino González Blanco, *Economía y sociedad en el Bajo imperio según San Juan Crisostomo,* Publicaciones de la Fundacíon universitaria española 17 (Madrid: Fundación universitaria española, 1980), 280–81. Harper gives a thorough analysis of the term *oiketēs;* Kyle Harper, *Slavery in the Late Roman World, AD 275–425* (New York: Cambridge University Press, 2011), 513–18.

One of the most famous remarks Chrysostom made about slavery is found in his *Homiliae in epistulam I ad Corinthios* 40.6, in which he advises his audience that they should be able to get along without any household slaves. But then, at the Rubicon of abolition, Chrysostom turns back and consoles the slaveholders thus: "One master only needs to employ one slave; or rather two or three masters one slave. . . . We will allow you to keep a second slave. But if you collect many, you no longer do it for the sake of benevolence, but to indulge yourself. . . . when you have purchased slaves and have taught them trades whereby to support themselves, let them go free."[3] Instead of abolition, then, Chrysostom recommends diminution and manumission.

Chrysostom's statements about the management of household slaves should be read within his broader program of pastoralizing the household and its slaves. This chapter will explore the implications of domestic pastoralization for household slaves in both agricultural and urban contexts. The pastoralization of the household had significant implications both for the character and role of the slave body, and for the number of slaves owned by a household. Chrysostom makes an important distinction between tactical slaveholding (owning only a few slaves) and strategic slaveholding (owning a large number of slaves). Thus this chapter will also consider the implications of the proliferation of tactical slaveholding for the display of status and power by the Roman elite.

THE NATURE AND DYNAMICS OF DOMESTIC PASTORALIZATION

The concept of pastoralization is based on Foucault's work on governmentality and biopolitics. It refers to a very specific type of governance in which the one who governs others is seen in the role of a shepherd (*pasteur*), and the governed as a flock. While these roles appear in the writings of Plato, the shepherd-flock model of government is based mainly on principles from the Hebrew Bible.[4] Foucault notes, however, that pastoral power was transformed into something completely different in Christian thought.[5] It became an institutionalized form of power and government with a distinct character. In Christian pastoralism the shepherd leads

3. *Hom. 1 Cor.* 40.6 (F2.515–16): Καὶ γὰρ ἑνὶ τὸν ἕνα χρῆσθαι δεσπότην οἰκέτῃ μόνον ἐχρῆν· μᾶλλον δὲ καὶ δύο καὶ τρεῖς δεσπότας ἑνὶ οἰκέτῃ. . . . εἰ δὲ καὶ ἀναγκαῖον, ἕνα που μόνον, ἢ τὸ πολὺ δεύτερον. . . . εἰ δὲ πολλοὺς συνάγεις, οὐ φιλανθρωπίας ἕνεκεν τοῦτο ποιεῖς, ἀλλὰ θρυπτόμενος. . . . ἀλλ᾽ ἀγοράσας, καὶ τέχνας διδάξας ὥστε ἀρκεῖν ἑαυτοῖς, ἄφες ἐλευθέρους.

4. Michel Foucault, *Security, Territory, Population: Lectures at the Collège De France 1977–1978*, ed. Michel Senellart et al., trans. Graham Burchell (New York: Palgrave Macmillan, 2009), 115–254. Foucault utilizes many authors from late antiquity, including Chrysostom, Ambrose, Cyprian, Jerome, and Cassian.

5. Foucault, *Security, Territory, Population*, 164–65.

and directs the flock to salvation, watches over and teaches them, and disciplines, corrects, and punishes them. Care and spiritual guidance are the central concerns of Christian pastoralism. Foucault quotes Chrysostom as saying: "The pastor must take care of the whole town and even of the *orbis terrarum*."[6] Thus, when I speak of the pastoralization of the household, I refer to the discursive practice in which the values, principles, structures, and especially the functions and operations of Christian pastoral power are carried over to and duplicated in the household.

Pastoral power tends to spread and duplicate itself. The reason for this is, as Foucault notes, that the shepherd does not wield power over a territory per se, but over a multiplicity of people in different territories.[7] Although I do believe that in late antiquity pastoral power became highly territorial[8]—a development that Foucault by and large neglects—especially with the distribution of episcopal sees and sacralization of religious places, the focus was still on governing the flock. But what is the relevance of pastoralism to slaves? Although pastoralism is communal in that the shepherd cares for the whole flock, governing a multiplicity, it is also an individualized governmentality, since the pastor must account for each sheep, and in a household the sheep would have included slaves. The logical avenue of distribution of pastoral power was the household; churches, after all, primarily consisted of households, and the metaphor of the household of God was also a primary metaphor for the church. And because of the dynamics of pastoral power, bishops were often intimately involved with households.

As a subset of their role as spiritual advisers, bishops often took the role of domestic advisers. Kristina Sessa's work on the influence of bishops on Roman households in the West yields some important insights.[9] Although the *dominus* and *paterfamilias* of the house still remained the primary domestic authority, households often availed themselves of the advice of bishops in certain ethical, legal, and spiritual matters. Sessa discerns three contexts where episcopal advice was most commonly sought: in marriage, in the administration of land and property, and of course, in slaveholding (the issues in all three contexts, of course, being inextricably connected). Domestic episcopal advice, then, related to the art and practice of *oikonomia* (household management), and the household was a space where men could fashion their masculinity, and where bishops and spiritual leaders could increase their influence.[10] As I will demonstrate in this chapter,

6. Ibid., 168.

7. Ibid., 125.

8. This is a point especially demonstrated by Christine Shepardson, *Controlling Contested Places: Late Antique Antioch and the Spatial Politics of Religious Controversy* (Berkeley: University of California Press, 2014).

9. Kristina Sessa, *The Formation of Papal Authority in Late Antique Italy: Roman Bishops and the Domestic Sphere* (New York: Cambridge University Press, 2011), 127–73.

10. Ibid., 3–5.

discussions about the pastoralization of the household and *oikonomia* inevitably touch on the issue of masculinity.

Chrysostom, however, was not simply an ad hoc adviser on various legal and religious issues. He had an organized vision for the households of the cities in which he ministered, both in Antioch and in Constantinople. "If we manage our households in this [Christian] way," Chrysostom explains, "we will also be qualified for the management of the church. For surely a house is a little church."[11] Chrysostom envisioned households as "little churches." The pastoralization of the household was *the* central strategy in Chrysostom's vision of the transformation of the city, which he considered immoral and degenerate.[12] Domestic pastoralization in Chrysostom, then, implies the transformation of the household into a space similar to that of the church. However, Chrysostom did not ultimately achieve everything he sought to change with this strategy. This point is notably stressed by Peter Brown: "John's ideal of the Christian household as a lay monastery, closed to the profane world, excluded too much of the life of the city outside its walls. It had little impact at the time."[13]

Although pastoralization did not transform the city as universally as Chrysostom hoped, it was not without effect, and I do not believe the strategy was a total failure. The research of both Kate Cooper[14] and Kristina Sessa[15] has shown that Christianity profoundly reshaped the Roman household. And it is my intent in this book similarly to show that Chrysostom's work reshaped Roman households, though perhaps on a more realistic scale than he wanted. Christianity in general, and Chrysostom in particular, influenced not only the spiritual and religious life of the household, but also its ephemeral operation.[16] In some instances the changes were considerable. If we look at agricultural landholdings of households, an interesting picture emerges. In one of his homilies, Chrysostom refers to the construction of a church building on the villa estate of what appears to be one of his congregants. With this reference, Chrysostom may also be trying to gain the favor of the rural aristocracy, or at least to increase his influence among such families. In her work on the Christianization of the aristocracy in the West, Michele Salzman has illustrated that the rural landowning aristocracy was particularly

---

11. *Hom. Eph.* 20.3 (F4.311–12): "Αν οὕτω τὰς οἰκίας διοικῶμεν τὰς ἑαυτῶν, καὶ πρὸς ᾽Εκκλησίας ἐπιστασίαν ἐσόμεθα ἐπιτήδειοι· καὶ ἡ οἰκία γὰρ ᾽Εκκλησία ἐστὶ μικρά. In his *Serm. Gen.* 6 (PG 54.607.27–28), Chrysostom tells his audience to turn their houses into churches.

12. Aideen M. Hartney, *John Chrysostom and the Transformation of the City* (London: Duckworth, 2004), 67–71.

13. Peter R. L. Brown, *The Body and Society: Men, Women, and Sexual Renunciation in Early Christianity* (New York: Columbia University Press, 1988), 320.

14. Kate Cooper, *The Fall of the Roman Household* (New York: Cambridge University Press, 2007).

15. Sessa, *Formation of Papal Authority.*

16. Hartney, *Transformation of the City,* 117–32.

resistant to processes of Christianization. When reading Chrysostom, it seems that some of the villa culture of the West was carried over to the East; there were villas in Daphne, and Libanius mentions rural landowners. Villa estates were perhaps not as widespread in the East as in the West, but the sources confirm their existence.[17] The urban aristocracy, however, saw religious affiliation as an opportunity to acquire imperial favor.[18] Also, many elite men, as a result of the crisis of Roman masculinity in the fourth century, fled to their villa estates to live the life of leisure (*otium*). Life in the countryside was all but leisurely for nonelites. This crisis of elite masculinity, noted by Mathew Kuefler, had significant implications for doulology in late antiquity.[19]

It was against this backdrop that the villa church arose, and its establishment was strategic; it was intended to keep a pastoral grip on an aristocracy that was suspicious of Christianity, and on men who no longer saw any reason to continue living in the stressful urban world. Although not primarily concerned with the spiritual guidance of slaves, the villa church played an important role in their spiritual welfare and that of free resident laborers (*kolōnes, coloni*) working on the villa estates. "Now this is the palace of Christ, the church you are building," Chrysostom explains. "Do not look at the cost, but calculate the fruit." The spiritual care of laborers was an important function of this church-in-the-fields, as Chrysostom notes, "The laborers cultivate your land, you must cultivate their souls; they bring your fruits to you, you must lead them up to heaven."[20] The concept introduced by Chrysostom here—idea of spiritual agriculture—was common in ancient literature. In return for their work in the fields, laborers received spiritual sustenance. Chrysostom also introduces a new spiritual economy and profitability for the estate. Whereas authors like Cato, Varro, and Columella advise landholders to run their estates for maximum profit, Chrysostom wants them to become spiritual farmers and focus on the spiritual profitability of their lands; this was also the initiative of Philo's treatise on agriculture. Chrysostom envisions that each villa estate should have a church. He even encourages the participation of laborers from neighboring estates, and, probably, villages. The small villages scattered over the vast countryside of the East may have benefited from villa churches. The

17. Libanius, *Or.* 30 (Foerster 3.87–118); I am indebted to Christine Shepardson for her comments on Eastern rural culture.

18. Michele R. Salzman, *The Making of a Christian Aristocracy: Social and Religious Change in the Western Roman Empire* (Cambridge, MA: Harvard University Press, 2004), 82–84.

19. Mathew Kuefler, *The Manly Eunuch: Masculinity, Gender Ambiguity, and Christian Ideology in Late Antiquity* (Chicago: University of Chicago Press, 2001), 55–67.

20. *Hom. Act.* 18.5 (PG 60.147.36–40): Νῦν οὖν βασίλειά ἐστι τοῦ Χριστοῦ, τῆς ἐκκλησίας ἡ οἰκοδομή. Μὴ τὸ ἀνάλωμα ἴδῃς, ἀλλὰ τὸν καρπὸν λόγισαι· γεωργοῦσιν ἐκεῖνοι τὴν γῆν, σὺ γεώργησον αὐτῶν τὰς ψυχάς· φέρουσί σοι καρποὺς ἐκεῖνοι, σὺ εἰς τὸν οὐρανὸν αὐτοὺς ἀνάγαγε. See Sessa, *Formation of Papal Authority*, 164.

pastoralization of the household, and the introduction of spiritual agriculture, were interwoven in the day-to-day running of the villa.

The villa church had its own priest and functioned in basically the same way as any other church.[21] The priest may have been appointed from the many monks living near villages and farms, or from the patronage network of the owner as a favor to one of his friends or clients. The input of a local *chōrepiskopos,* a bishop of a rural district but subordinate to the urban bishop, was probably sought in most cases. Frans van de Paverd confirms that there were rural Christians serving as priests who visited the city during feast days. In his analysis of *De statuis* 19 (*Epulis ss. martyrum*), Van de Paverd problematizes the identity of the so-called men from the country to which the homily refers, and concludes these men were probably ordained priests serving in such country churches.[22] Chrysostom gives the landlord the authority to appoint an active board of clergy, and like Columella, who advises absentee landholders to be involved with the physical agriculture of the farm, Chrysostom advises them to be cultivators of spiritual husbandry. "For ought not each believer build a church," Chrysostom asks, "[and] get a teacher to assist him ... support a teacher, support a deacon, and a sacerdotal body corporate."[23] Although it was customary for bishops to approve these appointments, the clergy appointed to minister in these churches were mostly under the supervision of the landowners.[24]

Chrysostom describes the villa church as being like a wife or daughter of the landowner, to whom he must give a dowry. Moreover, maintaining a healthy spiritual agriculture ensures that the real agriculture, the winepresses and orchards, will yield good fruit because of the blessing of God. The church will also bring God's protection to the field. Chrysostom describes God's protection as a defensive wall around the lands. This advice was also common in Roman agronomy—the

21. For more on the dynamics of such villa churches, see Sessa, *Formation of Papal Authority,* 163–70.

22. For the role and function of monks and other holy men living in the countryside of the East, see Peter R. L. Brown, "The Rise and Function of the Holy Man in Late Antiquity," *Journal of Roman Studies* 61 (1971): 80–101. On the issue of ordained priests serving in rural churches, see Frans van de Paverd, *St. John Chrysostom, The Homilies on the Statues: An Introduction,* Orientalia christiana analecta 239 (Rome: Pontificium Institutum Studiorum Orientalium, 1991), 277–93.

23. *Hom. Act.* 18.4 (PG 60.147.2–4, 17–18): Οὐ γὰρ ἐχρῆν ἕκαστον τῶν πιστῶν ἐκκλησίαν οἰκοδομεῖν, διδάσκαλον λαμβάνειν πρὸς τὸ συναίρεσθαι ... θρέψον διδάσκαλον, θρέψον διάκονον καὶ ἱερατικὸν σύστημα; see Kim Bowes, *Private Worship, Public Values, and Religious Change in Late Antiquity* (New York: Cambridge University Press, 2008), 157.

24. Bowes, *Private Worship, Public Values,* 157–58. Jones also notes that it often happened that these clergy on villa estates were *coloni,* who were meagerly paid and often had to perform other jobs in addition to working in the parish; see CTh. 16.2.33.398; Arnold H. M. Jones, *The Later Roman Empire, 284–602: A Social, Economic and Administrative Survey* (Baltimore: Johns Hopkins University Press, 1964), 2:908–9, 1379.

successful estate had to carefully conduct all the necessary religious rites, especially those related to fertility. Fertility was a very important religious discourse in agrarian contexts, and Chrysostom here assures his audience that the Christian God is also a God of fertility, and will ensure a blessed harvest. This seems to Chrysostom to be a remedy for the lack of spiritual nourishment that agricultural slaves experienced. Being removed from the city had its disadvantages:

> I wish it were possible to bring those slaves who are outside into the cities. "What then," you would say, "if he should also become wicked?" But why should he, I ask you? Because he has come into the city? But consider that being on the outside he will be much more wicked. For he who is wicked within the city, will be much more so outside. For here he will be exempted from necessary cares, his master taking that care upon himself; but there the worry about those things will distract him perhaps even from things more necessary and more spiritual.[25]

Chrysostom expects slaveholders to take responsibility for the pastoral care of their slaves. Chrysostom also seems to believe that urban slaveholders take better care of their slaves than rural ones—a point that may have some truth to it. Slaves on large agricultural estates did not always live in acceptable circumstances, even for slaves. This is an interesting inversion of a common ancient perception that the *vita rustica* is much more beneficial to slaves than city life. Normally, agricultural slaves were seen in a more positive light. In older Roman agronomical literature the *vita rustica*, in general, was seen as being more beneficial to the formation of virtue. Columella believes that constant city life has made the ruling class of Roman men soft and resulted in the degeneration of farming in the Roman Empire.[26] However, the masculinity of elite men who abandon their civic duties and retreat to their villas in the country is also questioned. Here the aristocratic *vita rustica* is equated with the life of leisure (*otium*) and is not fitting for a free man.

This was also the case in late antiquity.[27] Free elite men had to visit their estates often and use them to enhance their manhood so that they could perform their civic duties optimally, but they must not use their estates as an escape from their civic life. Chrysostom understands that the simplicity of the *vita rustica* is beneficial for one's spiritual formation, but when it comes to slaves, he may have seen the matter differently. Slaves did not have the luxury of such mobility. They were stuck in the fields they had to till, along with various other "free" laborers who had very

---

25. *Hom. Phlm.* arg. (F6.327–28): Εἴθε τοὺς ἔξωθεν εἰς τὰς πόλεις εἰσωθεῖν ἐνῆν. Τί οὖν, φησὶν, ἂν καὶ αὐτὸς φαῦλος γένηται; Διὰ τί, εἰπέ μοι, παρακαλῶ; ὅτι πρὸς πόλιν εἰσῆλθεν; Ἀλλ᾿ ἐννόει, ὅτι καὶ ἔξω ὢν φαυλότερος ἔσται· ὁ γὰρ ἔνδον φαῦλος γενόμενος, πολλῷ μᾶλλον ἔξω ὤν· ἐνταῦθα μὲν γὰρ καὶ τῆς ἀναγκαίας φροντίδος ἀπήλλακται, τοῦ δεσπότου μεριμνῶντος· ἐκεῖ δὲ ἡ περὶ τούτων φροντὶς ἴσως ἀπάξει αὐτὸν καὶ τῶν ἀναγκαιοτέρων καὶ πνευματικωτέρων.

26. Columella, *Rust.* 1. preface (Ash 4–5).

27. Kuefler, *Manly Eunuch*, 65–66.

little mobility themselves. In the later Roman Empire legislation was introduced that bound *coloni* as "slaves of the land from which they were born" (*servi terrae ipsius cui nati sunt*), restricted their freedom of movement, and gave the landowner power over them that was similar to that of a slaveholder (*dominus*) over a slave.[28]

Thus, in Chrysostom's thought, the city functions as a type of carceral-disciplinary space. When Chrysostom speaks of the "city" here, he is referring to Christian urban spaces like the church and the Christian household—spaces conducive to conversion and Christianization.[29] It seems that Chrysostom would rather risk having slaves in close proximity to ecclesiastical influence, notwithstanding the dangers of the theater and the baths, than far away and removed from such influence, working in the fields. Although Chrysostom often idealized rural Christians who visited the city,[30] with regard to slaves the city had more direct recourse to Christianization than the countryside. The villa church assured, even if only theoretically, that slaves in the countryside could have access to some form of pastoral care.

Furthermore, if Chrysostom's comments are accurate and his advice was followed, which may have been the case, the villa church would have hosted gatherings composed mainly of slaves, *coloni,* and perhaps villagers and monks from the surrounding area. The pressure from various sides on *domini* to provide pastoral care to their slaves supports the accuracy of these accounts. This villa church can therefore be understood as a type of heterotopia, a psychogeographical modalization and spatialization of Christian spirituality, where the slave is secure and isolated from the dangers of the *vita rustica*. Heterotopias are described by Foucault as "spaces of otherness," a geography that separates itself from all other sites that may surround it, whether physically or symbolically.[31] The villa church represents not only a physical space that is foreign to the rustic and has more in common with the urban, but also all those technologies of urban pastoralization, including both ritual and spiritual guidance. The establishment of the villa church was an overt act of colonizing the physical agricultural landscape and planting within it an agriculture of the spirit, a psychic husbandry.

But what can we say about the care and management of slaves in urban households, households more in reach of pastoral power? How did pastoral power take hold of the urban household and its slaves, and what were the effects of this usurpation of domestic power? Chrysostom's audience was rather mixed—some, as

---

28. *CJ* 52.1.393; see Jones, *The Later Roman Empire,* 796–801, 1328.

29. For more on the politics of place and space in Chrysostom, see Shepardson, *Controlling Contested Places.*

30. Shepardson, *Controlling Contested Places,* 129–62.

31. See Michel Foucault, "Of Other Spaces, Heterotopias," *Architecture, Mouvement, Continuité* 5 (1984): 46–49; Stuart Elden and Jeremy W. Crampton, "Space, Knowledge, and Power: Foucault and Geography," in *Space, Knowledge and Power: Foucault and Geography,* ed. Stuart Elden and Jeremy W. Crampton (Farnham: Ashgate, 2007), 1–18.

we saw above, probably did own large villa estates with many slaves, but the majority were simple householders who were not illustriously wealthy; his audience may have included businesspeople, people in civil service, and most certainly people from more impoverished households. Although there is still much uncertainty about the number of slaves in urban households, it is likely that the majority of Chrysostom's audience were slaveholders, and those too poor to afford slaves no doubt had contact with them on a regular basis. We also know from Chrysostom himself that some less privileged households also had a slave or two, and that slaves owned slaves from their *peculium*. Domestic slaves were also present at some of the gatherings Chrysostom addressed. The pastoralization Chrysostom sought to impose on urban households was complex in both its discursivity and its practical application. The household was pastoralized in two ways: through a hierarchized network of power and authority mirroring that of the church, and through a duplication of the liturgical and ritual dynamics of the church.

At this stage I should mention that there was an additional crucial operation of domestic pastoralization at work in the household—the pastoralization of sexuality. Sexuality is a domestic matter, and it was clearly targeted by agents of pastoralism like Chrysostom. The pastoralization of sexuality included the regulation and restructuring of slave sexualities, especially in the light of the common occurrence of sexual exploitation of slaves. I will discuss this issue in greater detail in chapter 6. For now I will focus on the hierarchy of pastoral power that was duplicated in the household, and then the liturgical and ritual aspects of domestic pastoralization.

What we have in the first instance, then, is a reproduction of the excess of pastoral power in the late ancient Roman household. The *paterfamilias* now reflected the character and authority of a priest and vice versa, and even the slave father, who had to preside over his family, had this authority. The wife, children, and slaves in a household were all assigned new roles that were related to Christian domestic hierarchy, teaching, liturgy, and ritual. To demonstrate both the conceptual particularity and potency of this reproduction, I refer to this process as the pastoralization of the domestic somatoscape. I use the term *somatoscape* in this instance not only to emphasize the corporeality of this migration of power, but also to illustrate how this power penetrated the performativity of bodies in the domestic sphere. It was quite different from building a church in the fields on a villa estate. Rather, it was a colonization of a different character, one that penetrated, to the very core, "those subtle interactions and negotiations that are grafted onto domestic flesh, somatic performances between the *corps domestique* and the *espace domestique*."[32] It influenced the distribution and mobility

32. Chris L. de Wet, "Between the Domestic and the Agoric Somatoscape: John Chrysostom on the Appearance of Female Roman Aristocrats in the Marketplace," *Religion & Theology* 20, nos. 3–4 (2013): 206.

of bodies in the household—for example, slaves were now allowed in certain spaces where they would not normally be welcome, such as at the table while scripture was being read. It even touched on sexual positions, coital decorum, and eugenics, as we will see in chapter 6, and the way people feasted and partied.

Both Peter Brown and Kim Bowes have noted Chrysostom's idealism, and its failure, when it came to the pastoralization of the household.[33] It was especially his encounters with Constantinopolitan households that caused most of his despondency—his stringent and idealistic commands to elite households along with his autocratic financial management may have been among the main reasons for his eventual alienation and deportation.[34] He may have had more success in Antioch. Yet Chrysostom dreamt of the household as untainted by the secular mire of the city. At the core of this ideal pastoralization there is the duplication of sacerdotal authority in the body of the *paterfamilias*. We have seen in the case of villa churches that Chrysostom allowed the lord of the estate to appoint and oversee the clerical body of the villa church, giving him duties similar to those of a bishop. The landholder also had to be personally involved in the spiritual agriculture of those laboring in the fields, like a priest or a deacon. The transmission of pastoral power to the urban domestic sphere may not have differed much, in principle, from its transference to the rustic sphere. In the urban household the *paterfamilias* also had to act as priest of the house—again not an alien notion in late ancient Roman *oikonomia*. In traditional Roman religion, the *paterfamilias* had to sacrifice on behalf of his household to the Lares, Penates, and Genius.[35] The church is the house (*oikos*) of God and represents the authority of God on earth, an authority embodied in the episcopate. This power is then transposed to patriarchy and kyriarchy, and the father-slaveholder emerges as the priest and teacher of his house.

Moreover, like Xenophon, Chrysostom also subscribed to the notion of holistic *oikonomia,* and assumed an isomorphism between political and ecclesiastical micro- and macrocosms:

Everyone's house is a city, and every man is a prince in his own house. It is clear that this is the character of the wealthy house, where there are both lands, and overseers, and rulers over rulers. But I am also saying that the house of the poor man is like a city. Since there are also offices of authority here; for instance, the husband has authority over the wife, the wife over the slaves, the slaves again over their own wives; again the wives and the husbands over the children. Does he not appear to you to be, as it were, a type of king, having so many authorities under his own authority? And

33. Brown, *Body and Society*, 319–20; Bowes, *Private Worship, Public Values*, 116–22.
34. Bowes, *Private Worship, Public Values,* 119–20.
35. Salzman, *Making of a Christian Aristocracy,* 155.

is it not crucial that he should be more skilled both in domestic and civic government than all the rest? For the one who knows how to manage these in their various
relations, will also know how to select the fittest people for offices, truly, and will
choose excellent ones. And in this way the wife will be a second king in the house,
lacking only the crown; and he who knows how to choose this king, will excellently
regulate all the others.[36]

The wife then becomes a surrogate of male authority, who is especially responsible
for the governance of children and slaves. When it came to slave management, it
was the mistress (*despoina, domina*) of the house who was most involved in its
daily operation, especially in the surveillance of slaves. In this regard, Foucault
rightly observes that the power of hierarchized surveillance operates like a "piece
of machinery," which produces power and distributes domestic bodies in a con-
tinuous field that is regulated by a series of "calculated gazes."[37] Chrysostom's
holistic oeconomical ideology assumes an isomorphism between the domestic
somatoscape and the church in terms of both hierarchical structure and regulatory
function. The domestic hierarchization is then reduplicated in slave families. The
sacerdotal authority of the slaveholder is also reduplicated in the slave father, and
as we know from other sources noted in chapter 2, slaves belonging to slaves also
had to answer to their enslaved masters.[38]

The reduplicated ecclesiastical hierarchy in the domestic sphere now enables
the second mode of reproduction of pastoral power in the household—that of liturgy and ritual. This second modalization is somewhat complex; since its very
beginning Christianity has been domestic, with many gatherings taking place in
house churches.[39] Slaves were mostly included in these gatherings, where they had
certain ritual obligations, like being baptized and partaking in the communal
meal. This was not unique to Christianity. Since slaves were part of the broader
familia, their participation in the domestic cult and household *collegium* was not
alien to Roman religion at all. Like the *paterfamilias,* slaves also had responsibili-

36. *Hom. Eph.* 22.1 (F4.335): Πόλις ἐστὶν ἡ ἑκάστου οἰκία, ἄρχων ἐστὶν ἕκαστος τῆς ἑαυτοῦ οἰκίας.
Καὶ ὅτι μὲν τοιαύτη ἡ τῶν πλουτούντων, εὔδηλον, ἔνθα καὶ ἀγροὶ καὶ ἐπίτροποι καὶ ἄρχοντες ἐπὶ
ἄρχουσιν· ἐγὼ δὲ καὶ τὴν τῶν πενήτων οἰκίαν φημὶ πόλιν εἶναι. Καὶ γὰρ καὶ ἐνταῦθά εἰσιν ἀρχαί· οἷον,
κρατεῖ τῆς γυναικὸς ὁ ἀνήρ, ἡ γυνὴ τῶν οἰκετῶν, οἱ οἰκέται τῶν ἰδίων γυναικῶν· πάλιν αἱ γυναῖκες
καὶ οἱ ἄνδρες τῶν παίδων. Ἆρα οὐ δοκεῖ σοι, καθάπερ τις βασιλεὺς εἶναι, τοσούτους ἔχων ἄρχοντας
ὑποτεταγμένους ἑαυτῷ, καὶ πάντων προσήκειν αὐτὸν οἰκονομικώτερον εἶναι καὶ πολιτικώτερον; Ὁ
γὰρ εἰδὼς διαφόρως κεχρῆσθαι τούτοις, οἶδε τοὺς ἐπιτηδείους ἄρχοντας αἱρεῖσθαι, καὶ αἱρήσεταί γε
λαμπρούς. Οὐκοῦν ἔσται βασιλεὺς ἕτερος ἡ γυνὴ ἐν οἰκίᾳ χωρὶς τοῦ διαδήματος, καὶ ὁ εἰδὼς τὸν
βασιλέα τοῦτον αἱρεῖσθαι, πάντα τὰ ἄλλα καλῶς διαθήσει. See *Hom. 1 Cor.* 34 (F2.427).

37. Michel Foucault, *Discipline & Punish: The Birth of the Prison,* trans. Alan Sheridan (New York:
Vintage, 1977), 177.

38. *Hom. Matt.* 58.6 (PG 58.571.16–572.1).

39. Carolyn Osiek, Margaret Y. MacDonald, and Janet H. Tulloch, *A Woman's Place: House
Churches in Earliest Christianity* (Minneapolis: Fortress Press, 2006).

ties in the household cult. Bowes notes that in certain areas of the Roman world, household shrines were most commonly found in service quarters like kitchens.[40]

We have, during the time of Chrysostom, a potent domestic Christianity, and a world in which slaves played a pivotal role in domestic devotional and cult activities. Thus, when bishops offer advice and guidelines for domestic liturgy and ritual, it is not so much a new framework that is being imposed, but rather an attempt at regulation and modification of the current cultic life of the *domus,* and such regulations had to include the role of slaves.[41]

Yet Chrysostom's vision for households in Antioch was still very idealistic, and his antagonistic encounters with Constantinopolitan households may have been more sobering. Many of the Constantinopolitan households that Chrysostom sought to regulate were aristocratic households, and shortly before his exile, we also see various aristocratic households lined up against him, and, according to Palladius, most notably those that were close to the empress Eudoxia—namely, the homes of the widows Marsa and Castricia, and Eugraphia.[42] It may have been the case that Chrysostom's ideal of a network of house churches, cells of purity and chastity, spread out across the city, his Antiochene dream, morphed into a political power play in his Constantinopolitan nightmare. Regulating domestic religion also had its financial advantages, in both urban households and villa churches.[43] So we must read Chrysostom's advice on how to turn one's house into a church in these contexts—the comments are sometimes idealized, and at other times they represent a more desperate attempt to regulate domestic power structures—not without effect.

Besides its regulatory function in the household, ritualized pastoral power had a corrective impetus, especially regarding slaves. Among the many rituals Chrysostom prescribes, the reading of scripture stands out as one of the fundamental practices of a Christian household. Other practices include fasting, the singing of spiritual songs (especially psalms), prayer, and installing a box in one's house for the purposes of almsgiving (the poor box).[44] Slaves also partook in Christian

40. Bowes, *Private Worship, Public Values,* 30.

41. At an earlier time, for instance, we hear Tertullian complaining and warning Christians to keep an eye on their slaves so that they may not import non-Christian religious practices secretly into the household; see Tertullian, *Idol.* 15 (PL 759.18–762.10); J. Albert Harrill, "The Domestic Enemy: A Moral Polarity of Household Slaves in Early Christian Apologies and Martyrdoms," in *Early Christian Families in Context: An Interdisciplinary Dialogue,* ed. David L. Balch and Carolyn Osiek, Religion, Marriage, and Family (Grand Rapids, MI: Eerdmans, 2003), 237.

42. See Palladius, *Dial.* 4.92–94 (SC 341.94–95); Bowes, *Private Worship, Public Values,* 118–20.

43. Bowes, *Private Worship, Public Values,* 118.

44. I am greatly indebted here to Blake Leyerle for her excellent treatment of household ritual in Chrysostom, as well as for our numerous discussions on the topic; Blake Leyerle, "'Turn Your House into a Church': Prescribed Domestic Rituals in the Preaching of John Chrysostom" (paper presented at the Annual Meeting of the Society of Biblical Literature, Chicago, 2012). For more on the poor box,

public processions, vigils, and festivities.[45] In his comments about the villa churches, Chrysostom highlights the rituals of prayer, hymns, and communion as vehicles of God's blessing on the land.[46] During his time in Antioch, Chrysostom remarks:

> Let us take all this to heart, then, dearly beloved, and on returning home let us serve a double meal, one of food and the other of sacred reading; while the husband reads what has been said, let the wife learn and the children listen, and let not even the slaves be deprived of the chance to listen. Turn your house into a church; you are, in fact, even responsible for the salvation both of the children and of the slaves. Just as we are accountable for you, so too each of you is accountable for your slave, your wife, your child.[47]

This passage clearly shows the reproduction of regulatory pastoral power in Christian domestic rituals, and there is no reason to believe that some households did not follow these guidelines. In Chrysostom's thinking, there needs to be symmetry between the church and domestic religious practices. Chrysostom advises his congregants to return home after attending the sermon, and to repeat the service in their homes. The *paterfamilias* becomes the mirror image of the preacher, and must read and explain the same scripture that was exposited in the service. This must be done in the presence of the whole *familia,* including the domestic slaves. The purpose is to duplicate and amplify the flow of pastoral power in the household, thereby tightening the doctrinal grip on domestic religious observance, and also to correct and instill virtue in those listening; the repetition of the church service in the house becomes an extension of the machinery of pastoralism.

The regulation of household rituals was not only corrective. Regulating domestic rituals served as a type of quarantine, an operation to keep the religious identity of the household pure from syncretistic tendencies. It therefore became a measure

---

see Chrysostom's *De eleemosyna* 4 (PG 51.266.16–38); see also Wendy Mayer, "John Chrysostom on Poverty," in *Preaching Poverty in Late Antiquity: Perceptions and Realities,* ed. Pauline Allen, Bronwen Neil, and Wendy Mayer, Arbeiten zur Kirchen- und Theologiegeschichte (Leipzig: Evangelische Verlagsanstalt, 2009), 103–4.

45. *Omn. mart.* 1 (Stavronikita 6.139r.12–22; *CPG* 4441.15): ἀντὶ σηρικῶν ἱματίων σάκκων . . . ἀντὶ μύρων σποδὸν ὑποστρωσαμένην . . . ἀντὶ ὑπογραφῆς ἐπιτριμμάτων. See Wendy Mayer, trans., *The Cult of the Saints,* Popular Patristics Series (Crestwood, NY: St. Vladimir's Seminary Press, 2006), 241. I would like to thank Wendy Mayer for providing me with the text of Stavronikita 6 (*CPG* 4441).

46. *Hom. Act.* 18.4 (PG 60.47.47–50.22).

47. *Serm. Gen.* 6 (PG 54.607.22–39): Ταῦτα οὖν ἅπαντα, ἀγαπητοί, διακρατῶμεν, καὶ οἴκαδε ἀναχωρήσαντες διπλῆν παραθῶμεν τὴν τράπεζαν, τὴν τῶν σιτίων, καὶ τὴν τῆς ἀκροάσεως, καὶ λεγέτω μὲν ἀνὴρ τὰ εἰρημένα, μανθανέτω δὲ γυνή, ἀκουέτω δὲ καὶ παιδία, μὴ ἀποστερείσθωσαν δὲ μηδὲ οἰκέται τῆς ἀκροάσεως ταύτης. Ἐκκλησίαν ποίησόν σου τὴν οἰκίαν· καὶ γὰρ καὶ ὑπεύθυνος εἶ καὶ τῆς τῶν παιδίων καὶ τῆς τῶν οἰκετῶν σωτηρίας· καὶ καθάπερ ἡμεῖς ὑπὲρ ὑμῶν ἀπαιτούμεθα λόγον. οὕτω καὶ ἕκαστος ὑμῶν καὶ ὑπὲρ οἰκέτου, καὶ ὑπὲρ γυναικὸς, καὶ ὑπὲρ παιδὸς ἀπαιτεῖται εὐθύνας. Translation (slightly modified): Robert C. Hill, trans., *St. John Chrysostom: Eight Sermons on the Book of Genesis* (Brookline, MA: Holy Cross Orthodox Press, 2004), 105.

of security, a drawing of religious borders and a social geography of exclusion. Pastoral power aimed to both seize and protect its prize from other opposing discursive forces. It is a social geography of exclusion, since Chrysostom not only includes the Christian rituals mentioned above, but he anathematizes other rituals like observing the Sabbath and other Jewish feasts,[48] as well as what he calls "Greek superstitions," like those for naming infants by burning candles.[49] This is important because it would complicate matters in intermarriages of Christian and non-Christian spouses.[50] In addition, many slaves in the households of Antioch and Constantinople were probably not Romans. The presence of barbarian slaves was a source of anxiety for many Romans. By keeping slaves close to the ritual operation of the Christian household, the danger of slaves importing non-Christian religious practices into the household might be limited. For example, Chrysostom refers to the superstition of wet nurses who mark the foreheads of children with mud to guard them from the evil eye.[51]

It seems that some Christian households also resisted efforts like those of Chrysostom to expunge the household of any non-Christian influence. Isabella Sandwell has convincingly shown how problematic Chrysostom considered the relations and allegiances between Christians, Jews, and Greeks in Antioch, in both social and religious contexts.[52] Chrysostom's concern also illustrates that the religious identity, and consequently the rituals, of these households were not monolithic. Sandwell uses Bourdieu's notion of habitus to explain the dynamics of religious identity of Christians, Jews, and Greeks in the time of Chrysostom.[53] They did not function according to religio-juridical lines of separation, like those Chrysostom proposed, but rather coexisted and influenced each other in a society that was perhaps more mutually inclusive than the sources often illustrate.

Finally, Chrysostom's ritualization of the household was also a totalizing discourse. He expected *familiae* not only to conduct rituals at times of religious observance. In Chrysostom's thought there is a universal colonization of domestic spatiality and temporality. This is most visible in his comments on prayer as a domestic ritual. All spaces and times are appropriate for prayer. "It is possible for a servant making purchases and running hither and yon, or standing in the

48. Christians adopting Jewish religious practices is Chrysostom's major headache in his homilies *Adv. Jud.*

49. See *Inan.* 48 (SC 188.146); *Hom. 1 Cor.* 12.13 (F2.146).

50. It is interesting that there is no legislation from the fourth century prohibiting "pagans" from marrying Christians, although Christians are specifically forbidden to marry Jews; see *C.Th.* 3.7.2, 9.7.5, 16.8.6; see Salzman, *Making of a Christian Aristocracy*, 315.

51. *Hom. 1 Cor.* 12.13 (F2.146–47); see also the discussion in chapter 4 on birth superstitions.

52. Isabella Sandwell, *Religious Identity in Late Antiquity: Greeks, Jews and Christians in Antioch* (New York: Cambridge University Press, 2007), 208–12.

53. Ibid., 17–33.

kitchen, when there is no possibility of going to church," Chrysostom says, "to pray attentively and ardently. Place is not something God is ashamed of."[54] Every space, every moment, every act of labor, the entire field of the domestic somatoscape, is ritualized and sacralized. Fasting, for instance, instills a particular health in the household, in that it removes the stress and busyness of cooks and servants running around and shouting, and, most importantly, curbs inebriation at the very core.[55] This totalized devotion must also act as a testimony to non-Christians, especially when it comes to feasting and avoiding drunkenness—the symposium must be transformed:

> And I say these things not thereby forbidding you to meet together or have supper at a common table, but to prevent you from behaving shamefully, and wanting indulgence to be proper indulgence, and not a punishment, or vengeance, or drunkenness and debauchery. Let the Greeks learn that Christians are the best at feasting! And to feast in an orderly way. For *rejoice*, it says, *in the Lord with trembling* [Ps. 2:11]. But how are we to rejoice? By reciting hymns, making prayers, introducing psalms in the place of those illiberal songs. So will Christ also be present at our table, and will fill the whole banquet with blessing, when you pray, when you sing spiritual songs, when you invite the poor to share in what is set before you, when you set much order and temperance over the banquet. And so you will turn the room into church, hymns to the master of all things in the place of ill-timed shouts and cheers.[56]

Christian households must set an example of holiness to outside eyes by introducing the rituals of prayer and the singing of hymns. Hymnodies and psalmodies must replace menial or illiberal songs in the Christian symposium. There must be no instance of clamoring or a drunken contretemps. This again assumes a polarized view of religious identity, an insider-outsider scheme that Chrysostom often sought to impose on his congregants. The table was a very important setting in early Christianity. Slaves were often included in the table rituals, and here Chrys-

---

54. *Anna* 4.6 (PG 54.668.8–12): ἔξεστιν οἰκέτῃ, καὶ ὠνουμένῳ, καὶ ἀναβαίνοντι καὶ καταβαίνοντι, καὶ μαγειρείῳ παρεστῶτι, ὅταν μὴ δυνατὸν εἰς ἐκκλησίαν ἐλθεῖν, εὐχὴν ποιεῖσθαι ἐκτενῆ καὶ διεγηγερμένην. Οὐκ ἐπαισχύνεται τόπον ὁ Θεός. Translation: Robert C. Hill, trans., *Homilies on Hannah, David and Saul,* St. John Chrysostom: Old Testament Homilies 1 (Brookline, MA: Holy Cross Orthodox Press, 2003), 120; see Leyerle, "'Turn Your House into a Church.'"

55. *Anna* 1.1 (PG 54.633.13–42); see Hill, *Homilies on Hannah, David and Saul,* 66.

56. *Hom. Rom.* 25[24].2 (F1.400): Ταῦτα δὲ λέγω, οὐ κωλύων συνιέναι οὐδὲ κοινῇ συνδειπνεῖν, ἀλλὰ κωλύων ἀσχημονεῖν, καὶ βουλόμενος τὴν τρυφὴν εἶναι τρυφήν, ἀλλὰ μὴ κόλασιν μηδὲ τιμωρίαν καὶ μέθην καὶ κῶμον. Μαθέτωσαν Ἕλληνες, ὅτι μάλιστα Χριστιανοὶ τρυφᾶν ἴσασι, καὶ τρυφᾶν μετὰ κόσμου. Ἀγαλλιᾶσθε γὰρ, φησὶ, τῷ Κυρίῳ ἐν τρόμῳ. Πῶς δὲ ἔστιν ἀγαλλιᾶσθαι; Ὕμνους λέγοντας, εὐχὰς ποιουμένους, ψαλμοὺς ἐπεισάγοντας ἀντὶ τῶν ἀνελευθέρων ἐκείνων ἀσμάτων. Οὕτω καὶ ὁ Χριστὸς τῇ τραπέζῃ παρέσται, καὶ εὐλογίας ἐμπλήσει τὴν εὐωχίαν ἅπασαν, ὅταν εὔχῃ, ὅταν ᾅδῃς πνευματικὰ, ὅταν πένητας ἐπὶ τῶν προκειμένων τὴν κοινωνίαν καλῇς, ὅταν εὐταξίαν πολλὴν καὶ σωφροσύνην ἐπιστήσῃς τῷ συμποσίῳ· οὕτω καὶ ἐκκλησίαν ἐργάσῃ τὸν τόπον, ἀντὶ τῶν ἀκαίρων κραυγῶν καὶ εὐφημιῶν τὸν τῶν ἁπάντων Δεσπότην ὑμνῶν.

ostom also encourages his members to invite the poor to their feast. The feast is then also transformed into a church through the addition of the rituals of prayer and hymns, and through the invitation of the poor. For Chrysostom, slaves are almost always present, whether they are praying silently in the kitchen or listening attentively to the repetition of the scripture reading in the hours after the church service. We will now examine the dynamics between slaves and other household members more closely by first looking at the differences between slaves and the wife and children of the household.

SLAVES AND THE WIFE AND CHILDREN OF A HOUSEHOLD

The term *familia* referred to those individuals in the household who were subject to the *patria potestas,* including household slaves. The common thread among wives, children, and slaves is that all of them were subject to the authority of the *paterfamilias.* But the dynamics of this domination were not uniform in all cases. For Chrysostom, a husband's rule over his wife was very different from his rule over a slave. The two main differences between the wife and the slave in their relationship to the *paterfamilias* derive from their places in the domestic hierarchy, which was based on principles from the biblical creation account, and the nature of the fear, or respect, they had to show the *paterfamilias.*

In the first instance, as we also noted in chapter 2, conjugal domination was a natural form of governance, while the domination of slaves was unnatural and the result of sin. "From the beginning, God made only one form of government, placing man over woman," we hear from Chrysostom, "but after our race ran aground into much disorder, other forms of rule appeared, that of slaveholders, that of secular governors."[57] Later in the same homily Chrysostom explains the hierarchical functioning of the household in very specific terms:

> Furthermore, in order that the one may be submissive and the other rule, for having equal honor often leads to fighting, he consecrated it not to be a democracy, but a monarchy. And as in an army, one may see this order in every household. In the rank of king, for instance, there is the husband; but in the rank of lieutenant and general, the wife; and the children too are given a third rank in rule. Then after these a fourth rule, that of the domestic slaves. For these also exercise power over their inferiors, and some of them are often set over the whole household, guarding the rank of the master, but still as a domestic slave. And with this again another rule, and among them the wives, the children, and among the children yet another, according to their

---

57. *Hom. 1 Cor.* 34.7 (F2.427): Καὶ ἐξ ἀρχῆς μὲν μίαν ἐποίησεν ἀρχήν, τὸν ἄνδρα ἐπιστήσας τῇ γυναικί· ἐπειδὴ δὲ εἰς πολλὴν ἐξώκειλεν ἀταξίαν τὸ γένος ἡμῶν, καὶ ἑτέρας κατέστησε, τὰς τῶν δεσποτῶν, τὰς τῶν ἀρχόντων·

age and sex. For among the children the female does not exercise equal power . . . . Therefore even before humanity was increased to a multitude, when there were only the first two, he commanded the male to rule, and the female to obey.[58]

We have here an integrated and functional domestic politic. Chrysostom is very clear about the nature of domestic governance—it is a monarchy (*basileia*), not a democracy (*dēmokratia*). Again we see Chrysostom's holistic oeconomical framework surfacing. In the terms of military and political organization, the natural role of the husband is that of a king, and the wife is the lieutenant and general. The term *homotimon* also denotes military status, often referring to generals who have equal honor in terms of their capacity to command troops. In other words, the authority of the husband and wife is not equal. This position of the wife is related to the governance of slaves, as seen above in *Homiliae in epistulam ad Ephesios* 22.1. Although the husband rules then as both king and priest, the wife manages the household slaves in the performance of their duties. Chrysostom was often very concerned about the way women treated their slaves. The wife ought to gain her husband's respect in the way she treated the slaves.[59]

This hierarchy was duplicated within the slave family—the slave husband had to take responsibility over his family. Chrysostom mentions that although slaves are often charged with managing the whole estate of the slaveholder, the slave remains a slave, again illustrating the limits of social mobility. It is interesting that Chrysostom makes some pedopsychological observations here—children also have implicit social hierarchies in terms of age and sex, and even here male children dominate young females. The social conditioning that supported distinctions between free males, females, and enslaved persons probably took place from early childhood.

Although Chrysostom rarely sees the wife in the same social light as a slave, he does describe marriage as a type of slavery. When advising women against marriage he states that marriage enslaves the wife to a certain measure, not only to the husband but also in terms of her obligations as domestic manager. Virginity is better because it excludes any type of submission: "For marriage truly is a chain, not only because of the multitude of its anxieties and daily worries, but also because it

---

58. *Hom. 1 Cor.* 34.6 (F2.425): Εἶτα ἵνα τὸ μὲν ὑποτάττηται, τὸ δὲ ἄρχῃ τὸ γὰρ ὁμότιμον οἶδε πολλάκις μάχην εἰσάγειν· οὐκ ἀφῆκε δημοκρατίαν εἶναι, ἀλλὰ βασιλείαν, καὶ καθάπερ ἐν στρατοπέδῳ, ταύτην ἄν τις ἴδοι τὴν διάταξιν καθ᾽ ἑκάστην οἰκίαν. Ἔστι γοῦν ἐν τάξει μὲν βασιλέως ὁ ἀνὴρ, ἐν τάξει δὲ ὑπάρχου ἡ γυνὴ καὶ στρατηγοῦ· καὶ οἱ παῖδες δὲ ἀρχὴν κεκλήρωνται τρίτην· εἶτα μετὰ ταῦτα ἀρχὴ τετάρτη ἡ τῶν οἰκετῶν· καὶ γὰρ καὶ οὗτοι κρατοῦσι τῶν ἐλαττόνων, καὶ εἷς τις πολλάκις τοῖς πᾶσιν ἐφέστηκε, τὴν τοῦ δεσπότου τάξιν διατηρῶν, πλὴν ὡς οἰκέτης. Καὶ μετὰ ταύτης ἑτέρα πάλιν ἀρχὴ καὶ ἐν αὐτοῖς ἡ τῶν γυναικῶν, ἡ τῶν παίδων, καὶ ἐν αὐτοῖς τοῖς παισὶ πάλιν ἑτέρα κατὰ τὴν ἡλικίαν καὶ κατὰ τὴν φύσιν· οὐδὲ γὰρ ἐν τοῖς παιδίοις ὁμοίως τὸ θῆλυ κρατεῖ. . . . Διὰ τοῦτο καὶ πρὶν εἰς πλῆθος ἐξενεχθῆναι τὸ γένος, δύο μόνων ὄντων τῶν πρώτων, τῷ μὲν ἄρχειν, τῇ δὲ ἄρχεσθαι ἐκέλευσε.

59. *Hom. Eph.* 15.2 (F4.259).

forces spouses to submit to one another, which is harsher than every other kind of servitude."[60] Chrysostom's remarks on marriage are complex, since he had to manage opinions thereof and act to avoid people falling into sin—virginity is better than marriage, yet being married is still better than risking fornication; it was a difficult balance to strike even for Chrysostom. So because of the submission involved in marriage, Chrysostom still sees it as a type of servitude that is inferior to virginity. Virginity is true freedom (despite virgins and monks still being slaves of Christ).

In the second instance, the fear and respect that the wife had to show her husband differed from that of the slave toward the *paterfamilias*. Fear lubricated the gears of the Roman domestic machine. It governed domestic behavior and insulated the control of the *paterfamilias* and the order he was expected to maintain. Fear was also something to be applied to children and slaves to inhibit their passions, and in Chrysostom it functioned as a very important pedagogical apparatus. Fear of punishment was one of the most effective utilizations of fear.[61] Fear of hell stood out as a potent phobic technology to control young adolescents[62] and slaves.[63] Infernal fear was, in general, a useful measure for social control.[64] But physical punishment also served as an excellent deterrent, especially in the case of slaves; Chrysostom recounts that, "often, by whipping one domestic slave, they make the rest more temperate out of fear."[65] Punishment of slaves was in most instances a public affair, or at least one where all those in the household who needed to get the message were present.[66] The fear that a slave had of the *paterfamilias* was based solely on the latter's ability to punish and, if he wished, drastically alter the quality of the slave's life through various deprivations.[67]

The fear that a wife ought to show her husband is quite different in Chrysostom's thought. In his homilies on the Ephesian household code (Eph. 5:22–6:9), Chrysostom explains this difference in some detail. The main difference between the wife and the slave in relation to the *paterfamilias* is based on their corporeal unity and separation. The husband and wife are one body, with the husband as

60. *Virg.* 41.1.11–15 (SC 125.236): Δεσμὸς γὰρ ὄντως ὁ γάμος, οὐ διὰ τὸν τῶν φροντίδων ὄχλον μόνον οὐδὲ διὰ τὰς λύπας τὰς καθημερινὰς ἀλλ᾽ ὅτι παντὸς οἰκέτου χαλεπώτερον ἀλλήλοις ὑποκεῖσθαι τοὺς γεγαμηκότας καταναγκάζει. Translation: Sally R. Shore, trans., *John Chrysostom: On Virginity; Against Remarriage* (Lewiston, NY: Edwin Mellen Press, 1983), 61.

61. Harper, *Slavery in the Late Roman World,* 219–48.

62. *Inan.* 41 (SC 188.138), 44 (SC 188.142).

63. *Hom. Phlm.* 3.2 (F6.346–53).

64. *Hom. Rom.* 6[5].6 (F1.66–67).

65. *Laz.* 3.7 (PG 48.1003.42–43): ἕνα πολλάκις μαστιγώσαντες οἰκέτην, τοὺς λοιποὺς σωφρονεστέρους ἐποίησαν τῷ φόβῳ.

66. For more on public punishment and especially whipping, see Jennifer A. Glancy, *Corporal Knowledge: Early Christian Bodies* (New York: Oxford University Press, 2010), 24–47.

67. See chapter 5.

head, as Christ is head of the church (Eph. 5:22–24). The metaphor of the body implies both hierarchy and concord.[68] According to Ephesians 5:33, the wife must also fear her husband. Fear, which is perhaps better translated as "respect" if one follows Chrysostom's reasoning, is embedded in any hierarchy. "The wife is a second ruler. She must then not expect equal honor (*tēn isotimian*), for she is under the head"; here Chrysostom highlights the hierarchical domestic politic, but it is also a symbiosis, and the husband must not "look down on her as being in subjection, for she is the body, and if the head despises the body, it will also perish."[69]

In response to the respect and obedience of the wife, the husband must show love. Love here is both mystical and a sign of the providence of the husband. It is mystical in that it is based on the mystical union of the bodies of husband and wife, which is like the union between Christ and the church.[70] But the husband also shows love by providing for the needs of the wife (similar to his provision for the needs of slaves). Although slaves were indeed considered surrogate bodies of their owners,[71] there is no mystical and corporeal unity between master and slave in Chrysostom's thought. The corporeal unity of the husband and wife is natural and ordered by God. Since this unity between husband and wife is natural, it must also be one of concord (*eirēnē*) and unity of the pair (*syzygia*).

The dynamics of the domestic body politic, in Chrysostom's thought, is based on an interchange between love, fear, and obedience.[72] The most intimate operation of the household is seen in the corporeal unity between husband and wife, which is totally absent between slaveholders and slaves, since the latter relationship and form of governance is not natural but a consequence of sin. The dynamics of fear and governance differ for anthropogenic and doulogenic reasons. Love and fear then are very different for wives and slaves, yet in Chrysostom love and fear seem to be two sides of the same coin. The curativity of conjugal and kyriarchal love is similar, the husband cares and corrects both his wife and his slaves; but whereas kyriarchal love also proves to be productive, conjugal love is more cooperative.

---

68. For an excellent discussion of the rhetoric of the body in early Christian discourse, see Dale B. Martin, *The Corinthian Body* (New Haven, CT: Yale University Press, 1995).

69. *Hom. Eph.* 20.2 (F4.308): Ἀρχὴ δευτέρα ἐστὶν ἡ γυνή. Μήτε οὖν αὕτη τὴν ἰσοτιμίαν ἀπαιτείτω· ὑπὸ γὰρ τὴν κεφαλήν ἐστι· μήτε ἐκεῖνος ὡς ὑποτεταγμένης καταφρονείτω· σῶμα γάρ ἐστι, κἂν καταφρονῇ τοῦ σώματος ἡ κεφαλὴ, καὶ αὐτὴ προσαπολεῖται.

70. For a more detailed discussion of Chrysostom's views on marriage and sexuality, see Elizabeth A. Clark, "Sexual Politics in the Writings of John Chrysostom," *Anglican Theological Review* 59, no. 1 (1977): 3–20; Clark, *Jerome, Chrysostom, and Friends: Essays and Translations* (Lewiston, NY: Edwin Mellen, 1979), 1–34; Shore, *Chrysostom: On Virginity; Against Remarriage*, vii–xlii; Brown, *Body and Society*, 305–22; Jo Ann C. Heaney-Hunter, "'Disobedience and Curse' or 'Affection of the Soul'? John Chrysostom, Marriage, and Sin," *Diakonia* 24 (1991): 171–86.

71. Glancy, *Slavery in Early Christianity*, 15–16.

72. *Hom. Eph.* 20.2 (F4.308).

But, then, what exactly is the nature of the fear that slaves should exhibit toward their masters? Chrysostom makes a very important point in this instance:

Slaves, [Paul] says, be obedient to your masters according to the flesh [Eph. 6:5]. Immediately he uplifts the wounded soul, immediately he consoles it. Do not be grieved, he says, because you are inferior to the wife and the children. Slavery is only a name. The domination is according to the flesh, brief and temporary; for whatever is of the flesh, is not permanent. With fear, he adds, and trembling. Do you see that he does not demand the same fear from slaves as from wives? For in that case he simply said, and the wife must fear her husband [Eph. 5:33]. In the case of slaves he expands the demand, with fear, he says, and trembling, in singleness of your heart, as unto Christ. He repeatedly says this. What are you saying, blessed Paul? He is a brother [Philem. 16], he enjoys the same benefits, he belongs to the same body. And, moreover, he became the brother, not only of the master himself, but also of the Son of God, he enjoys all the same advantages. Yet do you say, obey your masters according to the flesh, with fear and trembling? Yes, since he said it, I say it. For if I command free persons to submit to another in the fear of God, as he said above, submitting yourselves one to another in the fear of Christ [Eph. 5:21], if I order the wife to fear her husband, although she is his equal, much more is it the case with the domestic slave. For it is not a practice of low birth, but the highest nobility, to know how to humble ourselves, and to be moderate, and to be courteous to our neighbor. And the free have served the free with much fear and trembling.[73]

It was already noted that slaves ought to fear their masters because of earthly and possible heavenly punishment. We now see the rationale behind that statement. The apparent equality that husbands and wives, and slaveholders and slaves, were supposed to have in Christ (Gal. 3:28) made very little difference in the domestic context. Even the kinship language in which slaves are described as "brothers" is quite obsolete. Chrysostom is very clear about his own view regarding the submission of slaves—since Paul told slaves to be submissive, therefore

73. Hom. Eph. 22.1 (F4.330–31): Οἱ δοῦλοι, φησίν, ὑπακούετε τοῖς κυρίοις κατὰ σάρκα. Εὐθέως τὴν λελυπημένην ἀνέστησε ψυχήν, εὐθέως παρεμυθήσατο. Μὴ ἄλγει, φησὶν, ὅτι ἔλαττον ἔχεις καὶ τῆς γυναικὸς, καὶ τῶν παίδων· ὄνομα δουλείας ἐστὶ μόνον· κατὰ σάρκα ἐστὶν ἡ δεσποτεία, πρόσκαιρος καὶ βραχεῖα· ὅπερ γὰρ ἂν ᾖ σαρκικὸν, ἐπίκηρόν ἐστι. Μετὰ φόβου, φησὶ, καὶ τρόμου. Ὁρᾷς ὅτι οὐ τὸν αὐτὸν ἀπαιτεῖ παρὰ γυναικὸς καὶ δούλων φόβον; Ἐκεῖ μὲν γὰρ ἁπλῶς εἶπεν· Ἡ δὲ γυνὴ, ἵνα φοβῆται τὸν ἄνδρα· ἐνταῦθα δὲ μετ' ἐπιτάσεως, Μετὰ φόβου, φησὶ, καὶ τρόμου. Ἐν ἁπλότητι τῆς καρδίας ὑμῶν, ὡς τῷ Χριστῷ. Συνεχῶς τοῦτό φησι. Τί λέγεις, ὦ μακάριε Παῦλε; ἀδελφός ἐστι, τῶν αὐτῶν ἀπέλαυσεν, εἰς τὸ αὐτὸ σῶμα τελεῖ· μᾶλλον δὲ ἀδελφὸς ἐγένετο οὐ τοῦ κυρίου τοῦ ἑαυτοῦ, ἀλλὰ καὶ τοῦ Υἱοῦ τοῦ Θεοῦ, τῶν αὐτῶν ἀπολαύει πάντων, καὶ λέγεις, Ὑπακούετε τοῖς κατὰ σάρκα κυρίοις μετὰ φόβου καὶ τρόμου; Διὰ γὰρ τοῦτο, φησὶ, φημί. Εἰ γὰρ τοὺς ἐλευθέρους ἀλλήλοις ὑποτάσσεσθαι κελεύω διὰ τὸν τοῦ Θεοῦ φόβον, καθάπερ ἀνωτέρω ἔλεγεν· Ὑποτασσόμενοι ἀλλήλοις ἐν φόβῳ Θεοῦ· εἰ γὰρ τὴν γυναῖκα προστάσσω φοβεῖσθαι τὸν ἄνδρα, καίτοι αὕτη καὶ ὁμότιμός ἐστι· πολλῷ μᾶλλον τὸν οἰκέτην. Οὐ γὰρ δυσγένεια τὸ πρᾶγμά ἐστιν, ἀλλ' ἡ πρώτη εὐγένεια, τὸ εἰδέναι ἐλαττοῦσθαι, καὶ μετριάζειν, καὶ εἴκειν τῷ πλησίον. Καὶ ἐλεύθεροι ἐλευθέροις μετὰ πολλοῦ φόβου καὶ τρόμου ἐδούλευον.

Chrysostom says it (*dia gar touto, phēsi, phēmi*). He juxtaposes the spiritual equality between the wife, slave, and husband with the universal submission that Christianity in its labor ethic demands. Contrary to conventional wisdom, nobility does not lie in being served, but in submission and service to others—we already noted this in chapter 2, where rendering service was shown to be Christomorphic. Slaves are told here to continue fearing and submitting to their owners, since slavery is only a temporary state, and showing fear and submission is in fact a sign of nobility, not servility.

The household hierarchy that the New Testament describes in the household codes enforced the submission of slaves to masters. Since slavery is temporary, it is of lesser importance. Chrysostom also exposits that the addition of the term "with trembling" implies an intensification of fear. In principle, slaves ought to fear their masters more than wives fear, or respect, their husbands. The superiority of the wife over the slave is again emphasized—although the slave and the master are one in the body of Christ, they do not share in the corporeal unity that is between husband and wife.

The status of the slave and the child in the Roman household has been a matter of contention for some time, with some arguing that there was practically no distinction in status, and others emphasizing major differences.[74] In the passage cited above, Chrysostom clearly states a difference in rank. Yet some of the basic similarities between slaves and children are, for instance, linguistic (a slave is quite often called a *puer* or *pais,* indicating the slave's dependence on the master, and also in a derogatory sense indicating the slave's delinquency, puerility, and unmasculinity[75]), juridical (children and slaves could not legally own property and fell under the *patria potestas*[76]), and social (slaves could be freed and adopted as children in the household, and children could be sold as slaves). Regarding this last point, Chrysostom tells fathers to warn their children of the slippery slope between childhood and slavery—adolescents always need to behave as free persons. "Do you not see how many fathers have renounced their sons and have introduced slaves in their place?" a father should ask; he should also warn his son, "Be careful then that no such thing happens to you."[77] It did happen that freed persons were adopted by their former owners, since they had no legal line of personal kinship.[78]

74. Saller, "Hierarchical Household," 112–13.

75. See *Hom. Heb.* 28.4 (F7.320–21); *Inan.* 70 (SC 188.170).

76. Chrysostom, quoting Paul, notes that while an heir is a child, he is in this juridical sense no different than a slave (see Gal. 4:1–3); see *Comm. Gal.* 4.1 (F4.66).

77. *Inan.* 71.874–77 (SC 188.172–74): ῍Η οὐχ ὁρᾷς πόσοι πατέρες παῖδας μὲν ἀπεκήρυξαν, δούλους δὲ εἰς τὴν ἐκείνων τάξιν εἰσήγαγον; Σκόπει τοίνυν ὅπως μηδὲν τοιοῦτον γένηται·

78. See Jane F. Gardner, "The Adoption of Roman Freedmen," *Phoenix* 43, no. 3 (1989): 236–57; Hugh Lindsay, *Adoption in the Roman World* (New York: Cambridge University Press, 2009), 133–36.

Although there were many commonalities between slaves and children, there were also several important markers of difference between children and slaves. In Roman thought, the education, discipline, and punishment of children were supposed to be different from those of slaves.[79] Children should never, for instance, be whipped like slaves.[80] In his exegesis of Ephesians 6:4, Chrysostom makes a similar observation: "*Do not provoke your children to anger* [Eph. 6:4], as many do by disinheriting them, and disowning them, and treating them harshly, not as free persons, but as menial slaves."[81] Like most ancient rhetors, Chrysostom admonished fathers to train the *filiusfamilias* in the ways of free men, so that he would not exhibit servile behavior. Elite fathers should teach their privileged sons from an early adolescent age as follows:

> Teach him the principles of the natural order, and what is a slave, and what is a free man. Say to him: My child, there were no slaves in the olden days of our forefathers, but sin led to slavery. For when someone gave insult to his father, he suffered this judgement, to become the slave of his brothers [Gen. 9:21–25]. Take heed that you do not become the slave of your slaves. If you should be angry with them and your behavior is the same as theirs, if you should have no more virtue than them, you will have the same measure of worth as them. Endeavor then to be the master of your slaves and become so, not by behaving like a slave, but by your habits, so that while you are a freeborn man, you may never be found to be a slave of your slaves.[82]

The distinction between slave and free ought to be taught in the religious education of the child. The story of Joseph should be repeatedly told to the child.[83] Sons need to be taught the natural order of things. Chrysostom is not here referring to natural slavery, but the conventions of everyday life in his world, or at least the unnaturalness of slavery resulting from sin. We see here that a very strategic and pedagogical *doulogenia* is utilized by Chrysostom—slavery was born when sons no longer respected their fathers, and degenerated into disobedience. When referring to sons becoming slaves after disobeying their fathers, Chrysostom

79. For Chrysostom's views on raising children, see Blake Leyerle, "Appealing to Children," *Journal of Early Christian Studies* 5, no. 2 (1997): 243–70.

80. See Plutarch, *Lib. educ.* 8F.12 (Babbitt 40–41); Saller, "Hierarchical Household," 127.

81. *Hom. Eph.* 21.1 (F4.323): Μὴ παροργίζετε τὰ τέκνα ὑμῶν, οἷον οἱ πολλοὶ ποιοῦσιν, ἀποκληρονόμους ἐργαζόμενοι, καὶ ἀποκηρύκτους ποιοῦντες, καὶ φορτικῶς ἐπικείμενοι, οὐχ ὡς ἐλευθέροις, ἀλλ᾽ ὡς ἀνδραπόδοις.

82. *Inan.* 71 (SC 188.172): Δίδασκε αὐτὸν καὶ τὰ περὶ τῆς φύσεως, καὶ τί μὲν δοῦλος, τί δὲ ἐλεύθερος. Λέγε αὐτῷ· Παιδίον, οὐκ ἦσαν δοῦλοι τὸ παλαιὸν ἐπὶ τῶν προγόνων τῶν ἡμετέρων, ἀλλ᾽ ἡ ἁμαρτία τὴν δουλείαν εἰσήγαγεν. Ἐπειδὴ γάρ τις εἰς τὸν πατέρα ἐγένετο ὑβριστής, ταύτην ἔτισε τὴν δίκην, ὥστε δοῦλος γενέσθαι τῶν ἀδελφῶν. Ὅρα τοίνυν μὴ τῶν δούλων ᾖς δοῦλος. Ἂν γὰρ ὀργίζῃ καθάπερ ἐκεῖνοι καὶ πάντα πράττῃς τὰ αὐτὰ καὶ μηδὲν αὐτῶν πλέον ἔχῃς κατὰ τὴν ἀρετήν, οὐδὲ κατὰ τὴν ἀξίαν ἕξεις. Σπούδαζε τοίνυν κύριος αὐτῶν εἶναι καὶ γίγνεσθαι μὴ τούτῳ, ἀλλὰ τοῖς τρόποις, μήποτε αὐτὸς ἐλεύθερος ὢν δοῦλος τούτων εὑρεθῇς.

83. *Inan.* 61 (SC 188.158–60).

brings up the so-called curse of Ham (Canaan). In Genesis 9:25 Noah cursed Ham to become the slave of his brothers. As Eve was the cause of all women falling under submission to men, which Chrysostom also calls slavery, so too Ham was the cause of all slaves being in their current state of subjection. Chrysostom says that a slave may rightly ask: "Why on earth was it that when Ham was insolent to his father, the effects of sin were transmitted to the whole race?" The answer is that although Ham introduced this sin to the world, current slaves reinforced their status by their own sins.[84]

In Chrysostom's day, fathers could not legally sell their children into slavery, but they did have recourse to measures of disinheritance. However, despite the legal prohibition, it seems that the sale of children into slavery did occur, perhaps in some cases under the guise of rented labor, or even prostitution.[85] Sons needed to respect their fathers so as not to become physical or psychic slaves. Self-mastery was very important in this instance. In this sense, both slaves and children share a common space in ancient thought—both are unable to control their passions.[86] Both slaves and children should be taught to be virtuous and master their passions, but children should do so in a way that exemplifies their freedom. The difference is that boys should be raised to be not only good husbands and fathers, but also firm masters.

In Chrysostom's treatise on how to raise children, the free adolescent male, with his still inchoate masculinity, is differentiated from the slave with regard to (a) the spaces he occupies, (b) the people with whom he associates, (c) the way he takes care of himself, and (d) the words he hears and speaks. Chrysostom uses the identity and stereotype of the slave as a contrast to inform his image of the freeborn male. So, in the first instance, young men should not be allowed to go near the theater or any drunken revelry. "Most importantly, then, let us guide him away from shameful spectacles and songs," Chrysostom warns, "and never let a freeborn boy go up into the theater."[87] "My child," a father must say, "those spectacles are for the unfree, seeing naked women who speak shameful words."[88] Secondly, young boys should avoid

---

84. *Serm. Gen.* 5.1 (PG 54.599.26–28): Τί δήποτε, τοῦ Χαναὰν εἰς τὸν πατέρα ὑβρίσαντος, τὰ τῆς τιμωρίας εἰς ἅπαν διέβη τὸ γένος; Translation: Hill, *Sermons on the Book of Genesis,* 80. For more on the curse of Ham and slavery, see Stephen R. Haynes, *Noah's Curse: The Biblical Justification of American Slavery* (New York: Oxford University Press, 2002); David M. Goldenberg, *The Curse of Ham: Race and Slavery in Early Judaism, Christianity, and Islam* (Princeton, NJ: Princeton University Press, 2003).

85. Ville Vuolanto, "Selling a Freeborn Child: Rhetoric and Social Realities in the Late Roman World," *Ancient Society* 33 (2003): 169–207.

86. *Inan.* 76 (SC 188.178).

87. *Inan.* 77.923–25 (SC 188.178): Πρῶτον μὲν οὖν αὐτὸν θεαμάτων αἰσχρῶν καὶ ἀκουσμάτων ἀπάγωμεν, καὶ μηδέποτε εἰς θέατρον ἀναβαινέτω παῖς ἐλεύθερος.

88. *Inan.* 78.937–39 (SC 188.180): Ὦ τέκνον, ἀνελευθέρων τὰ θεάματα ἐκεῖνα, γυναῖκας ἰδεῖν γυμνουμένας, αἰσχρὰ φθεγγομένας.

the company of women,[89] especially slave women. The sexual dangers of associating with slave women are vivid in Chrysostom's mind. "Say that to be despised by the slave woman is only fitting for a slave," Chrysostom advises the fathers, "and that a young man has the greatest need of seriousness."[90] Sons should not fool around with or exploit slave girls, but focus on that which is important to become faithful Christian men—a freeborn man is a serious (*spoudē*) man, a man with religious fervor. *Spoudē* corresponds to the Roman ideal of *severitas*, which is related to austerity and self-restraint. Fathers should take care that their children are not exposed to simply any slave, but only those who are virtuous.[91] Thirdly, children should not be too dependent on slaves. Some tasks should never be done by a slave—for instance, assistance in bathing and dressing. "Let the slaves perform only such services that he cannot do for himself," Chrysostom says. "For instance, a free man cannot cook; for he must not occupy himself with such things and then neglect the deeds appropriate for a free man."[92] Finally, a child should listen only to words worthy of a free person, and his speech must not be like that of a slave.[93] By associating with every slave he encounters, the boy opens up his mind to superstition and gossip.[94]

Regarding daughters, Chrysostom instructs fathers to choose a husband very carefully—virtue ought to be the standard. Selecting a husband based on family allegiance, status, and, worst of all, wealth would be like selling the daughter into slavery. Chrysostom warns of the danger of this alluring possibility of marrying one's daughter off for wealth: "For if you seek a wealthier husband, not only will you not benefit her, but you will even disadvantage her, making her a slave instead of free. For the pleasure she will reap from her golden vessels will not be so great as the disgust that comes from her slavery."[95]

STRATEGIC AND TACTICAL SLAVEHOLDING

To this point I have shown, first, that Chrysostom's comments on domestic slaveholding, whether urban or agricultural, should be understood within his wider

---

89. *Inan.* 60 (SC 188.158).

90. *Inan.* 62.767–69 (SC 188.160): Λέγε ὡς δουλοπρεπὲς ὑπὸ τῆς δούλης καταφρονεῖσθαι καὶ ὅτι πολλῆς μάλιστα δεῖται τῆς σπουδῆς ὁ νέος.

91. *Inan.* 38 (SC 188.128–30).

92. *Inan.* 70.854–57 (SC 188.170): Ἐκεῖνα δὲ μόνον οἱ παῖδες ὑπηρετήτωσαν, ὅσα οὐχ οἷόν τε αὐτὸν ἑαυτῷ διακονήσασθαι· οἷον μαγειρεύειν οὐ δυνατὸν ἐλεύθερον· οὐ γὰρ χρὴ τῶν πόνων ἀφέμενον τῶν ἐλευθέρῳ προσηκόντων τούτοις ἑαυτὸν διδόναι.

93. *Inan.* 22 (SC 188.106–8), 28 (SC 188.114–18).

94. *Inan.* 38 (SC 188.128–30).

95. *Hom. Col.* 12.2 (F5.311): Πλουσιώτερον γὰρ ζητοῦσα, οὐ μόνον αὐτὴν οὐκ ὠφελήσεις, ἀλλὰ καὶ βλάψεις, δούλην ἀντ' ἐλευθέρας ποιοῦσα. Οὐ τοσαύτην γὰρ ἀπὸ τῶν χρυσίων καρπώσεται τὴν ἡδονήν, ὅσην ἀπὸ τοῦ δουλεύειν τὴν ἀηδίαν.

vision of domestic pastoralization. Second, as a result of this pastoralization, Chrysostom emphasized the differences between slaves and other members of the household who fell under the *patria potestas,* and thereby reinforced social distinctions between free and enslaved people. Children, especially, had to know and embody these differences. The final point that requires attention is the effect of pastoralization on the number of slaves a household should have. At the outset, we see a move toward the diminution of the number of slaves in the Christian household. Chrysostom gives the following advice to his congregation in Antioch:

> One master only needs to employ one slave; or rather two or three masters one slave. . . . We will allow you to keep a second slave. But if you collect many, you no longer do it for the sake of benevolence, but to indulge yourself. . . . when you have purchased slaves and have taught them trades whereby to support themselves, let them go free.[96]

In perhaps a more condescending tone, scolding them for their excessive luxury, he gives the elite Christians in Constantinople similar advice:

> But there is no one who lays down their abundance. For as long as you have many slaves, and garments of silk, these things are all abundances. Nothing is indispensable or necessary, without which we are able to live; these things are superfluous, and are simply add-ons. Let us then see, if you allow me, what we cannot live without. If we have only two slaves, we can live. For some live without slaves, what excuse do we have, if we are not satisfied with two? We can also have a house built with bricks with three rooms; and this is sufficient for us. For are there not some with children and a wife who have only one room? Let there also be, if you will, two serving boys.[97]

The advice is basically the same in both instances—a radical reduction in the number of slaves in the elite household (with owning no slaves being the ideal). Determining the number of slaves in late ancient households is difficult, especially since we have so little evidence from poorer households, and such biased evidence from elite contexts. Some elite households had many slaves, each with very specialized duties. In a typically exaggerated statement, Chrysostom states that the

---

96. *Hom. 1 Cor.* 40.6 (F2.515–16): Καὶ γὰρ ἑνὶ τὸν ἕνα χρῆσθαι δεσπότην οἰκέτῃ μόνον ἐχρῆν· μᾶλλον δὲ καὶ δύο καὶ τρεῖς δεσπότας ἑνὶ οἰκέτῃ. . . . εἰ δὲ καὶ ἀναγκαῖον, ἕνα που μόνον, ἢ τὸ πολὺ δεύτερον. . . . εἰ δὲ πολλοὺς συνάγεις, οὐ φιλανθρωπίας ἕνεκεν τοῦτο ποιεῖς, ἀλλὰ θρυπτόμενος. . . . ἀλλ' ἀγοράσας, καὶ τέχνας διδάξας ὥστε ἀρκεῖν ἑαυτοῖς, ἄφες ἐλευθέρους.

97. *Hom. Heb.* 28.4 (F7.320): 'Αλλ' οὐδείς ἐστιν οὐδὲ τὸ περίσσευμα καταβάλλων· ἕως γὰρ ἂν ἔχῃς οἰκέτας πολλοὺς καὶ ἱμάτια σηρικὰ, πάντα ταῦτα περιττεύματά ἐστιν. Οὐδὲν ἀναγκαῖον οὐδὲ τῆς χρείας, ὧν ἄνευ δυνάμεθα ζῆν· ταῦτα περιττὰ καὶ ἁπλῶς ἔξω πρόσκειται. Τίνος οὖν ἄνευ οὐ δυνάμεθα ζῆν ἴδωμεν, εἰ δοκεῖ. Κἂν δύο μόνους ἔχωμεν οἰκέτας, δυνάμεθα ζῆν· ὅπου γάρ εἰσί τινες χωρὶς οἰκετῶν ζῶντες, ποίαν ἡμεῖς ἔχομεν ἀπολογίαν, τοῖς δύο οὐκ ἀρκούμενοι; Δυνάμεθα καὶ ἐκ πλίνθων ἔχειν οἰκίαν τριῶν οἰκημάτων· καὶ τοῦτο ἀρκεῖ ἡμῖν. Εἰπὲ γάρ μοι, οὐκ εἰσί τινες μετὰ παίδων καὶ γυναικὸς ἕνα οἶκον ἔχοντες; Ἔστωσαν δὲ, εἰ βούλει, καὶ παῖδες δύο.

wealthy households of Antioch sometimes had one or two thousand slaves.[98] Having only two slaves was to many a sign of poverty. Chrysostom tells us that even the houses of the "poor" had slaves, often families of slaves. The meaning of the term "poor," in this instance, is perhaps very broad and more rhetorical than factual—he is probably not referring to the poorest of the poor.[99] We need to be cautious about the statements of the number of slaves in both wealthy and poor households—in most instances Chrysostom's depictions of rich and poor are polarized and hyperbolic. As noted, evidence about the occurrence of slavery in poor households is unfortunately very scant; the majority of records are from elite households. What is clear, however, is that slaveholding was not a privilege reserved only for the elite—it is very likely that "middling" and some poorer households had slaves.[100] We also know that freed persons and slaves themselves often owned other slaves.[101] Thus, I propose a scheme of strategic/tactical slaveholding in the following pages to help clarify some issues related to the quantity of slaves and to sidestep some of the difficulties presented by the lack of data.

We observed above that Chrysostom uses terms from military governance and organization to elucidate domestic relationships. In ancient thinking there has always been a close connection between slavery and the language of war, between doulology and polemology. At this point, and by using similar polemological concepts, I propose that the mode of slaveholding Chrysostom wants his audience to assume be termed tactical slaveholding, as opposed to an elite type of slaveholding that I will call strategic slaveholding.[102]

The difference between strategy and tactics is based on the utilization and distribution of power and resources. Michel de Certeau applies the concepts of the military theorist Carl von Clausewitz[103] to illustrate how strategic power is transformed into tactical power: "Power is bound by its very visibility"—thus, its representation.[104] Reduction of the number of slaves, then, reduces and limits the

---

98. *Hom. Matt.* 63.4 (PG 58.608.31). Of course, it is not impossible that some illustrious households owned such a large number of slaves.

99. For the rhetorical nature of Chrysostom's constructions of rich and poor, see Wendy Mayer, "Poverty and Generosity toward the Poor in the Time of John Chrysostom," in *Wealth and Poverty in Early Church and Society*, ed. Susan R. Holman, Holy Cross Studies in Patristic Theology and History (Grand Rapids, MI: Baker Academic, 2008), 140–58.

100. Harper, *Slavery in the Late Roman World*, 50–56.

101. Saller, "Hierarchical Household," 112–14.

102. I have already explored the concepts of tactical and strategic slaveholding in a basic sense in another article, but now wish to elaborate more on their nature and dynamics; see Chris L. de Wet, "John Chrysostom's Advice to Slaveholders," *Studia Patristica* 67 (2013): 359–65.

103. Carl P. G. von Clausewitz, *On War*, ed. Michael E. Howard, trans. Peter Paret (Princeton, NJ: Princeton University Press, 1989).

104. Michel de Certeau, *The Practice of Everyday Life*, trans. Steven F. Rendall (Berkeley: University of California Press, 1984), 37.

channels of mastery and the exhibition of wealth and status; thus, it reduces the visibility of power. In military terms, the more one's forces or resources are visibly reduced, the more strategy is transformed into tactics. De Certeau explains: "[A] tactic is determined by the *absence of power* just as a strategy is organized by the postulation of power."[105]

In the context of this discussion, we can consider slaves as nodes of power—that is, modulations through which the slaveholder can make his or her power visible and effective. Strategic power, in De Certeau's mind, is based on spatial utility, since resources are abundant. Strategy must utilize space to its full advantage. When one has a large army that occupies a vast space to overcome the enemy, the dynamics of the army are strategic. Tactics, because of the lack of visible resources, must cleverly utilize time. Smaller forces cannot play the game of space, and must therefore make use of time and often deception or trickery to overthrow their opponent. Strategy is then the utilization of spatial requirements, while tactics involve the utilization of temporal requirements. Once a large number of slaves—that is, strategic slaveholding—is reduced, we have tactical slaveholding. These modes of slaveholding should not be absolutized, they should be viewed as two poles on the social scale of slaveholding—some households lean more toward strategic slaveholding, and others tactical. It may be the case that more Roman households were already in a tactical mode of slaveholding. This depends on many factors, such as the type of household, the types of labor, geographical setting, male to female ratio, and so on. Chrysostom still allows for a slaveholder to have "one or two" slaves. In this case, the small number of slaves should be utilized to the most efficient extent, and according to Chrysostom's ascetic thinking, only for necessity (*anankē*) and need (*chreia*).

Strategic slaveholding was the elite mode of slaveholding, and an assault thereupon is indicative of the wider Christian reaction against excessive wealth. Chrysostom stops short of ordering his members to get rid of all their slaves, since this would have been an extremely rigorous ascetic command, which some might have considered heretical if we consider the canons of the Council of Gangra. It is likely that the objectification of the slave body—turning it into an object and possession—was probably more common and pronounced in strategic slaveholding contexts. By this I do not imply that it was necessarily less common in tactical slaveholding, but having fewer slaves may have entailed a more direct relationship between slaves and slaveholders. Slaves had representational value in such contexts. But the public display of slaves in numbers and splendor cannot simply be reduced to a display of economic power and status—it was part of a very complex structure within the habitus of the elite Roman lifestyle.

---

105. Ibid., 38 (De Certeau's emphasis).

This display was, of course, not at all limited to the marketplace or any other public spectacle. The dinner party, for instance, was also a perfect place to show off one's slaves. Chrysostom describes the wealthy dinner party as one filled with exotic slaves, prostitutes, and courtesans.[106] Noel Lenski has shown how slaves, especially banquet slaves, were literally objectified into household artifacts and artworks—the slaves, especially the symposium slaves, are transformed into tools, tray bearers, and light stands, illustrating the pervasive and denigrating nature of doulological reification often found in strategic slaveholding contexts.[107] Mass manumission was also a feature of strategic slaveholding. We should remember that mass manumissions were not uncommon in the Roman world. They were, however, a sign of benefaction, patronage, and status. Chrysostom wanted to transform the phenomenon of mass manumission by giving it an ascetic flair. By objectifying the slave body, it is possible to include the manumission of slaves in the category of wealth renunciation.

Tactical slaveholding was quite different. The majority of middling and poor households that did own slaves had to adopt a tactical mode of slaveholding. Both Carl von Clausewitz and Michel de Certeau note tactics as an "art of the weak"— that is, as a tactical polemology of the weak.[108] It is unlikely that the majority of elite households followed Chrysostom's radical advice, and if there were mass manumissions, they may have been more a display of status and wealth. And just because there was a mass manumission did not mean that the slaveholding mode became tactical. Chrysostom did not want people to manumit many slaves; they had to manumit all their slaves (except one or two). It seems that households that switched from strategic to tactical slaveholding were the exception rather than the rule. Perhaps the most famous example is that of Melania, who, according to tradition, manumitted thousands of slaves.[109] Such radical moves were highly unpopular, often among the slaves themselves, who did not always favor manumission. Large-scale manumission was not only costly but also risky.

The majority of illustrious and elite households probably continued in the strategic mode of slaveholding. Large-scale manumission of slaves on agricultural estates was even more unlikely, since such a move would seriously affect the functionality of the estate. The problem lies more within the middling or bourgeois households that owned anything between two and twenty slaves.[110] Such households had a mode of slaveholding that probably combined elements of both strategic and tactical slaveholding depending on the size of the property, its productivity, and number of

106. *Hom. Col.* 1.6 (F5.179–80).

107. Noel Lenski, "Working Models: Functional Art and Roman Conceptions of Slavery," in *Roman Slavery and Roman Material Culture*, ed. Michele George (Toronto: University of Toronto Press, 2013), 129–57.

108. De Certeau, *Practice of Everyday Life*, 37.

109. Harper, *Slavery in the Late Roman World*, 191–97.

110. Ibid., 40–60.

dependents. A household running on twenty slaves would be seriously challenged if the numbers were reduced to two or three. There is no evidence to suggest whether these households followed Chrysostom's advice, or to estimate the numbers of those that may have reduced their slave numbers. The low success level Chrysostom had in transforming households, especially in Constantinople, and his idealistic and, perhaps to some, unrealistic vision of domestic Christianity, can only add to the current speculation that few households reduced the number of their slaves. The *patria potestas* was also in a crisis, and one wonders whether men would want to limit the channels of mastery, and, in effect, the affirmation of their masculinity, even more by getting rid of their slaves. On the other hand, being self-sufficient and not dependent on slaves was a new hallmark of masculinity, so this point also remains speculative. Moreover, if one looks at the broader discourse of slavery in Chrysostom, where he mostly uses language that seems to sustain slaveholding practices, the occurrence of radical shifts from strategic to tactical slaveholding seems even more unlikely. Furthermore, tactical slaveholding could often simply be a matter of perspective—some may have considered owning twenty slaves strategic, others tactical. From Chrysostom's perspective, however, it is clear that anything over three or four slaves falls into the category of strategic slaveholding.

Thus, while there was no major shift from strategic to tactical slaveholding, but rather a scale where households leaned closer to one mode or the other, we do know that some households manumitted large numbers of slaves, and even though the majority of bourgeois households still had more slaves than Chrysostom wanted, it may be that some individuals took his advice seriously. So here we are then examining the exceptions rather than the rule. The other more serious problem we are faced with is the effect of Chrysostom's promotion of tactical slaveholding in the general study of slavery in early Christianity. Although few people probably listened to Chrysostom, he still advocated a radical shift to tactical slaveholding, and this is often viewed in a positive light and has led some to conclude that statements like those of Chrysostom were in fact ameliorative to the scourge of slavery. Some laud authors like Chrysostom and Gregory Nazianzus[111] for being similar in their rhetoric of tactical slaveholding to Gregory of Nyssa's[112] absolute renunciation of slavery.[113]

David Ford takes an extremely problematic stance, noting: "But from his [Chrysostom's] 'heavenly perspective,' and in the light of the culture in which he lived, his

111. The will of Gregory of Nazianzus is often cited in this regard. For a discussion of Gregory's will, see Harper, *Slavery in the Late Roman World*, 480–82. See also Ilaria Ramelli, "Gregory of Nyssa's Position in Late Antique Debates on Slavery and Poverty, and the Role of Asceticism," *Journal of Late Antiquity* 5, no. 1 (2012): 87–118.

112. See *Hom. Eccl.* 4 (SC 416.227ff.).

113. Paul Allard, "Slavery and Christianity," in *Catholic Encyclopedia* (New York: Robert Appleton Company, 1912), n.p., http://www.newadvent.org/cathen/14036a.htm.

somewhat conservative response to slavery is understandable. . . . Chrysostom is trying to permeate the entire master-slave relationship of his culture with a Christian spirit."[114] Such ameliorative views seem to ignore the fact that there were individuals, like Gregory of Nyssa, or groups, perhaps like the Eustathians, who were able to see the problems of slavery and denounce it. Such ameliorative views also seem to be based on a very selective reading of sources, focusing on those that can be read as ameliorative, and ignoring others, like Chrysostom's approval of physically punishing slaves. Such views are also ignorant of the carceral mechanics within seemingly "positive" aspects of slavery. I do believe that in Gregory of Nyssa we probably have the most admirable attack on slavery in the whole corpus of ancient literature. Although he subscribed to the concept of slavery to God, and thereby still perpetuated a rhetoric that sustained slaveholding, he was at least able to ethically separate institutional slavery from the metaphor, and highlight its oppressiveness.

But how close was Chrysostom's shift to tactical slaveholding to Gregory of Nyssa's quasi-abolitionary stance? And should we see Chrysostom's preference for tactical slaveholding as admirable and ameliorative? The answer to the first question is simple: although Chrysostom does show some discomfort at times regarding slavery, most of his rhetoric rather sustained slaveholding practices, and, most importantly, Chrysostom allows for people to have one or two slaves. The difference between having no slaves, as Gregory of Nyssa proposes, and having one or two is a major difference. Chrysostom was not ideologically close to Gregory of Nyssa at all. The second question requires more discussion, but in essence, I will argue that tactical slaveholding was not ameliorative at all to slavery, quite the opposite in fact. We cannot view a shift to tactical slaveholding as something good or something that paved the way or prepared the ground for abolitionist thinking. As I noted earlier, it may be that many households were by default more tactical in their slaveholding. To illustrate this point, we need to ask what the implications of tactical slaveholding would have been for slaves and slaveholders.

First, tactical slaveholding is not so much a reaction against the problem of slavery per se; it is a form of wealth renunciation, since slaves were considered property and part of the wealth of the slaveholder. The idea of promoting tactical slaveholding signifies a shift to a more ascetic lifestyle. It also influenced the social status of the slaveholder. This is clearly seen in the second quotation above from advice given to the elite of Constantinople. Chrysostom includes slaves among the wealth and "bling" of the Roman aristocracy, especially female aristocrats. I will return to this issue shortly in greater detail.

Furthermore, Chrysostom states in *Hom. 1 Cor.* 40.6 that to collect many slaves is not a matter of benevolence (*philanthrōpia*) anymore, but one of self-indulgence

114. David Ford, *Women and Men in the Early Church: The Full Views of St. John Chrysostom* (South Canaan, PA: St. Tikhon's Seminary Press, 1996), 154–55.

(*thryptō*). How can strategic slaveholding be an instance of *philanthrōpia*? This probably refers either to the *philanthrōpia* of the slaveholder, the need to care for himself and his dependents, or to the care of the slaveholder toward the slaves. It may be a combination of both. Perhaps some individuals saw the acquisition of slaves as a type of charity, in that they cared for the needs of the slave and the slave worked for them. We have already seen numerous instances where Chrysostom warns his audience that slaveholding is a great responsibility, and one that can be quite overwhelming, turning the slaveholder into the slave of the slaves. So it may be that some people saw strategic slaveholding as a way to fulfill their obligations to their wives and children and to the less fortunate enslaved ones too. The life of a slave might closely resemble the life of a poor person. Chrysostom, however, warns that such acts are pretentious and self-indulgent, and not truly philanthropic. The point is that tactical slaveholding was not a direct attack on slavery, but part of a very general rhetorical trend of wealth renunciation, and perhaps even a reaction against typical mass manumissions that were displays of status and wealth.

Second, we need to ask: what were the consequences of tactical slaveholding for the remaining slaves? The problem here is that attention is drawn to the (hypothetical) majority of slaves that may have been manumitted—who were not necessarily better off after being manumitted. But what about the slaves who remained? This is a significant question if most households did not own a large number of slaves. It stands to reason that slaves working in a tactical mode may have been pressed harder than those in a strategic mode. The fewer slaves in a household, the more work those slaves needed to do, and their work would not necessarily have been specialized. Having fewer slaves also intensified their discipline and surveillance, and thus the likelihood of punishment. If De Certeau is correct in stating that tactical power relies often on cunning and trickery, then it stands to reason that slaves in tactical modes may have resorted to similar deceptive measures out of compulsion and desperation, thereby increasing the chances of punishment and also feeding into the slave stereotype that saw slaves as dishonest and cheats.

Moreover, as a corollary to the Christian labor ethic we find in Chrysostom, he seems to suggest that the only work slaves ought to do was that which would be considered shameful for a free person to perform. For instance, slaves were expected to do the cooking for their masters,[115] but other menial duties certainly included cleaning and sewerage management. Susan Treggiari's work on the occupations of slaves, especially women, in the earlier days of the Roman Empire may also be relevant here—the majority of slaves had menial jobs, perhaps doorkeeping and cleaning, although many were also craftspersons.[116] Such menial work also

115. *Inan.* 70.855–56 (SC 188.170).
116. See Susan Treggiari, "Domestic Staff at Rome in the Julio-Claudian Period, 27 B.C. to A.D. 68," *Histoire Sociale* 6 (1973): 241–55; Treggiari, "Jobs for Women," *American Journal of Ancient History* 1

shows the limits of social mobility in ancient times, and also why some, like Marleen Flory and Dale Martin, prefer to focus on "managerial slaves" to make their arguments plausible.[117] Specialized and sought-after occupations like administrative and medical jobs are in the minority, especially since only a minority of slaves were literate. Chrysostom did not consider it a problem for a priest to own a slave for the purpose of performing these "shameful" tasks. He says that while the wealthy are building estates and still complaining about money, "if someone of the clergy . . . has an attendant, so that he may not be forced to act shamefully, they set it down as riches."[118] Chrysostom himself was probably served by slaves in service of the sees of Antioch and Constantinople, and may have owned slaves in his own personal capacity. He also groups slaves under the perceived "wealth" of a priest. Thus, the conditions of slaves in a tactical mode of slaveholding appear to have been worse than for those working in a strategic mode.

In conclusion, Chrysostom's vision for the pastoralization of the household advocated and idealized tactical slaveholding. Having fewer slaves would make the operations of pastoralization, like spiritual direction, participating in rituals, teaching, correcting, surveillance, discipline, and punishment, much easier. His advice to manumit slaves was not a reaction against the evil of slavery per se, but a device to promote domestic pastoralization. Yet, tactical slaveholding was perhaps the mode of slaveholding within which most households functioned. Strategic slaveholding was the privilege of the wealthy. Despite some exceptions, those elite households that owned large numbers of slaves probably never shifted to a tactical mode of slaveholding. And even if they did, it would not at all have been ameliorative to the institution of slavery. Slaves laboring under such circumstances endured difficult conditions. Promoting manumission, while still allowing for some to be enslaved, under worse circumstances, is a far cry from abolition or amelioration.

(1976): 76–104; Treggiari, "Questions on Women Domestics in the Roman West," in *Schiavitù, manomissione e classi dipendenti nel mondo antico,* ed. Maria Capozza (Rome: L'Erma di Bretschneider, 1979), 185–201.

117. Marleen B. Flory, "Family in *Familia*: Kinship and Community in Slavery," *American Journal of Ancient History* 3 (1978): 78–95; Dale B. Martin, *Slavery as Salvation: The Metaphor of Slavery in Pauline Christianity* (New Haven, CT: Yale University Press, 1990).

118. *Hom. Phil.* 10[9].2 (F5.104): ἂν δέ τις τῶν ἱερέων . . . τὸν διακονούμενον ἔχῃ, ἵνα μὴ ἀναγκάζηται αὐτὸς ἀσχημονεῖν, πλοῦτον τὸ πρᾶγμα τίθενται. The term Chrysostom uses here to describe those who attend to the priest is *diakoneō*, a term more likely describing a servant than a slave, although it may be a euphemism, and the purpose of this "attendant," —namely, performing "shameful" tasks—does support the idea that the term *diakoneō* may denote a slave. Allen translates the phrase more literally as "servant"; Pauline Allen, trans., *John Chrysostom, Homilies on Philippians,* Writings from the Greco-Roman World 16 (Atlanta: Society of Biblical Literature, 2013), 199. Harper also reads this expression as referring to a slave; Harper, *Slavery in the Late Roman World,* 104.

BONDAGE DIVESTED: PASTORALIZATION, WEALTH,
AND THE STATUS OF THE ELITE

As I noted at the start of this chapter, domestic pastoralization was an operation of pastoral power. Yet when one form of power asserts and duplicates itself, it has implications for other forms of power. Thus, the last issue we need to address relates to the implications of pastoralization and tactical slaveholding for elite status and power. We have already touched on this briefly. It is an issue that receives ample attention in Chrysostom's homilies. Slaves were more than just property or possessions in the simple sense of the term; slaves were also status markers, symbolic capital, and played an important role in the public display of elite power and wealth. Slaves were "bling" often decorated in gold and silk, but consisting of flesh and blood, bone and sinew.

Chrysostom had very specific guidelines for the use of slaves once they had been bought. It disturbed him that slaves were used to show off the economic power and social status of the slaveholder. To Chrysostom, this practice indicated that the slaveholder was dominated by vainglory, greed, and pride. The pride and pomp associated with slave processions were disconcerting to Chrysostom. And his concern about such displays extended even to manumission. Although manumission could be considered an act of philanthropy, a mass manumission could be seen as a display of wealth and status. This phenomenon was common at Roman funerals, where many slaves were usually manumitted.[119]

The use and display of slaves were issues of *repraesentatio* and *habitus* (in its traditional Latin sense), or what Chrysostom calls *schēma*. Chrysostom explains how he understands *schēma:* "Often some people, while depriving themselves of the necessities and wasting away from hunger, still worry about their possessions (*tōn skeuōn*). And if you ask them, they say: 'I must maintain my distinction.'" While I have translated *schēma* here as "distinction," in Bourdieu's sense,[120] it could also refer to social appearance; Chrysostom understands it more as pretension and ostentation. "What distinction, O man?" Chrysostom asks. "This is not the distinction of a person."[121] The sense of the term here is complex, encompassing several elements that make up one's social appearance and honor. These include material elements, like one's dress, house, the food one eats, one's slaves of course, and so on—in our

119. John Bodel, "Death on Display: Looking at Roman Funerals," in *The Art of Ancient Spectacle,* ed. Bettina Bergmann and Christine Kondoleon (New Haven, CT: Yale University Press, 1999), 259–81; Lauren H. Petersen, *The Freedman in Roman Art and Art History* (New York: Cambridge University Press, 2006), 117–25, 260.

120. Pierre Bourdieu, *Distinction: A Social Critique of the Judgement of Taste,* trans. Richard Nice (Cambridge, MA: Harvard University Press, 1984), 165–70.

121. *Inan.* 14.205–9 (SC 92–94): Πολλάκις τῶν ἀναγκαίων τινὲς ἑαυτοὺς ἀποστερήσαντες καὶ λιμῷ φθειρόμενοι τούτων οὐκ ἀμελοῦσι τῶν σκευῶν. Κἂν ἐρωτήσῃς αὐτούς, «τὸ σχῆμά μου, φησίν, ἔχειν ὀφείλω». Ποῖον σχῆμα, ἄνθρωπε; οὐκ ἔστι τοῦτο σχῆμα ἀνθρώπου.

modern patois, what is called "bling" and "keeping up with the Joneses." But the term also suggests the symbolic and habitual, like the way one talks, walks, sits, eats, stands, the people with whom one associates, one's gestures, charity, and so on. Chrysostom provides an entire pathology of pretentious *schēma*: "Those who are occupied by present things, those who consider riches something to be envied, those who disparage poverty, those pursuing power, those gaping after outward glory." Elite *schēma* was a major source of anxiety for the forces of pastoralization.

Chrysostom then continues with his pathology of elite *schēma*, and includes "those who consider themselves to be great when they raise lavish houses, and purchase expensive graves, and have herds of slaves, and surround themselves with a great swarm of eunuchs."[122] Slaves and eunuchs were important markers of social status, and even in death, one was expected to have *schēma*; it was displayed at one's funerary festivities and on one's sarcophagus. Chrysostom links *schēma* to one's possessions (*skeuoi*). This term can denote a number of possessions, including clothing, furniture, slaves, and sarcophagi; it can also simply mean "body," again highlighting the corporeal link between slavery, *schēma*, and *skeuos*. There is some irony in Chrysostom's accusation. Although their bodies waste away with hunger, their outward bodily appearance must be without blemish. Thus, the main characteristic of *schēma* is that it is highly somatic—*schēma* is one's sociocorporeal vernacular. It is the way one's body is projected in public, one's self-fashioning. *Schēma* is also relational; it is a condition for dealing with social superiors and inferiors, and very important for courting favor in Roman society.

Chrysostom's pathology of pretentious *schēma* included not only those seeking power and outward glory, but also possessions that were markers of elite distinction in ancient society, including a large number of slaves, many eunuchs, expensive homes, and a fine sepulcher. Yet for Chrysostom these markers of distinction are signs of decadence. Even the quasi philanthropy of acts of benefaction is problematic, since the motive behind such actions was vainglory (*kenodoxia*).[123]

The more exotic a slave was, the more distinction he or she provided to the owner. Although Roman slavery, unlike transatlantic slavery, was not based on racism and racial differentiation,[124] it did involve issues of ethnicity. Along with

122. *Hom. Rom.* 21[20].2 (F1.353): Οἱ πρὸς τὰ παρόντα ἐπτοημένοι πράγματα, οἱ πλοῦτον ζηλωτὸν εἶναι νομίζοντες, καὶ πενίαν ἐξευτελίζοντες, οἱ δυναστείαν διώκοντες, οἱ πρὸς τὴν δόξαν τὴν ἔξωθεν κεχηνότες, οἱ μεγάλους ἑαυτοὺς εἶναι νομίζοντες, ὅταν οἰκίας λαμπρὰς ἐγείρωσι, καὶ τάφους πολυτελεῖς πρίωνται, καὶ ἀνδραπόδων ἀγέλας ἔχωσι, καὶ πολὺν εὐνούχων περιφέρωσιν ἐσμόν.

123. For more on the patristic understanding of philanthropy, see Demetrios J. Constantelos, "The Hellenic Background and Nature of Patristic Philanthropy in the Early Byzantine Era," in *Wealth and Poverty in Early Church and Society*, ed. Susan R. Holman, Holy Cross Studies in Patristic Theology and History (Grand Rapids, MI: Baker Academic, 2008), 187–210.

124. Erich S. Gruen, *Rethinking the Other in Antiquity*, Martin Classical Lectures (Princeton, NJ: Princeton University Press, 2012), 210–11.

eunuchs, "barbarian" slaves, who might be of Germanic, Eastern, or African descent, were considered exotic members of one's slave entourage. "For the swarm of domestic slaves, and the barbarian slaves outfitted in gold, and the fawners and flatterers, and the silver-tinseled chariots, and the other absurdities greater than these," Chrysostom laments, "are not acquired for any pleasure's sake or necessity, but for mere vanity."[125] Barbarian slaves were listed with other extravagant and absurd vanities of the super-rich. Interestingly, the *NPNF* translation of this passage renders *barbaroi* as "black servants." One may speculate about the reason for this translation. The term would certainly include African slaves, but there were also numerous other "barbarian" slaves in late ancient Roman households, particularly Gothic slaves, and the presence of Germanic slaves in Chrysostom's social context should not be underestimated. Did transatlantic slavery perhaps inform the *NPNF* translator's view of slavery in Roman times?

Chrysostom therefore aims to change the character of elite *schēma*, and to do so via moral restructuring. He wants to change the dynamics of virtue in relation to public appearance, targeting in particular the possession and display of large numbers of slaves. This moral restructuring forms part of Chrysostom's promulgation of tactical slaveholding and his vision of pastoralization. Necessity is made a virtue.[126] Yet necessity had a very prominent doulological dimension. To offer an example, I will focus here on Chrysostom's comments in his *Homiliae in epistulam ad Hebraeos* 28.4–5, which specifically address the procession of female Roman aristocrats with its public display of "herds" of slaves.[127] While in this homily Chrysostom focuses on the interplay between distinctive symbolic capital and elite female identity, I will attempt to relate his discussion to that of elite male identity in other, corresponding sources.

Demonstrating his usual rhetorical prowess, Chrysostom depicts a scene that was common in the forums of Antioch and Constantinople:

> And how is it not shameful, you say, that a woman of nobility should walk out with only two slaves? It is no shame that a noble woman should walk around with two slaves but it is a shame if she should walk around with many. Perhaps you laugh when you hear this. Believe me, it is a shame! Do you think it is an important matter to go

---

125. *Hom. Rom.* 18[17].4 (F1.303): Ὁ γὰρ ἑσμὸς τῶν οἰκετῶν, καὶ οἱ χρυσοφοροῦντες βάρβαροι, καὶ οἱ παράσιτοι, καὶ οἱ κόλακες, καὶ τὰ ἀργυρένδετα ὀχήματα, καὶ τὰ ἄλλα τὰ τούτων καταγελαστότερα, οὐχ ἡδονῆς ἕνεκεν οὐδὲ χρείας τινὸς γίνεται, ἀλλ' ἢ κενοδοξίας μόνης. For an extensive discussion of the issue of "barbarian" slaves in Roman society, see Noel Lenski, "Captivity, Slavery and Cultural Exchange between Rome and the Germans from the First to the Seventh Century CE," in *Invisible Citizens: Captives and Their Consequences*, ed. Catherine M. Cameron (Salt Lake City: University of Utah Press, 2008), 80–109.

126. Virginia Burrus, *Begotten, Not Made: Conceiving Manhood in Late Antiquity*, Figurae: Reading Medieval Culture (Stanford, CA: Stanford University Press, 2000), 21–22.

127. See F7.320–22.

out with many slaves, like dealers in sheep, or dealers in slaves? This is pomp and vainglory, the other is philosophy and dignity. For a noble woman should not be known by the scores of slaves who attend to her. For what virtue is there in having many slaves? This does not belong to the soul, and whatever is not of the soul does not exhibit freedom. When she is satisfied with little, then is she a noble woman indeed; but when she needs many things, she is a slave and inferior to real slaves.[128]

What is Chrysostom's strategy in this passage with regard to wealth and elite status and power? First, he wants to redefine and restructure nobility, which is here described in terms of freedom (*eleutheria*). True nobility, true free status, lies in having fewer slaves, not more—nobility does not lie in extravagance but in simplicity and necessity. Tactical slaveholding is noble; strategic slaveholding is shameful. Necessity, in turn, is expressed in one's choice to wear simple clothes, not to live in a mansion, and to strive toward a life based on tactical rather than strategic slaveholding. Chrysostom does not insist that the free matron have no slaves at all, but allows her two or so, since they are still needed to guard her chastity and reputation when she appears in public.[129] In *Contra eos qui subintroductas habent virgines* 9.49–54, Chrysostom states that women are in more need of slaves than men due to their "soft" and "delicate" nature.

Chrysostom does make it clear that the marketplace is a place for men, and the home the place for women.[130] When the noblewoman appears in public, she cannot do so alone—the presence of slaves around her assures society that her intentions in public are honorable. Some women appear in public with large numbers of slaves, not only to demonstrate their wealth and status, but also to show that they are honorable. Chrysostom was very much against such displays of wealth and power. But he does not advise women to appear in public with no slaves—he understands the risk of such a move—a noble woman only needs to appear with two slaves. Chrysostom proposes a type of anopticism, where the woman is visible to her slaves, but inconspicuous to the envious eye of the public. The dynamics of anopticism have been highlighted by Cynthia Baker, who emphasizes that

128. *Hom. Heb.* 28.4 (F7.320–21): Καὶ πῶς οὐκ αἰσχύνη, φησὶν, ἐστὶ τὸ μετὰ δύο οἰκετῶν τὴν ἐλευθέραν βαδίζειν; "Απαγε, οὐκ ἔστι τοῦτο αἰσχύνη, μετὰ δύο οἰκετῶν τὴν ἐλευθέραν βαδίζειν, ἀλλ᾽ αἰσχύνη ἐστὶ τὸ μετὰ πολλῶν προϊέναι. Τάχα γελᾶτε τούτων ἀκούοντες. Πιστεύσατε, τοῦτό ἐστιν αἰσχύνη, τὸ μετὰ πολλῶν προϊέναι. "Ωσπερ οἱ προβατοπῶλαι, ἢ ὥσπερ οἱ τῶν ἀνδραπόδων κάπηλοι, οὕτω μέγα τι ἡγεῖσθε τὸ μετὰ πλειόνων οἰκετῶν προϊέναι. Τῦφος τοῦτο καὶ κενοδοξία· ἐκεῖνο φιλοσοφία καὶ σεμνότης. Τὴν γὰρ ἐλευθέραν οὐκ ἀπὸ τοῦ πλήθους τῶν ἀκολούθων φαίνεσθαι δεῖ· ποία γὰρ ἀρετὴ ἀνδράποδα ἔχειν πολλά; Τοῦτο οὐκ ἔστι ψυχῆς· ὅπερ δὲ οὐκ ἔστι ψυχῆς, οὐ δείκνυσιν ἐλευθέραν. "Οταν ὀλίγοις ἀρκῆται, τότε ἐστὶν ἐλευθέρα ὄντως· ὅταν δὲ πολλῶν δέηται, δούλη ἐστὶ καὶ ἀνδραπόδων χείρων.

129. See chapters 4 and 6.

130. *Virg.* 73.1.17–23 (SC 125.350). For a detailed study of Chrysostom's views on the marketplace, see Luke Lavan, "The Agorai of Antioch and Constantinople as Seen by John Chrysostom," *Bulletin of the Institute of Classical Studies* 50, no. 91 (2007): 157–67.

anopticism "requires only that the *subject* be disregarded and unperceived *as such*." She goes on to define anopticism as "a set of habits, regulations, and practices that, by and large, constitute a wife's identity—her 'housing' or 'house-ness,' if you will—through her disappearance."[131] Anopticism had to be part of the elite female's *schēma*. The role of slaves as a mobile carceral contingent for women and children also explains why Chrysostom believed that slaveholders were in fact "slaves" to their own slaves.

Second, Chrysostom elevates the discourse so that it operates solely on a moral level, and he also restructures the operation of virtue with regard to nobility and free status. While necessity remains at the center of his argument, he also juxtaposes the vices of pomp (*typhos*) and vainglory (*kenodoxia*) with "philosophy" (*philosophia*) and dignity (*semnotēs*). The term *philosophia* is in this instance a synonym for *sōphrosynē* (self-control, chastity), especially as it is coupled with *semnotēs* (dignity), which especially denoted sexual integrity.[132] So for the female aristocrat, the excessive adornment of the body with slaves and apparel signifies a move away from nobility, chastity, and female dignity. But Chrysostom applies exactly the same principles to men. In his advice on how to fashion a Christian *filiusfamilias*, he states that necessity and self-sufficiency should be the prime virtues of such a man. He should not be adorned with extravagant clothes or jewelry or be in need of many slaves. These are signs of femininity, which should not be present in a man.[133] Chrysostom, in fact, believed that luxury and extravagance often led to homoerotic passion,[134] and having many slaves was a mark of the unmanly.

Necessity then becomes a gendered discourse in Chrysostom—having fewer slaves and a simpler standard of living generally is indicative of the self-sufficient male and chaste female. Tactical slaveholding was a guarantor of masculinity, from which women could also benefit. If men did not conform to these standards, ironically they were not free, but actually slaves. In the following passage, Chrysostom presents a tirade similar to that in *Hom. Heb.* 28.4, only here it is directed at men:

---

131. Cynthia M. Baker, *Rebuilding the House of Israel: Architectures of Gender in Jewish Antiquity*, Divinations: Rereading Late Ancient Religion (Stanford, CA: Stanford University Press, 2002), 62 (Baker's emphasis). I want to express my gratitude to Cynthia Baker for pointing this out to me and clarifying the interesting phenomenon of anopticism.

132. See chapter 6.

133. See *Inan.* 5 (SC 188.78–80), 11 (SC 188.86–88), 16 (SC 188.96–98), 70–71 (SC 188.170–72).

134. He believed that luxury was the original sin of Sodom; *Hom. Gen.* 1.6 (PG 53.23.58–24.4); see *Hom. Rom.* 5[4].3 (F1.51); Chris L. de Wet, "John Chrysostom on Homoeroticism," *Neotestamentica* 48, no. 1 (2014): 187–218. I purposefully avoid using the term "homosexuality," because, as Brooten states, "'Homoeroticism' has a less fixed meaning than 'homosexuality' and is therefore better suited to studying the texts of a culture very different from the contemporary cultures of industrialized nations"; Bernadette J. Brooten, *Love between Women: Early Christian Responses to Female Homoeroticism* (Chicago: University of Chicago Press, 1996), 8.

And we build splendid tombs, and buy expensive houses, and lead herds of all kinds
of slaves with us, and decide on different managers for lands and houses, stewards of
money, and setting managers over managers. But not one word is spoken to us about
the management of the soul. And what will be the limit to this type of behavior? Do
we not fill one stomach, do we not clothe one body? Why so much tumult over business affairs? Why then and to what purpose do we butcher and rip the soul that we
have obtained to shreds by giving attention to the service of such things, contriving
for ourselves a terrible slavery? For the one that needs many things is the slave of
many things, although such a person appears to be their master. Now the master is
the slave even of his domestic slaves, and he introduces another and a worse type of
servitude. And in another way this person is also their slave, not daring to enter the
marketplace without them, nor the bath, nor the field, but they always go out and
about everywhere without him. He who seems to be the master does not even dare
to depart from his home if his slaves are not present, and if he even peeks out of his
house, he thinks he will be ridiculed.[135]

Chrysostom argues that the master is transformed into a slave—a transformation that I call doulomorphism. By appearing with herds of slaves in public, one
not only resembles the shameful slave-dealer, but also betrays the fact that one is a
moral slave and a slave to one's possessions—your possessions possess you. Thus,
Chrysostom again implements a stringent interiorization of slavery. It is no longer
the outward appearance that should display freedom and nobility, but the soul.
The myriad of slaves, costly clothing, jewelry, and big, expensive houses entrap
and enslave the soul. These possessions, and slaves in particular, are all seen as
extensions of the body of the elite. The luxurious adornment of the body signifies
an amplification and intensification of its power. If we again return to De Certeau's
distinction between strategic and tactical power, the pattern in Chrysostom's
thought becomes clear.[136] Strategic power is bound by its visibility and representation—the body adorned with gold and slaves deploys its strategic power visibly
and intensively. It shows that the elite body is powerful and has symbolic reach.
Such an elite body is also secure—it is protected not only by the slaves,[137] but by the

135. *Hom. Jo.* 80.3 (PG 59.436.21–41): Καὶ λαμπροὺς μὲν οἰκοδομοῦμεν τάφους, καὶ ὠνούμεθα
πολυτελεῖς οἰκίας, καὶ παντοδαπῶν οἰκετῶν ἀγέλας περισύρομεν, καὶ οἰκονόμους διαφόρους
ἐπινοοῦμεν, ἀγρῶν, οἰκιῶν, χρημάτων ἄρχοντας, καὶ ἄρχοντας ἀρχόντων καθιστῶντες· τῆς δὲ ψυχῆς
ἠρημωμένης οὐδεὶς ἡμῖν λόγος. Καὶ τί τούτων ἔσται τὸ πέρας; οὐχὶ μίαν γαστέρα πληροῦμεν; οὐχὶ ἓν
σῶμα περιβάλλομεν; τίς ὁ πολὺς τῶν πραγμάτων θόρυβος; τί δήποτε, καὶ διατί τὴν ψυχὴν, ἣν ἐλάχομεν,
κατακόπτομεν, σπαράττομεν εἰς τὴν τῶν τοιούτων λειτουργίαν, χαλεπὴν ἑαυτοῖς ἐπινοοῦντες
δουλείαν; Ὁ γὰρ πολλῶν δεόμενος, πολλῶν δοῦλός ἐστι, κἂν δοκῇ κρατεῖν τούτων. Ἐπεὶ καὶ τῶν
οἰκετῶν δοῦλός ἐστιν ὁ δεσπότης, καὶ θεραπείας ἕτερον εἰσφέρει τρόπον μείζονα· καὶ ἄλλως δὲ
δοῦλος, χωρὶς ἐκείνων οὐκ εἰς ἀγορὰν ἐμβαλεῖν τολμῶν. οὐκ εἰς βαλανεῖον, οὐκ εἰς ἀγρόν· οὗτοι δὲ
πολλάκις χωρὶς ἐκείνου πανταχοῦ περιίασιν. Ἀλλ' ὁ δοκῶν εἶναι κύριος, ἂν μὴ παρῶσιν οἱ δοῦλοι, οὐ
τολμᾷ προελθεῖν οἴκοθεν, ἀλλὰ κἂν προκύψῃ τῆς οἰκίας μόνος, καταγέλαστον ἑαυτὸν εἶναι νομίζει.
136. De Certeau, *Practice of Everyday Life*, 37.
137. For slaves acting as guards, see *Stat.* 2.4 (PG 49.39.38–43).

aura of social power emanating from it. But Chrysostom now inverts this logic and aims to divest the adorned body of its strategic power; he then invests this power in the body that lives by necessity, and promotes a tactical power of the body.

When the elite body is overly adorned with slaves, it actually assumes their subjectivity, which is highly shameful—you are what you wear. The strategic deployment of power, especially strategic slaveholding, implies that a person cannot take care of him- or herself. The care of the self was very important, as Foucault has repeatedly demonstrated. Strategic power is now redefined as weakness. The masters become slaves of their possessions and their lifestyle, their distinction enslaves them—such a person is a slave of reputation (*ho doxēs doulos*).[138] Chrysostom also argues that institutional slaves have more freedom of mobility than their masters, since the master cannot go out without his slaves. Thus Chrysostom departs on an extensive rhetorical campaign promoting tactical slaveholding and thereby reducing the effect of slaves as distinctive symbolic capital.

The rhetoric of tactical slaveholding had a number of consequences. It had an ascetic purpose. By reducing the number of one's slaves, one thereby shows that one is not dependent on money and luxury to live; fewer slaves signify a lifestyle based on necessity, not on status and luxury. It is again important to stress that slaves functioned in a cosmetic sense. Thus Chrysostom tells men and women to desist from adorning themselves with expensive clothing and jewelry, and excessive slaves. In this sense, tactical slaveholding is also decosmeticization. When men overdress they look like girls,[139] and when women overdress they look like prostitutes. Pornomorphism, when one resembles or becomes a prostitute, is a common target of invective in Chrysostom. Bear in mind that many prostitutes were also slaves. Unlike metaphorical slavery to God, pornomorphism is a negative type of doulomorphism—no one should ever resemble a slave-prostitute! Chrysostom states:

> Let us then dress in such clothing as is sufficient for our need. For what does a lot of gold mean? These things are fitting to actors on stage, this dress suits them—prostitutes, people who do everything to be seen. Let the one who is on the stage or in the dancing arena beautify herself, for she desires to attract all to her. But a woman who professes godliness, let her not beautify herself in this way, but in a different manner. You have a way of beautifying yourself that is far better. You also have a theater: for that theater make yourself beautiful, clothe yourself with that apparel. What is your theater? Heaven, the company of angels. I do not refer only to virgins, but also to those living in the world. All who believe in Christ have that theater. Let our speech

138. *Hom. Jo.* 20.3 (PG 59.165.22–30).
139. *Inan.* 16 (SC 188.96–98).

be of such a nature that we may please those spectators. Dress in such garments that you may satisfy them.[140]

Chrysostom proposes a new scopic economy, one that is based on heavenly not earthly distinction and perception. Having few or no slaves is in fact a type of moral and spiritual cosmetic, and such a woman departs from the realm of pornomorphism to one of virginity—she embodies the subjectivity of a virgin, the opposite of that of a prostitute.

It should be remembered in this instance that the call to the female Roman aristocrat to discard the majority of her slaves and to decosmeticize herself is necessarily a male discourse. We need to take note here that Chrysostom had many conflicts with some elite Roman women. There are two sides to this issue: first, the display of elite female power troubles Chrysostom, and he states that parading in public is a marker of shame and slave status rather than of dignity and freeborn status. The conditions of female class distinction are redefined. Dress and adornment, including adornment with slaves, are often discourses with the potential for competition and conflict. Karen Hansen describes dress and adornment as a "set of competing discourses, linked to the operation of power, that construct the body and its presentation," and that it "readily becomes a flash point of conflicting values, fuelling contests in historical encounters, in interactions across class, between genders and generations, and in recent global cultural and economic exchanges."[141]

Adornment, whether with a "dress" made from silk fabric or accessorized with slave bodies, is very performative. Furthermore, Alicia Batten notes that "elite males attack women for their elaborate adornment, they accuse them of greed and *luxuria* and attach moral and symbolic meanings to the women's dress when what may be fuelling this invective, at least in part, are worries about the economic power of the women who owned and wore such items."[142] By restructuring the principles of adornment, Chrysostom also restructures the very essence of public

140. *Hom. Heb.* 28.4 (F7.322–23): Τοιαῦτα τοίνυν φορῶμεν ἱμάτια, τὰ τὴν χρείαν πληροῦντα. Τί γὰρ βούλεται ὁ πολὺς χρυσός; τοῖς ἐπὶ σκηνῆς ταῦτα ἁρμόττει, ταῦτα ἐκείνων τὰ φορήματα, πορνῶν ἐστι γυναικῶν, πάντα πρὸς τὸ θεαθῆναι ποιουσῶν. Καλλωπιζέσθω ἐκείνη ἡ ἐπὶ τῆς σκηνῆς, ἡ ἐπὶ τῆς ὀρχήστρας· πάντας γὰρ βούλεται πρὸς ἑαυτὴν ἐπισπάσασθαι· ἡ δὲ ἐπαγγελλομένη θεοσέβειαν, μὴ οὕτω καλλωπιζέσθω, ἀλλὰ ἑτέρως ἔχει καλλωπισμὸν πολὺ ἐκείνης μείζονα. Ἔχεις καὶ σὺ θέατρον· πρὸς ἐκεῖνο καλλωπίζου τὸ θέατρον, ἐκεῖνον περιτίθεσο τὸν κόσμον. Ποῖόν σού ἐστι τὸ θέατρον; Ὁ οὐρανός, ὁ τῶν ἀγγέλων δῆμος· οὐχὶ τῶν παρθένων λέγω μόνον, ἀλλὰ καὶ τῶν κοσμικῶν· πᾶσαι, ὅσαι τῷ Χριστῷ πιστεύουσιν, ἐκεῖνο ἔχουσι τὸ θέατρον. Τοιαῦτα φθεγγώμεθα, ἵνα ἐκείνοις τέρπωμεν τοὺς θεατάς· τοιαῦτα περιτίθεσο, ἵνα ἐκείνους εὐφράνῃς.

141. Karen T. Hansen, "The World in Dress: Anthropological Perspectives on Clothing, Fashion, and Culture," *Annual Review of Anthropology* 33, no. 1 (2004): 370; Alicia J. Batten, "Carthaginian Critiques of Adornment," *Journal of Early Christian History* 1, no. 1 (2011): 5.

142. Batten, "Carthaginian Critiques of Adornment," 6.

appearance—he changes the rules of the game. The promotion of tactical slave-holding had significant implications for adornment.

Adornment in Roman society was dictated by numerous unspoken principles and, in the case of women especially, was directly related to honor concerns. Roman society was very much obsessed with public appearance, as it was so directly related to class conditioning and distinction. The display of remarkable adornment in the form of dress or slaves was part of the strategic public performance of Roman aris-tocratic women, and, as Kelly Olson observes, "Women were not ignorant cultural dopes, coerced into beautification, or passive narcissists; but rather knowledgeable and adept cultural actors."[143] This point underlines the wealth of some women dur-ing the late imperial period—Chrysostom was especially concerned about wealthy widows who behaved in a way contrary to what he advised.[144] Chrysostom's state-ments in the passages cited above are perfect examples of elite male criticism of female adornment, and tactical slaveholding played an important part in this criti-cism. This polemic forms part of the long-standing early Christian invective against extravagant female dress codes.[145] Christian women ought to adorn themselves with virtue and modesty rather than fine cosmetic commodities.[146] Moreover, the woman adorned with gold, silk, and many slaves draws the wrong type of attention, attention that often leads to the vices of vainglory and envy. In fact, Chrysostom accuses such women of wanting to cause envy in the eyes of other women.[147]

When it comes to men who overdress, Chrysostom directly attacks their mas-culinity. Such men are also associated with the theater. "A young man, who has his hair long behind, and effeminizes his nature," Chrysostom explains, "contentiously strives to turn into the likeness of a dainty girl, both in appearance, and in bodily purportment (tō schēmati), and in clothing, and generally in all ways."[148] Men who act like women are as disturbing to Chrysostom as women who display their social status publicly—Chrysostom attacks the masculinity of such men in the same way that he uses pornomorphic rhetoric against women who are extravagant.

Chrysostom's rhetoric against those who publicly flaunt their flamboyant ward-robes and huge troops of slaves also serves as a strategy to influence male actions

143. Kelly Olson, *Dress and the Roman Woman: Self-Presentation and Society* (London: Routledge, 2008), 111; Batten, "Carthaginian Critiques of Adornment," 10.

144. *Hom. Heb.* 28.5 (F7.322–23).

145. See, for instance, New Testament: 1 Tim. 2:9–15; 1 Pet. 3:1–6; Clement of Alexandria, *Paed.* 3.11 (Marrou 128–30); Tertullian, *Cult. fem.* (PL 1.1417–48); Cyprian, *Hab. virg.* (PL 4.439–64).

146. For more on early Christian dress codes, see Kristi Upson-Saia, *Early Christian Dress: Gender, Virtue, and Authority* (New York: Routledge, 2011).

147. *Hom. Heb.* 28.5 (F7.323)

148. *Hom. Matt.* 37.6 (PG 57.426.42–45): Ὁ μὲν γὰρ ὄπισθεν ἔχει κόμην νέος ὤν, καὶ τὴν φύσιν ἐκθηλύνων, καὶ τῷ βλέμματι, καὶ τῷ σχήματι, καὶ τοῖς ἱματίοις, καὶ πᾶσιν ἁπλῶς εἰς εἰκόνα κόρης ἁπαλῆς ἐκβῆναι φιλονεικεῖ. See *Inan.* 16 (SC 188.96–98).

and identity—it plays a part in the pastoralization of the household. In his rhetoric of tactical slaveholding, Chrysostom also has in his sight the female's husband or father, those who wield the *patria potestas*. Thus, the elite *despoina* plays the role of a catalyst that can either oppose the powers of pastoralization on the part of the authoritative male, or transfer the domestic agenda of bishops to the household and thereby influence her husband or father. Doulology therefore plays an important role in asserting episcopal influence in elite households. The body of the *despoina* is in this regard then a liminal space, a field where the games of honor, power, and influence are played among men.[149] By denying the elite *despoina* the privilege of strategic slaveholding and decosmeticizing her, Chrysostom indirectly tells men to get their houses in order—they must get with the program of pastoralization.

In fact, Chrysostom attempts to manipulate women by stating: "In this way you will be respected by your husband, when you do not need many things. For every man has confidence toward those who ask him for things; but when he sees that they have no need of him, then his pride subsides, and he converses with them as equals." This argument appears to be quite convincing, and Chrysostom continues: "When your husband sees that you have no need of him in anything, that you do not think much of the gifts that come from him, then, even though he is very confident, he will respect you more than if you were adorned in golden apparel. And you will no longer be his slave. For we are compelled to lower ourselves to those of whom we stand in need."[150] Thus, by denying her need for slaves and extravagant gifts, the elite female aristocrat liberates herself not only from slavery to her possessions and to vainglory, but also from slavery to her husband. She gains a modicum of independence, even equality. While from a superficial perspective it seems as if Chrysostom is providing some agency to these women, one should be careful to take this type of rhetoric at face value. He uses it as a manipulative strategy aimed at addressing issues of male governance and housecraft.[151]

Finally, since displaying excessive apparel and slaves in public is directly linked to pornomorphism, by renouncing flashy clothes and reducing the number of her slave attendants, the elite matron becomes an emblem of virginity. Doulology, especially the element of tactical slaveholding and the diminution of slaves as

---

149. De Wet, "Domestic and Agoric Somatoscape."

150. *Hom. Heb.* 28.4 (F7.323): Οὕτω γὰρ αἰδέσιμος ἔσῃ τῷ ἀνδρί, ὅταν μὴ πολλῶν δέῃ. Πᾶς γὰρ ἄνθρωπος εἴωθεν ἀκκίζεσθαι κατὰ τῶν δεομένων αὐτοῦ· ὅταν δὲ ἴδῃ μὴ χρείαν ἔχοντας, κατασπᾷ τὸ φρόνημα, ὥστε ὁμοτίμως διαλέγεται. Ὅταν ἴδῃ ὁ ἀνὴρ ὅτι οὐ χρείαν αὐτοῦ ἔχεις ἐν οὐδενί, ὅτι καταφρονεῖς τῶν παρ' αὐτοῦ δωρεῶν, κἂν σφόδρα ᾖ φρονηματιῶν, τότε σε αἰδεσθήσεται μᾶλλον, ἢ τὰ χρυσία περικειμένην· καὶ οὐκέτι ἔσῃ αὐτοῦ δούλη. Ὧν γὰρ χρείαν ἔχομεν, ὑποκύπτειν τούτοις ἀναγκαζόμεθα.

151. See Kate Cooper, "Insinuations of Womanly Influence: An Aspect of the Christianization of the Roman Aristocracy," *Journal of Roman Studies* 82 (1992): 150–64.

symbolic capital, played an important role in Chrysostom's views on virginity. By choosing to have fewer slaves in her procession, the female Roman aristocrat adopts one of the core values of virginity—anopticism. "For virginity of the body is but the accompaniment and shadow of the other, while that is the true virginity," he states, "I admonish you, let us enkindle a desire for those blessings, let us long for that bridegroom, let us be virgins of the true virginity. For the Lord desires the virginity of the soul."[152] Moral and spiritual virginity now become the true markers of chastity, status, and nobility.

I have spent a great deal of time on the female Roman aristocracy; but what were the implications of pastoralization and Chrysostom's brand of doulology for men? What were the implications for late ancient masculinities? Furthermore, while we have Chrysostom's rhetoric of pastoralization, a question arises: how do Chrysostom's comments match up with what may have been the reality of domestic relationships and household slavery? Rather than being read as descriptive—that is, stating what was going on in households—Chrysostom's rhetoric should perhaps be read as reactionary. His propatriarchal and prokyriarchal stance is a symptom and a sign of an unstable and eroded patriarchy and kyriarchy.

Kuefler has argued, convincingly in my opinion, that Roman masculinity was in crisis during the fourth century.[153] The growing power of the principate forced a change in men's civic participation; essentially, it came to be driven less by aristocratic competition than by imperial patronage and favoritism. Imperial and civic offices had less security because of the often dramatic changes in imperial leadership, and most of the traditional offices occupied by aristocratic men became honorific.[154] Military service in the army was also less appealing to men, because the majority of soldiers were non-Roman "barbarians."[155] So men could not necessarily depend on participation in government to affirm their masculinity and personal worth.[156] Ecclesiastical participation was an attractive alternative for some men, who saw it as a way to reestablish their patriarchy and kyriarchy.

Transforming the *paterfamilias* into a lay domestic "priest" already instilled a sense of masculinity. Pastoralization then also became a form of masculinization. There was a sharp decline in the *patria potestas* during Chrysostom's time.[157] The

152. *Hom. Heb.* 28.5 (F7.327–28): αὕτη γὰρ ἡ τοῦ σώματος ἐκείνης ἐστὶν ἐπακολούθημα καὶ σκιὰ, ἡ δὲ ἀληθὴς παρθενία ἐκείνη ἐστί . . . παρακαλῶ, λάβωμέν τινα πόθον ἐκείνων τῶν ἀγαθῶν, ποθήσωμεν ἐκεῖνον τὸν νυμφίον, ὦμεν παρθένοι τὴν ἀληθῆ παρθενίαν· τὴν γὰρ τῆς ψυχῆς παρθενίαν ἐπιζητεῖ ὁ δεσπότης.

153. Kuefler, *Manly Eunuch,* esp. 37–69.

154. Jones, *Later Roman Empire,* 1:523–606.

155. John W. G. H. Liebeschuetz, *Barbarians and Bishops: Army, Church, and State in the Age of Arcadius and Chrysostom* (Oxford: Clarendon Press, 1990), 1–88.

156. Kuefler, *Manly Eunuch,* 55.

157. Ibid., 70–102.

high standards of Roman masculinity were a challenge for those who were not always able to embody the virtues that moralists like Chrysostom prescribed. Traditional Roman masculinity, based on the principles of penetrability and impenetrability,[158] gave way to a different, Christian model of masculinity, based on chastity, endurance, and self-renunciation, values that had traditionally been seen as being more feminine.[159] Men had much less power over their wives. A wife could initiate a divorce, and her dowry remained her property, and there were also reverse dowries in this period. Legally speaking, a *paterfamilias* could be a woman.[160] Women also had the power to manage and bequeath inheritances and own property.[161] Men had less power over their children, particularly their sons, and they no longer had the power of death over a slave. Ecclesiastical leaders like Chrysostom expected men to relinquish most of their slaves, thereby reducing the channels of mastery and the self-fashioning of masculinity.

Therefore, in terms of hierarchy and male authority, despite Chrysostom's attempts to reproduce a patriarchal pastoralism in the domestic ranks, men's roles were less stable and women were not the submissive domestic dupes that Chrysostom so often describes. Male kyriarchy itself was not always that potent in direct domestic affairs. Chrysostom's own comments also attest to this—women had to manage the household slaves. If we were to ask who supervised the majority of slaves in the later Roman Empire, the answer would be the *dominae*. Women did wield power in the domestic sphere,[162] and although *oikonomia* was a masculine discourse, women utilized the opportunity to gain respect from their male counterparts. Chrysostom advises women to manage their slaves in way that will impress the men in their lives.[163] They had to manage slaves with self-control and strictness. Chrysostom himself grew up in such a household, where his widowed mother, Anthusa, had to manage the slaves.[164] In terms of household religious ritual, while Chrysostom envisions the *paterfamilias* taking the lead here, women were very active in ritual functions. Women ran their own scripture study groups, which may also have involved slaves.[165] This being said, society, and the church in

158. See Jonathan Walters, "Invading the Roman Body: Manliness and Impenetrability in Roman Thought," in *Roman Sexualities*, ed. Marilyn B. Skinner and Judith P. Hallet (Princeton, NJ: Princeton University Press, 1997), 29–46; Holt N. Parker, "The Teratogenic Grid," ibid., 47–65.

159. Burrus, *Begotten, Not Made*, 19–22. See also chapter 6.

160. Richard P. Saller, "Pater Familias, Mater Familias, and the Gendered Semantics of the Roman Household," *Classical Philology* 94, no. 2 (1999): 182–97.

161. Kuefler, *Manly Eunuch*, 70–73.

162. Susan Treggiari, *Roman Marriage: Iusti Coniuges from the Time of Cicero to the Time of Ulpian* (New York: Oxford University Press, 1991), 250–61; Jane Phillips, "Roman Mothers and the Lives of Their Adult Daughters," *Helios* 6 (1978): 69–80; Kuefler, *Manly Eunuch*, 70–71, 321.

163. *Hom. Eph.* 15.2 (F4.259).

164. *Sacr.* 1.5.1–14 (SC 272.88).

165. Bowes, *Private Worship, Public Values*, 189–90.

particular, were still patriarchal, but it was a desperate patriarchy, struggling to affirm and increase the eroded *patria potestas*. The neomasculinity that Christianity offered, a strong brand of which we find in Chrysostom, was seen as perhaps the last hope of reestablishing Roman masculinity.

. . .

In sum, doulology occupied a central place in the pastoralization of the household. Pastoralization influenced the nature of the slave body as distinct from the wife and children, and also, practically speaking, had implications for the number of slaves a household might have—tactical slaveholding was preferred. This last implication, in turn, had very serious consequences for the display of wealth and status by the Roman aristocracy, especially women. Regarding the character of the domestic slave, Chrysostom was outspoken about the differences between wives, children, and slaves, and their relationship to the *paterfamilias*. Although all belonged to the communal *familia* and all were part of the body of Christ, traditional Roman values of patriarchy and kyriarchy were affirmed in Chrysostom's homilies. Chrysostom insisted that free persons should never act or be treated like slaves, thus again reinforcing the stereotypes of slaves and free and the social boundaries between them. Nevertheless, slaves were included in the religious rituals of the household, and male slaves were granted a sacerdotal authority over their own wives, children, and slaves. As regards the number of slaves in a household, while it is very clear that Chrysostom nowhere objects outright to owning slaves in principle, he does object to the possession of an excessive number of slaves and proposes a tactical mode of slaveholding. He promotes tactical slaveholding not primarily because of the oppression of slavery; rather, his advice functions within his wider ideology of wealth renunciation and the transformation of social status. Slaveholding in this tactical sense permeated Chrysostom's entire socioeconomical framework, and functioned on levels related to elite power, social status, public appearance, gender, and various aspects of sexuality. Chrysostom's domestic pastoralization and rhetoric of tactical slaveholding were related to the suppression of female power and the redefinition of a masculinity in crisis. It is the link between doulology and this crisis and redefinition of masculinity and kyriarchy that will be the focus of the chapters that follow.

4

The Didactics of Kyriarchy

Slavery, Education, and the Formation of Masculinity

The education and discipline of children were central to their formation as future men and women of the Roman Empire. But these children also had to be taught how to be future slaveholders—a process called kyriarchization. Pedagogy itself was a very complex phenomenon, hardly monolithic. Most of the sources we have, including the Chrysostomic sources, depict elite pedagogy, where children were assigned nurses and pedagogues to nurture and guide them through the early stages of their lives, and to prepare them for adulthood. Poorer families did not always have the luxury of using nurses and pedagogues in the education of their children. Some schooled their children informally at home, or even gave them to monasteries. Furthermore, elite pedagogy is notably androcentric, focusing on how to make men out of boys; girls receive far less attention except in their preparation for marriage or virginity. Of course, the education of girls was equally important to the formation of masculinity, since they had to be habituated into the workings of patriarchy. This is where the nurse and pedagogue played an important role.

Kyriarchization lies at the core of the formation of masculinity in the Roman world and was one of the most prominent aspects of social reproduction in Chrysostom's pedagogical advice. Along with becoming a good husband and father, Chrysostom wants the young male adolescent to become a good master of his future slaves. Nurses and pedagogues, and other slaves involved in education, therefore, made a significant contribution to the creation and endurance of a slaveholding society—not only were they the objects of domination, but they also facilitated kyriarchal fashioning. It is important to remember that all Chrysostom's comments about slavery and education still operate within his vision of domestic pastoralization.

The aim of this chapter is to investigate the role of slaves in the education of children and the formation of masculinity as we understand it from Chrysostom's works. To elucidate the relationship between kyriarchization and masculinity, we will examine Chrysostom's comments both on the role of nurses, pedagogues, and slaves in the education of children, and on the education of slaves themselves.

KYRIARCHAL VAMPIRISM: THE SLAVE AS NURSE

It is ironic that despite the view that they were incompetent and degenerate, slaves played a major role in the rearing and education of elite children in the Roman household. Children had close contact with slaves from infancy. In ancient thought, education started at the breast. The wet nurse (*titthē, trophos, nutrix*) and the midwife (*maia, obstetrix*), who were often slaves or freedwomen,[1] played critical roles in child rearing in Roman times, especially as infant and maternal mortality rates were so high.[2] Yet nursing has been neglected in studies of ancient masculinity and slavery.[3] As this chapter will show, however, the nurse was the crucial first step in the creation of Roman masculinity, especially in teaching girls how to behave in a patriarchal society. Although some wet nurses were ex-slaves, their former owners still exercised some control over the nurses' bodies and periods of lactation—a further indication of the opaqueness of the boundary between enslavement and freed status. Nursing was considered a menial task, the last resort of poor, enslaved, and freed women, who sold the fruit of their bodies to sustain the growing elite class.[4] Chrysostom lists nurses among the lesser ranks of slaves and eunuchs, noting their low social status.[5]

But wet nursing was an exact science, in the ancient sense of the word. Medicographers like Soranus[6] and Oribasius[7] gave very specific advice on how to select a wet nurse. The wet nurse had to be close to the same age as the mother, and healthy, sober, and, most important, of good character. Ancient medical science promoted wet nursing. Although some ancients like Pliny recognized the medical

---

1. Keith R. Bradley, "Wet-Nursing at Rome: A Study in Social Relations," in *The Family in Ancient Rome: New Perspectives,* ed. Beryl Rawson (Ithaca, NY: Cornell University Press, 1987), 201–5; Sandra R. Joshel, "Nurturing the Master's Child: Slavery and the Roman Child-Nurse," *Signs* 12 (1986): 3–5.

2. For an interesting comparative study on this topic, see Valerie A. Fildes, *Breasts, Bottles, and Babies: A History of Infant Feeding* (Edinburgh: Edinburgh University Press, 1986), 105–11.

3. A notable exception here is the excellent study of Joshel, "Nurturing the Master's Child."

4. Joshel, "Nurturing the Master's Child," 5–6; Kyle Harper, *Slavery in the Late Roman World, AD 275–425* (New York: Cambridge University Press, 2011), 103–4.

5. *Hom. 1 Cor.* 7.18 (F2.85–86).

6. Soranus, *Gyn.* 2.12.19 (Temkin 90–94).

7. Oribasius, *Coll. med.* 33 (CMG 6.1.1.126–27); see Harper, *Slavery in the Late Roman World,* 110–12.

benefits of consuming human milk in general,[8] Soranus, for instance, advised against having a mother breastfeed immediately after birth.[9] This had to do with his views regarding colostrum, which is now recognized as having numerous nutritional benefits. Jennifer Glancy opines that the negative view of colostrum had to do with the notion that it was processed uterine blood, and hence not seen as being beneficial or pure; this view was shared by several early Christian authors, including Tertullian.[10] According to Susan Holman, wet nursing also distanced the child from the "unstable" body of the mother.[11]

The second-century philosopher Favorinus, however, is skeptical about using slaves as wet nurses, relying on the common doulological stereotypes that these women are barbarous, servile, and mostly inebriated. Using such women for the intimate and physical task of nursing endangers the physical and moral safety of the child.[12] Favorinus prefers that a child be suckled by the mother herself. He also believed that the semen of the father influences the milk: "The disposition of the nurse and the quality of the milk play a great role in character development; the milk is, from the beginning, tinged with the father's seed, and affects the baby from the mother's mind and body as well."[13]

The discourse of slavery and masculinity even penetrated the milk that flowed from the ancient female body. In drinking the milk of an immoral woman, the infant received the degeneracy ingrained in the semen of the woman's sex partner. This understanding supported the widespread idea in Roman society that one should employ only morally irreproachable women as wet nurses. Ancient writers were therefore quite opinionated about wet nursing and child rearing. According to his biographer, Plutarch, Cato had the eccentric habit of having his wife, Licinia, breastfeed not only their own children, but also the slaves' children in order to strengthen their bond of faith to their owner and his offspring: "For the mother nursed it [Cato's son] herself, and often gave suck also to the infants of her slaves,

8. According to Pliny, human milk cured fevers and also had curative ophthalmological effects; Pliny, *Hist. nat.* 28.21.72 (Jones 50–53); see Jennifer A. Glancy, *Corporal Knowledge: Early Christian Bodies* (New York: Oxford University Press, 2010), 112.

9. See Susan R. Holman, "Molded as Wax: Formation and Feeding of the Ancient Newborn," *Helios* 24 (1997): 85–88; Glancy, *Corporal Knowledge*, 112–13.

10. Tertullian, *Carn. Chr.* 20 (Evans 66–71); Glancy, *Corporal Knowledge*, 113–14.

11. Holman, "Molded as Wax," 84. For a discussion of the ancient views on the bodies of children, see Aline Rousselle, *Porneia: On Desire and the Body in Antiquity*, trans. Felicia Pheasant (New York: Barnes & Noble, 1996), 47–62.

12. Aulus Gellius, *Noct. Att.* 12.1.7 (Rolfe 354–55); see Joshel, "Nurturing the Master's Child," 6; Lynn Cohick, *Women in the World of the Earliest Christians: Illuminating Ancient Ways of Life* (Grand Rapids, MI: Baker Academic, 2009), 145–47.

13. Aulus Gellius, *Noct. Att.* 12.1.20 (Rolfe 358–59): quoniam videlicet in moribus inolescendis magnam fere partem ingenium altricis et natura lactis tenet, quae iam a principio imbuta paterni seminis concretione ex matris etiam corpore et animo recentem indolem configurat.

that they might come to cherish a brotherly affection for her son."[14] Here nursing is used as a technology to subjugate and condition slave children, and the link between nursing and moral formation in ancient thought becomes evident. The services of wet nurses were used after childbirth for the period of lactation, although some wealthy households used their own slaves if they were acceptable and, of course, lactating. Nurses of the elite household did not simply perform the biological function of breast-feeding; they were often the closest companions of the freeborn Roman female, and they especially had to guard the modesty of their mistress and the freeborn daughters of the house.[15] Wet nurses were often also sought out by monasteries to breast-feed abandoned infants.[16]

Chrysostom's comments on the nursing of children attest to the influence of nurses in society. The close proximity of the nurse to the parent and child calls for careful consideration regarding their selection and regulation. Chrysostom also notes that many mothers send their children to wet nurses for breast-feeding after the suffering of labor,[17] and lists the nurse along with the mother and other female slaves as the custodians of a girl-child's modesty and regulators of her public mobility: "A biological father has many things that make the custodianship of his daughter facile; for he has the mother, and nurse, and numerous female slaves who partake in helping the parent to keep the young girl safe."[18] This statement is typical of the literature describing nurses and their duties, which was written by free, elite males. A nurse had to care for an infant for the first two or three years of its life, and had to supervise the child in the most basic sense. Chrysostom speaks of the nurse directing the child in toilet training: "The nurse says to the child, when you relieve yourself, lift up your clothes, and do the same for as long as you sit."[19]

Like the other ancient authors mentioned above, Chrysostom was also very concerned about choosing the right nurse for a child—the wet nurse and nurse involved in raising the child were, of course, not necessarily the same. Chrysostom

14. Plutarch, *Cat. mai.* 20.3 (Perrin 360–61): αὐτὴ γὰρ ἔτρεφεν ἰδίῳ γάλακτι· πολλάκις δὲ καὶ τὰ τῶν δούλων παιδάρια τῷ μαστῷ προσιεμένη, κατεσκεύαζεν εὔνοιαν ἐκ τῆς συντροφίας πρὸς τὸν υἱόν. Plutarch also wrote a treatise on the topic of nursing, which is now lost; see Leofranc Holford-Strevens, *Aulus Gellius: An Antonine Scholar and His Achievement* (Oxford: Oxford University Press, 2003), 79.

15. See Bradley, "Wet-Nursing at Rome"; Harper, *Slavery in the Late Roman World,* 109–12.

16. Basil, *Ascet. magn.* 15 (PG 31.952–57); see Timothy S. Miller, "The Care of Orphans in the Byzantine Empire," in *Medieval Family Roles: A Book of Essays,* ed. Cathy J. Itnyre (New York: Garland, 1996), 121–36; Timothy S. Miller, *The Orphans of Byzantium: Child Welfare in the Christian Empire* (Washington, DC: Catholic University of America Press, 2003), 155–60.

17. *Hom. Matt.* 82.5 (PG 58.744.21–25); *Hom. 2 Tim.* 1.1 (F6.165).

18. *Sacr.* 3.13.37–41 (SC 272.214): Καὶ ὁ μὲν κατὰ σάρκα πατὴρ πολλὰ ἔχει τὰ ποιοῦντα αὐτῷ τὴν φυλακὴν εὔκολον τῆς θυγατρός· καὶ γὰρ καὶ μήτηρ καὶ τροφὸς καὶ θεραπαινῶν πλῆθος καὶ οἰκίας ἀσφάλεια συνανταλαμβάνεται τῷ γεννησαμένῳ πρὸς τὴν τῆς παρθένου τήρησιν.

19. *Hom. Col.* 4.4 (F5.220): ἡ τροφὸς τῷ παιδίῳ λέγει· Ὅταν ἀποπατῇς, ἀνάστειλόν σου τὰ ἱμάτια, καὶ μέχρι τοσούτου, ὅταν καθιζάνῃς.

associates two dangers with the selection of the wrong nurse. First, there is the danger of superstition, especially related to the evil eye. Chrysostom recounts the following practices:

> Then after the marriage, if perhaps a child is born, here again we will see the same foolishness and many symbolic practices full of ridiculousness. . . . What will one say about the amulets and the bells which are hung on the hand, and the scarlet cilia, and the other things filled with so much stupidity. Are the parents not supposed to envelop the child with nothing except the protection of the cross? . . . But the women in the bath, the nurses and slave girls, take mud and smear it with the finger and make a mark on the child's forehead. And if someone asks, "What does the mud and the clay mean?" "It repels the evil eye," they say, "and witchcraft and envy." . . . This is preposterous! A satanic comedy subjecting those who mistakenly believe such things not only to mockery but also to hell! . . . And when you ought to inscribe the cross on the forehead, which represents invincible protection, you eschew this, and fall into satanic foolishness? . . . Why should anyone speak about the other satanic observances related to labor-pains and childbirth, which the midwives introduce with wickedness on the head themselves?[20]

The period close to and during childbirth was an extremely stressful and traumatic time for a household. The lives of both the mother and the child were in danger, so the use of protective rituals and apotropaic devices related to pregnancy and birth were very common in antiquity. The nurse and the midwife played an important role in the events surrounding birth, both medically (midwives and nurses were the main sources for medical information for male doctors, who were not allowed have much physical access to female bodies) and in terms of religion and magic—we also should not see ancient medicine, religion, and magic as being mutually exclusive of one another. Midwives were also associated with abortifacient agents.[21] Chrysostom gives an entire list of other birth apotropaics, including amulets, bells, red woofs tied to the hands, and mud markings. The event of

---

20. *Hom. 1 Cor.* 12.13–14 (F2.146–48): Εἶτα μετὰ τὸν γάμον εἴποτε γένοιτο παιδίον, καὶ ἐνταῦθα πάλιν τὴν αὐτὴν ἄνοιαν ὀψόμεθα, καὶ πολλὰ σύμβολα γέλωτος γέμοντα. . . . Τί ἄν τις εἴποι τὰ περίαπτα καὶ τοὺς κώδωνας τοὺς τῆς χειρὸς ἐξηρτημένους καὶ τὸν κόκκινον στήμονα, καὶ τὰ ἄλλα τὰ πολλῆς ἀνοίας γέμοντα, δέον μηδὲν ἕτερον τῷ παιδὶ περιτιθέναι, ἀλλ᾿ ἢ τὴν ἀπὸ τοῦ σταυροῦ φυλακήν; . . . Βόρβορον αἱ γυναῖκες ἐν τῷ βαλανείῳ λαμβάνουσαι τροφοὶ καὶ θεραπαινίδες, καὶ τῷ δακτύλῳ χρίσασαι, κατὰ τοῦ μετώπου τυποῦσι τοῦ παιδίου· κἂν ἔρηταί τις, Τί βούλεται ὁ βόρβορος, τί δὲ ὁ πηλός; Ὀφθαλμὸν πονηρὸν ἀποστρέφει, φησί, καὶ βασκανίαν καὶ φθόνον. . . . Γέλως ταῦτα καὶ κωμῳδία σατανική, οὐκ εἰς χλευασίαν μόνον, ἀλλὰ καὶ εἰς γέενναν καταστρέφουσα τοὺς ἀπατωμένους . . . καὶ δέον τὸν σταυρὸν ἐπιγράφειν τῷ μετώπῳ, τὴν ἀσφάλειαν ἄμαχον παρέχοντα, σὺ δὲ ταῦτα ἀφεὶς, ἐπὶ τὴν σατανικὴν ἄνοιαν καταπίπτεις; . . . Τί ἄν τις εἴποι τὰς ἑτέρας παρατηρήσεις τὰς σατανικὰς ἐπὶ τῶν ὠδίνων καὶ τῶν τοκετῶν, ἃς αἱ μαῖαι ἐπὶ κακῷ τῆς ἑαυτῶν ἐπεισάγουσι κεφαλῆς;

21. Jean-Jacques Aubert, "Threatened Wombs: Aspects of Ancient Uterine Magic," *Greek, Roman and Byzantine Studies* 30, no. 3 (1989): 421–49. For more on contraception and abortion, see chapter 6.

childbirth was highly ritualized in the ancient world.[22] The nature of the amulets, for instance, is not directly mentioned in the text from Chrysostom, but it may relate to the figure of Baubo, the old woman who amused Demeter upon the loss of her daughter. The Greek goddesses Demeter and Artemis were associated with childbirth, and Baubo was often linked to midwives and nurses in the Graeco-Roman world.[23] Many figurines of Baubo functioned as amulets to protect the woman in labor—their appearance varied, but was normally that of a smiling woman with a large head, pronounced breasts and genitalia, sometimes sitting in a squatting position. Maurice Olender associates Baubo with Priapus, and also notes that the amulets of Baubo were used against the evil eye.[24] Midwives and nurses also often laid herbs around the area where the birth would take place to honor these goddesses.

Chrysostom recounts some of the other fears a prospective mother might have, such as giving birth to a deformed baby, or having a girl instead of a boy.[25] Pliny even prescribed certain herbs that pregnant women could take to assist them in having either a boy or a girl.[26] If a child was born into a traditional Roman household, the child received a *bulla*, a protective amulet.[27] *Bullae* were sometimes quite extravagant, made from gold and gems. Along with its apotropaic qualities, the *bulla* was a marker, an *insignia*, of free status—it separated the freeborn from the slave infant.[28] When the child was born, the father lifted the child up as a sign of welcoming him or her into the *familia*—for the baby this was an issue of life and death, nurture or exposure, since not all children were necessarily accepted into the family. After this, the most important ritual was for naming the child. A boy was named on the ninth day after birth, and a girl on the eighth—the *dies lustricus*. This occurred at the time when the umbilical cord was finally removed, and symbolized the child's biological separation from its mother; it was also the day when

22. Susan Wise, "Childbirth Votives and Rituals in Ancient Greece" (PhD diss., University of Cincinnati, 2007).

23. Early Christian authors like Clement of Alexandria (*Protrep.* 2.20.1–21.2 [SC 2.75]) and Arnobius (*Adv. gent.* 5.25–27 [PL 5.132.1–9]) refer to this myth; see Wise, "Childbirth Votives," 121–22.

24. Maurice Olender, "Aspects of Baubo: Ancient Texts and Contexts," in *Before Sexuality: The Construction of Erotic Experience in the Ancient Greek World*, ed. David M. Halperin, John J. Winkler, and Froma I. Zeitlin (Princeton, NJ: Princeton University Press, 1990), 83–114; Wise, "Childbirth Votives," 123–27.

25. *Hom. Jo.* 34.3 (PG 59.198.7–42); *Hom. Matt.* 18.5 (PG 57.270.32–59); *Virg.* 57.4.66 (SC 125.310–12); see Blake Leyerle, "Appealing to Children," *Journal of Early Christian Studies* 5, no. 2 (1997): 246.

26. Pliny, *Hist. nat.* 26.90.151–60 (Jones 376–81); see chapter 6.

27. Hagith Sivan, *Galla Placidia: The Last Roman Empress* (New York: Oxford University Press, 2011), 45–46.

28. Tim G. Parkin, "The Elderly Children of Greece and Rome," in *On Old Age: Approaching Death in Antiquity and the Middle Ages*, ed. Christian Krötzl and Katariina Mustakallio, Studies in the History of Daily Life (800–1600) (Turnhout: Brepols, 2011), 25–40.

a child received his or her social identity. During these days many deliberations and rituals took place for selecting the proper name. In *Homiliae in epistulam I ad Corinthios* 12.13, Chrysostom condemns naming rituals involving the burning of lamps, and advises parents to give their children the names of biblical heroes.

Furthermore, Chrysostom also condemns the ritual of marking the child's forehead with mud to ward off the evil eye and curb the danger of envy.[29] Midwives and nurses should avoid these "Greek" superstitions at all costs.[30] Chrysostom links these rituals and superstitions to the satanic. He also warns against other rituals, such as using bells, salt, ashes, and types of powders as protective charms for children.[31] While Chrysostom is negative about the use of amulets,[32] he does advise people to draw little crosses on the foreheads of their children (perhaps even as a replacement ritual for the donning of the *bulla*) as a type of spiritual armor.[33] In other instances, if a child is sick, he tells parents to hang a small gospel text around the child's neck.[34] It is important to note here that Chrysostom does not deny the existence of evil forces that may harm a child; he is simply critical of the protective measures. He does not denounce the power of apotropaics; he simply proposes the use of Christian apotropaics. The changes to these rites of passage did not occur immediately or extensively, but we do see some influence of Christianity in the following centuries, when traditional rites for naming and protection were replaced with Christianized versions along with, of course, the spread of infant baptism.[35] Chrysostom directly assaulted the non-Christian religious life and cultic customs of slaves and freedpersons, and proposed Christian substitutes, once again typical of his program of domestic pastoralization.

Second, there is the problem of hearing old wives' tales (*mythoi*) and gossip from nurses. This problem is obviously more relevant to children who have grown up. Chrysostom not only wanted to regulate and pastoralize the traditional religious practices of slaves, but he also sought to regulate the speech and narratives of slaves. He advises parents:

29. Chris L. de Wet, "John Chrysostom on Envy," *Studia Patristica* 47 (2010): 255–60.

30. *Hom. 1 Cor.* 12.14 (F2.146–47).

31. *Hom. Col.* 8.5 (F5.263).

32. Blake Leyerle, "'Keep Me, Lord, as the Apple of Your Eyes': An Early Christian Child's Amulet," *Journal of Early Christian History* 3, no. 2 (2013): 73–93.

33. *Hom. 1 Cor.* 12.14 (F2.147).

34. See *Hom. 1 Cor.* 12.7 (F2.142–43); *Stat.* 19.4 (PG 49.196.37–46); the most important studies on amulets and children in Chrysostom have been done by Leyerle; see her "Appealing to Children," 250; Leyerle "Children and 'the Child' in Early Christianity," in *The Oxford Handbook of Childhood and Education in the Classical World,* ed. Judith Evans Grubbs, Tim Parkin, and Roslynne Bell (New York: Oxford University Press, 2013), 559–79; Leyerle, "An Early Christian Child's Amulet."

35. Jaclyn L. Maxwell, *Christianization and Communication in Late Antiquity: John Chrysostom and His Congregation in Antioch* (New York: Cambridge University Press, 2009), 152.

Let children then hear nothing inappropriate from slaves or a pedagogue or nurses. But as plants require the greatest measure of care when they are mere seedlings, so too children. So let us have foresight in selecting good nurses that a good foundation from the ground up may be laid for the young ones, and that from the beginning they may receive nothing that is wicked. Thus do not let them listen to silly old wives' tales.[36]

Parents had to choose morally sound child attendants. Since both the nurse and, as we will shortly see, the pedagogue are intimately involved in raising children, parents ought to select them carefully. Chrysostom wanted parents to strictly control the contact children had with slaves, and he suggests that parents monitor the knowledge that may be passed on from nurse to child. He thinks it is best to teach children biblical stories from a very early age, and to avoid fables and myths. "When we receive children from the nurse, let us not accustom them to old wives' tales," he says. But his scriptural pedagogy is very specific and purposeful: "Let them learn from an early age that there is judgment, that there is punishment; let it be planted in their minds"[37]—these are the principles that children should understand from an early age. It should be stressed in this instance that biblical discourses of obedience and punishment represent very pervasive discourses of slavery, and by teaching children about judgment and punishment, one already instills a dominating and fearful disposition into the child. Children had to be taught the difference between slaves and free from an early age.

What is the purpose of this embedded doulology in Chrysostom's scriptural pedagogy? The answer is obvious: "This fear which is implanted in them produces great goodness. For a soul that has learned from an early age to be restrained by this anticipation will not soon shake off this lasting fear."[38] It produces a fear that will bridle the passions of the child. The control of the passions was a crucial element of masculinity. This same thinking applied to the education of slaves, as we will shortly see. Fear is a technology for moral control and regulation. This scriptural pedagogy based on fear and control of the passions is set over and against stories and myths children hear from nurses and other slaves. In fact, the whole

36. *Inan.* 37.469–38.476 (SC 188.128–30): Μηδὲν οὖν ἄτοπον ἀκουέτωσαν οἱ παῖδες μήτε παρὰ οἰκετῶν μήτε παρὰ παιδαγωγοῦ μήτε παρὰ τροφέων. Ἀλλὰ καθάπερ τὰ φυτὰ τότε μάλιστα πολλῆς χρείαν ἔχει τῆς ἐπιμελείας, ὅταν ἁπαλὰ ᾖ, οὕτω καὶ οἱ παῖδες· ὥστε τροφέων προνοῶμεν ἀγαθῶν, ἵνα αὐτοῖς ἐκ κρηπῖδος καλὸς θεμέλιος βάλληται καὶ μηδὲν ὅλως ἐξ ἀρχῆς παραδέχωνται πονηρόν. Μὴ τοίνυν, μηδὲ μύθους ἀκουέτωσαν ληρώδεις καὶ γραώδεις.

37. *Hom. 2 Thess.* 2.2 (F5.459): ἀπὸ τῆς τίτθης τὰ παιδία λαμβάνοντες, μὴ μύθοις γραϊκοῖς αὐτὰ ἐνεθίζωμεν, ἀλλ' ἐκ πρώτης ἡλικίας μανθανέτω, ὅτι κρίσις ἐστίν, ὅτι κόλασις· ἐμπηγνύσθω αὐτῶν τῇ διανοίᾳ.

38. *Hom. 2 Thess.* 2.2 (F5.459–60): οὗτος ὁ φόβος συρριζωθείς, μεγάλα ἐργάζεται ἀγαθά. Ψυχὴ γὰρ μαθοῦσα ἐκ πρώτης ἡλικίας τῇ προσδοκίᾳ ταύτῃ κατασείεσθαι, οὐ ταχέως ἀποσείσεται τοῦτο τὸ δέος.

household, and even enemies of the *paterfamilias,* must be regulated by these discourses of obedience, fear, and punishment: "Let us educate ourselves by these words, as well as our wives, slaves, children, friends, even our enemies if possible."[39] A man who aspires to excel as a teacher of the faith must start by teaching his children and slaves, and only then can he teach other adults.[40] The gendering and kyriarchization of knowledge were key to Chrysostom's pedagogy.

In another example, Chrysostom notes that mothers use threats and fear to silence their crying children; they threaten to throw them to the wolves to encourage discipline, although they will never truly abandon them.[41] Christ works in the same way with believers; fear and threats of punishment serve in the formation of obedience and the creation of a docile body. Chrysostom wanted this phobic scriptural pedagogy to replace other methods of raising children. He notes that "many wicked slaves show scary and ridiculous masks to children (the masks are not frightening by their nature, but they appear to be because of the children's simple minds), causing much laughter."[42]

Ghost stories and stories of demons among crypts, and souls of children enslaved to sorcerers, are also mythical tales used to scare children. Chrysostom denies the existence of ghosts, noting that a human soul cannot change its substance into that of a demon. Another person cannot enslave the soul—ghosts are no more than demons in disguise.[43] Such ghost stories, along with the use of amulets and other apotropaic devices, need to be avoided from the early days of a child's education; nurses and other slaves must be constantly regulated, and the child guarded against such influences. Over and against this, Chrysostom introduces an opposing symbolic reality, like christening children on their foreheads, and a scriptural pedagogy the objective of which is to master the passions and cultivate behaviors of domination—to achieve the habituation of masculine virtue. This is already the first indication, and we will consider many more in this chapter, that doulological discourse and practice were conditioned into children from a very young age. Masculinity and kyriarchy were molded in the cradle and at the breast.

If one has obtained a good nurse, Chrysostom argues, the children will prosper, and the children and other family members will love her. Good nurses also had to discipline children. This was done in cooperation with the parents. Nurses disciplined

---

39. *Hom. 2 Thess.* 2.2 (F5.460): Τούτοις τοῖς λόγοις καὶ ἡμᾶς αὐτοὺς ῥυθμίζωμεν, καὶ γυναῖκας καὶ δούλους καὶ τέκνα καὶ φίλους, εἰ δυνατόν, καὶ ἐχθρούς.

40. *Hom. Tit.* 2.4 (F6.276).

41. *Adv. Jud.* 3.1.8 (PG 48.863.25–28).

42. *Adv. Jud.* 1.3.7 (PG 48.848.34–38): τοῖς παιδίοις ἐκείνοις προσωπεῖα δεικνύντες φοβερὰ καὶ καταγέλαστα τῶν μιαρῶν οἰκετῶν πολλοὶ (οὐ γάρ ἐστι φύσει φοβερά, ἀλλὰ διὰ τὸ εὐτελὲς τῆς διανοίας τοιαῦτα φαίνεται) πολὺν κινοῦσι γέλωτα.

43. *Hom. Matt.* 28.3 (PG 57.353.17–37).

and punished children for minor offenses, while, as Chrysostom tells us, more serious offenses had to be handled by the parents.[44] This discipline and punishment also started at a very young age, even during breast-feeding. For instance, in a very elementary way, a suckling had to be taught some self-control. Chrysostom knows that babies can be greedy, and a good nurse needs to realize when she is feeding a child for the sake of hunger or excess—not entirely bad advice.[45] The masculine virtues of necessity and self-control should be conditioned into children from nonage. Furthermore, children should learn not to become dependent and lazy. The often-painful principle of abstinence and self-control is as crucial to children as it is to adults. Parents need to be strict in the same way that Christ is strict with his followers. For instance, a baby should not become too accustomed to being held; the nurse should promote moderation and abstinence at a child's early developmental stages:

> Do you not see, that we even admonish nurses not to make a habit of always carrying children, that they should not make them accustomed to it and so make them dependent? This is why those children that are raised under the supervision of their parents become weak, damaging their health both both inopportune and immoderate leniency. Even pain is a good thing in due proportion, care is also good, need is good—for they make us strong, and their opposites are also good. But each of these destroys us when they are excessive, one makes us soft, but the other breaks us.[46]

The avoidance of excess and luxury, and of course, total deprivation, were fundamental principles in Chrysostom's views on the formation of masculinity and mastery. Luxury makes people soft and effeminate, while, as he stated above, a moderate amount of pain and need makes them strong. Pain, too, was an important factor in the formation and performance of masculine identity. Chrysostom contrasts virile strength (*ischyros*) with unmanly weakness and flaccidity (*chaunoō*)—both terms have clear sexual connotations. The nurse plays a very important part here. Chrysostom was not ignorant on the topic, and often used techniques of breast-feeding and weaning as metaphors to illustrate spiritual principles. As Blake Leyerle notes, he knew that babies were often irate during breast-feeding, and that it was also a difficult endeavor for mothers and nurses. He commented about mock nursing and the transition to solid foods.[47]

---

44. *Hom. 1 Cor.* 15.2 (F2.174); *Hom. Heb.* 34.2 (F7.377–78).

45. *Hom. Matt.* 17.5 (PG 57.261.58–262.5).

46. *Hom. Act.* 54.3 (PG 60.378.45–54): Οὐχ ὁρᾷς, ὅτι καὶ τροφοῖς παρακελευόμεθα, μὴ διαπαντὸς βαστάζειν τὰ παιδία, ὥστε μὴ εἰς ἔθος αὐτὰ καθιστᾷν, μήτε ἐξίτηλα αὐτὰ ποιεῖν; Διὰ τοῦτο τὰ ἐπ' ὄψεσιν ἀνατρεφόμενα τῶν γονέων, ἀσθενέστερα γίνεται, τῆς φειδοῦς τῆς ἀκαίρου τε καὶ ἀμέτρου λυμαινομένης αὐτῶν τὴν ὑγίειαν. Καλὸν καὶ λύπη σύμμετρος, καλὸν καὶ φροντὶς, καλὸν καὶ ἔνδεια· ἰσχυροὺς γὰρ ἡμᾶς ποιεῖ καλὰ καὶ τὰ ἐναντία· ἕκαστον γὰρ αὐτῶν ἄμετρον γενόμενον ἀπόλλυσι, καὶ τὸ μὲν χαυνοῖ, τὸ δὲ διαρρήγνυσιν.

47. See *Hom. 1 Cor.* 4.6 (F2.43); *Hom. Matt.* 17.5–6 (PG 57.261–62); Leyerle, "Appealing to Children," 250–51.

Most of these examples are used as metaphors—milk was a very common metaphor in the New Testament and consequently in Chrysostom, and had a vibrant textual life. Milk is often considered a reference to doctrine, and nursing a metaphor for spiritual and pastoral care.[48] Those Christians who adhere to Jewish practices, for example, are abnormalized as being like adult men still suckling on their nurses.[49] With this metaphor of milk and nursing Chrysostom also attacks the masculinity of his opponents, especially followers of other religions and heretical movements. The metaphor of the nurse is common in Chrysostom's thought. He describes sleep as an excellent nurse that nourishes and refreshes the body.[50] The earth is also like a nurse in that it provides sustenance for its children.[51] The city too is seen as a nurse and parent.[52] Another common metaphor is that of Christ being like a nurse. An interesting and somewhat vampiric version of this metaphor is found in one of Chrysostom's homilies: "There are often mothers that after labor give out their children to other women as nurses; but Christ does not do this, but he himself feeds us with his own blood, and by all means permeates us with himself."[53] Christ is the nurse that feeds his children with his blood—blood and breast milk were always closely related in ancient medical and religious thought.[54] Milk, like semen, was viewed as blood "cooked" by the heat of the body.[55] This example of the nursing metaphor, like the others, illustrates the belief that breast-feeding, even in terms of Christ's blood, influenced moral formation.

The purpose of nursing metaphors like these was to demonstrate the love Christ has for his children. Paul is also depicted as a nurse. In 1 Thessalonians 2:7, Paul describes his relationship with the Thessalonian Christians in terms of a nurse caring for her children.[56] In his interpretation of this verse, Chrysostom states: "A teacher ought to be like this. Does the nurse flatter that she may gain glory? Does she ask for money from her little children? Is she disrespectful or onerous toward

---

48. See New Testament: 1 Cor. 3:2; Heb. 5:2; Chrysostom, *Hom. 1 Cor.* 8.1 (F2.89); *Hom. Eph.* 9.1 (F4.215); *Hom. Heb.* 7.2 (F7.89), 9.3 (F7.116); *Stat.* 9.3 (PG 49.105.16–22).

49. *Hom. 1 Tim.* 12.2 (F6.95).

50. *Hom. Gen.* 11.2 (PG 53.91.26–31).

51. *Hom. Gen.* 9.4 (PG 53.77.26–29); 11.4 (PG 53.92.20–22).

52. *Stat.* 2.2 (PG 49.35.33–39).

53. *Hom. Matt.* 82.5 (PG 58.744.5–9): Μητέρες πολλάκις εἰσὶ, καὶ μετὰ τὰς ὠδῖνας ἑτέραις ἐκδιδόασι τροφοῖς τὰ παιδία· αὐτὸς δὲ τοῦτο οὐκ ἠνέσχετο, ἀλλ' αὐτὸς ἡμᾶς τρέφει οἰκείῳ αἵματι, καὶ διὰ πάντων ἡμᾶς ἑαυτῷ συμπλέκει.

54. Denise Kimber Buell, *Making Christians: Clement of Alexandria and the Rhetoric of Legitimacy* (Princeton, NJ: Princeton University Press, 1999), 131–79.

55. Helen King, *Hippocrates' Woman: Reading the Female Body in Ancient Greece* (London: Routledge, 1998), 142–43.

56. The text in 1 Thess. 2:7 reads: "But we were gentle among you, as when a nurse takes care of her own children"; NA28: ἀλλ' ἐγενήθημεν νήπιοι ἐν μέσῳ ὑμῶν, ὡς ἐὰν τροφὸς θάλπῃ τὰ ἑαυτῆς τέκνα.

them? Are nurses not more indulgent to children than their mothers?"[57] All of these metaphors assume that nurses truly loved the children they nourished and raised, that they were close to these children, and that the children also loved their nurses. In one instance, Chrysostom lists the nurse with other close family members, such as parents, grandparents, brothers, sisters. He includes the nurse as a relationship of kinship (*syngeneia*).[58]

We must again be suspicious of such language of love and kinship. As with the slavery metaphors described in chapter 2 of this book, the metaphor of the nurse functions as doulological discourse that narrates the point of view of only the slaveholder and the freeborn children, not the slaves. Some nurses may have truly loved the children in their care, and then there is the possibility that these nurses saw free elite children as parasitic agents. We will never know exactly. The question is not whether nurses loved or were loved by these children. What is more important is that these metaphors and stereotypes of the good, loving nurse and the bad, superstitious nurse reflect the language of domination that was prevalent among the elite of late Roman society, and expose the fissures of that society. Even if the affection was genuine, it was an affection born out of oppression and paternalism. Nurses were subject to the same degrading and oppressive practices of correction and punishment as any other slave; perhaps even more so, since the body of the nurse is the one slave body that is closest to the corporeality of the elite. Many Roman authors describe the love that nurses have for their children,[59] but the love that male elite slaveholders saw in nurses may only have been a misreading of a desperation stemming from the inability to offer resistance to their masters or patrons.

Sandra Joshel compares the experiences of a Roman nurse to those of the black mammies of the American South. The picture that emerges is complex and illustrates that we cannot take such descriptions of affection at face value.[60] Having grown up under the cold shadow of apartheid in South Africa, I can also personally recall the "loving" relations between white people and their black subordinates in the midst of that oppressive regime. And it would be untrue to state that such exchanges of affection were false or insincere in all cases. The problem is that it was always a relationship in which reciprocity was based on the fear of oppression, punishment, and dehumanization. As in the case of the Roman nurse, the American

57. *Hom. 1 Thess.* 2.2 (F5.331): Μὴ ἡ τροφὸς κολακεύει, ἵνα δόξης τύχῃ; μὴ χρήματα αἰτεῖ παρὰ τῶν παίδων τῶν μικρῶν; μὴ βαρεῖα αὐτοῖς ἐστι καὶ φορτική; οὐχὶ μᾶλλον τῶν μητέρων εἰσὶ προσηνεῖς;

58. *Hom. 1 Cor.* 34.4 (F2.426).

59. Joshel, "Nurturing the Master's Child," 7–8.

60. Both Finley and Joshel criticize Vogt's positive evaluation of affectionate nurses as an attempt to highlight the "humanitarian" attitude of Roman society; see Moses I. Finley, *Ancient Slavery and Modern Ideology* (New York: Viking Press, 1980), 99–119; Joshel, "Nurturing the Master's Child," 4–5; Joseph Vogt, *Ancient Slavery and the Ideal of Man,* trans. Thomas Wiedemann (Cambridge, MA: Harvard University Press, 1975), 105–8.

black mammy, or the South African *bediende* or *ousie*,[61] any affectionate relationship was still the fruit of a poisonous tree.

The stereotypes of the good and the bad nurse are indicative of some of the problems of late Roman and Christian society. The good nurse becomes a discursive strategy to ensure loyalty at all costs, even at the cost of perhaps neglecting her own children for the sake of the elites. Its purpose is to inculcate, as we have seen, ideologies and behaviors of domination at a very young age. Habits of self-control and mastery had to be inseminated in early infancy, and even in the first years following infancy, the child needs to be disciplined in a scriptural pedagogy that affirms operations of domination and enslavement. We have, then, in the symbol of the good nurse a kyriarchization and masculinization of infancy and childhood, and this operation also spilled over and permeated into the Christian discourse of teaching and spiritual guidance. The metaphor of milk and nursing functioned to infantilize undesired spiritual growth or nonconformance to dominant ecclesiastical structures of power.

In Chrysostom's thought, the image of the bad nurse who introduces superstition, fables, and gossip also feeds into the pathologization of the slave in antiquity. Pastoral power makes a direct and overt assault on the non-Christian traditions and practices of these slave women; the traditions and practices are vilified with the subjectivity of the nurse. The image of the good and bad nurse functions in the same way as the image of the faithful and disloyal slave. By controlling the knowledge and behavior of the nurse, Chrysostom enforces the nurse's carceral state and thereby again introduces a language and practice that sustain slaveholding. Many women may have felt compelled to abandon their own traditions for Christian traditions and rituals in order to find work and support in Christian households; or at the least, they were forced to perform any private devotions out of sight of others, which was very difficult for a slave or a freedwoman. There is also the very real possibility of forced conversion to Christianity, which would also sustain the carceral state of the nurse. While it is uncertain to what extent Chrysostom's advice was followed, his comments do coincide with the general corrective rhetoric against nurses in Roman antiquity and the operations of pastoralization, and the result may have been that these women lived very incongruent religious lives with the constant fear of being persecuted, corrected, and punished—possibilities they saw looming in the very eyes of the children they suckled.

61. The Afrikaans word *bediende* is a more formal word that means "maid." *Ousie* has the same meaning, but it has a more derogatory sense and, along with the very offensive term *meit*, is often used to refer to black female workers in white households or black women generally. Such opprobrious language, along with a general racist mind-set that devalued anyone that was not white, could not be separated from these "affectionate" relationships between white and black people during apartheid. It shows how problematic the idea of loving relationships can be when they occur within oppressive systems like Roman slavery or apartheid.

Joshel notes that the image of the good nurse is an exposé of the disturbing symptoms of imperial society.[62] The discourse of nursing and surrogacy destabilized ancient frameworks of gender, parentage, and kyriarchy. This is evident in the divergent views of ancient authors, with some, like Favorinus, condemning wet nursing, and others, like pseudo-Chrysostom, noting nursing as a marker of shame not fit for the elite mother.[63] This discourse illustrated the anxieties about the degeneration of the elite household—men were concerned that women were no longer fulfilling their natural roles as mothers. Joshel rightly notes that the good nurse is the correlate of the bad mother, the mother concerned only with beauty and comfort (it was believed that breast-feeding caused premature aging[64])—nursing is therefore a symptom of elite decadence.[65] Another motivation for an elite woman to hire a wet nurse may have been to increase her chances of becoming pregnant again, as breast-feeding was viewed by some as contraceptive.[66] Nursing also highlights the neglect that the infant of the nurse herself may have experienced.

All of that duly noted, however, the activity of nurses also shaped and reproduced ancient Roman masculinity and femininity. Chrysostom believed that nurses had to guard the chastity of the young *filiafamilias*, to be a mobile carceral space. Wherever the girl went, the nurses and female slaves had to accompany her, watching over her and protecting her. In this way, the nurse transforms after breast-feeding into a guardian of female chastity, thus assuring that male honor remains unscathed by any form of disgrace—a very important task considering the fragile nature of Roman masculinity in late antiquity. In this way, nursing shaped and sustained Roman masculinity and subjugated femininity. Nursing itself, to some, may have become a marker of shame.[67] The failure of males and Roman masculinity generally is also seen in the discourse of nursing, where men are no longer able to properly regulate and master their wives and children. The unspoken dilemma of the sexual regulation and abuse of female slaves, who could also have been nurses, must also not be forgotten. Oribasius advised against having sex when breast-feeding, and slave women who nursed could be forced not to have sex with their own partners.[68] The contraceptive nature of breast-feeding may have encouraged sexual activity during the period of lactation.

With these problems related to masculinity, kyriarchy, in turn, is also destabilized. In the operation of nursing, the future slaveholder depends on and feeds off

62. Joshel, "Nurturing the Master's Child," 9–12.

63. *In Ps. 50* 1 (PG 55.572.35–37); see Harper, *Slavery in the Late Roman World*, 112.

64. King, *Hippocrates' Woman*, 143.

65. Joshel, "Nurturing the Master's Child," 10–11.

66. King, *Hippocrates' Woman*, 143.

67. Harper, *Slavery in the Late Roman World*, 111–12.

68. Oribasius, *Coll. med.* 33 (CMG 6.1.1.126–27); for the text and discussion, see Harper, *Slavery in the Late Roman World*, 112.

the slave body. The emphasis on the love of the good nurse for the slaveholder and the children then aims to ameliorate this problematic kyriarchal vampirism—the nurse is just as dependent on the slaveholder as the slaveholder is on the nurse. We have seen this type of paternalistic rhetoric frequently in Chrysostom. The dependency of the slaves on the master (who then becomes a slave himself, according to Chrysostom) simply disguises the dependence and decadence of the slaveholder. It also exposes the vulnerability of the slaveholding family.[69] Moreover, the domination over nurses, who were often freed slaves, also shows how slavery and the discourse of domination were perpetuated even when someone was freed. The grip of kyriarchy was desperate and not easily loosened. We therefore need to be critical of any doulological metaphor that proposes to be good and based on morally sound principles. Discourses of love, loyalty, and care cannot be taken at face value in these statements. They too had a carcerality that served to sustain slavery and strengthen Roman masculinity and kyriarchy.

MAKING MASTERS: THE ROLE OF THE PEDAGOGUE

Besides the nurse, the majority of elite Roman children, especially boys, had a slave companion almost like a tutor, called in Greek a *paidagōgos* (hence the Latin *paedagogus*), who accompanied the boy to school and back.[70] Lisa Maurice states that the pedagogue was always a slave in the early Empire,[71] although from Chrysostom's comments, this does not always seem to be the case. Generally, pedagogues were slaves or freedmen. Speaking to his elite households, Chrysostom envisions a few virtuous slaves participating in the education of the boy, and the pedagogue must be chosen from them. But if there are no slaves fitting for the role, the father must hire a freedman for this undertaking.[72] In some cases, elderly men served as pedagogues.[73] Despite the importance of his job, the pedagogue, like the nurse, was generally considered to do menial work, although there were some high-ranking and respected pedagogues active in the Roman education system.

69. Matthew J. Perry, *Gender, Manumission, and the Roman Freedwoman* (New York: Cambridge University Press, 2013), 51.

70. See Henri I. Marrou, *A History of Education in Antiquity,* trans. George Lamb, Wisconsin Studies in Classics (Madison: University of Wisconsin Press, 1982), 267–68; Cornelia B. Horn and John W. Martens, *"Let the Little Children Come to Me": Childhood and Children in Early Christianity* (Washington, DC: Catholic University of America Press, 2009), 29–30; Christian Laes, *Children in the Roman Empire: Outsiders Within* (New York: Cambridge University Press, 2011), 113–22.

71. Lisa Maurice, *The Teacher in Ancient Rome: The Magister and His World* (Lanham, MD: Lexington Books, 2013), 127.

72. *Inan.* 38.475–90 (SC 188.128–30); see Georg Kontoulis, *Problem der Sklaverei (ΔΟΥΛΕΙΑ) bei den kappadokischen Kirchenvätern und Johannes Chrysostomus* (Bonn: Habelt, 1993), 332–54.

73. Tim G. Parkin, *Old Age in the Roman World: A Cultural and Social History* (Baltimore: Johns Hopkins University Press, 2003), 220, 240.

Chrysostom recounts a very interesting tale of a monk who was convinced to take up the role of pedagogue for a boy in the city. Chrysostom visited the monk, who lived in the mountains, and asked the man "why, after having achieved such wisdom, he had lowered himself to take the position of a pedagogue." The monk himself was not very happy about having taken up this wordly task, and when Chrysostom asks him, he seems relieved that he "only had a little time left in the occupation."[74] By becoming a pedagogue, the monk humbled and shamed himself for the sake of schooling the young boy in the monastic life. We will return to this episode shortly.

Some pedagogues did enjoy more esteem than others; some were well known for their good teaching skills, and were sometimes even exchanged as gifts.[75] The pedagogue was more than a simple babysitter; he was a guardian and responsible for protecting the boy from outside influences, especially from the danger of pederasty and kidnapping. Chrysostom made it obvious—rather than spoiling the boy, a father should choose a good pedagogue for his son, and not clothe the boy in luxurious clothing. Certain physical features, like long hair and pierced ears, are unnatural qualities for a man.[76] A real man must look rugged and simple, and not in any instance resemble a woman in his demeanor. A man's physical appearance must be evidence of his own self-control and self-sufficiency. Chrysostom was very concerned that a young boy might assume an effeminized corporeality from his wealthy parents, which could even lead to homoeroticism. The pedagogue must guard against these dangers.

Pederasty was common in Chrysostom's time, despite much legislation aiming to protect the freeborn male child.[77] To return briefly to the issue of the *bulla,* young men were given a *bulla* at birth, an amulet protecting them not only from supernatural forces but also from physical ones. Along with the *toga praetexta,* the *bulla* serves as *insignia* showing that the child was freeborn, and thereby acts as a type of deterrent against sexual threats.[78] It also highlights the constant danger of sexual abuse faced by slave children. Chrysostom, however, is against decorating a boy with extravagant

---

74. *Adv. oppug.* 3.12 (PG 47.369.3–6): τὴν πρόφασιν ἐπεχείρουν μανθάνειν δι᾽ ἣν τοιαύτης ἐπειλημμένος σοφίας εἰς τὸν τῶν παιδαγωγῶν βίον καθῆκεν ἑαυτόν. . . . Ὁ δὲ μικρὸν ἔφησεν ἑαυτῷ λείπεσθαι χρόνον ἐν τούτῳ. Translation: David G. Hunter, trans., *A Comparison Between a King and a Monk; Against the Opponents of the Monastic Life: Two Treatises by John Chrysostom* (Lewiston, NY: Edwin Mellen, 1988), 152.

75. Libanius received a pedagogue as a gift from his friend Seleucus; *Ep.* 734.3 (Foerster 10.660); see Harper, *Slavery in the Late Roman World,* 114.

76. *Inan.* 16.239–56 (SC 188.96–100).

77. Kyle Harper, *From Shame to Sin: The Christian Transformation of Sexual Morality in Late Antiquity* (Cambridge, MA: Harvard University Press, 2013), 144–57.

78. Robert E. A. Palmer, "*Bullae insignia ingenuitatis,*" *American Journal of Ancient History* 14 (1989): 1–69.

bullae and *togae*, or any type of excessive jewelry, like earrings. While these may be signs of freeborn status and wealth, Chrysostom sees them as dangerous devices that make a boy look effeminate and only increase the love of wealth and vainglory. Long hair, jewels, and fine clothing are unnatural for a man and create a gender ambiguity that disturbs Chrysostom. Child sexuality was a source of great anxiety for Chrysostom, especially the sexuality of boys, and anything that might stimulate a child sexually, including such adornments, but also mingling with women, especially slave women, was unacceptable. It was more important for a father to choose a good pedagogue to guard the child and focus on raising the child in virtue.

Chrysostom contrasts the allure of the kidnapper with the strictness of the pedagogue: "Oftentimes kidnappers, when they intend to steal and kidnap little children, do not promise them beatings and whippings, or any other thing that is similar, but offer them cakes and sweetmeats." This in contrast to fathers who appoint a pedagogue as a surrogate and extension of paternal authority, who disciplines and punishes the child, but also protects him: "Fathers at least behave in an opposite way to kidnappers. When they send their children to school, they appoint pedagogues over them, threaten them with beatings, and wall them in with fear."[79] The pedagogue is supposed to protect the boy from external sexual threats, as well as from the boy's own sexual salacity. Pedagogues were, ironically, central in the early childhood development of masculinity and especially kyriarchy. Much like nurses, pedagogues were the biological apparatuses that milled Roman masculinity and sustained kyriarchy.

Conflict and status confusion in the relations between pedagogues and their freeborn students were quite common, especially as the child started growing into a slaveholder.[80] Libanius is open about this status confusion: "Thus, thrashing and throttling and torturing, and all the things which masters use against their slaves, are also deemed fitting for those who are set over their sons."[81] Libanius also complains about the abuse good pedagogues often suffered at the hands of their pupils, and ranks some pedagogues only slightly behind the honorable professors of the schools in Antioch.[82] Some did not share these sentiments; for example, there is the much earlier legend of the staunch traditionalist Cato, who did not allow a slave to teach his son because he felt education was too important to be left to the

---

79. *Stat.* 16.4 (PG 49.168.3–6, 16–19): Ἀνδραποδισταὶ πολλάκις παιδία μικρὰ συλῶντες καὶ κλέπτοντες, οὐ πληγὰς καὶ μάστιγας, οὐδ᾽ ἄλλο τι τῶν τοιούτων ὑπισχνοῦνται, ἀλλὰ πλακοῦντας καὶ τραγήματα.... Οἱ γοῦν πατέρες ἀπεναντίας τοῖς ἀνδραποδισταῖς ποιοῦσιν· ὅταν εἰς διδασκαλεῖον πέμπωσι τὰ παιδία, παιδαγωγοὺς ἐφιστῶσι, πληγὰς ἀπειλοῦσι, φόβον ἐπιτειχίζουσι.

80. Maurice, *Teacher in Ancient Rome*, 127.

81. Libanius, *Prog.* 3.2.9 (Foerster 8.77): διὰ τοῦτο γὰρ καὶ παίειν καὶ ἄγχειν καὶ στρεβλοῦν καὶ ἃ τῶν δεσποτῶν πρὸς τοὺς οἰκέτας, ταῦτα καὶ τῶν υἱέων τοῖς ἐφεστῶσιν ἀξιοῦσιν ὑπάρχειν. Translation: Harper, *Slavery in the Late Roman World*, 114.

82. Libanius, *Or.* 58.7–20 (Foerster 4.184–91); see Harper, *Slavery in the Late Roman World*, 115.

servile classes.[83] Such negative slave stereotypes, as we saw and will see in numerous sources, were still present in late antiquity.

The pedagogue also played an important part in the moral formation of the child.[84] Like the nurse, the pedagogue could punish the child if he deserved it, and the pedagogue also provided auxiliary education alongside the schoolteacher. The pedagogue had to coach a boy until he was ready to assume the *toga virilis*—that is, until his entry into manhood and citizenship. Some girls had pedagogues,[85] who were responsible, along with nurses, for the safety, education, and marriage preparation of the *filiafamilias*. As Raffaella Cribiore has shown well, those expensive pedagogues and slaves who had the ability to read and write were very active in the education of children in the Roman Empire.[86]

In late Roman antiquity, the distinction between the pedagogue and the free professional teacher, the *magister* and *professor*, became more pronounced.[87] Many pedagogues, however, were literate and also served a secondary role as a type of teacher.[88] Some pedagogues, and other literate slaves, were probably taught in *paedagogia*, a type of school for slave children. The precise nature, dynamics, and prevalence of the *paedagogium*, however, are unclear. There were imperial *paedagogia* and also some in illustrious households.[89] Another institution related to the care of slaves was the slave infirmary (*valetudinarium*)—a dormitory or outbuilding used for the medical care of slaves.[90] Besides the elusive ancient insti-

---

83. Plutarch, *Cat. mai.* 20.3–4 (Perrin 360–61): "As soon as the boy [Cato's son] showed signs of understanding, his father took him under his own charge and taught him to read, although he had an accomplished slave, Chilo by name, who was a school-teacher and taught many boys. Still, Cato thought it not right, as he tells us himself, that his son should be scolded by a slave, or have his ears tweaked when he was slow to learn, still less that he should be indebted to his slave for such a priceless thing as education"; ἐπεὶ δ' ἤρξατο συνιέναι, παραλαβὼν αὐτὸς ἐδίδασκε γράμματα. καίτοι χαρίεντα δοῦλον εἶχε γραμματιστὴν ὄνομα Χίλωνα, πολλοὺς διδάσκοντα παῖδας· οὐκ ἠξίου δὲ τὸν υἱόν, ὥς φησιν αὐτός, ὑπὸ δούλου κακῶς ἀκούειν ἢ τοῦ ὠτὸς ἀνατείνεσθαι μανθάνοντα βράδιον, οὐδέ γε μαθήματος τηλικούτου [τῷ] δούλῳ χάριν ὀφείλειν.

84. See Marrou, *History of Education*, 144–46; W. Martin Bloomer, "The Ancient Child in School," in Grubbs et al., *The Oxford Handbook of Childhood and Education in the Classical World*, 444–63. For an overview of the role and function of moral education in Chrysostom, see Ottorino Pasquato, "La priorità dell'educazione morale in Giovanni Crisostomo," in *Spiritualità del lavoro nella catechesi dei Padri del III-IV secolo*, ed. Sergio Felici (Rome: LAS, 1986), 105–39.

85. William V. Harris, *Ancient Literacy* (Cambridge, MA: Harvard University Press, 1991), 239.

86. Raffaella Cribiore, *The School of Libanius in Late Antique Antioch* (Princeton, NJ: Princeton University Press, 2007), 118–48.

87. Maurice, *Teacher in Ancient Rome*, 7–8, 127–28.

88. Stanley F. Bonner, *Education in Ancient Rome: From the Elder Cato to the Younger Pliny* (Berkeley: University of California Press, 1977), 39.

89. Harris, *Ancient Literacy*, 247–49.

90. Andrew T. Crislip, *From Monastery to Hospital: Christian Monasticism and the Transformation of Health Care in Late Antiquity* (Ann Arbor: University of Michigan Press, 2005), 125–28.

tution known as the *paedagogium,* there were very few other avenues of formal education and care for slave children, with the exception of the monastery—most slaves were educated in households.[91] There is of course always the possibility that some slaves were self-taught.[92] The inclusion of slaves in Christian households in the ritual of scripture reading may also have contributed to their literacy.[93]

So despite their official differences, at times the distinction between pedagogues and teachers is not very clear, showing their close functional relationship. In numerous instances Chrysostom refers to pedagogues and teachers (*didaskaloi*) simultaneously, often without clear differentiation—their roles were inseparable.[94] Sometimes a slave damaged the writing instruments of a child, and it was then, Chrysostom argues, that a father should teach the young *filiusfamilias* to control his temper. Fathers must say: "If you see that your slave has broken one of your pencils or damaged a pen, do not be angry or insulting but forgiving and gentle." We can infer something about the behavior of elite children toward their slaves in Chrysostom's observation that "children become cantankerous when such items are damaged and tend rather to lose their soul than to let the offender go unpunished."[95] Children were involved in the punishment of slaves from a very young age. There are elementary school exercises in which a small child is taught to read a text in which he threatens a slave with crucifixion.[96] Chrysostom is more concerned about the control of the child's anger and his attachment to material possessions, than he is about the child's involvement in punishment and domination. Chrysostom is against harsh punishment that is not thought through, but he does not rule out punishment of slaves in general. Children were supposed to be taught under what circumstances to have a slave punished. That is what makes a good slaveholder.

Although the pedagogue was not on the same social level as the professional teacher, the pedagogue had to ensure that the child did the homework lessons

91. For a detailed discussion of children and monasticism, see Carrie Schroeder, "Children and Egyptian Monasticism," in *Children in Late Ancient Christianity,* ed. Cornelia B. Horn and Robert R. Phenix, Studien und Texte zu Antike und Christentum 58 (Tübingen: Mohr Siebeck, 2009), 317–38.

92. For more on the relationship between slavery and literacy, see Pieter J. J. Botha, *Orality and Literacy in Early Christianity* (Eugene, OR: Cascade Books, 2012), 49–86.

93. See Chris L. de Wet, "'If a Story Can So Master the Children's Soul': Christian Scriptural Pedagogy, Orality and Power in the Writings of John Chrysostom," *Oral History Journal of South Africa* 2, no. 1 (2014): 121–42.

94. *Ex. Ps.* 1.3 (PG 55.43.2–4); *Hom. Matt.* 81.1 (PG 58.738.2–3); *Hom. Act.* 14.4 (PG 60.117.33–34).

95. *Inan.* 73.891–93, 895–98 (SC 188.174–76): «"Αν ἴδῃς ἢ γραφίδα ἀπολωλυῖαν ἢ κάλαμον διακλασθέντα ὑπὸ τοῦ οἰκέτου, μὴ ὀργίζου μηδὲ ὑβρίσῃς, ἀλλ' ἔσο συγγνωμονικός, ἔσο εὐπαραίτητος.» ... Χαλεποὶ γὰρ ἐν ταῖς τῶν τοιούτων ἀπωλείαις οἱ παῖδες καὶ μᾶλλον ἂν τὴν ψυχὴν πρόοιντο ἢ τὸν περὶ ταῦτα γενόμενον κακὸν ἀτιμώρητον ἀφεῖεν ἄν.

96. *Colloq. Harl.* 18 (CGL 3.642); for a discussion of this source, see Harper, *Slavery in the Late Roman World,* 344–45.

assigned by the teacher, and had the special role of instilling a love of rhetoric and language in a young boy. Pedagogues joined children in the classroom and almost everywhere else.[97] They had to guard a youth against malicious lovers, and were often too close for comfort in the life of a young boy.[98] In essence, the pedagogue was a mobile carceral contingent, a biological panopticon that monitored and corrected the child. Chrysostom provided direct advice for the pedagogue regarding the mobility of the boy. He was not to be brought near women, especially slave women; he had to stay very far away from the theater; and generally, he had to be shielded from undesirables.[99] The greatest enemy of a young boy, according to Chrysostom, is his own pubescent lust. Pedagogues accompanied boys to the baths, and they had to ensure that boys did not bathe in the company of women.[100]

A pedagogue, therefore, had to fashion the morality of a child. He directed the child in the corporeal vernacular that made up the habitus of freeborn status, especially in terms of the performance of masculinity. This included how to walk in public and behave in the marketplace, how to speak, sit, eat, drink, laugh, and behave toward women and other slaves[101]—the entire social grammar of Roman freeborn masculinity. Authors like Chrysostom and Libanius stress the importance of the pedagogue in developing the language and rhetorical skills of a child,[102] skills fundamental especially in the preparation for manhood. The boy had to be taught *disciplina,* those behavioral reproductions that would prepare him for manhood and citizenship—most important, this *disciplina* would brace him for the pinnacle of Roman masculinity, the *vita militaris.*

Pedagogues also had a reputation for their sternness and recourse to punish a disobedient child.[103] The pedagogue had to teach a child fear as well as dignity. Fear was a crucial element in the functioning of the pedagogue, and Chrysostom was very vocal about the benefits of fear: "If fear was not good, fathers would not have appointed pedagogues over their children."[104] Fear was the most common feature of the relationship between a boy and his pedagogue.[105] To understand this dynamic, it should be recognized that slaves were somatic surrogates for their

97. Maurice, *Teacher in Ancient Rome,* 128–30. Centuries earlier in his typical satyrical and exaggerated style, Plautus has one of his adolescent characters complain that he cannot even kiss a girl without the pedagogue being present; *Bacch.* 122–68 (Barsby 38–41); Maurice, *Teacher in Ancient Rome,* 127.

98. For a useful evaluation of pedagogues in the works of Libanius, see Raffaella Cribiore, *Gymnastics of the Mind: Greek Education in Hellenistic and Roman Egypt* (Princeton, NJ: Princeton University Press, 2005), 50–51; Cribiore, *School of Libanius.*

99. *Inan.* 60.754–56 (SC 188.158), 78.937–40 (SC 188.180–82), 90.1058–70 (SC 188.196).

100. *Inan.* 60.754–56 (SC 188.158).

101. Maurice, *Teacher in Ancient Rome,* 129. See also Chrysostom, *Bab. Jul. gent.* 70.1–7 (SC 362.184).

102. Cribiore, *School of Libanius,* 118–29.

103. *Stag.* 1.6 (PG 47.442.3–13); *Hom. Act.* 42.4 (PG 60.301.48–50).

104. *Stat.* 15.2 (PG 49.154.17–19): Εἰ μὴ καλὸν ἦν ὁ φόβος, οὐκ ἂν πατέρες παιδαγωγοὺς τοῖς παισὶν.

105. *Stat.* 17.2 (PG 49.172.24–28).

masters.[106] The fear the boy had for his pedagogue is the most telling feature of the surrogacy of patriarchy in the body of the pedagogue. The body of the pedagogue was seized by patriarchy and permeated with the *patria potestas*. "And as with sick persons, when the ill child kicks and turns away from the food given by the physicians, the assistants call the father or the pedagogue," Chrysostom explains, "and ask them to take the food from the physician's hands and bring it to the child, so that out of fear toward them he may take it and be quiet."[107] There is an isomorphism between paternal and pedagogical power. It was not so much the subjectivity of the pedagogue himself that inspired fear, but his patriarchal surrogacy.

As boys grew up, however, and realized their superiority, they challenged and even rebuked their pedagogues. Although the pedagogue represented paternal power, such challenges did not threaten the father directly. Moreover, fathers could defend a pedagogue if need be, and we will see that Chrysostom himself told fathers to carefully scrutinize a boy when he rebukes a slave or pedagogue. When the boy develops into a man, the paternal power that the body of the pedagogue catalyzed is used against the pedagogue and any other slave. Chrysostom complains about the laxity of freeborn children in his time, the delinquency of the youth, and contends that "fathers are to blame, while they force the horse-breakers to discipline their horses with much care . . . but their own young they neglect." The youth, in Chrysostom's opinion, had lost their *disciplina*, their self-control (*sōphrosynē*), "going around for a long time unrestrained, and without self-control, putting themselves to shame by fornications, and gambling, and entertainment in the lawless theaters."[108]

In fact, one focus of Chrysostom's treatise *De inani gloria* is the role and responsibility of the virtuous pedagogue. But fathers have neglected to consider this in selecting a pedagogue, and so their sons have fallen into ruin, Chrysostom argues. He considers choosing a pedagogue an art form, and describes the pedagogue as a sculptor, a pilot,[109] someone who fashions virtue and masculinity.[110] "But if we have appointed a pedagogue over a child's soul, we select hastily and randomly whoever

106. Jennifer A. Glancy, *Slavery in Early Christianity* (Minneapolis: Fortress Press, 2006), 15–16.

107. *Hom. 1 Cor.* 12.1 (F2.132): Καὶ καθάπερ ἐπὶ τῶν καμνόντων, ὅταν λακτίζῃ τὸ παιδίον τὸ ἀρρωστοῦν καὶ ἀποστρέφηται τὰ προσφερόμενα σιτία παρὰ τῶν ἰατρῶν, τὸν πατέρα ἢ τὸν παιδαγωγὸν καλέσαντες οἱ προσεδρεύοντες, παρὰ τῶν τοῦ ἰατροῦ χειρῶν λαβόντας τὰ σιτία προσάγειν κελεύουσιν, ὥστε ἐκ τοῦ φόβου τοῦ πρὸς ἐκείνους δέξασθαι καὶ ἡσυχάσαι.

108. *Hom. Matt.* 59.7 (PG 58.582.55–583.3): Αἴτιοι δὲ οἱ πατέρες, οἳ τοὺς μὲν πωλοδάμνας ἀναγκάζουσι τοὺς ἵππους τοὺς ἑαυτῶν μετὰ πολλῆς ῥυθμίζειν τῆς ἐπιμελείας . . . τοὺς δὲ αὐτῶν νέους ἐπὶ πολὺ περιορῶσιν ἀχαλινώτους περιόντας καὶ σωφροσύνης ἐρήμους, πορνείαις καὶ κύβοις καὶ ταῖς ἐν τοῖς παρανόμοις θεάτροις διατριβαῖς καταισχυνομένους.

109. *Hom. Matt.* 81.5 (PG 58.737.18–23).

110. See also Cribiore, *School of Libanius,* 131.

comes our way," Chrysostom grumbles, "and yet there is no greater art than this. For what is equal to training the soul, and forming the mind of someone that is young? For the person who has this skill must be more perfectionistic than any painter or any sculptor."[111] Ironically, by neglecting to choose a good pedagogue to shape a boy's masculinity, fathers have turned their sons into slaves, as Chrysostom frets: "Our foolishness is great in this case; here the free are more shameful than slaves. For slaves we correct, if not for their sake, then for our own. But the free do not even enjoy the benefit of this care, but are more repulsive to us than these slaves."[112] Here again the boundaries between moral and institutional slavery are blurred. Nature is turned upside down by the ill discipline of the free. Institutional slaves, like nurses and pedagogues, are used as shaming devices in Chrysostom's rhetoric to combat moral slavery among the freeborn.

A pedagogue remained with a boy for several years, and there was no specific age when a pedagogue was no longer appropriate.[113] A boy received the *toga virilis* around the age of sixteen, entered the army at seventeen, and started on the *cursus honorum* in his twenties.[114] The donning of the *toga virilis* may have been a watershed for some boys to finally release their pedagogues; it was when the boy became an *adulescens*—that is, late adolescence. Some pedagogues remained with their pupils for many years after the formal tutoring relationship ended. Chrysostom believed that most pedagogues left their pupils far too early, during the period when lust is most fierce, thereby perhaps supporting the period of late adolescence for the expected departure of the pedagogue.

Chrysostom compares the human life cycle to an ocean, with each period of life representing a certain type of sea. The first thalassic age is that of childhood (*to tēs paidikēs hēlikias*). This is the time when pedagogues are appointed. It is a sea "having much tempestuousness, because of its lack of mindfulness, its ease, because it is not stable." As with any ship that finds itself in stormy waters, "we appoint pedagogues and teachers over it, through care adding what is lacking in nature, there as by the skill of a pilot." This then reflects the period of early childhood, when the pedagogue is most active. "After this age follows the sea of the puberty," Chrysos-

---

111. *Hom. Matt.* 59.7 (PG 58.584.13–19): ἂν δὲ ψυχῇ παιδὸς ἐπιστῆσαι δέῃ παιδαγωγὸν, ἁπλῶς καὶ ὡς ἔτυχε τὸν ἐπελθόντα αἱρούμεθα. Καίτοιγε τῆς τέχνης ταύτης οὐκ ἔστιν ἄλλη μείζων. Τί γὰρ ἴσον τοῦ ῥυθμίσαι ψυχήν, καὶ διαπλάσαι νέου διάνοιαν; Καὶ γὰρ παντὸς ζωγράφου καὶ παντὸς ἀνδριαντοποιοῦ τὸν ταύτην ἔχοντα τὴν ἐπιστήμην ἀκριβέστερον διακεῖσθαι χρή.

112. *Hom. Matt.* 59.7 (PG 58.584.3–8): Ἐντεῦθεν πολλὴ ἡ ἄνοια· ἐντεῦθεν τῶν δούλων οἱ ἐλεύθεροι ἀτιμότεροι. Τοῖς μὲν γὰρ δούλοις, εἰ καὶ μὴ δι' αὐτούς, ἀλλὰ δι' ἡμᾶς αὐτοὺς ἐπιτιμῶμεν· οἱ δὲ ἐλεύθεροι οὐδὲ ταύτης ἀπολαύουσι τῆς προνοίας, ἀλλὰ καὶ τούτων ἡμῖν εἰσιν εὐτελέστεροι.

113. Laes, *Children in the Roman Empire*, 115.

114. Fanny Dolansky, "*Togam Virilem Sumere*: Coming of Age in the Roman World," in *Roman Dress and the Fabrics of Roman Culture*, ed. Jonathan Edmondson and Alison Keith (Toronto: University of Toronto Press, 2009), 47–52.

tom explains, "where the gales are as turbulent as in the Aegean, with lust increasing in us." We have here the age of youth, of puberty (*meirakieia*). This period is even worse than the former, since "this age is especially bereft of discipline ... because his mistakes are not corrected, for both teacher and pedagogue withdraw at this time."[115] Chrysostom is concerned that pedagogues left at the time they were most required—when puberty was in full swing. It is the period when the sexual drive of the young male is reaching its peak. This was Chrysostom's main problem with the formation of masculinity in early childhood. This issue will be discussed in more detail in chapter 6, where the problem of slavery and sexuality is examined.

After this period, according to Chrysostom, comes the time when a man starts his own household. So the period between the departure of the pedagogue and the marriage of the young man is Chrysostom's greatest concern. The only solution is to guide the boy into an early marriage so as to avoid fornication, or at least to entrust him to monks, who should school him in the monastic life.[116] The period of late adolescence is the time when a young man must demonstrate his *sōphrosynē*, his self-control. In Roman thought, the pedagogue was a fundamental accoutrement for virtue formation. Chrysostom recounts: "Since also with a child, if he is guided by some pedagogue whom he fears, and lives with self-control and virtuously, it is no surprise, for all attribute the self-control of the youth to his fear of the pedagogue." However, when the pedagogue departs, then the boy may show that he is truly a man, "when he continues to behave appropriately, after the bridle from that period is removed, then everyone recognizes him for the self-control of his earlier age."[117] To provide an exemplum of virtue, Chrysostom tells fathers to narrate the story of Jacob. When he was young and in exile, Jacob traveled without a pedagogue or a nurse, but still remained faithful to God.[118] Boys, then, should not become dependent on their pedagogues for their own virtue.

The two main offenses the *filiusfamilias* had to avoid at all costs were adultery and pederasty. With regard to the latter, the danger of being penetrated was always looming for both freeborn and slave boys alike. The freeborn boy wore his *bulla*

---

115. *Hom. Matt.* 81.5 (PG 58.737.18–738.3): πολὺν ἔχον τὸν σάλον διὰ τὸ ἀνόητον, διὰ τὴν εὐκολίαν, διὰ τὸ μὴ πεπηγέναι. Διὰ τοῦτο καὶ παιδαγωγοὺς καὶ διδασκάλους ἐφιστῶμεν, τὸ λεῖπον τῇ φύσει διὰ τῆς ἐπιμελείας εἰσφέροντες, ὥσπερ ἐκεῖ διὰ τῆς τέχνης τῆς κυβερνητικῆς. ... Μετὰ ταύτην τὴν ἡλικίαν ἡ τοῦ μειρακίου διαδέχεται θάλαττα, ἔνθα σφοδρὰ τὰ πνεύματα, καθάπερ ἐν τῷ Αἰγαίῳ, τῆς ἐπιθυμίας ἡμῖν αὐξανομένης ... ἀλλὰ καὶ διὰ τὸ τὰ ἁμαρτήματα μὴ ἐλέγχεσθαι· καὶ γὰρ καὶ διδάσκαλος καὶ παιδαγωγὸς λοιπὸν ὑπεξίστανται.

116. *Inan.* 61.757–75 (SC 188.158–60), 81.984–95 (SC 188.186–88).

117. *Stat.* 17.2 (PG 49.172.24–31): Ἐπεὶ καὶ παιδίον, ἕως μὲν ἂν ὑπὸ παιδαγωγοῦ τινος ἄγηται φοβεροῦ, καὶ μετὰ σωφροσύνης καὶ ἐπιεικείας ζῇ, θαυμαστὸν οὐδέν, ἀλλὰ τῷ τοῦ παιδαγωγοῦ φόβῳ τὴν σωφροσύνην τοῦ νέου λογίζονται πάντες· ὅταν δὲ ἀποθέμενος τὴν ἐκεῖθεν ἀνάγκην, ἐπὶ τῆς αὐτῆς μένῃ σεμνότητος, τότε καὶ τὴν ἐπὶ τῆς προτέρας ἡλικίας σωφροσύνην αὐτῷ πάντες λογίζονται.

118. *Inan.* 46.660–76 (SC 188.144).

and the *toga praetexta* to distinguish him from slave boys and to show possible pedophiles that he was free. There was much legislation in place that protected the freeborn boy from pederasty, although it does not mean it was not prevalent.[119] The pedagogue had to protect the boy from the danger of pederasty, yet in a vehement tirade against pederasty Chrysostom says: "No benefit comes from law courts or laws or pedagogues or parents or attendants or teachers." He gives the whole spectrum of personae that had to guard the young boy—yet they offer no security. "Some are corrupted by money, others are concerned only about their pay."[120] Status and power, according to Chrysostom, played an important part in the violation of children, and he blames, among others, corrupt pedagogues. It seems that the older man who had his sights set on a boy may often have used his power, wealth, and influence to intimidate the parents and pedagogue. Young slave boys were probably even more abused in lecherous practices.

Of course, same-sex passion between young boys and men was not always involuntary. Both André-Jean Festugière and Aline Rousselle argue that a boy's sexual initiation took place at the age of ten, about four to six years prior to receiving the *toga virilis,* and point out that this is also the age that Chrysostom recommends that a boy enter into the care of a monk or monastery if he was to be raised in the monastic life.[121] The age of ten was also considered the year that marked the child's ability to distinguish between right and wrong and to be held accountable for sin. More generally, the sexual life of boys was celebrated, especially their first ejaculation, and the festival of the Liberalia, when the *bulla* and *toga praetexta* were shed. In his illuminating history of the penis, David Friedman states: "A Roman citizen's body was private property, off-limits to penetration, but his penis worked for the Empire. Not the Christian penis. It broke the worldly chain of Rome and replaced it with a new spiritual connection."[122]

Chrysostom's advice, however, perhaps not pertains to protecting boys from pederasty and same-sex passion. Ten was also the age when a boy was to be groomed for

---

119. For more on homoeroticism and pederasty in Chrysostom, see Bernadette J. Brooten, *Love between Women: Early Christian Responses to Female Homoeroticism* (Chicago: University of Chicago Press, 1996), esp. 344–48; Harper, *From Shame to Sin,* 22–31, 95–99, 144–48; Chris L. de Wet, "John Chrysostom on Homoeroticism," *Neotestamentica* 48, no. 1 (2014): 187–218.

120. *Adv. oppug.* 3.8 (PG 47.361.18–21): Οὐδὲν ὄφελος δικαστηρίων, οὐδὲ νόμων, οὐδὲ παιδαγωγῶν, οὐ πατέρων, οὐκ ἀκολούθων, οὐ διδασκάλων· τοὺς μὲν γὰρ ἴσχυσαν διαφθεῖραι χρήμασιν, οἱ δ᾽ ὅπως αὐτοῖς μισθὸς γένοιτο μόνον ὁρῶσι. Translation: Hunter, *Two Treatises,* 140. See also *Hom. Rom.* 5[4] (F1.44–52); Brooten, *Love between Women,* 344–48.

121. *Adv. oppug.* 3.17 (PG 47.378.32–48); see André-Jean Festugière, *Antioche païenne et chrétienne: Libanius, Chrysostome et les moines de Syrie,* Bibliothèque des Écoles françaises d'Athènes et de Rome 194 (Paris: De Boccard, 1959), 202–6; Hunter, *Two Treatises,* 165; Rousselle, *Porneia,* 133–36.

122. David M. Friedman, *A Mind of Its Own: A Cultural History of the Penis* (New York: Simon and Schuster, 2001), 34. See also Hanne Blank, *Virgin: The Untouched History* (New York: Bloomsbury Publishing, 2007), 122.

marriage—so Chrysostom provides two possible solutions for the problem of cele-brated pubescent lust and the danger of homoeroticism. Either boys prepare for marriage at an early age or start to follow the monastic lifestyle. The move to have young men marry at an early age demonstrates a haste to place them in positions of mastery, and if they should leave their hometowns, a measure to keep them faithful and chaste. It could imply that Chrysostom wanted men to marry at the same age as women, in their late teens or early twenties. Traditionally, Roman men married at a later age than women. But Roman masculinity was quite unstable during late antiq-uity. Men not only had less control over wives and slaves, but the congenital relation-ship between fathers and sons had also eroded. Although many sons lost their fathers at an early age, the *filiusfamilias* was still legally bound under the *patria pot-estas* while the father was alive.[123] Traditionally, it was expected of a son to enter military or civil service when he reached maturity. This would also give him some independence from the father. However, in Chrysostom's time, many elite men were not so inclined to enter military service, and may have pursued other career avenues.

Conservative fathers may have wanted their sons to be prepared for the *vita mili-taris,* and the *disciplina paedagogi* had to prepare the boy for his military career. Chrysostom was not altogether dismissive of military service. In contrast to some Christian pacifist writers, Chrysostom took a more moderate view. He advises fathers to "make [their son] attentive of political affairs within his power and without having sin." In the case of duty in the army, Chrysostom counseled, "let him learn not to profit shamefully from it if he defends those who have suffered injustice, or any sim-ilar situation."[124] However, in a case like this, the father must "introduce his bride to him immediately and . . . not wait for him to serve as a soldier or participate in polit-ical affairs"—advice that again showed Chrysostom's preference for a very early mar-riage age for men.[125] Married Christian soldiers needed to behave honorably and manly. Prior to this, the pedagogue must teach the boy self-mastery and honor. There were, of course, alternatives. Some men did not want to go into military service, and a career in the church or monastery was an attractive alternative. The wide use of the metaphor of Christian spiritual soldiery, especially in Chrysostom,[126] attests to the fact that ascetic neomasculinity was an attractive option for men to affirm their

123. See Richard P. Saller, "*Patria Potestas* and the Stereotype of the Roman Family," *Continuity and Change* 1, no. 1 (1986): 7–22; Saller, "Men's Age at Marriage and Its Consequences in the Roman Family," *Classical Philology* 82, no. 1 (1987): 21–34.

124. *Inan.* 89.1053–57 (SC 188.194–96): Ποιῶμεν δὲ αὐτὸν καὶ πραγμάτων ἄπτεσθαι πολιτικῶν τῶν κατὰ δύναμιν, τῶν οὐκ ἐχόντων ἁμαρτήματα. Ἄν τε γὰρ στρατεύηται, μαθέτω μὴ κερδαίνειν αἰσχρῶς· ἄν τε τοῖς ἀδικουμένοις συναγορεύῃ, ἄν τε ὁτιοῦν τοιοῦτον.

125. *Inan.* 81.984–86 (SC 188.186–88): ταχέως ἄγαγε τὴν νύμφην, μηδὲ περιμείνῃς, ὥστε αὐτὸν στρατεύεσθαι ἢ πολιτικῶν ἅψασθαι πραγμάτων καὶ τότε·

126. See *Inan.* 23.325–24.353 (SC 188.108–10); *Compar. reg. mon.* 2 (PG 47.388.30–389.41); see Hunter, *Two Treatises,* 71.

manliness. It is quite evident from *Inan.* that Chrysostom wants the pedagogue to teach a boy Christian ascetic discipline. This discipline is explicated in the language of the contest (*agōn*). Chrysostom exclaims: "Raise an athlete for Christ and teach him although he is in the world to be pious from an early age."[127]

But Chrysostom does admit that he prays for many parents to raise young men fit for the monastic life, and for them to send them to the desert.[128] Mathew Kuefler has shown, convincingly, that the monk became the new epitome of Christian masculinity in late antiquity.[129] Chrysostom tells the story of a mother who asked a monk to assume the role of pedagogue for her son. The main reason for this radical request was that she feared the father would "enslave the child in the bonds of life prematurely, that he would deprive him of this zeal, that he would lead him into the army, and that he would render the child unable to live an upright life afterwards."[130] We have here a mother who wanted her child to enter the monastic life. She fears that the traditional course the child might have to take—namely, marriage and the *vita militaris*—would rob the child of his spiritual zeal and any possibility of being a soldier of Christ. There is a conflict here, a polarization of two very different views of masculinity. There is the father, who would have his son conform to traditional standards of Roman masculinity, and the mother, who sees more value in the ascetic masculinity of the monastic life. Marriage and military service will corrupt the boy. So she assumes a preventive agency, commences to deceive the father, and asks a monk to lower himself to the role of a slave pedagogue to "take him away alone to another place, where you can enjoy full freedom to form him without interference from his father or any of the household, and where you can make him live as if he were in a monastery."[131] With the monk as the pedagogue, the channels of the *patria potestas* become limited; the boy is also shielded from being influenced by other members of the household, like siblings or slaves. The mother's proposition demonstrates the point that the whole household was involved in pedagogy.[132]

127. *Inan.* 19.286–87 (SC 188.104): Θρέψον ἀθλητὴν τῷ Χριστῷ καὶ ἐν κόσμῳ ὄντα δίδαξον εὐλαβῆ ἐκ πρώτης ἡλικίας.

128. *Inan.* 19.286–87 (SC 188.104).

129. Mathew Kuefler, *The Manly Eunuch: Masculinity, Gender Ambiguity, and Christian Ideology in Late Antiquity* (Chicago: University of Chicago Press, 2001), 105–298.

130. *Adv. oppug.* 3.12 (PG 47.369.16–21): πρὸ ὥρας αὐτὸν ἤδη καταδήσῃ τοῖς τοῦ βίου σχοινίοις, καὶ ταύτης αὐτὸν ἀποστήσας τῆς σπουδῆς, ἐπὶ τὴν ζώνην ἀγάγοι, καὶ τὴν ἐξ ἐκείνης ῥαθυμίαν ἅπασαν, καὶ ἀδύνατον αὐτῷ τὴν μετὰ ταῦτα κατασκευάσῃ διόρθωσιν. Translation: Hunter, *Two Treatises*, 152.

131. *Adv. oppug.* 3.12 (PG 47.369.31–34): καταμόνας αὐτὸν ἔχων λοιπὸν ἐπὶ τῆς ἀλλοτρίας, οὔτε τοῦ πατρὸς ἐνοχλοῦντος, οὔτε τῶν οἰκείων τινὸς, μετὰ πολλῆς αὐτὸν τῆς ἐξουσίας διαπλάσαι δυνήσῃ, καὶ καθάπερ ἐν μοναστηρίῳ διάγοντα, οὕτω ποιῆσαι ζῆν. Translation: Hunter, *Two Treatises*, 152.

132. See Andrzej Uciecha, "Rodzina miejscem wychowania w traktacie pedagogicznym o wychowaniu dzieci Jana Chryzostoma," *Slaskie Studia Historyczno-Teologiczne* 19/20 (1986): 65–92; Wulf Jaeger, "Sklaverei bei Johannes Chrysostomus" (PhD diss., Christian-Albrechts-Universität zu Kiel, 1974), 62–82; Kontoulis, *Problem der Sklaverei*, 344–45.

Furthermore, the alternative the mother proposes is also a way to determine if the child is fit for the monastic life. Although it seems that the boy desired to go into the desert, he was persuaded, for the safety of himself, his mother, and other monks, to remain in the city and study rhetoric and in some way please his father, who did not approve of the lifestyle the son had chosen. This interesting story illustrates the familial tensions that may have been present in some households, where one spouse was a devoted Christian, and both had differing views on pedagogy and masculinity. Such alternative pedagogies were certainly present in Chrysostom's time, but they were probably the exception rather than the rule. But this is Chrysostom's ideal pedagogy. "If someone even now should show me such a soul, if he should provide such a pedagogue, if he should promise that everything else will be taken care of in the same way," Chrysostom explains, "I would pray a thousand times that this might happen, even more than the parents themselves."[133]

This type of pedagogy also occurred in households and among children who were less privileged. Carrie Schroeder notes that ancient monasteries were "teeming with children."[134] Many children were donated or abandoned to monasteries, rather than being subjected to a life of poverty or slavery in the city.[135] Chrysostom also speaks of children being raised in monasteries for ten or twenty years.[136] Some monasteries, of course, also cared for sick children.[137] Ironically, many of the same doulological discourses from mainstream Roman society are also seen in the treatment of such children in monasteries. Children were sometimes donated to monasteries out of desperation, or because parents who were infertile made a promise to God to devote the child to the monastery if he allowed them to conceive. Thus, many children in the late Roman Empire and early Byzantium, especially in Egypt and the East, were educated in monasteries.[138]

In some cases such children lived under dire circumstances in the monasteries, often as quasi slaves. Children were sometimes "sold" to monasteries when parents could not afford to care for them, and in such cases the price of the child was determined in the same way as that of a slave. Although it is not always explicitly mentioned that such a child is regarded as a slave, the agreement often implies that the

---

133. *Adv. oppug.* 3.12 (PG 47.370.49–53): "Ὥστε εἴ τίς μοι ψυχὴν καὶ νῦν ἐδείκνυ τοιαύτην, καὶ παιδαγωγὸν παρεῖχε τοιοῦτον, καὶ τὰ ἄλλα πάντα ὁμοίως [ἐπιμελεῖσθαι] ἐπηγγείλατο, μυριάκις ἂν ηὐξάμην τοῦτο γενέσθαι μᾶλλον τῶν γεννησαμένων αὐτῶν. Translation: Hunter, *Two Treatises,* 154.

134. Schroeder, "Children and Egyptian Monasticism," 317.

135. See John Boswell, *The Kindness of Strangers: The Abandonment of Children in Western Europe from Late Antiquity to the Renaissance* (Chicago: University of Chicago Press, 1998).

136. *Adv. oppug.* 3.18 (PG 47.380.14–23); see Hunter, *Two Treatises,* 167.

137. For more on monasteries and health care, see Crislip, *From Monastery to Hospital.*

138. For the dynamics of childhood in Christian asceticism, see Ville Vuolanto, "Family and Asceticism: Continuity Strategies in the Late Roman World" (PhD diss., University of Tampere, Finland, 2008).

child owes his or her life's labor to the monastery. This most likely reflects Roman legislative procedures that stated that a foundling (*threptos, alumnus*) might be raised as either a child or a slave.[139] Thus, some contracts emphasize the ownership of the child's body by the monastery, and if someone wanted to take a child from a monastery, they had to pay between thirty and thirty-six pieces of gold, which accounts for the child spending his or her entire life in the monastery.[140] In some cases the Coptic words *schmschal* and *sayon* are used to describe the legal condition of the child in relation to the monastery, and the same terms were used to refer to a servant or a slave.[141] Moreover, children were sometimes treated with violence and even sexually abused in these contexts.[142]

Many children, however, received a quality education and care; some returned to mainstream society, while others remained and became monks. Along with a strict disciplinary regime, children in monasteries received instruction in reading both classical and Christian sources and in writing, accompanied by many other disciplinary exercises, chores, and spiritual direction.[143] These positive aspects of monastic education were firmly rooted in Chrysostom's mind. The problem here is that there is much ambiguity about the status and integration of children, as well as slaves, in the context of monasteries and the broader ascetic landscape. We will return to the issue of slaves in monasteries later in this chapter.

PEDAGOGY AS METAPHOR

Despite his constant emphasis on the poor, Chrysostom mostly speaks to elite and bourgeois households in his homilies, and when he speaks of pedagogy, he depicts the standard pedagogical practices of elite households, and less frequently pedagogy in ascetic and monastic contexts. Like nursing, pedagogy also served as a

---

139. Boswell, *Kindness of Strangers*, 116–19.

140. Cécile Morrisson and Jean Claude Cheynet, "Prices and Wages in the Byzantine World," in *The Economic History of Byzantium: From the Seventh through the Fifteenth Century*, ed. Angeliki E Laiou and Charalampos Bouras, Dumbarton Oaks Studies 39 (Washington, DC: Dumbarton Oaks Research Library and Collection, 2002), 847.

141. The Coptic terms ϩⲙ̄ϩⲁⲗ (v. ϩⲁⲗ) and 6ⲁⲩⲟⲛ, in this context, convey the sense of a temple slave or hierodule; Arietta Papaconstantinou, "Notes sur les actes de donation d'enfant au monastère thébain de Saint-Phoibammon," *Journal of Juristic Papyrology* 32 (2002): 92. See also Maria C. Giorda, "De la direction spirituelle aux règles monastiques: Péchés, penitence et punitions dans le monachisme pachômien (IVe-Ve siècles)," *Collectanea Christiana Orientalia* 6 (2009): 95–113; Schroeder, "Children and Egyptian Monasticism," 335–36.

142. John W. Martens, "'Do Not Sexually Abuse Children': The Language of Early Christian Sexual Ethics," in *Children in Late Ancient Christianity*, ed. Cornelia B. Horn and Robert R. Phenix, Studien und Texte zu Antike und Christentum 58 (Tübingen: Mohr Siebeck, 2009), 227–54; Harper, *From Shame to Sin*, 143–46.

143. Giorda, "De la direction spirituelle."

convenient metaphor, and it was this elite brand of pedagogy that was metaphorized by Chrysostom.

Chrysostom saw the primary task of the pedagogue as teaching *sōphrosynē*. It then often happens that techniques of spiritual discipline are called pedagogues of the soul. Chrysostom describes fasting and hunger,[144] for instance, as psychic pedagogues. Even Satan can be a pedagogue.[145] The most common pedagogical metaphor in early Christianity, however, is the one that refers to the Law of Moses as a pedagogue. This is a very early tradition in Christian thought. In Galatians 3:24–26, Paul writes: "So then, the law was our pedagogue until Christ came, in order that we might be justified by faith. But now that faith has come, we are no longer under a pedagogue, for in Christ Jesus you are all sons of God, through faith."[146] J. Albert Harrill rightly reads this statement in the context of Roman pedagogy and the coming of age of the child in the ancient Mediterranean world.[147] According to Paul, the Law is the temporary pedagogue of the faithful, but when they become Christians, they shed the nomic pedagogue, and through their faith they become sons of God and heirs—a spiritual *liberalia*. In Galatians 3:27, with reference to baptism, Paul admonishes his readers to clothe themselves with Christ, probably referring to the donning of the *toga virilis*.

In his own interpretation of the verse, Chrysostom sees the Law as the pedagogue and Christ as the teacher (*didaskalos*). The metaphor immediately affords Christ a higher and more authoritative status than the Law, and like the metaphor of the nurse's milk, it is used to defame Jewish identity. Chrysostom states:

> But the pedagogue is not opposed to the teacher, but works with him, purging the youth of all vice, and preparing him with all leisure for receiving lessons from his teacher. But when he has become trained, then the pedagogue leaves him. . . . If the Law then was our pedagogue, and we were guarded under his authority, it is not the opponent of grace, but the fellow laborer. But if grace has come, and it continues to hold us down, then it becomes an opponent; for if it shuts in those who ought to go forward to grace, then it destroys our salvation. . . . Those then are the greatest

---

144. *Hom. Gen.* 2.3 (PG 53.27.1620); *Stat.* 14.4 (PG 49.145.27–31).

145. This is said in reference to 1 Cor. 5:5, where Paul instructs his congregants to hand a sinful man over to the devil for chastisement; see *Hom. 1 Cor.* 15.3 (F2.173).

146. NA28: ὥστε ὁ νόμος παιδαγωγὸς ἡμῶν γέγονεν εἰς Χριστόν, ἵνα ἐκ πίστεως δικαιωθῶμεν· ἐλθούσης δὲ τῆς πίστεως οὐκέτι ὑπὸ παιδαγωγόν ἐσμεν. Πάντες γὰρ υἱοὶ θεοῦ ἐστε διὰ τῆς πίστεως ἐν Χριστῷ Ἰησοῦ·

147. J. Albert Harrill, "Coming of Age and Putting on Christ: The *Toga Virilis* Ceremony, Its Paranaesis, and Paul's Interpretation of Baptism in Galatians," *Novum Testamentum* 44, no. 3 (2002): 252–77. For similar approaches with a different emphasis, see David J. Lull, "'The Law Was Our Pedagogue': A Study in Galatians 3:19–25," *Journal of Biblical Literature* 105, no. 3 (1986): 481–90; Michael J. Smith, "The Role of the Pedagogue in Galatians," *Bibliotheca Sacra* 163, no. 650 (2006): 197–214.

slanderers of the Law, those who still keep it. For then the pedagogue makes a youth laughable, by keeping him under his care when time calls for his departure.[148]

Chrysostom diverges somewhat from the original intention of Paul in his interpretation. For Paul, Christ is not so much the teacher as he is the coming of the age of manhood, which is why baptism is like putting on the *toga Christi*. But Chrysostom makes Christ the teacher. It has been noted earlier in this chapter that in late antiquity the difference between teachers and pedagogues became more pronounced than in the early Empire, and this may be why Chrysostom's first instinct is to make Christ the teacher. Moreover, Chrysostom does not elaborate further on the teacher metaphor. He simply asserts that just as there is cooperation between a pedagogue and a teacher, so too there is cooperation between Christ and the Law[149]—the Law prepared humanity for the Christic manhood that superseded Judaism. Chrysostom chooses to emphasize the departure of the pedagogue—in other words, the obsoleteness of the Law and Jewish customs.[150] Because the Jews still observe the Law, they in fact make themselves the enemies of their own Law.

The tutor is seen as one who essentially and ironically enslaves the child until he has reached manhood, whereupon the tutor is supposed to depart. A pedagogue that remains with a boy during manhood is an obstruction to the child's development. The use of this metaphor also betrays the obsoleteness of pedagogues in ancient times. Their use was limited. The metaphor infantilizes and, indirectly, feminizes Judaism and, in turn, masculinizes and kyriarchizes Christianity—Christianity is seen as adulthood or manhood, and Judaism as childhood. There is also an embedded feminization of Jewish identity in the use of this metaphor. Men had slaves only for a short while, but women always had slaves

---

148. *Comm. Gal.* 3.25–26 (F4.64–65): Ὁ δὲ παιδαγωγὸς οὐκ ἐναντιοῦται τῷ διδασκάλῳ, ἀλλὰ καὶ συμπράττει, πάσης κακίας ἀπαλλάττων τὸν νέον, καὶ μετὰ πάσης σχολῆς τὰ μαθήματα παρὰ τοῦ διδασκάλου δέχεσθαι παρασκευάζων· ἀλλ' ὅταν ἐν ἕξει γένηται, ἀφίσταται λοιπὸν ὁ παιδαγωγός. . . . Εἰ τοίνυν ὁ νόμος παιδαγωγός, καὶ ὑπ' αὐτὸν ἐφρουρούμεθα συγκεκλεισμένοι, οὐκ ἐναντίος τῆς χάριτος, ἀλλὰ καὶ συνεργός· εἰ δὲ ἐλθούσης τῆς χάριτος ἐπιμένοι κατέχων, τότε ἐναντίος. Ἂν γὰρ ὀφείλοντας ἐξελθεῖν πρὸς αὐτὴν συγκλείῃ, τότε τὴν ἡμετέραν λυμαίνεται σωτηρίαν. . . . Οἱ τοίνυν αὐτὸν τηροῦντες νῦν, οὗτοι μάλιστα αὐτὸν διαβάλλουσι. Καὶ γὰρ ὁ παιδαγωγὸς τότε καταγέλαστον ποιεῖ τὸν νέον, ὅταν καιροῦ καλοῦντος αὐτὸν ἀποστῆναι, παρ' ἑαυτῷ κατέχῃ.

149. For more on the dynamics between Christ and the Law in Chrysostom's thought, see Joshua Garroway, "The Law-Observant Lord: John Chrysostom's Engagement with the Jewishness of Christ," *Journal of Early Christian Studies* 18, no. 4 (2010): 591–615. On the problem of Christ's Jewishness and that of Paul, see Andrew S. Jacobs, "A Jew's Jew: Paul and the Early Christian Problem of Jewish Origins," *Journal of Religion* 86 (2006): 258–86.

150. See Robert L. Wilken, *John Chrysostom and the Jews: Rhetoric and Reality in the Late 4th Century* (Eugene, OR: Wipf & Stock, 2004), 150–51.

with them.[151] Jews are also seen as being slaves to the Law, in Chrysostom's thought, but Christians are free. "Do you see by how many means he leads them away from the error of Judaism?" Chrysostom asks, "showing first that it was extreme foolishness for those who had become free instead of slaves to desire to become slaves instead of free."[152] Of course, Chrysostom is quite inconsistent in his applications of the slave metaphor, since it is acceptable for Christians to be slaves of God, but not acceptable for Jews to have the Law as pedagogue.

Chrysostom also abnormalizes Jewish identity, since he now depicts those who are faithful to the Law as grown men still under their pedagogues—a shameful and abnormal position. There was a similar pathologization in Chrysostom's use of the nurse metaphor. In that instance Jews were depicted as grown men still suckling on a nurse, and here they are men still under a pedagogue. According to Chrysostom, Jews are incomplete men who will never achieve the manhood of Christianity, the age of honor and virtue. Jews are therefore not only textually and doctrinally immature, as evident from the metaphor of the milk, but they are also inferior in terms of virtue and thus are lesser men spiritually speaking.[153] It is the age of the Spirit, where the child is no longer in need of pedagogical guidance. Chrysostom explains: "How does someone who has become a perfect example by his own accord need a pedagogue? Nor does someone who is a philosopher need a grammarian." In other words, by adherence to the Law, people lower themselves to the level of children, when they should be philosophers. "Why then do you embarrass yourselves," Chrysostom asks, paraphrasing Paul, "by now adhering to the Law, when you previously gave yourselves to the Spirit?"[154] This disturbing rhetoric is similar to that of the image of the milk. A grown man has no need for milk, and a boy who has become an heir no longer needs a pedagogue.

Finally, in Chrysostom's De Babyla contra Julianum et gentiles 70, he compares the relics and shrine of the martyr Babylas to a pedagogue.[155] As a pedagogue

---

151. Gendered invective and the rhetoric of feminization are common in Chrysostom's vilification of the Jews; see Ross S. Kraemer, "The Other as Woman: An Aspect of Polemic among Pagans, Jews, and Christians," in The Other in Jewish Thought and History: Constructions of Jewish Culture and Identity, ed. Laurence J. Silberstein and Robert L. Cohn, New Perspectives in Jewish Studies (New York: New York University Press, 1994), 121–44; Susanna Drake, Slandering the Jew: Sexuality and Difference in Early Christian Texts, Divinations (Philadelphia: University of Pennsylvania Press, 2013), 88–98.

152. Comm. Gal. 5.1 (F4.77): Ὁρᾷς δι' ὅσων αὐτοὺς ἀπάγει τῆς Ἰουδαϊκῆς πλάνης; Πρῶτον δεικνὺς, ὅτι ἐσχάτης ἀνοίας ἐλευθέρους ἀντὶ δούλων γενομένους δούλους ἀντ' ἐλευθέρων ἐπιθυμεῖν εἶναι.

153. Drake, Slandering the Jew, 78–98.

154. Comm. Gal. 5.18 (F4.89): Τῷ γὰρ οἴκοθεν κατορθοῦντι τὰ μείζω, ποῦ χρεία παιδαγωγοῦ; οὐδὲ γὰρ γραμματιστοῦ τις δεῖται φιλόσοφος ὤν. Τί τοίνυν ἑαυτοὺς ἐξευτελίζετε, τῷ πνεύματι πρότερον ἑαυτοὺς ἐκδόντες, καὶ νῦν προσκαθήμενοι τῷ νόμῳ;

155. Bab. Jul. gent. 70.1–7 (SC 362.184–85).

watches over youths at a party, ensuring that they follow proper decorum when they eat, drink, and laugh, so too the martyr monitors those arriving at Daphne, compelling them to behave piously. Again, the image of the pedagogue is synonymous with discipline and decorum.[156]

There is much conceptual continuity in Chrysostom's views on the nurse and the pedagogue. Both the nurse and the pedagogue occupy a central role in early childhood development, and both become catalysts of paternal power. Like the nurse, the pedagogue is also a modalization of a paternality that is decadent and dysfunctional. Although the father has a supervisory role in the pedagogy of the child, it is the body of the pedagogue that is closest to the body of the child. The pedagogue also suckles a boy, but here with the milk of andromorphism. The task of the pedagogue is to make a man out of the boy. There is then a doulological vampirism present in the operations of the nurse and the pedagogue—both surrender and subjugate their bodies, by force, to the power catalysis of patriarchy and kyriarchy. Roman masculinity was defined and reproduced by slavery. The notion of the good pedagogue mirrors that of the good nurse. Whereas the good nurse reflects bad motherhood, the good pedagogue reflects the problem of bad and absentee fathers. The body of the pedagogue affirms Roman masculinity by its reproduction, but it also destabilizes it, and represents a point of kyriarchal disorientation. The freeborn child fears the slave (or freed) pedagogue, but also constantly tests the boundaries of his domination. The pedagogue assists the boy then to become not only a good man and soldier, but also a good slaveholder. The more the boy becomes kyriarchized, the more unstable and confusing his relationship with the pedagogue becomes. Finally, when the cycle of masculinization and kyriarchization is complete, the boy sheds his pedagogue like a snake that outgrows its own skin. The *filiusfamilias* no longer needs the pedagogue's catalyzed patriarchal power, since this same power has come to fruition in the boy entering manhood. This was the ideal, of course—we have heard Chrysostom complain that free men act like slaves and dismiss their pedagogues too soon. Chrysostom is thus all too aware of the fissures in the production of Christian and Roman masculinity within the field of doulological pedagogy.

CORPOREAL GEOGRAPHIES: THE SLAVE BODY AS SITE FOR THE FORMATION OF MASCULINITY

Based on our findings above regarding nurses and pedagogues, we can conclude that the bodies of the nurse and the pedagogue functioned as sites and instruments for the formation of masculinity and the making of mastery. But nurses and pedagogues were not the only slaves involved in a child's education. Education was

156. *Stat.* 9.3 (PG 49.105.16–22).

the task of the entire household. Speaking to elite households that had many slaves, Chrysostom warns the father that he must carefully screen those slaves that will be involved in the child's education. "They must not be allowed to mingle with all the slaves," Chrysostom cautions, "but allow the remarkable ones, just as though they were approaching a revered statue."[157]

Virtuous slaves need to set an example to the free boy: "And If we should have slaves with self-control (*sōphronountas*), let us also take examples from them, saying how ridiculous it is to have so self-controlled a slave, while the free person is more base than him in behavior."[158] The slaves with *sōphrosynē* should set the example for the child (in the chapters that follow, the dynamics of *sōphrosynē* and slavery will be explored in greater depth). In his remarks on the education of young men, there is a meticulous somatography of kyriarchization—the slave body becomes a training ground for virtue. Just as the boy practices his letters on a sheet of parchment, so too the slave body becomes a parchment on which the boy writes his masculinity according to the methods, rules, and laws of kyriarchy. Michel de Certeau muses, "What is at stake is the relation between the law and the body—a body is itself defined, delimited, and articulated by what writes it. There is no law that is not inscribed on the body. Every law has a hold on the body."[159] In Chrysostom's thought, there are three important corporeal geographies of the slave body. The slave body is a space where, first, the boy learns self-sufficiency; second, where the boy learns to control his anger; and third, where the danger of lust is quarantined.

In the first instance, ironically, the boy must learn that he does not really need slaves. In Chrysostom, authentic kyriarchy is based on its material renunciation. This is part of Chrysostom's labor ethic—a man should be self-sufficient and do his own work. Having many slaves is nothing more than a disgraceful spectacle of vainglory and softness. "And often, although he can take care of himself," Chrysostom complains, "he buys a slave, not because he needs him but that he may not look shameful when taking care of himself."[160] Later in the same treatise, Chrysostom notes that a boy should use slaves only for menial tasks like cooking.[161] Chrysostom considered cooking a very base task. In a rabid attack against "fire-worshippers,"

157. *Inan.* 38.480–83 (SC 188.128–30): μηδὲ γὰρ πᾶσιν ἐξέστω τοῖς οἰκέταις ἀναμίγνυσθαι, ἀλλ' ἔστωσαν φανεροί, ὥσπερ ἀγάλματι προσιόντες φανεροί.

158. *Inan.* 79.949–52 (SC 188.182): Εἰ δὲ καὶ οἰκέτας ἔχοιμεν σωφρονοῦντας, καὶ ἀπὸ τούτων ἔστω τὰ παραδείγματα· ὅτι σφόδρα ἄτοπον τὸν μὲν οἰκέτην οὕτως εἶναι σώφρονα, τὸν δὲ ἐλεύθερον ἐκείνου φαυλότερον γενέσθαι.

159. Michel de Certeau, *The Practice of Everyday Life*, trans. Steven F. Rendall (Berkeley: University of California Press, 1984), 139.

160. *Inan.* 13.177–79 (SC 188.90): καὶ πολλάκις ἑαυτῷ διακονήσασθαι δυνάμενος οἰκέτην ὠνήσατο οὐ χρείας ἔνεκεν, ἀλλ' ὥστε μὴ δόξαι ἠτιμῶσθαι ἑαυτῷ διακονούμενος.

161. *Inan.* 70.855–56 (SC 188.170).

probably directed against devotees of Vesta and the hearth, Chrysostom denigrates the goddess by saying that she meets only with cooks and slaves, since they are the ones serving at the fire. So if people really want to devote themselves to Vesta, they should lower themselves and become cooks.[162] But cooks were also important in the formation of masculinity, since regimen was directly related to sexuality and masculinization.[163] A man had to watch what he ate, since food affected the soul, and this assumes that some cook slaves may have been knowledgeable in the realm of regimen. Interestingly enough, most ascetic diets have a preference for a raw, dry, and uncooked regimen (with the exception of dried bread, or *paxamatia*)—according to ancient medical knowledge, an uncooked and "light" regimen reduced the production of semen by cooling and drying the body, and thus curbed sexual desire.[164] Thus, if a man follows a truly rigorous ascetic regimen, with ample fasting, he would rarely have to cook, thereby also eliminating the need for slaves, as opposed to having countless slaves for every type of culinary specialty.

When it comes to taking care of his own body, such as getting dressed and bathing, the young man should not accept assistance from a slave.[165] Doulology was fundamental to ancient concepts of the care of the self. Chrysostom states that the majority of people get along without slaves—clearly attacking elite decadence—thereby implying that slaves are not a necessity, hence their unnatural and sinful anthropogonical position. This again seems to be Chrysostom's ideal—namely, having no slaves.

Yet, in reality, and perhaps knowing that none of the elite households will follow his advice, he makes a compromise and lets a boy have a slave to do only the menial and shameful tasks, similar to his recommendation to priests. He advises a scheme of tactical slaveholding. By doing this, the boy not only learns to be self-sufficient, but at the same time, he will not become too attached to his possessions, including slave bodies. Teaching a boy to shun material wealth is a very important element in Chrysostom's pedagogy. It was also seen in the event of a slave damaging the boy's writing utensils.[166] The renunciation of wealth and devaluation of material possessions are the new conditions for Christian masculinity. This was also one of the characteristics of the young man who had the monk as a pedagogue—he lived only on the bare necessities, without much food and only basic clothing.[167] In this way, the boy will also prove that he will never become a slave to his slaves. Christian masculinity therefore implies a type of household management in which the man

162. *Hom. Eph.* 12.1 (F4.230–32).

163. Teresa M. Shaw, *The Burden of the Flesh: Fasting and Sexuality in Early Christianity* (Minneapolis: Fortress Press, 1998), 129–60.

164. Ibid., 12–15, 116–23.

165. *Inan.* 70.849–63 (SC 188.170).

166. *Inan.* 73.891–93 (SC 188.174).

167. *Adv. oppug.* 3.12 (PG 47.370.10–49); see Hunter, *Two Treatises*, 153–54.

is not overwhelmed by organizational duties and responsibilities. Having excessive slaves shows that the man cannot take care of himself, which Chrysostom considers shameful and effeminate. Having many material possessions and slaves does not belong to the *schēma* or *habitus* of Christian masculinity.[168] These are all strategies of habitualization[169]—principles that need to function in the daily performance of masculinity.

Second, and this point is certainly the most prominent in Chrysostom's thought, slaves are very useful in helping a boy to control his anger. "So too let the slaves provoke him justly or unjustly," Chrysostom advises, "so that he may learn to always control his passion."[170] It becomes very important for the boy to know when to administer violence against a disobedient slave, and whenever this is necessary, the boy must also not forget his own faults. This is a crucial element in kyriarchization—learning the ability to be a stern yet just master. Controlling one's anger and the just administration of violence were not in any sense new advice in the fashioning of Roman masculinity.[171] Chrysostom continues:

> When he is angry with his slave, remind him of his inner condition, when he is harsh toward a slave, if the slave was not in the wrong, let him behave in these circumstances as in the former. If you see him beating a slave, demand an explanation for this, and again if he is insulting a slave. Do not let him be too lenient nor harsh, so that he may be both a man and fair.[172]

This is part of the mastery of the passions—a man who loses his temper is not at all manly. In a different homily, Chrysostom says that it is more common for women to lose their temper.[173] Men need to be in control of their passions, not slaves thereof. We see here that the father needs to train the boy in managing his slaves. When he punishes or strikes a slave, he needs to give account. This was very important in a world where dominicide and slave revolts often took place. Slavery is more sustainable when it is managed in emotional moderation; it is also why arguments like those above regarding the fair treatment of slaves, and any argument calling for the

---

168. *Inan.* 14.205–9 (SC 188.92–94)

169. For more on the Christianization of habits, see Maxwell, *Christianization and Communication,* 144–68.

170. *Inan.* 68.822–24 (SC 188.166): Οὕτω δὴ καὶ οἱ παῖδες αὐτὸν παροξυνέτωσαν συνεχῶς καὶ δικαίως καὶ ἀδίκως, ὥστε μανθάνειν πανταχοῦ κρατεῖν τοῦ πάθους.

171. John T. Fitzgerald, "The Stoics and the Early Christians on the Treatment of Slaves," in *Stoicism in Early Christianity,* ed. Tuomas Rasimus, Troels Engberg-Pedersen, and Ismo Dunderberg (Grand Rapids, MI: Baker Academic, 2010), 154–62.

172. *Inan.* 69.829–34 (SC 188.168): Ὅταν ὀργίζηται, ἀναμίμνησκε αὐτὸν τῶν οἰκείων παθημάτων, ὅταν πρὸς τὸν παῖδα χαλεπαίνῃ, εἰ μηδὲν αὐτὸς ἥμαρτεν καὶ οἷος ἂν ἦν ἐν τούτοις ὢν αὐτός. Κἂν ἴδῃς τύπτοντα τὸν παῖδα, τούτου δίκην ἀπαίτησον· κἂν ὑβρίζοντα, καὶ τούτου πάλιν. Μήτε δὲ μαλθακὸς ἔστω μήτε ἄγριος, ἵνα καὶ ἀνὴρ ᾖ καὶ ἐπιεικής.

173. *Hom. Eph.* 15.2 (F4.258–60).

humane treatment of slaves, are carceral mechanisms serving the interest of the institution and the slaveholding community, not the interest of the slaves. Chrysostom describes the ideal slaveholder—he is a "man" and he is "fair." Chrysostom here seems to follow Stoic tradition, which blames slave rebellions on abusive masters.[174]

Finally, slaves also play a role in mastering adolescent lust. In this case, it is the absence of the slave body that is crucial, and unlike learning to control one's anger, here the slave must not at all tempt the boy. While this topic will be discussed further in chapter 6, some preliminary observations should be made here. Chrysostom clearly understands the sexual dangers of slavery. One of the more common duties of slaves, especially females and younger men, was to satisfy the sexual needs of the owner.[175] Such duties are unacceptable in Chrysostom's eyes, and therefore he limits the contact boys have with females in general, especially female slaves. It is not only slaves of poor moral repute who need to be distanced from the child, but slave women in general, with the exception of very old women. This exception is based on the ancient notion that the elderly were lacking in sexual appetites and physical beauty. "Never let a slave girl approach him or serve him," Chrysostom commands, "except if it is a slave of advancing years, an old woman."[176] Furthermore, Chrysostom's prescriptions for the tasks a slave should not do for a boy also merit comment here. A slave should not do any tasks that are related to the care of the body, washing the feet, bathing, and getting dressed.[177] Chrysostom has multiple intentions with this statement—not only do they serve to teach the boy self-sufficiency, but they also limit any possible sexual temptation or titillation arising from the services performed. Self-sufficiency therefore also guards against lust. Slaves were, however, allowed to care for ill people, and Chrysostom advises his audience to send their slaves in their stead to attend to the sick.[178]

---

174. See J. Albert Harrill, *The Manumission of Slaves in Early Christianity*, Hermeneutische Untersuchungen zur Theologie 32 (Tübingen: Mohr Siebeck, 1998), 97–98; Keith R. Bradley, *Slavery and Rebellion in the Roman World, 140 B.C.–70 B.C.* (Bloomington: Indiana University Press, 1989). I would like to thank J. Albert Harrill for pointing out Chrysostom's adherence to Stoic tradition regarding abusive masters and slave revolts.

175. See Jennifer A. Glancy, "Obstacles to Slaves' Participation in the Corinthian Church," *Journal of Biblical Literature* 117, no. 3 (1998): 481–501; Carolyn Osiek, "Female Slaves, *Porneia*, and the Limits of Obedience," in *Early Christian Families in Context: An Interdisciplinary Dialogue*, ed. David L. Balch and Carolyn Osiek, Religion, Marriage, and Family (Grand Rapids, MI: Eerdmans, 2003), 255–76; Harper, *Slavery in the Late Roman World*, 281–325.

176. *Inan.* 79.944–46 (SC 188.182): μηδέποτε κόρη προσίτω μηδὲ διακονείτω, ἀλλ' ἤδη προβεβηκυῖα παιδίσκη, γυνὴ γηραλέα. See *Anna* 1.6 (PG 54.642.25–33).

177. *Inan.* 70.849–63 (SC 188.170).

178. *Hom. Eph.* 13.4 (F4.243).

EDUCATING SLAVES

The education of slaves in antiquity is a more ambiguous issue, although it stands to reason that the manner in which slaves were educated also served the interests of kyriarchy. Chrysostom is often lauded for advising slaveholders to teach their slaves virtue and a trade, and then to manumit them.[179] The idea of teaching slaves virtue will be discussed in chapter 5. Yet this type of advice was neither new nor radical in the Roman Empire. Seneca gave the same advice to the slaveholders to whom he was writing, since teaching a slave virtue and giving him or her an education would benefit both the slave and the master.[180] Some slaves were also educated prior to their enslavement, which obviously increased their value, especially those who were doctors, actors, teachers, and specialized craftspersons. In general, however, slaves received their primary education in the household.[181] Some illustrious villa estates had *paedagogia* where slaves received training. The exact dynamics of these *paedagogia* are unclear—some sources indicate that they were like a school for slaves, while others sources speak of them as simple living quarters. They may have differed from estate to estate. It is also not entirely clear whether the villa churches on some estates had contact with *paedagogia* or whether such churches served to educate rural slaves.

A slave was taught a trade in the daily dynamics of the household, since most households in ancient Rome were almost always productive in some form or another. Along with learning the basic skills of working in the domestic sphere, some households also had a family business, and in many cases, slaves were trained in the various skills it required. This training had several advantages, as Henrik Mouritsen has pointed out;[182] first, in an economy that had an underdeveloped labor market, training one's own slaves was the most efficient means of sustaining productivity. Second, it was in the owner's interest to have people working for him that were under his own authority and over whom he had absolute control, and who may also have been more trustworthy than outsiders. An authorized slave could also act on behalf of the master when it came to doing business. Finally, slaves are educated, their value also increases, and when an owner sells them, the owner still makes a profit. Educating slaves in a trade was in the interest of the household and helped increase its business interests. The instances of successful freedmen in

---

179. *Hom. 1 Cor.* 40.6 (F2.515).

180. Seneca, *Ben.* 3.19.2 (Griffin and Inwood 70–71); see Keith R. Bradley, "Seneca and Slavery," *Classica et Medievalia* 37 (1986): 161–72.

181. See S. L. Mohler, "Slave Education in the Roman Empire," *Transactions of the American Philological Association* 71 (1940): 262–80; Alan D. Booth, "The Schooling of Slaves in First-Century Rome," *Transactions of the American Philological Association* 109 (1979): 11–19; Harris, *Ancient Literacy*, 255–57.

182. Henrik Mouritsen, *The Freedman in the Roman World* (New York: Cambridge University Press, 2011), 219.

the Roman Empire attest to the fact that slaves were educated and manumitted from their households.[183] Aaron Kirschenbaum and Henrik Mouritsen emphasize that training and then manumitting the slave was also a form of upward mobility and reward.[184] Many freedpersons remained in the service of their former masters and perhaps had more important tasks and leadership roles assigned to them. So when Chrysostom tells his audience to teach the slave virtue and a trade, and then to manumit the slave, it does not imply that the slave will leave the household or fall outside the influence and authority of the former owner, who is now simply a patron. We should also not rule out the fact that some slaves were self-educated and used this agency to advance in society. Another concern that should be raised here is that with tactical slaveholding, there seems to be a general despecialization of slave labor, unlike the case of strategic slaveholding, where slaves often occupied highly specialized positions in households. A manumitted slave with a specialized skill could be in high demand, thus increasing the chances of making a decent, even affluent, living. Slaves manumitted from tactical slaveholding contexts, with few specialized skills, may have faced more challenges making a living.

The fact that the education of freeborn and enslaved children often happened simultaneously also illustrates the point that children were made aware of their status distinctions already in infancy. While young freeborn boys were conditioned into the habitus of Roman masculinity, enslaved children were taught the poetics of subjugation. When fathers are told to make their sons aware of their free status, it is implied that slaves are reminded of their enslaved status. This occurred both formally, such as when a father explains Genesis 1–2 and the origins of slavery to his son or teaches him to punish a slave, and also habitually, as when a child is kept away from certain slaves or has a slave cook for him. Education was based on imitation—the father had to set an example for the child; imitation was the very machinery of kyriarchization and masculinization.

W. Martin Bloomer has shown, for instance, how infants and children in the elite echelons of Roman society learned from a very young age to imitate and rehearse the role of the *paterfamilias* and his interactions with other members of the *familia*. Subordination and domination were taught by imitation.[185] Jonathan Edmondson has also pointed this out in his discussion of Cato's eccentricity in having his own free children and slave children play together—a type of play where the social dynamics of slave and slaveholder may already have been

---

183. Ibid., 219–20.

184. Aaron Kirschenbaum, *Sons, Slaves, and Freedmen in Roman Commerce* (Washington, DC: Catholic University of America Press, 1987), 127–30; Mouritsen, *Freedman in the Roman World*, 219–12.

185. W. Martin Bloomer, "Schooling in Persona: Imagination and Subordination in Roman Education," *Classical Antiquity* 16, no. 1 (1997): 57–78.

rehearsed.[186] Imitation is also a strategy that Chrysostom employs—children need to imitate both their fathers and the heroes of the biblical stories, but never slavish behavior (unless the slave is virtuous, of course). All scriptural pedagogy must be imitative pedagogy.

One of the main facets of slave education was literacy and numeracy, and William Harris notes that many high-ranking teachers were slaves or freedmen.[187] In the case of the later Roman Empire, there may be some changes in this regard. As we have seen above, by the fourth century the distinction between pedagogues and teachers was much more pronounced, although Libanius, for instance, speaks highly of enslaved persons in the teaching profession.[188] And again, a literate and numerate slave was highly beneficial not only for the running of the household and the teaching of children, but also because the master could communicate and interact with such a slave more sensibly. Slaves were taught literacy and numeracy in both households and *paedagogia*,[189] and the inclusion of the slave in scripture reading may also have contributed to their literacy.

Finally, slaves were also educated in monasteries, although the precise nature of this education is difficult to reconstruct exactly. An adult slave could also be sent to a monastery either under the direction of the master or as one seeking asylum. One of the problems here is that there is little or no literary or archaeological evidence from monasteries in late antiquity in the East, not including Egypt, that systematically describes their position on slavery. Chrysostom believed that the monastery was a space free from social status and distinction, although this was perhaps more idealistic than realistic. Chrysostom describes the very nature of the monastery thus: "To go to the monastery of a holy man is to pass, as it were, from earth to heaven. You do not see there what is seen in a private house. That company is free from all impurity. . . . No one calls for his slave, for each person serves himself."[190] The monastery is the image of perfected domestic pastoralization. For Chrysostom, the monastery is a realized eschatological space, a heavenly colonization of earthly space where there is no concept of private and personal property. Elizabeth Clark, however, has noted that some monasteries seem to have maintained class distinctions: Jerome tells us about Paula's monastery, which separated nuns according to nobility, and it seems that some of the high-ranking

186. Jonathan Edmondson, "Slavery and the Roman Family," in *The Cambridge World History of Slavery*, vol. 1, *The Ancient Mediterranean World*, ed. Keith Bradley and Paul Cartledge (New York: Cambridge University Press, 2011), 358.

187. Harris, *Ancient Literacy*, 255–56.

188. Libanius, *Or.* 58.7–20 (Foerster 4.184–91); see Harper, *Slavery in the Late Roman World*, 115.

189. Harris, *Ancient Literacy*, 255–59.

190. *Hom. 1 Tim.* 14.2 (F6.120): ὥσπερ ἀπὸ γῆς εἰς τὸν οὐρανὸν, οὕτως ἐστὶν εἰς μοναστήριον ἀνδρὸς ἁγίου καταφυγεῖν. Οὐχ ὁρᾷς ἐκεῖ ταῦτα ἅπερ ἐν τῇ οἰκίᾳ· πάντων καθαρὸς ὁ χορὸς ἐκεῖνος. . . . Καὶ οὐκ ἔστιν, ὥσπερ ἐπὶ τῆς οἰκίας, ῥέγχουσιν οἱ οἰκέται.

virgins were allowed to have a few slaves, although not those who formerly served them. According to Palladius, Chrysostom's female friend Olympias took fifty of her own slaves into her monastery, while Melania the Younger also kept some of her slaves with her when she became an ascetic.[191]

There is evidence suggesting that some poor monks were originally slaves,[192] and it also seems that monasteries were indeed used as asylum for runaway slaves.[193] The legislation surviving from antiquity for the latter, however, comes only from the Council of Chalcedon in 451 C.E.[194] There is also an important shift during the mid-fifth century, after Chalcedon, when the monastery became legally independent of lay ownership.[195] It is therefore problematic to apply fifth-century developments to monasteries earlier than this period. Moreover, the issue of providing asylum to slaves all but negates their status, and although such slaves certainly had to labor in the monastery, as in the case of abandoned children, the extent to which they may have been educated is not clear. If they were there only temporarily, they probably did not receive much education.

The councils and canons before Chalcedon are notoriously difficult to interpret regarding the issue of slave status and asylum. The silence of some other councils and canons is deafening, such as canon 7 of the Council of Sardica (346–347 C.E.), which gave the bishop power to intervene in cases of widows, orphans, and those subject to deportation who were treated violently or unjustly. There is no mention of slaves who have suffered the same fate.[196] The Council of Carthage (401 C.E.) is equally ambiguous and refers only to *manumissio in ecclesia*. It must also be remembered that Chalcedon rejected the asylum offered to slaves, and stipulated that such slaves be returned to their masters. Chrysostom himself, in his commentary on the Epistle to Philemon, admonishes runaway slaves, or any slave for that matter, to return or remain with their legal owners.[197]

It is only in the sixth century during the period of Justinian that a shift in policy becomes more or less evident. During this period, the church or monastery received

191. Elizabeth A. Clark, "Asceticism, Class, and Gender," in *Late Ancient Christianity*, ed. Virginia Burrus, A People's History of Christianity 2 (Minneapolis: Fortress Press, 2005), 39.

192. See Gervase Corcoran, *St. Augustine on Slavery*, Studia ephemeridis Augustinianum (Rome: Patristic Institute Augustinianum, 1985); Pauline Allen and Edward Morgan, "Augustine on Poverty," in *Preaching Poverty in Late Antiquity: Perceptions and Realities*, ed. Pauline Allen, Bronwen Neil, and Wendy Mayer (Leipzig: Evangelische Verlaganstalt, 2009), 148.

193. Youval Rotman, *Byzantine Slavery and the Mediterranean World*, trans. Jane Marie Todd (Cambridge, MA: Harvard University Press, 2009), 144–50.

194. Glancy, *Slavery in Early Christianity*, 90.

195. Kate Cooper, *The Fall of the Roman Household* (New York: Cambridge University Press, 2007), 236.

196. Rotman, *Byzantine Slavery*, 144.

197. *Hom. Phlm.* arg. (F6.325–28); see Glancy, *Slavery in Early Christianity*, 91; Chris L. de Wet, "Honour Discourse in John Chrysostom's Exegesis of the Letter to Philemon," in *Philemon in Perspective: Interpreting a Pauline Letter*, ed. D. Francois Tolmie (Berlin: De Gruyter, 2010), 317–32.

permission to accept slaves who wanted to become clergymen or monks on the condition that they had not committed any crime prior to their flight. So at this point we can say that slaves received a very elaborate education to prepare them to serve as clergy. But this was a later development and in Chrysostom's time probably not a possibility for slaves. Slaves (and various other classes) were officially excluded from service in the priesthood for a number of reasons, including the fact that owners still had power over slaves, the general negative social stereotyping of slaves, and also because positions in ecclesiastical leadership were highly coveted.[198] Kuefler has also argued that because of the high masculinity embedded in the character of the priest or bishop, slaves were excluded from participation in the priesthood.[199]

Even during the sixth century masters still had a claim on slaves serving as clergy. Owners could reclaim slaves who became clerics within a year of their service, and owners had three years to reclaim slaves who became monks. What is more, the monastery could not free slaves; this right was still reserved for the church and state authorities.[200] Cases of slaves in monasteries and their manumission were therefore still rerouted through the channels of *manumissio in ecclesia,* which assumed status boundaries between slave and master.[201] None of these instances above show a tendency toward either a negation of status in the monastery or a clear educational program for slaves prior to the sixth century.

Furthermore, the passage quoted above from Chrysostom about slaves in the monastery does not necessarily signal the absence of nonclerical slaves in the monastery; it simply means that the individual monks in the monastery were not supposed to use slaves for their own purposes. The churches and clergymen of late antiquity owned slaves, and there is no reason to doubt that the monastery, which was in itself a staunchly hierarchical entity, also collectively owned slaves. If one reads Chrysostom's discussions of slavery and necessity, it is clear that the communal owning of a slave, that is, one slave for two or three masters, was not out of the question. Chrysostom also states that priests are allowed to own a slave in order to perform those shameful duties, especially related to sewerage-management, cooking, and so on. If a priest could own a slave, one or two slaves per monk would not violate the monastic concept of necessity in Chrysostom's eyes.

The notion of the monastery as a household also supports rather than opposes the idea that slave status was recognized in monasteries.[202] It indicates that slaves

198. Jean Gaudemet, *L'Église dans l'empire romain (IVe-Ve siècles),* ed. Gabriel Le Bras, Histoire du droit et des institutions de l'Église en Occident 3 (Paris: Sirey, 1958), 136–40.

199. Kuefler, *Manly Eunuch,* 154–56.

200. Rotman, *Byzantine Slavery,* 145.

201. Harper, *Slavery in the Late Roman World,* 465–85.

202. Else M.W. Pedersen, "The Monastery as a Household within the Universal Household," in *Household, Women, and Christianities in Late Antiquity and the Middle Ages,* ed. Anneke Mulder-Bakker and Jocelyn Wogan-Browne (Turnhout: Brepols, 2005), 167–90.

probably received an education in monasteries that was similar to the education slaves received in households, in terms of labor, crafts, and literacy, since they had to contribute to the productivity of the monastery. The spatiality of the monastery is therefore not a socially neutral zone, as Chrysostom imagines it. The hierarchical dynamics of slave domesticity were still present. The strong collectivism found in monastic communities allowed for slaves to be owned and used within the group. An individual monk living in a monastery might have no need of a slave while he was at there, but the monastic community, like the church, might need slaves for its day-to-day operations, and so educating and training slaves in a monastery was also to its benefit.

· · ·

The body of the slave, whether a nurse, pedagogue, or any other slave, functioned as a site and apparatus for the formation of masculinity and the development of mastery in the freeborn from a very young age. Slaves played a crucial role in the education of children, but pedagogy itself was a very complex and polymorphous phenomenon. The two central figures in this process were the nurse and the pedagogue, although numerous other slaves were involved in early childhood education. Chrysostom realized how great the influence of the nurse and the pedagogue was, and therefore he provided very strict guidelines for how to select and regulate these slaves in the household. Most importantly, slaves were central to the formation of masculine identity and female chastity in Chrysostom's thought. From infancy, a *filiusfamilias* had to be taught principles of self-control and moderation, whether it was how much milk he could drink or how long he could be held; every action had to contribute to making the *filiusfamilias* a better man and master. The dynamics in the household itself may have been more organic and natural and less rigid than what Chrysostom describes—the point is, however, that the formation of kyriarchy started very early.

This task of kyriarchal fashioning was carried over to the role of the pedagogue, who had to prepare the boy for manhood. The duties of the pedagogue were related to the reproduction of the habitus of Roman masculinity; in other words, the pedagogue had to ensure that the boy's corporeal habituation was in the interest of kyriarchy. This included directing the boy in how to sit, eat, drink, laugh, speak, and, most importantly, interact with women and other slaves. The pedagogue's main aim was to teach the boy virtue, especially self-control. In this pedagogy there is a very potent process of kyriarchization—Chrysostom wants young men to become better husbands, fathers, and especially masters. Slaves were central in the reproduction of mastery.

When it came to the education of slaves, the process was less formal. Regarding the case of teaching slaves a trade, there is nothing novel or exemplary in Chrysostom's recommendations. His comments fall squarely within the bounds of social practice in Roman times. Slaves were taught trades in the households where they lived and often participated in the family business. Although it may seem admirable, educating one's slaves also contributed to sustaining the institution of slavery and functioned primarily to the benefit of the master. Methods of slave education are difficult to reconstruct. While pedagogies of kyriarchization were very active in the education of the freeborn male child, the education of slave children conditioned them into their future roles of subjugation—the distinctions between slaves and free persons were established at a very early age. Chrysostom wants fathers to teach their young boys the difference between slave and free, and he proscribes a scriptural pedagogy that will ensure that the child behaves as a free person, not a slave. The point of continuity and convergence in the education of both slave and free, in Chrysostom's thought, is the teaching of virtue, what I will call aretagogy. Both slave and free required training in virtue, and this had serious implications for the identity of slaves in late antiquity, which is the topic of the next chapter.

5

Whips and Scriptures

On the Discipline and Punishment of Slaves

"For both among themselves, and everywhere, it is admitted that the race of slaves is inordinate, not open to impression, stubborn, and does not show much aptitude for being taught virtue," Chrysostom says in one of his sermons.[1] Yet, in several other instances, he admonishes slaveholders to teach their slaves virtue.[2] It was not an easy task, Chrysostom believed, but it had to be done. Ancient stereotypes of slaves emphasized the idea that slaves were not only social outsiders, but that they were in many cases also delinquent and degenerate, requiring stern discipline and training in order to be effective and safe for society. For many people, slaves were not considered men in the ancient sense of the word. The doulological frameworks of both Xenophon and Aristotle systematically pathologized the subjectivity of the slave. Aristotle saw them as naturally inferior "unmen," while authors like Xenophon and Thycidides banned slaves from military service on account of their servility, unmanliness, cowardice, and disloyalty—in short, their alterity.[3] It was a stereotype that endured throughout late antiquity. The animalization of the slave in ancient as well as transatlantic doulologies attests to this pathologization and dehumanization. A common term for a slave, *andrapodon*, one that Chrysostom

---

1. *Hom. Tit.* 4.1 (F6.298): Καὶ γὰρ καὶ παρ' αὐτοῖς, καὶ πανταχοῦ τοῦτο διωμολόγηται, ὅτι τὸ τῶν δούλων γένος ἰταμόν πώς ἐστι, δυσδιατύπωτον, δυστράπελον, οὐ σφόδρα ἐπιτήδειον πρὸς τὴν τῆς ἀρετῆς διδασκαλίαν.

2. See *Hom. 1 Cor.* 40.6 (F2.515); *Hom. Eph.* 22.2 (F4.336–37); *Hom. Phlm.* arg. (F6.325–28); *Hom. Tit.* 4.1 (F6.298–99).

3. Peter Hunt, *Slaves, Warfare and Ideology in the Greek Historians* (Cambridge: Cambridge University Press, 2002), 144–46.

often uses, could literally mean a "man-footed animal."[4] It differentiates the slave from a four-footed animal, a *tetrapous*. Karl Jacoby has thus argued that slavery can be understood as the domestication of the animalized human, especially since many techniques used to domesticate animals, such as whipping, branding, and confinement, were also used on slaves.[5] The animalization of the slave therefore set the precedent for a system of structural abuse and oppression. However, the humanization of the slave, often considered positive by some, equally patholo-gized the slave. The idea of the humanity of the slave in antiquity (or in modern times, for that matter) is in itself a technology of repression and carcerality. It sim-ply gave slaveholders recourse to more "human" measures of oppression, like the rationing of food, forced marriages, the regulation of sex, and the threat of split-ting up families by manumission.

Thus, the education, discipline, and punishment of slaves, whether slaves were seen as animal or human, or both, were central to their identity as enslaved beings, and in order to sustain a slave-based economy, the strict surveillance and punish-ment of slaves were fundamental. This chapter investigates the role of aretagogy, discipline, and punishment in Chrysostomic doulology. I will argue here, first, that Chrysostom had a very explicit and Christianized program of reform for slaves, centering on the teaching of virtue—a process I will call aretagogy. The focus on virtue also implies a continuation of the theme of masculinity. What, then, are the implications of teaching slaves virtue? What is at stake in this discussion is the very nature of kyriarchal dynamics: by teaching slaves virtue, one teaches them, in essence, how to become men. How does this affect our understanding of kyriarchy and technologies of kyriarchization? In addition, the question of how virtue was taught to slaves also deserves attention. Second, Chrysostom's comments on the discipline and surveillance of slaves will be examined. We will look especially at the interiorization of surveillance, or self-surveillance, as well as Chrysostom's utiliza-tion of the Christic panopticon to regulate slave bodies, and the counter-surveillance provided by slaves. Finally, we will look at the issue of the punishment of slaves. How was punishment justified theologically and socially? Under what circum-stances should masters punish slaves, and how should they be punished?

SLAVERY, MASCULINITY, AND ARETAGOGY

Chrysostom's advice to masters to guide their slaves to virtue was not novel in the ancient world. Ancient Greek authors like Plato and even Aristotle believed that it

---

4. See *Bab. Jul. gent.* 30.16 (SC 362.130); *Hom. Gen.* 34.1 (PG 53.313.43); *Hom. Matt.* 58.3 (PG 58.570.24).

5. Karl Jacoby, "Slaves by Nature? Domestic Animals and Human Slaves," *Slavery & Abolition* 15, no. 1 (1994): 89–99.

was useful to teach slaves a small measure of virtue.[6] This view was also found in Stoicism,[7] and many early Christian authors also recommended teaching slaves virtue. Despite the common stereotype that the slave was delinquent and not capable of virtue, many authors saw value in teaching virtue to slaves.

In examining aretagogy, or the teaching of virtue, we must ask, first, what is virtue, and then, how does virtue differ for the slaveholder and the slave? In ancient Roman thought, virtue was inseparable from manliness.[8] Classical Greek philosophy portrays virtue (*aretē*) as a door swinging on four hinges—the four cardinal virtues, which are prudence (*phronēsis*), moderation (*sōphrosynē*), justice (*dikaiosynē*), and fortitude (*andreia*). While only *andreia* linguistically corresponds to manliness, the whole framework of virtue was androcentric. This is even more pronounced in Latin, at least linguistically. The Christian author Lactantius, for instance, defines gender categories primarily in terms of virtue.[9] He provides an etymological framework for these gender differences: the male (*vir*), who possesses superior virtue (*virtus*) and power (*vis*), is contrasted to the female (*mulier*), whose prime characteristic is softness (*mollitia*).[10] Chrysostom also defined gender roles in terms of virtue.[11] The woman must be submissive to the man because of her past disobedience in Eden. Chrysostom's theopolitical framework dictates that the man has rulership over the woman because of her lack of virtue and obedience, and because she allowed sin to enter into the world.[12]

While these gender differences seem clear and pronounced in Lactantius and Chrysostom, the dynamics between virtue and gender in the late Roman Empire are quite complex and difficult to define. For one thing, the modern distinction between sex and gender was absent in the ancient world. Thomas Laqueur calls the

---

6. Plato, *Leg.* 778a (Bury 176–79); Aristotle, *Pol.* 1260a33-b5 (Rackham 60–65).

7. See Dio Chrysostom, 2 *Serv. lib.* 15.29 (Cohoon 170–71); Seneca, *Ep.* 47.10ff. (Basore 306–8); see Peter Garnsey, *Ideas of Slavery from Aristotle to Augustine* (Cambridge: Cambridge University Press, 1996), 128–56; Garnsey, "The Middle Stoics and Slavery," in *Hellenistic Constructs: Essays in Culture, History, and Historiography,* ed. Paul Cartledge, Peter Garnsey, and Erich S. Gruen (Berkeley: University of California Press, 1997), 159–74.

8. Mathew Kuefler, *The Manly Eunuch: Masculinity, Gender Ambiguity, and Christian Ideology in Late Antiquity* (Chicago: University of Chicago Press, 2001), 19–42.

9. Lactantius, *Opif.* 10–13 (PL 7.40–60); see Virginia Burrus, *Begotten, Not Made: Conceiving Manhood in Late Antiquity,* Figurae: Reading Medieval Culture (Stanford, CA: Stanford University Press, 2000), 31–32.

10. See Burrus, *Begotten, Not Made,* 32; Kuefler, *Manly Eunuch,* 21–30.

11. Elizabeth A. Clark, *Jerome, Chrysostom, and Friends: Essays and Translations* (Lewiston, NY: Edwin Mellen, 1979), 1–34; Efthalia M. Walsh, "Overcoming Gender: Virgins, Widows, and Barren Women in the Writings of St. John Chrysostom" (PhD diss., Catholic University of America, 1994); David Ford, *Women and Men in the Early Church: The Full Views of St. John Chrysostom* (South Canaan, PA: St. Tikhon's Seminary Press, 1996), 90–114.

12. See *Serm. Gen.* 4.1–2 (PG 54.593–595.26); *Hom. Eph.* 20 (F4.299–321).

ancient system of gender difference a one-sex model,[13] in contrast to the modern two-sex model, but it is perhaps more accurate to speak of an opposite or inverted model of sexual differentiation. In this model of sexual differentiation, women were inverted men. In the one-sex model, the uterus is considered an inverted penis, and the ovaries (or in some cases, the womb[s]) are simply internal testicles.[14] Thus, there is only one gender—namely, the masculine.[15] This was not necessarily the only model of sexual differentiation present in Roman antiquity. Helen King has recently reevaluated Laqueur's propositions, and found that ancient sexual difference was much more complex than previously proposed.[16]

The extent to which Chrysostom shared in the belief of an inverted model of sex is difficult to determine, and I do not think we should simply force Laqueur's model on Chrysostom's thinking, as there are no clear indications of such a model in the sources; further research on this matter is required. Moreover, Chrysostom's views on the body and sexual differentiation were primarily influenced by his theological foundations, and not only by ancient medical knowledge. Although Chrysostom often acts as a medical philosopher,[17] his medical framework, like those of the Hippocratics and proponents of Galenism, was informed and shaped by his own religious convictions.[18] But whatever model of sexual differentiation we may find in Chrysostom, he does share the view that masculine virtue was the superior norm to which individuals, both men and women, should aspire. Masculinity was the general standard by which all people were measured, and all strived to attain it. It was performative—women and slaves could have been manly if they acted in such a manner within the bounds of certain social expectations.[19]

13. Thomas W. Laqueur, *Making Sex: Body and Gender from the Greeks to Freud* (Cambridge, MA: Harvard University Press, 1990), 25–62.

14. Aline Rousselle, *Porneia: On Desire and the Body in Antiquity*, trans. Felicia Pheasant (New York: Barnes & Noble, 1996), 5–46.

15. This is a point that Monique Wittig has also made in a more general sense: "There is only one [gender]: the feminine, the 'masculine' not being a gender. For the masculine is not the masculine but the general"; Wittig, "The Point of View: Universal or Particular," *Feminist Issues* 3 (1983): 64. See Kuefler, *Manly Eunuch*, 1–15.

16. Helen King, *The One-Sex Body on Trial: The Classical and Early Modern Evidence,* The History of Medicine in Context (Farnham: Ashgate, 2013).

17. Wendy Mayer, "Medicine in Transition: Christian Adaptation in the Later Fourth-Century East," in *Shifting Genres in Late Antiquity*, ed. Geoffrey Greatrex and Hugh Elton (Farnham: Ashgate, 2015), 11–26; Mayer, "Chrysostom's Last Word on Treating the Soul" (paper presented at the North American Patristics Society Annual Meeting, Chicago, 2014). I thank Wendy Mayer for providing me with this paper.

18. Helen King, *Hippocrates' Woman: Reading the Female Body in Ancient Greece* (London: Routledge, 1998), 99–113.

19. Judith Butler describes the discursivity of gender as one that produces and reproduces itself: "Acts, gestures and desire produce the effect of an internal core of substance, but produce this *on the surface of the body.* . . . Such acts, gestures, enactments, generally construed, are *performative* in the

For instance, in Chrysostom's interpretation of the narrative of the Maccabean martyrs, he describes the mother of the Maccabees as a virtuous and manly woman, specifically in the sense that she overcame her age and weaker maternal instinct—that is, love for her sons.[20] Andromorphism—the enunciation, imitation, and performance of masculinity by men, women, and slaves alike—therefore also reflects the fixity and normativity of the ancient gender scale. Gender and sex in antiquity, therefore, represent less a natural status than one's position on the scale of masculinity. But this scale should not be seen as inherently ascribing virtue to men and not to women or slaves. Most men of the late Roman Empire found it very difficult to meet the high standards of Roman masculinity; hence, late Roman masculinity was in crisis. Attaining virtue was therefore a process of subjectivation and habitualization; it was andromorphic, but also represented a way to take care of oneself, to achieve happiness, and to know and embrace one's place in the social hierarchy. In chapters 1 and 2 of this book we have already noted the close link between practices of aretagogy and operations of subjectivation, where slavery, especially in the case of the Stoics and Christians, was often seen as one's state relating to virtuosity rather than an institutional status.

Masculinity itself was very complex in antiquity—it is certainly more appropriate to speak of masculinities,[21] and hegemonic masculinities were often replaced by subordinated masculinities.[22] Michel Foucault noted that the rise of Christianity profoundly changed traditional Roman masculinity, with the result that the *vir* became more closely linked to the *virgo*.[23] Foucault viewed Christianization as the feminization of Roman masculinity. Such a totalization is, however, problematic. Foucault's views have been critiqued by Elizabeth Clark, who has demonstrated that Christianity still employed highly masculine images to describe virtue.[24] Rather than a total program of feminization, we see the promotion of certain fem-

sense that the essence or identity that they otherwise purport to express are *fabrications* manufactured and sustained through corporeal signs and other discursive means"; *Gender Trouble: Feminism and the Subversion of Identity* (New York: Routledge, 2006), 173 (Butler's emphasis).

20. *Macc.* 1 (PG 50.617.17–624.3); see Raphaëlle Ziadé, *Les martyrs Maccabées: De l'histoire juive au culte chrétien; Les homélies de Grégoire de Nazianze et de Jean Chrysostome*, Supplements to Vigiliae Christianae 80 (Leiden: Brill, 2007), 155–79, 313–22; Chris L. de Wet, "Claiming Corporeal Capital: John Chrysostom's Homilies on the Maccabean Martyrs," *Journal of Early Christian History* 2, no. 1 (2012): 3–21.

21. Page DuBois, "Ancient Masculinities," in *New Testament Masculinities*, ed. Stephen D. Moore and Janice C. Anderson, Semeia Studies 45 (Atlanta: Society of Biblical Literature, 2003), 319–24.

22. Raewyn W. Connell, *Gender and Power: Society, the Person, and Sexual Politics* (Stanford, CA: Stanford University Press, 1987), 183–90.

23. Michel Foucault, *The Use of Pleasure*, trans. Robert Hurley, vol. 2 of *The History of Sexuality* (New York: Vintage, 1985), 82–93.

24. Elizabeth A. Clark, "Foucault, the Fathers, and Sex," *Journal of the American Academy of Religion* 56, no. 4 (1988): 619–41.

inine qualities, such as patience and endurance (*hypomonē, patientia*),[25] which are then subsumed into a new hegemonic masculinity. We also find numerous competing masculinities in the ancient texts.[26]

However, despite the fact that men, women, and slaves strived to reach the pinnacle of the masculine scale of virtue, virtue was defined in very specific but also relative terms for men, women, and slaves. Each group had one defining virtue that validated its status as virtuous, and the same virtue might have a different meaning depending on whether one was a man, woman, or slave. A virtue like *sōphrosynē*, or in Latin *pudicitia*, had different meanings for men, women, and slaves. The concept of *sōphrosynē* has a wide semantic scope in Greek literature.[27] In the context of sexuality, for a free man it implied moderation and especially self-control (related to *enkrateia*, that is, self-mastery), while for a free woman it implied chastity and sexual abstinence at least until she married.[28] Slaves, however, had very little recourse to *sōphrosynē*—they were controlled by another, and they had no legal right to chastity. But for Chrysostom, while slaves also had to strive to be modest, a slave exhibited *enkrateia* when he or she endured or suffered violation for the sake of Christ.[29] Chrysostom also firmly believed that slaves had to be trained in *sōphrosynē*.[30] Thus, *sōphrosynē* and *enkrateia* for slaves were more related to both sexual integrity and overall obedience to the slaveholder. Virtue was therefore relative to one's social status. Chrysostom in particular encouraged fathers to teach their sons virtue, which would make them good slaveholders. Aretagogy was then a process of masculinization in a very wide but also very relative sense.

With this basic understanding of the nature, dynamics, and complexities of aretagogy in Roman antiquity, we can explore how Chrysostom understands the process of teaching slaves virtue. Since aretagogy is an operation of masculinization, we can begin by asking why Chrysostom tells slaveholders to make men of their slaves, and then consider what this tells us about the dynamics of kyriarchization. Teaching slaves virtue presupposes that slaves *could* be men. Male slaves were to become men, but in a very different sense of masculinity than that of freeborn men. I propose three reasons for Chrysostom's endorsement of teaching slaves virtue. First, such instruction had a regulatory function and provided a measure of security; second, it was necessary for reproducing and sustaining Roman

25. Burrus, *Begotten, Not Made*, 19–22.

26. Ibid., 106.

27. See G. J. De Vries, "ΣΩΦΡΟΣΥΝΗ en grec classique," *Mnemosyne* 11 (1943): 81–101; Foucault, *Use of Pleasure*, 61–64; Kyle Harper, *From Shame to Sin: The Christian Transformation of Sexual Morality in Late Antiquity* (Cambridge, MA: Harvard University Press, 2013), 41–53.

28. Harper, *From Shame to Sin*, 41–45.

29. *Hom. Tit.* 4.1 (F6.298–99).

30. See *Hab. eun. spir.* 3.7 (PG 51.287.4–8); *Adv. Jud.* 2.124ra.

kyriarchy; third, it amplified and intensified the operation of kyriarchy. In treating this last point, I will discuss the problem of fugitive slaves in Chrysostom, since the fugitive is seen as the complete opposite of the virtuous and disciplined slave.

The first reason for teaching slaves virtue is that it is a means of regulating them, creating docile slave bodies, and thereby protecting free society. If mastery was the defining virtue for a freeborn man, and chastity for a freeborn woman, then the defining virtue for a slave was to be submissively obedient (*hypotassō, akouō*). Chrysostom expresses this obedience (*akoē, gnōmosynē*) in terms of the respect the slave should show to the master;[31] slavery comes from sons, like Ham, showing disobedience (*anēkoïa, anēkoeō*) and imprudence (*agnōmosynē*) toward their fathers. When Chrysostom links slavery to sin, he does so in terms of obedience and disobedience. This incalcitrance is the cause of slavery, so its corrective, for Chrysostom, is obedience: "The institution of slavery was the fruit of sin, of rebellion against fathers. Let children listen carefully to this, that whenever they are disobedient to their fathers, they deserve to be slaves."[32]

Sin and disobedience are inextricably linked, as the legend of the curse of Ham demonstrates. Obedience was a crucial element in most ancient masculinities. The free male, for instance, had to be obedient as a soldier in the army. But here obedience functions in the sense of self-discipline, which was taught to him from childhood (in many instances, ironically, by slaves). Military discipline and obedience should therefore stem from a mastery of the self. The obedience of the slave is not based on self-mastery—although slaves can, of course, embody the virtue of self-mastery; rather, it is based on the mastery exercised over the slave by the master. Hence Chrysostom's link between the obedience of slaves and children—the body of the child, like that of the slave, is as yet incapable of mastery, so it must be mastered by the father and pedagogue.[33] This obedience, however, is not obedience in the general sense, but obedience according to the precepts of Christian doctrine. Chrysostom complains about slaveholders who do not teach their slaves true obedience:

> And if you want to hear the principles regarding slaves, listen to what I said about children up to now. Teach them to be pious, and everything else will follow from necessity. But now, when someone is going to the theater, or going off to the bath, he drags all his slaves behind him; but when he goes to church, not for a moment; nor does he admonish them to attend and listen. Now how will your slave listen, when

31. This is especially the case in his *Hom. Phlm.* (F6.326–53); Chris L. de Wet, "Honour Discourse in John Chrysostom's Exegesis of the Letter to Philemon," in *Philemon in Perspective: Interpreting a Pauline Letter*, ed. D. Francois Tolmie (Berlin: De Gruyter, 2010), 317–32.

32. *Hom. Eph.* 22.1 (F4.334): Ἁμαρτία τὸ πρᾶγμα ἔτεκεν, ἡ εἰς τοὺς πατέρας ὕβρις. Ἀκουέτωσαν οἱ παῖδες, ὅτι δοῦλοί εἰσιν ἄξιοι εἶναι, ὅταν εἰς τοὺς πατέρας ἀγνώμονες ὦσιν. The same type of reasoning is also present in Basil (*Spir.* 20 [SC 17.204–6]) and Ambrose (*Jac.* [CSEL 32.2.3–70]).

33. Rousselle, *Porneia*, 58–62.

you, his master, are busy with other things? First of all make it clear what God wants him to do, to be kind towards his fellow slaves, and to take virtue very seriously.[34]

Teaching a slave virtue and obedience is the purpose of religious pedagogy. Slaves and slaveholders owe their primary obedience to God, so the slave should be obedient to the master only if the slave's obedience falls within the scope of what pleases God. Chrysostom tells slaveholders to teach their slaves to be pious (*eulabeis*; the term has the sense of godly fear or reverence) and to take virtue (*aretē*) seriously. The *paterfamilias* then also takes up the role of shepherd and reformer (pastoralization)—he needs to provide spiritual and aretagogical guidance to his slaves. There are limits to the obedience of slaves—they may not obey a command if it violates God's commands.[35] The perfect obedience that a slave ought to show becomes an exemplum for Chrysostom of how Christians ought to obey God. "But if Paul admonishes slaves to show such obedience," Chrysostom states, "think of what ought to be our attitude toward our Master, who brought us into existence out of nothing, and who feeds and clothes us."[36] The same devotion that slaves ought to show their masters is required from Christians, so "let us at least serve him as our slaves serve us."[37] The obedient slave becomes a model of imitation: "But I especially encourage you to imitate slaves; only in that they work out of fear of their masters, let us do the same out of the fear of God."[38] While the degenerate behavior of slaves should never be mimicked, their absolute obedience should indeed serve as a model for one's religious identity.

This positive doulomorphism functions on the level of metaphorical slavery. People ought to become good slaves of God by embodying obedience. The basis of this type of reasoning, especially in the case of Chrysostom, lies in the instructions found in the Deutero-Pauline household codes. Ephesians 6:5, Colossians 3:22, 1 Timothy 6:1–2, and Titus 2:9–10 demand that slaves show obedience to their masters. Of course, Chrysostom notes that wives and children also need to show

---

34. *Hom. Eph.* 22.2 (F4.334–35): εἰ δὲ βούλεσθε πρότερον τὰ περὶ τῶν οἰκετῶν ἀκοῦσαι, ἀκούσατε τέως τὰ περὶ τῶν παίδων. Διδάσκετε αὐτοὺς εἶναι εὐλαβεῖς, καὶ πάντως πάντα ἕπεται. Νῦν δὲ εἰς μὲν θέατρον ἀνιών, καὶ εἰς βαλανεῖον ἀπιών τις, πάντας ἐπισύρεται τοὺς παῖδας· εἰς δὲ ἐκκλησίαν, οὐκέτι, οὐδὲ ἀναγκάζει παρεῖναι καὶ ἀκούειν. Πῶς δὲ ὁ οἰκέτης ἀκούσεται, σοῦ τοῦ δεσπότου ἑτέροις προσέχοντος; Ἠγόρασας, ἐπρίω τὸν δοῦλον; ἐπίταττε πρότερον αὐτῷ τὰ κατὰ Θεὸν, ὥστε πρὸς τοὺς συνδούλους εἶναι ἤπιον, ἀρετῆς πολὺν ποιεῖσθαι λόγον.

35. *Hom. Eph.* 22.2 (F4.334–35); *Hom. 1 Tim.* 16.2 (F6.141–42).

36. *Hom. 1 Tim.* 16.2 (F6.143): Εἰ δὲ τοῖς δούλοις οὕτως ἐπέταττε τοσαύτῃ κεχρῆσθαι τῇ ὑπακοῇ, ἐννοήσατε πῶς ἡμᾶς πρὸς τὸν δεσπότην διακεῖσθαι χρή, τὸν ἐκ τοῦ μὴ ὄντος εἰς τὸ εἶναι ἡμᾶς παραγαγόντα, τὸν τρέφοντα, τὸν ἐνδιδύσκοντα.

37. *Hom. 1 Tim.* 16.2 (F6.144): Εἰ καὶ μηδαμῶς οὖν ἑτέρως, κἂν ὡς οἱ οἰκέται οἱ ἡμέτεροι, δουλεύσωμεν αὐτῷ.

38. *Hom. 1 Tim.* 16.2 (F6.144): Ἐγὼ δὲ κἂν τοὺς οἰκέτας μιμήσασθαι παραινῶ· ὅσα ἐκεῖνοι διὰ τὸν φόβον τὸν ἡμέτερον πράττουσι, κἂν τοσαῦτα διὰ τὸν τοῦ Θεοῦ φόβον ἡμεῖς πράττωμεν. See *Hom. 1 Cor.* 26.3 (F2.310–12).

obedience. But their obedience is natural, while the slave's obedience comes from social custom (*synētheia*) and governance (*archē*) due to the consequences of sin. Chrysostom explains:

> Next Paul comes to the third kind of authority [related to slaves and masters]. Here there is also a certain love, but no more resulting from nature, as in the one above [with husbands and wives, parents and children], but from social custom, and from governance itself, and the works done. Since the range of love is more limited here, obedience is increased, and he elaborates on this, desiring to give to these from their obedience what the first have from nature. Thus, that which he discusses solely with the slaves is not for the sake of their masters, but also for their own sake, so that they may become desirable on their own for their masters.[39]

The obedience slaves ought to show their masters must be based on love and fear. Obedience is required because there is no natural and mystical bond of love as in the case of husbands and wives. But as we have seen in chapter 3, love here is a measure of security. Obedience is also a sign of loyalty and trust, and slaves should pledge loyalty to one master alone, and not have divided interests.[40] The obedient slave devotes his or her life entirely to the slaveholder without resistance.[41] The stereotype of the obedient slave also romanticizes kyriarchy, as it normally highlights the "good and humane" treatment of the obedient slave. Chrysostom argues the obvious—the more obedient a slave is, the better he or she will be considered in the eyes of the master. Of course, an obedient slave is not only safer, but also more productive. So obedience regulates the slave body, makes it more productive, and serves the interest of the security of the slaveholder and the slaveholding community. Obedience to God and the slaveholder is the primary marker of virtue for the slave.

The second reason for teaching slaves virtue is that it reproduces and sustains Roman kyriarchy. Slaves need to be virtuous because they are involved in the education of elite Roman children, especially boys. In Chrysostom's thought, only virtuous male slaves may be allowed near boys.[42] So in the formation of future virtuous slaveholders, in the reproduction of kyriarchy, the virtuous slave plays a central part. But aretagogy also sustained kyriarchy in late antiquity. Juxtaposed to the image of the good and virtuous slave is that of the fair and righteous slaveholder.

---

39. *Hom. Col.* 10.1 (F5.277): Εἶτα ἐπὶ τρίτην ἦλθεν ἀρχὴν. Ἐνταῦθα ἔστι μέν τι καὶ φίλτρον, ἀλλ᾽ οὐκέτι φυσικὸν, καθάπερ ἄνω, ἀλλὰ συνηθείας, καὶ ἀπ᾽ αὐτῆς τῆς ἀρχῆς, καὶ ἀπὸ τῶν ἔργων. Ἐπεὶ οὖν ἐνταῦθα τὸ μὲν τοῦ φίλτρου ὑποτέτμηται, τὸ δὲ τῆς ὑπακοῆς ἐπιτέταται, τούτῳ ἐνδιατρίβει, βουλόμενος, ὅπερ οἱ πρῶτοι ἔχουσιν ἀπὸ τῆς φύσεως, τοῦτο δοῦναι τούτοις ἀπὸ τῆς ὑπακοῆς. Ὥστε οὐχ ὑπὲρ τῶν δεσποτῶν τοῖς οἰκέταις μόνοις διαλέγεται, ἀλλὰ καὶ ὑπὲρ αὐτῶν, ἵνα ποθεινοὺς ἑαυτοὺς ἐργάζωνται τοῖς δεσπόταις.

40. *Hom. Jo.* 42.3 (PG 59.243.51–60).

41. *Hom. 1 Tim.* 16.2 (F6.143–44).

42. *Inan.* 38.475–90 (SC 188.128–30).

Virtuous masters should cultivate virtuous slaves, but good slaves also result in good masters. "Paul teaches us not to be ashamed of our slaves," Chrysostom states, "if they are virtuous."[43] The honor of the virtuous slave reflects back onto the slaveholder, resulting in admirable social rapport for the master.

On the other hand, Chrysostom also believes that the reason the majority of slaves are not virtuous is because of their masters. The body of the slave, in Chrysostom's thought, becomes a mirror and map of the honor of the slaveholder. In a very important passage, Chrysostom explains why most slaves are degenerate and difficult to train in virtue:

> For both among themselves, and everywhere, it is admitted that the race of slaves is inordinate, not open to impression, stubborn, and does not show much aptitude for being taught virtue, not from their nature, it cannot be, but from their bad upbringing, and the neglect of their masters. For those who rule over them care about nothing but their own service, and if they do give attention to their morals, they do it only to avoid the distress that would be their part when they fornicate, rob, or become drunk; and since they are so neglected and having no one to care for them, they obviously descend to the depths of wickedness. For if those under the tutelage of a father and mother, a pedagogue, an attendant, and teacher, with suitable companions, with the honor of a free condition, and many other advantages, find it difficult to depart from doing evil things, what can we expect from those who are bereft of all these, and are mixed up with wicked people, and associate fearlessly with whomever they want to, with no one concerned about their friendships—what type of people do we expect them to be? Because of this it is difficult for any slave to be good, especially when they do not have the advantage of being taught either by those outside or by ourselves. They do not engage in conversation with free persons who behave appropriately, who have a great regard for their reputation. For all these reasons it is a difficult and surprising thing that there should ever be a good slave.[44]

---

43. *Hom. Phlm.* arg. (F6.328): Διδάσκει ἡμᾶς μὴ ἐπαισχύνεσθαι τοὺς οἰκέτας, εἰ ἐνάρετοι εἶεν.

44. *Hom. Tit.* 4.1 (F6.298): Καὶ γὰρ καὶ παρ' αὐτοῖς, καὶ πανταχοῦ τοῦτο διωμολόγηται, ὅτι τὸ τῶν δούλων γένος ἰταμόν πώς ἐστι, δυσδιατύπωτον, δυστράπελον, οὐ σφόδρα ἐπιτήδειον πρὸς τὴν τῆς ἀρετῆς διδασκαλίαν, οὐ διὰ τὴν φύσιν, μὴ γένοιτο, ἀλλὰ διὰ τὴν ἀνατροφὴν καὶ τὴν ἀμέλειαν τὴν παρὰ τῶν δεσποτῶν. Ἐπειδὴ γὰρ πανταχοῦ οὐδενὸς ἑτέρου, ἀλλὰ τῆς αὐτῶν διακονίας οἱ κρατοῦντες αὐτῶν φροντίζουσιν· εἰ δέ που καὶ τῶν τρόπων ἐπιμεληθεῖεν, καὶ τοῦτο πάλιν διὰ τὴν αὐτῶν ἀνάπαυσιν πράττουσιν, ὥστε μὴ πράγματα αὐτοῖς παρέχειν ἢ πορνεύοντας, ἢ κλέπτοντας, ἢ μεθύοντας· εἰκότως ἠμελημένοι, καὶ οὐδένα τὸν πολυπραγμονοῦντα ἔχοντες, εἰς αὐτὰ τῆς κακίας τὰ βάραθρα καταποντίζονται. Εἰ γὰρ, ἔνθα πατὴρ ἐφέστηκε, καὶ μήτηρ, καὶ παιδαγωγὸς, καὶ τροφεὺς, καὶ διδάσκαλος, καὶ ἡλικιῶται, καὶ αὐτὴ ἡ τῆς ἐλευθερίας δόξα περικειμένη, καὶ πολλὰ ἕτερα, μόλις ἄν τις διαφύγοι τὰς τῶν πονηρῶν συνουσίας· τί οἴει τοὺς πάντων τούτων ἐρήμους ὄντας, καὶ μιαροῖς ἀναμιγνυμένους, καὶ μετὰ ἀδείας οἷς ἂν ἐθέλωσι συγγινομένους, οὐδενὸς ὄντος τοῦ τὰς φιλίας αὐτῶν πολυπραγμονοῦντος, τί οἴει τοὺς τοιούτους ἔσεσθαι; Διὰ τοῦτο δύσκολον δοῦλον γενέσθαι ἀγαθόν. Ἄλλως δὲ οὐδὲ διδασκαλίας ἀπολαύουσιν, οὔτε τῶν ἔξωθεν οὔτε τῶν παρ' ἡμῖν· οὐ συναναστρέφονται ἀνδράσιν ἐλευθέροις, κοσμίοις, πολλὴν τῆς αὐτῶν δόξης ποιουμένοις φροντίδα. Διὰ ταῦτα πάντα δύσκολον καὶ θαυμαστὸν, χρήσιμον οἰκέτην γενέσθαι ποτέ.

This passage exposes many of the fissures of kyriarchal society. Chrysostom attributes the degenerate character of slaves not to nature, as Aristotle would have it, but to bad upbringing (*anatrophē*) and neglect (*ameleia*) of the masters. Nurture, not nature, has corrupted the slave. In this passage Chrysostom practically excoriates every negative facet of slavery. Basically he says that the oppressive deprivation and domination of the institution of slaveholding result in degenerate slaves (!)—but his answer is not to scrap the system, but to simply amend and rectify the *conditions* of domination and deprivation both for slaves and for slaveholders. Rather than focusing on the depravity of the system, he sees only the nefarious children of its shame, those who dominate and those who are dominated, those accouched by the institution; sadly, he misses the forest for the trees.

Chrysostom's critique of slaveholders is not entirely novel. We find a similar critique of slaveholders in Philodemus. In his treatise on household management Philodemus not only asks how an estate can be profitable, but he also explores the idea of the virtuous landowner.[45] Both Philodemus and Chrysostom, centuries apart from each other, scold slaveholders for being concerned only with the labor and profitability of their slaves, with little consideration for their virtue. Wicked slaves are a sign of a bad and inconsiderate slaveholder—the masculinity of the master is depreciated by the bad behavior of his slaves, since their behavior shows that he is unable to control and discipline his subordinates. "For if we refuse to be called the masters of our bad slaves, and give up on them," Chrysostom explains, "and if any one comes to us and says, 'so-and-so does countless evils, he is your slave, is he not?' We immediately say, 'certainly not!'" Chrysostom continues that slaveholders give this response "in order to spare us the shame, for a slave has a close relationship with his master, and the disgrace passes from the one to the other."[46]

Wicked masters also treat their slaves with derision, while the virtuous man "will be more gentle toward his wife, children, and slaves."[47] As an example, Chrysostom points to the repugnance of men attending the theater—upon returning from the theatrical den of iniquity, "he will look upon his wife with more

---

45. For more on Philodemus's views on household management, slavery, and virtue, see Elizabeth Asmis, "Epicurean Economics," in *Philodemus and the New Testament World,* ed. John T. Fitzgerald, Dirk Obbink, and Glen S. Holland (Leiden: Brill, 2004), 133–76; David L. Balch, "Philodemus, 'On Wealth' and 'On Household Management': Naturally Wealthy Epicureans against Poor Cynics," ibid., 177–96; Voula Tsouna, *Ethics of Philodemus* (New York: Oxford University Press, 2007); Tsouna, *Philodemus, On Property Management,* Writings from the Greco-Roman World (Atlanta: Society of Biblical Literature, 2012), xxx–xxxi.

46. *Hom. Heb.* 24.7 (F7.274–75): Εἰ γὰρ ἡμεῖς παραιτούμεθα καλεῖσθαι δεσπόται πονηρῶν ἡμῶν δούλων, καὶ ἀφίεμεν αὐτούς· κἂν εἴπῃ τις προσελθών, ὁ δεῖνα μυρία ἐργάζεται κακά, ἆρα σὸς δοῦλός ἐστιν; εὐθέως φαμέν, ὅτι οὐδαμῶς, ἀποτριβόμενοι τὸ ὄνειδος· σχέσις γάρ ἐστι τῷ δούλῳ πρὸς τὸν δεσπότην, καὶ διαβαίνει ἡ ἀδοξία καὶ εἰς τοῦτον ἀπ' ἐκείνου.

47. *Hom. Act.* 42.4 (PG 60.302.8–9): πρὸς γυναῖκα, πρὸς παιδία, πρὸς τοὺς οἰκέτας ἔσονται ἐπιεικέστεροι.

contempt, he will be cantankerous with his domestics, irritated with his children, and vicious towards all."[48] The shame of the slave body, as we can see, is transposed onto the body of the slaveholder. It is because of the degeneration of the slaveholding class that slaves are so wicked. Finally, Chrysostom believes that slaves are flagitious because of their alienation from their family, their mothers and fathers, and also because they do not have a formal education system. Ironically, slaves are not virtuous because they lack pedagogues and proper education—a vicious cycle.

Chrysostom goes even further in some instances. "Hence our stupidity is manifold; hence the free are less honored than the slaves," he laments. Why are slaves more honored than the free? "For slaves we castigate, if not for their sake, then for our own," Chrysostom says, "but the free do not have the advantage of this care, but are even more appalling to us than these slaves."[49] The rhetoric of this passage is clear—Chrysostom uses extreme opposites to make his point—namely, that the slaveholders themselves no longer care about their own virtue or their children's aretagogy. In chapter 4, we noted that Chrysostom complains about pedagogues departing too early from the children they were guiding. Here, he suggests that the times and the *mores* have become so wicked that the social order itself is inverted. The free act like slaves, and slaves like the free.

A virtuous slave, on the other hand, can teach his or her owner righteousness,[50] and also has many advantages for the slaveholder and the household: "And virtue is so exceptional, that even a slave often benefits a whole family together with the master." The virtuous slave is also the one who often needs to manage the household, but the slaveholder needs to train such a slave. "And I know of many households, that they have greatly profited by the virtue of their slaves," Chrysostom intimates. "But if a slave placed under authority is able to educate the master," he continues, "much more can the master educate his slaves."[51]

When a slave is virtuous, Chrysostom believes, the master also shows respect to the slave and enables him to speak with more confidence, providing him with some agency. "In the case of slaves in large households, when any of those placed over the household are very highly respected, and manage everything themselves,"

<hr>

48. *Hom. Act.* 42.4 (PG 60.302.9–12): ['Αλλ' ἀπὸ τοῦ θεάτρου οὐχ οὕτως,] ἀλλ' ἀηδέστερον ὄψεται τὴν γυναῖκα, καὶ δυσχερὴς πρὸς τοὺς οἰκείους ἔσται, παροξυνθήσεται πρὸς τὰ παιδία, ἐκθηριωθήσεται πρὸς πάντας.

49. *Hom. Matt.* 59.7 (PG 58.584.3–8): 'Εντεῦθεν πολλὴ ἡ ἄνοια· ἐντεῦθεν τῶν δούλων οἱ ἐλεύθεροι ἀτιμότεροι. Τοῖς μὲν γὰρ δούλοις, εἰ καὶ μὴ δι' αὐτούς, ἀλλὰ δι' ἡμᾶς αὐτοὺς ἐπιτιμῶμεν· οἱ δὲ ἐλεύθεροι οὐδὲ ταύτης ἀπολαύουσι τῆς προνοίας, ἀλλὰ καὶ τούτων ἡμῖν εἰσιν εὐτελέστεροι.

50. See *Hom. Tit.* 4.1 (F6.298); *Hom. Eph.* 22.1 (F4.335).

51. *Hom. 2 Thess.* 5.3 (F5.494): καὶ τοσαύτη τῆς ἀρετῆς ἡ ὑπερβολή, ὥστε καὶ δοῦλος πολλάκις ὁλόκληρον ὠφέλησεν οἰκίαν μετὰ τοῦ δεσπότου.... Καὶ οἶδα πολλὰς οἰκίας, ὅτι μεγάλα ἐκέρδαναν ἀπὸ τῆς τῶν δούλων ἀρετῆς. Εἰ δὲ οἰκέτης ὑπ' ἐξουσίαν κείμενος τὸν δεσπότην ῥυθμίσαι δύναιτ' ἄν, πολλῷ μᾶλλον δεσπότης οἰκέτας.

Chrysostom notes that they benefit the master greatly, and confirms that they "can use great freedom of speech toward their masters,"[52] and that "the words of slaves can overturn the decision of their master."[53] Aretagogy therefore opens up more possibilities for upward social mobility and freedom of speech (*parrhēsia*) for slaves—they may receive more important tasks and perhaps have a better chance of manumission, which Chrysostom himself acknowledges.[54] Moreover, Chrysostom also suggests to slaves:

> For if you serve your master with good intentions, yet the cause of this service commences from your fear of God, so the one who serves with such great fear, will receive the greater reward. For if a slave does not control his hand, or his undisciplined tongue, how will the Greek admire the doctrine that is among us? But if they see their slave, who has been taught the philosophy of Christ, showing more self-mastery than their own philosophers, and serving with all meekness and good intentions, he will admire the power of the gospel in every way. For the Greeks do not judge doctrines by the doctrine itself, but they make the practice and lifestyle the test of the doctrines.[55]

Neglecting to teach slaves virtue not only affects masters in a negative way, but it can also damage the reputation of Christianity. The honor of the good Christian slave reflects back onto the master and the church, and serves as a mark of distinction to outsiders. "For if the unbeliever sees slaves behaving imperiously on account of the faith," Chrysostom warns, "he will blaspheme, as if the doctrine caused insubordination. But when he sees that they are persuaded to be obedient, he will be more persuaded."[56] Even slaves have the responsibility to guard the reputation of their religion. As we have seen above, Chrysostom has stated that Christian slaves should exhibit more self-mastery (*enkrateia*) than the philosophers of the Greeks, and he continues, "Therefore, let women and slaves be their teachers by their domestic lifestyle."[57] Similarly, Chrysostom describes the house

---

52. *Hom. Heb.* 24.6 (F7.273): Οἷον ἐπὶ τῶν ἐν ταῖς μεγάλαις οἰκίαις, ὅταν τινὲς εὐδοκιμῶσι τῶν προεστηκότων τῆς οἰκίας, καὶ σφόδρα εὐδοκιμῶσι, καὶ πάντα αὐτοὶ διέπωσι, καὶ πολλὴν πρὸς τοὺς δεσπότας τὴν παρρησίαν ἔχωσιν.

53. *Hom. Phlm.* 1.1 (F6.330): [οἶδε γὰρ πολλάκις καὶ] ῥήματα δούλων ἀνατρέψαι τὸν δεσπότην.

54. *Hom. 1 Cor.* 40.6 (F2.515).

55. *Hom. Tit.* 4.1 (F6.297–98): Κἂν γὰρ τῷ δεσπότῃ διακονῇς μετ' εὐνοίας, ἀλλ' ἡ πρόφασις ἀπὸ τοῦ φόβου τοῦ θεοῦ τὴν ἀρχὴν ἔχει. Ὥστε ὁ μετὰ τοσούτου φόβου ἐκείνῳ διακονῶν, μεγίστων ἐπιτεύξεται τῶν μισθῶν. Εἰ γὰρ χειρὸς μὴ κρατεῖ, μηδὲ γλώττης ἀκολάστου, πόθεν θαυμάσεται ὁ Ἕλλην τὸ δόγμα τὸ παρ' ἡμῖν; Εἰ δὲ τὸν δοῦλον θεάσοιτο τὸν ἐν Χριστῷ φιλοσοφοῦντα, τῶν παρ' αὐτοῖς φιλοσοφησάντων μείζονα τὴν ἐγκράτειαν ἐπιδεικνύμενον, καὶ μετὰ πολλῆς τῆς ἐπιεικείας καὶ τῆς εὐνοίας διακονούμενον, παντὶ τρόπῳ θαυμάσεται τὴν δύναμιν τοῦ κηρύγματος. Οὐ γὰρ ἀπὸ δόγματος δόγματα, ἀλλ' ἀπὸ πραγμάτων καὶ βίου τὰ δόγματα κρίνουσιν Ἕλληνες.

56. *Hom. 1 Tim.* 16.2 (F6.141): Ὁ γὰρ ἄπιστος, ἂν μὲν ἴδῃ διὰ τὴν πίστιν αὐθαδῶς προσφερομένους, βλασφημήσει πολλὰ ὡς στάσιν ἐμποιοῦν τὸ δόγμα· ὅταν δὲ ἴδῃ πειθομένους, μᾶλλον πεισθήσεται.

57. *Hom. Tit.* 4.1 (F6.298): Ἔστωσαν οὖν αὐτοῖς καὶ γυναῖκες καὶ δοῦλοι διδάσκαλοι διὰ τῆς οἰκείας ἀναστροφῆς.

that is suffused with virtue, where "every word the husband speaks is full of philosophy . . . and even slaves and women speak like philosophers."[58] Philosophy
(*philosophia*), in this context a close equivalent of *sōphrosynē* and *enkrateia*, and
the discourse of philosophization in this instance act as an apparatus for masculinization. By exhibiting the speech and self-control of philosophers, their virtue,
slaves and women are able to act like men.[59]

The third reason for teaching slaves virtue is that it amplifies and intensifies the
operation of kyriarchy. Although slaves occupied a position in which they were
controlled and dominated, slave men were themselves husbands and fathers who
had to control their own wives and children; slaves often owned other slaves.[60] The
slave must therefore be taught virtue in order to master his own family and slaves.
Chrysostom explains the chain of command: "The husband has authority over the
wife, the wife over the slaves, the slaves again over their own wives; again the wives
and the husbands over the children."[61] The slave who cannot control his own subordinates is also a threat to the security of the entire household. The basic dynamics of the reproduction of pastoral power also apply to male slaves. The male
slave needs to care for his wife, children, and slaves as a replica of the sacerdotal
paterfamilias. In duplicating pastoral power in the body of the male slave, aretagogy amplifies and intensifies the functioning of kyriarchy. The slave becomes a
master.

This final reason for teaching slaves virtue is related to the very nature of kyriarchy. It demonstrates that the operation of kyriarchal power is not based on simple binarisms—such as that there is only one who exercises power and one on
whom it is exercised. Kyriarchy is better understood as a complex network of
power flows and interactions on multiple hierarchical levels simultaneously. It is
multiphasic. It can be reproduced in every sphere of domestic and familial interaction. Within it, bodies can be transposed from being dominated to dominating.
The institution of slavery was pervasive—permeating those whom it oppressed,
and turning the oppressed into oppressors.

A PLAGUE OF THE HOUSE: THE RUNAWAY SLAVE

Chrysostom recounts a very interesting story that he heard through the grapevine
about a widow who had a slave couple, where the husband was wicked, but the

58. *Hom. Act.* 42.4 (PG 60.301.14–15, 17): πάντα φιλοσοφίας γέμοντα ῥήματα ἐφθέγξατο . . . καὶ
οἰκεῖοι καὶ γυναῖκες φιλοσοφοῦσι.

59. Gillian Cloke, *This Female Man of God: Women and Spiritual Power in the Patristic Age, AD
350–450* (London: Routledge, 1995), 67–69.

60. See *Hom. Matt.* 58.6 (PG 58.571.16–572.1); *Hom. 1 Cor.* 34.6 (F2.427); *Hom. Eph.* 22.1 (F4.335).

61. *Hom. Eph.* 22.1 (F4.335): κρατεῖ τῆς γυναικὸς ὁ ἀνήρ, ἡ γυνὴ τῶν οἰκετῶν, οἱ οἰκέται τῶν ἰδίων
γυναικῶν· πάλιν αἱ γυναῖκες καὶ οἱ ἄνδρες τῶν παίδων.

wife righteous (I will use the terms "husband" and "wife" here in a very loose sense, as the problem of slave marriages will be discussed in the next chapter):

> There was a certain slave girl coupled with a wicked man, some despicable runaway slave; after her husband committed many crimes, she was about to be sold by her mistress. For the crimes were too serious to pardon, and the woman was a widow, and was not able to punish him who plagued her house, and therefore decided to sell him. Then considering that it was an unholy thing to separate the husband from the wife, although the girl was useful, the mistress resolved to sell her along with him to avoid separating them.[62]

The story illustrates the dilemma a "useful" (*chrēsimē*) slave girl could face if her husband was not virtuous. Despite the ambiguity of slave marriages, the Christian widow considered the couple's relationship as spousal, and realized that the unrighteous slave husband was a danger and a shame to her house. Being a runaway, he may have been liable for criminal charges along with his other crimes. The slave husband is described in all the worst terms. He was wicked, vile, a plague of the house, and worst of all, a runaway. He had no obedience or loyalty, and no virtue. The virtue of the slave wife made no difference in the affair. The husband had to be virtuous. The husband here clearly resisted the imposed kyriarchy and subjugating aretagogy, but his resistance also influenced and compromised the position of his wife. The establishment of slave marriages and families complicated acts of resistance. The story also illustrates that although women were central in the management of household slaves, a woman like this widow could have difficulty with some aspects of slave management if a male was not in the house.

We have here an image of the slave that exemplifies the complete opposite of the virtuous and disciplined slave—the fugitive (*drapetēs, fugitivus*). This was no trivial matter—according to Chrysostom, virtuous slaves did not run away, but not teaching a slave virtue increased the possibility of flight. The contrast between the virtuous and the runaway slave is common in Chrysostom's thought. Not all slaves passively accepted their fate of enslavement. Escape was an option that many considered. While flight was considered a serious crime, it seems to have been rather banal and managed by the lower echelons of the Roman legal system.[63] Escape

---

62. *Hom. 1 Thess.* 11.3 (F5.436–37): Παιδίσκη τις ἀνδρὶ πονηρῷ συνεζευγμένη, μιαρῷ, δραπέτῃ τινὶ, αὕτη, πολλὰ τοῦ ἀνδρὸς ἡμαρτηκότος, καὶ μέλλοντος ἀπεμπολεῖσθαι παρὰ τῆς δεσποίνης· καὶ γὰρ μείζονα συγγνώμης ἦν τὰ ἁμαρτήματα, καὶ χήρα ἦν ἡ γυνὴ, καὶ κολάζειν αὐτὸν λυμαινόμενον αὐτῆς τὴν οἰκίαν οὐκ ἴσχυεν, ἀλλ᾽ ἔγνω ἀποδόσθαι· εἶτα ἀνόσιον εἶναι νομίζουσα ἡ δέσποινα διασπάσαι τῆς γυναικὸς τὸν ἄνδρα, κατεδέξατο καὶ χρησίμην οὖσαν τὴν κόρην, ὑπὲρ τῆς ἀπαλλαγῆς τῆς ἐκείνου συναπεμπολῆσαι.

63. For more on the legal aspects of flight, see William W. Buckland, *The Roman Law of Slavery: The Condition of the Slave in Private Law from Augustus to Justinian* (Cambridge: Cambridge University Press, 1908), 30–69, 267–74; Heinz Bellen, *Studien zur Sklavenflucht im römischen Kaiserreich,* Forschungen zur antiken Sklaverei 4 (Wiesbaden: Franz Steiner, 1971); Georg Klingenberg, *Corpus der*

was a major risk to the slaveholder. Not only did it mean that certain steps had to be taken to get the slave back, it also came at a cost to the slaveholder. The value of a fugitive slave was less than that of those who did not flee, and when selling a slave the trader was bound by law to disclose whether the slave had ever been a fugitive.[64]

Slave flight is a complex matter in itself. Many slaves fled in order to escape a harsh master, and to seek a life of freedom outside the constraints of kyriarchal power.[65] However, slave flight is often linked with various other crimes in the sources, notably theft and banditry.[66] Ecclesiastical structures also opposed any form of flight. The third canon of the Council of Gangra makes the church's opposition clear: "If any one shall teach a slave, under pretext of piety, to despise his master and to run away from his service, and not to serve his own master with goodwill and all honor, let him be anathema."[67] Chrysostom shared this view—he was against any slave fleeing from his or her master, and considered flight a punishable crime. It took great courage and tenacity for a slave to flee, and there was always the fear of being caught and punished.[68] Slaves were often chained to prevent them from fleeing.[69] Fugitives were a cause for anxiety among free people, since such slaves could blend in with society.[70] They could be difficult to dispose of once they were linked to the household, as we saw in the case of the widow who eventually had to sell both the runaway and his docile wife.[71]

Early Christian views regarding fugitive slaves were influenced by the statements in Paul's Letter to Philemon. In this letter, Paul intercedes on behalf of a slave, Onesimus, with his master, a wealthy Christian man called Philemon. Chrysostom's interpretation of this document is key to understanding why he views the flight of slaves as not only illegal, but also blasphemous. Since Paul advised Onesimus to return to his owner, so does Chrysostom urge all runaways

römischen Rechtsquellen zur antiken Sklaverei, Teil X: Juristisch speziell definierte Sklavengruppen, 6: Servus fugitivus, Forschungen zur antiken Sklaverei—Beihefte 16 (Stuttgart: Steiner, 2005); Keith R. Bradley, "Resisting Slavery at Rome," in The Cambridge World History of Slavery, vol. 1, The Ancient Mediterranean World, ed. Keith Bradley and Paul Cartledge (New York: Cambridge University Press, 2011), 362–84.

64. Buckland, Roman Law of Slavery, 30–41.

65. Kyle Harper, Slavery in the Late Roman World, AD 275–425 (New York: Cambridge University Press, 2011), 256–57.

66. Bellen, Studien zur Sklavenflucht, 95–105; Thomas Grunewald, Bandits in the Roman Empire: Myth and Reality (London: Routledge, 2004), 10.

67. See Jennifer A. Glancy, Slavery in Early Christianity (Minneapolis: Fortress Press, 2006), 90.

68. Stag. 3.1 (PG 47.474.57).

69. Lib. repud. 2.1 (PG 51.218.55–219.2); Stat. 9.3 (PG 49.108.7–12); see Harper, Slavery in the Late Roman World, 256.

70. Hom. Matt. 35.3 (PG 57.409.44–46)

71. Hom. 1 Thess. 11.3 (F5.436–37).

to return to their masters. The act of flight was a contravention not only of law, but of scripture. Fugitives were the worst kind of slaves, often seen to be thieves and bandits,[72] and the terms *drapetēs* (a male runaway) and *drapetria* (a female runaway) were sometimes used as profanities against slaves—a personification of their dereliction of virtue.[73]

In his homiletic series on Philemon,[74] Chrysostom immediately starts with the assumption that Onesimus was a runaway and a miscreant. Onesimus has broken the bonds of his carcerality and even committed the crime of theft (Philem. 18) according to Chrysostom. The dissoluteness of the fugitive Onesimus is matched only by the wholesomeness of the slaveholder, Philemon. Chrysostom's homilies on Philemon are an excellent example of the biased nature of writing about slavery in the late ancient world. Onesimus is the (former) antagonist, while Paul and especially Philemon are the protagonists. Chrysostom provides a summary of the plot of this epistle:

> First, it is necessary to explain the argument of the epistle, then also the issues that are sought from it. What then is the argument? There was a certain man, Philemon, a faithful and noble man. That he was a remarkable man is evident from the fact that his entire household consisted of believers, and of so many believers that it is even called a church. Therefore Paul says in this epistle, *And to the church that is in your house* [Philem. 2]. He also testifies to Philemon's great obedience, and that the *spirits of the faithful are refreshed* [Philem. 7] in him. And Paul himself in this epistle asked Philemon to prepare a lodging for him. It seems to me therefore that Philemon's house was in general a residence for believers. This remarkable man, then, had a certain slave named Onesimus. This Onesimus, having stolen something from his master, had run away. For we know that he had stolen something—hear what Paul says, *If he has wronged you, or owes you anything, I will repay you* [Philem. 18]. Going then to Paul in Rome, and having found him in prison, and having enjoyed the advantage of his teaching, he also received baptism there. The fact that he received the gift of baptism there is clear from Paul saying, *Whom I have begotten in my bonds* [Philem. 10]. Paul therefore writes, recommending Onesimus to his master, that on every account he should forgive him, and receive him as someone now reborn.[75]

---

72. *Hom. Col.* 7.3 (F5.252); *Hom. Rom.* 18[17].2 (F1.307); *Theod. laps.* 13, 18 (SC 117.152–60, 190–99).

73. *Hom. Eph.* 15.2 (F4.259).

74. See F6.325–53.

75. *Hom. Phlm.* arg. (F6.325–26): Πρῶτον ἀναγκαῖον τὴν ὑπόθεσιν εἰπεῖν τῆς ἐπιστολῆς, εἶτα καὶ τὰ ζητούμενα. Τίς οὖν ἡ ὑπόθεσις; Ἀνήρ τις Φιλήμων τῶν πιστῶν καὶ γενναίων ἀνδρῶν. Ὅτι γὰρ θαυμαστὸς ἦν, δῆλον ἀπὸ τοῦ καὶ τὴν οἰκίαν αὐτοῦ πᾶσαν εἶναι πιστήν, καὶ οὕτω πιστῶν, καὶ οὕτω πιστῶν, ὡς καὶ ἐκκλησίαν αὐτὴν ὀνομάζεσθαι. Διὰ τοῦτο καὶ γράφων ἔλεγε· Καὶ τὴν κατ᾽ οἶκόν σου ἐκκλησίαν. Μαρτυρεῖ δὲ αὐτῷ καὶ πολλὴν ὑπακοήν, καὶ ὅτι τὰ σπλάγχνα τῶν ἁγίων ἀνεπέπαυτο εἰς αὐτόν. Καὶ αὐτὸς δὲ γράφων ἐν ταύτῃ τῇ ἐπιστολῇ παρήγγελλεν αὐτῷ ἑτοιμάσαι ξενίαν. Οὕτω μοι δοκεῖ καταγώγιον εἶναι ἁγίων ἡ οἰκία ἐκείνου πάντων ἕνεκεν. Οὗτος δὴ οὖν ὁ θαυμαστὸς ἀνὴρ τις ὤν, παῖδά

Chrysostom starts by expanding on the previous carceral space of Onesimus—that is, the household of Philemon. Chrysostom notes that Philemon's household served as lodging for traveling Christians, and Philemon is depicted by Chrysostom as quite a "remarkable man" (*ho thaumastos anēr*).[76] It is interesting to see how Chrysostom describes the ideal Christian slaveholder in this homily. Philemon's house is more than just a house; it is referred to as a church. This is Chrysostom's ideal household, a household that is also a church. If Philemon's house is a church, it stands to reason that Chrysostom would consider Philemon a type of pastor for this *familia*. Chrysostom therefore strategically reconstructs the historical background of the epistle to reflect his view of the ideal pastoralized Christian household and the quintessential Christian slaveholder. It is also evident from Chrysostom's reading of Philemon 7 that "the spirits of the believers are refreshed in him,"[77] that he considered Philemon to occupy an active role in teaching and spiritual guidance of his household.

Philemon, the model Christian slaveholder according to Chrysostom, is then contrasted with Onesimus, the typical degenerate slave. Chrysostom now uses the same strategy that he used to exemplify the honor and virtue of Philemon to highlight the disgrace and devilry of Onesimus.[78] He was the worst kind of slave in Chrysostom's mind; a thief and a runaway. It should be noted that none of these details are mentioned explicitly in the text of the epistle; Chrysostom uses the stereotypes of his day to fill in the gaps in the *historia* of the text—he presupposes Onesimus is a malicious runaway.

Chrysostom's homilies on Philemon have received ample scholarly attention, especially regarding the legal status of Onesimus and of fugitive slaves in general. In an interesting scholarly dialogue, Margaret Mitchell and Allen Callahan debate Chrysostom's exegesis of Philemon and the origin of the opinion that Onesimus was in fact a *fugitivus*—a point of assumption.[79] Callahan argues, quite unconventionally, that Onesimus was not a slave at all, but Philemon's estranged brother. He

---

τινα εἶχεν Ὀνήσιμον. Ὁ τοίνυν Ὀνήσιμος οὗτος κλέψας τι παρὰ τοῦ δεσπότου, ἐδραπέτευσεν. Ὅτι γὰρ ἔκλεψεν, ἄκουσον τί φησιν· Εἰ δέ τι ἠδίκησέ σε, ἢ ὀφείλει, ἐγὼ ἀποτίσω. Ἐλθὼν τοίνυν πρὸς τὸν Παῦλον εἰς τὴν Ῥώμην, καὶ εὑρὼν αὐτὸν ἐν τῷ δεσμωτηρίῳ, καὶ ἀπολαύσας τῆς παρ᾽ αὐτοῦ διδασκαλίας, καὶ τοῦ βαπτίσματος ἔτυχεν ἐκεῖ. Ὅτι γὰρ ἐκεῖ ἔτυχε τῆς τοῦ βαπτίσματος δωρεᾶς, δῆλον ἐκ τοῦ εἰπεῖν· Ὃν ἐγέννησα ἐν τοῖς δεσμοῖς μου. Ὁ τοίνυν Παῦλος γράφει συνιστῶν αὐτὸν πρὸς τὸν δεσπότην, ὥστε πάντων ἕνεκεν λύσιν γενέσθαι, καὶ προσίεσθαι αὐτὸν ὡς ἀναγεννηθέντα νῦν.

76. *Hom. Phlm.* arg. (F6.325).
77. NA28: ὅτι τὰ σπλάγχνα τῶν ἁγίων ἀναπέπαυται διὰ σοῦ.
78. De Wet, "John Chrysostom's Exegesis of Philemon."
79. Margaret M. Mitchell, "John Chrysostom on Philemon: A Second Look," *Harvard Theological Review* 88, no. 01 (1995): 135–48; Allen D. Callahan, "Paul's Epistle to Philemon: Toward an Alternative Argumentum," *Harvard Theological Review* 86 (1993): 357–76; Callahan, "John Chrysostom on Philemon: A Response to Margaret M. Mitchell," *Harvard Theological Review* 88 (1995): 149–56.

continues to argue that Chrysostom is the first case in the *Wirkungsgeschichte* of the epistle in which the *fugitivus* reading is favored. Mitchell convincingly challenges Callahan's hypothesis. I do not wish to resume this debate, although I have difficulty agreeing with Callahan that Onesimus and Philemon are brothers. The point here is that Chrysostom had no reservations with regard to the status of Onesimus. He believes Onesimus was a runaway slave (*drapetēs*), and bases the rest of his exposition and his characterizations on this hypothesis.

There are several other hypotheses regarding the legal status of Onesimus; the scholarship seems to be quite divided. Chrysostom's view has been described as the "traditional view," that Onesimus was a *fugitivus*, a criminal and runaway slave—but we should note that the Greek term *drapetēs* does not necessarily have to assume the exact legal conditions of the Latin *fugitivus*. There are also several other views, like John Knox's interesting speculation that Onesimus was in fact the slave of Archippus, mentioned in Philemon 2, and that Paul wanted to use his influence on Philemon to persuade Archippus to spare Onesimus.[80] Peter Lampe has challenged the view that Onesimus was a *fugitivus*, since a *fugitivus* was not able to return to his master's household.[81] Lampe and Peter Arzt-Grabner rather note that Onesimus's legal status was that of an *erro*, an "absconder," someone who has carried out an escape but still has the option to return.[82] Scott Elliot, in turn, has argued that Onesimus was sent to Paul by Philemon as a gift, which Paul refused.[83]

80. John Knox, *Philemon among the Letters of Paul: A New View of Its Place and Importance* (Chicago: University of Chicago Press, 1935). Knox's hypothesis was revised by Winter, who also believed that Philemon was not a runaway, but actually sent by the church of Colossae to serve Paul; Sara C. Winter, "Paul's Letter to Philemon," *New Testament Studies* 33 (1987): 1–15.

81. The ambiguity of the legal terms *fugitivus* and *erro* has been a matter of scholarly contention for years. Peter Lampe originally used these terms, found in Roman jurists, to interpret Philemon; Peter Lampe, "Keine 'Sklavenflucht' des Onesimus," *Zeitschrift für die Neutestamentliche Wissenschaft* 76 (1985): 133–37. Thereafter, Rapske elaborated on Lampe's thesis that Onesimus was an *erro*, focusing especially on the idea of friendship in the letter; Brian M. Rapske, "The Prisoner Paul in the Eyes of Onesimus," *New Testament Studies* 37 (1991): 187–203. Lampe and Rapske's theories became very influential in the scholarly debate. It was then challenged by J. Albert Harrill, quite convincingly, who proposed that the social and juridical boundaries between a *fugitivus* and an *erro* were ambiguous at best, and that utilizing Roman jurists for the interpretation of the epistle is problematic; J. Albert Harrill, "Using Roman Jurists to Interpret Philemon," *Zeitschrift für die Neutestamentliche Wissenschaft* 90 (1999): 135–38; see also John Byron, *Recent Research on Paul and Slavery* (Sheffield: Sheffield Phoenix, 2008); Tobias Nicklas, "The Letter to Philemon: A Discussion with J. Albert Harrill," in *Paul's World*, ed. Stanley E. Porter, PAST 4 (Leiden: Brill, 2008), 201–20; Norman R. Petersen, *Rediscovering Paul: Philemon and the Sociology of Paul's Narrative World* (Philadelphia: Fortress Press, 1985).

82. Peter Arzt-Grabner, "Onesimus *Erro*: Zur Vorgeschichte des Philemonbriefes," *Zeitschrift für die Neutestamentliche Wissenschaft* 95 (2004): 131–43.

83. Scott S. Elliot, "'Thanks, but No Thanks': Tact, Persuasion, and Negotiation of Power in Paul's Letter to Philemon," *New Testament Studies* 57 (2010): 51–64.

My own view is consonant with that of J. Albert Harrill[84]—the problem is that the terms *fugitivus* and *erro* are based on ancient Roman legislative categories, which are often based on fictive court cases with conflicting and ambiguous definitions. Nor does Chrysostom seem to differentiate between *fugitivus* and *erro;* rather, he seems to use popular parlance related to runaways. Thus, I would argue that Chrysostom's views are difficult to use as legal bases for understanding *fugitivi* in the Letter to Philemon or later Roman society. The context is not juridical, and the term *drapetēs* does not necessarily differentiate between a *fugitivus* and an *erro*. D. François Tolmie is correct in noting: "What has become clear, in general, is that, to outsiders—like us—who read Paul's correspondence to Philemon, the letter yields *an incomplete picture* regarding Onesimus' status."[85] And even in Chrysostom's time, almost four centuries later, this picture was still quite unclear.

So we cannot use Chrysostom as a definitive witness to the legal status of Onesimus, since his audience is part of the masses, and his speech functions within ancient slave literary types and stereotypes. The important question here is why Chrysostom's first inclination would be to consider Onesimus a *drapetēs*. As I have noted above, we should be cautious about reading Chrysostom's comments in a strictly legal sense—the term *drapetēs* is connected to popular views on slave flight, and Chrysostom seems to use it in a more general sense as referring to running away. The focus is on the action, not the legal status. So the picture regarding the status of Onesimus was not clearer in Chrysostom's time than for scholars today, and the almost four centuries between Chrysostom and Paul can hardly be called close hermeneutical proximity. Chrysostom's use of the term *drapetēs* is not necessarily based on sound exegesis of the text either. He bases his argument for the runaway status of Onesimus solely on what is written in Philemon 8–19. Chrysostom's negative stereotyping of slaves inexplicitly influences Chrysostom's choice. It also shows that the seemingly neat legal and social lines of difference between an *erro* and a *fugitivus* were not clear, even to someone like Chrysostom. He, like most other ancients, expected the worst from slaves—that they would break the bonds of their carceral state; in this case, Onesimus ran away after committing theft.

Chrysostom therefore polarizes the situation and, essentially, rewrites the text of Philemon to suit the general view of kyriarchal society. Philemon and Onesimus represent opposite poles: the best kind of master and the worst kind of slave, the *drapetēs*. Polarization is an effective rhetorical strategy, in that it serves to highlight the point of the argument through the interplay of extreme opposites, and the

---

84. Harrill, "Using Roman Jurists," 135–36.

85. D. François Tolmie, "Tendencies in the Research on the Letter to Philemon," in *Philemon in Perspective: Interpreting a Pauline Letter,* ed. D. Francois Tolmie (Berlin: De Gruyter, 2010), 3 (Tolmie's emphasis).

Letter to Philemon lends itself quite conveniently to this rhetorical polarization. Chrysostom's views on fugitive slaves were based on literary stereotyping and polarization. Slaves who posed such resistance were vilified in the worst way, and it is important to understand that the view of fugitive slaves that we have from ancient sources, such as Chrysostom, is from the perspective of kyriarchy. The wicked runaway found in the sources may very well be one of many human beings who simply could not and did not accept the oppression of slavery, and seized his or her freedom by resisting an oppressive kyriarchal regime, not unlike the leaders of modern struggles.

THE MECHANICS OF ARETAGOGY

The next question that arises concerns the method of teaching virtue. How should slaves be taught virtue according to Chrysostom? In ancient thought, one of the main reasons people did not bother to teach slaves virtue was that virtue was something reserved for the elite male rulers of the city, and it was also temporally intensive—it took a great amount of time and effort. Aristotle believed that time and leisure were needed for the development of virtue and participation in politics. Virtue was an elite discourse and practice.[86] In the *Apophthegmata laconica*, Plutarch relates an anecdote about the Lacedaemonian Anaxandridas: "When someone inquired why they put their fields in the hands of the Helots, and did not take care of them themselves, he said, 'It was by not taking care of the fields, but of ourselves, that we acquired those fields.'"[87] The Spartan reasoning is clear here: the reason they have slaves is so that they do not have to be concerned with tilling the fields, but can spend their time cultivating virtue. Aretagogy, therefore, had a price—it required an investment of time and effort. But it also had certain benefits. Unlike these ancient philosophers, Chrysostom believed that virtue was much less time- and labor-intensive than vice: "How facile is virtue, and it has much benefit! How arduous is vice!"[88]

Chrysostom highlights three ways that virtue may be taught: (1) through fear of violence, confinement, deprivation, and punishment; (2) through imitation of a master who is a model of virtue; (3) through participation in Christian pastoral

---

86. Aristotle, *Pol.* 1328b37–1329a3 (Rackham 574–75); see Garnsey, *Ideas of Slavery,* 36.

87. Plutarch, *Mor.* 3. *Apoph. Lac.* 217a1–3 (Babbitt 296–97): Πυνθανομένου δέ τινος διὰ τί τοῖς εἵλωσι τοὺς ἀγροὺς ἐγχειρίζουσι καὶ οὐκ αὐτοὶ ἐπιμελοῦνται, 'ὅτι' ἔφη 'οὐ τούτων ἐπιμελούμενοι ἀλλ' αὐτῶν αὐτοὺς ἐκτησάμεθα.' See Michel Foucault, *The Hermeneutics of the Subject: Lectures at the Collège De France, 1981–1982,* ed. François Ewald and Alessandro Fontana, trans. Graham Burchell (New York: Picador, 2006), 31.

88. *Hom. Phlm.* 1.2 (PG 62.707.22–23): πῶς εὔκολον ἡ ἀρετὴ καὶ πολλὴν ἔχον ὠφέλειαν! πῶς ἐργῶδες ἡ κακία! The Field text (F6.333–34) omits πῶς ἐργῶδες ἡ κακία, and expands the phrase into an interrogative, showing that aretagogy does not require the aid of money or friends.

power and ritual. The first is the most prominent in Chrysostom's thought—virtue is taught by means of fear. It is not always successful, Chrysostom admits: "For someone will be able to bind down a slave by fear; no, not even him; for he will soon run away and disappear."[89] There must also be some form of compassion and love accompanying the fear. The use of fear is very important in regulating slaves. Chrysostom contrasts the fear that slaves have for their masters, which results in their good behavior, and the lack of fear Christians have for their heavenly slave-holder. "And this same temperance from the fear of their master, someone enforces on the slaves," Chrysostom states, "and rarely will you see a slave robbing or injuring a fellow slave." Chrysostom knew how effective fear was as a technology of virtue. "But among free men this is the opposite," he complains, "we bite and devour one another, we do not fear our master; we rob and ravage our fellow slaves, we beat them, and this in his very sight."[90]

To Chrysostom, there is nothing more natural than a slave fearing his master and thereby behaving appropriately. This is why the lack of the fear of God among believers is so disturbing and unnatural to Chrysostom. Masters can resort to violent punitive measures to teach their slaves virtue—in fact, this was a very common assumption in Chrysostom's thought. Chrysostom also seems fond of the principle of quarantine. For instance, boys had to be taught virtue by separating and shielding them from women and bad slaves. But there are also instances where slaves were locked up and subjected to strict discipline in order to reform them. Chrysostom describes the disciplining of a licentious slave girl thus:

> And when a noble and free man has an incontinent slave woman, who lures in all the bystanders for licentious purposes, he does not allow her to go out into the street, or to be seen in the alley, or to burst into the marketplace; rather, he confines her to the house, and binding her with fetters, he commands her to stay inside permanently, so that the restriction of the place and the constraint of the chains will be her starting point for modesty.[91]

89. *Hom. Eph.* 20.1 (F4.302): Οἰκέτην μὲν γὰρ φόβῳ τις ἂν καταδῆσαι δυνήσεται, μᾶλλον δὲ οὐδὲ ἐκεῖνον· ταχέως γὰρ ἀποπηδήσας οἰχήσεται.

90. *Hom. 1 Tim.* 16.2 (F6.145): Καὶ ταῦτα ἴδοι τις ἂν ἐν οἰκέταις διὰ τὸν τῶν δεσποτῶν φόβον παραφυλαττόμενα· καὶ σπανίως ἂν ἴδοις οἰκέτην τὰ τοῦ οἰκέτου ἁρπάζοντα, ἢ λυμαινόμενον. Παρὰ δὲ ἀνθρώποις ἐλευθέροις τὰ ἐναντία τούτων γίνεται· ἀλλήλους δάκνομεν, κατεσθίομεν, οὐ δεδοίκαμεν τὸν δεσπότην, τὰ τῶν συνδούλων ἁρπάζομεν, κλέπτομεν, τύπτομεν, ὁρῶντος αὐτοῦ.

91. *Adv. Jud.* 2.124ra (Wendy Pradels, Rudolf Brändle, and Martin Heimgartner, "Das bisher vermisste Textstück in Johannes Chrysostomus, *Adversus Judaeos*, Oratio 2," *Zeitschrift für antikes Christentum* 5 [2001]: 36): Καὶ καθάπερ ἀνὴρ εὐσχήμων καὶ ἐλεύθερος δούλην ἔχων ἀκόλαστον, ἅπαντας τοὺς παριόντας πρὸς τὴν ἑαυτῆς ἀσέλγειαν ἐπισπωμένην, οὐκ εἰς ἄμφοδον ἀφίησιν ἐξελθεῖν, οὐκ ἐν στενωπῷ φανῆναι, οὐκ εἰς ἀγορὰν ἐμβαλεῖν, ἀλλ' ἄνω καθείρξας ἐπὶ τῆς οἰκίας καὶ σιδήρῳ πεδήσας κελεύει μένειν ἔνδον διαπαντός, ἵνα καὶ ἡ τοῦ τόπου στενοχωρία καὶ ἡ τῶν δεσμῶν ἀνάγκη σωφροσύνης ὑπόθεσις αὐτῇ γένηται.

Aretagogy was not reserved only for male slaves. Females also had to be virtuous.[92] In the passage above, a slaveholder has a lubricious slave girl. The tale does not appear to be historical, but rather an explanation of what would seem to be the natural and ordinary correction of a female slave. In a different homily, while referring to the interrogation of one's conscience, Chrysostom says that one should discipline the soul like one would whip an unchaste and restless slave girl.[93] A slave girl can be taught only "when she no longer resists her mistress, but is docile, responsive and obedient, restraining the impulses of nature and keeping within proper limits."[94] Although both of these incidents may be extreme cases, Chrysostom still uses them as examples from everyday life, which may illustrate that such cases of abuse behind the façade of aretagogy were not uncommon, and that the correction of sexual vice could be particularly brutal.

In his advice on raising boys in *De inani gloria*, Chrysostom admits that teaching sexual virtue is the most difficult form of aretagogy.[95] Here Chrysostom gives us an interesting glimpse of how slave mobility was controlled. Just as boys are to be shielded from slave girls, this unfortunate female slave is not allowed to appear in public, neither in the streets nor in the marketplace. She is imprisoned in the house itself, in a very confined space (*stenochōria*), with chains stopping her from running away. According to Chrysostom, it is only by quarantine, by seclusion and solitary confinement, that one is able to train an unchaste female slave in sexual modesty (*sōphrosynē*). While the slave girl is claustrophobically chained indoors, the boy can enjoy walking around in public.

Slave women residing in Christian households also had to be taught *sōphrosynē*, especially since they were involved in the care of the *filiafamilias* of the slaveholder, if he had one. This instruction was also indirectly a protective measure that reduced the possibility of the *filiusfamilias* committing fornication with the slave girl. Just as male slaves had to demonstrate virtue to young freeborn boys, female slaves had to be examples of modesty to young women. Chrysostom therefore does not rule out the use of moderate violence and abuse for the purposes of teaching virtue.

---

92. For some general comments on female slaves in households, see Sarah B. Pomeroy, *Goddesses, Whores, Wives and Slaves: Women in Classical Antiquity* (New York: Random House, 1975), 423–50; Jennifer A. Glancy, "Obstacles to Slaves' Participation in the Corinthian Church," *Journal of Biblical Literature* 117, no. 3 (1998): 481–501; Harper, *Slavery in the Late Roman World*, 69–78.

93. *Hom. Matt.* 42.3 (PG 57.455.7–10).

94. *Hom. Gen.* 2.1 (PG 53.27.13–16): ὅτε οὐκ ἔτι κατεξανίσταται τῆς κυρίας ἡ δούλη, ἀλλ' εὐήνιος γενομένη πολλὴν τὴν πειθὼ καὶ τὴν ὑπακοὴν ἐπιδείκνυται, τὰ σκιρτήματα τῆς σαρκὸς καταστορέσασα, καὶ ἐπὶ τῶν οἰκείων ὅρων μένουσα. Translation: Robert C. Hill, trans., *St. John Chrysostom: Homilies on Genesis 1–17*, The Fathers of the Church 74 (Washington, DC: Catholic University of America Press, 1999), 30.

95. *Inan.* 58–61 (SC 188.156–60).

The second method of teaching virtue is imitation of the virtuous master. The slaveholder needs to set an example for the slaves in his own life. Virtuous slaves with shameful masters was an inversion of the social order. Imitation was a very powerful aretagogical method. In his interpretation of Paul's Letter to Philemon, Chrysostom especially recommends Paul, Philemon, and Onesimus as models worthy of imitation. Slaveholders should imitate both Paul and Philemon, while slaves should mimic the attitude and behavior of the reformed slave, Onesimus: "For if Paul shows such care for a runaway, a thief, and a robber, and neither refuses to send him back with such praises, nor is ashamed, much more should we not be careless in such matters." Paul is used as a model for how masters ought to treat even the most delinquent slaves. "We ought not to give up on the race of slaves, even if they have progressed to extreme wickedness," Chrysostom pleads.[96]

That Paul cared for Onesimus's well-being and virtue and did not show him any cruelty or rejection, despite the fact that Onesimus was the worst kind of slave, should also inspire a curative disposition among slaveholders. Even the most wicked slaves should not be abandoned. While it seems admirable to be concerned with the well-being and virtue of degenerate slaves, the means by which one might correct them could be extreme and quite violent.

Finally, slaves are to be taught virtue through participation in the operations of ecclesiastical power and rituals. The slave is part of the household and also part of the church, and therefore he or she is also subject to the demands of pastoral are-tagogy. A virtuous Christian slave upheld the good reputation of the household and church. In his reading of 1 Timothy 6:2, Chrysostom even notes that the office of the bishop has a responsibility to teach and exhort slaves. "What does the bishop have to do with slaves?" people may ask. "Surely a lot" is the answer; "he should exhort and teach even slaves." Like Paul, the bishop must constantly be "showing them the ways of submission, and treating them with much regard."[97] Slaves also fell within the pastoral care of the church, but church leaders had to actively culti-vate processes of subjugation and kyriarchization—they had to teach slaves sub-mission and obedience. Chrysostom was very harsh with masters who took their slaves to the theater but never thought of bringing them to church.[98]

---

96. *Hom. Phlm.* arg. (F6.327): Εἰ γὰρ Παῦλος ὑπὲρ δραπέτου, ὑπὲρ λῃστοῦ καὶ κλέπτου τοσαύτην ποιεῖται πρόνοιαν, καὶ οὐ παραιτεῖται μετὰ τοσούτων αὐτὸν ἐγκωμίων παραπέμψαι, οὐδὲ αἰσχύνεται, πολλῷ μᾶλλον οὐδὲ ἡμᾶς προσήκει ῥαθύμους εἶναι περὶ τὰ τοιαῦτα ... τὸ δουλικὸν γένος οὐ δεῖ ἀπογινώσκειν, κἂν εἰς ἐσχάτην ἐλάσῃ κακίαν.

97. *Hom. 1 Tim.* 16.2 (PG 62.588.52–58): Καὶ τί τοῦτο πρὸς τὸν ἐπίσκοπον; Καὶ πάνυ, ἵνα παραινῇ, ἵνα καὶ τούτους διδάσκῃ ... τρόπους ὑποταγῆς ὑποδεικνύντα, καὶ πολὺν αὐτῶν ποιούμενον λόγον. It must be noted here that the Field text (F6.142) omits the teaching of obedience (ἵνα καὶ τούτους διδάσκῃ ... τρόπους ὑποταγῆς ὑποδεικνύντα), but does include the bishop in the exhortation of slaves along with their masters.

98. *Hom. Eph.* 22.2 (F4.335).

While elaborating on the story of the jailor who had his whole family baptized in Acts 16:29–31, Chrysostom complains: "Yes, not like most men these days, who allow both slaves and wives and children to go unbaptized!"[99] From the earliest days of Christianity, slaves were included in the rite of baptism as catechumens. The baptismal formula of Galatians 3:28 supports this practice.[100] Chrysostom explains that if a slave wishes to join the army, "he is rejected"; and he continues: "The king of heaven does not regard status, but accepts slaves into his army."[101] When slaves are taught virtue they are endowed with a new type of masculinity and thereby become soldiers of Christ.[102] The traditional Roman precepts of masculinity no longer apply. We know this was, of course, very limited for slaves. They could still not join the army officially,[103] although some slaves did desert to non-Roman bands and armies.[104] Nor could slaves become clergy, although they could serve in influential political offices, like Eutropius, who was a freedman and eunuch. The same type of rhetoric is used in the discussion of martyrdom and asceticism—both are often described in terms of the contest (*agōn*). While slaves were excluded from participating in earthly games, the heavenly *agōn* was open to anyone regardless of status.[105] Since Paul did not hesitate to teach Onesimus, who "enjoyed the benefit of his teaching," Chrysostom adds, "he there also received baptism." Chrysostom also explains why he says this: "For that he obtained there

99. *Hom. Eph.* 8.2 (F4.185): ἀλλ' οὐχ ὡς νῦν οἱ πλείους περιορῶσι καὶ δούλους καὶ γυναῖκας καὶ παῖδας ἀμυήτους τυγχάνοντας. Some concessions were made for slaves whose masters forbade baptism—the ninth canon of Hippolytus states that such slaves will not be excluded posthumously from the gift of salvation; see Everett Ferguson, *Baptism in the Early Church: History, Theology, and Liturgy in the First Five Centuries* (Grand Rapids, MI: Eerdmans, 2009), 466. The church did not, however, force masters to baptize their slaves.

100. Pauline N. Hogan, *No Longer Male and Female: Interpreting Galatians 3:28 in Early Christianity*, Library of New Testament Studies (London: T&T Clark, 2008), 21–46, 122–64.

101. *Catech. illum.* 2.3 (PG 49.236.18–20): ἂν γὰρ δοῦλός τις ᾖ, ἐκβάλλεται· ὁ δὲ τῶν οὐρανῶν βασιλεὺς οὐδὲν τοιοῦτον ἐπιζητεῖ, ἀλλὰ καὶ δούλους δέχεται εἰς τὸ αὐτοῦ στρατόπεδον

102. Kuefler, *Manly Eunuch*, 105–24.

103. See *CTh.* 7.13.8 (29.1.380); see John W. G. H. Liebeschuetz, *Barbarians and Bishops: Army, Church, and State in the Age of Arcadius and Chrysostom* (Oxford: Clarendon Press, 1990), 26. For a discussion of slaves belonging to soldiers, as well as the involvement of slaves and freedmen in the army (although focusing on an earlier period, and especially looking at funerary inscriptions), see Natalie B. Kampen, "Slaves and *Liberti* in the Roman Army," in *Roman Slavery and Roman Material Culture*, ed. Michele George (Toronto: University of Toronto Press, 2013), 180–98.

104. See Bellen, *Studien zur Sklavenflucht*; Liebeschuetz, *Barbarians and Bishops*, 38, 61, 76–77; Grunewald, *Bandits in the Roman Empire*, 10–11.

105. *Macc.* 1.4 (PG 50.619.35–49); see Wendy Mayer, trans., *The Cult of the Saints*, Popular Patristics Series (Crestwood, NY: St. Vladimir's Seminary Press, 2006), 139. For a study of how the motifs of the contest (*agōn*) and endurance (*hypomonē*) were incorporated into Christian thought, especially martyrdom, see Ceslas Spicq, "Ὑπομονή, Patientia," *Revue des Sciences Philologiques* 19 (1930): 95–106; Brent D. Shaw, "Body/Power/Identity: Passions of the Martyrs," *Journal of Early Christian Studies* 4, no. 3 (1996): 269–312.

the gift of baptism is manifest from his saying, *whom I have begotten in my bonds* [Philem. 10]."[106] Once again Paul's treatment of Onesimus serves as an example of how masters should treat their slaves.

Finally, as we saw in chapter 3, slaves were included in the household rituals of prayer, scripture reading, and so on. In the case of slaves, as with young boys, scriptural pedagogy was linked to the teaching of virtue.[107] The teaching of eschatological doctrines like judgment, reward, punishment, and the resurrection had the ability to reform slaves through fear. Chrysostom's focus here is preaching (*kērygma*)—slaves are reformed through the power of preaching. It is the preaching of the faith that habitualizes slaves, making them docile, obedient, and complacent. The extent to which slave women were present in Chrysostom's church services is difficult to determine, but some may have attended with their mistresses, especially since they were expected to be virtuous and display modesty. Hence the importance of including slaves in Christian rituals and bringing them to church to hear the sermon. Preaching played a major role in supporting slavery with its call for obedience from slaves. The influence of preaching should not be underestimated especially in its capacity for habitualization.[108] Aretagogy, as a subset of preaching, was also a direct assault against any sin that might be present in the life of the slave—it was directed against pleasures.

SURVEILLANCE AND THE CHRISTIC PANOPTICON

The surveillance, discipline, and aretagogy of slaves went hand in hand. In Michel Foucault's *Discipline and Punish,* the French word used to refer to discipline is *surveiller,*[109] illustrating the conceptual overlap of discipline and surveillance. A slaveholding culture is inevitably a discipline-intensive surveillance culture. The purpose of this surveillance was to ensure optimal labor and productivity, as well as to monitor behavior—surveillance represented the gaze of the kyriarchal machine.[110] In ancient treatises on household and agricultural management, like

106. *Hom. Phlm.* arg. (F6.326): ἀπολαύσας τῆς παρ' αὐτοῦ διδασκαλίας, καὶ τοῦ βαπτίσματος ἔτυχεν ἐκεῖ. "Ὅτι γὰρ ἐκεῖ ἔτυχε τῆς τοῦ βαπτίσματος δωρεᾶς, δῆλον ἐκ τοῦ εἰπεῖν· "Ὃν ἐγέννησα ἐν τοῖς δεσμοῖς μου.

107. *Hom. Tit.* 4.1 (F6.298–99).

108. Jaclyn L. Maxwell, *Christianization and Communication in Late Antiquity: John Chrysostom and His Congregation in Antioch* (New York: Cambridge University Press, 2009), 144–68.

109. This was Foucault's own choice, as indicated by the English translator of the work; Michel Foucault, *Discipline & Punish: The Birth of the Prison,* trans. Alan Sheridan (New York: Vintage, 1977), translator's note. It is also in this work that Foucault utilized Bentham's notion of the panopticon to explain the disciplinary gaze one finds in institutions of power. The notion of panopticism, as Foucault utilized it, is also central to this section of the chapter.

110. Stefano Fenoaltea, "Slavery and Supervision in Comparative Perspective: A Model," *Journal of Economic History* 44, no. 3 (1984): 635–68.

those of Xenophon, pseudo-Aristotle, Cato, Varro, and Columella, we see that the surveillance of slaves had developed into a fine-tuned art. Xenophon believed in the surveillance and regulation of slaves in order to avoid laziness, unauthorized breeding, and theft;[111] pseudo-Aristotle emphasized the minute and precise surveillance of slaves. "Accordingly we must keep watch over our workers, suiting our dispensations and indulgences to their desert," he notes, "whether it be food or clothing, leisure or chastisement that we are apportioning."[112] Surveillance was also a means of care—it ensured that slaves always had proper provisions. In the agricultural context, both Cato and Varro had very specific directions for the *vilicus* regarding the monitoring of slaves. The *vilicus* had to make sure that slaves worked and were healthy, and that their needs were addressed.[113] However, it is Columella who makes clear how immensely important proper surveillance of slaves was. Columella was inherently suspicious of *vilici*,[114] and he advised landowners to visit their estates more frequently and conduct their own surveillance.[115] The *diligens dominus* should make surprise visits to his estate to ensure that all was well and that the villa was productive.[116] We also find an emphasis on surveillance in the New Testament, where God now monitors slaves alongside the slaveholder, demonstrating the centrality of surveillance even in a religious movement claiming to see no difference between slave and free.

All these surveillance strategies were common in Chrysostom's time, both in households and on agricultural estates.[117] Surveillance of new slaves was especially important. "A new slave is not entrusted with anything in a house," Chrysostom says, "till he has given proof of his character, having undergone many trials."[118] This period of probation was known as the examination or scrutiny (*dokimasia*). Surveillance therefore ensured that slaves behaved well and worked hard. "If a slave fights, it is not when his master sees him," Chrysostom says. "If he speaks arrogantly, it is not when his master hears him."[119] In practice it was the mistress, the *despoina* (or *kyria*; Latin *domina*), who probably conducted most of the

---

111. Xenophon, *Mem.* 2.1.9 (Marchant 86–87); *Oec.* 9.5, 21.10–11 (Marchant 440–41, 524–25).

112. *Oec.* 1344b1 (Armstrong 336–37).

113. See Cato, *Agr.* 2.1–4, 5.1–3 (Hooper 1–11); Varro, *Rust.* 1.17.4–7 (Hooper and Ash 226–27); see Jesper Carlsen, *Vilici and Roman Estate Managers until AD 284* (Rome: L'Erma di Bretschneider, 1995), 57–124; Ulrike Roth, *Thinking Tools: Agricultural Slavery between Evidence and Models,* Bulletin of the Institute of Classical Studies Supplement (London: Institute of Classical Studies, School of Advanced Study, University of London, 2007).

114. *Rust.* 1.arg.3, 1.1.20–2.1 (Ash 4–5, 38–39).

115. *Rust.* 1.arg.3, 1.8.16–19 (Ash 92–95).

116. *Rust.* 1.arg.3, 1.8.16–18 (Ash 92–95).

117. Harper, *Slavery in the Late Roman World,* 242–46.

118. *Hom. 1 Tim.* 11.1 (F6.85): εἰς μὲν οἰκίαν νεώνητον οἰκέτην μὴ πρότερον ἐγχειρίζεσθαί τι τῶν ἔνδον, πρὶν ἂν διὰ πολλῆς τῆς πείρας τῆς αὐτοῦ γνώμης πολλὰ τεκμήρια δῷ.

119. *Hom. 1 Tim.* 11.1 16.2 (F6.145): κἂν τύπτῃ, μὴ ὁρῶντος τοῦ δεσπότου, κἂν ὑβρίζῃ, μὴ ἀκούοντος.

surveillance, since she often had to practically enforce mastery, *despoteia,* in the household. Chrysostom carefully describes the well-ordered household under the watchful gaze of the *despoina:* "The mistress of the house is seated on her chair with all comeliness, and the slave women weave silently, and each of the domestics has his appointed task in hand."[120] This is a typical image of the Roman household, with the watchful mistress, the silent spinsters, and the obedient slaves. Chrysostom believed outsiders closely monitored Christian slaves, and they had to behave in a way that would not dishonor the household or church. Slaves had to be monitored by their owners as a matter of precaution.

But in Christian thinking in general, and in Chrysostom in particular, we witness a unique development regarding the surveillance of slaves—namely, the notion of the Christic panopticon, or divine surveillance. Divine surveillance assumes the heteronomy of the body. Since all bodies are made to be ruled, all bodies are under surveillance. In the household codes of the New Testament, pseudo-Paul advises slaves not to work in order to be seen by their masters, but because the heavenly slaveholder is watching them. In Ephesians 6:5-7 we read that slaves should obey their masters "with a sincere heart, as you would Christ, not by the way of eye-service, as people-pleasers, but as slaves of Christ, doing the will of God from the soul."[121] The parallel verse in Colossians 3:22 is practically identical. Christic panopticism presumes that whatever a person does, Christ will be watching. Since Christ is the heavenly slaveholder, it is only natural that he monitors his slaves. Chrysostom elaborates thus: "Make, Paul says, your service, which is required by the law, come from the fear of Christ. Since, when your master does not see you, and if you perform your duty and what is necessary for his honor, it is clear that you do it because of the sleepless eye."[122] This notion of divine surveillance is applied to both slaves and their masters, although the bulk of the advice is reserved for slaves; Chrysostom also states that the service of slaves is required by law, thereby justifying it. Yet divine surveillance is still surveillance, and the usual goals of surveillance apply—to optimize labor, increase obedience and loyalty, and promote virtuous behavior. Shadi Bartsch has shown the prevalence of panopticism in Roman "scopic paradigms," noting that "the Roman gaze is generative as well as repressive; it produces behaviors that conform to definitions of *virtus* and in doing so contributes to the entire Roman machinery of

120. *Hom. 1 Cor.* 36.8 (F2.459): καὶ γὰρ ἡ κυρία τῆς οἰκίας ἐπὶ τοῦ θρόνου κάθηται μετὰ εὐσχημοσύνης ἁπάσης, καὶ αἱ θεραπαινίδες μετὰ τῆς ἡσυχίας ὑφαίνουσι, καὶ τῶν οἰκετῶν ἕκαστος τὸ ἐπιταχθὲν μετὰ χεῖρας ἔχει.
121. NA28: ἐν ἁπλότητι τῆς καρδίας ὑμῶν ὡς τῷ Χριστῷ, μὴ κατ᾽ ὀφθαλμοδουλίαν ὡς ἀνθρωπάρεσκοι ἀλλ᾽ ὡς δοῦλοι Χριστοῦ ποιοῦντες τὸ θέλημα τοῦ θεοῦ ἐκ ψυχῆς,
122. *Hom. Col.* 10.1 (F5.277): Ποίησον, φησί, τὴν ἀπὸ τοῦ νόμου δουλείαν ἀπὸ τοῦ φόβου γίνεσθαι τοῦ Χριστοῦ. Κἂν γὰρ μὴ ὁρῶντος ἐκείνου πράττῃς τὰ δέοντα καὶ τὰ πρὸς τιμὴν τοῦ δεσπότου, δηλονότι διὰ τὸν ἀκοίμητον ὀφθαλμὸν ποιεῖς.

literary and philosophical self-shaping."[123] The disciplinary technology of panopticism, in doulological terms, meant that a slave should imagine Christ or Epicurus or Cato as a type of *censor*, monitoring him, and thus behave as would be pleasing to the *censor*. Cicero saw the office of the *censor* as one that guarded the *pudor* of the citizens.[124]

The Christic panopticon has two important effects. First, it interiorizes surveillance. Since Christ is watching, slaves need to watch themselves and how they serve. The interiorization of surveillance is especially evident in the phrases "sincerity of heart" (*en haplotēti tēs kardias*) and "doing God's will from the soul" (*poiountes to thelēma tou theou ek psychēs*) found in Ephesians 6:5–7. This psychic disposition will ensure loyalty and obedience. "Many slaves in numerous instances surreptitiously maltreat their masters," Chrysostom explains, but "this maltreatment Paul expels" when using this interiorizing terminology.[125] "He wants to have them freed not only from hypocrisy, but also from laziness," Chrysostom notes.[126] The interiorization of surveillance, in Chrysostom's view, will result in greater productivity. It also helps ensure that the subjectivity of the slave is consistent—the slave behaves appropriately whether under physical surveillance or not. "For that is not singleness, but hypocrisy, to hold one thing, and act another," Chrysostom says, "to appear one way when the master is present, but another when he is absent."[127] The interiorization of surveillance therefore ensures behavioral stability and integrity, and fights hypocrisy. It is of course based on the stereotype that slaves are hypocritical and prone to laziness and other vices when they are not watched. This obsession with surveillance also reveals the paranoia of kyriarchy, where the hold of power on the slave body is so great that its surveillance becomes universal, total, and permanent. Interiorized surveillance is also where the issue of corporeal heteronomy again surfaces, yet here the very real consequences of corporeal heteronomy are clear.

The second effect of the Christic panopticon is the devaluation of external surveillance. Surveillance by Christ gains priority over surveillance by human slaveholders. In noting this devaluation Chrysostom refers to "eye-service" or "slavery to the eyes" (*ophthalmodoulia*), as well as to "people-pleasers" (*anthrōpareskoi*). The eyes of people are superseded "by the sleepless eye" (*dia ton*

---

123. Shadi Bartsch, *The Mirror of the Self: Sexuality, Self-Knowledge, and the Gaze in the Early Roman Empire* (Chicago: University of Chicago Press, 2006), 136; see also 115–82. I also thank J. Albert Harrill for his insights on slavery and the gaze, which he shared in conversation.

124. Bartsch, *Mirror of the Self*, 136.

125. *Hom. Eph.* 22.1 (F4.331–32): λανθάνουσι γὰρ πολλοὶ πολλὰ περὶ τοὺς δεσπότας κακουργοῦντες τοὺς αὐτῶν. Καὶ ταύτῃ ἀναιρεῖ τὴν κακουργίαν.

126. *Hom. Col.* 10.1 (F5.277): Οὐ μόνον ὑποκρίσεως, ἀλλὰ καὶ ἀργίας αὐτοὺς ἀπηλλάχθαι βούλεται.

127. *Hom. Col.* 10.1 (F5.277): Ἐκεῖνο γὰρ οὐχ ἁπλότης, ἀλλ᾿ ὑπόκρισις, ἕτερον ἔχειν καὶ ἕτερον ποιεῖν· ἄλλον μὲν παρόντος φαίνεσθαι τοῦ δεσπότου, ἄλλον δὲ ἀπόντος.

akoimēton ophthalmon) of Christ. The devaluation of external surveillance also implies that the slave gets a measure of freedom (*eleutheria*) and agency (*proairesis*). "He has made them free instead of being slaves, when they do not need the dominion of their master," Chrysostom explains, "for the expression *from the soul* means, with good intentions, not with a slavish necessity, but with freedom and choice."[128] According to Chrysostom, Christic panopticism thus relativizes and even negates the state of slavery. The fear of Christ replaces any fear of human masters.

What are the implications of Christic panopticism for the dynamics of kyriarchy? At first sight Christic panopticism seems to work against kyriarchy;[129] however, this is simply not the case. Like the metaphorization of slavery, Christic panopticism intensifies the power of kyriarchy and the carcerality of slavery. In absorbing the divine and the spiritual, kyriarchal power is expanded. The slaveholder is simply removed from his reclining couch and placed on the throne of Christ, and even assumes his divine identity. And although Chrysostom sees this move as giving the slave agency, the Christic panopticon and the interiorization of surveillance rob the slave of the last strand of agency he or she may have had in psychological or spiritual terms, increasing the slave's carceral state and creating a powerful spiritual carcerality with no means of escape. The forces of kyriarchy also colonize the psychic and spiritual life of the slave. This occurs under the guise of pastoralism and pastoral guidance based on authoritative scriptures; after all, the primary duty of the shepherd is to keep watch.[130] And the devaluation of external surveillance is only professed; in reality, external surveillance is intensified when slaves are convinced that Christ is watching them. This development yields greater benefits for slaveholders than for slaves, despite the fact that Christ also watches masters. Hence Christic supervision and human supervision have the same purpose—to increase productivity and ensure good behavior. And the Christic panopticon turns out to be one of the most pervasive, oppressive, and intrusive strategies of kyriarchal power yet.

Furthermore, the Christic panopticon compels the slave to perform a measure of self-examination. There is now a shift from the kyriarchal technology of surveillance to *examination*—this shift signals the return and intensification of *dokimasia*. The slave now needs to examine him- or herself in order to behave like the ideal slave and to become (it is indeed a becoming, a subjectivation) both the ideal

---

128. *Hom. Col.* 10.1 (F5.278): Ἐλευθέρους αὐτοὺς ἐποίησεν ἀντὶ δούλων, ὅταν μὴ δέωνται τῆς τῶν δεσποτῶν ἐπιστασίας· τὸ γὰρ, "ἐκ ψυχῆς," τοῦτό ἐστι, τὸ μετ᾽ εὐνοίας, μὴ μετὰ δουλικῆς ἀνάγκης, ἀλλὰ μετ᾽ ἐλευθερίας καὶ προαιρέσεως.

129. This seems to be the view of Ford, *Women and Men in the Early Church*, 153–61.

130. Michel Foucault, *Security, Territory, Population: Lectures at the Collège de France, 1977–1978*, ed. Michel Senellart, François Ewald, Alessandro Fontana, and Arnold I. I. Davidson, trans. Graham Burchell (New York: Palgrave Macmillan, 2009), 115–90.

slave and the ideal master. The gaze of Christ and the slaveholder becomes aligned with the interior gaze of the slave. By means of this self-examination, the slave becomes his or her own slaveholder, and the enslaved body dominates itself—all borders between physical and moral slavery fade, and *psychē* becomes *despotēs* and *censor* in the fullest sense. This alignment of dominating and dominated motions in the body of the slave, the kyriarchal eclipse, is the pinnacle of kyriarchal power.

Finally, slaves were not only the objects of surveillance; they were also the eyes and ears of patriarchy and kyriarchy. Slaves in the ancient household mostly lived within the physical confines of its walls. It was an exception, mostly limited to large agricultural estates or illustrious homes, for slaves to live in large slave barracks.[131] In some cases slaves also lived in smaller buildings, like stalls and barns outside of the home,[132] or in cellars.[133] Some ancient houses may have had specific rooms for slaves, since objects like chains have been found in certain rooms.[134] In most cases, however, slaves probably slept throughout the house, wherever there was space.[135] Slaves had to guard the doors of the house and introduce visitors.[136] This is a significant point, stressed by Paul Veyne in his work on private life in antiquity. Veyne observes: "Remember that these people had slaves constantly at their beck and call and were never alone. They were not allowed to dress themselves or put on their own shoes. . . . The omnipresence of slaves was tantamount to constant surveillance."[137] Even bedroom privacy was rare—slaves often slept very close to the bed of the mistress, and always at the door of the bedchamber as guards.[138] Martial naughtily tells of the slaves masturbating at the bedchamber door when Hector and Andromache had sex.[139] Slaves are often depicted in scenes of Roman lovemak-

---

131. Michele George, "Slavery and Roman Material Culture," in Bradley and Cartledge, *Cambridge World History of Slavery*, 1:386–88.

132. See *Virg.* 70.2.19–30 (SC 125.346); *Hom. Act.* 45.4 (PG 60.319.52–53); *Hom. 1 Tim.* 16.2 (F6.142–43); for a general discussion of the slave in domestic places, see Michele George, "*Servus* and *Domus*: The Slave in the Roman House," in *Domestic Space in the Roman World: Pompeii and Beyond*, ed. Ray Laurence and Andrew Wallace-Hadrill, Journal of Roman Archaeology Supplementary Series 22 (Portsmouth, RI: JRA, 1997), 15–24.

133. Patrizia Basso, "Gli alloggi servili," in *Subterraneae domus: Ambienti residenziale di servizio nell'edilizia privata romana*, ed. Patrizia Basso and Francesca Ghedini, Sottosuolo nel mondo antico 4 (Verona: Cierre, 2003), 443–63.

134. Ibid., 455; Jonathan Edmondson, "Slavery and the Roman Family," in Bradley and Cartledge, *Cambridge World History of Slavery*, 1:346.

135. Edmondson, "Slavery and the Roman Family," 346–47.

136. *Ex. Ps.* 4.2 (PG 55.42.35–37).

137. Paul Veyne, *A History of Private Life*, vol. 1, *From Pagan Rome to Byzantium*, ed. Paul Veyne, trans. Arthur Goldhammer (Cambridge, MA: Belknap Press of Harvard University Press, 2000), 72–73.

138. Edmondson, "Slavery and the Roman Family," 346.

139. Martial, *Epig.* 11.104 (Bailey 84–85); see Stephen Hinds, *Allusion and Intertext: Dynamics of Appropriation in Roman Poetry* (New York: Cambridge University Press, 1998), 133–134.

ing.[140] When household members, especially women and young men went out, as we often hear from Chrysostom, they always had slaves with them.

Slaves were also monitored by other slaves, especially the *vilicus* or head slave of the household. The constant voyeurism of eavesdropping slaves (*oricularii servi*) was a main source of information for the outside world.[141] Slaves became the eyes of the outside world, taking part in the intense surveillance within ancient households and offering a window into life there.[142] Chrysostom himself says that he could get information about a household by asking the slaves.[143] All household members were under surveillance. Nurses and other female slaves watched over infants and young girls,[144] and pedagogues had to constantly accompany young boys.[145] Slaves represented a mobile carcerality for female and child members of elite households. Just as the *despoina* watched the slaves, the slaves had to watch the *despoina*. Slaves represented the patriarchal gaze. Chrysostom describes the troubles a married woman might experience as a result of surveillance:

> There are constant threats, gross insults, abuse—whether from a husband hurt without reason or from coarse servants—surveillance and spying. All is full of trembling and fear. For not only are her comings and goings the objects of curiosity, even her words and glances are carefully scrutinized. She must be more quiet than a stone and endure everything in silence, confined to her apartment no better than a prisoner. Or if she desires to speak and to sigh and to go out, she must supply a reason for everything, and give account to those corrupt judges, I mean the servants and group of domestics. . . . Who among the domestics will dare spy on his master and not immediately be thrown into the pit? So she will not be able to console herself with these devices, or in fact vent her anger through words.[146]

140. Patricia Clark, "Women, Slaves, and the Hierarchies of Domestic Violence: The Family of St. Augustine," in *Women and Slaves in Greco-Roman Culture: Differential Equations,* ed. Sandra R. Joshel and Sheila Murnaghan (New York: Routledge, 1998), 109–29; Edmondson, "Slavery and the Roman Family," 346.

141. Edmondson, "Slavery and the Roman Family," 346.

142. For more on the surveillance of the ancient Roman household, see Kate Cooper, "Closely Watched Households: Visibility, Exposure and Private Power in the Roman Domus," *Past & Present* 197, no. 1 (2007): 3–33.

143. *Serm. Gen.* 7.1 (PG 54.608.14–16).

144. *Sacr.* 3.13.1–19 (SC 272.210–12).

145. See chapter 4.

146. *Virg.* 52.5.76–87 (SC 125.294), 52.7.101–5 (SC 125.296): Ἀπειλαὶ καὶ ὕβρεις καὶ λοιδορίαι διὰ παντός—αἱ μὲν παρὰ τοῦ τετρωμένου μάτην ἀνδρός, αἱ δὲ παρὰ τῶν μιαρῶν θεραπόντων—φυλακαί, προφυλακαί, καὶ ἅπαντα δέους καὶ τρόμου μεστά. Οὐ γὰρ εἴσοδοι καὶ ἔξοδοι πολυπραγμονοῦνται μόνον ἀλλὰ καὶ ῥήματα καὶ βλέμματα καὶ στεναγμὸς μετὰ πολλῆς βασανίζεται τῆς ἀκριβείας καὶ ἀνάγκη ἢ τῶν λίθων ἀκινητοτέραν εἶναι καὶ σιγῇ πάντα φέρειν καὶ τῷ θαλάμῳ προσηλῶσθαι διαπαντὸς δεσμώτου χεῖρον. Ἢ βουλομένην φθέγγεσθαι καὶ στένειν καὶ ἐξιέναι πάντων εὐθύνας ὑπέχειν καὶ λόγον ἐν τοῖς διεφθαρμένοις ἐκείνοις δικασταῖς, ταῖς θεραπαινίσι λέγω καὶ τῷ πλήθει τῶν οἰκετῶν. . . . Τίς δὲ τὸν δεσπότην τολμήσει παρατηρεῖσθαι τῶν οἰκετῶν καὶ οὐκ εὐθέως ἐπὶ τὸ

Although Chrysostom paints this sad picture with his usual broad rhetorical brushstrokes, it provides some idea of the intense "surveillance and spying" (*phylakai, prophylakai*) that occurred in some households. Spying on the *despotēs* might be dangerous for slaves (and yet it still happened),[147] but it was expected of them to monitor the *despoina* of the house. Chrysostom portrays slaves as channels of domestic information to both the *paterfamilias* and the outside world (including the bishop). He even states that some slaves get involved in the quarrels of married couples, and then make up stories to exacerbate the argument.[148] Again such descriptions presume the delinquency of slaves in general, especially with regard to gossip. Nevertheless, because of their involvement in household affairs, some slaves probably served as channels of information.

One may speculate about whether slaves used their knowledge of household affairs to show some resistance to their slaveholders. For his part, Chrysostom does think that slaves used gossip as a means of resistance. Chrysostom notes that "the mistreated servant in circumstances such as these, since he has no other way of wreaking vengeance on the one who abuses him, does so by his tongue, by secret accusations." Yet he qualifies this statement by remarking that it "is natural for a servant so insulted who has this comfort alone, his own evil words, against the person who harasses him."[149] The problem with this type of sporadic resistance, or rebelliousness, as Keith Bradley has rightly noted, is that it was not part of a sustainable program of radical social restructuring—it was not organized resistance—making Roman slave resistance and its effects difficult to verify empirically.[150]

To return briefly to the passage above, the carcerality of the mistress of the household is emphasized in Chrysostom's characterization of her as a prisoner (*desmōtēs*) in her own home. A married woman was not, of course, confined to the house alone. However, Chrysostom considers nondomestic public spaces male

---

βάραθρον ἀπαχθήσεται; Οὔτε οὖν τούτοις δυνήσεται ἑαυτὴν παραμυθήσασθαι τοῖς μηχανήμασιν οὔτε γοῦν τὴν ὀργὴν διὰ τῶν ῥημάτων ἐξενεγκεῖν. Translation: Sally R. Shore, *Chrysostom: On Virginity; Against Remarriage* (Lewiston, NY: Edwin Mellen Press, 1983), 83–84.

147. Slaves were at times tortured for information about their masters, and this was the only type of testimony from slaves that was legally valid; see *Hom. Eph.* 16.1 (F4.264); *Iter. conj.* 271–79 (SC 138.184); Peter A. Brunt, "Evidence Given under Torture in the Principate," *Zeitschrift der Savigny-Stiftung für Rechtsgeschichte* 97 (1980): 256–65; Keith R. Bradley, *Slavery and Society at Rome* (New York: Cambridge University Press, 1994), 165–70; Edmondson, "Slavery and the Roman Family," 346.

148. *Virg.* 52.4.57–70 (SC 125.292); see also *Iter. conj.* 271–79 (SC 138.184).

149. *Subintr.* 10.16–24 (Dumortier 79–80): οἰκέτης γὰρ ὑβρισθεὶς, καὶ ὑπὲρ τοιούτων πραγμάτων, ἐπεὶ μηδενὶ τρόπῳ τὸν ὑβρικότα ἀμύνασθαι ἔχει, διὰ τῆς γλώττης τοῦτο ποιεῖ καὶ τῆς λαθραίας κατηγορίας ... μεθ' ὅσης εἰκὸς οἰκέτην ὄντα, καὶ τοιαῦτα ὑβρισμένον, καὶ ταύτην ἔχοντα μόνην παραμυθίαν τῶν οἰκείων κακῶν κατὰ τοῦ λελυπηκότος. Translation: Clark, *Jerome, Chrysostom, and Friends*, 193.

150. Bradley, *Slavery and Society*, 128–31.

spaces.[151] As we saw in chapter 3, the appearance of women in public was a source of great anxiety for Chrysostom, especially if it was accompanied by a display of wealth and power.[152] A woman could appear in public, but not with too many slaves, only one or two. Her mode of surveillance was anoptic, but the carceral gaze of slave eyes was never absent. Again the pervasiveness of kyriarchy is exposed; it seizes and controls the slave body in manifold ways. It dominates it, but also uses it to dominate others. The slave body is both the object of the kyriarchal gaze, but also a crucial and extended apparatus of that gaze. It is in this sense that the pastoralized household was both an observatory and a reformatory.

"WE ARE OF THE BOUND, NOT THE BINDERS": REWARD AND PUNISHMENT

"But, you say, the whole race of slaves becomes intolerable when it is treated with leniency. Yes, I know this myself," Chrysostom remarks.[153] Chrysostom believed that slaves required strict discipline and regulation, and that punishment was an important part of teaching them virtue. The fear of punishment was an incentive to act virtuously, while the act of punishment was supposed to make the slave body docile and more receptive to future correction. Reward functioned with the same purpose in mind, although it was written in a different but not necessarily less oppressive way onto the slave body. In some cases the difference between reward and punishment was clear. A good slave perhaps received a better ration of food or some wine,[154] or clothing,[155] or was allowed to have sex.[156] A reward might simply be the opportunity to enjoy basic necessities. Chrysostom notes, for instance, that a mistress might deprive her slave girl of food until her work was finished (apparently, pedagogues did the same to their pupils).[157] Slaves generally had a very poor diet. Some ate only bread, Chrysostom tells us.[158] Thus having better-quality food or wine would have been very appealing, and a reward, for a slave.[159]

---

151. *Virg.* 73.1.17–23 (SC 125.350).

152. *Hom. Heb.* 28.4–5 (F7.320–21).

153. *Hom. Eph.* 15.2 (F.4.259): Ἀλλ' ἀφόρητον, φησὶν, ἀνέσεως τυχὸν τὸ δουλικὸν γένος. Οἶδα κἀγώ·

154. See pseudo-Aristotle, *Oec.* 1344a35–1344b12 (Armstrong 336–37).

155. See Cato, *Agr.* 5.1–3, 59 (Hooper 12–15, 72–73); Lactantius, *Ir.* 5.12 (SC 289.108); see Harper, *Slavery in the Late Roman World,* 124.

156. See Xenophon, *Oec.* 9.5 (Marchant 440–41); Jerome, *Ep.* 79.8 (PL 30.730); see Harper, *Slavery in the Late Roman World,* 336.

157. *Stat.* 14.4 (PG 49.145.11–15).

158. *Hom. 1 Tim.* 16.2 (F6.141–43).

159. Regulating the diet of slaves, especially whether it was permitted for them to have some wine, was a contested matter in Roman antiquity. Food, at least, was a more common reward for obedient slaves; see pseudo-Aristotle, *Oec.* 1344a35 (Armstrong 336–37); Cato, *Agr.* 5.1–3 (Hooper 12–15); Varro,

Slaves were expected to be grateful for such treatment, while masters were not expected to show any gratitude to slaves. Chrysostom notes the common practice that masters do not give thanks to their slaves: "Do we return thanks to our slaves for serving us? Certainly not."[160] With this example he shows how good God is toward his slaves, since God thanks his slaves by showing them mercy and blessing. Chrysostom then points out, while referring to Christ the slaveholder, that it "is the glory of a master, to have grateful slaves," and adds that it is also "the glory of a master, that he should thus love his slaves."[161] Masters do not thank their slaves, but slaves should thank their masters for "loving" them and taking care of them— the paternalism is again very clear, and aims to cast the owner in a good and caring light. Yet, what we need to understand here is that punishment and reward operate within the same kyriarchal framework of behavioral control and manipulation, and they should not be seen as opposites but rather correlates. Both annex those subtly human characteristics of the slave body to coerce it into submission and action; reward and punishment differ in their deployment but are equally oppressive carceral mechanisms.

Chrysostom believed that disobedient slaves should be punished, and he justifies the reward and punishment of slaves in a theological manner. Since God punishes and rewards his slaves, so should people on earth punish their slaves.[162] Punishment is, in fact, a sign of goodness and care, while not punishing is cruel to the disobedient slave. By means of punishment, God stops the good from becoming bad. Punishment of slaves was a Christian duty. Chrysostom was in favor of slaves being punished when they deserved it, and he even justified the use of violence against slaves. It is the fear of punishment, however, that best ensures good behavior from slaves:

> They receive many insults from fear of us, and silently endure them with the patience of philosophers. They are subjected to our violence justly or unjustly, and they do not resist, but entreat us, even though they have often done nothing wrong. They are

---

Rust. 1.17.6–7 (Hooper and Ash 226–27); Philodemus, *Oec.* 9.26–44 (Tsouna 25–27); Libanius, *Decl.* 32.24 (Foerster 7.68); Theodoret, *Prov.* 7 (PG 83.677.15–680.30); Peter Garnsey, "Mass Diet and Nutrition in the City of Rome," in *Nourrir la plèbe: Actes du colloque tenu à Genèvre les 28 et 29. IX. 1989 en hommage à Denis van Berchem,* ed. Adalberto Giovannini (Basel: F. Reinhardt, 1991), 67–101; Bradley, *Slavery and Society,* 81–95; Phyllis P. Bober, *Art, Culture, and Cuisine: Ancient and Medieval Gastronomy* (Chicago: University of Chicago Press, 1999), 183; Sandra R. Joshel, *Slavery in the Roman World* (New York: Cambridge University Press, 2010), 131–32; Harper, *Slavery in the Late Roman World,* 237–38.

160. *Hom. Phlm.* 2.2 (PG 62.713.33–34): Μὴ χάριν ἴσμεν τοῖς οἰκέταις ἡμῶν διακονουμένοις ἡμῖν; Οὐδαμῶς. The Field text (F6.344) omits Οὐδαμῶς, and leaves the question open. The same answer is expected.

161. *Hom. Phlm.* 2.2 (F6.345): Καὶ γὰρ καὶ τοῦτο δόξα δεσπότου, τὸ οἰκέτας ἔχειν εὐγνώμονας· καὶ τοῦτο δόξα δεσπότου, τὸ οὕτω φιλεῖν αὐτὸν τοὺς δούλους.

162. For the theological justification of punishment, see *Hom. Tit.* 4.1 (F6.298); *Hom. Phlm.* 3.2 (F6.346–53); see also chapter 2; and for reward, see *Hom. Col.* 10.1 (F5.277–78).

satisfied to receive no more than they need and often less; with straw for their bed, and only bread for their food, they do not complain or murmur at their hard life, but because of their fear of us they are restrained from impatience. When they are entrusted with money, they return all of it. For I am not speaking of the bad slaves, but of those that are moderately good. If we threaten them, they are immediately humbled.[163]

In this passage, we find a description of the ideal character of the slave—a description of utter submission, with no resistance, only silence. Slaves should not resist, but display only an attitude of service and thankfulness. Fear is the defining characteristic of the relationship between the slave and slaveholder. The slaveholder can insult the slave, and the slave must passively endure the insults. The term *hybrizomai* is used, indicating the worst type of personal assault against one's dignity and status, often with connotations of violence.[164] Slaves are the subjects of violence, and Chrysostom says that just and unjust (*dikaiōs kai adikōs*) violence was applied to slaves. He justifies the use of violent punishment. It is what defined the slave body as such. Furthermore, administering moderate violence was a factor in affirming the masculinity of the slaveholder.[165]

Chrysostom also describes the living conditions of most slaves—they receive less than what they need, they sleep on straw on the ground, and eat only bread.

163. *Hom. 1 Tim.* 16.2 (F6.144): Ἐκεῖνοι διὰ τὸν φόβον τὸν ἡμέτερον ὑβρίζονται μυριάκις, καὶ παντὸς φιλοσόφου μᾶλλον ἐστήκασι σιγῶντες· ὑβρίζονται καὶ δικαίως καὶ ἀδίκως, καὶ οὐκ ἀντιλέγουσιν, ἀλλὰ παρακαλοῦσιν, ἀδικοῦντες οὐδὲν πολλάκις. Οὐδὲν πλέον τῆς χρείας λαμβάνοντες, πολλάκις δὲ καὶ ἔλαττον στέργουσι· καὶ ἐπὶ στιβάδος καθεύδοντες, καὶ ἄρτου μόνον πληρούμενοι, καὶ τὴν ἄλλην πᾶσαν δίαιταν ἔχοντες εὐτελῆ, οὐκ ἐγκαλοῦσιν, οὐδὲ δυσχεραίνουσιν ἐκεῖνοι διὰ τὸν παρ' ἡμῶν φόβον. Ἐμπιστευόμενοι χρήματα, πάντα ἀποδιδόασι· μὴ γάρ μοι τοὺς μοχθηροὺς εἴπῃς τῶν οἰκετῶν, ἀλλὰ τοὺς μὴ λίαν κακούς· ἂν ἀπειλήσωμεν, εὐθέως συστέλλονται.

164. See chapter 6 for a more detailed discussion of the use of *hybrizomai* and *hybris* in the discourse of slavery.

165. Violence played an important role in the fashioning of traditional Roman masculinity despite some Christian authors' adoption of an attitude of nonviolence. Violence was evident in many facets of daily life, whether beating one's slave, participating in military battles, enjoying the violence of the arena, or sports like wrestling; see Louis Swift, "St. Ambrose on Violence and War," *Transactions and Proceedings of the American Philological Association* 101 (1970): 533–43; Keith Hopkins, *Death and Renewal* (Cambridge: Cambridge University Press, 1983), 1–30; Michael Poliakoff, *Combat Sports in the Ancient World: Competition, Violence, and Culture* (New Haven, CT: Yale University Press, 1987); Joseph Joblin, *L'église et la guerre: Conscience, violence, pouvoir* (Paris: Desclée de Brouwer, 1988); Michael Gaddis, *There Is No Crime for Those Who Have Christ: Religious Violence in the Christian Roman Empire* (Berkeley: University of California Press, 2005), 151–250; Thomas Sizgorich, *Violence and Belief in Late Antiquity: Militant Devotion in Christianity and Islam*, Divinations: Rereading Late Ancient Religion (Philadelphia: University of Pennsylvania Press, 2009), 81–143; Hendrik F. Stander, "Violence in Chrysostom's Commentary on the Psalms," *Ekklesiastikos Pharos* 95 (2013): 258–65. For general remarks on the psychology of manliness and violence, see Robert Muchembled, *A History of Violence: From the End of the Middle Ages to the Present*, trans. Jean Birrell (Cambridge: Polity Press, 2012), 1–30.

They cannot complain, again because of fear. They are entrusted with their master's goods and have to manage them well. They live a life of constant threats and angst. Chrysostom shows only distanced pity and mediocre empathy for slaves here. He does not campaign for them as he does for the poor, and this seems strange, since the life of a slave and that of someone in extreme poverty could be quite similar. In his fight for the poor Chrysostom completely neglected the fate of slaves. This is perhaps because he believed that slaves were better off than the poor because of the care provided to them by their masters. We know, however, that slaves did not have easy lives, and during times of famine, it was slaves who died of hunger first.

"Thus, to discipline and punish ignorant slaves is a great accolade, and not a perchance commendation," Chrysostom exclaims, "when one can drive out wickedness using domestic violence against those who are the most evil."[166] The words discipline (*paideuō*) and punish (*sōphronizō*) are used explicitly here—the idea is to correct slaves, who are, like children, ignorant of virtue. The word for "punish" here, *sōphronizō*, is related to mastery as well as to teaching someone self-control and modesty (*sōphrosynē*), again showing how interrelated punishment and aretagogy are in Chrysostom's thought. We remember here the licentious slave girl who had to be taught *sōphrosynē* by means of violent correction and punishment. Thus, not only does Chrysostom allow for domestic violence (*dia tēs oikeias sphodrotētos*) against disobedient slaves, but he states that such punishment is commendable and a great accolade (*engkōmion megiston*) for the slaveholder. The best slaveholders, Chrysostom argues, are those who use punitive violence against disobedient slaves.

But while Chrysostom approves of punitive violence, he objects to unjust cruelty, excessive violence, and crimes committed against slaves. This is significant because slaves were not legal persons in their own right. Chrysostom warns slaveholders not to think "that what is done toward a slave, God will thus forgive, since it is done to a slave." Excessive and unjust violence against slaves is completely uncalled for, in Chrysostom's view. "Foreign laws indeed recognize a difference between these kinds of people," Chrysostom continues, "since they are the laws of human beings." He then juxtaposes non-Christian laws that exclude slaves from civil protection, with the laws of God, which consider all equal. "But the law of the common Lord and Master of all, which does good to all alike, and doling out the same privileges to all, knows no such difference,"[167] states Chrysostom, in a possible allusion to Galatians

166. *Hab. eun. spir.* 3.7 (PG 51.287.4–8): καθάπερ οἰκέτας ἀγνώμονας παιδεύειν καὶ σωφρονίζειν, ἀλλὰ καὶ ἐγκώμιον μέγιστον, καὶ οὐχ ὁ τυχὼν ἔπαινος, ὅτι τοὺς πρὸς τοσαύτην κατενεχθέντας κακίαν ἠδυνήθη διὰ τῆς οἰκείας σφοδρότητος ἀπαλλάξαι τῆς πονηρίας.

167. *Hom. Eph.* 22.1 (F4.333–34): Μὴ νομίσῃς, φησὶν, ὅτι τὰ εἰς τὸν δοῦλον, ὡς εἰς δοῦλον γινόμενα, οὕτως ἀφήσει. Οἱ μὲν γὰρ ἔξωθεν νόμοι διαφορὰν ἴσασι τούτων τῶν γενῶν, ἅτε ἀνθρώπων ὄντες νόμοι· ὁ δὲ νόμος ὁ τοῦ κοινοῦ Δεσπότου οὐδεμίαν οἶδε διαφοράν, ἅτε κοινῇ πάντας εὖ ποιῶν, καὶ πᾶσι τῶν αὐτῶν μεταδιδούς.

3:28. Furthermore, people who compel slaves to commit crimes are guilty of a double offense.[168] The call for just treatment of slaves is not unique to Christianity. Authors like Xenophon and the Roman agronomists promoted fair treatment of slaves to ensure good work and prevent possible revolts. John Fitzgerald has also shown how closely linked Stoic and early Christian views on the treatment of slaves were—both gave some informal protection to slaves and both condemned unjust punishment and cruelty.[169]

Unjust punishment was a common and important trope in early Christian rhetoric. The discourse of the slave who suffers unjustly is a central hermeneutical key to understanding early Christian subjectivity. Christ is depicted as the slave of God who suffers unjustly.[170] Thus when slaves are urged to endure unjust violence, they are being encouraged to be more like Christ—the endurance of unjust violence is a potent technology of Christomorphism. As Judith Perkins has noted, suffering was a crucial discourse in the construction of early Christian identity,[171] and the discourse of the slave who suffers unjustly was an important part of that more general discourse. Chrysostom states:

> For the one who suffers wrong in abundance claims an act for himself that he did not initiate, by allowing himself to be beaten on the other cheek as well, and not simply by enduring the first blow. For this last act may perhaps resemble cowardice, but it is in fact a mark of a high philosophy. In this way you will show that it was for the sake of wisdom that you also endured the first blow. And so in the case at hand, show here too that you bear slavery also willingly.[172]

Urging slaves to accept unjust suffering was, in fact, a very useful discourse that could help prevent revolt and resistance. Chrysostom urges slaves to accept violence willingly and not to pose any resistance—thus giving the slave agency. Furthermore, the promotion of suffering and submission reinforced the passive Christian virtues of endurance, patience, and pacifism. Chrysostom explicitly states here, as well as in *Homiliae in epistulam I ad Timotheum* 16.2, that to suffer

168. *Hom. Phlm.* 1.2 (F6.332).

169. John T. Fitzgerald, "The Stoics and the Early Christians on the Treatment of Slaves," in *Stoicism in Early Christianity*, ed. Tuomas Rasimus, Troels Engberg-Pedersen, and Ismo Dunderberg (Grand Rapids, MI: Baker Academic, 2010), 154–62. See also Keith R. Bradley, "Seneca and Slavery," *Classica et Medievalia* 37 (1986): 161–72; Garnsey, "Middle Stoics and Slavery."

170. This is a common theme in Phil. 2:1–11 and especially in 1 Pet. 2:13–25; see Chris L. de Wet, "The Discourse of the Suffering Slave in 1 Peter," *Ekklesiastikos Pharos* 95 (2013): 15–24.

171. Judith Perkins, *The Suffering Self: Pain and Narrative Representation in the Early Christian Era* (London: Routledge, 1995).

172. *Hom. Eph.* 22.1 (F4.332): Ὁ γὰρ ἐπιδαψιλευσάμενος τῷ παθεῖν κακῶς, καὶ ὅπερ οὐκ ἦν αὐτοῦ, ἐποίησεν ἑαυτοῦ τῷ ῥαπισθῆναι καὶ τὴν ἄλλην σιαγόνα, μὴ τῷ μόνον ἐνεγκεῖν. Τοῦτο μὲν γὰρ ἴσως δόξει καὶ φόβου εἶναι, ἐκεῖνο δὲ φιλοσοφίας πολλῆς. Καὶ ἔδειξας, ὅτι καὶ τοῦτο διὰ φιλοσοφίαν ἤνεγκας. Ὥστε καὶ νῦν δεῖξον τοῦτο, ὅτι καὶ ταύτην ἑκοντὶ φέρεις τὴν δουλείαν.

and endure violence passively is not a mark of cowardice, but a sign of the true philosophy—that is, Christian masculinity. When the passive virtues of suffering and endurance become the norm, slavery becomes acceptable, since the formerly subordinated mode of masculinity now becomes hegemonic. Bearing slavery "willingly" (hekonti)—receiving a second blow to the cheek—is a demonstration of agency, and Chrysostom shows that controlling one's actions and reactions— that is, one's passions—is not unmanly or cowardly, but a sign of true freedom and masculinity. Chrysostom is exceptionally Stoic in this regard. Of course, there is no real agency for the slave here, only violence.

Chrysostom also suggests that unjust suffering creates a kind of rewards account with God. He suggests the same about almsgiving.[173] Both almsgiving and suffering unjustly make God one's debtor. Thus the slave who suffers unjustly earns heavenly and spiritual capital. Chrysostom acknowledges that Christian slaves may suffer under non-Christian masters, but this is in fact a blessing, since it increases their eschatological reward with God: "For as they who receive a benefit, when they make no return, make God a debtor to their benefactors; so too, I say, do masters, if, when served well by you, they fail to repay you, repay you even more, by making God your debtor."[174]

In his argument regarding divine euergetism, Chrysostom also indirectly says that when earthly masters fail to reward slaves, they in fact increase their slaves' heavenly reward; this failure on the part of earthly masters compels God to reward slaves. Chrysostom's sociotheological manipulative strategies are very clear. Eschatologically speaking, God's judgment also then implies a correction of social inequalities and violence, and assumes that there will be compensation for unjust suffering. The suffering slave becomes the slave who will receive the greatest reward during the final judgment. Of course, the implication here is also that it is better not to be rewarded on earth, since the heavenly reward is better. Such an argument would not have made life any easier for slaves, but certainly had benefits for slaveholders and the well-being of kyriarchal structures. Punishment becomes the reward; the theology of a heavenly reward wrote its precepts on the body of the slave with the whip, the chain, and scripture.

But Chrysostom does not oppose "rightful" punitive violence. He lauds slaveholders who punish their slaves for injustice and disobedience. Punishing slaves was a daily duty of the slaveholder. "In the household the master judges the slaves day by day, calls them to account for their transgressions, he punishes some and forgives

173. See Hom. Matt. 15.9, 11 (PG 57.235.47, 238.36–37), 24.2 (PG 57.323.3), 66.5 (PG 58.632.30–31); Hom. 2 Tim. 1.2 (F6.171); Hom. Phlm. 1.2 (F6.334).

174. Hom. Eph. 22.1 (F4.333): Καθάπερ γὰρ οἱ καλῶς πάσχοντες, ὅταν μὴ ἀμείβωνται τοὺς εὐεργέτας, τὸν θεὸν αὐτοῖς ὀφειλέτην ποιοῦσιν· οὕτω δὴ καὶ οἱ δεσπόται, ἂν παθόντες εὖ παρὰ σοῦ μὴ σε ἀμείψωνταί, μᾶλλον ἠμείψαντο, τὸν θεὸν ὀφειλέτην σοι καταστήσαντες.

others," Chrysostom proclaims.[175] He compares the role of the slaveholder to the role of God—punishing slaves becomes a divine act in the same way that accepting punishment and suffering is Christomorphic. The slaveholder becomes the hand of God.

But punishing and correcting slaves were laborious tasks. For this reason Chrysostom advises the *despoina* not to have too many slave girls, since "what is more troublesome still, namely, the daily effort required to correct their laziness, to root out their villainy, to put an end to their ingratitude, and to correct all their other bad behavior," does not add quality to one's life.[176] Chrysostom remembers his own mother having to constantly correct and punish her domestic slaves,[177] and we also recall the widow who was unable to discipline and punish the runaway slave husband of one of her slave girls. This is another advantage of tactical slaveholding—it eases the tasks of discipline and punishment. Punishing slaves was mostly the duty of the *despoina* of the household and was often not administered directly by the slaveholder. Often, as Chrysostom notes, a friend mediated punishment, and at that time the slaveholder withdrew from the disobedient slave.[178] It was often the case that another slave acted as flogger (*mastiktōr*) and meted out the lashes—on villa estates, for instance, the *vilicus* had to punish disobedient slaves.[179] If a slave became too troublesome for the *despoina* to control, she could sell the slave, as in the case of the widow in *Homiliae in epistulam I ad Thessalonicenses* 11.3. Chrysostom also tells us that a "caring" master would often apply ointment to the wounds of a slave after whipping him.[180]

Chrysostom was also concerned about the emotional state of the slaveholder, especially when it came to punishment. It was important for the slaveholder to control his or her temper (*thymos*) when anger (*orgē*) was involved. This was a common notion in ancient thought, and it is found in almost every treatise focusing on the punishment of slaves.[181] Mastering one's anger was even more important than punishing the slave. For instance, Plutarch noted of the Spartan Charillus

---

175. *Hom. 2 Tim.* 3.3 (F6.188): Ἐν οἰκίᾳ μὲν γὰρ ὁ δεσπότης δούλοις δικάζει καθ᾽ ἑκάστην ἡμέραν, καὶ τῶν ἁμαρτημάτων αὐτοὺς ἀπαιτεῖ εὐθύνας, καὶ τὰ μὲν κολάζει, τὰ δὲ ἀφίησιν.

176. *Virg.* 67.6–9 (SC 125.336): καὶ τὰ τούτων ἔτι χαλεπώτερα, οἷον τὸ καθ᾽ ἑκάστην διατείνεσθαι τὴν ἡμέραν ῥαθυμίαν ἐπιστρέφουσαν, κακουργίαν ἐκκόπτουσαν, ἀχαριστίας παύουσαν, τὴν ἄλλην πᾶσαν αὐτῶν κακίαν παιδαγωγοῦσαν. Translation: Shore, *Chrysostom: On Virginity; Against Remarriage*, 103.

177. *Sacr.* 1.2.46–50 (SC 272.66–68).

178. *Hom. 1 Cor.* 14.1 (F2.161).

179. Carlsen, *Vilici and Roman Estate Managers*, 75.

180. *Serm. Gen.* 3.2 (PG 54.593.11–13).

181. See, for instance, Seneca, *Ir.* 2.26.6, 3.4.4 (Basore 222–23, 262–63); Plutarch, *Cohib. ir.* 458–64 (Helmbold 128–59); William Fitzgerald, *Slavery and Roman Literary Imagination*, Roman Literature and Its Contexts (Cambridge: Cambridge University Press, 1996), 34–41; Lieve Van Hoof, "Strategic Differences: Seneca and Plutarch on Controlling Anger," *Mnemosyne* 60 (2007): 74–76; Harper, *Slavery in the Late Roman World*, 230–31; Joshel, "Slavery and the Roman Literary Culture," in Bradley and Cartledge, *Cambridge World History of Slavery*, 1:232–33.

that "when one of the Helots conducted himself rather boldly toward him, he said, 'If I were not angry, I would kill you.'"[182] It was important that the slaveholder show emotional consistency in his behavior. He should not lose control of his temper or show mercy too soon. This was not an easy task, and so Chrysostom also dissuades the slaveholder from making an oath out of anger to punish a slave. This can cause great domestic strife. "Thus, often when we are dining at home, and one of the slaves makes a mistake," Chrysostom explains, "the wife swears that he will be flogged, and then the husband swears the opposite, resisting, and not allowing it."[183] The problem they then face is that one of them will be guilty of perjury. A slaveholder must therefore never swear to punish a slave, since the respective husband or wife may swear the contrary, or perhaps feel pity for the slave. Slaves also had to guard against further enraging the slaveholder, since the punishment of one slave might result in the punishment of many.[184] This is why other slaves often scorned the disobedient slave.[185] Slaveholders sometimes even chased slaves around the house with a whip—an indication of how common it may have been for a slaveholder to lose his or her patience and temper when punishing slaves.[186]

Chrysostom cites Paul as the best example of someone who managed his anger. Whenever Chrysostom tells slaveholders to bridle their rage, he refers to Paul's disposition toward Onesimus.[187] "Have you ordered your slave to be put in bonds, and were you angry, and exasperated?" Chrysostom asks. Then, in one of his most eloquent admonitions, Chrysostom tells slaveholders: "Remember Paul's bonds, and you will immediately stay your fury." He then beautifully reminds them of the central Christian value of suffering and pacifism: "Remember that we are of the bound, not the binders, of the bruised in heart, not the bruisers."[188] Chrysostom also often reminds slaveholders about the chains of Paul.[189] Before punishing a

---

182. Plutarch, *Mor.* 3. *Apoph. Lac.* 232c5–6 (Babbitt 394–95): Τῶν δὲ εἱλώτων τινὸς θρασύτερον αὐτῷ προσφερομένου, 'εἰ μὴ ὠργιζόμην' εἶπε, 'κατέκτανον ἄν σε.'

183. *Stat.* 14.3 (PG 49.145.2–5): Πολλάκις γοῦν ἐπὶ τῆς οἰκίας ἀριστοποιουμένων ἡμῶν, καὶ τῶν οἰκετῶν τινος διαμαρτόντος, ὤμοσε μαστιγώσειν ἡ γυνή· εἶτα ἀντώμοσεν ὁ ἀνὴρ, τὰ ἐναντία ἐπιφιλονεικῶν καὶ οὐκ ἐκτρέπων.

184. *Serm. Gen.* 3 (PG 54.592.29–35); see Robert C. Hill, trans., *St. John Chrysostom: Eight Sermons on the Book of Genesis* (Brookline, MA: Holy Cross Orthodox Press, 2004), 57–58.

185. *Virg.* 46.4.37–40 (SC 125.260).

186. *Hom. Gen.* 17.2 (PG 53.136.40–46).

187. *Hom. Phlm.* 2.1 (F6.335–37).

188. *Hom. Col.* 12.1 (F5.301): Ἐκέλευσας δεσμευθῆναι παῖδα, καὶ ὠργίσθης καὶ παρωξύνθης; μνημόνευε τῶν Παύλου δεσμῶν, καὶ εὐθέως παύσεις τὴν ὀργήν· ἀναμνήσθητι ὅτι τῶν δεδεμένων ἡμεῖς, ἀλλ' οὐ τῶν δεόντων, τῶν συντετριμμένων τὴν καρδίαν, ἀλλ' οὐ τῶν συντριβόντων. Translation: *NPNF* (the translation in *NPNF* successfully reproduces the poise of the text).

189. See *Stat.* 16.3–4 (PG 49.164–67); *Hom. Eph.* 8.7–8 (F4.202–5); Margaret M. Mitchell, *The Heavenly Trumpet: John Chrysostom and the Art of Pauline Interpretation* (Louisville, KY: Westminster John Knox Press, 2002), 176–86.

slave, the slaveholder should also reflect on his own faults and remember that he is also subject to punishment from God. This was one of the first principles a father had to teach his son—to control his anger and examine his own flaws before punishing a slave.[190] Losing one's temper was a shameful display.

Since the *despoina* was the primary manager of household slaves, Chrysostom expected her to control her temper, especially when it concerned female slaves. In this, he masculinizes the mistress. Traditionally, and especially in Chrysostom's thought, women were seen as not having the ability to control their emotions.[191] Good female slaveholders were considered manly, since they successfully dominated and controlled themselves and their subordinates. The appearance of the mistress was very important. Households were not entirely "private spaces," but rather, in Kate Cooper's words, "closely-watched" spaces,[192] governed by a strict politic of appearance. This may be because in cities houses were built in close proximity to each other. Chrysostom actually advised people to monitor not only themselves, but also their neighbors.[193]

Chrysostom recounts the following scene in Antioch: "Women, when they are angry with their female slaves, fill the whole house with their own shouting." Moreover, "if the house is perhaps built along a narrow street, then all those who are present hear the mistress screaming, and the maid wailing," which then leads other women to gossip, and "all the women around immediately peek inside and say, 'So-and-so is beating her own slave!'" Such a scene reaches its disgraceful climax when "some have come to such an extreme of vulgarity as to unveil the head, and to drag their slave girls by the hair." This unveiling of the slave girl in a fit of rage is a disgrace to both the slave and the mistress. Rather than resorting to this extreme, Chrysostom tells the free women in his audience to "punish her then with the rod and with stripes," if necessary; however, before doing this, the mistress must not forget about her own faults. Most importantly, however, the mistress must always try to win the respect and admiration of her husband in the just and gentle treatment of slave girls: "If you should learn these things in your household regarding the female slaves, to be tolerant and not harsh, much more will it be like this with your husband." Of course, it is the husband's approval and opinion that matter most: "So will the exemplary discipline in your relation with your female slaves benefit you in gaining the goodwill of your

190. *Inan.* 67.803–12 (SC 188.164–66), 73.889–908 (SC 188.174–76).

191. *Macc.* 1.6 (PG 50.620.10–621.20); see Mayer, *Cult of the Saints*, 140–41.

192. See Cooper, "Closely Watched Households"; Cooper, *The Fall of the Roman Household* (New York: Cambridge University Press, 2007), 122–33.

193. For more on Chrysostom's advice to monitor one's neighbors, see Christine Shepardson, *Controlling Contested Places: Late Antique Antioch and the Spatial Politics of Religious Controversy* (Berkeley: University of California Press, 2014), 102–4.

husbands."[194] So not only does the mistress become manly through such behavior, but she gains male favor.

It is clear, in the first instance, that the problem for Chrysostom is not so much the verbal and physical abuse of a female slave as it is the mistress's loss of control of her temper and the public unveiling and exposure of women in general. As in his comments on the rearing of boys, here too slaves become a training ground for learning virtue—not for the boy this time—but for the mistress. Slaves become objects to negotiate spousal favor. The mistress can win the favor of her husband by showing him that she can control her anger, especially toward female slaves. This does not rule out physical punishment. She must just avoid punishing a slave as a stimulus response to anger. One cannot lose control of the passions, since one then becomes their slave.[195]

Chrysostom also condemns sexual humiliation in the punishment of female slaves. "For they will strip the girls, and call their husbands for the purpose," Chrysostom laments, "and oftentimes tie them to the pallets." This type of behavior, like the unveiling of a female slave, dishonors the *despoina*. "Do you strip your slave girl, and expose her to your husband?" Chrysostom asks, "and are you not ashamed, lest he should condemn you for it?" This disturbing passage depicts the utter powerlessness of female slaves in the Roman world, especially the corporal humiliation they had to endure. Now, Chrysostom continues, the anger of the *despoina* also infects her husband, and the episode of physical punishment and verbal abuse (*kraugē*) intensifies. "And then do you exasperate him yet more, and threaten to put her in chains," Chrysostom says, "having first taunted the wretched and pitiable woman with ten thousand reproachful names, and called her 'Thessalian witch, runaway, and whore?'"[196] In describing the profanity of the mistress here, Chrysostom reaches back to several stereotypes that link female slavery to prostitution, and slavery in general to unfaithfulness and degeneration. Chrysostom's use of the word *proïstēmi* also suggests a link between the forced exhibition-

---

194. *Hom. Eph.* 15.2 (F4.258, 260): αἵ, ὅταν ὀργίζωνται ταῖς θεραπαινίσι, τὴν οἰκίαν ἅπασαν τῆς κραυγῆς πληροῦσι τῆς ἑαυτῶν . . . πολλάκις δὲ καὶ εἰ παρὰ στενωπὸν τυγχάνοι ᾠκοδομημένη ἡ οἰκία, καὶ οἱ παριόντες ἅπαντες ἀκούουσιν αὐτῆς βοώσης, καὶ τῆς θεραπαινίδος ὀλολυζούσης . . . καὶ πᾶσαι εὐθέως διακύψασαι, ἡ δεῖνα, φησὶ, τὴν δούλην τύπτει τὴν αὐτῆς. . . . [Νῦν δὲ] εἰς τοσοῦτό τινες ἀτοπίας ἥκουσιν, ὡς ἀποκαλύπτειν τὴν κεφαλὴν, καὶ ἀπὸ τριχῶν σύρειν τὰς θεραπαινίδας . . . Ῥάβδῳ καὶ πληγαῖς σωφρόνισον. . . . Ἐὰν ἐν οἰκίᾳ ταῦτα παιδευθῇς ἐπὶ τῆς θεραπαινίδος, καὶ προσηνὴς ᾖς, καὶ μὴ χαλεπὴ, πολλῷ μᾶλλον ἐπὶ τοῦ ἀνδρὸς ἔσῃ τοιαύτη. . . . Ὥστε ἡ περὶ τὰς θεραπαινίδας φιλοσοφία μέγιστα ὑμᾶς εἰς τὴν τῶν ἀνδρῶν εὔνοιαν ὠφελεῖ.

195. See chapter 2.

196. *Hom. Eph.* 15.2 (F4.258–59): Γυμνώσασαι γὰρ τὰς κόρας, καὶ τὸν ἄνδρα ἐπὶ τοῦτο καλέσασαι, δεσμοῦσι πολλάκις πρὸς τοῖς σκίμποσιν . . . ἀλλὰ γυμνοῖς τὴν παιδίσκην, καὶ δεικνύεις τῷ ἀνδρί; καὶ οὐκ αἰσχύνη μή σου καταγνῷ; καὶ ἐπιπλέον αὐτὸν παροξύνεις, καὶ ἀπειλεῖς δήσειν, μυρία πρότερον λοιδορησαμένη τῇ ἀθλίᾳ καὶ ταλαιπώρῳ, Θεσσαλίδα, δραπέτριαν, προεστῶσαν καλοῦσα. See also chapter 6.

ism of the girl and her status as a prostitute. As noted, calling a slave a runaway (*drapetria*) was a common form of invective to show the sedition of a slave. The tempestuous jeremiad of the mistress is further expanded with the term "Thessalian" (*Thessalida*). The *NPNF* translation uses the phrase "Thessalian witch," which I have retained. This term of invective has a long history in Greek,[197] and had become a stereotypologism for trickery, fraud, and sorcery, thereby including, in a double stereotype, both the insubordination and fraud of the slave and her inclination toward superstition and sorcery. In Roman thought, Thessalian women were synonymous with witchcraft and demonry.[198]

If we compare this account to that of the chained profligate slave girl in *Adversus Judaeos* 2, as well as to the reference to the promiscuous one in *In Matthaeum* 42.3, we find many similarities.[199] In both accounts the slave girls are chained up, incarcerated, and flogged for their behavior and character, and both illustrate the dynamics between sexual vice and harsh physical punishment. Sexual slander against slave women seems to have been especially common because the close connection between slavery, sexual abuse, and prostitution—the topic of chapter 6. This behavior is unacceptable to Chrysostom for two reasons: the mistress's inability to control her anger, which leads to excessive punishment and coarse verbal abuse; and the sadistic sexual exposure and humiliation of the slave girl, who is unveiled and even stripped. While Chrysostom's view is biased in that it is based on the stereotype that women cannnot control their passions, there is no reason to doubt that such incidents took place in households, whether perpetrated by male or female slaveholders.

Slaves were punished for various other reasons besides lickerish conduct. A cook might be chastised for preparing a bad meal,[200] while a slave speaking lewdly in front of the son of the slaveholder had to be punished immediately.[201] "And your slave, if he says anything rude while you are listening, will receive innumerable stripes," Chrys-

---

197. According to the twelfth-century author Eustathius, Euripides's phrase Θεσσαλὸν σόφισμα, the "Thessalian trick," was widespread; see Euripides, *Phoen.* 1408 (Kovacs 359); Eustathius, *Comm. Hom. Il.* 1.517.22–28 (Stallbaum 400). The phrase is very common in Greek and Latin literature of the Roman world, with a wide range of references denoting sorcery (especially related to lunar magic), trickery, and fraud; see Anne-Marie Tupet, *La magie dans la poésie latine: Des origines à la fin du règne d'Auguste*, Études anciennes serie latine (Paris: Les Belles Lettres, 1976), 90–102; D. E. Hill, "The Thessalian Trick," *Rheinisches Museum für Philologie* 116 (1973): 221–38; Oliver Phillips, "The Witches' Thessaly," in *Magic and Ritual in the Ancient World*, ed. Paul Mirecki and Marvin Meyer, Religions in the Graeco-Roman World 141 (Leiden: Brill, 2001), 378–86.

198. Glen W. Bowersock, "Zur Geschichte des römischen Thessaliens," *Rheinisches Museum für Philologie* 108 (1965): 277.

199. See *Adv. Jud.* 2.124ra; *Hom. Matt.* 42.3 (PG 57.455.7–10).

200. *Virg.* 69.1–19 (SC 125.318–20).

201. *Inan.* 53.706–9 (SC 188.152).

ostom says.[202] Theft and laziness were also infractions that merited punishment.[203] Of course, slaves who ran away or murdered a family member received the harshest punishment.[204] Methods of punishment included deprivation of food,[205] house arrest,[206] sale,[207] binding with chains,[208] and, of course, whipping.[209] In the case of murder, the guilty slave(s) as well as other domestic slaves were executed. Despite his call for the merciful and moderate treatment of slaves, if the situation called for it, Chrysostom approved at some point all of the measures listed above.

Scars from flogging were the defining marks of the slave body; they were signs of social dishonor. Glancy is correct in noting that whipping "played a pedagogic and ultimately epistemological function, imparting knowledge of degradation and dishonorable submissiveness."[210] Whipping demonstrated the total domination of the slaveholder over the slave.[211] Whipping was a public affair, at least one that happened in front of other slaves in order to deter them from any possible ill behavior. "Scourging one slave," Chrysostom explains, "often makes the rest more disciplined out of fear."[212] The whip used was called a *mastix,* or in Latin, *flagellum;* it was made from leather with several protruding thongs that often had nails or other weights tied to the edges. As we saw in several instances above, both males and females were whipped with this instrument. Chrysostom tells us that a serious lashing could include between thirty and fifty lashes,[213] while some lashings seemed endless.[214] Slaves who committed less serious crimes were whipped by the master, a friend, or one of the other household slaves, although serious floggings were later carried out by the public *mastiktōr* (*flagellator*).[215]

Beating the slave of another, however, was considered a major faux pas, and seen as a direct insult against the owner. It could be considered damage of property, or an

202. *Hom. Matt.* 37.5 (PG 57.425.54–55): Καὶ ὁ μὲν οἰκέτης αἰσχρόν τι φθεγγόμενος ἀκούοντός σου, μυρίας λήψεται μάστιγας.

203. *Hom. Phlm.* 2.1 (F6.335–37); *Sacr.* 1.2.46–50 (SC 272.66); *Virg.* 67.1.1–22 (SC 125.306–8).

204. *Hom. Phlm.* 3.2 (F6.346–53).

205. *Stat.* 14.4 (PG 49.145.11–15).

206. *Adv. Jud.* 2.124ra.

207. *Hom. 1 Thess.* 11.3 (F5.436–37).

208. *Hom. 1 Cor.* 40.6 (F2.515); *Lib. repud.* 2.1 (PG 51.218.55–57); *Stat.* 9.3 (PG 49.108.7–12); *Virg.* 41.2.15–29 (SC 125.236–38).

209. *Hom. Matt.* 42.3 (PG 57.455.7–10); *Hom. Eph.* 15.2 (F4.258–59); *Hom. Phlm.* 2.2 (F6.344).

210. Jennifer A. Glancy, *Corporal Knowledge: Early Christian Bodies* (New York: Oxford University Press, 2010), 30.

211. *Hom. Goth.* 8.6 (PG 63.509.18–19).

212. *Laz.* 3.8 (PG 48.1003.42–43): ἕνα πολλάκις μαστιγώσαντες οἰκέτην, τοὺς λοιποὺς σωφρονεστέρους ἐποίησαν τῷ φόβῳ.

213. *Adv. Jud.* 8.6.7–8 (PG 48.936.56–937.4).

214. *Stat.* 20.5 (PG 49.206.37–39).

215. Graeme R. Newman, *The Punishment Response* (New Brunswick, NJ: Transaction Publishers, 1985), 58.

indirect assault against the owner, since slaves were also surrogate bodies of the owners. "If we should beat the slave of another," Chrysostom says, "the master is incensed, and calls the act an insult."[216] Excessive flogging, however, was discouraged, and it became illegal to flog a female slave in such an excessive way that she died within thirty days.[217] This was most likely a strategy to deflect some of the shame of punishment away from the slaveholder and onto the state apparatus represented by the *flagellator.*[218] As Chrysostom also notes, it was not so much the number of lashes that was significant, but the amount of pain inflicted on the slave body. "Accordingly, after inflicting countless lashings upon some of the domestic slaves, they might hold fast saying that they most surely did not commit an offense," Chrysostom relates, "and because the pain which results from the lashings proves to be unbearable, they decide to stay the rest of the blows."[219] Whipping makes the slave beg and plead for mercy, arguing for innocence, and the pain inflicted becomes sufficient to halt the rest of the scourges. This was probably a common scene in Roman households.

Pain was an important aspect of Roman slavery; our term *pain* derives from the Latin *poena,* meaning "punishment," usually of the divine kind. In terms of the different Greek terms for pain, Helen King notes that the wide lexical and sematic scope of pain constructed a very specific medico-cultural framework for pain. Pain has a narrative; pain both tells a story and is a story in itself. A term like *ponos* often referred to a pain that should be borne, while one such as *odynē,* which is used by Chrysostom above, points to a destructive pain that requires attention. While *ponos* was generally regarded as constructive pain, *odynē* was dangerous and destructive.[220] Elaine Scarry's influential study of pain illustrates that it had two functions: those of "unmaking" and "making" one's reality. The piercing pain of whipping, as Chrysostom describes it here, was therefore not like *ponos* or *lypē,* the honorable pains a man had to endure in war or the labor pains of women; the pain of whipping had a sole purpose—to coerce the slave body into submission and/or to shame and destroy it—the pain of whipping and the torture of slaves were an unmaking of the slave's body and world. Most importantly, as Scarry notes, the objectification (and, in my opinion, the quantification) of someone's

216. *Stat.* 20.4 (PG 49.202.43–45): κἂν τυπτήσωμεν ἀλλότριον οἰκέτην, ὁ δεσπότης ἀγανακτεῖ, καὶ ὕβριν εἶναί φησι τὸ πρᾶγμα.

217. Newman, *Punishment Response,* 58.

218. For a general discussion of the deflection of the shame of punishment, see Foucault, *Discipline & Punish,* 3–31.

219. *Stelech.* 2.4 (PG 47.417.20–24): καθάπερ τῶν οἰκετῶν οἱ μυρία ἐργασάμενοι δεινά, ὅτι μὲν οὐχ ἥμαρτον οὐκ ἂν ἔχοιεν εἰπεῖν, διὰ δὲ τὸ τὴν ὀδύνην ἀφόρητον εἶναι τὴν ἀπὸ τῶν μαστίγων, ἀξιοῦσιν ἀνεθῆναι λοιπὸν τῶν πληγῶν.

220. King, *Hippocrates' Woman,* 122–27; see also Roselyne Rey, *The History of Pain,* trans. Louise Elliott Wallace, J. A. Cadden, and S. W. Cadden (Cambridge, MA: Harvard University Press, 1993), 21–22.

pain, as we see in Chrysostom's account of a slave whipping above, is translated into the insignia of power. The *odynē* of whipping unmakes the world and body of the slave, but at the same time it makes and empowers the kyriarchal body. The narrative of *odynē* is one of complete domination. In this sense, doulological *odynē* then indeed does become necessary for the honor of free men and the making of masculinity in general, but only when it is applied to the slave body.[221]

In general, however, Chrysostom did not approve of physical violence against slave girls, except perhaps in the case of extreme licentiousness. When it came to the disciplining of women, he preferred interventions and exercises rather than violent signs of punishment. In fact, whipping a slave girl reflected shame back onto the slaveholder. The marks on a slave girl's back told the story of the slaveholder's cruelty, particularly when he had beaten the girl so badly that bruises remained for some time. "Then if she should have permission to go out to the bath," Chrysostom says, "there are bruises visible on her back when she is naked, and she carries the marks of your cruelty around."[222] Instead of flogging the girl, he advises the *despoina* to investigate the cause of the disobedience of the slave girl. He intimates that it is often the result of drunkenness. Although inebriation formed part of the slave stereotype, it would not be surprising if alcohol abuse was common among ancient slaves, considering their circumstances; the prevalence of the debate on giving wine to slaves in ancient literature seems to support this. In such a case, the slave girl must be deprived of wine or whatever caused her inebriation.[223] It is at least somewhat encouraging to see that, in Chrysostom's view, the slave body was no longer unconditionally open to violence, and that it was especially shameful to violently abuse a woman, whether slave or free. Chastising domestic bodies was ultimately the task of the *paterfamilias*, but we saw that the mistress punished slaves, and slaves punished children and other slaves. Punishment was primarily determined by one's status. The worst a husband could do to a wife was slapping her on the cheek.[224] Children, especially sons, required punishment, but it was very important to Chrysostom that sons be punished in the manner of freeborn persons, and not whipped like slaves.[225]

---

221. Elaine Scarry, *The Body in Pain: The Making and Unmaking of the World* (New York: Oxford University Press, 1985), 27–59. See also Susanna Elm, "Roman Pain and the Rise of Christianity," in *Quo Vadis Medical Healing: Past Concepts and New Approaches,* ed. Susanna Elm and Stefan N. Willich, International Library of Ethics, Law, and the New Medicine 44 (Berlin: Springer, 2009), 41–54.

222. *Hom. Eph.* 15.2 (F4.259): Εἶτα ἐν βαλανείῳ ἐὰν δέῃ προελθεῖν, μώλωπες κατὰ τῶν νώτων γυμνουμένης αὐτῆς, καὶ τεκμήρια περιφέρει τῆς ὠμότητος.

223. *Hom. Eph.* 15.2 (F4.259).

224. For Chrysostom's views on domestic violence and spousal abuse, see Joy A. Schroeder, "John Chrysostom's Critique of Spousal Violence," *Journal of Early Christian Studies* 12, no. 4 (2004): 413–42. Patricia Clark's "Women, Slaves, and the Hierarchies of Domestic Violence" is also very useful.

225. *Inan.* 30–31.407–41 (SC 188.120–24); this was common advice in Roman antiquity. Whipping a freeborn child would basically reduce his status to that of a slave in the child's own eyes and the eyes of his peers; see Richard P. Saller, "Corporal Punishment, Authority, and Obedience in the Roman

Punishment is a very potent social discourse, and has several dimensions. Two of the most common corollaries to punishment are proportionality and celerity.[226] In the first instance, in very few cases of the punishment of slaves was the punishment proportionate to the crime. Punishment here was not at all a question of retribution or even justice per se, but an instance of total degradation and terror, not only devaluing the body of the slave, but also pathologizing it, often sexually, as in the case of the slave girl being stripped and whipped. It turned the body of the female slave into a sadistic object of prurience,[227] which enraged the mistress even more, and also objectified the slave body. The excessive punishment of slaves had to show the total domination of the slaveholder over the body of the slave, and the terror it caused served to keep slaves submissive. Nothing so clearly demonstrates the kyriarchal grip on the slave body as the disproportionate means of punishment. At times, when slaves died, this grip had become so robust that the slave body completely collapsed under its hold.

Second, punishment had to be swift. Chrysostom himself advocated swift punishment of slaves. The celerity of punishment, especially public punishment, aims to ensure spectators of the close connection between the crime and the penalty that results from it. The punishment of slaves then exposes the fissures of the dysfunctional Roman household, fissures that posed a considerable problem for pastoral power, especially in the relationship between husband and wife—an understandable consequence when a system like slavery, which justifies physical and sexual oppression, has permeated the essential and relational dynamics of a household without any resistance from the pastoral powers that ought to have protected the household and addressed slavery. Authors like Chrysostom saw the problems related to slavery, as is evident from the discussion above, yet believed that the dominant powers of government had too much to lose if slavery were abolished, or that slavery had become so banal that it was seen as a problem that simply had to be managed rather than abrogated.

. . .

The aretagogy, discipline, and punishment of slaves highlight how intensive the processes of masculinization and kyriarchization were in late antiquity. The increased hold on the slave body, and the obsession with virtue and discipline, were signs and symptoms of a masculinity in crisis. Roman masculinity, as we have it in Chrysostom at least, distributed its power by making "men" out of women

Household," in *Marriage, Divorce, and Children in Ancient Rome,* ed. Beryl Rawson (Oxford: Clarendon Press, 1991), 144–65.

226. Newman, *Punishment Response,* 152–54.

227. For a discussion of the links between prurience, suffering, and punishment in the context of Christian martyrdom, see David Frankfurter, "Martyrology and the Prurient Gaze," *Journal of Early Christian Studies* 17, no. 2 (2009): 215–45.

and slaves, thereby also complicating the dynamics of kyriarchy. The distinction between the dominator and the dominated disappeared. The processes of masculinization and kyriarchization propagated themselves through the technologies of education, as we saw in chapter 4, and through discipline and punishment, as we have seen in this chapter.

Teaching slaves virtue, similarly to masculinizing them, served the purpose of reducing instances of resistance or revolts. It was also important to teach slaves virtue because of their role in the education of children, especially males, and in the protection of the chastity and honor of freeborn women. Since slaves were often also husbands, fathers, and masters themselves, they also had to embody kyriarchal power. Aretagogy involved very strict procedures of discipline and surveillance that often violated the body of the slave. Theological strategies like the Christic panopticon claimed to give slaves a sense of agency, but in fact deprived them of agency altogether. Even the "rewards" slaves received can hardly be seen as positive gestures. Reward and punishment were equally oppressive and functioned in the same framework for distributing kyriarchal power; they differed only in their application. Foucault speaks of the two requirements in the ritual and liturgy of punishment. It must mark the body of the victim, and it must be public and spectacular.[228] In the case of the punishment of slaves, the punishment always outweighed the crime. Even in cases of dominicide, it was not only the murderer who was executed, but also all of the other household slaves. Punishment was public and excessive. Thus, the punishment of slaves was not solely retributive, but was used to demonstrate the extreme kyriarchal grip on the slave body, terrifying other enslaved onlookers, and displaying the apparent "triumph" of an eroded masculinity over vice. Sexualized punishment humiliated, objectified, and pathologized the slave body. The public and excessive punishment of the slave demonstrated the total, all-encompassing victory of kyriarchal power over the slave body, where the kyriarchal grip was so forceful that the slave body was destroyed.

The problem, as Foucault also notes, is that the shame of punishment is reflected back onto the one who punishes, and being punished then becomes a type of glorious martyrdom.[229] This is exactly what happened in early Christianity, and this unsettles Chrysostom. To Chrysostom, Christian identity was founded in being scourged, not flinging the whip. Public and spectacularly violent punishment reflected the degradation of ancient Roman society—a society founded on the brutality of slavery. The harsh punishment of slaves further destablized masculinity, hence Chrysostom's strict measures to regulate and redistribute the means of punishment. Yet one had to strike a fine balance—one must punish unruly slaves in order to teach them virtue, but one must never make them suffer unjustly, and

228. Foucault, *Discipline & Punish*, 34–35.
229. Ibid., 9–10.

one must preferably use only moderate violence, and only as a last option. A Christian who punished a slave unjustly and with excessive violence was a shameful spectacle, while the slave who suffered this punishment was considered admirable.

Thus, already in the fourth and fifth centuries we see a move to dole out punishment with less apparent horror. Slaveholders were becoming less directly involved in punishment. Chrysostom recommends the whip and chain only in extreme cases, advising slaveholders to use more pervasive and less visible means of punishment, such as spiritual and moral exercises based on scripture. Punishment is manipulated to become anoptic. This is not an ameliorative move—punishment and violation remain; they are just transformed into aretagogical exercises rather than violent signs. Kyriarchal oppression was swept under the carpet, but the practice of slaveholding continued because it appeared to be less violent. Occurring alongside these changes in the discipline and punishment of slaves was a desperate restructuring of slave sexualities, which is the subject of the next chapter.

6

Exploitation, Regulation, and Restructuring

Managing Slave Sexuality

When it comes to the study of slavery in antiquity, there are few issues as contentious or as ambiguous as the sexuality of slaves. In many cases, slaves were the sex objects of their owners, and had no recourse to legal protection against sexual violation or rape. Slaves were often also forced and incentivized to "breed" to increase the property of the owner through their offspring; at other times sexual activity for slaves was prohibited. Sexual honor was practically nonexistent for slaves.[1] For instance, the Greek word for a freeborn woman, *eleuthera,* was practically synonymous with sexual honor, demure, and modesty, and often denoted a married *matrona* or *kyria.* Yet the exploitation of slave sexuality runs even deeper than this—it was woven into the very fabric of Roman society, and was part of its essential functioning. Slave sexuality was central to concepts such as the coming of age, marriage, adultery, family life, law, and entertainment in Roman life. Furthermore, the impact of prostitution on slave sexuality should not be underestimated; the majority of prostitutes were slaves or freedwomen. In many ways, prostitution defined slave sexuality, whether a slave was a public prostitute working in a brothel, or a slave girl or boy involved in what the Romans viewed as "private prostitution,"

1. See Fridolf Kudlien, *Die Sklaven in der griechischen Medizin der klassischen und hellenistischen Zeit,* Forschungen zur antiken Sklaverei 2 (Wiesbaden: F. Steiner, 1969); Jennifer A. Glancy, "Obstacles to Slaves' Participation in the Corinthian Church," *Journal of Biblical Literature* 117, no. 3 (1998): 481–501; Glancy, *Slavery in Early Christianity* (Minneapolis: Fortress Press, 2006), 21–27, 49–53; Kyle Harper, *From Shame to Sin: The Christian Transformation of Sexual Morality in Late Antiquity* (Cambridge, MA: Harvard University Press, 2013); Edward E. Cohen, "Sexual Abuse and Sexual Rights: Slaves' Erotic Experience at Athens and Rome," in *A Companion to Greek and Roman Sexualities,* ed. Thomas K. Hubbard, Blackwell Companions to the Ancient World (Chichester: Wiley-Blackwell, 2014), 184–98.

in the household of a master. The eunuch, one who often destabilized notions of masculinity and sexuality, should also be mentioned in this context. In sum, the slave body, whether male or female, was defined by its susceptibility to sexual regulation and exploitation, and itself influenced the definition of Roman sexuality, informing both its ideals and anxieties. Through investigation of slave sexuality, one gains a better understanding of how kyriarchal power in Roman society functioned, and sees more clearly some of the fissures of the slaveholding system. Foucault refers to sexuality as a "dense transfer point for relations of power."[2] Sexuality shapes society, and vice versa; however, sexuality also manages to sustain varied social tensions and points of disorientation precisely because of its instrumentality in power relations. In addition to shaping society, sexuality, because of its very nature, also destabilizes social power structures, power relations, and power knowledge.

A tension exists, for instance, between the treatment of the slave body as property, which could be used as a sex object if desired, and the representation of the chastity and corporeal integrity of all human bodies in Christian discourse. The honor and integrity of the slave body, including its sexual integrity, reflected back onto the slaveholder. This tension, in turn, also disturbed traditional Roman views of chastity, marriage, and adultery. Some saw slaves as neutral ground, morally speaking, with slaves being used as sexual outlets for the freeborn. In Chrysostom's sources it is clear that the sexual abuse of slaves was a common occurrence, but not without risks for the owner. There was always the danger of reprisals, or of slaves abusing the slaveholder, such as in "disastrous contracts for him, to exploit him sexually, and even to assault or kill him."[3] Spouses who abused their domestic slaves always had to be cautious of the gaze of their partner, and of course, there was always the risk of unwanted offspring with a slave. Furthermore, while slaves were the objects of sexual abuse and systematic exploitation, they often owned other slaves, and it is highly probable that slaves also sexually abused or exploited their own slaves.

The sexual exploitation and regulation of slaves should therefore be seen as a sign and symptom of a society inherently destabilized by the wider operation of slave sexuality in relation to the powers of kyriarchy and the changing face of masculinity with the rise of Christianity. The sexual exploitation and regulation of slaves also help explain why Chrysostom felt compelled to discuss the restructuring of slave sexuality. In this chapter we will examine Chrysostom's views on slave sexuality, particularly its exploitation, regulation, and restructuring. Chrysostom's

2. Michel Foucault, *The History of Sexuality: An Introduction*, trans. Robert Hurley, vol. 1 of *The History of Sexuality* (New York: Vintage, 1978), 103.

3. Alan Watson, *Roman Slave Law* (Baltimore: Johns Hopkins University Press, 1987), 1. See Cohen, "Sexual Abuse and Sexual Rights," 184.

discussion of slave sexuality in Roman society focuses on the following: (1) the issue of the sexual abuse of slaves in relation to marriage, sexual shame, and adultery; (2) the problem of prostitution, and (3) the anxieties caused by eunuchs and castration. All three represent a form of sexual exploitation of the slave body that Chrysostom now wants to regulate and restructure in light of his universal sexual ethic, in which only marriage, sexual renunciation, and virginity are viable options for one's sexual fashioning. Most importantly, Chrysostom's comments on the regulation and restructuring of slave sexuality function within his wider vision of the pastoralization of the household.

BETWEEN SHAME AND MODESTY: MARRIAGE, ADULTERY, AND SEXUAL DISHONOR

Marriage was the most important form of social regulation in the Roman world. It was both the channel by which freeborn legitimate heirs were produced to carry on the legacy of the family and the Roman people, and the condition for the transfer of property between families. Marriage was, of course, also an important political apparatus that elite families used to strengthen their social and economic position, and to increase their political influence. Besides all these exchanges of power, people also found love and companionship in the institution of marriage. The perfect combination of these elements was known as the *digna condicio*—a match not only between the social status of the husband and that of the wife, but also that of their families. Marriages were often arranged at a very early age, at times even during infancy. Strictly speaking, girls were marriageable shortly after menarche, although most girls in late ancient Roman society married in their mid- to late teens. There may have been some cases, depending on the region, where girls married at a very young age.[4] Men married at an older age, usually in their mid-twenties,[5] although Chrysostom wanted men to marry at a younger age. For her entire life the freeborn woman had slaves to guard her chastity. When she was young and unmarried, the girl's slaves had to ensure that that she was not violated and her virginity remained intact, and when she was married, they still had to ensure that she was not involved in an adulterous or shameful relationship.

The chastity (*sōphrosynē, pudicitia*) of the married woman was a constant source of anxiety for the Roman patriarchy, and it was strictly regulated. A person could basically be guilty of two sexual crimes: adultery (*moicheia, adulterium*) and sexual dishonor (*phthora, stuprum*). In the first instance, Susan Treggiari has

---

4. Antti Arjava, *Women and Law in Late Antiquity* (New York: Oxford University Press, 1996), 31.

5. See Walter Scheidel, "Roman Age Structure: Evidence and Models," *Journal of Roman Studies* 91 (2001): 1–26; Kyle Harper, "Marriage and Family," in *The Oxford Handbook of Late Antiquity*, ed. Scott F. Johnson (New York: Oxford University Press, 2012), 670–72.

shown that the Roman concept of adultery was initially formulated on the basis of a married woman having an affair, and thus, was biased against women rather than men. Although men of course could also be charged with adultery, the point of departure was the violation of the free married woman (*eleuthera*).[6] In point of fact, adultery was seen as a crime not against the female per se, but against the man under whose authority she was—either her father, husband, or guardian. The offense of *stuprum*—a term that does not have an English equivalent, has to do with sexual misconduct with an unmarried woman, either a virgin or a widow.[7] *Pudicitia* in the traditional sense therefore had different meanings for men and women, as we have already noted. For a woman it meant keeping her virginity intact until marriage, remaining chaste. For a man, it referred to mastering one's passions and practicing moderation—notably, it also meant avoiding *adulterium*, but it did not mean universal sexual abstinence, as in the case of women. Men could use prostitutes or slave girls in moderation without damaging their *pudicitia*. However, the unmarried man could not simply have sex with any slave girl he fancied—sexually violating another man's slave could make the perpetrator guilty of *stuprum*. *Stuprum* was a legal offense, initially not as serious as *adulterium*, but punishable with a fine, although in more serious circumstances, like violating a freeborn boy or virgin girl, the punishment was more severe.[8] But having sex with a prostitute or one's own slave did not hold the risk of engaging in *stuprum*. While women could also be found guilty of *stuprum*,[9] men had much more sexual freedom than women in these contexts.

Free Roman masculinity was essentially defined by two characteristics: a man's ability to dominate and master his wife, children, slaves, and his passions—in short, his *dominium* or *despoteia;* and the inviolability of a man's status by other men.[10] Holt Parker has portrayed Roman masculinity in what he calls the teratogenic grid.[11] The grid is fundamentally based on the principles of activity and passivity. Masculinity is defined by activity, while femininity is essentially passivity. Any confusion of these roles results in gender and status abnormality and antitypicality. The Latin term for the normal active male is *vir,* and for the normal passive female,

6. Susan Treggiari, *Roman Marriage: Iusti Coniuges from the Time of Cicero to the Time of Ulpian* (New York: Oxford University Press, 1991), 163–64.

7. William Smith, *A Dictionary of Greek and Roman Antiquities* (London: John Murray, 1875), 23.

8. See Smith, *Dictionary of Greek and Roman Antiquities,* 23, 302, 585, 884; Mathew Kuefler, *The Manly Eunuch: Masculinity, Gender Ambiguity, and Christian Ideology in Late Antiquity* (Chicago: University of Chicago Press, 2001), 92–95, 213; Harper, *From Shame to Sin,* 52–54, 148–49.

9. Arjava, *Women and Law in Late Antiquity,* 217–27.

10. Jonathan Walters, "Invading the Roman Body: Manliness and Impenetrability in Roman Thought," in *Roman Sexualities,* ed. Marilyn B. Skinner and Judith P. Hallet (Princeton, NJ: Princeton University Press, 1997), 29–46.

11. Holt N. Parker, "The Teratogenic Grid," in Skinner and Hallet, *Roman Sexualities,* 47–65.

femina or *puella*. The antitypes that Parker identifies are the abnormal passive man (*cinaedus*) and the abnormal active female (*virago, tribas, moecha*). These sociosexual roles to a large extent governed everyday life between men and women in the Roman world, both juridically and culturally, and also informed notions of homoeroticism. Having sex with slaves, whether male or female, was acceptable, since being sexually available to the master was seen as a basic duty of a slave, whether the slave was male or female.[12] Of course, it was a highly shameful and serious crime for a free woman to be penetrated by a male slave. In a case like this the woman would lose all her possessions and be sent into exile, while the slave would be killed.[13] The teratogenic grid serves as a useful schema for understanding something about the formation of elite Roman sexuality in the late Republic and high Empire. It does have its limits, however, since it is unclear to what extent the schema was applicable in nonelite contexts. Nonelite men who did not have their own slave girls as sexual outlets resorted mostly to prostitution, which Kyle Harper rightly calls "the poor man's piece of the slave system."[14]

We have noted the difference between *adulterium* and *stuprum,* and the freedom implicit in male sexuality, as well as the importance of the inviolablity of men to Roman masculinity. In the later Roman Empire, these concepts underwent dramatic changes with important implications for understanding slave sexuality. While early on *stuprum* was seen as a crime punishable by a fine, in later Roman legislation the punishment was death.[15] By the fifth century we see a much stronger juridical influence on male sexuality,[16] and by the fourth century this influence is already very pronounced, especially in Chrysostom's thought. Chrysostom is representative of the early Christian tradition that expanded the scope of sexual crimes—a development that is evident in the Christian interpretation of "fornication" (*porneia*),[17] and the widespread adoption of sexual renunciation.[18] As the New Testament is surprisingly silent on the issue of the sexual abuse of slaves,[19]

12. Craig A. Williams, *Roman Homosexuality* (New York: Oxford University Press, 2009), 15–40.

13. *C.Th.* 9.9.1; in Arjava, *Women and Law in Late Antiquity,* 225–27.

14. Harper, *From Shame to Sin,* 49.

15. Smith, *Dictionary of Greek and Roman Antiquities,* 585.

16. Kuefler, *Manly Eunuch,* 91–93.

17. See Aline Rousselle, *Porneia: On Desire and the Body in Antiquity,* trans. Felicia Pheasant (New York: Barnes & Noble, 1996), 129–40; Kuefler, *Manly Eunuch,* 165–66; Jennifer W. Knust, *Abandoned to Lust: Sexual Slander and Ancient Christianity* (New York: Columbia University Press, 2006), 51–54.

18. Peter R. L. Brown, *The Body and Society: Men, Women, and Sexual Renunciation in Early Christianity* (New York: Columbia University Press, 1988).

19. For the issue of slave sexual abuse in the New Testament, see Glancy, "Obstacles to Slaves' Participation"; Carolyn Osiek, "Female Slaves, *Porneia,* and the Limits of Obedience," in *Early Christian Families in Context: An Interdisciplinary Dialogue,* ed. David L. Balch and Carolyn Osiek, Religion, Marriage, and Family (Grand Rapids, MI: Eerdmans, 2003), 255–76.

Chrysostom had to be inventive in order to make the scriptures relevant for addressing the problem of slave sexuality.

REGULATING SLAVE SEXUALITY

Chrysostom deploys three key discursive operations to address sexual exploitation of slaves: the desexualization of the slave body, the criminalization of its sexual violation, and its honorification. All three strategies should be viewed within the context of Chrysostom's vision of domestic pastoralization, since sexuality is a domestic matter. The pastoralization of sexuality did not exclude the slave body; in fact it gave the slave body a great deal of attention, since it was such a common object of exploitation and sexual sin.

When I speak of the desexualization of the slave body, I refer to a discursive process in which the slave body no longer serves as a morally and juridically neutral site that can be used as a sexual outlet for the free. The desexualization of the slave body takes place within Chrysostom's universal sexual ethic, which favors marriage, sexual renunciation, and virginity (or widowhood) as the sole avenues for sexual expression. The majority of the new sexual conditions that Chrysostom placed on slave bodies were in fact applicable to all persons—for instance, avoiding premarital or adulterous sex, and general sexual abstinence—but the implications of these conditions for the sexuality of slaves were quite different than for the sexuality of the free. In early Christian thought, marriage was necessary for two reasons: to produce legitimate heirs and to curb lust. "So marriage was granted for the sake of procreation, but an even greater reason was to quench the fiery passion of our nature," says Chrysostom, but "after the earth and sea and all the world has been inhabited, only one reason remains for it: the suppression of licentiousness and debauchery."[20]

Virginity, however, is a higher calling in Chrysostom's universal sexual ethic. It had numerous benefits over marriage; in the case of virginity there was no anxiety about managing slaves or being a "slave" to one's husband or wife.[21] Chrysostom directly applied the discourse of virginity to the body of the slave—virginity was no longer something reserved only for the freeborn, or an exoticism when found in a slave body. Slave women could and should also embody virginal honor; they must strive to be both physical and/or spiritual virgins.

---

20. *Virg.* 19.1.2–3, 11–13 (SC 125.156–58): Ἐδόθη μὲν οὖν καὶ παιδοποιίας ἕνεκεν ὁ γάμος· πολλῷ δὲ πλέον ὑπὲρ τοῦ σβέσαι τὴν τῆς φύσεως πύρωσιν . . . ὕστερον δὲ πληρωθείσης καὶ τῆς γῆς καὶ τῆς θαλάττης καὶ τῆς οἰκουμένης πάσης μία λείπεται πρόφασις αὐτοῦ μόνη, ἡ τῆς ἀκολασίας καὶ ἡ τῆς ἀσελγείας ἀναίρεσις. Translation: Sally R. Shore, trans., *John Chrysostom, On Virginity; Against Remarriage* (Lewiston, NY: Edwin Mellen, 1983), 27. See Brown, *Body and Society*, 308–9.

21. See *Virg.* 52 (SC 125.290), 56–57 (SC 125.332–38), 75.3 (SC 125.360–62).

Most importantly, the true test of virginity was not the intactness of the hymen (which is a modern, Western biomedical definition of virginity), but the presence of *sōphrosynē*. Chrysostom expected slave women to have *sōphrosynē*, and their owners to teach it to them.[22] For Chrysostom, there was a direct correlation between teaching slave women *sōphrosynē*, and their desexualization and embodiment of virginity. The key here is *sōphrosynē*—female slaves were no longer exempt from corporeal and spiritual chastity. Slave women were not objects of sexual access anymore; they had to be vessels of honor, exemplars of *sōphrosynē*. Even if women were not physical virgins, Chrysostom believed that the virginity of the soul, psychic virginity, carried equal weight in God's eyes. "For the pure soul is a virgin," Chrysostom explains, "although she has a husband, she is a virgin as to that which is real virginity indeed, that which is worthy of admiration." Any woman is now capable of being a psychic virgin, including slave women: "For virginity of the body is but the accompaniment and shadow of the other, while that is the true virginity."[23] If Chrysostom believed that a slave girl, whether a physical or spiritual virgin, could exhibit *sōphrosynē*, then the implication is that her honor could be violated. Thus, for Chrysostom, sexually violating a slave girl is an act of *stuprum*, and as we will shortly see, also adultery. Along with the spiritualization of virginity, we see a spiritualization of sexual dishonor—*stuprum* or, in Greek, *phthora*—in Chrysostom's thought. The true virgin is he or she whose soul is not violated (*aphthoros psychēn*). The slave body is absorbed into the rhetoric and practice of sexual honor and chastity, both physically and spiritually.

Virgin slave girls were already a sought-after commodity in the ancient Roman slave trade. Their price was much higher than the price for nonvirgins. The reasons for wanting a virgin slave girl were varied. Some wanted virgin slaves simply to violate them, while others preferred virgin slaves because of their chastity and good character, especially if the slave was to guard the chastity of a wife or daughter. A good master might raise slave girls as virgins, while a wicked one might force them into prostitution.[24] Yet, attaching the value of virginity to the slave body had a moral impetus. Chrysostom disapprovingly describes the virginity testing that some slave girls, and free virgins as well, had to endure, especially when virgins

22. See *Hab. eun. spir.* 3.7 (PG 51.287.4–8); *Adv. Jud.* 2.124ra.

23. *Hom. Heb.* 28.5 (F7.327): Ἡ γὰρ ἄφθορος ψυχὴν παρθένος ἐστὶ, κἂν ἄνδρα ἔχῃ· παρθένος τὴν ὄντως παρθενίαν, τὴν θαυμαστήν· αὕτη γὰρ ἡ τοῦ σώματος ἐκείνης ἐστὶν ἐπακολούθημα καὶ σκιὰ, ἡ δὲ ἀληθὴς παρθενία ἐκείνη ἐστί. The concept of psychic virginity was very popular in late ancient Christian discourse; see Susanna Elm, *Virgins of God: The Making of Asceticism in Late Antiquity* (Oxford: Clarendon Press, 1994), 115–24, 142–43; Teresa M. Shaw, *The Burden of the Flesh: Fasting and Sexuality in Early Christianity* (Minneapolis: Fortress Press, 1998), 81–92.

24. Jennifer A. Glancy, "Slavery and the Rise of Christianity," in *The Cambridge World History of Slavery*, vol. 1, *The Ancient Mediterranean World*, ed. Keith Bradley and Paul Cartledge (New York: Cambridge University Press, 2011), 467.

lived with men not related to them, and midwives went to virgins' houses "in order to discern who is violated and who is untouched, just as people do with their slaves they purchase."[25] The precise details of the virginity test remain sketchy. It was not necessarily, as we may think from a modern perspective, checking the hymen. In her study of virginity in the medieval period, Kathleen Kelly has shown that there were numerous methods of testing virginity, "such as examining the urine, observing the effects of certain decoctions and fumigations, and even reading astrological signs."[26] In patristic thought, the hymen seems to be more of a metaphorical invention, something that has to be sealed.[27] According to Chrysostom, some virgins consented to such tests, and others did not; he believed that virgins had to demonstrate their virginity by their character. Both midwives and physicians probably undertook the task of determining virginity.[28] For Chrysostom, virgin slaves had to be of sound moral character as a test of their virginity.[29] Chrysostom notes that one's status is not by any means a hindrance to virginity and good character: "Even if she is not free, even this status does not spoil her betrothal. It is enough to display a beautiful soul and to attain first rank."[30] In a different homily, Chrysostom makes the same point: "Even if a virgin be a slave, let her abide in modesty."[31]

The slave body is further desexualized by its quarantine, by removing it from the vicinity of possible violators—in other words, young freeborn Roman males. Generally speaking, husbands and wives had to be careful with whom they associated among the slaves, as Chrysostom warns: "Let neither demand a great measure of service from the slaves, neither the husband from the slave girl, nor the wife from the male slave; for even these things are enough to beget suspicion."[32] Free persons had to be aware of how they interacted with slaves, especially of the opposite sex, since the walls of the ancient household had many eyes and ears.

25. *Fem. reg.* 2.36–38 (Dumortier 100): ἀλλ' ὥστε διαγνῶναι καθάπερ ἐπὶ τῶν ὠνουμένων θεραπαινίδων, τίς μὲν ἡ διεφθαρμένη, τίς δὲ ἡ ἀνέπαφος. Translation: Elizabeth A. Clark, *Jerome, Chrysostom, and Friends: Essays and Translations* (Lewiston, NY: Edwin Mellen, 1979), 213. There is a similar reference in Ambrose, where a midwife is called to examine the virginity of a slave girl, and even after the examination her status was unclear; *Ep.* 56.8 (CSEL 82.88); see Kyle Harper, *Slavery in the Late Roman World, AD 275–425* (New York: Cambridge University Press, 2011), 294–95.

26. Kathleen Coyne Kelly, *Performing Virginity and Testing Chastity in the Middle Ages*, Routledge Research in Medieval Studies (London: Routledge, 2000), 12.

27. Ibid., 1–39.

28. *Sacr.* 4.2.16–24 (SC 272.240–42).

29. Kelly, *Performing Virginity and Testing Chastity*, 35–36.

30. *Virg.* 60.1.7–9 (SC 125.320): Κἂν γὰρ μηδὲ ἐλευθέρα οὖσα τύχῃ, οὐδὲ τοῦτο αὐτῆς λυμαίνεται τὴν μνηστείαν, ἀλλὰ ἀρκεῖ ψυχὴν ἐπιδείξασθαι καλὴν καὶ τῶν πρωτείων τυχεῖν. Translation: Shore, *On Virginity*, 97.

31. *Hom. Col.* 12.2 (F5.307): Κἂν δούλη τις ᾖ παρθένος, ἐν σωφροσύνῃ μενέτω.

32. *Hom. Eph.* 20.6 (F4.313): Μηδεὶς πέρα τοῦ μέτρου τῶν οἰκετῶν ἀντιποιείσθω, μήτε τῆς κόρης ὁ ἀνὴρ, μήτε τοῦ οἰκέτου ἡ γυνή· καὶ γὰρ ταῦτα ἱκανὰ τεκεῖν ὑποψίας.

Furthermore, Chrysostom also wanted male adolescents to marry early. He applied the same strategy that was used to guard female chastity—marrying at a young age—to young men.[33] A boy had to remain separated from all women, especially slaves, and he had to avoid the theater at all costs.[34] Chrysostom was well aware of the sexual dangers related to slave girls: "Let us take this precaution with the young people, too, and not draw their attention to where there are loose housemaids, immodest damsels, licentious slave girls." We have here the entire vocabulary related to female slaves: "Let us give instructions and advice if we have such a housemaid or such a neighbor or anyone else of that kind," Chrysostom advises, "not to enter into conversation with the young lest a spark fall from it and engulf the soul of the youngster."[35] In this way, the lust of the boy can be managed, and the risk of committing *phthora* is dramatically reduced. The movements of the boy were strictly regulated, and his pedagogue also had to ensure that his bathing habits were free from the presence of females.[36]

It is interesting to note that some of the tasks Chrysostom advises the boy to do himself are duties that are very close to the body. So while a slave may cook for a boy, slaves should not be involved in any duties related to the physical care of the boy's body. "If, however, the boy would wash his feet, never let a slave do this, but let him do it for himself," Chrysostom says, and "do not let a slave hand him his cloak, and do not let him expect another to serve him in the bath."[37] All the duties that Chrysostom lists imply physical contact with the body of the boy—foot washing (a very common job reserved for slaves),[38] bathing, and dressing. Taking on these tasks would not only teach a boy self-sufficiency, but would help him avoid possible sexual contact with a slave, or at least to avoid any occurrence of lustful thoughts or flirting.

Slaves were involved in the most intimate aspects of the daily lives of their owners. For instance, slaves often slept in the same room as their mistress. Slave girls

---

33. *Inan.* 61.757–75 (SC 188.158–60), 81.984–82.1009 (SC 188.186–90).

34. *Inan.* 60.755 (SC 188.158), 78.937–40 (SC 188.180–82), 90.1058–70 (SC 188.196).

35. *Anna* 1.6 (PG 54.642.25–33): ταύτην καὶ ἐπὶ τῶν παιδίων τὴν πρόνοιαν ἔχωμεν, καὶ μὴ παράγωμεν αὐτῶν τὰς ὄψεις, ἔνθα θεραπαινίδες ἀσελγεῖς, ἔνθα κόραι ἄσωτοι, ἔνθα δοῦλαι ἀκόλαστοι, ἀλλὰ κελεύωμεν, καὶ παρεγγυῶμεν, κἂν θεραπαινίδα τοιαύτην ἔχωμεν, κἂν γείτονα, κἂν ἁπλῶς ἑτέραν τινὰ τοιαύτην, μήτε εἰς ὄψιν, μήτε εἰς συνουσίαν λόγων τοῖς νέοις ἔρχεσθαι, ὥστε μὴ σπινθῆρα ἐκεῖθεν ἐκπεσόντα ὁλόκληρον ἀνάψαι τοῦ παιδίου τὴν ψυχήν. Translation: Robert C. Hill, trans., *Homilies on Hannah, David and Saul*, St. John Chrysostom: Old Testament Homilies 1 (Brookline, MA: Holy Cross Orthodox Press, 2003), 80.

36. *Inan.* 60.754–56 (SC 188.158).

37. *Inan.* 70.849–63 (SC 188.170).

38. See *Hom. Phil.* 8[7].1 (F5.75–76) for Chrysostom's comments on foot washing, especially on the role of Jesus, who took on the form and work of a slave and washed his disciples' feet; see Pauline Allen, trans., *John Chrysostom, Homilies on Philippians*, Writings from the Greco-Roman World 16 (Atlanta: Society of Biblical Literature, 2013), 116–19.

assisted in dressing their mistress, and prepared her perfume and makeup.[39] An additional advantage of tactical slaveholding was, then, that it limited the risk of *phthora* among the free members of the household. In his treatise on virginity, Chrysostom explains the disadvantages and risks of having too many slave girls in the household. One of the greatest risks

> is the presence of an attractive girl among the group—and this is bound to happen with many servants since the wealthy class is just as eager to have pretty ones as it is for many of them. So whenever a servant girl happens to stand out, if she captures her master's fancy and puts him under her spell or has more influence over him beyond being admired, the distress felt by the mistress of the house is the same: she has been surpassed, if not in love, at least in youthfulness and admiration.[40]

The appearance of slaves mattered to their owners. Attractive slave girls and eunuchs might cost more than others, and like the golden ornaments and jewel-encrusted vessels, attractive slaves were yet another symbol of status, wealth, and Roman decadence. The beautiful slave girl in the passage above posed a very real sexual threat to the mistress of the household, even leading to sexual infidelity on the part of the husband. Strangely, Chrysostom does not say much about the close proximity of attractive female slaves to free women (or men to men, for that matter)—his concern is heteroerotic penetration, and he probably does not see two women or men together as that much of a danger (or simply does not think about it or ever mention it). In one of Chrysostom's harangues on the decadence of the wealthy in comparison to the simplicity of the poor, he puts forward the image of a dinner table—the table of the wealthy had "many servants, outfitted with clothes not inferior to that of the guests, and brightly clothed, and wearing exotic trousers, beautiful to behold, in the very prime of life, stout and well-built." The table of the poor had "only two servants, treading all that vanity under foot."[41] Yet, even tables of poor households had slaves and servants attend to them—this is clearly not a reference to the indigent, but probably the moderately poor. The description of the servants and slaves at the wealthy table is remarkable—Chrysostom describes

39. *Stelech.* 2.1 (PG 47.412.18–29).

40. *Virg.* 67.9–19 (SC 125.336): ὅπερ μάλιστα ἐν τῷ πλήθει τῆς τοιαύτης θεραπείας συμβαίνειν εἴωθεν, ὅταν ἐν τῇ τῶν θεραπαινίδων ἐκείνων ἀγέλῃ εὐπρεπής τις οὖσα τύχῃ. Ἀνάγκη γὰρ τοῦτο πάντως ἐν τῷ πλήθει συμπεσεῖν· οὐδὲ γὰρ ὥστε πολλὰς κτήσασθαι μόνον, ἀλλ' ὥστε καὶ εὐειδεῖς ἐξ ἴσης οἱ πλουτοῦντες σπουδάζουσιν. Ὅταν οὖν συμβῇ τινα διαλάμπειν ἐν αὐταῖς, ἄν τε ἕλῃ τὸν δεσπότην τῷ φίλτρῳ ἄν τε μηδὲν περαιτέρω τοῦ θαυμασθῆναι ἰσχύσῃ, τὰ τῆς ὀδύνης ἴσα γίνεται τῇ δεσποίνῃ παρευδοκιμουμένῃ εἰ καὶ μὴ τῷ πόθῳ ἀλλὰ τῇ τοῦ σώματος ὥρᾳ καὶ τῷ θαύματι. Translation: Shore, *On Virginity,* 103–4.

41. *Hom. Col.* 1.2 (F5.179): Πάλιν ἐνταῦθα μὲν ἔστωσαν διάκονοι πολλοί, τῶν κατακειμένων οὐχ ἧττον κεκοσμημένοι τοῖς ἱματίοις, καὶ ἐνδεδυμένοι λαμπρῶς, καὶ ἀναξυρίδας ἔχοντες, καλοὶ μὲν ἰδεῖν, αὐτὸ ἄγοντες τῆς ἡλικίας τὸ ἄνθος, σφριγῶντες καὶ εὐσωματοῦντες· ἐκεῖ δὲ δύο μόνοι ἔστωσαν διάκονοι, πάντα τὸν τῦφον τοῦτον πεπατηκότες.

their beauty, but there are also some sexual nuances in the description. The servants and slaves are physically attractive and well built. The exotic trousers (*anaxyrides*) seem to indicate an Eastern style of dress, as the term used may be related to a Persian word. Clothing was a very important social code in Roman society.[42] The slaves are not only physically beautiful and fashionably dressed, but they also seem to be exotic, similar to the cuisine set on the table—everything suggests decadence, excess, and exclusivity. The servants and slaves of the poor were few and simply clothed—the display of one's slaves was also an ascetic trait and a symbol of wealth renunciation. And it was not only women who worried about slaves' attractions. Chrysostom also refers to paranoid and jealous men who suspect their wives of committing sexual crimes with the male slaves in the household.[43]

Sex with slave girls was seen as an especially pleasure-centered experience. Besides the simple titillation of regularly being with a new sexual partner, sex with slaves may have been seen as being particularly pleasurable because of Roman coital decorum and eugenics. Peter Brown notes the Roman belief that sexual positions had a direct influence on conception and development, and that the "adoption of a variety of sexual positions was a form of playing around in the face of mankind's great Mother, 'Nature': men invented other positions as a result of wantonness, licentiousness and intoxication."[44] The extent to which married couples followed this tradition of coital order is, of course, open to speculation. Yet, sex with a slave or prostitute meant that the decorum of the marriage bed no longer applied, and the physical act of sex could be more liberal and pleasurable. Traditionally, at least, pleasure was not the primary purpose of lovemaking for spouses; rather, it was successful conception and eugenics that gained priority.

Chrysostom, however, rejects the idea that having sex with a slave girl was more pleasurable. Being with one's freeborn wife was much more pleasurable and honorable[45]—and "if someone seeks pleasure, let him especially avoid intercourse with a prostitute!"[46] Chrysostom therefore also desexualizes the slave body by removing all pleasure from the sexual encounter with a slave. These are the multiple strategies for desexualizing the slave body and guarding the slaveholder from possible *phthora*.

The second discursive operation Chrysostom uses in his consideration of the sexual exploitation of slaves—the criminalization of the slave body's sexual

---

42. Mary Harlow, "Clothes Maketh the Man: Power Dressing and Elite Masculinity in the Later Roman World," in *Gender in the Early Medieval World: East and West, 300–900*, ed. Leslie Brubaker and Julia M. H. Smith (New York: Cambridge University Press, 2004), 44–70.

43. *Virg.* 52.1.1–28 (SC 125.288–90); see Shore, *On Virginity*, 83–84.

44. Brown, *Body and Society*, 21.

45. *Propt. fornic.* 5 (PG 51.217.6–8).

46. *Propt. fornic.* 5 (PG 51.217.13–14): εἴ τις ἡδονὴν διώκει, οὗτος μάλιστα φευγέτω τὴν πρὸς τὰς πόρνας ὁμιλίαν.

violation—is very closely linked to the first. The sexual exploitation of the slave body becomes a criminal act in Chrysostom's rhetoric. We have already seen above that Chrysostom expands the notion of *stuprum/phthora* to include the sexual violation of a slave girl. His assault on sexual sin, especially the sexual abuse of slave women and frequenting prostitutes, formed part of a systematic program of redefining and reconstructing sexuality and sexual sin in the broad framework of marriage, adultery, and virginity. Not only did Chrysostom expand the conceptual spectrum of *phthora,* but he also merged it with adultery (*moicheia*). In a homily solely devoted to the problem of fornication and adultery (referring to 1 Cor. 7:2), Chrysostom states:

> For we are not ignorant of the fact that many consider it adultery only when someone should sexually violate a married woman. But I, myself, am saying that it is adultery all the same when one has sex with any woman—whether she is openly a prostitute, a slave girl, or any other woman without a husband—it is wicked and concupiscent. For it is surely not only from the ones who are being violated, but also from the ones who violate, that the accusation of adultery is contracted. And do not mention to me now extraneous laws that drag wives who have been adulterized into courts of law demanding an account, but not demanding an account when those having husbands and wives are seduced by the slave girls. But I will read to you the law of God, which is similarly displeased with both wives and husbands, saying that the act is adultery. . . . For even those from the domestic slaves are favored, that if a master receives chattels, he should violate none of them.[47]

The sphere of adultery is now expanded, and not only includes violating a married woman, but even a professional prostitute (*dēmosia*) or a slave girl (*therapainis*). Chrysostom's contemporary, Ambrose, had the same view: "Any sexual offense (*stuprum*) is adultery (*adulterium*), it is lawful neither for a husband or a wife."[48] The rhetoric also shows how prevalent the sexual abuse of female slaves was in late antiquity, despite the risks and measures to curb it. Conveniently, however, Chrysostom emphasizes that it is the married partner who is seduced by the

---

47. *Propt. fornic.* 4 (PG 51.213.48–214.5, 214.18–20): Οὐκ ἀγνοοῦμεν γὰρ ὅτι πολλοὶ μοιχείαν νομίζουσιν, ὅταν τις ὕπανδρον φθείρῃ γυναῖκα μόνον· ἐγὼ δὲ κᾶν δημοσίᾳ πόρνῃ, κᾶν θεραπαινίδι, κᾶν ἄλλῃ τινὶ γυναικὶ ἄνδρα οὐκ ἐχούσῃ πρόσχῃ κακῶς καὶ ἀκολάστως, ἔχων γυναῖκα, μοιχείαν τὸ τοιοῦτον εἶναί φημι. Οὐ γὰρ δὴ μόνον ἀπὸ τῶν ὑβριζομένων, ἀλλὰ καὶ ἀπὸ τῶν ὑβριζόντων τὸ τῆς μοιχείας συνίσταται ἔγκλημα. Μὴ γάρ μοι τοὺς ἔξωθεν νόμους εἴπῃς νῦν, οἳ τὰς μὲν γυναῖκας μοιχευομένας εἰς δικαστήριον ἕλκουσι καὶ εὐθύνας ἀπαιτοῦσιν, ἄνδρας καὶ γυναῖκας ἔχοντας καὶ θεραπαινίσι προφθειρομένους οὐκ ἀπαιτοῦσιν εὐθύνας· ἀλλ’ ἐγώ σοι τὸν τοῦ Θεοῦ νόμον ἀναγνώσομαι, ὁμοίως καὶ ἐπὶ τῆς γυναικὸς καὶ ἐπὶ τοῦ ἀνδρὸς ἀγανακτοῦντα, καὶ μοιχείαν εἶναι τὸ πρᾶγμα λέγοντα. . . . μηδὲ παραφθειρέτω· καὶ γὰρ τῶν οἰκετῶν ἐκεῖνος εὔνους λέγεται, ὃς ἂν τὰ δεσποτικὰ δεξάμενος χρήματα, μηδὲν ἐξ αὐτῶν διαφθείρῃ.

48. Ambrose, *Abr.* 1.4.25 (PL 14.452): *Omne stuprum adulterium est, nec viro licet quod mulieri non licet.* See William J. Dooley, *Marriage according to St. Ambrose* (Washington, DC: Catholic University of America Press, 1948).

slave girl (*therapainisi prophtheiromenous*), not vice versa, again illustrating the prejudice against the sexual integrity of slaves. Chrysostom believes that the reason that many men have intercourse with slave girls and prostitutes is because they had a deficient upbringing. Chrysostom again says that "even if the one who corrupts the married man is a prostitute, it is a case of adultery," but also adds that after marriage "they betake themselves to women who are whores, because they did not practice self-control (*sōphronein*) before marriage."[49] He believes that the sexual abuse of slaves is conditioned and habituated into men at a very young age, and that may indicate that slave sexual abuse started, in some instances, while men were very young, probably at adolescence. Even some young boys sexually abused their slaves.

To press the argument, Chrysostom asserts that God's law overrides Roman law. While the Roman legal system was traditionally biased against the violation of free married women, the law of God does not favor status and is impartial.[50] Chrysostom uses two terms for sexual violation in this instance: *phtheirō* (and various compounds of it, like *diaphtheirō* and *prophtheirō*; all verbal forms of *phthora*) and *hybrizō*. The term *hybrizō* has a broad linguistic-doulological scope in Chrysostom. It can refer to an insult in the general sense, as when a son insults his father and causes his enslavement,[51] or extreme punishment and physical maltreatment,[52] and sexual violation (often related to rape, abuse, or prostitution).[53] At times it is difficult to determine whether Chrysostom uses the word to denote sexual violation or simply excessive verbal and physical abuse.[54] In his comments on punishment, Chrysostom objects when reasonable punishment (*sōphronizō*) becomes violation (*hybrizō*), and he also states that the man who sexually violates slave girls also insults (*kathybrizō*) his wife.[55] In classical Greek literature *hybrizō* and *hybris* function quite often as euphemisms for sexual abuse. Both *phthora* and *hybris* are used interchangeably by Chrysostom to denote sexual dishonor (*stu-*

---

49. *Anna* 1.6 (PG 54.642.56–643.3): κἂν πόρνη ᾖ ἡ προσφθειρομένη τῷ γεγαμηκότι, μοιχεία τὸ πρᾶγμά ἐστι ... πρὸς τὰς ἑταιριζομένας γυναῖκας τρέχουσιν, ἐπειδὴ πρὸ τοῦ γάμου σωφρονεῖν οὐκ ἐμελέτησαν. Interestingly enough, a different manuscript reads κἂν πόρνη μὴ ᾖ, "even if she is *not* a prostitute," thereby also including women outside of the ranks of prostitutes; see PG 54.642 note [d; Colb.]; Hill, *Homilies on Hannah, David and Saul*, 144.

50. *Propt. fornic.* 4 (PG 51.214.39–40).

51. *Hom. Eph.* 22.1 (F4.334); *Inan.* 71.867–69 (SC 188.172).

52. See *Hel. vid.* (PG 51.339.32); *Phoc.* 6 (PG 50.702.5); *Stat.* 20.4 (PG 49.202.43–45).

53. See *Bern. Pros. Domn.* 3 (PG 50.630.37); *Hom. 1 Cor.* 12.12 (F2.146–47); *Hom. Matt.* 6.7 (PG 57.72.16–18); *Fem. reg.* 11.90 (Dumortier 135). In his invective against female homoeroticism, Chrysostom says that "women violated other women"; *Hom. Rom.* 5[4] (F1.47): αἵ τε γὰρ γυναῖκες γυναῖκας ὕβριζον. See Bernadette J. Brooten, ed., *Love between Women: Early Christian Responses to Female Homoeroticism* (Chicago: University of Chicago Press, 1996), 345.

54. See, for instance, the reference in *Subintr.* 10.16–24 (Dumortier 79–80); see chapter 5.

55. *Propt. fornic.* 4 (PG 51.214.51–54).

prum), which is now also considered an act of adultery. In earlier times, the concept of *hybris* was important in Athenian law, and protected any individual, whether male or female, slave or free, from this type of violation. Chrysostom's deployment of the term closely resembles its use in Demosthenes,[56] whose rhetoric may have been influential in this case, since Chrysostom may have been taught by Libanius or someone similarly schooled in Greek literature.[57] Demosthenes quotes the Athenian law of *hybris,* that "if anyone commits an insult against anyone . . . whether slave or free, or does anything illegal to any of these people," there is reason for legal action. "Listen, men of Athens, to how benevolent this law is," writes Demosthenes. "It states that not even slaves deserve to suffer insult."[58]

In Chrysostom's view, the law of God holds people who violate slaves liable not simply for *phthora* then, but for the highest form of *hybris—moicheia*. In this way the sexual violation of the slave is criminalized—anyone who abuses a slave, whether a prostitute or a domestic, not only sins,[59] but is also guilty of committing a crime (*paranomos*): adultery.[60] The Latinized version of Greek *moicheia* is *moechia,* a term first used by Tertullian,[61] and later deployed to refer to extramarital sex in the general sense. A *moechus* was a man who had sex with a woman besides his wife. The use of the Latin terms *moechia* and *moechus* is indicative of the change in late Roman sociocultural opinion and legislation regarding adultery and sexual violation.[62] Chrysostom's rhetoric functions within this shift in the perception of

56. See David Cohen, "Sexuality, Violence, and the Athenian Law of *Hybris,*" *Greece & Rome* 38, no. 2 (1991): 171–88; Cohen, "Sexual Abuse and Sexual Rights," 185–88.

57. For more on Demosthenes's influence on Chrysostom, see P. J. Ryan, "Chrysostom—A Derived Stylist?," *Vigiliae Christianae* 36, no. 1 (1982): 5–14. Chrysostom was aware of ancient Athenian law, as his comments against pederasty in *Hom. Rom.* 5[4].2 (F1.48) attest.

58. Demosthenes, *Mid.* 47.1–2, 48.1–2 (Butcher 36–37): Ἐάν τις ὑβρίζῃ εἴς τινα . . . τῶν ἐλευθέρων ἢ τῶν δούλων, ἢ παράνομόν τι ποιήσῃ εἰς τούτων τινά. . . . Ἀκούετ', ὦ ἄνδρες Ἀθηναῖοι, τοῦ νόμου τῆς φιλανθρωπίας, ὃς οὐδὲ τοὺς δούλους ὑβρίζεσθαι ἀξιοῖ. See Douglas MacDowell, "Hybris in Athens," *Greece & Rome* 23 (1976): 14–31; Nick R. E. Fisher, "Hybris and Dishonour I," ibid., 177–93; Fisher, "Hybris and Dishonour II," *Greece & Rome* 26 (1979): 32–47; Fisher, "*Hybris,* Status and Slavery," in *The Greek World,* ed. Anton Powell (London: Routledge, 1995), 44–84. Not all classical authors shared these precise sentiments. Xenophon, for instance, does recognize the right of a master to use his slaves sexually, although he believes that sex with a person of inferior status is not as rewarding as with one's wife; *Oec.* 10.8 (Marchant 450–51); see Marilyn B. Skinner, *Sexuality in Greek and Roman Culture* (Malden, MA: Blackwell, 2005), 144–45.

59. *Propt. fornic.* 4 (PG 51.215.13).

60. *Propt. fornic.* 2 (PG 51.211.5); Demosthenes also uses this term with regard to violating a slave (*Mid.* 47.1–2 [Butcher 36–37]).

61. See Tertullian, *Pud.* 3–5 (PL 2.985–88); see William P. Le Saint, trans., *Treatises on Penance: On Penitence and On Purity,* Ancient Christian Writers 28 (Westminster: Newman Press, 1959), 41–130; Kuefler, *Manly Eunuch,* 329–30.

62. See Alexander Souter, *A Glossary of Later Latin to 600 A.D.* (Oxford: Clarendon Press, 1964), 254; Kuefler, *Manly Eunuch,* 82, 86, 329–30.

sexuality in general, and more specifically, the sexual violation of slave bodies. In the end Chrysostom reaches back to the most archaic meaning of *hybris,* as an insult against God. The reason the status of the person violated makes no difference is because the crime is not against the slave in the first instance, but against God. "So that even if you should violate the empress, or even your own female slave who has a husband, the transgression is the same," Chrysostom explains. "Why? Because he does not avenge the persons that are harmed, but himself. For you are equally polluted, you have equally insulted God."[63] Even if it is not adultery, but fornication, it remains an insult against God in Chrysostom's mind. Adultery is also extended to apply to slave marriages despite their legal ambiguity. The slave marriage is vulnerable to adultery in Chrysostom's eyes. It also tells us that although slave marriages did not enjoy official legal status, there was probably some unofficial yet significant and important recognition of slave unions in society. The popular and habitual status that slave unions enjoyed shows the limits of using legislation to understand everyday social relations in late antiquity.

Interestingly enough, when the story of Abraham, Sarah, and Hagar (Gen. 16) is discussed Chrysostom needs to do some careful explaining as to why it was *not* a case of adultery. Chrysostom believed that what made their story unique was the fact that there was no jealousy or lust involved—in fact, Chrysostom praises Sarah for making such a great sacrifice in having her husband sleep with Hagar. It was a sign of the greatest affection to Chrysostom. Abraham did not take Hagar out of his own volition or lust—it is not, in this case, then the act of intercourse that is the problem, but the passions that lead to it. Abraham also never loved Hagar; his love was always for Sarah. The circumstances were different—Abraham had no lust and gained no pleasure from it. Hence neither was guilty of adultery. Chrysostom is oblivious to the plight of Hagar, who had no say in the matter at all—she simply had to be sexually available.[64]

Furthermore, although he often affirms and applies the teratogenic grid when it suits his argument, Chrysostom ultimately overturns it, negating the normalizing and abnormalizing tendencies of male activity and female passivity respectively. Chrysostom states: "For it is surely not only from the ones who are being violated, but also from the ones who violate, that the accusation of adultery is contracted."[65] In this statement Chrysostom makes both the active (*tōn hybrizontōn*) and the passive (*tōn hybrizomenōn*) party culpable for adultery and sexual dishonor—teratogenicity is no longer based on active or passive sexual activity. The teratogenic grid of the

63. *Hom. 1 Thess.* 5.2 (F5.369–70): Ὥστε κἂν τὴν βασιλίδα διαφθείρῃς, κἂν τὴν δούλην τὴν σὴν ὕπανδρον οὖσαν, ὅμοιον τὸ ἔγκλημα. Διὰ τί; Ὅτι οὐ τὰ ἀδικούμενα ἐκδικεῖ πρόσωπα, ἀλλ' ἑαυτόν · σὺ γὰρ ὁμοίως ἐμολύνθης, ὁμοίως τὸν Θεὸν ὕβρισας

64. *Hom. Gen.* 38.1–2 (PG 53.351–53); *Hom. Eph.* 20.6 (F4.313–14).

65. *Propt. fornic.* 4 (PG 51.213.53–54): Οὐ γὰρ δὴ μόνον ἀπὸ τῶν ὑβριζομένων, ἀλλὰ καὶ ἀπὸ τῶν ὑβριζόντων τὸ τῆς μοιχείας συνίσταται ἔγκλημα.

early empire is therefore no longer applicable in the context of slave sexuality. This restructuring of sexual teratogenicity seems to have been a general tendency in late antiquity. Mathew Kuefler uses an example from Ausonius to illustrate the same point, only in the context of same-sex passion—Ausonius writes that both those who commit sexual misconduct (*stuprum committunt*) and those against whom sexual misconduct is committed (*stuprum perpetiuntur*) are guilty of an offense (*crimen*).[66] Thus, masculinity, in Chrysostom's view, is no longer determined by mastering and penetrating the bodies of social inferiors. The same standards of *sōphrosynē* (as modesty) that were applicable to females are now also applicable to males. There are twelve occurrences of *sōphrosynē* (or its derivatives) in the homily *Propter fornicationes*, and in four instances the term is coupled with the notion of dignity (*semnotēs, dignitas*)[67]—Chrysostom is probably alluding to 1 Timothy 3:4, which reads: "A man must manage his own household well . . . with all dignity."[68]

This coupling is significant. In Roman law, if a person was guilty of a crime, especially a sexual offense, that person lost his or her *dignitas*, which made it difficult for the person to participate in certain civic activities, such as being a witness in court or holding certain offices—*dignitas* was a very important aspect of free masculinity. It was especially linked to prostitution, as Thomas McGinn has pointed out; in Chrysostom, losing one's *semnotēs* implies that one's sexual status is akin to that of a prostitute.[69] The loss of *dignitas* because of sexual misconduct was linked to infamy (*atimia, infamia*).[70] *Infamia* could include a number of dishonorable acts, including cowardice in the army and arranging double marriages, and, as Kuefler notes, it was often linked to unmanliness.[71] Most importantly, as with *dignitas*, *infamia* was linked to both female and male prostitution.[72] Chrysostom, in this case, speaks of dishonoring someone "by means of infamous behavior."[73] The combination of *sōphrosynē* and *semnotētos* denotes sociosexual integrity, which is epitomized by being corporeally unified with one's wife and corporeally separate from any other woman or man. Chrysostom repeatedly

---

66. Ausonius, *Epigr.* 43 (Kay 50); see Kuefler, *Manly Eunuch*, 92.

67. *Propt. fornic.* 4 (PG 51.214.15, 48, 59; 215.40).

68. NA28: τοῦ ἰδίου οἴκου καλῶς προϊστάμενον . . . μετὰ πάσης σεμνότητος.

69. Thomas A. J. McGinn, *Prostitution, Sexuality, and the Law in Ancient Rome* (New York: Oxford University Press, 1998), 336.

70. For more on the legal background of *infamia*/ἀτιμία, see Smith, *Dictionary of Greek and Roman Antiquities*, 533–36.

71. Kuefler, *Manly Eunuch*, 30.

72. See Otto Karlowa, "Zur Geschichte der Infamia," *Zeitschrift für Rechtsgeschichte* 9 (1870): 204–37; Smith, *Dictionary of Greek and Roman Antiquities*, 536; Abel H. J. Greenidge, Infamia: *Its Place in Roman Public and Private Law* (Oxford: Clarendon Press, 1894); Max Kaser, "Infamia und ignominia in den römischen Rechtsquellen," *Zeitschrift der Savigny-Stiftung für Rechtsgeschichte* 73 (1956): 220–78; McGinn, *Prostitution, Sexuality, and the Law*, 65–70; Harper, *From Shame to Sin*, 150–53.

73. *Propt. fornic.* 2 (PG 51.211.23–24): διὰ τῆς ἀτίμου πομπῆς.

makes use of Paul's argument of corporeal unity in relation to marriage found in 1 Corinthians 7:4.[74] And to show that the slave body is sexually out of bounds, Chrysostom rewrites 1 Corinthians 7:4 with a new doulological emphasis. "How does God's law then introduce here the same retribution for those in slavery and those in positions of mastery?" Chrysostom asks; and then as an answer he provides the new rereading of 1 Corinthians 7:4: "And accordingly the husband is the *master* (*despotēs*) of his wife's body, and the wife is the *mistress* (*despoina*) of her husband's body."[75] The husband and wife possess sexual dominion only over each other's bodies, negating any possible sexual domination they may claim over the slave body—the retribution is equal (*isotimia*) whether one violates slave or free.[76]

This strategy of criminalization is then also related to Chrysostom's final discursive operation—the honorification of the slave body; the slave body becomes a site that is no longer morally neutral, but has the capacity to cause honor, or shame if exploited. This is a very powerful strategy, since honor was a very valuable symbolic commodity in ancient times. The honor or shame of the slaves now reflects back onto the owner,[77] hence the importance of teaching slaves *sōphrosynē*. Slave men had to be taught virtue so that they could control their own families, which was to the advantage of the owner's household.[78] Teaching sexual virtue was especially important to Chrysostom. A slaveholder may even resort to intensive and violent punitive measures to curb sexual vice. "Rip her to shreds with the scourge, like some unruly and lascivious slave girl," Chrysostom says about the wicked conscience.[79] As we also saw in chapter 5, a licentious slave girl could be chained and confined in the owner's household.

The sexuality of slave girls was therefore strictly regulated, even to the point of testing their virginity (in the ancient sense). It formed part of the very complex

74. *Propt. fornic.* 4 (PG 51.214.15–16, 21–28; 218.11–13).

75. My emphasis; *Propt. fornic.* 4 (PG 51.214.39–40, 44–46): Πῶς οὖν ἐνταῦθα ἴσην ἀντίδοσιν δουλείας καὶ δεσποτείας εἰσήγαγε; . . . Καὶ καθάπερ ἐκεῖνος δεσπότης ἐστὶ τοῦ σώματος αὐτῆς, οὕτω καὶ αὕτη δέσποινα τοῦ ἐκείνου σώματος.

76. *Propt. fornic.* 4 (PG 51.214.46–47).

77. See *Hom. Act.* 42.4 (PG 60.301.14–15, 17); *Hom. Eph.* 15.2 (F4.259); *Hom. Phlm.* arg. (F6.328); *Hom. 1 Tim.* 16.2 (F6.141); *Hom. Tit.* 4.1 (F6.298); see chapter 5.

78. Studies on slave families include Iza Bieżuńska-Małowist, "La vie familiale des esclaves," *Index* 8 (1978): 140–43; Marleen B. Flory, "Family in *Familia*: Kinship and Community in Slavery," *American Journal of Ancient History* 3 (1978): 78–95; Bradley, *Slaves and Masters in the Roman Empire: A Study in Social Control* (New York: Oxford University Press, 1987), 47–80; Dale B. Martin, "Slave Families and Slaves in Families," in Balch and Osiek, *Early Christian Families in Context: An Interdisciplinary Dialogue*, 207–30; Glancy, *Slavery in Early Christianity*, 45–47; Jonathan Edmondson, "Slavery and the Roman Family," in Bradley and Cartledge, *Cambridge World History of Slavery*, 1:347–51; Harper, *Slavery in the Late Roman World*, 261–73.

79. *Hom. Matt.* 42.3 (PG 57.455.8–10): κατάξαινε μαστίζων αὐτὴν, καθάπερ τινὰ θεραπαινίδα μετέωρον καὶ πορνευομένην. See also *Adv. Jud.* 124ra.

system that comprised domestic honor. When Chrysostom expanded the concept of adultery to include all other sexual offenses, he made domestic honor even more fragile. This may also be one of the reasons why slave marriages and family life received some informal recognition in the household and society. Chrysostom uses the terms *zeugnymi* and *syzeugnymi* when speaking of slave unions, known as *contubernia* in Roman law, which convey a sense of informality (over and against *gameō*). The use of this terminology was a choice; others, like Basil, used the term *gamos* to refer to a slave marriage. And Chrysostom acknowledged slave unions as subject to adultery. This recognition was not necessarily a widespread sentiment— the choice to allow slaves to have certain familial relations was still the owner's, and there is evidence that slave families were often split up, especially parents from children.[80] At times, slaves were also forced into certain relationships. Chrysostom laments: "In this way many have forced their domestics and slaves. Some have drawn them into marriage against their will, and others have forced them to perform disgraceful services, perverse sexual deeds, acts of theft, financial fraud, and violence."[81] Yet Chrysostom himself suggests that a licentious woman might be given in marriage to a husband in order to limit her recourse to fornication. "What if she is a prostitute?" someone may ask, and Chrysostom replies: "Yoke her to a husband, remove the opportunities for her to commit fornication."[82] Although we cannot know for certain, I believe that the rudimentary recognition of slave marriages and the attribution of modesty to the slave body—that is, the sophrosynic factor—as evidenced in Chrysostom, may also have implied that slave sex should exhibit the kind of decorum found among married couples, especially in terms of eugenics and ensuring good offspring from slaves. Statements like those of Chrysostom, and the practical consequences I have outlined, may have physically changed the way two slave bodies coalesced in lovemaking, showing the extent to which pastoralization possibly influenced some households. Just as feasting around the table had to be orderly,[83] so too did sex.

Masters had immense control over the relationships of slaves, and the honor of the master overrode the happiness of the slave. We have already heard of the widow slaveholder who sold her slave girl because of the wickedness of the girl's husband.[84] The *paterfamilias* had the authority to arrange a marriage for any of his

80. Bradley, "On the Roman Slave Supply and Slavebreeding," in *Classical Slavery*, ed. Moses I. Finley (London: Routledge, 1987), 53–81.

81. *Hom. Phlm.* 1.2 (F6.333): Πολλοὶ πολλοὺς οἰκέτας ἠνάγκασαν, καὶ παῖδας· οἱ μὲν εἰς γάμους εἵλκυσαν μὴ βουλομένους, οἱ δὲ ὑπηρετήσασθαι διακονίαις ἀτόποις, καὶ ἔρωτι μιαρῷ, καὶ ἁρπαγαῖς καὶ πλεονεξίαις καὶ βίαις.

82. *Hom. Eph.* 15.2 (F4.259–60): Τί οὖν, φησίν, ὅταν πορνεύῃ; Ζεῦξον ἀνδρί, περίελε τῆς πορνείας τὰς ὑποθέσεις.

83. *Hom. Rom.* 25[24].2 (F1.400–401); see chapter 3.

84. *Hom. 1 Thess.* 11.3 (F5.436–37).

subordinates, including his children and slaves. Slaves were not allowed to "marry" without the consent of the master—yet another measure to protect domestic honor. Basil of Caesarea was very clear about this. He did not allow slaves to enter into secret marriages, which could be seen as an act of resistance or a desperate move for familial stability and security; Basil still affirmed the dominion of the owner over the relationships of the slave: "It is a grave fault even on the part of a slave to give herself away in secret wedlock and fill the house with impurity, and, by her wicked life, to wrong her owner."[85] The sanction of the master also determined the rules of fornication and adultery for slave marriages. It is only a marriage, and thus not adultery, if the owner recognizes and authorizes the marriage. In slave marriages, the fiat of the slaveholder assumes the function of law. If the owner approves of the marriage, however, it is not a sin if slaves have sex, since it is not extramarital. "The woman who yields to a man against her master's will commits fornication," Basil warns, "but if afterwards she accepts free marriage, she marries. The former case is fornication; the latter marriage. The covenants of persons who are not independent (*tōn hypexousiōn*) have no validity."[86] The word of the slaveholder is therefore the determining factor in whether slaves commit fornication or not, and the word of the owner solemnizes a slave marriage.[87] Bernadette Brooten rightly notes that besides the recognition of slave marriages by church leaders, and the sexual regulations imposed upon them, we know very little about the actual interrelational dynamics of these unions.[88] If we take all this into account, it seems clear that slaveholders principally used slave relationships to manage their honor. The point that needs to be made here is that Chrysostom affirms the potential of the slave body as a denominator in domestic honor, and sexual exploitation always poses a risk to the honor of the household.

The implementation of this new universal sexual ethic, which did not differentiate between slave and free, is yet another aspect of the pervasive operation of domestic pastoralization. Sexuality is essentially a domestic matter. We saw in

85. Basil, *Ep.* 199.18.21–23 (Courtonne 162): Μέγα μὲν ἁμάρτημα καὶ δούλην λαθραίοις γάμοις ἑαυτὴν ἐπιδιδοῦσαν φθορᾶς ἀναπλῆσαι τὸν οἶκον καὶ καθυβρίζειν διὰ τοῦ πονηροῦ βίου τὸν κεκτημένον. Translation: *NPNF.* For an excellent analysis of the role of female slaves in Basil's letters, see Bernadette Brooten, "Enslaved Women in Basil of Caesarea's Canonical Letters: An Intersectional Analysis," in *Doing Gender, Doing Religion: Case Studies on Intersectionality in Early Judaism, Christianity and Islam,* ed. Ute Eisen, Christine Gerber, and Angela Standhartinger, Wissenschaftliche Untersuchungen zum Neuen Testament 302 (Tübingen: Mohr Siebeck, 2013), 325–55.

86. Basil, *Ep.* 199.40.1–5 (Courtonne 163): ῾Η παρὰ γνώμην τοῦ δεσπότου ἀνδρὶ ἑαυτὴν ἐκδιδοῦσα ἐπόρνευσεν, ἡ δὲ μετὰ ταῦτα πεπαρρησιασμένῳ γάμῳ χρησαμένη ἐγήματο. ῞Ωστε ἐκεῖνο μὲν πορνεία, τοῦτο δὲ γάμος. Αἱ γὰρ συνθῆκαι τῶν ὑπεξουσίων οὐδὲν ἔχουσι βέβαιον. Translation: *NPNF;* see Harper, *Slavery in the Late Roman World,* 273.

87. Geoffrey S. Nathan, *The Family in Late Antiquity: The Rise of Christianity and the Endurance of Tradition* (London: Routledge, 2000), 173.

88. Brooten, "Enslaved Women in Basil," 331–33.

chapter 3 that slaves were included in all aspects of domestic pastoralization, whether embodying sacerdotal authority as a priest over an enslaved family, or sharing in the religious rituals of the household. The pastoralization of sexuality likewise implied the inclusion of slave sexuality. But the efforts of Chrysostom's vision of pastoralization had to be radical; hence we see that the slave body is desexualized, its violation criminalized, and it became a site for the transposition of honor or disgrace.

DISGRACE COMMODIFIED: DOULOLOGY AND PROSTITUTION

One of the greatest threats to pious domestic sexuality was prostitution. The sexuality of slaves and prostitution were closely linked both socially and economically. It is not possible to determine the exact numbers, but we know that many prostitutes were also slaves, and even those who were not slaves did not always have much agency in their own affairs.[89] According to LSJ, there may be a direct etymological link between slavery and prostitution—the Greek words *pornē* (prostitute) and *porneuō* (prostitution) may be related to the term *pernēmi* (to be bought and sold, or exported as a slave), emphasizing the fungibility of both slavery and prostitution. However, the language of prostitution does not always refer to those in the actual profession. It is often the case that the term "prostitute" simply refers to a libidinous woman (or man). And sexual promiscuity was a stereotype very often associated with slave girls, especially by Chrysostom, so it is not difficult to see why the line between prostitution and the sexual promiscuity of female slaves is blurred.[90]

Although prostitutes were often slaves or freedwomen, and slave girls were often thought of as private prostitutes, the actual profession of prostitution was clearly distinguished from the "domestic" sexual duties of slaves.[91] Ulpian distinguishes between women involved in *adulterium* and *stuprum* and the *prostituta;* he

89. See Vittorio Citti, "Πόρνη καὶ δούλη: Una coppia nominale Lisia," in *Schiavi e dipendenti nell'ambito dell' "oikos" e della "familia": Atti del XXII Colloquio GIREA, Pontignano (Siena), 19–20 Novembre 1995*, ed. Mauro Moggi and Giuseppe Cordiano, Studi e testi di storia antica (Pisa: ETS, 1997), 91–96; McGinn, *Prostitution, Sexuality, and the Law*, 266–67; McGinn, *The Economy of Prostitution in the Roman World: A Study of Social History and the Brothel* (Ann Arbor: University of Michigan Press, 2004), 67–92; Edward E. Cohen, "Free and Unfree Sexual Work: An Economic Analysis of Athenian Prostitution," in *Prostitutes and Courtesans in the Ancient World*, ed. Christopher A. Faraone and Laura K. McClure (Madison: University of Wisconsin Press, 2006), 95–124.

90. *Hom. Eph.* 15.2 (F4.259–60); for more on the links between sexual promiscuity and the life of slavery, see René Martin, "La vie sexuelle des esclaves d'après les Dialogues Rustiques de Varron," in *Varron: Grammaire antique et stylistique latine*, ed. Christian Bruel, Publications de La Sorbonne (Paris: Les Belles Lettres, 1978), 113–26.

91. Perry, *Gender, Manumission, and the Roman Freedwoman*, 29–37.

also notes the public (*palam*) nature of the profession of prostitution, and does not limit it to the brothel, but includes inns and taverns. Although he emphasizes the venality of prostitution, a woman could be seen as a prostitute even without accepting money if she made herself publicly available for sex.[92] It does seem that many people who owned brothels often made use of slaves for their labor requirements. Ulpian refers to such slave prostitutes as *instrumenti*.[93] The clothing of free women and regular slave women was also different from that of prostitutes. Prostitutes wore a *toga*.[94]

Chrysostom also differentiates between the abuse of a domestic slave girl, often using the term *therapainis*, and a public prostitute, *dēmosia* or *pornē pandēmos*.[95] The close link between slavery and prostitution in Chrysostom can be seen in his use of prostitution as a metaphor:

> Earlier they were members of a prostitute, but Christ has made them members of his own body. Therefore, you have no authority over them anymore. Serve (*douleue*) him that has set you free [note the paradox again]. For if you had a daughter, and from extreme madness had rented her out to a pimp, and made her a prostitute, and then a king's son happens to pass by and liberate her from that slavery, and marry her himself, you have no right then to ever take her back to the brothel. For you have given her away, once and for all, and you have sold her. It is also the same with us. We rented out our own flesh to the devil, that terrible pimp; Christ saw it and set it free, and removed it from that evil tyranny. It is no longer then ours but belongs to the one who set it free. If you wish to use it as a king's bride, nothing stops you; but if you take it to where it was before, you will suffer just as those who are guilty of such outrages deserve.[96]

This fairy-tale-esque passage exhibits all the elements that were also present in Chrysostom's metaphor of slavery to God. Chrysostom uses the example of child prostitution in fact, which is interesting in itself. It shows that parents still had complete control over their children, and they could, and did, force them into a life of prostitution. Coerced prostitution such as the case above was outlawed in 428

---

92. *Dig.* 23.2.43.pr-3; see Perry, *Gender, Manumission, and the Roman Freedwoman*, 29–33.

93. *Dig.* 23.2.43.9; see McGinn, *Prostitution, Sexuality, and the Law*, 54–55.

94. McGinn, *Prostitution, Sexuality, and the Law*, 159–60.

95. *Propt. fornic.* 4 (PG51.213.48–50); *Laed.* 6.78–81 (SC 103.92).

96. *Hom. 1 Cor.* 18.3 (F2.209): Πόρνης ἦν μέλη πρὸ τούτου, καὶ ὁ Χριστὸς ἐποίησεν αὐτὰ μέλη τοῦ ἰδίου σώματος. Οὐκ ἄρα αὐτῶν ἐξουσίαν ἔχεις λοιπόν· ἐκείνῳ δούλευε τῷ ἐλευθερώσαντι. Οὐδὲ γάρ, εἰ θυγατέρα ἔχων, ἐκ πολλῆς τῆς ἀνοίας ἐξεμίσθωσας αὐτὴν πορνοβοσκῷ, καὶ πορνεύεσθαι ἐποίησας, εἶτα βασιλέως υἱὸς παριὼν ἠλευθέρωσέ τε αὐτὴν τῆς δουλείας ἐκείνης καὶ συνῆψεν ἑαυτῷ, κύριος ἧς λοιπὸν ἄγειν αὐτὴν ἐπὶ τὸ πορνεῖον· ἅπαξ γὰρ ἔδωκας καὶ ἐπώλησας. Τοιοῦτόν ἐστι καὶ τὸ ἡμέτερον· Ἐξεμισθώσαμεν τὴν σάρκα τὴν ἑαυτῶν τῷ διαβόλῳ, τῷ χαλεπῷ πορνοβοσκῷ· ἰδὼν ὁ Χριστός, ἐρρύσατο αὐτὴν καὶ ἀπήλλαξε τῆς πονηρᾶς τυραννίδος ἐκείνης· οὐ τοίνυν ἐστὶν ἡμετέρα λοιπόν, ἀλλὰ τοῦ ῥυσαμένου. Ἐὰν ἐθέλῃς ὡς νύμφῃ βασιλέως κεχρῆσθαι, οὐδεὶς ὁ κωλύων· ἐὰν δὲ ἐπὶ τὰ πρότερα ἀγάγῃς, πείσῃ ταῦτα, ἃ τοὺς τοιαῦτα ὑβρίζοντας εἰκός.

by Theodosius II—an indication that it may have been quite prevalent at the time.[97] In 439 Theodosius also ejected all pimps from Constantinople and stopped collecting tax from them, as this was used as a justification of their continuing in their trade. Nothing is said of prostitutes, however, and for several decades tax was still collected from prostitutes inside and from procurers outside Constantinople.[98] It seemed at least common enough for Chrysostom to use it as a spiritual example. In the example, the girl is sold to a pimp (*pornoboskos*) into a life of prostitution, and is then ransomed by a prince. Chrysostom makes it very clear that the parents have absolutely no authority over her anymore—she has been sold (*epōlēsas*)—nor can she be taken back to the brothel after being married to the prince. The heteronomy of the body is once again clear in this passage. At no point is the girl truly free; she belongs to her parents, then to the pimp, and then to the prince. Her agency is only passive, various types of servitude are chosen for her, and her body is vendible, evident in the use of the word *pōleō*, meaning "sell." In the metaphor, before meeting Christ, one's body is like that of a harlot, and salvation is seen as ransoming the harlot from the pimp, who is the devil in this case, and becoming the property of Christ. Although this may be one of the more extreme cases, it also shows the risks of being a female, especially a nonelite female, in Roman society, and the very close links between slavery and prostitution both materially and metaphorically.

By the same token, the concept of freedom (*eleutheria, libertas*) also had numerous sexual connotations—it denoted a state associated with sexual honor and chastity. Chrysostom contrasts the prostitute with two women in Roman society, the free wife and the virgin. The body of the prostitute was seen as the polar opposite of the *matrona* and the *virgo*. The free *materfamilias* was the embodiment of virtue and chastity, female *dignitas* and *pudicitia*. Chrysostom believed that prostitutes could not in any way match the benefits of the free *materfamilias*. "A free wife offers at the same time pleasure and security, joy and honor, order and a good conscience,"[99] Chrysostom assures his audience. The inherent risks in frequenting a prostitute stand in contrast to the benefits of remaining with one's wife. The *materfamilias* should be a symbol of the honor of her husband. While complaining about men who visit the theater, Chrysostom states: "How then will your wife look at you after this, when you have returned from such malfeasance (*paranomia*)?" The sight of the free wife puts her husband to shame: "How will she receive you?

---

97. *C.Th.* 15.8.2; see Harper, *From Shame to Sin*, 184–85; Jill Harries, "Men without Women: Theodosius' Consistory and the Business of Government," in *Theodosius II: Rethinking the Roman Empire in Late Antiquity*, ed. Christopher Kelly, Cambridge Classical Studies (New York: Cambridge University Press, 2013), 83–84.

98. See McGinn, *Prostitution, Sexuality, and the Law*; Harper, *From Shame to Sin*, 183–86.

99. *Propt. fornic.* 5 (PG 51.217.6–8): Ἐπὶ γὰρ τῆς ἐλευθέρας γυναικὸς ὁμοῦ καὶ ἡδονὴ καὶἀσφάλεια καὶ ἄνεσις καὶ τιμὴ καὶ κόσμος καὶ συνειδὸς ἀγαθόν. See *Fem. reg.* 7.62 (Dumortier 120).

How will she speak to you after you have so publicly disgraced the common nature of femaleness (*gynaikeia*)," Chrysostom asks, "and are made by such a spectacle the slave of a prostitute?"[100] Prostitutes and slave girls are no longer morally neutral ground—it is shameful to have sex with them, and one's whole household is brought into dishonor.

The idea that slaves and prostitutes were morally neutral outlets for male sexual desire was common in Roman society.[101] Chrysostom emphasizes the incompatibility of the free *materfamilias* with the status of the prostitute further when he tells the men in his audience to imagine the women of the theater are their wives. The licentiousness of the theater and prostitutes in fact shame the very essence of femaleness (*gynaikeia*), and men ought to feel ashamed when seeing women exploited in the theater, since they share the same nature as their wives. In Greek medical literature, *gynaikeia* has a wide range of meanings, from referring specifically to the menstrual period to being a term for diseases of women[102]—Chrysostom's use here is more general, but we must not overlook the corporeality implied in the term. The dancing bodies and exposed flesh of the women in the theater are a disgrace to ideal female corporeality, quintessential *gynaikeia,* which is synonymous, for Chrysostom, with modesty, chastity, and reticence. "Tell me then, with what eyes will you look at your wife at home," Chrysostom asks, "having seen her insulted there?" The antics of prostitutes in the theater therefore insult all women. "Or how do you not blush being reminded of the partner of your home, when you see her same nature disgraced?"[103] Chrysostom reminds men that both the prostitute and the free *materfamilias* share the same corporeal nature—hence, treating a *woman* like a prostitute is shameful, since she has the same nature (*physis*), the same body (*sōma*), as a free *materfamilias.* "Both the prostitute and the free woman share the same nature and the same body," Chrysostom reminds his male audience members.[104] So while he builds on the distinction between the *materfamilias* and the prostitute, he also negates the distinction with an appeal to recognize their common femaleness. He acknowledges the social differences between the wife and

100. *Hom. Matt.* 6.7 (PG 57.72.41–46): Πῶς οὖν ὄψεταί σε λοιπὸν ἡ γυνὴ ἀπὸ τῆς τοιαύτης ἐπανελθόντα παρανομίας; πῶς δέξεται; πῶς προσερεῖ, οὕτως ἀτίμως τὸ κοινὸν τῆς γυναικείας παραδειγματίσαντα φύσεως, καὶ αἰχμάλωτον ὑπὸ τῆς τοιαύτης ὄψεως καὶ δοῦλον γεγενημένον τῆς πορνευθείσης γυναικός;

101. See Treggiari, *Roman Marriage,* 301; Glancy, *Slavery in Early Christianity,* 50–51; Harper, *Slavery in the Late Roman World,* 310–14.

102. Helen King, *Hippocrates' Woman: Reading the Female Body in Ancient Greece* (London: Routledge, 1998), 23.

103. *Hom. Matt.* 6.7 (PG 57.71.56–60): Ποίοις οὖν ὀφθαλμοῖς, εἰπέ μοι, λοιπὸν τὴν γυναῖκα ἐπὶ τῆς οἰκίας ὄψει, ἰδὼν αὐτὴν ὑβριζομένην ἐκεῖ; Πῶς δὲ οὐκ ἐρυθριᾷς ἀναμιμνησκόμενος τῆς συνοίκου, ἡνίκα ἂν τὴν φύσιν αὐτὴν παραδειγματιζομένην ἴδῃς;

104. *Hom. Matt.* 6.7 (PG 57.72.22–23): ἡ αὐτὴ φύσις καὶ σῶμα τὸ αὐτὸ καὶ τῆς πόρνης καὶ τῆς ἐλευθέρας.

the prostitute, and emphasizes their natural and engendered similarity. The shared corporeal nature of all womankind therefore changes the game of sexual honor and shame for free men. Of course, the conversion of a prostitute, a major theme in late ancient Christianity, was very commendable.[105] By turning to Christ and forsaking her old ways, the harlot gained dignity (*semnotēs*).[106]

Chrysostom refutes the idea that by promoting prostitution, one avoids adultery. Rather he believes that fornication and prostitution could increase incidents of adultery. Speaking to the younger people in his audience, and showing that this may have been a popular idea among young males, Chrysostom explains: "The one who has not learned to commit fornication will also not know how to commit adultery." Fornication does not prevent adultery, but actually prepares people for it. "But the one who wallows among prostitutes will quickly also go forward into adultery," Chrysostom adds, "and will destroy himself altogether, if not with the married, then with those who do not have such ties."[107] Prostitution was a social danger to Chrysostom—so while he states that when married men sleep with women other than their wives, including slaves and prostitutes, they commit adultery, he emphasizes that when unmarried youths do the same, they prepare themselves for adultery. Thus, such behavior is then not a sign of masculinity, but of weakness.

There is also a strict government of vision in this instance, based on the words of Jesus in Matthew 5:27–28: "You have heard that it was said, 'You will not commit adultery.' But I am saying to you that everyone who looks at a woman lustfully has already committed adultery with her in his heart."[108] This interiorization of adultery was very influential in early Christianity, and played a major part in expanding the scope of adultery to include prostitutes and slave women. Chrysostom speaks of "touching with the eyes," which insults both the wife of the man who does it, and the one who is being desired. "For even though you have not touched her with your hand, you have fondled her with your eyes, and thereby it is considered adultery."[109] Chrysostom believed in the purification of one's vision; while

---

105. This cultural motif was very popular in late antiquity, and Chrysostom himself refers to a famous prostitute who turned to the Christian life; see *Hom. Matt.* 67.3–4 (PG 58.636.48–637.5); for an extensive discussion of the idea of the penitent prostitute, see Harper, *From Shame to Sin*, 191–236.

106. *Hom. Matt.* 6.5 (PG 57.69.7–9).

107. *Hom. 1 Thess.* 5.1 (5.371): Ὁ μὴ μαθὼν πορνεύειν, οὐδὲ μοιχεύειν εἴσεται· ὁ δὲ ἐκείναις ἐγκαλινδούμενος, καὶ ἐπὶ τοῦτο ταχέως ἥξει· κἂν μὴ ὑπάνδροις, ἀλλὰ λελυμέναις συμφθαρῇ γυναιξί.

108. NA28: Ἠκούσατε ὅτι ἐρρέθη· οὐ μοιχεύσεις. ἐγὼ δὲ λέγω ὑμῖν ὅτι πᾶς ὁ βλέπων γυναῖκα πρὸς τὸ ἐπιθυμῆσαι αὐτὴν ἤδη ἐμοίχευσεν αὐτὴν ἐν τῇ καρδίᾳ αὐτοῦ.

109. *Hom. Matt.* 17.2 (PG 57.257.24–26): Εἰ γὰρ καὶ μὴ ἥψω τῇ χειρί, ἀλλ᾽ ἐψηλάφησας τοῖς ὀφθαλμοῖς· διὰ τοῦτο καὶ τοῦτο μοιχεία νενόμισται. For more on Chrysostom's reading of the Sermon on the Mount, see Jaroslav Pelikan, *Divine Rhetoric: The Sermon on the Mount as Message and as Model in Augustine, Chrysostom and Luther* (Crestwood, NY: St. Vladimir's Seminary Press, 2001), 67–150.

instructing catechumens he warns them of the danger of beholding the mysteries of Christ, and then with the same eyes lusting after a prostitute and commiting adultery.[110] Blake Leyerle has shown that one's sight and soul were closely connected in the Chrysostom's thought. The pollution of the eyes also implied the pollution of the soul.[111]

The subjectivity of the virgin is also informed by that of the prostitute. The impenetrable corporeality of the virgin in particular is contrasted to the corporeal availability of the prostitute.[112] Yet, Chrysostom complains that "if a virgin should meet a man, he says the day becomes unprofitable; but if a prostitute should meet him, it is auspicious, and profitable, and full of much business."[113] While Chrysostom emphasizes the shared nature and body of the *materfamilias* and virgin with those of prostitutes when it serves his argument, he also makes use of their well-known social differences. He especially dislikes the vainglorious fashion trends of wives and virgins, and compares them to those of prostitutes. "We can no longer distinguish between prostitutes and virgins; look at how indecent they have become!" Chrysostom laments. "A virgin's attire should consist of only what is necessary, plain and applied without effort," he notes, commenting specifically on the trouble to which prostitutes go to market themselves.[114] Virgins had to be socially invisible—they should not be exposed to fondling either by hands or by the eyes. They should adorn themselves inwardly. Now their anopticism has faded, and they have become all but inconspicuous, in Chrysostom's view. He says the same about free women parading themselves in the marketplace.[115]

The accusation that free women and virgins appear to be prostitutes is, first, an example of rhetorical animadversion. What Chrysostom means is that free women and virgins have now also begun to have the same corporeal vernacular, the same habitus, as prostitutes. Interestingly, in Chrysostom's discussions of penitent prostitutes, it is not only their renunciation of sexual vice that draws attention, but, even more, their avoidance of wealth and prodigality, showing that some prostitutes, whether slave, freed, or free, made good money from their trade. Penitent prostitutes especially eschew excessive ornamentation and makeup. They exchange "sackcloth for silken clothes, smeared with ash instead of perfume," appearing like

110. *Illum. catech.* 2.2 (PG 49.234.17–20).

111. Blake Leyerle, "John Chrysostom on the Gaze," *Journal of Early Christian Studies* 1, no. 2 (1993): 159–74.

112. *Hom. Matt.* 71.2 (PG 58.665.28–32).

113. *Illum. catech.* 2.5 (PG 49.240.8–10): Ἐὰν ἀπαντήσῃ παρθένος, φησὶν, ἄπρακτος ἡ ἡμέρα γίνεται· ἐὰν δὲ ἀπαντήσῃ πόρνη, δεξιὰ καὶ χρηστὴ καὶ πολλῆς ἐμπορίας γέμουσα.

114. *Hom. 1 Tim.* 8.3 (F6.67): Οὐκέτι διαγινώσκομεν τὰς πόρνας καὶ οὐδὲ τὰς παρθένους. Ὅρα εἰς πόσην ἀσχημοσύνην ἐξήγαγον ἑαυτάς. Ἀνεπιτήδευτον εἶναι χρὴ τὴν παρθένον, ἁπλῶς καὶ εἰκῆ κειμένην.

115. *Hom. Heb.* 28.4 (F7.320–21).

corpses with no "makeup and rouge."[116] Everything about the life of the prostitute troubled Chrysostom, not just that they engaged in adultery with married men and in other sexual vices. He often associated the life of the prostitute with fast money, parties, and the entertainment of the theater—this explains why the motif of the penitent prostitute was such a powerful image to Chrysostom. Free women who lived such lives were not so different from prostitutes in Chrysostom's mind—they were all part of the invective strategy of pornomorphism, a strategy readily applied by the patriarchy to subdue any form of female agency or power. Generally, however, sexual vice, whether prostitution or homoeroticism, was in almost all instances linked to luxury and material affluence in Chrysostom's thought.

But there is also a second dimension to Chrysostom's pornomorphism in this case, extending beyond his usual invective against wealth. There may have been actual confusion of matrons and prostitutes in Chrysostom's time. Prostitutes did not always wear their togas, and so the distinctions between matrons and prostitutes were not always clear in Roman society; men had to be very careful whom they accosted in public.[117] Makeup and other forms of accessorizing were also associated with prostitutes, which explains Chrysostom's slur.[118] For Chrysostom, dressing up and putting one's body on display in public is equal to an act of prostitution. "Do not please your husband by those means which prostitutes use," Chrysostom advises, "but by those ways worthy of free wives."[119]

As in the case of boys being overly adorned and effeminized, Chrysostom was especially worried that the filiafamilias might pick up the bad dressing habits of her mother. In the limited guidance given to mothers and daughters in his treatise on vainglory, this advice stands out: "Let the mother learn to educate her girl by these principles," he says, "to guide her away from extravagance and personal

116. *Omn. mart.* 15 (Stavronikita 6.144v.15–30; *CPG* 4441.15): ἀντὶ σηρικῶν ἱματίων σάκκων . . . ἀντὶ μύρων σποδὸν ὑποστρωσαμένην . . . ἀντὶ ὑπογραφῆς ἐπιτριμμάτων. Translation: Wendy Mayer, trans., *The Cult of the Saints,* Popular Patristics Series (Crestwood, NY: St. Vladimir's Seminary Press, 2006), 252.

117. Kelly Olson, "*Matrona* and Whore: Clothing and Definition in Roman Antiquity," in Faraone and McClure, *Prostitutes and Courtesans,* 197.

118. For more on the issue of makeup, desire, and the gaze, see Amy Richlin, "Making Up a Woman: The Face of Roman Gender," in *Off with Her Head! The Denial of Women's Identity in Myth, Religion, and Culture,* ed. Howard Eilberg-Schwartz and Wendy Doniger (Berkeley: University of California Press, 1995), 185–213; McGinn, *Prostitution, Sexuality, and the Law,* 160; Carlin Barton, "Being in the Eyes: Shame and Sight in Ancient Rome," in *The Roman Gaze: Vision, Power, and the Body,* ed. David Fredrick (Baltimore: Johns Hopkins University Press, 2002), 216–35; Olson, "*Matrona* and Whore"; Kristi Upson-Saia, *Early Christian Dress: Gender, Virtue, and Authority* (New York: Routledge, 2011), 33–58.

119. *Hom. Col.* 10.2 (F5.286): μὴ ἀπὸ τούτων ἄρεσκε τῷ ἀνδρί, ἀφ' ὧν καὶ αἱ πόρναι, ἀλλ' ἀπὸ τούτων μᾶλλον, ἀφ' οὗ αἱ γυναῖκες αἱ ἐλεύθεραι.

246 EXPLOITATION, REGULATION, AND RESTRUCTURING

embellishment and all similar vanities that are the mark of prostitutes."[120] In fact, when women adorn themselves like prostitutes, they share the responsibility when their husbands start admiring prostitutes, and this is one of the greatest risks of pornomorphism: "Let us not teach our husbands to admire mere outward appearance." The danger, to Chrysostom, is obvious: "For if your adornment is of this nature, the habit of looking at your face will make it easy for him to be enamoured of a prostitute."[121] Free, especially virginal, feminine decorum was very important to Chrysostom, and women who plunged themselves into "the indecorum (aschēmosynē) of prostitutes," even without having intercourse, would receive the same judgment, since they would attract the male gaze like a prostitute.[122]

Advice like this on public dress was much more than simply a strategy of habituation—Susanna Elm has shown that during Chrysostom's time in Constantinople there were intense "style" wars, especially in the public processions of orthodox and Arian groups. Arians were well known for their lavish processions. Yet there were also great orthodox processions through the city, and the empress Eudoxia's famous appearance in nothing but a slave's garb stood out as a highlight for Chrysostom: "She followed after the saints looking like a slave girl."[123] Eudoxia embodied the very essence of askēsis, and by shunning her imperial attire, she made manifest her solidarity with monks and other ascetics. Virgins and matrons should avoid dolling themselves up like prostitutes, but should rather assume the type of simplicity seen in a slave girl. Simplicity was the new mark of distinction—less was more.

Chrysostom then also uses the discourse of prostitution and pornomorphism as ascetic strategies. Along with his admonitions against vainglory, he linked prostitution to the love of money. Chrysostom was disturbed by the excessive wealth of some prostitutes, especially in light of the poverty in other areas of society. Some of the less fortunate in his assembly might be troubled by the fact that prostitutes made more money than they did and wore more expensive clothes.[124] Chrysostom was also very bothered by the fact that men preferred to give their money to pros-

---

120. *Inan.* 90.1058–60 (SC 188.196): Καὶ ἡ μήτηρ δὲ μαθέτω τὴν αὐτῆς κόρην τούτοις παιδεύειν καὶ πολυτελείας ἀπάγειν καὶ κόσμου καὶ τῶν ἄλλων ἁπάντων, ἅπερ ἐστὶ πορνῶν γυναικῶν. See *Hom. Col.* 10.3 (F5.286).

121. *Hom. 1 Tim.* 4.2 (F6.40): Μὴ παιδεύωμεν τοὺς ἄνδρας ὄψεις μόνας φιλεῖν· ἂν γὰρ ᾖς οὕτω κοσμουμένη, ταχέως ὑπὸ τῆς ἑταιρηκυίας, μελετήσας ἐν τῇ ὄψει τῇ σῇ, ἁλίσκεται.

122. *Fem. reg.* 1 (Dumortier 97): τῶν πορνευομένων γυναικῶν ἀσχημοσύνην. Translation: Clark, *Jerome, Chrysostom, and Friends,* 210. See also Upson-Saia, *Early Christian Dress,* 47.

123. *Dict. rel. mart.* 2.1 (PG 63.469.10): ὥσπερ θεραπαινὶς παρηκολούθει τοῖς ἁγίοις. See Susanna Elm, "What the Bishop Wore to the Synod: John Chrysostom, Origenism, and the Politics of Fashion at Constantinople," *Adamantius* 19 (2013): 156–69.

124. *Laed.* 6.77–97 (SC 103.92); *Hom. 1 Tim.* 2.3 (F6.18).

titutes instead of to the poor.[125] Ironically, the whore chaser, in Chrysostom's mind, was nothing more than a slave to lust, and a slave to the prostitute herself.[126]

Most importantly, Chrysostom associated prostitution with the loss of *semnotēs*, not only for the prostitute, but also for the client. The sexual disgrace of prostitution was spread by three means: by adultery, by possible reproduction, and simply by association. As we have already seen, Chrysostom includes prostitution in the scope of adulterous behavior; he makes prostitution a domestic matter. The implication is that the social indignity of the prostitute is now transferred onto her client, whether he is slave or free. Disgrace becomes a type of socially transmitted disease,[127] resulting from the man becoming one flesh with the prostitute.[128]

There is, of course, also the danger of gaining shame by reproduction—birth control was not what it is today, and it was not uncommon for prostitutes to become pregnant by their clients. Issues of conception, contraception, and abortion are therefore directly related to the doulology, since slaves were considered reproductive capital.[129] The issue of reproductive capital is often discussed in terms of the domestic "breeding" of slaves, and the rewards for enslaved mothers who had many children. After all, it was from natural reproduction that the Roman slave supply was sustained. But when we look at the problem of reproduction in the context of prostitution, we again see how complex and fissured the concept of slaves as reproductive capital was, and Chrysostom provides an interesting account of what reproductive capital entailed in terms of prostitution, and slavery in general. Reproductive capital was not simply an issue of natural reproduction and supply and demand. It was part of a very complex cultural code, and entailed much more than simply rewarding slave mothers for having children. Chrysostom's comments offer us a glimpse of the "underworld" of slave reproduction, one that merits some discussion here.

Children born from slaves, in most cases, became slaves themselves. Being a child of a "slave and a prostitute" was a status of great disgrace.[130] Unwanted offspring were often exposed, picked up, and introduced into slavery.[131] In a very

125. *Hom. Jo.* 42.4 (PG 59.244.22–24).

126. *Hom. Matt.* 6.7 (PG 57.72.43–46), 48.5 (PG 58.493.36–39).

127. Chrysostom specifically calls fornication a disease (νόσος); see *Hom. Jo.* 63.4 (PG 59.353.33–354.39).

128. *Hom. 1 Cor.* 18 (F2.205–14).

129. Marianne B. Kartzow, "Navigating the Womb: Surrogacy, Slavery, Fertility—and Biblical Discourses," *Journal of Early Christian History* 2, no. 1 (2012): 38–54.

130. *Hom. Jo.* 28.3 (PG 59.165.22–23); *Mansuet.* 1 (PG 63.554.12–14 [Sp.]); see Cohen, "Free and Unfree Sexual Work," 103.

131. For more on child exposure in the Roman Empire, see William V. Harris, "Child-Exposure in the Roman Empire," *Journal of Roman Studies* 84 (1994): 1–22; Judith Evans Grubbs, "Church, State, and Children: Christian and Imperial Attitudes toward Infant Exposure in Late Antiquity," in *The Power of Religion in Late Antiquity*, ed. Andrew Cain and Noel Lenski (Farnham: Ashgate, 2009), 119–31.

important passage, Chrysostom gives a very sobering account of the danger of having progeny with prostitutes:

> For even if a child is born, it also brings disgrace on you, and because of you an injustice has been done to it in being born illegitimate and of low status. And even if you leave it a large sum of money, there is still disgrace at home, disgrace in the city, disgrace in a court of law, and it is still the offspring of a prostitute and a slave. You will also stand disgraced, while you are alive, and when you have died. For even when you have passed away, the memorials of your shame remain. Why then bring disgrace in all these ways? Why sow where the soil purposefully destroys the fruit? Where there are many efforts to ensure contraception? Where there is murder [i.e., abortion] before the birth? For even the prostitute no longer remains a prostitute, but you also make her a murderess. Do you see how drunkenness leads to fornication, fornication to adultery, adultery to murder; or to something even worse than murder? For I do not know what to call it, since it does not remove the pregnancy, but even prevents birth. Why then do you violate the gift of God, and fight with his laws, and seek what is a curse as if it is a blessing, and turn the chamber of procreation into a chamber of murder, and prepare the woman that was given for childbearing for murder? For in order to make more money by being pleasing and desirable to her lovers, she will not even hesitate to do this, in so doing heaping a great pile of coals on your head. For even if the shameless act is of her choosing, its cause is still yours. This also results in idolatry. For many people who wish to become attractive conjure spells, and libations, and love-charms, and a myriad other devices. But still after such disgrace, after murders, after idolatries, many consider it to be a matter of indifference, and many that have wives too. And so the mélange of evil is even greater. For witchcraft is further applied, not to the womb that is prostituted, but to the injured wife, and there are numerous schemes and invocations of demons, and necromancies, and daily fights, and unresolved arguments, and familial jealousy.[132]

132. *Hom. Rom.* 25[24].3–4 (F1.401–2): Κἂν γὰρ τεχθῇ παιδίον, καὶ σὲ ᾔσχυνε, καὶ αὐτὸ ἠδίκηται διὰ σὲ νόθον καὶ δυσγενὲς γενόμενον. Κἂν μυρία αὐτῷ καταλίπῃς αὐτῷ χρήματα, ἄτιμος ἐν οἰκίᾳ, ἄτιμος ἐν πόλει, ἄτιμος ἐν δικαστηρίῳ καὶ ὁ ἐκ πόρνης καὶ ὁ ἐκ δούλης· ἄτιμος δὲ καὶ σὺ.πάλιν, καὶ ζῶν καὶ τετελευτηκώς· κἂν γὰρ ἀπέλθῃς, μένει τὰ ὑπομνήματα τῆς ἀσχημοσύνης. Τί τοίνυν ἅπαντα καταισχύνεις; Τί σπείρεις ἔνθα ἡ ἄρουρα σπουδάζει διαφθεῖραι τὸν καρπόν; ἔνθα πολλὰ τὰ ἀτόκια; ἔνθα πρὸ τῆς γενέσεως φόνος; καὶ γὰρ καὶ τὴν πόρνην οὐκ ἀφίης μεῖναι πόρνην μόνον, ἀλλὰ καὶ ἀνδροφόνον ποιεῖς. Εἶδες ἀπὸ μέθης πορνείαν, ἀπὸ πορνείας μοιχείαν, ἀπὸ μοιχείας φόνον; μᾶλλον δὲ καὶ φόνου τι χεῖρον· οὐδὲ γὰρ ἔχω πῶς αὐτὸ καλέσω· οὐ γὰρ τεχθὲν ἀναιρεῖ, ἀλλὰ καὶ τεχθῆναι κωλύει. Τί τοίνυν καὶ τοῦ Θεοῦ τὴν δωρεὰν ὑβρίζεις, καὶ τοῖς αὐτοῦ μάχῃ νόμοις, καὶ ὅπερ ἐστὶ κατάρα, τοῦτο σὺ ὡς εὐλογίαν μεταδιώκεις, καὶ τὸ ταμιεῖον τῆς γενέσεως ταμιεῖον ποιεῖς σφαγῆς, καὶ τὴν πρὸς παιδοποιΐαν δοθεῖσαν γυναῖκα πρὸς φόνον παρασκευάζεις; "Ἵνα γὰρ ἀεὶ τοῖς ἐρασταῖς εὐχάριστος ᾖ καὶ ποθεινὴ, καὶ πλέον ἀργύριον ἕλκῃ, οὐδὲ τοῦτο παραιτεῖται ποιῆσαι, μέγα ἐπὶ τὴν σὴν κεφαλὴν ἐντεῦθεν σωρεύουσα τὸ πῦρ· εἰ γὰρ καὶ ἐκείνης τὸ τόλμημα, ἀλλὰ σὴ ἡ αἰτία γίνεται. Ἐντεῦθεν καὶ εἰδωλολατρεῖαι. Πολλαὶ γὰρ ὥστε ἐπιχαρεῖς γενέσθαι, καὶ ἐπῳδὰς καὶ σπονδὰς καὶ φίλτρα καὶ μυρία ἕτερα μηχανῶνται. Ἀλλ᾽ ὅμως μετὰ τοσαύτην ἀσχημοσύνην, μετὰ φόνους, μετὰ εἰδωλολατρείας, πολλοῖς ἀδιάφορον τὸ πρᾶγμα εἶναι δοκεῖ, πολλοῖς καὶ γυναῖκας ἔχουσιν· ἔνθα καὶ πλείων ὁ φορυτὸς τῶν κακῶν. Καὶ γὰρ φαρμακεῖαι λοιπὸν κινοῦνται, οὐκ ἐπὶ τὴν νηδὺν τὴν πορνευομένην, ἀλλ᾽ ἐπὶ

Chrysostom considers prostitution one link in a chain of serious vices, all set on destroying the most important social unit in Roman society—the household. Although Roman law did not do much initially to curb the sexual exploitation of slave women, it did face the problem of illegitimate children. Excluding some exceptional cases involving adrogation, generally, men were not allowed to adopt their illegitimate children.[133] In this way the patrimony belonging to legitimate heirs remained secure. Mixed-status reproduction was therefore something juridically regulated, yet it remained complex and problematic.[134] Chrysostom is very clear about this: having illegitimate children with slaves and prostitutes introduces an all-encompassing disgrace (*atimia*) for the male; there is disgrace in the household, in the city, and in the courts. Even money cannot buy the child a better status. There is also an additional dimension to this shame—since Romans believed that they gained immortality and honor by producing legitimate heirs, the disgrace of illegitimate children would also endure. This passage also portrays the slippery slope of vice—drunkenness leads to prostitution, which leads to murder and idolatry. The body of the woman, which was made to bear children (*paidopoiïa*), now becomes a space for murder (*phonos*)—that is, abortion and contraception. In principle, Chrysostom did not differentiate between contraception and abortion; they were essentially the same thing in his view; contraception was proactive abortion, and, like many ancient authors, Chrysostom considers slave women and prostitutes as custodians of knowledge about abortion—which may have been a real possibility.[135] Chrysostom's use of the terms *atokion* (technically referring to contraception or "not-breeding") and *phonos* (abortion, but literally meaning "murder") to distinguish between contraception and abortion is consonant with the gynecological views of Soranus.[136]

The use of magic and superstition was not limited to the event of birth and infancy only, as noted in chapter 4—measures for contraception and abortion were inextricably interwoven with the magical arts, which was idolatry to Chrysostom. Uterine magic was used either for safeguarding a fetus, ensuring a safe

---

τὴν ἠδικημένην γυναῖκα, καὶ ἐπιβουλαὶ μυρίαι, καὶ δαιμόνων κλήσεις, καὶ νεκυομαντεῖαι, καὶ πόλεμοι καθημερινοὶ, καὶ ἄσπονδοι μάχαι, καὶ σύντροφοι φιλονεικίαι.

133. Jane F. Gardner, "The Adoption of Roman Freedmen," *Phoenix* 43, no. 3 (1989): 236–57.

134. For an extensive discussion of mixed-status sex and offspring in late antiquity, see Harper, *Slavery in the Late Roman World*, 442–55.

135. See John Scarborough, "The Pharmacology of Sacred Plants, Herbs, and Roots," in *Magika Hiera: Ancient Greek Magic and Religion*, ed. Chris A. Faraone and Dirk Obbink (New York: Oxford University Press, 1991), 144–45; Bruce W. Frier, "Natural Fertility and Family Limitation in Roman Marriage," *Classical Philology* 89 (1994): 318–33; King, *Hippocrates' Woman*, 136, 144.

136. Soranus, *Gyn.* 1.60 (Temkin 62). Soranus was the main influence on gynecology in late antiquity; see King, *Hippocrates' Woman*, 134, 231.

birth and healthy offspring, or for the purposes of contraception and abortion.[137] While Chrysostom struggles to find the correct terminology, the term *atokia* is used to refer to medicines and magic that serve as contraceptives and abortifacients. As Helen King notes, "Since conception was a gradual process taking place over several months, the line between abortion and contraception was also drawn at a point different from our own."[138] Many methods of contraception were used in ancient times, including amulets made from a stone called hematite,[139] apotropiacs containing herbs and animal matter,[140] plants like saffron, and even fetuses.[141] Chrysostom specifically notes the magic spells, love elixirs, and libations that are applied to the wombs and fetuses of all women, especially prostitutes. There are hundreds of different spells and remedies concerning conception, contraception, abortion, and birth in the Roman world. Pliny, for instance, identifies mandrake seeds and artemisia as useful for purging the uterus and removing a dead fetus. They are also useful when dealing with excessive menstruation. Pliny also mentions two unknown herbs, *arsenogonon* and *thelygonon,* which can result in the birth of a boy or a girl, respectively.[142] Most importantly, we need to remember that ovulation was a modern discovery, and so was totally unknown to the ancients.[143] In the context of slavery and prostitution, it is important to take the cultural context of ancient contraception, abortion, and drug use into consideration. In Chrys-

---

137. A helpful study of the issue of uterine magic and abortion is Jean-Jacques Aubert, "Threatened Wombs: Aspects of Ancient Uterine Magic," *Greek, Roman and Byzantine Studies* 30, no. 3 (1989): 421–49. See Georg Petzl and Hasan Malay, "A New Confession-Inscription from the Katakekaumene," *Greek, Roman and Byzantine Studies* 28 (1987): 459–72; Angelos Chaniotis, "Drei kleinasiatische Inschriften zur griechischen Religion," *Epigraphica Anatolica* 15 (1990): 127–33; Georg Petzl, "Die Beichtinschriften Westkleinasiens," *Epigraphica Anatolica* 22 (1994): 1–174; John M. Riddle, *Contraception and Abortion from the Ancient World to the Renaissance* (Cambridge, MA: Harvard University Press, 1994), 19, 65, 109–15; Riddle, *Eve's Herbs: A History of Contraception and Abortion in the West* (Cambridge, MA: Harvard University Press, 1997); Daniel Ogden, *Magic, Witchcraft, and Ghosts in the Greek and Roman Worlds: A Sourcebook* (New York: Oxford University Press, 2002), 243–44; David Frankfurter, "Fetus Magic and Sorcery Fears in Roman Egypt," *Greek, Roman and Byzantine Studies* 46 (2006): 37–62; John M. Riddle, *Goddesses, Elixirs, and Witches: Plants and Sexuality throughout Human History* (New York: Palgrave Macmillan, 2010). For a collection of modern anthropological case studies, see Thomas Buckley and Alma Gottlieb, eds., *Blood Magic: Explorations in the Anthropology of Menstruation* (Berkeley: University of California Press, 1988). The works of Riddle provide an overview of contraception and abortion in the ancient world, but also note King's critique of Riddle's approach; King, *Hippocrates' Woman,* 145–46.

138. King, *Hippocrates' Woman,* 134.

139. Aubert, "Threatened Wombs," 434.

140. Riddle, *Contraception and Abortion,* 96–97.

141. Frankfurter, "Fetus Magic and Sorcery Fears." For general comments on child sacrifice in the context of early Christianity, see Rousselle, *Porneia,* 107–21.

142. Pliny, *Hist. nat.* 26.90.151–60 (Jones 376–81); for *arsenogonon* and *thelygonon,* see *Hist. nat.* 26.91.162 (Jones 382–83); see Riddle, *Goddesses, Elixirs, and Witches,* 70.

143. King, *Hippocrates' Woman,* 143.

ostom's statements on contraception, abortion, and witchcraft (as well as all the other elements in his vice list), we encounter a typical male anxiety about the control of fertility—by visiting a prostitute, Chrysostom implies, the male relinquishes his power over fertility and legitimate reproduction. Men were supposed to decide which infants lived and which infants died, since it was the man who planted the seed, while the woman was only the field in which the seed grew. Again, King's observation is important to note here: "The myth of effective plant-based contraceptives may thus be a male expression of a fear that women hold the knowledge which could enable them to control the fertility of the household."[144]

Wine was of course a very important elixir, not only for birth and abortion, but for sexuality in general; hence we find Chrysostom's references to drunkenness in the list of vices associated with prostitution. Wine was *the* dominant psychotropic in Roman times, associated with Dionysus, and related to bodily heat and thus, sexual activity.[145] Once again Pliny links various ancient cultivars of wine to both contraception and madness: "Even wine contains miraculous properties. One grown in Arcadia is said to produce the ability to bear children in women and madness in men," Pliny explains, "whereas in Achaia, particularly in the neighborhood of Carynia, there is a wine that is reported to prevent child-bearing, and this even if women eat the grapes when they are pregnant, although these do not differ in taste from ordinary grapes."[146]

The lore of contraception and abortion was widespread. In entering the world of prostitution, the client also inevitably enters a world of drunkenness, adultery, murder, and sorcery. Although Roman laws regulated sorcery, there existed no specific law against contraception, despite numerous other laws on marriage, sexuality, and children.[147] Regarding abortion, Chrysostom is not alone in his specific condemnation of drinks that apparently cause abortion and act as contraceptives.[148] Jerome, who bemoans the state of virgins who have fallen from the church and become pregnant, states that they take potions for contraceptive and abortifacient purposes.[149]

Like Chrysostom, Jerome also compiles a whole list of vices that accompany contraception and abortion. While methods of contraception and abortion may

144. Ibid., 156.

145. Harper, *From Shame to Sin*, 57–58.

146. Pliny, *Hist. nat.* 14.22.116–17 (Rackham 262–63): Sunt et in vino prodigia. dicitur in Arcadia fieri quod fecunditatem feminis inportet, viris rabiem; at in Achaia maxime circa Caryniam abigi partum vino, atque etiam si uvam edant gravidae, cum differentia in gustatu non sit. See Riddle, *Goddesses, Elixirs, and Witches*, 70.

147. Riddle, *Eve's Herbs*, 85–87.

148. Riddle, *Contraception and Abortion*, 86–87.

149. Jerome, *Ep.* 22.13 (PL 22.401.36–402.3); see Riddle, *Eve's Herbs*, 87; Robert Jütte, *Contraception: A History* (Cambridge: Polity, 2008), 22–25.

have been quite prevalent among prostitutes and slave girls who were in danger of sexual violation, Chrysostom notes that spells were also placed on the wombs of free wives—this is probably a reference to the measures some men took to ensure that only their wife became pregnant (or not). The spell was supposed to ensure that the wife's womb was only accessible to the husband's semen.[150] The purpose of most potions and spells, however, was to cause abortion by means of menstruation or menorrhagia. Lunar cycles were also carefully monitored to help cause or prevent abortion.[151] The necromancy and invocations of demons that Chrysostom mentions are probably references to the use of fetuses in witchcraft and similar rituals. Newborns, stillborns, and aborted fetuses played a prominent role in certain ancient rites.[152] Such rituals were used as love spells and also divination. Chrysostom's earlier mention of a slave girl being called a Thessalian witch may also be a reference to the use in Thessalian witchcraft of rituals involving fetuses or spells involved in conception, contraception, and abortion.[153] Along with the drunkenness, adultery, murder, and satanic rituals and sorcery comes the problem of domestic disagreements, fights, and jealousy. In Chrysostom's description, this is the world in which a man enters when he frequents prostitutes. Yet it also suggests an aspect of the slave body as reproductive capital that is important to take note of here, especially because of the threat posed by the slave body to Roman society and Christian identity, notably in terms of who controls fertility—it was not simply about multiplying the number of slaves. The slave body as reproductive capital was also a problem that had to be managed by elite slaveholders.

Finally, the sexual disgrace of prostitution was spread simply by association. As the discussion above makes clear, prostitution was simply one station in a network of sin and vice. By associating with a prostitute, a man came into close corporeal proximity with undesirables. "Tell me, should you and your slave go to the same woman? And I wish it were only your slave, and not also the executioner!" says Chrysostom. He continues: "And you could not possibly bear to take the executioner by the hand; but the woman that has become one in body with him you embrace and kiss."[154] In Chrysostom's view, he who lies with a prostitute not only becomes one body with her, but also shares her body with individuals from the lower strata of society, including fugitive slaves, gladiators, and the deformed

---

150. Aubert, "Threatened Wombs," 426–27.

151. Ibid., 447–48.

152. See Anne-Marie Tupet, *La magie dans la poésie latine: Des origines à la fin du règne d'Auguste*, Études anciennes serie latine (Paris: Les Belles Lettres, 1976), 82–91; Aubert, "Threatened Wombs," 435–37; Frankfurter, "Fetus Magic and Sorcery Fears," 37–62.

153. *Hom. Eph.* 15.2 (F4.259); see chapter 5.

154. *Hom. 1 Thess.* 5.4 (F5.374): Εἰπέ μοι, πρὸς τὴν αὐτὴν καὶ σὺ καὶ ὁ οἰκέτης ὁ σός; καὶ εἴθε ὁ οἰκέτης μόνον, ἀλλὰ καὶ ὁ δῆμιος. Καὶ χεῖρας μὲν τοῦ δημίου οὐκ ἂν ἀνάσχοιο κατασχεῖν· τὴν δὲ ἐν ἐκείνῳ σῶμα γενομένην περιπλέκῃ καὶ καταφιλεῖς.

and ugly—perhaps even the executioner![155] Impurity and defilement are transmitted from one body to another. It makes no difference to the prostitute who approaches her; as long as they have money, she does not care about their status or appearance, and the free man is treated in the same way as the menial slave: "And this is the unique nature of prostitutes, that they are his who gives the gold." Prostitution makes all men equal, since "whether he is a slave, a gladiator, or whomever, yet if he makes a proposition, they receive him," Chrysostom says, "but the free, even if they are more noble than anyone else, they do not entertain without gold."[156]

Those who partake in prostitution not only associate with the bodies of lower-class people, but also find themselves in spaces ridden with vice. In particular, Chrysostom draws attention to the connection between prostitution and the theater. Actors and actresses were often associated with prostitution. Although they were not always slaves, there would have been slave prostitutes around the theater. Many restrictions were placed on people whose profession was acting, such as not being able to marry into the aristocracy; and the legislation of both Leo I and Theodosius II had implications for prostitutes involved in the theater.[157] Chrysostom saw the theater as a place for wicked people and menial slaves. "For surely both adulteries and stolen marriages are there, and there are women prostituting themselves, male courtesans, young people being effeminized," Chrysostom notes. "All that is there is extreme lawlessness, all sorcery, all shame."[158] Here we have yet another list of vices, this time linking the theater with both male and female prostitution,[159] adultery, the corruption of the youth, homoeroticism, and again, sorcery. The same is said about the hippodrome.[160] In his invective against Julian, Chrysostom often employed these images. During the feast of Aphrodite, Chrysostom states that "male pimps and female procurers formed a circle with the

155. *Hom. Matt.* 71.3 (PG 58.665.21–32); *Hom. Rom.* 25[24].3–4 (F1.401); *Hom. 1 Thess.* 5.1 (5.371).

156. *Hom. Heb.* 15.3 (F7.190): Καὶ τοῦτο δὲ τῶν πορνῶν ἴδιόν ἐστιν, ὅτι τοῦ τὸ χρυσίον διδόντος εἰσί· κἂν γὰρ δοῦλος ᾖ, κἂν μονομάχος, κἂν ὁστισοῦν, προτείνῃ δὲ τὸν μισθὸν, καταδέχονται· τοὺς δὲ ἐλευθέρους, κἂν πάντων ὦσιν εὐγενέστεροι, χωρὶς τοῦ ἀργυρίου οὐ προσίενται.

157. See Anne Duncan, "Infamous Performers: Comic Actors and Female Prostitutes in Rome," in Faraone and McClure, *Prostitutes and Courtesans*, 252–73; Harper, *From Shame to Sin*, 48, 186, 218–19.

158. *Hom. Matt.* 37.6 (PG 57.426.63–427.4): Καὶ γὰρ καὶ μοιχεῖαι, καὶ γάμων ἐκεῖ κλοπαὶ, καὶ γυναῖκες ἐκεῖ πορνευόμεναι, ἄνδρες ἡταιρηκότες, νέοι μαλακιζόμενοι, πάντα παρανομίας μεστὰ, πάντα τερατωδίας πάντα αἰσχύνης. See *Hom. Matt.* 32.7 (PG 57.388.19–22), 88.4 (PG 58.780.15–17); for a more detailed discussion of the link between prostitution and the theater, see Blake Leyerle, *Theatrical Shows and Ascetic Lives: John Chrysostom's Attack on Spiritual Marriage* (Berkeley: University of California Press, 2001), 67–71; see also Aideen M. Hartney, *John Chrysostom and the Transformation of the City* (London: Duckworth, 2004), 90–107, 138–39.

159. For more on male prostitution, see Craig A. Williams, *Roman Homosexuality* (New York: Oxford University Press, 2009), 40–50.

160. *Stat.* 17.2 (PG 49.176.2–10).

emperor in the middle, prancing through the marketplace and speaking and laughing in the way of people of that profession."[161]

Chrysostom also denounces the presence of prostitutes at the wild parties, wedding receptions, and symposia of the rich. Such prostitutes may have come from the local brothel, or were slave girls in service of their owner—in many instances, however, these women were courtesans, upmarket prostitutes. The presence of courtesans at Roman dinner parties and weddings is an interesting phenomenon that exposes many of the gender anxieties of Roman society, especially men's concern to control women's freedom.[162] Chrysostom states:

> But those prostitutes, what is the meaning of them attending the wedding? They ought to hide their faces when there is a marriage; they ought to be buried, prostitution is the corruption of marriage, yet we introduce them at marriage ceremonies. . . . For this is the nature of the prostitute. When you are preparing perfume, you do not allow any bad smell to come near. Marriage is perfume. Why then do you introduce the rotting stench of the dunghill into the preparation of the perfume? What are you saying? Shall the virgin dance, and not be a disgrace before her bedfellow? For she ought to have more dignity than them, she comes from the nurse's arm, and not from the palaestra. For the virgin ought not to appear publicly at all at a marriage feast.[163]

A few general comments about the presence of prostitutes at Roman feasts are warranted here. Two types of prostitutes may have been present at such events—the regular, common prostitute (*pornē*) and the upmarket courtesan (*hetaira*). If it was an elite feast, most of the prostitutes would have been courtesans, but we do read of many domestic slave girls also being present at such feasts and fulfilling sexual duties. Courtesans were regarded as having a higher status than common prostitutes. Sharon James has shown that the presence of such courtesans at feasts destabilized dominant male power, since courtesans were not on the same level as pros-

---

161. *Bab. Jul. gent.* 77.14–18 (SC 362.196): πορνοβόσκοι δὲ ἄνδρες καὶ γυναῖκες προαγωγοὶ καὶ πᾶς ὁ τῶν ἡταιρηκότων χορὸς τὸν βασιλέα κυκλώσαντες εἶχον ἐν μέσῳ διὰ τῆς ἀγορᾶς βαδίζοντες καὶ τοιαῦτα φθεγγόμενοι καὶ οὕτως ἀνακακχάζοντες ὡς τοὺς ἐκ τῆς ἐργασίας ἐκείνης εἰκὸς ἦν.

162. For more on courtesans, see Elizabeth S. Cohen, "'Courtesans' and 'Whores': Words and Behaviour in Roman Streets," *Women's Studies* 19 (1991): 201–8; James N. Davidson, *Courtesans and Fishcakes: The Consuming Passions of Classical Athens* (Chicago: University of Chicago Press, 1998); McGinn, *Economy of Prostitution,* 206–27; Sharon L. James, "A Courtesan's Choreography: Female Liberty and Male Anxiety at the Roman Dinner Party," in Faraone and McClure, *Prostitutes and Courtesans,* 224–51; Sean Corner, "Sumposion," in *A Companion to Greek and Roman Sexualities,* ed. Thomas K. Hubbard, Blackwell Companions to the Ancient World (Chichester: Wiley-Blackwell, 2014), 210–11.

163. *Hom. Col.* 12.4 (F5.306): Αἱ δὲ πόρναι, διὰ τί; Δέον αὐτὰς ἐγκαλύπτεσθαι ὅταν γάμος ᾖ, δέον αὐτὰς κατορύττεσθαι· φθορὰ γὰρ γάμου πορνεία· ἡμεῖς δὲ ἄγομεν αὐτὰς εἰς γάμους . . . τοῦτο γὰρ ἡ πόρνη. Ὅταν μύρον κατασκευάζητε, οὐδὲν δυσῶδες ἀφίετε πλησιάζειν. Μύρον ἐστὶν ὁ γάμος· τί τοίνυν τὴν τοῦ βορβόρου δυσωδίαν ἐπεισάγεις τῇ τοῦ μύρου κατασκευῇ; Τί λέγεις; ὀρχεῖται ἡ παρθένος, καὶ οὐκ αἰσχύνεται τὴν ὁμήλικα; Ταύτης γὰρ σεμνοτέραν αὐτὴν εἶναι δεῖ· ἐξ ἀγκάλης γε, οὐκ ἐκ παλαίστρας ἐξῆλθε. Φαίνεσθαι γὰρ ὅλως ἐν γάμοις τὴν παρθένον οὐ δεῖ.

titutes, and preferred gifts and favors to payment.[164] They were also more difficult to control than slave girls and prostitutes. Chrysostom was especially troubled by the presence of both prostitutes and courtesans at dinner parties and wedding feasts—and he purposely makes no distinction between a *porne* and a *hetaira*—to him, they are the same. Their presence at weddings is particularly troubling, since the wedding represents the rite of passage from virginity to married life, again showing the contrast between prostitution and marriage or virginity. Chrysostom was also very concerned about newlywed virgins acting like prostitutes at these feasts.

For Chrysostom, the female body had to be under male control at all times—this is why he advises that the bride not even appear publicly at her own wedding. She should be the epitome of dignity. Having prostitutes present at the wedding shames both the bride and the groom. These women stand for everything Chrysostom is against: not only prostitution, but also the freedom of women—that is, women not under the direct and structured authority of a father and husband. The olfactory metaphor sums it all up—sweet and rotten smells simply cannot mix, the rancid will overwhelm the sweet. The character of prostitutes, and especially their speech, offend the sacrality of a wedding.[165] The virgin comes from the nurse's arm, symbolic of the structured care and carceral space provided by the patriarchy, while the courtesan comes from the palaestra, a sporting venue often associated with the sex trade.[166] Chrysostom approves of technologies of slavery like the nurse's arm, as long as they are in line with the operations of the patriarchy, but a doulological operation such as prostitution and courtesanship disturbs him.

The typical symposium scene troubles Chrysostom because it displays the excess and decadence of the elite class, and such gatherings lead only to destruction. The perfect example, to Chrysostom, of the consequences of such wild living is found in the narrative of Herodias's striptease and the decapitation of John the Baptist.[167] Herodias is the virgin who was forced to become a harlot, and her actions lead to murder and damnation. In fact, Chrysostom says that it was not Herodias who was dancing, but the devil who beset her. And there is a lesson to be learned from this story: "For it is not a head in a tray that the dancers now ask, but the souls of those who recline at the feast." The price partygoers pay is much greater: "For when they make them slaves, and leading them to unlawful love, and beseiging them with prostitutes, they do not cut off the head, but slaughter the soul, making them adulterers, and effeminate, and prostitutes."[168] The symposium transforms its

---

164. James, "Courtesan's Choreography," 224–30.

165. See *Hom. Col.* 1.6 (F5.179–80).

166. McGinn, *Economy of Prostitution*, 212–14.

167. *Hom. Matt.* 48 (PG 58.487–96).

168. Ibid. (PG 58.493.34–39): Οὐ γὰρ κεφαλὴν αἰτοῦσιν ἐπὶ πίνακι οἱ νῦν ὀρχούμενοι, ἀλλὰ τὰς ψυχὰς τῶν ἀνακειμένων. "Οταν γὰρ δούλους αὐτοὺς ποιῶσι, καὶ εἰς παρανόμους ἔρωτας ἄγωσι, καὶ

attendees, ironically, into slaves, and they lose their souls. Again Chrysostom provides a list of those who exemplify sexual vice—they are adulterers, effeminate, slaves, and prostitutes themselves. Such men are described as effeminate probably because they are dominated and manipulated, in Chrysostom's eyes, by women like courtesans and prostitutes. The dishonor spread by prostitution through adultery, reproduction, and association is not only domestic, civic, social, and juridical disgrace; engaging in prostitution also leads to damnation since prostitution, in Chrysostom's thinking, is not only related to fornication, but specifically to adultery, drunkenness, revelry, murder, and sorcery.

CASTRATED SOULS: EUNUCHISM, CASTRATION, AND SLAVERY

One of the worst forms of sexual exploitation of slaves was probably the forced castration of male slaves, which made them eunuchs. The eunuch (*eunouchos*) occupied a central but ambiguous place in the exploitation of slave sexuality and was a complex figure in Chrysostom's doulology.[169] Whereas Chrysostom constantly attempts to stabilize slave sexuality by including slaves in the politics of adultery, marriage, and sexual disgrace, the elusive character of the eunuch proved difficult to stabilize and orient even for Chrysostom. When it came to sexuality, Chrysostom was thoroughly Roman in that he depended principally on the absoluteness of male and female difference. This formed the basis for his views on masculinization and kyriarchization, and informed his depiction of the operation of virtue and vice. Gender ambiguity was a problem for Chrysostom. Even though he lauds women who act virtuously like men, in his eyes women still have to know their place in the patriarchal hierarchy, and although they may act virtuously like men, they still remain women.

In addition, the presence of eunuchs in the household contributed to Chrysostom's and others' anxiety over the role of the *paterfamilias,* while the presence and influence of eunuchs in the imperial courts were also a point of discomfort.[170] Chrysostom also had to deal with a freed court eunuch, named Eutropius, who had fallen out of favor politically.[171] Eventually, however, Christian authors includ-

---

πόρνας ἐπιτειχίζωσιν, οὐχὶ τὴν κεφαλὴν ἀναιροῦσιν, ἀλλὰ τὴν ψυχὴν σφάττουσι, μοιχοὺς ἐργαζόμενοι καὶ θηλυδρίας καὶ πόρνους.

169. Latin uses the terms *eunuchus, spado,* and *castratus* interchangeably (some other appellations will also be highlighted).

170. Dirk Schlinkert, "Der Hofeunuch der Spätantike: Ein gefährlicher Außenseiter?," *Hermes* 122 (1994): 342–59; Walter Stevenson, "The Rise of Eunuchs in Greco-Roman Antiquity," *Journal of the History of Sexuality* 5, no. 4 (1995): 505–8.

171. For background on Chrysostom's dealings with Eutropius, see John N. D. Kelly, *Golden Mouth: The Story of John Chrysostom—Ascetic, Preacher, Bishop* (Ithaca, NY: Cornell University Press, 1998), 105–11, 145–55.

ing Chrysostom adopted the idea of spiritual castration, which became an important symbol in the Christian neomasculinity of the later Roman Empire. The presence of the eunuch also challenged Chrysostom's understanding of male-female difference, masculinization, and of course slave sexuality, especially virginity. Coerced castration, however, still remained one of the cruelest and inhumane crimes perpetrated against unfree bodies.[172]

The majority of eunuchs in Roman society were either slaves or freedpersons,[173] and the details of their castration are murky. Roman law was very much against the practice of castration, and there were numerous laws in place to prosecute not only those who were responsible for performing castration, but also those who voluntarily accepted it.[174] With reference to the formulations of Ulpian, Walter Stevenson and Mathew Kuefler have shown that despite the complexity of the issue of castration and eunuchs in Roman law, a somewhat structured terminology existed to deal with it.[175] Roman law identified three types of eunuchs: eunuchs by nature (*natura spadones*), people who have been made eunuchs (*thlibiae thlasiae*), and other eunuchs (*aliud genus spadonum*). These terms are probably Graecisms that slipped into legislation, not too different from what developed in the language of adultery— each term denotes the method of castration. *Thlibiae thlasiae* is probably related to the Greek term *thlibō*, meaning to "press hard," which refers to the procedure of tying up the scrotum and severing the vas deferens, while *spado* was derived from *spaō*, meaning "sever or tear," here referring to the surgical removal or simply cutting off of the testicles. "Natural eunuchs" were probably men with underdeveloped or injured sex organs from birth or adolescence, or perhaps intersex persons.

Regarding their religious duties in Roman society,[176] eunuchs were mostly associated with the cult of the Magna Mater, which had its adherents even in late antiquity;[177] it was supported by both Elagabalus and Julian.[178] Central to this cult

---

172. For a discussion of cruelty and castration, see Anthony Adams, "'He Took a Stone Away': Castration and Cruelty in the Old Norse *Sturlunga Saga*," in *Castration and Culture in the Middle Ages*, ed. Larissa Tracy (Cambridge: D. S. Brewer, 2013), 188–209.

173. Peter Guyot, *Eunuchen als Sklaven und Freigelassene in der griechisch-römischen Antike* (Stuttgart: Klett-Cotta, 1980).

174. Kuefler, *Manly Eunuch*, 32–33.

175. Stevenson, "Rise of Eunuchs," 476–78; Kuefler, *Manly Eunuch*, 33.

176. For instances of religious castration outside of the Greek and Roman world, see Arthur D. Nock, "Eunuchs in Ancient Religion," *Archiv für Religionswissenschaft* 23 (1925): 25–33. Many eunuch slaves may have been imported from outside the Roman Empire, considering the ban on castration. For a general overview of eunuchs in biblical literature, see F. P. Retief, J. F. G. Cilliers, and S. P. J. K. Riekert, "Eunuchs in the Bible," *Acta Theologica* 26, no. 2 (2006): 247–58; Sean D. Burke, *Queering the Ethiopian Eunuch: Strategies of Ambiguity in Acts*, Emerging Scholars (Minneapolis: Fortress Press, 2013).

177. Jacob Latham, "'Fabulous Clap-Trap': Roman Masculinity, the Cult of Magna Mater, and Literary Constructions of the *Galli* at Rome from the Late Republic to Late Antiquity," *Journal of Religion* 92, no. 1 (2012): 84–122.

178. Kuefler, *Manly Eunuch*, 246–47.

was the *gallus*, a eunuch priest who severed his genitals on the *dies sanguinis* (the Day of Blood, 24 March) as a fertility rite and perhaps as a sign of personal dedication to a female deity.[179] Several Christian authors, including Prudentius, Lactantius, and Augustine,[180] protested this cultic practice.[181]

Chrysostom notes that most people who have themselves castrated do so because they believe it will curb their lust. The numerous condemnations of Christian self-castration indicate that some indeed practiced it.[182] One of the most famous examples is probably Origen, who had himself discreetly castrated in his early twenties.[183] Castration and becoming (like) a eunuch, it should be remembered, are instances of doulomorphism—even if some eunuchs were not slaves, the act was fertile (excuse the pun) with the symbolism of slavery. The more famous episode in the Bible involving a eunuch is the story of Philip and the Ethiopian eunuch (Acts 8:26–40); however in his interpretation of this narrative, Chrysostom hardly makes note of the court official's status as a eunuch; rather Chrysostom lauds the eunuch's love of scripture and his religious zeal.[184] In his discussion of the most influential biblical verse regarding castration, Matthew 19:12 (which Origen, despite his inclination to allegory, took literally),[185] Chrysostom explains:

179. Rousselle, *Porneia*, 122–23.

180. See Prudentius, *Perist.* 10, lines 1059–75; Lactantius, *Div. inst.* 1.17; Augustine, *Civ.* 7.24; texts and translations: Kuefler, *Manly Eunuch*, 379–80.

181. See Mary Beard and John Henderson, "With This Body I Thee Worship: Sacred Prostitution in Antiquity," in *Gender and the Body in the Ancient Mediterranean,* ed. Maria Wyke (Oxford: Blackwell, 1998), 56–79; Kuefler, *Manly Eunuch,* 249; Shaun Tougher, *The Eunuch in Byzantine History and Society* (London: Routledge, 2009), 35–39.

182. Self-castration may have been common from the earliest years of Christianity; see Henry Chadwick, ed., *The Sentences of Sextus* (Cambridge: Cambridge University Press, 1959), 109–12; Rousselle, *Porneia,* 121–28; Brown, *Body and Society,* 168–70; Stevenson, "Rise of Eunuchs," 506–9; Kuefler, *Manly Eunuch,* 245–82. Another important study is that of Daniel F. Caner, "The Practice and Prohibition of Self-Castration in Early Christianity," *Vigiliae Christianae* 51, no. 4 (1997): 396–415.

183. See Eusebius, *Hist. eccl.* 6.8.2–3 (Oulton 28–29); Chadwick was not convinced of the historicity of this event, although Brown does allow for its possibility, and I am in agreement with Brown's view; see Henry Chadwick, *Early Christian Thought and the Classical Tradition* (Oxford: Oxford University Press, 1966), 67; Brown, *Body and Society,* 168–69.

184. *Hom. Act.* 19 (PG 60.149–58); for a discussion of the religious zeal and bibliophilia of the Ethiopian eunuch in this homily, see Chris L. de Wet, "'If a Story Can So Master the Children's Soul': Christian Scriptural Pedagogy, Orality and Power in the Writings of John Chrysostom" *Oral History Journal of South Africa* 2, no. 1 (2014): 121–42.

185. The text reads: "For there are eunuchs who have been so from their mother's womb, and there are eunuchs who have been made eunuchs by people, and there are eunuchs who have made themselves eunuchs for the sake of the kingdom of heaven. Let the one who is able to receive this receive it"; NA28: εἰσὶν γὰρ εὐνοῦχοι οἵτινες ἐκ κοιλίας μητρὸς ἐγεννήθησαν οὕτως, καὶ εἰσὶν εὐνοῦχοι οἵτινες εὐνουχίσθησαν ὑπὸ τῶν ἀνθρώπων, καὶ εἰσὶν εὐνοῦχοι οἵτινες εὐνούχισαν ἑαυτοὺς διὰ τὴν βασιλείαν τῶν οὐρανῶν. ὁ δυνάμενος χωρεῖν χωρείτω.

For the severing of a body part is not able to repress such waves, and to calm them, like the strap of reason; actually, it is only reason that can achieve this. . . . But when he says, that *they made themselves eunuchs* [Matt. 19:12], he does not mean the excision of the genitals, far from it, but the severance of evil thoughts. So the one who has severed his genitals, in fact, is subject even to a curse, as Paul says, *I wish those who trouble you would emasculate themselves* [Gal. 5:12]. And understandably so! For such a person is busy with the deeds of murderers, and giving ear to those who slander God's creation, and opens the mouths of the Manichaeans, and is guilty of the same maleficent acts as those who mutilate themselves among the Greeks. For to cut off our body parts has been a demonic act from the very beginning, and a satanic plot, so that they may defame the work of God, and maim this living creature, and not allowing for freedom of choice, but to the nature of our members, so the greater part of them may sin safely, as being irresponsible. And they doubly harm this living creature, both by mutilating the members, and by suppressing the zeal of free choice on behalf of good deeds.[186]

There are three important discursive operations in this passage. First, Chrysostom removes lust from the area of the genitalia and places it in the seat of reason. More accurately, following a Platonic division of the soul, Chrysostom probably believed that lust resided in the liver, the seat of the irascible part of the soul, which had to be controlled by the rational part of the soul, located in the brain. Second, he spiritualizes castration, opening up the possibility of becoming moral eunuchs. Third, Chrysostom uses castration as a vilifying technology, a strategy of othering against social outsiders like the Jews and Manichaeans.

First, then, Chrysostom separates lust from the function of the genitals; he "degenitalizes" lust—essentially, lust does not originate from the genitalia but from free will (*proairesis*)—even eunuchs can still choose to lust. Like many other early Christian thinkers, Chrysostom does not suggest that desire be eradicated from the soul, but that it be directed toward proper objects, like one's husband or wife, or Christ. This is a very important move for Chrysostom, since he places his argument in line with a long tradition that addressed the problem of lust in eunuchs—his view is not unique. It was traditionally believed that castration had two aims—to return to a state of childhood (or to become like an angel), and

186. *Hom. Matt.* 62.3 (PG 58.599.42–600.7): Οὐ γὰρ οὕτως ἐκτομὴ μέλους, ὡς λογισμοῦ χαλινός, τὰ τοιαῦτα οἶδε καταστέλλειν κύματα, καὶ γαλήνην ποιεῖν· μᾶλλον δὲ λογισμὸς μόνος. . . . Ὅταν δὲ λέγῃ, ὅτι Εὐνούχισαν ἑαυτούς, οὐ τῶν μελῶν λέγει τὴν ἐκτομήν· ἄπαγε· ἀλλὰ τῶν πονηρῶν λογισμῶν τὴν ἀναίρεσιν. Ὡς ὅ γε τὸ μέλος ἐκτεμών, καὶ ἀρᾷ ἐστιν ὑπεύθυνος, καθὼς ὁ Παῦλός φησιν· Ὄφελον καὶ ἀποκόψονται οἱ ἀναστατοῦντες ὑμᾶς. Καὶ μάλα εἰκότως. Καὶ γὰρ τὰ τῶν ἀνδροφόνων ὁ τοιοῦτος τολμᾷ, καὶ τοῖς τοῦ Θεοῦ διαβάλλουσι τὴν δημιουργίαν δίδωσιν ἀφορμήν, καὶ τῶν Μανιχαίων ἀνοίγει τὰ στόματα, καὶ τοῖς παρ' Ἕλλησιν ἀκρωτηριαζομένοις τὰ αὐτὰ παρανομεῖ. Τὸ γὰρ ἀποκόπτειν τὰ μέλη, δαιμονικῆς ἐνεργείας καὶ σατανικῆς ἐπιβουλῆς ἐξ ἀρχῆς γέγονεν ἔργον· ἵνα τοῦ Θεοῦ τὸ ἔργον διαβάλλωσιν· ἵνα τὸ ζῶον τοῦτο λυμήνωνται· ἵνα μὴ τῇ προαιρέσει, ἀλλὰ τῇ τῶν μελῶν φύσει τὸ πᾶν λογισάμενοι, οὕτως ἀδεῶς ἁμαρτάνωσιν αὐτῶν οἱ πολλοί, ἅτε ἀνεύθυνοι ὄντες· καὶ διπλῇ παραβλάψωσι τὸ ζῶον τοῦτο, καὶ τῷ τὰ μέλη πηροῦν, καὶ τῷ τῆς προαιρέσεως τὴν ὑπὲρ τῶν ἀγαθῶν προθυμίαν κωλύειν.

to prevent loss of the vital *pneuma*. The *pneuma* was seen as highly concentrated blood, and one's essential and invaluable life essence. Adherents of the latter view believed that if the *pneuma* is not lost by the transmission of sperm, it transforms into psychic *pneuma*, thereby strengthening the moral and spiritual dimension of one's existence. Castration was not, initially, focused on inhibiting sexual desire, but on remaining infertile and cultivating spiritual fertility—eunuch priests of the cult of Cybele could still achieve erections.[187] The fact that eunuchs, like the *galli*, were still sexually active (the *galli* are supposed to have even practiced a type of sacred prostitution), did puzzle Graeco-Roman society, since their ability to be sexually active went against what seemed to be conventional wisdom at the time. There was now a clear distinction, medically, between the flow and distribution of *pneuma* for the sake of fertilization, and the simple act of ejaculation.[188]

The symbolic link with early childhood probably also informed popular belief about the lack of sexual drive in eunuchs. Moreover, the practice of self-castration may also have been angelomorphic, a sign of an almost prelapsarian restoration in which people will become like asexual angels,[189] where there truly is "no more male or female" (Gal. 3:28); it also negates any chance of circumcision or reproduction of slave offspring, thereby also fulfilling the promise of "no more Jew or Greek," and "no more slave or free." Some may have regarded eunuchism as a higher natural state, a state of perfection. Paul was an example to Chrysostom of someone who was totally impervious to natural lust, and so also resembling the angelic or spiritual eunuch state.[190] Coincidentally, Chrysostom believed angels were also slaves of God.[191]

But Chrysostom warns against this, and notes that castration goes against nature. In fact, the reason castration is punished is because it is unnatural. Chrysostom uses the same reason to argue for the prosecution of same-sex passion—both castration and homoeroticism are unnatural to Chrysostom and therefore subject to punishment. "Ask for what reason the legislators punish those who

187. Rousselle, *Porneia*, 122–23.
188. Ibid., 123.
189. There is also the curious case of an eleventh-century manuscript of the homilies of Chrysostom that was drafted as an imperial gift (Coislin 79). The miniatures in the manuscript represent the emperor and the empress Maria of Alania, with Chrysostom on the one side and the archangel Michael on the other. The monk Sabas is also displayed, with the typical façade of a eunuch—no beard, with a smooth and soft face. There is also a curious miniature of the scribe or painter (γραφεύς) of the manuscript, in a supplicatory position facing the archangel Michael, signifying that Michael is the intercessor. At that stage angels were seen as the patrons of eunuchs, again illustrating the close conceptual links between the state of the eunuch, child, and the angel; for an extensive discussion, with images, of this manuscript, see Carmen-Laura Dumitrescu, "Remarques en marge du 'Coislin 79': Les trois eunuques et le problème du donateur," *Byzantion* 57, no. 1 (1987): 32–45; Tougher, *Eunuch in Byzantine History*, 113–14.
190. See *Laud.* 1.9 (SC 300.126).
191. *Serm. Gen.* 2.1–2 (PG 54.588.37–589.11).

make men eunuchs," Chrysostom says, "and you will see that it is for no other reason than the fact that they mutilate nature."[192] The view that eunuchs were immune to lust was still very common in the fourth century, and it prompted Basil of Ancyra to warn virgins against the dangers of eunuchs. Basil states that castrated men actually burn with more desire and are less restrained because they know they have no risk of making a woman pregnant.[193] This type of advice was relevant especially for elite Christian households in which eunuchs were both a safeguard for the chastity of unmarried girls and something of an exotic commodity—the physical beauty of eunuchs is often emphasized in the sources.[194]

Chrysostom often refers to elite masters who own "swarms of eunuchs."[195] The exoticism of eunuchs is a particular sign of decadence to Chrysostom—in referring to the inner adornment of saints, he excludes a whole list of elite luxuries: "It is not from bracelets, or from necklaces, or from their eunuchs either, and their slave girls, and gold-embroidered dresses, but from their labor for the sake of the truth."[196] For Chrysostom lust is not a problem of the genitals but a problem of reason and the will; lust does not rest in the loins. "But it is not so with respect to lust, but many who have been made eunuchs have not been freed from the fire that burned within them," Chrysostom explains, "for the desire lies in other organs [perhaps the liver and brain], imprinted inwardly in our nature."[197]

In *Homiliae in Matthaeum* 62.3, Chrysostom states that only the "strap" (*chalinos*) of reason can "repress" (*katastellein*) the waves of lust. His choice of words suggests a pun, first with the term *chalinos,* which alludes to the straps used to tie up the testicles, and then with the term *katastellō,* which can also mean "repress, reduce, or restrain." Chrysostom's argument here about the seat of lust is Platonic—it is reason (*logismos*), or the rational part of the soul, that controls lust, which is usually located

192. *Hom. Rom.* 5[4].3 (F1.49): ἐρώτησον τίνος ἔνεκεν τοὺς εὐνούχους ποιοῦντας κολάζουσιν οἱ νομοθέται, καὶ εἴσῃ, ὅτι δι' οὐδὲν ἕτερον, ἢ ὅτι τὴν φύσιν ἀκρωτηριάζουσι. Same-sex passion was even worse than prostitution in Chrysostom's view, since to him prostitution was at least natural albeit sinful; see *Hom. Rom.* 5[4].3 (F1.48–49).

193. Basil of Ancyra, *Virg.* 61 (PG 30.793.5-796.51); see Rousselle, *Porneia,* 123; Brown, *Body and Society,* 169.

194. Shaun Tougher, "The Aesthetics of Castration: The Beauty of Roman Eunuchs," in Tracy, *Castration and Culture,* 48–72.

195. See *Hom. Eph.* 20.6 (F4.314); *Hom. Jo.* 28.3 (PG 59.166.21–23); *Hom. Rom.* 21[20].2 (F1.353); *Stat.* 13.2 (PG 49.138.17–27).

196. *Hom. Rom.* 32[31] (F1.474): οὐκ ἀπὸ τῶν ψελλίων, οὐδὲ ἀπὸ τῶν ὁρμίσκων, οὐδὲ ἀπὸ τῶν εὐνούχων καὶ τῶν θεραπαινίδων καὶ τῶν χρυσοπάστων ἱματίων, ἀλλ'ἀπὸ τῶν ὑπὲρ τῆς ἀληθείας ἱδρώτων.

197. *Hom. Tit.* 5.2 (F6.306): Ἐπὶ δὲ τῆς τῶν σωμάτων ἐπιθυμίας οὐχ οὕτως, ἀλλὰ καὶ εὐνουχισθέντες πολλοὶ τὴν ἔνδον ἐνοχλοῦσαν πυρὰν οὐκ ἀπέβαλον· ἡ γὰρ ἐπιθυμία ἐν ἑτέροις κεῖται ὀργάνοις, ἔνδον ἐν τῇ φύσει ἐγκειμένη.

in the irascible part of the soul.[198] The link between castration and sexual restraint inevitably boils over into the debate about virginity. Some believed that eunuchs were virgins par excellence, since they had severed any physicality that could lead to sexual intercourse. But Chrysostom refutes this point as well: "No one would praise eunuchs for virginity because they do not marry ... the mutilation of their bodies deprives them of this virtue."[199] The prime reason for marriage—to produce legitimate heirs—is not an option for eunuchs. Here again the focus is not on their lackluster libido, but their sterility.

After he degenitalizes lust, Chrysostom introduces a discourse of spiritual castration.[200] It is not the physical act of castration that is a mark of distinction, but when one becomes a spiritual eunuch, one has removed vice from one's nature. Chrysostom rightly notes that most people who become eunuchs did not have any choice in the matter, since they were slaves—physical castration is thus juxtaposed to the doctrine of free moral agency. Whether one is a physical eunuch or not, one retains free will (*proairesis*) when choosing the path of spiritual castration, and this is much more admirable to Chrysostom. This was also true in the case of Chrysostom's other doulomorphic metaphors.[201] Ironically, most of the Christian slave metaphors professed to grant the institutional slave agency.

The promotion of spiritual castration had two purposes. First, spiritual castration served as an antitype to Christians who had performed physical self-castration and was an attempt to deter others from doing the same—it thereby served to counterbalance the uncomfortable gender ambiguity of physical eunuchs. Second, as Kuefler has shown, it represented the new ideal of Christian masculinity, especially embodied in the figure of the manly eunuch, and more generally, in monasticism. Kuefler states that "the eunuch served as a symbol not only of the dangers of traditional Roman masculinity but also of its Christian transformation."[202] Chrysostom used the same strategy of interiorization with regard to virginity;[203] spiritual castration is simply another version of Chrysostom's strategy of spiritual

---

198. The Platonic theory of the tripartite soul was quite influential in Christian circles; Shaw, *The Burden of the Flesh*, 32. For Chrysostom's use of selected Platonic concepts and imagery, see Konstantinos Bosinis, "Two Platonic Images in the Rhetoric of John Chrysostom: 'The Wings of Love' and the 'Charioteer of the Soul,'" *Studia Patristica* 41 (2006): 433–38; Raymond J. Laird, *Mindset, Moral Choice and Sin in the Anthropology of John Chrysostom* (Strathfield: St. Paul's, 2012).

199. *Virg.* 8.5.56–61 (SC 125.118): τοὺς εὐνούχους οὐδεὶς ἂν ἐπαινέσειεν εἰς παρθενίας λόγον ὅτι μὴ γαμοῦσιν ... τοὺς εὐνούχους ἡ τοῦ σώματος πήρωσις τῆς ἐπὶ τῷ πράγματι φιλοτιμίας ἐξέβαλεν. Translation: Shore, *On Virginity*, 11. See also *Stag.* 2.12 (PG 47.470.17–23); *Virg.* 13.3.28–29 (SC 125.136), 36.2.28–30 (SC 125.212–14), 49.6.92–94 (SC 125.280).

200. For an extensive discussion of spiritual castration in Christian authors from the West, see Kuefler, *Manly Eunuch*, 260–82.

201. See chapter 2.

202. Kuefler, *Manly Eunuch*, 245.

203. *Hom. Heb.* 28.5 (F7.327)

virginity, and an element of the universal framework of slavery to God. In this sense, Chrysostom also incorporates the metaphor of the court eunuch and his king—Christ: "Eunuchs especially ought to stand by the king." Chrysostom then qualifies the statement: "By eunuchs, I mean those who are of sound mind, having no wrinkle or blemish, high-minded, having the perspective of the soul, gentle and quick-sighted, energetic and accomplished, not sleepy or supine, full of the utmost freedom."[204] Spiritual eunuchs are not enslaved like many physical eunuchs, but are free.

Finally, Chrysostom uses the motif of castration as an alterizing invective strategy. Here we especially see the anxiety surrounding the gender ambiguity caused by castration coming to the fore. Chrysostom does not refer to natural eunuchs here, but to those who have performed self-castration. Castration is both denaturalized and demonized in Chrysostom's rhetoric—castration becomes a form of blasphemy against God as the creator of nature.[205] Castration, as noted above, is also the epitome of the renunciation of free moral agency: it has a servile nature. Examples from various heretical movements support this extreme pathologization. As a resolution to the confusion Matthew 19:12 may cause, Chrysostom posits Paul's words from Galatians 5:12, and thereby concludes that castration is in fact a curse, not a religious blessing. Castration is associated with Jewish circumcision, as is evident in Chrysostom's reference to its association with murder—Chrysostom refers to the Jews as murderers of Christ and worse.[206] Circumcision becomes castration, mutilation, and a curse.

It was not the first time that opponents of Judaism accused Jews of genital mutilation. The emperor Hadrian also considered circumcision a form of castration, and banned it under Roman law that forbade castration;[207] this despite the fact that Judaism outrightly rejected castration.[208] In fact, the Christian reaction against castration was not unique, but rather the result of an intersection of Jewish, Christian, and Graeco-Roman attitudes toward the practice.[209] Jews owning Christian slaves was a major problem for Christians in late antiquity. A Christian slave

204. *Hom. Heb.* 17.5 (F7.212): Τοὺς εὐνούχους μάλιστα δεῖ παρεστάναι τῷ βασιλεῖ· εὐνούχους λέγω τοὺς τὴν διάνοιαν λευκούς, μηδένα ἔχοντας ῥύπον μηδὲ σπῖλον, ὑψηλοὺς τῇ διανοίᾳ, τὸ ὄμμα ἥμερον τῆς ψυχῆς ἔχοντας καὶ ὀξυδερκές, εὐπερίστροφον καὶ γοργόν, ἀλλὰ μὴ ὑπνηλὸν μηδὲ ὕπτιον, ἐλευθερίας γέμον πολλῆς.

205. Caner, "Practice and Prohibition of Self-Castration," 407–8.

206. *Adv. Jud.* 1.6.3 (PG 48.852.12); *Hom. Jo.* 55.1 (PG 59.302.51–56); *Hom. 1 Tim.* 2.2 (F6.17).

207. Shaye J. D. Cohen, *From the Maccabees to the Mishnah* (Louisville, KY: Westminster John Knox, 2006), 25.

208. Mathew Kuefler, "Castration and Eunuchism in the Middle Ages," in *Handbook of Medieval Sexuality*, ed. Vern L. Bullough and James A. Brundage (New York: Routledge, 1996), 282–84.

209. Jack Collins, "Appropriation and Development of Castration as Symbol and Practice in Early Christianity," in Tracy, *Castration and Culture*, 73–86.

owned by a Jewish family might experience numerous difficulties, since Jewish law required slaves to be circumcised, but Christian law forbade it.[210] Constantine already forbade this practice of circumcising Christian slaves, but this does not mean it ceased. It was perhaps just as troubling to be a Jewish slave in a Christian family. Due to these regulations, however, it is likely that Christians and Jews tried to avoid purchasing slaves with opposite religious affiliations. In the fourth century there were numerous legislative acts banning proselytism of Christian slaves by Jews, until Justinian totally banned Jews from owning Christian slaves.[211]

In the same breath, Chrysostom uses the negative slave metaphor of eunuchism and castration against the Manichaeans, showing how doulology was used as an invective strategy. The centrality of freedom and free moral choice in Chrysostom's invective demonstrates how he again contrasts moral freedom with moral slavery. Both his references to slandering against nature and God's creation, as well as the idea of self-mutilation, are directed to the Manichaeans along with the Jews.[212] Self-castration and eunuchism are central to Chrysostom's invective against Manichaeism. Chrysostom also links the Jews' circumcision and the Manichaeans' self-mutilation in his interpretation of Galatians 1:4.[213] Chrysostom was acquainted with Manichaeism, albeit from a position of animosity, and refutes Manichaean doctrine by trying to show that creation and the human body are not inherently evil (this would be in conflict with Chrysostom's notions of free will). The fact that there is goodness and virtue in the world, as embodied by ordinary human beings like the apostle Paul, shows that creation is not inherently evil. Rather, it is "the depraved moral agency" (*tēn proairesin tēn diephtharmenēn*) that causes hardship and suffering.[214] The strict Manichaean disciplinary regime is vilified by Chrysostom and is called self-mutilation.

The Manichaeans did have a negative view of the body, but Chrysostom's view that they lacked proper spiritual discipline is simply not accurate, since they incorporated the same strict discipline in their religious and spiritual practices.[215] Their practices were aimed at psychic purification in service of their migration to the

---

210. Kuefler, "Castration and Eunuchism," 282.

211. Amnon Linder, "The Legal Status of Jews in the Byzantine Empire," in *Jews in Byzantium: Dialectics of Minority and Majority Cultures*, ed. Robert Bonfil et al. (Leiden: Brill, 2011), 168–72.

212. For Chrysostom's rhetoric against the Manichaeans, see Maria G. Mara, "Aspetti della polemica antimanichea di Giovanni Crisostomo," in *Atti dell'undicesimo simposio Paolino: Paolo tra Tarso e Antiochia; Archeologia/storia/religione*, ed. Luigi Padovese (Rome: Pontificia Università Antonianum, 2008), 195–99; Chris L. de Wet, "Paul, Identity-Formation and the Problem of Alterity in John Chrysostom's Homilies *In Epistulam ad Galatas Commentarius*," *Acta Theologica Supplementum* 19 (2014): 18–41.

213. *Comm. Gal.* 1.4 (F4.11–13); see De Wet, "Problem of Alterity," 30–36.

214. *Comm. Gal.* 1.4 (F4.9–10).

215. Jason BeDuhn, *The Manichaean Body: In Discipline and Ritual* (Baltimore: Johns Hopkins University Press, 2000), 25–125.

divine realm.[216] In his interpretation of Galatians, Chrysostom again notes that the Manichaeans practiced self-castration. There is a possibility that Chrysostom is correct, since they did exhibit a highly oppositional stance against sexual intercourse—it is very difficult to verify though, since I am not aware of any Manichaean author who refers to Manichaean castration, although the myth of Uranus's castration was influential.[217] There are later instances of self-castration by Manichaeans during the Muslim period—for instance the case of the radical ascetic Mᵉṣallyāne—but these were exceptions rather than the rule, and other Manichaeans rejected such behavior.[218] Chrysostom is then probably referring to Manichaean radicals or relying on folkloristic traditions that speak of Manichaean castration—otherwise this is simply a form of extreme sexual slander against Manichaeism.

Since castration functions here as invective rhetoric with a very broad sematic range, Chrysostom may also be referring to the Manichaeans' negative view of marriage and reproduction (not sexual intercourse) and their contraceptive efforts. Manichaean cosmological formulations led to a very negative view of marriage and procreation, but not necessarily sex.[219] The Manichaean elect were not allowed to have sex, while all other members were forbidden to have children. Various contraceptive and probably abortifacients were employed to guard against unwanted progeny, including having women wash out their vagina after intercourse, fellatio, herbal contraceptives, and barrier methods.[220] But the point Chrysostom constantly emphasizes is that evil is not seated in a physical part of the body, but lies in the corrupt part of the soul and in the evil volition.

The final element in this invective conglomeration is what Chrysostom refers to as the custom of the "Greeks." Without a doubt this refers to the cult of Cybele the Magna Mater, and to the legends of the castration of Attis. Chrysostom specifically refers to the *galli*, who, along with the Jews, Manichaeans, and anyone else practicing self-castration, not only mutilate the body, the creation of God, but also mar free moral choice. The invective of self-mutilation and castration should also be

216. Jason BeDuhn, "The Metabolism of Salvation: Manichaean Concepts of Human Physiology," in *The Light and the Darkness: Studies in Manichaeism and Its World*, ed. Paul Mirecki and Jason BeDuhn, Nag Hammadi and Manichaean Studies 50 (Leiden: Brill, 2001), 18–33.

217. See Alexander of Lycopolis, *Manich. opinion.* 10.16.9–20; cited in Samuel N.C. Lieu, *Manichaeism in the Later Roman Empire and Medieval China*, Wissenschaftliche Untersuchungen zum Neuen Testament 63 (Tübingen: Mohr Siebeck, 1992), 160.

218. Michael G. Morony, *Iraq after the Muslim Conquest* (Piscataway, NJ: Gorgias, 2005), 459.

219. For an extensive discussion of Augustine's response to Manichaean views on contraception, see John K. Coyle, *Manichaeism and Its Legacy*, Nag Hammadi and Manichaean Studies 69 (Leiden: Brill, 2009), 283–95.

220. Vern L. Bullough, ed., "Augustine, Saint (d. 430)," in *Encyclopedia of Birth Control* (Santa Barbara, CA: ABC-CLIO, 2001), 24–26.

seen as leaning toward feminization. Chrysostom recurrently uses the slander of effeminacy to shame his opponents[221]—it is a direct assault on their masculinity; the physical mutilation of men, whether it is circumcision or self-castration, is in Chrysostom's mind a sign and symbol of everything that is abnormal, unnatural, effeminate, and morally depraved in pagan, Jewish, and heretical Christian culture. This is also why eunuchism is central to Chrysostom's polemic against homoeroticism.

We have seen thus far that Chrysostom envisions a type of spiritual castration, which is seen as severing vice from one's life. This metaphor is a positive use of the metaphor of castration and the eunuch; however, Chrysostom also uses the metaphor of eunuch slaves in a negative sense against those monks living with virgins in "spiritual marriage," and here again the problem of gender ambiguity surfaces. In his polemic against syneisaktism, or so-called spiritual marriage, Chrysostom laments:

> The men receive the women at the door, strutting as if they had been transformed into eunuchs, and when everyone is looking, they guide them with enormous pride. Nor do they slink away, but go so far as to glory in their performance. Even at that most awesome hour of the mysteries, they are much occupied with waiting on the virgins' pleasure, providing many of the spectators with occasion for offense.[222]

We can see here that Chrysostom disapproves of any "unnatural" gender hierarchization that these relationships display, and the invective of gynaecodouly is also implied in this context, perhaps with even more vigor than in previous instances.[223] Here, the virgins abandon their "natural" gender roles and adopt the façade of the masculine. The males are seen as effeminate and slavish.[224] Chrysostom describes these monks as men who resemble "effeminate soldiers who throw away their shields and sit down with a spindle and a basket," and now they have the reputation "above all slaves of women, because we have dashed to the ground all the nobility given us from above and exchanged it for earthly servility and shabbiness."[225] We again find the term *gynaikodouloi*, along with other

---

221. Susanna Drake, *Slandering the Jew: Sexuality and Difference in Early Christian Texts*, Divinations (Philadelphia: University of Pennsylvania Press, 2013), 78–98.

222. *Subintr.* 10.38–45 (Dumortier 80–81): Ἀπό τε γὰρ τῶν θυρῶν αὐτὰς ἔξωθεν δεχόμενοι, καὶ ἀντὶ τῶν εὐνούχων γινόμενοι σοβοῦσιν, καὶ προηγούμενοι μέγα φρονοῦσιν, ὁρώντων ἁπάντων, καὶ οὐ καταδύονται, ἀλλὰ καὶ ἐπαγάλλονται· καὶ ἐν αὐτῷ δὲ τῷ φρικωδεστάτῳ τῶν μυστηρίων καιρῷ πολλὰ πρὸς τὴν ἐκείνων ἀρεσκείαν διακονοῦνται, πολλοῖς τῶν ὁρώντων λαβὰς παρέχοντες. Translation: Clark, *Jerome, Chrysostom, and Friends*, 194.

223. *Hom. Matt.* 62.6 (PG 58.603.3–8); see chapter 2.

224. Blake Leyerle, *Theatrical Shows and Ascetic Lives: John Chrysostom's Attack on Spiritual Marriage* (Berkeley: University of California Press, 2001), 124–34.

225. *Subintr.* 6.28–29, 35–38 (Dumortier 64): καθάπερ στρατιῶται μαλακοὶ τὴν ἀσπίδα, ἠλακάτη παρακάθησθε καὶ καλαθίσκῳ . . . γυναικοδούλων πανταχοῦ δόξαν λαμβάνομεν, ὅτι χαμαὶ τὴν εὐγένειαν

homoerotic terms of invective like *malakoi* and *douloprepeia* (men resembling a slavish disposition).[226] We also saw in chapter 2 that Chrysostom used different types of slave metaphors to differentiate various forms of moral slavery. In the previous examples he referred to sick, overworked slaves, slaves owned by slaves, and prostitutes.

But here, Chrysostom compares such a monk not only to a slave (specifically, a pseudo-male slave and, ironically, a man-footed animal, an *andrapodon*), but also to a eunuch. Why are these men compared to eunuchs? Because eunuchs were viewed with a great deal of suspicion in Roman society on account of their gender ambiguity. Eunuchs were often stereotyped as sexually perverse and untrustworthy. The eunuch represented a threat to conventional masculinities; hence the move toward spiritual castration.[227] These male slaves of lust abandon natural gender roles; they are compared to eunuch slaves, emasculated slaves. Since the men in these spiritual marriages fail to embody traditional masculine roles expected in Roman society, they destabilize Christian masculinity. They are dominated by women, *gynaikodouloi*. They are denigrated as being soft, effeminate, irrational, and slavish.[228]

. . .

The discourse of sexuality was one of the most common technologies of subjectivation in the ancient world. Who you were, your status, your civic and religious participation, were influenced by sexuality. Most importantly, the discourse of sexuality lent itself to strategies of pathologization and abnormalization. Chrysostom recommended strict regulation of slave sexuality, and vehemently warned his audience against the sexual exploitation of slaves. His many admonitions against the sexual abuse of slaves, even to such an extent that he, along with various others, restructured the whole terminology and conceptual framework related to slave sexuality, is indicative of the prevalence of the sexual exploitation of slaves in Roman society. This restructuring forms part of his program of domestic pastoralization—in fact, the pastoralization of sexuality, especially slave sexuality, may have been one of the most important discursive operations of pastoral power. Advice such as what we see in Chrysostom did seem to have an impact, since later

---

ἅπασαν ῥίψαντες τὴν ἄνωθεν δοθεῖσαν ἡμῖν, ἀντικαταλλαττόμεθα τὴν ἀπὸ τῆς γῆς δουλοπρέπειάν τε καὶ εὐτέλειαν. Translation: Clark, *Jerome, Chrysostom, and Friends*, 180–81. See *Subintr.* 6.42–47 (Dumortier 65); Clark, 181.

226. See Drake, *Slandering the Jew*, 78–98.

227. Kuefler, *Manly Eunuch*, 31–36. See also Leyerle, *Theatrical Shows and Ascetic Lives*, 129–30.

228. *Subintr.* 11 (Dumortier 83–86); see Aideen M. Hartney, "Manly Women and Womanly Men: The *Subintroductae* and John Chrysostom," in *Desire and Denial in Byzantium*, ed. Liz James, *Papers from the Thirty-First Spring Symposium of Byzantine Studies, University of Sussex, Brighton, March 1997* (Aldershot: Ashgate Variorum, 1999), 46.

legislation does reflect the changes in sexual offenses that bishops like Chrysostom and Ambrose envisaged. Whether this advice led to a decline in the sexual abuse of slaves is another question. The very fact that it was later written into legislation may prove the contrary, that Chrysostom's advice was not entirely followed. Furthermore, what we should not forget is that everything we know about slave sexuality comes from the pens of nonslaves—Chrysostom would not have been able to write from a slave's perspective, so the sources are biased.

What is also clear is that Chrysostom simply replaces one form of sexual regulation with another. There is no reason to believe that this new ethos of slave sexuality was any less oppressive or ameliorative—it may have simply added to the technologies of sexual exploitation and pathologization common to slave corporeality. The regulation and conceptual restructuring of slave sexuality may simply have involved the substitution of one form of exploitation for another. The new regulations made no difference to the slave's carceral state—in fact, the strict repression may have even intensified the carceral state of the slave. Nowhere is the slave body afforded any sexual liberation. New regulations may also have increased the grip of kyriarchal power on the sexual life of the slave, since slaves were now forced, violently at times, to exhibit *sōphrosynē*, a value structured for free, not enslaved society. And as we saw, *sōphrosynē* was often written very violently onto the slave body. Unwanted marriages may also have been arranged, or happy ones dissolved, along with the separation of children from parents. The criminalization of the slave body's sexual violation may also have intensified abuse, intimidation, and manipulation, since the slaveholder could be found guilty of a significant offense.

The two slave sexualities that expose the most significant fissures in masculinity and kyriarchy are prostitution and eunuchism. In late antiquity we see very strict regulation of, even an assault on, prostitution. This is another sign of the intense pastoralization of the domestic sphere and its sexuality—prostitution was a threat to domestic integrity and honor, and served as a front of resistance against men who aimed to control the fertility of females to whom they had sexual access. Prostitution no longer deterred men from adultery, but became a manifestation of it; slave sexuality was increasingly measured by the standards of free sexuality. Slaves found the standards of free masculinity difficult to meet without the structures and support systems to which free persons had access.

All these shifts are indicative of the changing face of Roman masculinity with the rise of Christianity. In this crisis of masculinity, the basic concept of Roman sexuality, including the role of slavery in sexual discourse, had to be rethought. A new universal sexual ethic had to be implemented, one that did not distinguish, in principle, between slave and free. The various transformations of sexuality during this period manifest the interests of the new guarantors of power—namely, the agents of pastoralism. The inclusion of sexual transgression in the domain of sin was in itself significant.[229] Sexuality had always been a religious matter, and sexualities considered to be deviant were now subject to both social and religious pathologization; hence Chrysostom's inclusion of prostitution and castration among other serious sins, such as drunkenness, adultery, heresy, idolatry, murder, blasphemy, and sorcery.

But it was the sexuality of the eunuch that stood out as an example of gender destabilization and a source of anxiety to authors like Chrysostom. It was repeatedly emphasized that the gender ambiguity of eunuchs upset the systems of masculine power in Roman society, and both the obsession to outlaw castration and the promotion of spiritual castration aimed to reshape the sexuality of the eunuch and transform it into a new standard of masculinity. However, perhaps there was a more pervasive operation of power than the (de- and re-)masculinization of the subjectivity of the eunuch. If we examine the discourse of eunuchism and castration in Chrysostom, there is a very apparent philosophical and social disinvestment in the castrated slave body itself. No questions are raised about the violence and mutilation that slaves had to endure without a choice in the matter. Rejection of castration was the true operation of free moral choice for Chrysostom, but the issue of the corporeal disfigurement of slaves who had no choice in the first place rarely surfaces. Although Roman legislation addressed the problem of castration (or rather imposed a policy of "out-of-sight-out-of-mind"), it took no action against eunuchism itself; people still owned eunuchs, and they were prominent in most structures of Roman society. As in the case of slavery in general, castration became a matter of indifference, and the church again attempted to draw the attention away from this violent mutilation of human beings by positing a spiritual castration, a spiritual mutilation.

Pastoral power reserved the right to act against coerced castration and the making of eunuchs. It took a stand against castration as a violation of masculinity and nature, but took no action to abolish it as a form of violence particularly aimed at the slave body. As is appropriate near the conclusion of this book, we may look at the body of the eunuch as telling the story of the power of kyriarchy, and it is clear that that story has come full circle; castration represents the inscription of domination in the worst sense, standing out as a pillar in the history of calamities.[230] Despite the masculinity inscribed by spiritual eunuchism, the real eunuch is physically no longer a "man" according to Roman standards—physical castration is demasculinization in the utmost and final sense. Eunuchs have no chance of producing offspring but are still sexually pathologized for what society sees as a

---

229. For an extensive discussion of this phenomenon, see Harper, *From Shame to Sin.*

230. For castration and eunuchism as elements in the history of calamities (a term taken from Abelard), see Larissa Tracy, "Introduction: A History of Calamities: The Culture of Castration," in Tracy, *Castration and Culture*, 1–28.

clumsy, reckless, and dangerous sexual drive. At no point does anyone address the inhumanity of forced castration on the unfree, or object to the fact that eunuchs, an exotic and useful commodity, can still be bought at the slave market. Owning eunuchs was rather a mark of distinction to some, and decadence to others. Chrysostom was less concerned about the forced castration of slaves than he was about the eunuch as a sign of decadence. Eunuchism was just as embedded in society as slavery, but rather than giving sense and value to the body of the slave, and proposing the abolishment of coerced castration, Chrysostom offered spiritual castration as an alternative, an alternative showing a disturbing indifference to perhaps the most extreme and inhumane violence perpetrated against slave bodies.

7

Conclusion

Preaching Bondage and the Legacy
of Christian Doulology

When it is therefore visible that the power of preaching, which restrains a
race so reckless, and so stubborn, has rendered them well behaved and gentle,
their masters, however unreasonable they may be, will accept a high opinion
of our doctrines. . . . For the more wicked they are, the more astonishing is
the power of that preaching.[1]

The problem of slavery never became one of the great theological controversies of late antiquity, nor did it receive the attention that many other theological topics did. Yet, Chrysostom's preaching about slavery probably had more of a direct impact on the daily life of his congregants than many other theological topics. Chrysostom's homilies were instruments for transmitting a Christianized doulology to later Roman society. We should not underestimate the impact of some of his homilies. Chrysostom used metaphors and stereotypes of the slave strategically in his homilies to shape Christian identity and the identity of outsiders. Rather than addressing the problem of slavery, Chrysostom's preaching used slavery for its own benefit, and even became somewhat accustomed to and even dependent on doulology.

What then do Chrysostom's homilies tell us about the effects of Christianization on the discourse of slavery in the later Roman world? What changed, and what remained the same, and what were the consequences for slaves and slaveholders? Christianity did not offer an entirely novel response to slavery. Chrysostom himself was influenced by various ideologies regarding slavery. His views on

1. *Hom. Tit.* 4.1 (F6.298–99): "Ὅταν οὖν ἴδωσιν, ὅτι τὸ γένος τὸ οὕτως ἴταμον, τὸ οὕτως αὔθαδες ἡ τοῦ κηρύγματος δύναμις χαλινὸν περιθεῖσα πάντων εἰργάσατο κοσμιώτερον καὶ ἐπιεικέστερον, κἂν σφόδρα πάντων ὦσιν ἀλογώτεροι οἱ δεσπόται, λήψονται ἔννοιαν μεγάλην περὶ τῶν δογμάτων τῶν παρ' ἡμῖν . . . ὅσῳ γὰρ ἂν ὦσι κακοὶ, τοσούτῳ μάλιστα θαυμάζεται τοῦ κηρύγματος ἡ ἰσχύς."

slavery have a strong Stoic and Pauline character. Like the Stoics, Chrysostom believed that slavery was nothing but a label—it was transitory and fleeting. He showed the same indifference toward slavery that the Stoices did; like the Stoics, he was much more concerned about the condition of the human soul. By Chrysostom's time, slavery had been extensively denaturalized and interiorized through centuries of Christian ethical and theological formulations. Chrysostom was not a slave. He could not know what it felt like to be a slave. Perhaps his experience and views changed during the time of his exile, when he was under the domination of another, had very limited agency, and lived in harsh circumstances where safety was never guaranteed—but we will never know.

The homilies exhibit very little empathy toward slaves. Chrysostom showed much more concern for people who were slaves of sin and slaves to the passions—"real" slaves in his mind. Chrysostom readily employed the metaphor of slavery to press the argument of the nature of sin and governance. He needed to convince his audience of an important point—the heteronomy of their bodies; if they could not identify themselves as slaves of Christ, then they were slaves to sin. Free moral agency could be found only in being a slave of Christ, and by being a slave of Christ, one was truly free. People had to master their passions, and not become enslaved to them, as this signified a loss of agency. Free will could be regained only through obedience to Christ, since sin was disobedience, and disobedience spawned slavery. The metaphor of slavery came in many garbs—Chrysostom uses the metaphors of regular domestic slaves, slaves belonging to other slaves, nurses, pedagogues, prostitutes, eunuchs, and even slave dealers; each metaphor with its very own special edge and emphasis. Unfortunately the more the metaphor of slavery was developed and spread in Christian theology, the more insouciant and blasé Christian attitudes became toward institutional slavery.

These findings are important for scholarship because they show how crucial it is to understand the theological metaphor of slavery in relation to its real, institutional counterpart. Institutional slavery informed the metaphor, and the metaphor sustained the institution. Admittedly, Chrysostom shows much discomfort with slavery at times, and he does indeed come close to abolishing it—yet in not one instance does he succeed in looking past the banality of slavery to see its oppressive and destructive social effects. Slavery was the elephant in the room, and rather than addressing it directly, the discourse was elevated to a spiritual plane that universalized and totalized slavery—rather than promoting abolition and making no one a slave, everyone now became slaves, either of God or of sin and the passions. Thus, the spiritual modalization of slavery and freedom exposed institutional slaves to even more oppression, since acts like violent and intrusive correction, punishment, and general pathologization were recommended and authorized by the metaphor. Most importantly, the metaphor of slavery had scriptural support, whereas abolition had none.

The metaphorization of slavery also complexified concepts like virtue, freedom, and love—concepts that seem to be positive, yet act very pervasively as mechanisms that reinforce the carceral state of institutional slaves. All of the positive metaphors of slavery to God claimed that they gave the slave a measure of agency and free choice, yet in reality, slaves had little agency in the oppression they had to endure. As a result of the theological metaphorization of slavery, we find an intensive labor ethic in Chrysostom's thought, one that assumed universal submission by both slaves and masters. This ethic of submission was less concerned about status, and more about mutual service with Christ as the heavenly slaveholder. Everyone had to be slaves of each other. Yet what this universal ethic of submission promoted was far from equality in status; it rather suggested that Christian slaves should be "better" slaves than non-Christians, and hardly removed any authority from the slaveholder. In fact, it gave more authority to the slaveholder, since he or she was now designated by God to dominate. The real effects of doulological metaphorization and interiorization were felt by slaves in their domestic contexts.

The study of doulology also assists us in understanding Chrysostom's pastoral agenda and how he implements domestic pastoralization. Essentially, doulology informed and shaped the Roman ideology of masculinity. Masculinity was in crisis in late antiquity—the analysis of late ancient doulology attests to this. Slavery in this period both displayed the strategies used to fashion and reproduce masculinity, and exposed the fissures in the eroding patriarchy. Chrysostom, like many other Christian authors, had a vision for a new type of man, a serious man, a man of *spoudē*, who was husband, father, and master in a distinctly Christian sense. In a very limited sense, male slaves could become men, and female slaves could exhibit *sōphrosynē* and other masculine virtues. The Christian slave woman was also affected, as she was awarded sexual dignity, which she had not previously enjoyed, yet this inscription of honor in reality often entailed violent discipline, forced conversion, regulation of sexual activity, and an even tighter carceral grip on her body, since it became a catalyst for honor or disgrace.

The new Christian man was schooled in methods of masculinization and kyriarchization that were different from those of earlier centuries, and Christian women, children, and slaves had to comply with the demands of this new masculinity. The new Christian man had to dominate others, as priest over his subordinates, and some male slaves could even assume this agency over their own families and slaves. This new man was educated in a new social curriculum of kyriarchization, where he represented the authority of God over his slaves, with the right to educate, discipline, and punish. He had to teach his son to be a just slaveholder. He was not supposed to own too many slaves, nor use them in any display that might show luxury, decadence, or effeminacy. He should never look like a slave of his slaves. He had to be a self-sufficient man; a slave of God.

Ideally, this man should marry at a young age, and had the option to join the military; but choosing the monastic life was the pinnacle. If he chose marriage, he always had to embody marital fidelity and never commit adultery or be involved in any form of sexual disgrace. Under no circumstances could he sexually exploit a slave, whether one in his house or a prostitute. As a slaveholder-priest, he was charged with teaching his slaves moderation and chastity, by means of spiritual exercises or even by moderately violent means, as a last resort. As for his children, he could choose a suitable husband or wife for his slaves, and he had to manage their sexuality in an honorable way. Physically, he had to embody the habitus of masculinity, but he had to strip all passion from his soul. The making of this new Christian man, along with the new façades of the wife, children, and slaves, was fundamental to Chrysostom's program of domestic pastoralization.

These elements defined masculinity, and although it was the *despoina* who mostly managed the slaves, Chrysostom says very little about the female slave-holder. In Chrysostom's mind, she is out of place—burdened with the many yokes of marriage, slaveholding being one of the heaviest. If she found herself in that position, many of the standards of masculinity were also applicable to her. She had to teach virtue to her slaves, but she also had to guard her own virtue and chastity, by never losing her temper with slaves and desisting from arrogantly flaunting them in public. She had to monitor the slaves, although they were also her monitors, the eyes and ears of the house. The elite *despoina* could hardly escape the carcerality of slave bodies around her—they guarded and observed her modesty, suckled her children, taught her sons and daughters, cooked her food, and protected her at night while she slept.

As a domestic adviser, Chrysostom did not alter the structure of the traditional Roman *familia*. He rather stressed the differences between the husband, wife, children, and slaves. Yet, Chrysostom did have a vision for households in Antioch and Constantinople. He desired to tighten the grip of pastoralism on the household by introducing numerous strategies of pastoralization into the domestic sphere. Some households accepted the recommendations, while others resisted. In this program of pastoralization, the *paterfamilias* had to become a lay priest of the household. The hierarchical structure of the household remained intact, but the father had to assume responsibility for the spiritual growth of those under his roof. Chrysostom wanted the entire *familia* to attend church services, and he also advised people to reenact and revise the sermon at home in order to learn more from it and to habituate any principles that may have been given. Slaves were not excluded from this; along with attending church services and public processions, they were also to be included in the household rituals of prayer, scripture reading, and hymn singing. They were also supposed to be baptized, and some even worked for the priests.

The obedient and devoted Christian slave was a testimony to the devotion of the master, and it is very likely that among the many forms of oppression slaves had to endure, forced conversion was among the most common. Chrysostom took a very aggressive stance against what he referred to as superstitions and religious rites and myths related to slaves. The slave culture of the Roman world had its own constructed symbolic reality—a reality in which slaves chose certain deities and supernatural forces that, for some reason, gave them meaning in their existence and contributed to the identity they had to simply accept. It was a variegated socioreligious milieu that often spilled over into the lives of slaveholders. This "slave underworld," as Chrysostom viewed it, was seen as yet another pathology in the subjectivity of the slave—and it was a reality that owners had to constantly suppress. Some slaves did find solace in Christianity, and accepted its rule, while others may have only acted the part.

But one of the most important reasons that slaves had to be regulated and normalized was because of their central role in the education of children. In some cases slaves were just as involved as parents in the raising of a child. Nurses had to take care of infants and freeborn daughters, while pedagogues guided the *filiusfamilias* into manhood. Chrysostom saw the potential in this instance, and in his sermons he gives very practical advice to his audience regarding the activities of nurses and pedagogues. Freeborn children had to be conditioned into the dynamics of kyriarchy from a very young age. Even newborns were subject to the forces of kyriarchization. Nurses and pedagogues had the children perform exercises that would assist them in becoming good slaveholders—this is how kyriarchy reproduced itself, via the intermediary of the slave, at the breast of the nurse and by the rod of the pedagogue. However, Chrysostom's comments about nurses and pedagogues also expose the dysfunctionality of the Roman household. Images of the good nurse and pedagogue presume that the parents were absent and incapable of raising their children. Chrysostom did preach to these parents on how to raise their children; the most important action was to make children aware of the difference between slaves and free. Slaves also functioned as training grounds for virtue, didactic tools the parent or pedagogue could use to shape the boy's masculinity or ingenue's femininity and by which the child might learn to control his or her passions.

However, to sustain his vision of the virtuous and useful Christian slave in the household, Chrysostom prescribed a strict regime of discipline, surveillance, and punishment. Chrysostom gave some very concrete and practical guidelines for this regime. First, slaves had to be taught virtue. The teaching of virtue, or aretagogy, ensured that the slave remained obedient to the master, but also that he or she set a good example for non-Christian outsiders. Rather than liberating Christian slaves, Chrysostom sought to impress non-Christians by showing them that the church and Christians were better at mastering and controlling their slaves than non-Christians. Christian slaves were also expected to work harder than their non-Christian counterparts, and to endure suffering and abuse without resistance or revolt, knowing that God would some day reward them when they were in heaven. To stimulate good behavior and optimum productivity, Chrysostom promulgated a biblical framework for slave surveillance—the Christic panopticon. In this framework, surveillance was interiorized and absolutized. The slaves now had the eyes of Christ, and the slaveholder focused on them. The purpose of Christic panoptical surveillance was the same as that of regular surveillance—it had to ensure that slaves behaved well and worked hard. This was a highly pervasive technology of kyriarchy. Chrysostom also preached to his audience about the punishment of slaves. Wicked slaves *had* to be punished—it was not only a prerogative, but a Christian duty. Since God punishes his slaves, Christian slaveholders ought to punish theirs. The punishment could be violent, but it must not be excessive, abusive, or unreasonable. It was expected that good slaves would be rewarded. Chrysostom rightly admits that it is the social environment of slavery that results in the lapse of a slave's character—being neglected as infants, abused as children, having no formal education, no recognized familial structure, limited friendships, and likely being prone to alcohol abuse. But rather than abolishing slavery, he aims to restructure the conditions of oppression in an attempt to reform and regulate slaves.

However, it was difficult to regulate slave sexuality, especially with the high levels of sexual exploitation of slaves in Roman society. The problem Chrysostom faced was that his world had been fashioned by years of systematic and institutionalized abuse against slaves, including sexual abuse. He knew that it was common even for boys in their pubescent years, as well as married men, to violate slave girls and prostitutes. In order to address this problem, and this was a trend throughout the late ancient church, Chrysostom restructures the very foundations of Roman sexuality and marriage. First, Chrysostom expects slaves to exhibit sexual modesty and self-control (*sōphrosynē*), and he attempts to guard the sexual integrity of the slave body by desexualizing it, criminalizing its sexual violation, and instilling a sense of honor in it. Overturning the teratogenic grid, he expanded the scope of sexual shame and adultery to include sexual violations against slaves. Slaves were no longer morally neutral ground—having sex with a slave while being married was an act of adultery, and if unmarried, fornication. Slave unions received informal recognition. Chrysostom's preaching actively set out to guard the chastity of slaves. Thus, slaves had to endure yet another regulatory framework that was not necessarily less oppressive than the previous one. Slaves still had no sexual agency, had to adhere to a standard of modesty and self-control without the advantages of the free, and faced harsh physical punishment if they failed in any of these respects.

Prostitution was even more problematic to Chrysostom. But having sex with a prostitute is also criminalized in Chrysostom's framework, despite being legal according to Roman imperial legislation. Whoever frequents a prostitute suffers social, religious, and civic disgrace. Not only does he risk the well-being of his household and insult his wife, but he also runs the risk of being involved in a whole spectrum of other sins and vices, including drunkenness, unplanned pregnancy, abortion, idolatry, and sorcery. In Chrysostom's thought, sin does not function in pockets of isolation; it is dynamic and a slippery slope—one sin easily leads to another and another. Chrysostom was also disturbed by the practice of castration and eunuchs, but rather than addressing the oppressive practice of coerced castration directly, he falls back on an argument for spiritual castration to get rid of vice, again showing nothing but indifference to the plight of male slaves who were being forcefully castrated to become eunuchs. The analysis of prostitution in Chrysostom illustrated the complexities of slaves as reproductive capital. It was not simply a case of maintaining a high birthrate among slaves to sustain the slave supply. The slave body as reproductive capital had numerous cultural, social, religious, and legal complications that Chrysostom does not hesitate to mention. Chrysostom wanted men to retain their control of fertility and reproduction, and by frequenting slave girls and prostitutes, a man was in danger of losing this control.

Chrysostom's preaching about slaveholding is also part of his rhetoric concerning the management and renunciation of wealth. Like most of his audience members, Chrysostom also saw slaves as property and thus part of the wealth of his audience. How they utilized this wealth was very important to Chrysostom. When it came to the possession and use of slaves, less was more, and the principle of necessity had to govern the need for slaves. Chrysostom did believe that it was best not to have any slaves, not because of the injustice and oppressive nature of slavery, but because people should be able to care for themselves. He was more bothered by luxury and decadence than by slavery itself. Avoiding any sign of ascetic rigorism, Chrysostom tells his audience that the acceptable situation was to own between two and four slaves, but no more. Thus, he promoted a tactical mode of slaveholding, based on smaller numbers, over and against strategic slaveholding, which was based on a large number of slaves. Households that had large numbers of slaves probably did not reduce their numbers drastically—most households in late antiquity were in any case already close to a tactical mode of slaveholding. While some households may have reduced the number of slaves they had, tactical slaveholding was not ameliorative to slavery—it worsened conditions for slaves. Slaves were often showcased in public as symbols of status and power, in a kabuki of wealth and domination, if you will. It was a spectacle that nauseated Chrysostom, to say the least. He openly attacked the public display of slaves, especially by female Roman aristocrats, and added that a noble person should not appear in public with more than two slaves.

However, Chrysostom advised people to purchase slaves, teach them a trade and virtue, and then to manumit them. This advice would not have appeared radical to his audience—it was common practice in Roman times to teach slaves a trade, usually related to the family business, and then to manumit them in order to increase their usefulness and opportunities for upward social mobility. Even after being freed, however, the owner still had power over the freed person in various degrees. Not all slaves necessarily had better lives after manumission; some had it worse, again showing how oppressive the institution of slavery was. Yet, the worst thing a slave could do was run away. Any form of resistance was rejected by Chrysostom as being unlawful and even blasphemous. Slaves had to accept their status and remain enslaved. Chrysostom's views on fugitive slaves is based in particular on his reading of Paul's Letter to Philemon, where Paul advises Onesimus to return to his owner after running away.

The power of Chrysostom's preaching resided in its ability to cultivate habits among his listeners, and to creatively interpret scripture to be relevant for every aspect of slaveholding. From the analysis given in this book, I must conclude by saying that Chrysostom's homilies did indeed cultivate certain behaviors among both slaveholders and slaves in the assembly. Unfortunately very few of these behaviors improved conditions for slaves—in many instances one form of oppression was simply supplanted by another, for instance in the case of restructuring slave sexuality, and in other cases older forms of domination were only given a Christian content, while their execution remained practically the same, as, for instance, in the case of discipline and punishment.

· · ·

The purpose of this book was to examine how the discourse of slavery operated in Chrysostom's homilies. This involved looking not only at slavery as an institution, but also at its metaphorization, and how the dynamics between these two manifestations of slavery worked. As we also saw in this investigation of Chrysostom's doulology, slavery expresses itself in a very particular way. What makes slavery such a problematic discourse to analyze is that it expresses itself in a language that professes to negate it. In Chrysostom's homilies, concepts like freedom, kinship, humanity, religious devotion, marriage, reward, and even manumission often did not function as concepts exposing the evil that is institutional slavery; in most cases, these seemingly benevolent ideas functioned as carceral mechanisms that enforced the state of the enslaved. These were the greatest weapons of kyriarchy. Freedom was one of the most common carceral mechanisms in Chrysostom's homilies—the freedom that Chrysostom preached kept slaves in their state of bondage. This occurs when freedom is elevated to a metaphysical level. Chrysostom often speaks of "true" freedom, a liberty that is indifferent to the social status of its subject. Kinship too was a carceral mechanism. Slaves were to be considered as spiritual equals and brothers and sisters, yet in practice such distinctions probably carried little weight. Chrysostom's homilies, in fact, show very little use of the old Pauline language of the spiritual kinship of slaves; discourses of division and exclusion were much more commonplace. Ancient authors often emphasized the humanity of slaves, yet this too was a carceral mechanism. So the challenge to the scholar of doulology is to be aware of this subversive enunciation of slavery; it seems at face value to be positive, yet it is highly inhuman and tyrannical. The dark night of slavery is not yet over; freedom has not fully dawned—the legacy of this doulology presents itself in our contemporary society daily, whether in human trafficking, the abuse of women and children, racism, homophobia, or economic oppression.

Writing about slavery is difficult. It is painful. It constantly reminds us of that great failure of humanity. It testifies to how often we are completely unable to identify oppression, and how we are even less able—or should I say, willing—to do something about it. Despite all our advances as human beings, the stain of slavery remains, and although the light of humanity and its wisdom can be so splendorous, and we must never lose trust in this, I ask, along with Hannah More, whose poem opened this book, *Why are thy genial beams to parts confin'd?*

Alterity	A state of otherness or difference.
Anopticism	A term used by Cynthia Baker to describe the presence of a subject, usually a female, in a determined spatial setting, in terms of that subject's invisibility or inconspicuousness.
Antikinship	A concept used by the anthropologist Paul Bohannan, referring to slavery as the total inversion of and absolute alienation from natal or familial ties. Antikinship is different from nonkinship, which is not essentially set against familial ties and could include business partners, etc.
Aretagogy	The teaching of virtue, especially as related to "masculinization" (see below).
Carcerality and Carceral Mechanisms	Carcerality refers to a state of confinement, quarantine, or imprisonment (incarceration), while carceral mechanisms refer to those concepts or processes that serve to keep someone in a state of confinement.
Christic Panopticon	The unending and all-encompassing surveillance thought to be performed by the divine Christ on slaves and slaveholders both of their outward actions and inner thoughts and feelings.
Christomorphism	The imitative act of taking on or being given the subjectivity and identity of Christ, usually in a symbolic, moral, and especially religious sense—that is, becoming like Christ.
Decosmeticize	To reverse beautification, usually the external type that relies on cosmetics or apparel.

Degenitalize	To negate the influence and prominence of the physical genitals with regard to a certain issue—e.g., when lust is degenitalized it is not generated from or sustained by the genitals.
Desexualization	Specifically in the context of slavery, the process by which the slave body no longer serves as a morally and juridically neutral site that can be used as a sexual outlet for the free.
Discourse and Discursivity	In this book, these terms are used specifically as conceived by Michel Foucault. Discourse refers to the dynamic way knowledge and the meaning of an idea (e.g., the idea of slavery) are constituted and enunciated, a type of language in practice, as well as how different forms of knowledge relate to each other, focusing on the role, operation, and effect of discourse with regard to social and cultural practices, forms of subjectivity, and relations of power. Discursivity refers to the nature of something that produces and presents itself as a discourse in the just-mentioned sense of the word.
Doulogenia	The origins or birth of slavery.
Doulology	The discourse of slavery; more specifically, when slavery as a constitution of knowledge, a language, and a social practice is enunciated and used to produce and reproduce meanings and behaviors in various related contexts (see also "discourse" above).
Doulomorphism	The imitative act of taking on or being given the subjectivity and identity of a slave, usually in a symbolic and moral sense—that is, becoming a slave or like a slave.
Gynaecodouly	From the Greek word *gynaikodoulos* (literally, "a slave of women"); a term used by John Chrysostom to refer to the moral enslavement of men to women, especially in the context of syneisaktism.
Habitus	A notion developed by the sociologist Pierre Bourdieu. Bourdieu defined habitus as "a durable, transposable system of definitions" (*Logic of Practice,* 53), a structured corporeal vernacular, learned by a young child in the home from both the conscious and the unconscious behaviors and practices of the family and close companions.
Hamartigenia	The origins or birth of sin.
Heteronomy	The state of being unable to rule or govern oneself; the exclusion of the freedom of autonomy. In the early Christian context, human bodies are referred to as heteronomous, in the sense that they are always subject to the rule and domination of a higher power, such as God, sin, the devil, a slaveholder, etc.

Interiorization	The process by which a concept, value, or behavior is made part of one's inner nature, and related to one's inner thought and emotion.
Kyriarchy and Kyriarchization	Kyriarchy is a term coined by Elizabeth Schüssler Fiorenza, which she understands as an appellation for the intersectional structures of domination, and those processes by which a dominant subjectivity exercises power over a subordinated subjectivity. Kyriarchization refers to the formation of attitudes and behaviors of mastery—that is, the creation of masters.
Kyriophorism	The naming of a slave by a slaveholder, specifically when the slave receives the name of the master.
Masculinization	The process of making someone or something masculine or manly in character, behavior, or appearance; in antiquity masculinization gives a person social worth and prominence (for masculinization and virtue, see "aretagogy" above).
Medicalization	The expression of something in medical terms, or the use of medical language to characterize something that is not essentially a medical problem or issue.
Metaphorization	The process of turning something into a metaphor.
Naturalization	In two senses that are often related, this term can refer to (a) the attribution of something to the provenance of nature—e.g., natural slavery; (b) the process of making someone or something natural, and consequently, normal, or "in line with nature" in character, behavior, or appearance—that is, by that person's or thing's imitation of values and practices thought to be blue-printed in nature or within the natural "order."
Pastoralization	The process by which the values, principles, structures, and especially the functions and operations of Christian pastoral power (pastoralism) are carried over to and duplicated in another structure, such as the household.
Pathologization	The process of treating an individual or group, especially with regard to personal characteristics and behavior, as socially and psychologically abnormal, deviant, or diseased (also referred to as abnormalization).
Polemology	The discourse of war and warfare.
Pornomorphism	The imitative act of taking on or being given the subjectivity and identity of a prostitute, usually in a symbolic and moral sense—that is, becoming a prostitute or like a prostitute or a sexually immoral person.
Psychic	Relating to the soul (from the Greek *psychē*); a term mostly used to refer to the interiorized mechanisms of characterization and

self-governance (e.g., "psychic virgin"—that is, a virgin of
the soul).

Reproductive Capital   A term referring to the understanding of the slave body as
property or capital of the owner, and as such exhibiting the
potential for biological reproduction or multiplication, thereby
increasing the wealth of the owner.

Somatic   Relating to the body (from the Greek *sōma*).

Somatography   A term derived from the work of Michel de Certeau, and
referring to a social and/or juridical principle or operation that
"writes" itself on the body; in other words, the direct corporeal
effects of an institution or law—e.g., through punishment,
reward, confinement, recognition, etc.

Somatoscape   A certain space, with an emphasis on its occupants as bodies,
and the movements and interactions of those bodies based on
the conditions of the particular space—e.g., the household as a
somatoscape distributes bodies in a very specific way, and also
has social conditions that govern how different domestic bodies
interact with each other.

Subjectivation   A term used by Michel Foucault to refer to the construction of
an individual identity (that is, a subject or "self"), and sometimes
expanded to refer to the construction of group identity or
collective "self."

Thaumatic   In the case of a phenomenon or statement, having shock value or
inducing astonishment or wonder.

BIBLIOGRAPHY

ABBREVIATIONS

ANF	*Ante-Nicene Fathers* series.
BAGD	Bauer, W., W. F. Arndt, F. W. Gingrich, and F. W. Danker. *A Greek-English Lexicon of the New Testament and Other Early Christian Literature.* Chicago: University of Chicago Press, 1957.
CC	Corpus Christianorum: Series latina. Turnhout: Brepols, 1953–.
CGL	Corpus glossariorum latinorum. Leipzig: Teubner, 1892–.
CMG	Corpus medicorum graecorum. Leipzig: Teubner, 1928–.
CPG	*Clavis patrum graecorum.* Turnhout: Brepols, 1974–.
CSEL	Corpus scriptorum ecclesiasticorum latinorum. Vienna, 1866 –.
F	Field, Frederick. *Ioannis Chrysostomi interpretatio omnium epistularum Paulinarum.* 7 vols. Oxford: J. H. Parker, 1854–62.
LCL	Loeb Classical Library. Cambridge, MA: Harvard University Press.
LSJ	Liddell, H. G., R. Scott, H. S. Jones, and R. McKenzie. *A Greek-English Lexicon.* Oxford: Clarendon Press, 1996.
NA28	*Nestle-Aland Novum Testamentum Graece.* Institute for New Testament Textual Research. 28th ed. Stuttgart: Deutsche Bibelgesellschaft, 2012.
NIV	New International Version [Bible].
NPNF	*Nicene and Post-Nicene Fathers* series.
PG	Patrologiae cursus completus: Series graeca. Edited by Jacques-Paul Migne. 162 vols. Paris, 1857–86.
PL	Patrologiae cursus completus: Series ecclesiae latinae. Edited by Jacques-Paul Migne. 217 vols. Paris, 1844–64.
PS	Patrologia syriaca (Patrologia orientalis). Edited by R. Graffin et al. 49 vols. Paris: Firmin-Didot, 1894–.
SC	Sources chrétiennes. Paris: Cerf, 1943–.

PRIMARY SOURCES

Ambrose. *De Abraham.* PL 14.419–500.

———. *De Jacob.* C. Schenkl (ed.). CSEL 32.2. Vienna, 1897.

———. *De officiis ministrorum.* PL 16.23–184.

———. *De virginitate.* PL 16.265–302.

———. *Epistulae.* O. Faller (ed.). CSEL 82. Vienna, 1968.

Ambrosiaster. *Commentarius in Epistulam ad Corinthios prima.* H. J. Vogels (ed.). CSEL 81.2. Vienna, 1968.

Ante-Nicene Fathers. A. Roberts et al. (eds.). 10 vols. Reprint, Grand Rapids, MI: Hendrickson, 1885–.

Aphrahat, *Demonstrationes.* PS 1.1–747.

Aristotle. *Politica.* H. Rackham (ed.). *Aristotle: Politics.* LCL 264. Cambridge, MA: Harvard University Press, 1932.

Arnobius. *Disputationum adversus gentes.* PL 5.349–66.

Augustine. *De civitate Dei.* B. Dombart and A. Kalb (eds.). CC 47–48. Turnhout: Brepols, 1955.

———. *Epistulae*.* J. Divjak (ed.). CSEL 88. Vienna, 1981.

Aulus Gellius. *Noctes Atticae.* J.C. Rolfe (ed.). *Aulus Gellius: Attic Nights.* Vol. 2. LCL 200. Cambridge, MA: Harvard University Press, 1927.

Ausonius. *Epigrammata.* N. Kay (ed.). *Ausonius: Epigrams.* Duckworth Classical Essays. London: Bristol Classical Press, 2001.

Basil of Ancyra. *De virginitate.* PG 30.669–809.

Basil of Caesarea. *Asceticon magnum sive Quaestiones (regulae fusius tractatae).* PG 31.901–1052.

———. *De spiritu sancto.* B. Pruche (ed.). *Basile de Césarée: Sur le Saint-Esprit.* SC 17. Paris: Cerf, 1968.

———. *Epistulae.* Y. Courtonne (ed.). *Lettres.* 3 vols. Paris: Les Belles Lettres, 1957–66.

Cato. *De agricultura.* W.D. Hooper and H.B. Ash (eds.). *Cato and Varro: On Agriculture.* LCL 283. Cambridge, MA: Harvard University Press, 1993.

Cicero. *De legibus.* C.W. Keyes (ed.). *Cicero: De re publica, De legibus.* LCL 213. Cambridge, MA: Harvard University Press, 1928.

Clement of Alexandria. *Paedagogus.* C. Mondésert, C. Matray, and H.-I. Marrou (eds.). *Clément d'Alexandrie: Le pédagogue.* SC 70, 108, 158. Paris: Cerf, 1960–70.

———. *Protrepticus.* C. Mondésert and A. Plassart (eds.). *Clément d'Alexandrie: Protrepticus.* SC 2. Paris: Cerf, 1949.

Colloquium Harleianum. G. Goetz (ed.). Corpus glossariorum latinorum 3. Leipzig: Teubner, 1892.

Columella. *De re rustica.* H.B. Ash (ed.). *Columella: On Agriculture.* 3 vols. LCL 361, 407, 407. Cambridge, MA: Harvard University Press, 1941–54.

Cyprian. *Ad Quirinum testimonia adversus Judaeos.* PL 4.675–780.

———. *Liber de habitu virginum.* PL 4.439–64.

Demosthenes. *In Midiam.* S.H. Butcher (ed.). *Demosthenis orationes.* Vol. 2.1. Oxford: Clarendon Press, 1907.

Dio Chrysostom. *De servitute et libertate II (Oratio 15).* J.W. Cohoon (ed.). *Dio Chrysostom: Discourses 12–30.* LCL 339. Cambridge, MA: Harvard University Press, 1939.

Epictetus. *Dissertationes.* W. A. Oldfather (ed.). *Epictetus: Discourses, Books 1–2.* LCL 131. Cambridge, MA: Harvard University Press, 1925.

Euripides. *Phoenissae.* D. Kovacs (ed.). *Euripides: Helen, Phoenician Women, Orestes.* LCL 11. Cambridge, MA: Harvard University Press, 2002.

Eustathius. *Commentarii ad Homeri Iliadem.* J. G. Stallbaum (ed.). *Eustathii: Commentarii ad Homeri Iliadem.* Vol. 1. Cambridge Library Collection. New York: Cambridge University Press, 2010.

Fronto and Marcus Aurelius. *M. Cornelii Frontonis et M. Aurelii epistulae.* C. R. Haines (ed.). *Fronto: Correspondence.* Vol. 1. LCL 112. Cambridge, MA: Harvard University Press, 1919.

Gregory of Nazianzus. *De pauperem amore (oratio 14).* PG 35.857–909.

Gregory of Nyssa. *Homiliae in Ecclesiasten.* P. Alexander (ed.). *Grégoire de Nysse: Homélies sur l'Ecclésiaste.* SC 416. Paris: Cerf, 1996.

Ignatius. *Epistulae.* B. D. Ehrman (ed.). *Apostolic Fathers.* Vol. 1. LCL 24. Cambridge, MA: Harvard University Press, 2003.

Jerome. *Adversus Jovinianum libri II.* PL 23.205–384.

———. *Epistulae.* PL 30.325–1224.

John Chrysostom. *Ad illuminandos catecheses.* PG 49.223–40.

———. *Ad populum Antiochenum de statuis.* PG 49.15–222.

———. *Ad Stagirium a daemone vexatum.* PG 47.423–94.

———. *Ad Stelechium de compunctione.* PG 47.411–22.

———. *Ad Theodorum lapsum.* J. Dumortier (ed.). *Jean Chrysostome: À Théodore.* SC 117. Paris: Cerf, 1966.

———. *Adversus Judaeos.* PG 48.843–942.

———. *Adversus Judaeos (oratio 2).* W. Pradels et al. (eds.). "Das bisher vermisste Textstück in Johannes Chrysostomus, *Adversus Judaeos,* Oratio 2." *Zeitschrift für antikes Christentum* 5 (2001): 22–49.

———. *Adversus oppugnatores vitae monasticae.* PG 47.319–86.

———. *Comparatio regis et monachi.* PG 47.387–92.

———. *Contra eos qui subintroductas habent virgines.* J. Dumortier (ed.). *Les cohabitations suspectes; Comment observer la virginité.* Paris: Les Belles Lettres , 1955.

———. *De Anna.* PG 54.631–76.

———. *De Babyla contra Julianum et gentiles.* M. A. Schatkin et al. (eds.). *Jean Chrysostome: Discours sur Babylas.* SC 362. Paris: Cerf, 1990.

———. *De eleemosyna.* PG 51.261–72.

———. *De inani gloria et de educandis liberis.* A.-M. Malingrey (ed.). *Jean Chrysostome: Sur la vaine gloire et l'éducation des enfants.* SC 188. Paris: Cerf, 1972.

———. *De laudibus sancti Pauli apostoli.* A. Piédagnel (ed.). *Jean Chrysostome: Panégyriques de S. Paul.* SC 300. Paris: Cerf, 1982.

———. *De Lazaro.* PG 48.963–1054.

———. *De libello repudii.* PG 51.217–26.

———. *De Maccabeis.* PG 50.617–28.

———. *De mutatione nominum.* PG 51.113–56.

———. *De non iterando conjugio.* B. Grillet and G. H. Ettlinger (eds.). *Jean Chrysostome: À une jeune veuve; Sur le marriage unique.* SC 138. Paris: Cerf, 1968.

——. *De sacerdotio.* A.-M. Malingrey (ed.). *Jean Chrysostome: Sur le sacerdoce.* SC 272. Paris: Cerf, 1980.

——. *De sanctis Bernice et Prosdoce.* PG 50.629–40.

——. *De sancto hieromartyre Phoca.* PG 50.699–706.

——. *De virginitate.* B. Grillet (ed.). *Jean Chrysostome: La virginité.* SC 125. Paris: Cerf, 1966.

——. *Expositiones in Psalmos.* PG 55.39–498.

——. *Homilia dicta postquam reliquiae martyrum.* PG 63.467–72.

——. *Homiliae in epistulam ad Colossenses.* F5.172–312.

——. *Homiliae in epistulam ad Ephesios.* F4.104–365.

——. *Homiliae in epistulam ad Galatas commentarius.* F4.1–103.

——. *Homiliae in epistulam ad Hebraeos.* F7.1–384.

——. *Homiliae in epistulam ad Philemonem.* F6.325–53.

——. *Homiliae in epistulam ad Philippenses.* F5.1–171.

——. *Homiliae in epistulam ad Romanos.* F1.1–495.

——. *Homiliae in epistulam ad Titum.* F6.264–324.

——. *Homiliae in epistulam I ad Corinthios.* F2.1–555.

——. *Homiliae in epistulam I ad Thessalonicenses.* F5.313–442.

——. *Homiliae in epistulam II ad Thessalonicenses.* F5.443–96.

——. *Homiliae in epistulam I ad Timotheum.* F6.1–161.

——. *Homiliae in epistulam II ad Timotheum.* F6.162–263.

——. *In acta apostolorum.* PG 60.13–384.

——. *In Genesim (homiliae).* PG 53.21–385, 54.385–580.

——. *In Genesim (sermones).* PG 54.581–630.

——. *In Heliam et viduam.* PG 51.337–48.

——. *In illud: Habentes eundem spiritum.* PG 51.187–208.

——. *In illud: Propter fornicationes autem unusquisque suam uxorem habeat.* PG 51.271–302.

——. *In Joannem.* PG 59.23–482.

——. *In martyres omnes.* Stavronikita 4. *CPG* 4441.

——. *In Matthaeum.* PG 57.13–472, 58.471–794.

——. *In principium Actorum.* PG 51.65–112.

——. *Quod nemo laeditur nisi a se ipso.* A.-M. Malingrey (ed.). *Jean Chrysostome: Lettre d'exil.* SC 103. Paris: Cerf, 1964.

——. *Quod regulares feminae viris cohabitare non debeant.* J. Dumortier (ed.). *Les cohabitations suspectes; Comment observer la virginité.* Paris: Les Belles Lettres, 1955.

Lactantius. *De ira Dei.* C. Ingremeau (ed.). *Lactance: La colère de Dieu.* SC 289. Paris: Cerf, 1982.

——. *De opificio Dei.* PL 7.9–78.

——. *Divinae institutiones.* S. Brandt (ed.). CSEL 19.1. Vienna, 1890.

Libanius. *Declamationes.* Richard Foerster (ed.). *Libanii opera.* Vols. 5–7. Leipzig: Teubner, 1909–13.

——. *Epistulae.* Richard Foerster (ed.). *Libanii opera.* Vols. 10–11. Leipzig: Teubner, 1921–22.

——. *Orationes.* Richard Foerster (ed.). *Libanii opera.* Vols. 1–4. Leipzig: Teubner, 1903–8.

——. *Progymnasmata.* Richard Foerster (ed.). *Libanii opera.* Vol. 8. Leipzig: Teubner, 1915.

Martial. *Epigrammaton libri*. D. R. Shackleton Bailey (ed.). *Martial: Epigrams*. Vol. 3. LCL 480. Cambridge, MA: Harvard University Press, 1993.

New Testament. B. Aland et al. (eds.). *Nestle-Aland Novum Testamentum Graece*. 28th ed. Stuttgart: Deutsche Bibelgesellschaft, 2012.

Nicene and Post-Nicene Fathers. P. Schaff et al. (eds.). 38 vols. Reprint, Whitefish, MT: Kessinger, 1887–.

Oribasius. *Collectiones medicae*. J. Raeder (ed.). *Oribasii collectionum medicarum reliquiae*. Corpus medicorum graecorum 6.1.1. Leipzig: Teubner, 1928.

Origen. *Fragmenta ex commentariis in epistulam i ad Corinthios (in catenis)*. C. Jenkins. "Documents: Origen on I Corinthians." *Journal of Theological Studies* 9 (1907–8): 29–51.

Palladius. *Dialogus de vita Joannis Chrysostomi*. A.-M. Malingrey (ed.). *Palladios: Dialogue sur la vie de Jean Chrysostome*. Vol. 1. SC 341. Paris: Cerf, 1988.

Philo. *De agricultura*. A. C. Geljon and D. Runia (eds.). *Philo of Alexandria: On Cultivation; Introduction, Translation and Commentary*. Philo of Alexandria Commentary 4. Leiden: Brill, 2012.

———. *De cherubim*. F. H. Colson and G. H. Whitaker (eds.). *Philo*. Vol. 2. LCL 227. Cambridge, MA: Harvard University Press, 1929.

———. *De Josepho*. F. H. Colson and G. H. Whitaker (eds.). *Philo*. Vol. 2. LCL 227. Cambridge, MA: Harvard University Press, 1929.

———. *Quod omnis probus liber*. F. H. Colson and G. H. Whitaker (eds.). *Philo*. Vol. 9. LCL 363. Cambridge, MA: Harvard University Press, 1941.

Philodemus. *De oeconomia*. V. Tsouna (ed.). *Philodemus: On Property Management*. Writings from the Greco-Roman World. Atlanta: Society of Biblical Literature, 2012.

Plato. *Alcibiades*. N. Denyer (ed.). *Plato: Alcibiades*. Cambridge Greek and Latin Classics. New York: Cambridge University Press, 2001.

———. *Leges*. R. G. Bury (ed.). *Plato: Laws*. 2 vols. LCL 187, 192. Cambridge, MA: Harvard University Press, 1926.

Plautus. *Bacchides*. J. Barsby (ed.). *Plautus: Bacchides*. Classical Texts. Chicago: Aris & Phillips, 1986.

Pliny the Elder. *Historia naturalis* 14. H. Rackham (ed.). *Pliny: Natural History*. Vol. 4. LCL 370. Cambridge, MA: Harvard University Press, 1945.

———. *Historia naturalis* 26. W. H. S. Jones and A. C. Andrews (eds.). *Pliny: Natural History*. Vol. 7. LCL 393. Cambridge, MA: Harvard University Press, 1956.

———. *Historia naturalis* 28. W. H. S. Jones and A. C. Andrews (eds.). *Pliny: Natural History*. Vol. 8. LCL 418. Cambridge, MA: Harvard University Press, 1963.

Plutarch. *Cato maior*. B. Perrin (ed.). *Plutarch: Lives; Themistocles and Camillus, Aristides and Cato Major, Cimon and Lucullus*. Vol. 2. LCL 47. Cambridge, MA: Harvard University Press, 1914.

———. *De cohibenda ira (Moralia)*. W. C. Hembold (ed.). *Plutarch: Moralia*. Vol. 6. LCL 337. Cambridge, MA: Harvard University Press, 1939.

———. *Moralia*. F. C. Babbitt et al. (eds.). *Plutarch: Moralia*. 15 vols. LCL 197, 245. Cambridge, MA: Harvard University Press, 1927–69.

Prudentius. *Liber peristephanon*. PL 60.275–596.

Pseudo-Aristotle. *Oeconomica*. G. C. Armstrong (ed.). *Aristotle: Metaphysics, Books 10–14, Oeconomica, Magna Moralia*. LCL 287. Cambridge, MA: Harvard University Press, 1935.

Pseudo-John Chrysostom. *De mansuetudine sermo.* PG 63.549–56.

———. *In Psalmum 50 (homilia 1).* PG 55.565–75.

Seneca. *De beneficiis.* M. Griffin and B. Inwood (eds.). *Seneca: On Benefits.* Chicago: University of Chicago Press, 2011.

———. *De ira.* J. W. Basore (ed.). *Seneca: Moral Essays.* Vol. 1. LCL 214. Cambridge, MA: Harvard University Press, 1928.

———. *Epistulae.* R. M. Gummere (ed.). *Seneca: Epistles 1–65.* Vol. 4. LCL 75. Cambridge, MA: Harvard University Press, 1917.

Soranus. *Gynaeciorum.* O. Temkin (ed.). *Soranus' Gynecology.* Baltimore: Johns Hopkins University Press, 1956.

Tertullian. *Adversus Marcionem.* PL 2.239–524.

———. *De carne Christi.* E. Evans (ed.). *Tertullian's Treatise on the Incarnation.* London: SPCK, 1956.

———. *De cultu feminarum.* PL 1.1303–34.

———. *De idolatria.* PL 1.661–96.

———. *De pudicitia.* PL 2.979–1030.

Theodoret. *De providentia.* PG 83.556–773.

Varro. *Rerum rusticarum.* W. D. Hooper, and H. B. Ash (eds.). *Cato and Varro: On Agriculture.* LCL 283. Cambridge, MA: Harvard University Press, 1993.

Xenophon. *Memorabilia.* E. C. Marchant (ed.). *Xenophontis opera omnia.* Oxford: Clarendon Press, 1921.

———. *Oeconomicus.* E. C. Marchant (ed.). *Xenophontis opera omnia.* Oxford: Clarendon Press, 1921.

SECONDARY SOURCES

Adams, Anthony. "'He Took a Stone Away': Castration and Cruelty in the Old Norse *Sturlunga Saga.*" In *Castration and Culture in the Middle Ages,* edited by Larissa Tracy, 188–209. Cambridge: D. S. Brewer, 2013.

Allard, Paul. "Slavery and Christianity." In *Catholic Encyclopedia,* n.p. New York: Robert Appleton Company, 1912. http://www.newadvent.org/cathen/14036a.htm.

Allen, Pauline, trans. *John Chrysostom, Homilies on Philippians.* Writings from the Greco-Roman World 16. Atlanta: Society of Biblical Literature, 2013.

Ambler, Wayne. "Aristotle on Nature and Politics: The Case of Slavery." *Political Theory* 15, no. 3 (1987): 390–410.

Anderson, James. *Paradox in Christian Theology: An Analysis of Its Presence, Character, and Epistemic Status.* Paternoster Theological Monographs. Eugene, OR: Wipf & Stock, 2007.

Ankum, Hans. "*Mancipatio* by Slaves in Classical Roman Law." *Acta Juridica* 1 (1976): 1–18.

Arjava, Antti. *Women and Law in Late Antiquity.* New York: Oxford University Press, 1996.

Arzt-Grabner, Peter. "Onesimus *Erro*: Zur Vorgeschichte des Philemonbriefes." *Zeitschrift für die Neutestamentliche Wissenschaft* 95 (2004): 131–43.

Asmis, Elizabeth. "Epicurean Economics." In *Philodemus and the New Testament World,* edited by John T. Fitzgerald, Dirk Obbink, and Glen S. Holland, 133–76. Leiden: Brill, 2004.

Aubert, Jean-Jacques. "Threatened Wombs: Aspects of Ancient Uterine Magic." *Greek, Roman and Byzantine Studies* 30, no. 3 (1989): 421–49.

Avalos, Hector. *Slavery, Abolitionism, and the Ethics of Biblical Scholarship*. The Bible in the Modern World 38. Sheffield: Sheffield Phoenix, 2011.

Baker, Cynthia M. *Rebuilding the House of Israel: Architectures of Gender in Jewish Antiquity*. Divinations: Rereading Late Ancient Religion. Stanford, CA: Stanford University Press, 2002.

Balch, David L. "Philodemus, 'On Wealth' and 'On Household Management': Naturally Wealthy Epicureans against Poor Cynics." In *Philodemus and the New Testament World*, edited by John T. Fitzgerald, Dirk Obbink, and Glen S. Holland, 177–96. Leiden: Brill, 2004.

Bartchy, S. Scott. ΜΑΛΛΟΝ ΧΡΗΣΑΙ: *First Century Slavery and 1 Corinthians 7:21*. SBL Dissertation Series. Missoula, MT: Society of Biblical Literature, 1973.

Barton, Carlin. "Being in the Eyes: Shame and Sight in Ancient Rome." In *The Roman Gaze: Vision, Power, and the Body* edited by David Fredrick, 216–35. Baltimore: Johns Hopkins University Press, 2002.

Bartsch, Shadi. *The Mirror of the Self: Sexuality, Self-Knowledge, and the Gaze in the Early Roman Empire*. Chicago: University of Chicago Press, 2006.

Basso, Patrizia. "Gli alloggi servili." In *Subterraneae domus: Ambienti residenziale di servizio nell'edilizia privata romana*, edited by Patrizia Basso and Francesca Ghedini, 443–63. Sottosuolo nel mondo antico 4. Verona: Cierre, 2003.

Batten, Alicia J. "Carthaginian Critiques of Adornment." *Journal of Early Christian History* 1, no. 1 (2011): 3–21.

Beard, Mary, and John Henderson. "With This Body I Thee Worship: Sacred Prostitution in Antiquity." In *Gender and the Body in the Ancient Mediterranean*, edited by Maria Wyke, 56–79. Oxford: Blackwell, 1998.

BeDuhn, Jason. *The Manichaean Body: In Discipline and Ritual*. Baltimore: Johns Hopkins University Press, 2000.

———. "The Metabolism of Salvation: Manichaean Concepts of Human Physiology." In *The Light and the Darkness: Studies in Manichaeism and Its World*, edited by Paul Mirecki and Jason BeDuhn, 5–37. Nag Hammadi and Manichaean Studies 50. Leiden: Brill, 2001.

Bellen, Heinz. *Studien zur Sklavenflucht im römischen Kaiserreich*. Forschungen zur antiken Sklaverei 4. Wiesbaden: Franz Steiner, 1971.

Bergadá, Maria M. "La condemnation de l'esclavage dans l'homélie IV." In *Gregory of Nyssa, Homilies on Ecclesiastes: An English Version with Supporting Studies*, edited by Stuart G. Hall, *Proceedings of the Seventh International Colloquium on Gregory of Nyssa (St. Andrews, 5–10 September 1990)*, 185–96. Berlin: De Gruyter, 1994.

Berger, Klaus. *Identity and Experience in the New Testament*. Translated by Charles Muenchow. Minneapolis: Fortress Press, 2003.

Berrouard, Marie-François. "Un tournant dans la vie de l'église d'Afrique les deux missions d'Alypius en Italie à la lumière des lettres 10*, 15*, 16*, 22* et 23*A de saint Augustin." *Revue des Études Augustiniennes* 31 (1985): 46–70.

Bieżuńska-Małowist, Iza. "La vie familiale des esclaves." *Index* 8 (1978): 140–43.

Blank, Hanne. *Virgin: The Untouched History*. New York: Bloomsbury Publishing, 2007.

Bloomer, W. Martin. "The Ancient Child in School." In *The Oxford Handbook of Childhood and Education in the Classical World,* edited by Judith Evans Grubbs, Tim Parkin, and Roslynne Bell, 444–63. New York: Oxford University Press, 2013.

———. "Schooling in Persona: Imagination and Subordination in Roman Education." *Classical Antiquity* 16, no. 1 (1997): 57–78.

Bober, Phyllis P. *Art, Culture, and Cuisine: Ancient and Medieval Gastronomy.* Chicago: University of Chicago Press, 1999.

Bodel, John. "Death on Display: Looking at Roman Funerals." In *The Art of Ancient Spectacle,* edited by Bettina Bergmann and Christine Kondoleon, 259–81. New Haven, CT: Yale University Press, 1999.

———. "Slave Labour and Roman Society." In *The Cambridge World History of Slavery,* vol. 1, *The Ancient Mediterranean World,* edited by Keith Bradley and Paul Cartledge, 311–36. New York: Cambridge University Press, 2011.

Boersma, Hans. *Embodiment and Virtue in Gregory of Nyssa: An Anagogical Approach.* New York: Oxford University Press, 2013.

Bohannan, Paul J. *Social Anthropology.* New York: Holt, Rinehart and Winston, 1963.

Bonner, Stanley F. *Education in Ancient Rome: From the Elder Cato to the Younger Pliny.* Berkeley: University of California Press, 1977.

Booth, Alan D. "The Schooling of Slaves in First-Century Rome." *Transactions of the American Philological Association* 109 (1979): 11–19.

Bosinis, Konstantinos. "Two Platonic Images in the Rhetoric of John Chrysostom: 'The Wings of Love' and the 'Charioteer of the Soul.'" *Studia Patristica* 41 (2006): 433–38.

Boswell, John. *The Kindness of Strangers: The Abandonment of Children in Western Europe from Late Antiquity to the Renaissance.* Chicago: University of Chicago Press, 1998.

Botha, Pieter J. J. *Orality and Literacy in Early Christianity.* Eugene, OR: Cascade Books, 2012.

Bourdieu, Pierre. *Distinction: A Social Critique of the Judgement of Taste.* Translated by Richard Nice. Cambridge, MA: Harvard University Press, 1984.

———. *The Logic of Practice.* Translated by Richard Nice. Cambridge: Polity Press, 1990.

Bowersock, Glen W. "Zur Geschichte des römischen Thessaliens." *Rheinisches Museum für Philologie* 108 (1965): 277–89.

Bowes, Kim. *Private Worship, Public Values, and Religious Change in Late Antiquity.* New York: Cambridge University Press, 2008.

Bradley, Keith R. "On the Roman Slave Supply and Slavebreeding." In *Classical Slavery,* edited by Moses I. Finley, 53–81. London: Routledge, 1987.

———. "Resisting Slavery at Rome." In *The Cambridge World History of Slavery,* vol. 1, *The Ancient Mediterranean World,* edited by Keith Bradley and Paul Cartledge, 362–84. New York: Cambridge University Press, 2011.

———. "Seneca and Slavery." *Classica et Mediaevalia* 37 (1986): 161–72.

———. *Slavery and Rebellion in the Roman World, 140 B.C.–70 B.C.* Bloomington: Indiana University Press, 1989.

———. *Slavery and Society at Rome.* New York: Cambridge University Press, 1994.

———. "Slavery in the Roman Republic." In *The Cambridge World History of Slavery*, vol. 1, *The Ancient Mediterranean World*, edited by Keith Bradley and Paul Cartledge, 241–64. New York: Cambridge University Press, 2011.

———. *Slaves and Masters in the Roman Empire: A Study in Social Control.* New York: Oxford University Press, 1987.

———. "Wet-Nursing at Rome: A Study in Social Relations." In *The Family in Ancient Rome: New Perspectives,* edited by Beryl Rawson, 201–29. Ithaca, NY: Cornell University Press, 1987.

Brooten, Bernadette J., ed. *Beyond Slavery: Overcoming Its Religious and Sexual Legacies.* New York: Palgrave Macmillan, 2010.

———. "Enslaved Women in Basil of Caesarea's Canonical Letters: An Intersectional Analysis." In *Doing Gender, Doing Religion: Case Studies on Intersectionality in Early Judaism, Christianity and Islam,* edited by Ute Eisen, Christine Gerber, and Angela Standhartinger, 325–55. Wissenschaftliche Untersuchungen zum Neuen Testament 302. Tübingen: Mohr Siebeck, 2013.

———. *Love between Women: Early Christian Responses to Female Homoeroticism.* Chicago: University of Chicago Press, 1996.

Brown, Peter R. L. *The Body and Society: Men, Women, and Sexual Renunciation in Early Christianity.* New York: Columbia University Press, 1988.

———. "The Rise and Function of the Holy Man in Late Antiquity." *Journal of Roman Studies* 61 (1971): 80–101.

Brunt, Peter A. "Evidence Given under Torture in the Principate." *Zeitschrift der Savigny-Stiftung für Rechtsgeschichte* 97 (1980): 256–65.

Bruun, Christer. "Greek or Latin? The Owner's Choice of Names for *Vernae* in Rome." In *Roman Slavery and Roman Material Culture,* edited by Michele George, 19–42. Toronto: University of Toronto Press, 2013.

Buckland, William W. *The Roman Law of Slavery: The Condition of the Slave in Private Law from Augustus to Justinian.* Cambridge: Cambridge University Press, 1908.

Buckley, Thomas, and Alma Gottlieb, eds. *Blood Magic: Explorations in the Anthropology of Menstruation.* Berkeley: University of California Press, 1988.

Buell, Denise Kimber. *Making Christians: Clement of Alexandria and the Rhetoric of Legitimacy.* Princeton, NJ: Princeton University Press, 1999.

Bullough, Vern L., ed. "Augustine, Saint (d. 430)." In *Encyclopedia of Birth Control,* 24–26. Santa Barbara, CA: ABC-CLIO, 2001.

Burke, Sean D. *Queering the Ethiopian Eunuch: Strategies of Ambiguity in Acts.* Emerging Scholars. Minneapolis: Fortress Press, 2013.

Burrus, Virginia. *Begotten, Not Made: Conceiving Manhood in Late Antiquity.* Figurae: Reading Medieval Culture. Stanford, CA: Stanford University Press, 2000.

Butler, Judith. *Gender Trouble: Feminism and the Subversion of Identity.* New York: Routledge, 2006.

Byron, John. *Recent Research on Paul and Slavery.* Sheffield: Sheffield Phoenix, 2008.

———. *Slavery Metaphors in Early Judaism and Pauline Christianity: A Traditio-Historical and Exegetical Examination.* Wissenschaftliche Untersuchungen zum Neuen Testament 162. Tübingen: Mohr Siebeck, 2003.

Callahan, Allen D. "John Chrysostom on Philemon: A Response to Margaret M. Mitchell." *Harvard Theological Review* 88 (1995): 149–56.

————. "Paul's Epistle to Philemon: Toward an Alternative Argumentum." *Harvard Theological Review* 86 (1993): 357–76.

Caner, Daniel F. "The Practice and Prohibition of Self-Castration in Early Christianity." *Vigiliae Christianae* 51, no. 4 (1997): 396–415.

Carandini, Andrea. "La villa romana e la piantagione schiavistica." In *Storia di Roma*, edited by Aldo Schiavone and Andrea Giardina, 4:101–200. Turin: Einaudi, 1990.

Carlsen, Jesper. "Subvilicus: Subagent or Assistant Bailiff?" *Zeitschrift für Papyrologie und Epigraphik* 132 (2000): 312–16.

————. "Varro, Marcus Terentius." In *The Historical Encyclopedia of World Slavery*, vol. 2, *L-Z*, edited by Junius P. Rodriguez, 669–70. Santa Barbara, CA: ABC-CLIO, 1997.

————. *Vilici and Roman Estate Managers until AD 284*. Rome: L'Erma di Bretschneider, 1995.

Chadwick, Henry. *Early Christian Thought and the Classical Tradition*. Oxford: Oxford University Press, 1966.

————, ed. *The Sentences of Sextus*. Cambridge: Cambridge University Press, 1959.

Champion, Craige. "Columella's *De Re Rustica*." In *The Historical Encyclopedia of World Slavery*, vol. 1, *A-K*, edited by Junius P. Rodriguez, 174–75. Santa Barbara, CA: ABC-CLIO, 1997.

Chaniotis, Angelos. "Drei kleinasiatische Inschriften zur griechischen Religion." *Epigraphica Anatolica* 15 (1990): 127–33.

Citti, Vittorio. "Πόρνη καὶ δούλη: Una coppia nominale Lisia." In *Schiavi e dipendenti nell'ambito dell' "oikos" e della "familia": Atti del XXII Colloquio GIREA, Pontignano (Siena), 19–20 Novembre 1995*, edited by Mauro Moggi and Giuseppe Cordiano, 91–96. Studi e testi di storia antica. Pisa: ETS, 1997.

Clark, Elizabeth A. "Asceticism, Class, and Gender." In *Late Ancient Christianity*, edited by Virginia Burrus, 27–45. A People's History of Christianity 2. Minneapolis: Fortress Press, 2005.

————. "Foucault, the Fathers, and Sex." *Journal of the American Academy of Religion* 56, no. 4 (1988): 619–41.

————. "Ideology, History and the Construction of 'Woman' in Late Ancient Christianity." In *A Feminist Companion to Patristic Literature*, edited by Amy-Jill Levine and Maria M. Robbins, 101–24. London: T&T Clark, 2008.

————. *Jerome, Chrysostom, and Friends: Essays and Translations*. Lewiston, NY: Edwin Mellen, 1979.

————. *Reading Renunciation: Asceticism and Scripture in Early Christianity*. Princeton, NJ: Princeton University Press, 1999.

————. "Sexual Politics in the Writings of John Chrysostom." *Anglican Theological Review* 59, no. 1 (1977): 3–20.

Clark, Patricia. "Women, Slaves, and the Hierarchies of Domestic Violence: The Family of St. Augustine." In *Women and Slaves in Greco-Roman Culture: Differential Equations*, edited by Sandra R. Joshel and Sheila Murnaghan, 109–29. New York: Routledge, 1998.

Cloke, Gillian. *This Female Man of God: Women and Spiritual Power in the Patristic Age, AD 350–450*. London: Routledge, 1995.

Cohen, Boaz. "Peculium in Jewish and Roman Law." *Proceedings of the American Academy for Jewish Research* 20 (1951): 135–234.

Cohen, David. "Sexuality, Violence, and the Athenian Law of *Hybris.*" *Greece & Rome* 38, no. 2 (1991): 171–88.

Cohen, Edward E. "Free and Unfree Sexual Work: An Economic Analysis of Athenian Prostitution." In *Prostitutes and Courtesans in the Ancient World,* edited by Christopher A. Faraone and Laura K. McClure, 95–124. Madison: University of Wisconsin Press, 2006.

———. "Sexual Abuse and Sexual Rights: Slaves' Erotic Experience at Athens and Rome." In *A Companion to Greek and Roman Sexualities,* edited by Thomas K. Hubbard, 184–98. Blackwell Companions to the Ancient World. Chichester: Wiley-Blackwell, 2014.

Cohen, Elizabeth S. "'Courtesans' and 'Whores': Words and Behaviour in Roman Streets." *Women's Studies* 19 (1991): 201–8.

Cohen, Shaye J. D. *From the Maccabees to the Mishnah.* Louisville, KY: Westminster John Knox, 2006.

Cohick, Lynn. *Women in the World of the Earliest Christians: Illuminating Ancient Ways of Life.* Grand Rapids, MI: Baker Academic, 2009.

Collins, Jack. "Appropriation and Development of Castration as Symbol and Practice in Early Christianity." In *Castration and Culture in the Middle Ages,* edited by Larissa Tracy, 73–86. Cambridge: D. S. Brewer, 2013.

Connell, Raewyn W. *Gender and Power: Society, the Person, and Sexual Politics.* Stanford, CA: Stanford University Press, 1987.

Constantelos, Demetrios J. "The Hellenic Background and Nature of Patristic Philanthropy in the Early Byzantine Era." In *Wealth and Poverty in Early Church and Society,* edited by Susan R. Holman, 187–210. Holy Cross Studies in Patristic Theology and History. Grand Rapids, MI: Baker Academic, 2008.

Conzelmann, Hans. *1 Corinthians: A Commentary on the First Epistle to the Corinthians.* Translated by James Waterson Leitch. Hermeneia. Philadelphia: Fortress Press, 1975.

Cooper, Kate. "Closely Watched Households: Visibility, Exposure and Private Power in the Roman Domus." *Past & Present* 197, no. 1 (2007): 3–33.

———. *The Fall of the Roman Household.* New York: Cambridge University Press, 2007.

———. "Insinuations of Womanly Influence: An Aspect of the Christianization of the Roman Aristocracy." *Journal of Roman Studies* 82 (1992): 150–64.

Corner, Sean. "Sumposion." In *A Companion to Greek and Roman Sexualities,* edited by Thomas K. Hubbard, 199–214. Blackwell Companions to the Ancient World. Chichester: Wiley-Blackwell, 2014.

Coyle, John K. *Manichaeism and Its Legacy.* Nag Hammadi and Manichaean Studies 69. Leiden: Brill, 2009.

Cribiore, Raffaella. *Gymnastics of the Mind: Greek Education in Hellenistic and Roman Egypt.* Princeton, NJ: Princeton University Press, 2005.

———. *The School of Libanius in Late Antique Antioch.* Princeton, NJ: Princeton University Press, 2007.

Crislip, Andrew T. *From Monastery to Hospital: Christian Monasticism and the Transformation of Health Care in Late Antiquity.* Ann Arbor: University of Michigan Press, 2005.

Dal Lago, Enrico, and Constantina Katsari. "Ideal Models of Slave Management in the Roman World and in the Ante-Bellum American South." In *Slave Systems: Ancient and Modern,* edited by Enrico Dal Lago and Constantina Katsari, 187–213. New York: Cambridge University Press, 2008.

———. "The Study of Ancient and Modern Slave Systems: Setting an Agenda for Comparison." In *Slave Systems: Ancient and Modern,* edited by Enrico Dal Lago and Constantina Katsari, 3–31. New York: Cambridge University Press, 2008.

Davidson, James N. *Courtesans and Fishcakes: The Consuming Passions of Classical Athens.* Chicago: University of Chicago Press, 1998.

De Certeau, Michel. *The Practice of Everyday Life.* Translated by Steven F. Rendall. Berkeley: University of California Press, 1984.

De Vries, G. J. "ΣΩΦΡΟΣΥΝΗ en grec classique." *Mnemosyne* 11 (1943): 81–101.

De Wet, Chris L. "Between the Domestic and the Agoric Somatoscape: John Chrysostom on the Appearance of Female Roman Aristocrats in the Marketplace." *Religion & Theology* 20, nos. 3–4 (2013): 202–17.

———. "Claiming Corporeal Capital: John Chrysostom's Homilies on the Maccabean Martyrs." *Journal of Early Christian History* 2, no. 1 (2012): 3–21.

———. "The Discourse of the Suffering Slave in 1 Peter." *Ekklesiastikos Pharos* 95 (2013): 15–24.

———. "Honour Discourse in John Chrysostom's Exegesis of the Letter to Philemon." In *Philemon in Perspective: Interpreting a Pauline Letter,* edited by D. Francois Tolmie, 317–32. Berlin: De Gruyter, 2010.

———. "'If a Story Can So Master the Children's Soul': Christian Scriptural Pedagogy, Orality and Power in the Writings of John Chrysostom." *Oral History Journal of South Africa* 2, no. 1 (2014): 121–42.

———. "John Chrysostom and Slavery: The *Status Quaestionis.*" *Journal of Early Christian History* 4, no. 2 (2014): 31–39.

———. "John Chrysostom on Envy." *Studia Patristica* 47 (2010): 255–60.

———. "John Chrysostom on Homoeroticism." *Neotestamentica* 48, no. 1 (2014): 187–218.

———. "John Chrysostom on Slavery." *Studia Historiae Ecclesiasticae* 34, no. 2 (2008): 1–13.

———. "John Chrysostom's Advice to Slaveholders." *Studia Patristica* 67 (2013): 359–65.

———. "Paul and Christian Identity-Formation in John Chrysostom's Homilies *De Laudibus Sancti Pauli Apostoli.*" *Journal of Early Christian History* 3, no. 2 (2013): 34–47.

———. "Paul, Identity-Formation and the Problem of Alterity in John Chrysostom's Homilies *In Epistulam ad Galatas Commentarius.*" *Acta Theologica Supplementum* 19 (2014): 18–41.

———. "Sin as Slavery and/or Slavery as Sin? On the Relationship between Slavery and Christian Hamartiology in Late Ancient Christianity." *Religion & Theology* 17, nos. 1–2 (2010): 26–39.

———. "The Vilification of the Rich in John Chrysostom's Homily 40 *On First Corinthians.*" *Acta Patristica et Byzantina* 21, no. 1 (2010): 82–94.

Dolansky, Fanny. "*Togam Virilem Sumere:* Coming of Age in the Roman World." In *Roman Dress and the Fabrics of Roman Culture,* edited by Jonathan Edmondson and Alison Keith, 47–70. Toronto: University of Toronto Press, 2009.

Donald, Leland. *Aboriginal Slavery on the Northwest Coast of North America.* Berkeley: University of California Press, 1997.

Dooley, William J. *Marriage according to St. Ambrose.* Washington, DC: Catholic University of America Press, 1948.

Drake, Susanna. *Slandering the Jew: Sexuality and Difference in Early Christian Texts.* Divinations. Philadelphia: University of Pennsylvania Press, 2013.

DuBois, Page. "Ancient Masculinities." In *New Testament Masculinities,* edited by Stephen D. Moore and Janice C. Anderson, 319–24. Semeia Studies 45. Atlanta: Society of Biblical Literature, 2003.

Dumitrescu, Carmen-Laura. "Remarques en marge du 'Coislin 79': Les trois eunuques et le problème du donateur." *Byzantion* 57, no. 1 (1987): 32–45.

Duncan, Anne. "Infamous Performers: Comic Actors and Female Prostitutes in Rome." In *Prostitutes and Courtesans in the Ancient World,* edited by Christopher A. Faraone and Laura K. McClure, 252–73. Madison: University of Wisconsin Press, 2006.

Edmondson, Jonathan. "Slavery and the Roman Family." In *The Cambridge World History of Slavery,* vol. 1, *The Ancient Mediterranean World,* edited by Keith Bradley and Paul Cartledge, 337–61. New York: Cambridge University Press, 2011.

Elden, Stuart, and Jeremy W. Crampton. "Space, Knowledge, and Power: Foucault and Geography." In *Space, Knowledge and Power: Foucault and Geography,* edited by Stuart Elden and Jeremy W. Crampton, 1–18. Aldershot: Ashgate, 2007.

Elliot, Scott S. "'Thanks, but No Thanks': Tact, Persuasion, and Negotiation of Power in Paul's Letter to Philemon." *New Testament Studies* 57 (2010): 51–64.

Elm, Susanna. "Augustine, Romans, and Late Roman Slavery." Paper presented at the Society of Biblical Literature Annual Meeting, Baltimore, 2013.

———. "Roman Pain and the Rise of Christianity." In *Quo Vadis Medical Healing: Past Concepts and New Approaches,* edited by Susanna Elm and Stefan N. Willich, 41–54. International Library of Ethics, Law, and the New Medicine 44. Berlin: Springer, 2009.

———. *Virgins of God: The Making of Asceticism in Late Antiquity.* Oxford: Clarendon Press, 1996.

———. "What the Bishop Wore to the Synod: John Chrysostom, Origenism, and the Politics of Fashion at Constantinople." *Adamantius* 19 (2013): 156–69.

Emig, Rainer, and Oliver Lindner. Introduction to *Commodifying (Post)Colonialism: Othering, Reification, Commodification and the New Literatures and Cultures in English,* edited by Rainer Emig and Oliver Lindner, vii–xxiv. Cross/Cultures 127: ASNEL Papers 16. Amsterdam: Rodopi, 2010.

Engberg-Pedersen, Troels. *The Stoic Theory of Oikeiosis: Moral Development and Social Interaction in Early Stoic Philosophy.* Aarhus: Aarhus University Press, 1990.

Fee, Gordon D. *The First Epistle to the Corinthians.* New International Commentary on the New Testament. Grand Rapids, MI: Eerdmans, 1987.

Fenoaltea, Stefano. "Slavery and Supervision in Comparative Perspective: A Model." *Journal of Economic History* 44, no. 3 (1984): 635–68.

Fentress, Elizabeth. "Spinning a Model: Female Slaves in Roman Villas." *Journal of Roman Archaeology* 21 (2008): 419–22.

Ferguson, Everett. *Baptism in the Early Church: History, Theology, and Liturgy in the First Five Centuries.* Grand Rapids, MI: Eerdmans, 1986.

Festugière, André-Jean. *Antioche païenne et chrétienne: Libanius, Chrysostome et les moines de Syrie.* Bibliothèque des Écoles françaises d'Athènes et de Rome 194. Paris: De Boccard, 1959.

Fildes, Valerie A. *Breasts, Bottles, and Babies: A History of Infant Feeding.* Edinburgh: Edinburgh University Press, 1986.

Findlay, Ronald. "Slavery, Incentives, and Manumission: A Theoretical Model." *Journal of Political Economy* 83, no. 5 (1975): 923–33.

Finley, Moses I. *Ancient Slavery and Modern Ideology.* New York: Viking Press, 1980.

Fisher, Nick R. E. "Hybris and Dishonour I." *Greece & Rome* 23 (1976): 177–93.

———. "Hybris and Dishonour II." *Greece & Rome* 26 (1979): 32–47.

———. "*Hybris*, Status and Slavery." In *The Greek World,* edited by Anton Powell, 44–84. London: Routledge, 1995.

Fitzgerald, John T. "The Stoics and the Early Christians on the Treatment of Slaves." In *Stoicism in Early Christianity,* edited by Tuomas Rasimus, Troels Engberg-Pedersen, and Ismo Dunderberg, 154–62. Grand Rapids, MI: Baker Academic, 2010.

Fitzgerald, William. *Slavery and the Roman Literary Imagination.* Roman Literature and Its Contexts. Cambridge: Cambridge University Press, 1996.

Flory, Marleen B. "Family in *Familia*: Kinship and Community in Slavery." *American Journal of Ancient History* 3 (1978): 78–95.

Ford, David. *Women and Men in the Early Church: The Full Views of St. John Chrysostom.* South Canaan, PA: St. Tikhon's Seminary Press, 1996.

Fortenbaugh, William W. "Aristotle on Slaves and Women." In *Articles on Aristotle,* vol. 2, edited by Jonathan Barnes, Malcolm Schofield, and Richard Sorabji, 135–39. London: Duckworth, 1975.

Foucault, Michel. *The Archaeology of Knowledge and the Discourse on Language.* Translated by Alan M. Sheridan Smith. New York: Pantheon, 1971.

———. *The Care of the Self.* Translated by Robert Hurley. Vol. 3 of *The History of Sexuality.* New York: Vintage, 1988.

———. *Discipline & Punish: The Birth of the Prison.* Translated by Alan Sheridan. New York: Vintage, 1977.

———. *The Hermeneutics of the Subject: Lectures at the Collège de France, 1981–1982.* Edited by François Ewald and Alessandro Fontana. Translated by Graham Burchell. New York: Picador, 2006.

———. *The History of Sexuality: An Introduction.* Translated by Robert Hurley. Vol. 1 of *The History of Sexuality.* New York: Vintage, 1978.

———. "Of Other Spaces, Heterotopias." *Architecture, Mouvement, Continuité* 5 (1984): 46–49.

———. *Security, Territory, Population: Lectures at the Collège de France, 1977–1978.* Edited by Michel Senellart, François Ewald, Alessandro Fontana, and Arnold I. I. Davidson. Translated by Graham Burchell. New York: Palgrave Macmillan, 2009.

———. *The Use of Pleasure.* Translated by Robert Hurley. Vol. 2 of *The History of Sexuality.* New York: Vintage, 1985.

Frankfurter, David. "Fetus Magic and Sorcery Fears in Roman Egypt." *Greek, Roman and Byzantine Studies* 46 (2006): 37–62.

———. "Martyrology and the Prurient Gaze." *Journal of Early Christian Studies* 17, no. 2 (2009): 215–45.

Freierman, Steven. "African Histories and the Dissolution of World History." In *Africa and the Disciplines: The Contributions of Research in Africa to the Social Sciences and Humanities,* edited by Robert H. Bates, V. Y. Mudimbe, and Jean F. O'Barr, 167–212. Chicago: University of Chicago Press, 1993.

Friedman, David M. *A Mind of Its Own: A Cultural History of the Penis.* New York: Simon and Schuster, 2001.

Frier, Bruce W. "Natural Fertility and Family Limitation in Roman Marriage." *Classical Philology* 89 (1994): 318–33.

Gaddis, Michael. *There Is No Crime for Those Who Have Christ: Religious Violence in the Christian Roman Empire.* Berkeley: University of California Press, 2005.

Gardner, Jane F. "The Adoption of Roman Freedmen." *Phoenix* 43, no. 3 (1989): 236–57.

———. "Slavery and Roman Law." In *The Cambridge World History of Slavery*, vol. 1, *The Ancient Mediterranean World*, edited by Keith Bradley and Paul Cartledge, 414–37. New York: Cambridge University Press, 2011.

Garnsey, Peter. *Ideas of Slavery from Aristotle to Augustine.* Cambridge: Cambridge University Press, 1996.

———. "Mass Diet and Nutrition in the City of Rome." In *Nourrir la plèbe: Actes du colloque tenu à Genèvre les 28 et 29. IX. 1989 en hommage à Denis van Berchem*, edited by Adalberto Giovannini, 67–101. Basel: F. Reinhardt, 1991.

———. "The Middle Stoics and Slavery." In *Hellenistic Constructs: Essays in Culture, History, and Historiography*, edited by Paul Cartledge, Peter Garnsey, and Erich S. Gruen, 159–74. Berkeley: University of California Press, 1997.

Garroway, Joshua. "The Law-Observant Lord: John Chrysostom's Engagement with the Jewishness of Christ." *Journal of Early Christian Studies* 18, no. 4 (2010): 591–615.

Garver, Eugene. "Aristotle's Natural Slaves: Incomplete Praxeis and Incomplete Human Beings." *Journal of the History of Philosophy* 32, no. 2 (1994): 173–95.

Gaudemet, Jean. *L'Église dans l'empire romain (IVe-Ve siècles).* Edited by Gabriel Le Bras. Histoire du droit et des institutions de l'Église en Occident 3. Paris: Sirey, 1958.

Geljon, Albert C., and David T. Runia, eds. *Philo of Alexandria, On Cultivation.* Leiden: Brill, 2013.

George, Michele. "*Servus* and *Domus*: The Slave in the Roman House." In *Domestic Space in the Roman World: Pompei and Beyond*, edited by Ray Laurence and Andrew Wallace-Hadrill, 15–24. Journal of Roman Archaeology Supplementary Series 22. Portsmouth, RI: JRA, 1997.

———. "Slavery and Roman Material Culture." In *The Cambridge World History of Slavery*, vol. 1, *The Ancient Mediterranean World*, edited by Keith Bradley and Paul Cartledge, 385–413. New York: Cambridge University Press, 2011.

Gigante, Marcello. *Philodemus in Italy: The Books from Herculaneum.* Translated by Dirk Obbink. Ann Arbor: University of Michigan Press, 2002.

Giorda, Maria C. "De la direction spirituelle aux règles monastiques: Péchés, penitence et punitions dans le monachisme pachômien (IVe-Ve siècles)." *Collectanea Christiana Orientalia* 6 (2009): 95–113.

Glancy, Jennifer A. "Christian Slavery in Late Antiquity." In *Human Bondage in the Cultural Contact Zone: Transdisciplinary Perspectives on Slavery and Its Discourses*, edited by Raphael Hörmann and Gesa Mackenthun, 63–80. Münster: Waxmann, 2010.

———. *Corporal Knowledge: Early Christian Bodies.* New York: Oxford University Press, 2010.

———. "Obstacles to Slaves' Participation in the Corinthian Church." *Journal of Biblical Literature* 117, no. 3 (1998): 481–501.

―――. "Slavery and the Rise of Christianity." In *The Cambridge World History of Slavery*, vol. 1, *The Ancient Mediterranean World*, edited by Keith Bradley and Paul Cartledge, 456–81. New York: Cambridge University Press, 2011.

―――. "Slavery in *Acts of Thomas.*" *Journal of Early Christian History* 2, no. 2 (2012): 3–21.

―――. *Slavery in Early Christianity.* Minneapolis: Fortress Press, 2006.

Goldenberg, David M. *The Curse of Ham: Race and Slavery in Early Judaism, Christianity, and Islam.* Princeton, NJ: Princeton University Press, 2003.

González Blanco, Antonino. *Economía y sociedad en el Bajo imperio según San Juan Crisostomo.* Publicationes de la Fundacíon universitaria española 17. Madrid: Fundación universitaria española, 1980.

Goodrich, Peter. "Anti-Teubner: Autopoiesis, Paradox, and the Theory of Law." *Social Epistemology* 13, no. 2 (1999): 197–214.

Greenidge, Abel H. J. Infamia: *Its Place in Roman Public and Private Law.* Oxford: Clarendon Press, 1894.

Grey, Cam. "Slavery in the Late Roman World." In *The Cambridge World History of Slavery*, vol. 1, *The Ancient Mediterranean World*, edited by Keith Bradley and Paul Cartledge, 482–509. New York: Cambridge University Press, 2011.

Grubbs, Judith Evans. "Church, State, and Children: Christian and Imperial Attitudes toward Infant Exposure in Late Antiquity." In *The Power of Religion in Late Antiquity*, edited by Andrew Cain and Noel Lenski, 119–31. Farnham: Ashgate, 2009.

Gruen, Erich S. *Rethinking the Other in Antiquity.* Martin Classical Lectures. Princeton, NJ: Princeton University Press, 2012.

Grunewald, Thomas. *Bandits in the Roman Empire: Myth and Reality.* London: Routledge, 2004.

Guyot, Peter. *Eunuchen als Sklaven und Freigelassene in der griechisch-römischen Antike.* Stuttgart: Klett-Cotta, 1980.

Hansen, Karen T. "The World in Dress: Anthropological Perspectives on Clothing, Fashion, and Culture." *Annual Review of Anthropology* 33, no. 1 (2004): 369–92.

Harlow, Mary. "Clothes Maketh the Man: Power Dressing and Elite Masculinity in the Later Roman World." In *Gender in the Early Medieval World: East and West, 300–900*, edited by Leslie Brubaker and Julia M. H. Smith, 44–70. New York: Cambridge University Press, 2004.

Harper, Kyle. *From Shame to Sin: The Christian Transformation of Sexual Morality in Late Antiquity.* Cambridge, MA: Harvard University Press, 2013.

―――. "Marriage and Family." In *The Oxford Handbook of Late Antiquity*, edited by Scott F. Johnson, 667–714. New York: Oxford University Press, 2012.

―――. "Slave Prices in Late Antiquity (and in the Very Long Term)." *Historia* 59 (2010): 206–38.

―――. *Slavery in the Late Roman World, AD 275–425.* New York: Cambridge University Press, 2011.

Harries, Jill. "Men without Women: Theodosius' Consistory and the Business of Government." In *Theodosius II: Rethinking the Roman Empire in Late Antiquity*, edited by Christopher Kelly, 67–89. Cambridge Classical Studies. New York: Cambridge University Press, 2013.

Harrill, J. Albert. "Coming of Age and Putting on Christ: The *Toga Virilis* Ceremony, Its Paranaesis, and Paul's Interpretation of Baptism in Galatians." *Novum Testamentum* 44, no. 3 (2002): 252–77.

———. "The Domestic Enemy: A Moral Polarity of Household Slaves in Early Christian Apologies and Martyrdoms." In *Early Christian Families in Context: An Interdisciplinary Dialogue,* edited by David L. Balch and Carolyn Osiek, 231–54. Religion, Marriage, and Family. Grand Rapids, MI: Eerdmans, 2003.

———. *The Manumission of Slaves in Early Christianity.* Hermeneutische Untersuchungen zur Theologie 32. Tübingen: Mohr Siebeck, 1998.

———. "The Psychology of Slaves in the Gospel Parables: A Case Study in Social History." *Biblische Zeitschrift* 55 (2011): 63–74.

———. *Slaves in the New Testament: Literary, Social, and Moral Dimensions.* Minneapolis: Fortress Press, 2005.

———. "Using Roman Jurists to Interpret Philemon." *Zeitschrift für die Neutestamentliche Wissenschaft* 90 (1999): 135–38.

———. "The Vice of Slave Dealers in Greco-Roman Society: The Use of a Topos in 1 Timothy 1:10." *Journal of Biblical Literature* 118, no. 1 (1999): 97–122.

Harris, William V. *Ancient Literacy.* Cambridge, MA: Harvard University Press, 1991.

———. "Child-Exposure in the Roman Empire." *Journal of Roman Studies* 84 (1994): 1–22.

Hart, D. Bentley. "The 'Whole Humanity': Gregory of Nyssa's Critique in Light of His Eschatology." *Scottish Journal of Theology* 54, no. 1 (2001): 51–69.

Hartman, Saidiya V. *Scenes of Subjection: Terror, Slavery, and Self-Making in Nineteenth-Century America.* New York: Oxford University Press, 1997.

Hartney, Aideen M. *John Chrysostom and the Transformation of the City.* London: Duckworth, 2004.

———. "Manly Women and Womanly Men: The *Subintroductae* and John Chrysostom." In *Desire and Denial in Byzantium,* edited by Liz James, 41–48. *Papers from the Thirty-First Spring Symposium of Byzantine Studies, University of Sussex, Brighton, March 1997.* Aldershot: Ashgate Variorum, 1999.

Haynes, Stephen R. *Noah's Curse: The Biblical Justification of American Slavery.* New York: Oxford University Press, 2002.

Heaney-Hunter, Jo Ann C. "'Disobedience and Curse' or 'Affection of the Soul'? John Chrysostom, Marriage, and Sin." *Diakonia* 24 (1991): 171–86.

Heath, Malcolm. "Aristotle on Natural Slavery." *Phronesis* 53 (2008): 243–70.

Heine, Ronald E. *The Commentaries of Origen and Jerome on St. Paul's Epistle to the Ephesians.* Oxford Early Christian Studies. Oxford: Oxford University Press, 2002.

Herrmann-Otto, Elizabeth. *Ex Ancilla Natus: Untersuchungen zu den "hausgeborenen" Sklaven und Sklavinnen im Westen des römischen Kaiserreiches.* Forschungen zur antiken Sklaverei 24. Stuttgart: Steiner, 1994.

Hershbell, Jackson P. "Epictetus: A Freedman on Slavery." *Ancient Society* 26 (1995): 185–204.

Hezser, Catherine. *Jewish Slavery in Antiquity.* New York: Oxford University Press, 2006.

Hill, D. E. "The Thessalian Trick." *Rheinisches Museum für Philologie* 116 (1973): 221–38.

Hill, Robert C., trans. *Homilies on Hannah, David and Saul.* St. John Chrysostom: Old Testament Homilies 1. Brookline, MA: Holy Cross Orthodox Press, 2003.

————, trans. *St. John Chrysostom: Eight Sermons on the Book of Genesis.* Brookline, MA: Holy Cross Orthodox Press, 2004.

————, trans. *St. John Chrysostom: Homilies on Genesis 1–17.* The Fathers of the Church 74. Washington, DC: Catholic University of America Press, 1999.

Hinds, Stephen. *Allusion and Intertext: Dynamics of Appropriation in Roman Poetry.* New York: Cambridge University Press, 1998.

Hogan, Pauline N. *No Longer Male and Female: Interpreting Galatians 3:28 in Early Christianity.* Library of New Testament Studies. London: T&T Clark, 2008.

Holford-Strevens, Leofranc. *Aulus Gellius: An Antonine Scholar and His Achievement.* Oxford: Oxford University Press, 2003.

Holman, Susan R. "Molded as Wax: Formation and Feeding of the Ancient Newborn." *Helios* 24 (1997): 77–95.

Hopkins, Keith. *Death and Renewal.* Cambridge: Cambridge University Press, 1983.

Horn, Cornelia B., and John W. Martens. *"Let the Little Children Come to Me": Childhood and Children in Early Christianity.* Washington, DC: Catholic University of America Press, 2009.

Hunt, Peter. "Slaves in Greek Literary Culture." In *The Cambridge World History of Slavery,* vol. 1, *The Ancient Mediterranean World,* edited by Keith Bradley and Paul Cartledge, 23–47. New York: Cambridge University Press, 2011.

————. *Slaves, Warfare and Ideology in the Greek Historians.* Cambridge: Cambridge University Press, 2002.

Hunter, David G., trans. *A Comparison between a King and a Monk; Against the Opponents of the Monastic Life: Two Treatises by John Chrysostom.* Lewiston, NY: Edwin Mellen, 1988.

Jacobs, Andrew S. "A Jew's Jew: Paul and the Early Christian Problem of Jewish Origins." *Journal of Religion* 86 (2006): 258–86.

Jacoby, Karl. "Slaves by Nature? Domestic Animals and Human Slaves." *Slavery & Abolition* 15, no. 1 (1994): 89–99.

Jaeger, Wulf. "Die Sklaverei bei Johannes Chrysostomus." PhD diss., Christian-Albrechts-Universität zu Kiel, 1974.

James, Sharon L. "A Courtesan's Choreography: Female Liberty and Male Anxiety at the Roman Dinner Party." In *Prostitutes and Courtesans in the Ancient World,* edited by Christopher A. Faraone and Laura K. McClure, 224–51. Madison: University of Wisconsin Press, 2006.

Joblin, Joseph. *L'église et la guerre: Conscience, violence, pouvoir.* Paris: Desclée de Brouwer, 1988.

Jones, Arnold H. M. *The Later Roman Empire, 284–602: A Social, Economic and Administrative Survey.* 2 vols. Baltimore: Johns Hopkins University Press, 1986.

Joshel, Sandra R. "Geographies of Slave Containment and Movement." In *Roman Slavery and Roman Material Culture,* edited by Michele George, 99–128. Toronto: University of Toronto Press, 2013.

————. "Nurturing the Master's Child: Slavery and the Roman Child-Nurse." *Signs* 12 (1986): 3–22.

————. "Slavery and the Roman Literary Culture." In *The Cambridge World History of Slavery,* vol. 1, *The Ancient Mediterranean World,* edited by Keith Bradley and Paul Cartledge, 214–40. New York: Cambridge University Press, 2011.

————. *Slavery in the Roman World.* New York: Cambridge University Press, 2010.

Jütte, Robert. *Contraception: A History.* Cambridge: Polity Press, 2008.

Kampen, Natalie B. "Slaves and *Liberti* in the Roman Army." In *Roman Slavery and Roman Material Culture,* edited by Michele George, 180–98. Toronto: University of Toronto Press, 2013.

Karlowa, Otto. "Zur Geschichte der Infamia." *Zeitschrift für Rechtsgeschichte* 9 (1870): 204–37.

Kartzow, Marianne B. "Navigating the Womb: Surrogacy, Slavery, Fertility—and Biblical Discourses." *Journal of Early Christian History* 2, no. 1 (2012): 38–54.

Kaser, Max. "Infamia und ignominia in den römischen Rechtsquellen." *Zeitschrift der Savigny-Stiftung für Rechtsgeschichte* 73 (1956): 220–78.

Kelly, John N. D. *Golden Mouth: The Story of John Chrysostom—Ascetic, Preacher, Bishop.* Ithaca, NY: Cornell University Press, 1998.

Kelly, Kathleen Coyne. *Performing Virginity and Testing Chastity in the Middle Ages.* Routledge Research in Medieval Studies. London: Routledge, 2000.

King, Helen. *Hippocrates' Woman: Reading the Female Body in Ancient Greece.* London: Routledge, 1998.

————. *The One-Sex Body on Trial: The Classical and Early Modern Evidence.* The History of Medicine in Context. Farnham: Ashgate, 2013.

Kirschenbaum, Aaron. *Sons, Slaves, and Freedmen in Roman Commerce.* Washington, DC: Catholic University of America Press, 1987.

Klingenberg, Georg. *Corpus der römischen Rechtsquellen zur antiken Sklaverei, Teil X: Juristisch speziell definierte Sklavengruppen, 6: Servus fugitivus.* Forschungen zur antiken Sklaverei—Beihefte 16. Stuttgart: Steiner, 2005.

Knox, John. *Philemon among the Letters of Paul: A New View of Its Place and Importance.* Chicago: University of Chicago Press, 1935.

Knust, Jennifer W. *Abandoned to Lust: Sexual Slander and Ancient Christianity.* New York: Columbia University Press, 2006.

Kontoulis, Georg. *Zum Problem der Sklaverei (ΔΟΥΛΕΙΑ) bei den kappadokischen Kirchenvätern und Johannes Chrysostomus.* Bonn: Habelt, 1993.

Kraemer, Ross S. "The Other as Woman: An Aspect of Polemic among Pagans, Jews, and Christians." In *The Other in Jewish Thought and History: Constructions of Jewish Culture and Identity,* edited by Laurence J. Silbertein and Robert L. Cohn, 121–44. New Perspectives in Jewish Studies. New York: New York University Press, 1994.

Kronenberg, Leah. *Allegories of Farming from Greece and Rome: Philosophical Satire in Xenophon, Varro, and Virgil.* New York: Cambridge University Press, 2009.

Kudlien, Fridolf. *Die Sklaven in der griechischen Medizin der klassischen und hellenistischen Zeit.* Forschungen zur antiken Sklaverei 2. Wiesbaden: F. Steiner, 1969.

Kuefler, Mathew. "Castration and Eunuchism in the Middle Ages." In *Handbook of Medieval Sexuality,* edited by Vern L. Bullough and James A. Brundage, 279–306. New York: Routledge, 1996.

————. *The Manly Eunuch: Masculinity, Gender Ambiguity, and Christian Ideology in Late Antiquity.* Chicago: University of Chicago Press, 2001.

Laes, Christian. *Children in the Roman Empire: Outsiders Within.* New York: Cambridge University Press, 2011.

Laird, Raymond J. *Mindset, Moral Choice and Sin in the Anthropology of John Chrysostom.* Early Christian Studies 15. Strathfield: St. Paul's, 2012.

Lampe, Peter. "Keine 'Sklavenflucht' des Onesimus." *Zeitschrift für die Neutestamentliche Wissenschaft* 76 (1985): 133–37.

Laqueur, Thomas W. *Making Sex: Body and Gender from the Greeks to Freud.* Cambridge, MA: Harvard University Press, 1990.

Latham, Jacob. "'Fabulous Clap-Trap': Roman Masculinity, the Cult of Magna Mater, and Literary Constructions of the *Galli* at Rome from the Late Republic to Late Antiquity." *Journal of Religion* 92, no. 1 (2012): 84–122.

Lavan, Luke. "The Agorai of Antioch and Constantinople as Seen by John Chrysostom." *Bulletin of the Institute of Classical Studies* 50, no. S91 (2007): 157–67.

Lenski, Noel. "Captivity, Slavery and Cultural Exchange between Rome and the Germans from the First to the Seventh Century CE." In *Invisible Citizens: Captives and Their Consequences,* edited by Catherine M. Cameron, 80–109. Salt Lake City: University of Utah Press, 2008.

———. "Constantine and Slavery: Libertas and the Fusion of Roman and Christian Values." *Atti dell'Accademia Romanistica Costantiniana* 19 (2011): 235–60.

———. "Working Models: Functional Art and Roman Conceptions of Slavery." In *Roman Slavery and Roman Material Culture,* edited by Michele George, 129–57. Toronto: University of Toronto Press, 2013.

Le Saint, William P., trans. *Treatises on Penance: On Penitence and On Purity.* Ancient Christian Writers 28. Westminster: Newman Press, 1959.

Levin, Michael. "Aristotle on Natural Subordination." *Philosophy* 72, no. 280 (1997): 241–57.

Leyerle, Blake. "Appealing to Children." *Journal of Early Christian Studies* 5, no. 2 (1997): 243–70.

———. "Children and 'the Child' in Early Christianity." In *The Oxford Handbook of Childhood and Education in the Classical World,* edited by Judith Evans Grubbs, Tim Parkin, and Roslynne Bell, 559–79. New York: Oxford University Press, 2013.

———. "John Chrysostom on the Gaze." *Journal of Early Christian Studies* 1, no. 2 (1993): 159–74.

———. "'Keep Me, Lord, as the Apple of Your Eyes': An Early Christian Child's Amulet." *Journal of Early Christian History* 3, no. 2 (2013): 73–93.

———. *Theatrical Shows and Ascetic Lives: John Chrysostom's Attack on Spiritual Marriage.* Berkeley: University of California Press, 2001.

———. "'Turn Your House into a Church': Prescribed Domestic Rituals in the Preaching of John Chrysostom." Paper presented at the Society of Biblical Literature Annual Meeting, Chicago, 2012.

Liebeschuetz, John W. G. H. *Barbarians and Bishops: Army, Church, and State in the Age of Arcadius and Chrysostom.* Oxford: Clarendon Press, 1990.

Lieu, Samuel N. C. *Manichaeism in the Later Roman Empire and Medieval China.* Wissenschaftliche Untersuchungen zum Neuen Testament 63. Tübingen: Mohr Siebeck, 1992.

Linder, Amnon. "The Legal Status of Jews in the Byzantine Empire." In *Jews in Byzantium: Dialectics of Minority and Majority Cultures,* edited by Robert Bonfil, Oded Irshai, Guy G. Stroumsa, and Rina Talgam, 149–218. Leiden: Brill, 2011.

Lindsay, Hugh. *Adoption in the Roman World*. New York: Cambridge University Press, 2009.

Lord, Carnes, trans. *Aristotle's Politics*. Chicago: University of Chicago Press, 2013.

———. "On the Early History of the Aristotelian Corpus." *American Journal of Philology* 107, no. 2 (1986): 137–61.

Lull, David J. "'The Law Was Our Pedagogue': A Study in Galatians 3:19–25." *Journal of Biblical Literature* 105, no. 3 (1986): 481–90.

Lunn-Rockliffe, Sophie. *Ambrosiaster's Political Theology*. Oxford Early Christian Studies. New York: Oxford University Press, 2007.

MacDowell, Douglas. "Hybris in Athens." *Greece & Rome* 23 (1976): 14–31.

MacMullen, Ramsay. "Late Roman Slavery." *Historia* 36 (1987): 359–82.

———. "The Preacher's Audience (AD 350–400)." *Journal of Theological Studies* 40, no. 2 (1989): 503–11.

Malosse, Pierre-Louis. "Jean Chrysostome a-t-il été l'élève de Libanios?" *Phoenix* 62 (2008): 273–80.

Mara, Maria G. "Aspetti della polemica antimanichea di Giovanni Crisostomo." In *Atti dell'undicesimo simposio Paolino: Paolo tra Tarso e Antiochia; Archeologia/storia/religione*, edited by Luigi Padovese, 195–99. Rome: Pontificia Università Antonianum, 2008.

Marazano, Annalisa. *Roman Villas in Central Italy: A Social and Economic History*. Leiden: Brill, 2007.

Maróti, Egon. "The Vilicus and the Villa System in Ancient Italy." *Oikumene* 1 (1976): 109–24.

Marrou, Henri I. *A History of Education in Antiquity*. Translated by George Lamb. Wisconsin Studies in Classics. Madison: University of Wisconsin Press, 1982.

Martens, John W. "'Do Not Sexually Abuse Children': The Language of Early Christian Sexual Ethics." In *Children in Late Ancient Christianity*, edited by Cornelia B. Horn and Robert R. Phenix, 227–54. Studien und Texte zu Antike und Christentum 58. Tübingen: Mohr Siebeck, 2009.

Martin, Dale B. *The Corinthian Body*. New Haven, CT: Yale University Press, 1995.

———. *Sex and the Single Savior: Gender and Sexuality in Biblical Interpretation*. Louisville, KY: Westminster John Knox Press, 2006.

———. "Slave Families and Slaves in Families." In *Early Christian Families in Context: An Interdisciplinary Dialogue*, edited by David L. Balch and Carolyn Osiek, 207–30. Religion, Marriage, and Family. Grand Rapids, MI: Eerdmans, 2003.

———. *Slavery as Salvation: The Metaphor of Slavery in Pauline Christianity*. New Haven, CT: Yale University Press, 1990.

Martin, René. "La vie sexuelle des esclaves d'après les Dialogues Rustiques de Varron." In *Varron: Grammaire antique et stylistique latine*, edited by Christian Bruel, 113–26. Publications de La Sorbonne. Paris: Les Belles Lettres, 1978.

Mattern, Susan P. *Galen and the Rhetoric of Healing*. Baltimore: Johns Hopkins University Press, 2008.

Maurice, Lisa. *The Teacher in Ancient Rome: The Magister and His World*. Lanham, MD: Lexington Books, 2013.

Maxwell, Jaclyn L. *Christianization and Communication in Late Antiquity: John Chrysostom and His Congregation in Antioch*. New York: Cambridge University Press, 2009.

Mayer, Wendy. "Chrysostom's Last Word on Treating the Soul." Paper presented at the North American Patristics Society Annual Meeting, Chicago, 2014.

———. trans. *The Cult of the Saints.* Popular Patristics Series. Crestwood, NY: St. Vladimir's Seminary Press, 2006.

———. "Homiletics." In *The Oxford Handbook of Early Christian Studies,* edited by Susan A. Harvey and David G. Hunter, 565–83. New York: Oxford University Press, 2008.

———. *The Homilies of St John Chrysostom—Provenance: Reshaping the Foundations.* Orientalia Christiana Analecta 273. Rome: Pontificio Istituto Orientale, 2005.

———. "John Chrysostom: Extraordinary Preacher, Ordinary Audience." In *Preacher and Audience: Studies in Early Christian and Byzantine Homiletics,* edited by Mary B. Cunningham and Pauline Allen, 105–37. A New History of the Sermon 1. Leiden: Brill, 1998.

———. "John Chrysostom on Poverty." In *Preaching Poverty in Late Antiquity: Perceptions and Realities,* edited by Pauline Allen, Bronwen Neil, and Wendy Mayer, 69–118. Arbeiten zur Kirchen- und Theologiegeschichte. Leipzig: Evangelische Verlagsanstalt, 2009.

———. "Medicine in Transition: Christian Adaptation in the Later Fourth-Century East." In *Shifting Genres in Late Antiquity,* edited by Geoffrey Greatrex and Hugh Elton, 11–26. Farnham: Ashgate, 2015.

———. "Poverty and Generosity toward the Poor in the Time of John Chrysostom." In *Wealth and Poverty in Early Church and Society,* edited by Susan R. Holman, 140–58. Holy Cross Studies in Patristic Theology and History. Grand Rapids, MI: Baker Academic, 2008.

———. "Who Came to Hear John Chrysostom Preach?" *Ephemerides Theologicae Lovanienses* 76, no. 1 (2000): 73–87.

McCormick, Michael. "New Light on the 'Dark Ages': How the Slave Trade Fuelled the Carolingian Economy." *Past & Present* 177, no. 1 (2002): 17–54.

———. *Origins of the European Economy: Communications and Commerce, A.D. 300–900.* New York: Cambridge University Press, 2001.

McGinn, Thomas A. J. *The Economy of Prostitution in the Roman World: A Study of Social History and the Brothel.* Ann Arbor: University of Michigan Press, 2004.

———. *Prostitution, Sexuality, and the Law in Ancient Rome.* New York: Oxford University Press, 1998.

McKeown, Niall. "Resistance among Chattel Slaves in the Classical Greek World." In *The Cambridge World History of Slavery,* vol. 1, *The Ancient Mediterranean World,* edited by Keith Bradley and Paul Cartledge, 153–75. New York: Cambridge University Press, 2011.

———. "The Sound of John Henderson Laughing: Pliny 3.14 and Roman Slaveowners' Fear of Their Slaves." In *Fear of Slaves—Fear of Enslavement in the Ancient Mediterranean,* edited by Anastasia Serghidou, 265–79. *Actes du XXIXe colloque international du groupe international de recherches sur l'esclavage dans l'antiquité.* Besançon: Presses universitaires de Franche-Comté, 2007.

Meijer, Piet A. *Stoic Theology: Proofs for the Existence of the Cosmic God and of the Traditional Gods (including a Commentary on Cleanthes' Hymn on Zeus).* Delft: Eburon, 2007.

Miller, Timothy S. "The Care of Orphans in the Byzantine Empire." In *Medieval Family Roles: A Book of Essays,* edited by Cathy J. Itnyre, 121–36. New York: Garland, 1996.

———. *The Orphans of Byzantium: Child Welfare in the Christian Empire.* Washington, DC: Catholic University of America Press, 2003.

Milnor, Kristina. *Gender, Domesticity, and the Age of Augustus: Inventing Private Life*. New York: Oxford University Press, 2005.

Mitchell, Margaret M. *The Heavenly Trumpet: John Chrysostom and the Art of Pauline Interpretation*. Louisville, KY: Westminster John Knox Press, 2002.

———. "John Chrysostom on Philemon: A Second Look." *Harvard Theological Review* 88, no. 1 (1995): 135–48.

Möhler, Johann A. "Bruchstücke aus der Geschichte der Aufhebung der Sklaverei." In *Gesammelte Schriften und Aufsätze*, vol. 2, edited by Johann J. I. Von Döllinger, 54–140. Regensburg: Manz, 1939.

Mohler, S. L. "Slave Education in the Roman Empire." *Transactions of the American Philological Association* 71 (1940): 262–80.

Moriarty, Rachel. "Human Owners, Human Slaves: Gregory of Nyssa, *Hom. Eccl. 4*." *Studia Patristica* 27 (1993): 62–69.

Morley, Neville. "Slavery under the Principate." In *The Cambridge World History of Slavery*, vol. 1, *The Ancient Mediterranean World*, edited by Keith Bradley and Paul Cartledge, 265–86. New York: Cambridge University Press, 2011.

Morony, Michael G. *Iraq after the Muslim Conquest*. Piscataway, NJ: Gorgias, 2005.

Morrisson, Cécile, and Jean Claude Cheynet. "Prices and Wages in the Byzantine World." In *The Economic History of Byzantium: From the Seventh through the Fifteenth Century*, edited by Angeliki E. Laiou and Charalampos Bouras, 815–78. Dumbarton Oaks Studies 39. Washington, DC: Dumbarton Oaks Research Library and Collection, 2002.

Mouritsen, Henrik. *The Freedman in the Roman World*. New York: Cambridge University Press, 2011.

Muchembled, Robert. *A History of Violence: From the End of the Middle Ages to the Present*. Translated by Jean Birrell. Cambridge: Polity Press, 2012.

Natali, Carlo. "*Oikonomia* in Hellenistic Political Thought." In *Justice and Generosity: Studies in Hellenistic Social and Political Philosophy*, edited by André Laks and Malcolm Schofield, 95–128. New York: Cambridge University Press, 1995.

Nathan, Geoffrey S. *The Family in Late Antiquity: The Rise of Christianity and the Endurance of Tradition*. London: Routledge, 2000.

Newman, Graeme R. *The Punishment Response*. New Brunswick, NJ: Transaction Publishers, 1985.

Nicklas, Tobias. "The Letter to Philemon: A Discussion with J. Albert Harrill." In *Paul's World*, edited by Stanley E. Porter, 201–20. PAST 4. Leiden: Brill, 2008.

Nisbet, R. G. "The Festuca and the Alapa of Manumission." *Journal of Roman Studies* 8 (1918): 1–14.

Nock, Arthur D. "Eunuchs in Ancient Religion." *Archiv für Religionswissenschaft* 23 (1925): 25–33.

Ogden, Daniel. *Magic, Witchcraft, and Ghosts in the Greek and Roman Worlds: A Sourcebook*. New York: Oxford University Press, 2002.

Olender, Maurice. "Aspects of Baubo: Ancient Texts and Contexts." In *Before Sexuality: The Construction of Erotic Experience in the Ancient Greek World*, edited by David M. Halperin, John J. Winkler, and Froma I. Zeitlin, 83–114. Princeton, NJ: Princeton University Press, 1990.

Olson, Kelly. *Dress and the Roman Woman: Self-Presentation and Society*. London: Routledge, 2008.

———. "*Matrona* and Whore: Clothing and Definition in Roman Antiquity." In *Prostitutes and Courtesans in the Ancient World*, edited by Christopher A. Faraone and Laura K. McClure, 186–206. Madison: University of Wisconsin Press, 2006.

Osiek, Carolyn. "Female Slaves, *Porneia*, and the Limits of Obedience." In *Early Christian Families in Context: An Interdisciplinary Dialogue*, edited by David L. Balch and Carolyn Osiek, 255–76. Religion, Marriage, and Family. Grand Rapids, MI: Eerdmans, 2003.

Osiek, Carolyn, Margaret Y. MacDonald, and Janet H. Tulloch. *A Woman's Place: House Churches in Earliest Christianity*. Minneapolis: Fortress Press, 2006.

Pagels, Elaine. "The Politics of Paradise: Augustine's Exegesis of Genesis 1–3 versus That of John Chrysostom." *Harvard Theological Review* 78, no. 1–2 (1985): 67–99.

Palmer, Robert E. A. "*Bullae insignia ingenuitatis*." *American Journal of Ancient History* 14 (1989): 1–69.

Papaconstantinou, Arietta. "Notes sur les actes de donation d'enfant au monastère thébain de Saint-Phoibammon." *Journal of Juristic Papyrology* 32 (2002): 83–105.

Parker, Holt N. "The Teratogenic Grid." In *Roman Sexualities*, edited by Marilyn B. Skinner and Judith P. Hallet, 47–65. Princeton, NJ: Princeton University Press, 1997.

Parkin, Tim G. "The Elderly Children of Greece and Rome." In *On Old Age: Approaching Death in Antiquity and the Middle Ages*, edited by Christian Krötzl and Katariina Mustakallio, 25–40. Studies in the History of Daily Life (800–1600). Turnhout: Brepols, 2011.

———. *Old Age in the Roman World: A Cultural and Social History*. Baltimore: Johns Hopkins University Press, 2003.

Pasquato, Ottorino. "La priorità dell'educazione morale in Giovanni Crisostomo." In *Spiritualità del lavoro nella catechesi dei Padri del III-IV secolo*, edited by Sergio Felici, 105–39. Rome: LAS, 1986.

Patterson, Orlando. *Slavery and Social Death: A Comparative Study*. Cambridge, MA: Harvard University Press, 1982.

———. "Slavery, Gender, and Work in the Pre-Modern World and Early Greece: A Cross-Cultural Analysis." In *Slave Systems: Ancient and Modern*, edited by Enrico Dal Lago and Constantina Katsari, 32–69. New York: Cambridge University Press, 2008.

Pedersen, Else M. W. "The Monastery as a Household within the Universal Household." In *Household, Women, and Christianities in Late Antiquity and the Middle Ages*, edited by Anneke Mulder-Bakker and Jocelyn Wogan-Browne, 167–90. Turnhout: Brepols, 2005.

Pelikan, Jaroslav. *Divine Rhetoric: The Sermon on the Mount as Message and as Model in Augustine, Chrysostom and Luther*. Crestwood, NY: St. Vladimir's Seminary Press, 2001.

Perkins, Judith. *The Suffering Self: Pain and Narrative Representation in the Early Christian Era*. London: Routledge, 1995.

Perry, Matthew J. *Gender, Manumission, and the Roman Freedwoman*. New York: Cambridge University Press, 2013.

Pervo, Richard I. *The Making of Paul: Constructions of the Apostle in Early Christianity*. Minneapolis: Fortress Press, 2010.

Petersen, Lauren H. *The Freedman in Roman Art and Art History*. New York: Cambridge University Press, 2006.

Petersen, Norman R. *Rediscovering Paul: Philemon and the Sociology of Paul's Narrative World*. Philadelphia: Fortress Press, 1985.

Petzl, Georg. "Die Beichtinschriften Westkleinasiens." *Epigraphica Anatolica* 22 (1994): 1–174.

Petzl, Georg, and Hasan Malay. "A New Confession-Inscription from the Katakekaumene." *Greek, Roman and Byzantine Studies* 28 (1987): 459–72.

Phillips, Jane. "Roman Mothers and the Lives of Their Adult Daughters." *Helios* 6 (1978): 69–80.

Phillips, Oliver. "The Witches' Thessaly." In *Magic and Ritual in the Ancient World*, edited by Paul Mirecki and Marvin Meyer, 378–86. Religions in the Graeco-Roman World 141. Leiden: Brill, 2001.

Poliakoff, Michael. *Combat Sports in the Ancient World: Competition, Violence, and Culture*. New Haven, CT: Yale University Press, 1987.

Pomeroy, Sarah B. *Goddesses, Whores, Wives and Slaves: Women in Classical Antiquity*. New York: Random House, 1975.

———. "Slavery in the Greek Domestic Economy in the Light of Xenophon's *Oeconomicus*." *Index* 17 (1989): 11–18.

———, trans. *Xenophon, Oeconomicus: A Social and Historical Commentary*. Oxford: Clarendon Press, 1995.

Pradels, Wendy, Rudolf Brändle, and Martin Heimgartner. "Das bisher vermisste Textstück in Johannes Chrysostomus, *Adversus Judaeos*, Oratio 2." *Zeitschrift für antikes Christentum* 5 (2001): 22–49.

Prakash, Gyan. *After Colonialism: Imperial Histories and Postcolonial Displacements*. Princeton, NJ: Princeton University Press, 1994.

Quadrato, Renato. "*Beneficium manumissionis e obsequium*." *Index* 24 (1996): 341–53.

Raaflaub, Kurt A. *The Discovery of Freedom in Ancient Greece*. Translated by Renate Francisono. Chicago: University of Chicago Press, 2004.

Ramelli, Ilaria. "Gregory of Nyssa's Position in Late Antique Debates on Slavery and Poverty, and the Role of Asceticism." *Journal of Late Antiquity* 5, no. 1 (2012): 87–118.

Rapske, Brian M. "The Prisoner Paul in the Eyes of Onesimus." *New Testament Studies* 37 (1991): 187–203.

Reay, Brendon. "Agriculture, Writing, and Cato's Aristocratic Self-Fashioning." *Classical Antiquity* 24, no. 2 (2005): 331–61.

Retief, F. P., J. F. G. Cilliers, and S. P. J. K. Riekert. "Eunuchs in the Bible." *Acta Theologica* 26, no. 2, Acta Theologica Supplementum 7 (2006): 247–58.

Reumann, John. "The Use of Oikonomia and Related Terms in Greek Sources to about A.D. 100 as a Background for Patristic Applications." PhD diss., University of Pennsylvania, 1957.

Rey, Roselyne. *The History of Pain*. Translated by Louise Elliott Wallace, J. A. Cadden, and S. W. Cadden. Cambridge, MA: Harvard University Press, 1993.

Richlin, Amy. "Making Up a Woman: The Face of Roman Gender." In *Off with Her Head! The Denial of Women's Identity in Myth, Religion, and Culture*, edited by Howard Eilberg-Schwartz and Wendy Doniger, 185–213. Berkeley: University of California Press, 1995.

Richter, Gerhard. *Oikonomia: Der Gebrauch des Wortes Oikonomia im Neuen Testament, bei den Kirchenvätern und in der theologischen Literatur bis ins 20. Jahrhundert*. Berlin: De Gruyter, 2005.

Richter, Will. "Seneca und die Sklaven." *Gymnasium* 65 (1958): 196–218.

Riddle, John M. *Contraception and Abortion from the Ancient World to the Renaissance.* Cambridge, MA: Harvard University Press, 1994.

———. *Eve's Herbs: A History of Contraception and Abortion in the West.* Cambridge, MA: Harvard University Press, 1997.

———. *Goddesses, Elixirs, and Witches: Plants and Sexuality throughout Human History.* New York: Palgrave Macmillan, 2010.

Rihll, Tracey E. "Classical Athens." In *The Cambridge World History of Slavery,* vol. 1, *The Ancient Mediterranean World,* edited by Keith Bradley and Paul Cartledge, 48–73. New York: Cambridge University Press, 2011.

Rocca-Serra, Guillaume. "Le stoicisme pré-imperial et l'esclavage." *CRDAC* 8 (1976): 205–22.

Roth, Ulrike. "Food, Status, and the *Peculium* of Agricultural Slaves." *Journal of Roman Archaeology* 18 (2005): 278–92.

———. "No More Slave-Gangs: Varro, *De Re Rustica* 1.2.20–1." *Classical Quarterly* 55 (2005): 310–15.

———. *Thinking Tools: Agricultural Slavery between Evidence and Models.* Bulletin of the Institute of Classical Studies Supplement. London: Institute of Classical Studies, School of Advanced Study, University of London, 2007.

Rotman, Youval. *Byzantine Slavery and the Mediterranean World.* Translated by Jane Marie Todd. Cambridge, MA: Harvard University Press, 2009.

Rousselle, Aline. *Porneia: On Desire and the Body in Antiquity.* Translated by Felicia Pheasant. New York: Barnes & Noble, 1996.

Ryan, P. J. "Chrysostom—A Derived Stylist?" *Vigiliae Christianae* 36, no. 1 (1982): 5–14.

Saller, Richard P. "Corporal Punishment, Authority, and Obedience in the Roman Household." In *Marriage, Divorce, and Children in Ancient Rome,* edited by Beryl Rawson, 144–65. Oxford: Clarendon Press, 1991.

———. "The Hierarchical Household in Roman Society: A Study of Domestic Slavery." In *Serfdom and Slavery: Studies in Legal Bondage,* edited by Michael L. Bush, 112–29. London: Routledge, 1996.

———. "Men's Age at Marriage and Its Consequences in the Roman Family." *Classical Philology* 82, no. 1 (1987): 21–34.

———. "Pater Familias, Mater Familias, and the Gendered Semantics of the Roman Household." *Classical Philology* 94, no. 2 (1999): 182–97.

———. "*Patria Potestas* and the Stereotype of the Roman Family." *Continuity and Change* 1, no. 1 (1986): 7–22.

Salzman, Michele R. *The Making of a Christian Aristocracy: Social and Religious Change in the Western Roman Empire.* Cambridge, MA: Harvard University Press, 2004.

Sandwell, Isabella. *Religious Identity in Late Antiquity: Greeks, Jews and Christians in Antioch.* New York: Cambridge University Press, 2007.

Santos, Narry F. *Slave of All: The Paradox of Authority and Servanthood in the Gospel of Mark.* London: Sheffield Academic Press, 2003.

Scarborough, John. "The Pharmacology of Sacred Plants, Herbs, and Roots." In *Magika Hiera: Ancient Greek Magic and Religion,* edited by Chris A. Faraone and Dirk Obbink, 138–74. New York: Oxford University Press, 1976.

Scarry, Elaine. *The Body in Pain: The Making and Unmaking of the World*. New York: Oxford University Press, 1985.

Scheidel, Walter. "Free-Born and Manumitted Bailiffs in the Graeco-Roman World." *Classical Quarterly* 40, no. 02 (1990): 591–93.

———. "Quantifying the Sources of Slaves in the Early Roman Empire." *Journal of Roman Studies* 87 (1997): 156–69.

———. "Real Slave Prices and the Relative Cost of Labour in the Greco-Roman World." *Ancient Society* 35 (2005): 1–17.

———. "Roman Age Structure: Evidence and Models." *Journal of Roman Studies* 91 (2001): 1–26.

———. "The Roman Slave Supply." In *The Cambridge World History of Slavery*, vol. 1, *The Ancient Mediterranean World*, edited by Keith Bradley and Paul Cartledge, 287–310. New York: Cambridge University Press, 2011.

Schlinkert, Dirk. "Der Hofeunuch der Spätantike: Ein gefährlicher Außenseiter?" *Hermes* 122 (1994): 342–59.

Schofield, Malcolm. "Ideology and Philosophy in Aristotle's Theory of Slavery." In *Aristoteles' "Politik": Akten Des XI. Symposium Aristotelicum*, edited by Günter Patzig, 1–27. Göttingen: Vandenhoeck & Ruprecht, 1990.

Schroeder, Carrie. "Children and Egyptian Monasticism." *Children in Late Ancient Christianity*, edited by Cornelia B. Horn and Robert R. Phenix, 317–38. Studien und Texte zu Antike und Christentum 58. Tübingen: Mohr Siebeck, 2009.

Schroeder, Joy A. "John Chrysostom's Critique of Spousal Violence." *Journal of Early Christian Studies* 12, no. 4 (2004): 413–42.

Schumacher, Leonard. "Einleitung." In *Corpus der römischen Rechtsquellen zur antiken Sklaverei*, pt. 6, *Stellung des Sklaven im Sakralrecht*, edited by Leonard Schumacher, 1–4. Forschungen zur antiken Sklaverei—Beihefte 3.6. Stuttgart: Franz Steiner, 2006.

Schüssler Fiorenza, Elizabeth. "Introduction: Exploring the Intersections of Race, Gender, Status, and Ethnicity in Early Christian Studies." In *Prejudice and Christian Beginnings: Investigating Race, Gender, and Ethnicity in Early Christian Studies*, edited by Laura Nasrallah and Elizabeth Schüssler Fiorenza, 1–25. Minneapolis: Fortress Press, 2010.

Sessa, Kristina. *The Formation of Papal Authority in Late Antique Italy: Roman Bishops and the Domestic Sphere*. New York: Cambridge University Press, 2011.

Shaw, Brent D. "Body/Power/Identity: Passions of the Martyrs." *Journal of Early Christian Studies* 4, no. 3 (1996): 269–312.

Shaw, Teresa M. *The Burden of the Flesh: Fasting and Sexuality in Early Christianity*. Minneapolis: Fortress Press, 1998.

Shepardson, Christine. *Controlling Contested Places: Late Antique Antioch and the Spatial Politics of Religious Controversy*. Berkeley: University of California Press, 2014.

Shore, Sally R., trans. *John Chrysostom: On Virginity; Against Remarriage*. Lewiston, NY: Edwin Mellen Press, 1983.

Sirks, A. J. Boudewijn "Informal Manumission and the Lex Iunia." *Revue Internationale des Droits de l'Antiquité* 28 (1981): 247–76.

Sivan, Hagith. *Galla Placidia: The Last Roman Empress*. New York: Oxford University Press, 2011.

Sizgorich, Thomas. *Violence and Belief in Late Antiquity: Militant Devotion in Christianity and Islam*. Divinations: Rereading Late Ancient Religion. Philadelphia: University of Pennsylvania Press, 2009.

Skinner, Marilyn B. *Sexuality in Greek and Roman Culture*. Malden, MA: Blackwell, 2005.

Smith, Michael J. "The Role of the Pedagogue in Galatians." *Bibliotheca Sacra* 163, no. 650 (2006): 197–214.

Smith, William. *A Dictionary of Greek and Roman Antiquities*. London: John Murray, 1875.

Snyder, H. Gregory. *Teachers and Texts in the Ancient World: Philosophers, Jews, and Christians*. London: Routledge, 2000.

Souter, Alexander. *A Glossary of Later Latin to 600 A.D.* Oxford: Clarendon Press, 1964.

Spicq, Ceslas. "'Ὑπομονή, Patientia." *Revue des Sciences Philologiques* 19 (1930): 95–106.

Stander, Hendrik F. "Violence in Chrysostom's Commentary on the Psalms." *Ekklesiastikos Pharos* 95 (2013): 258–65.

Stevenson, Walter. "The Rise of Eunuchs in Greco-Roman Antiquity." *Journal of the History of Sexuality* 5, no. 4 (1995): 495–511.

Strauss, Leo. *Xenophon's Socratic Discourse: An Interpretation of the "Oeconomicus."* Ithaca, NY: Cornell University Press, 1970.

Sweat, Laura C. *The Theological Role of Paradox in the Gospel of Mark*. London: T&T Clark, 2013.

Swift, Louis. "St. Ambrose on Violence and War." *Transactions and Proceedings of the American Philological Association* 101 (1970): 533–43.

Thiselton, Anthony C. *The First Epistle to the Corinthians*. New International Greek Testament Commentary. Grand Rapids, MI: Eerdmans, 2000.

Thurmond, David L. "Some Roman Slave Collars in CIL." *Athenaeum* 82, no. 72 (1994): 459–78.

Tiersma, Peter M. "Rites of Passage: Legal Ritual in Roman Law and Anthropological Analogues." *Journal of Legal History* 9, no. 1 (1988): 3–25.

Tolmie, D. François. "Tendencies in the Research on the Letter to Philemon." In *Philemon in Perspective: Interpreting a Pauline Letter*, edited by D. Francois Tolmie, 1–28. Berlin: De Gruyter, 2010.

Torelli, Mario. "La formazione della villa." In *Storia di Roma*, edited by Arnaldo Momigliano and Aldo Schiavone, 2:123–32. Turin: Einaudi, 1990.

Tougher, Shaun. "The Aesthetics of Castration: The Beauty of Roman Eunuchs." In *Castration and Culture in the Middle Ages*, edited by Larissa Tracy, 48–72. Cambridge: D.S. Brewer, 2013.

———. *The Eunuch in Byzantine History and Society*. London: Routledge, 2009.

Toynbee, Arnold J. *Hannibal's Legacy: Rome and Her Neighbours after Hannibal's Exit*. Vol. 2. Oxford: Oxford University Press, 1965.

Tracy, Larissa. "Introduction: A History of Calamities: The Culture of Castration." In *Castration and Culture in the Middle Ages*, edited by Larissa Tracy, 1–28. Cambridge: D.S. Brewer, 2013.

Treggiari, Susan. "Domestic Staff at Rome in the Julio-Claudian Period, 27 B.C. to A.D. 68." *Histoire Sociale* 6 (1973): 241–55.

———. "Jobs for Women." *American Journal of Ancient History* 1 (1976): 76–104.

———. "Questions on Women Domestics in the Roman West." In *Schiavitù, manomissione e classi dipendenti nel mondo antico,* edited by Maria Capozza, 185–201. Rome: L'Erma di Bretschneider, 1979.

———. *Roman Marriage: Iusti Coniuges from the Time of Cicero to the Time of Ulpian.* New York: Oxford University Press, 1991.

Tsang, Sam. *From Slaves to Sons: A New Rhetoric Analysis on Paul's Slave Metaphors in His Letter to the Galatians.* Studies in Biblical Literature 81. New York: Peter Lang, 2005.

Tsouna, Voula. *The Ethics of Philodemus.* New York: Oxford University Press, 2007.

———, trans. *Philodemus, On Property Management.* Writings from the Greco-Roman World. Atlanta: Society of Biblical Literature, 2012.

Tupet, Anne-Marie. *La magie dans la poésie latine: Des origines à la fin du règne d'Auguste.* Études anciennes serie latine. Paris: Les Belles Lettres, 1976.

Uciecha, Andrzej. "Rodzina miejscem wychowania w traktacie pedagogicznym o wychowaniu dzieci Jana Chryzostoma." *Slaskie Studia Historyczno-Teologiczne* 19/20 (1986): 65–92.

Upson-Saia, Kristi. *Early Christian Dress: Gender, Virtue, and Authority.* New York: Routledge, 2011.

Van de Paverd, Frans. *St. John Chrysostom, The Homilies on the Statues: An Introduction.* Orientalia Christiana Analecta 239. Rome: Pontificium Institutum Studiorum Orientalium, 1991.

Van Hoof, Lieve. "Strategic Differences: Seneca and Plutarch on Controlling Anger." *Mnemosyne* 60 (2007): 59–86.

Vera, Domenico. "Essere 'schiavi della terra' nell'Italia tardoantica: Le razionalitá di una dipendenza." *Studia Historica* 25 (2007): 489–505.

Veyne, Paul. *A History of Private Life.* Vol. 1, *From Pagan Rome to Byzantium.* Edited by Paul Veyne. Translated by Arthur Goldhammer. Cambridge, MA: Belknap Press of Harvard University Press, 2000.

———. *Seneca: The Life of a Stoic.* Translated by David Sullivan. New York: Routledge, 2003.

Vogt, Joseph. *Ancient Slavery and the Ideal of Man.* Translated by Thomas Wiedemann. Cambridge, MA: Harvard University Press, 1975.

Von Clausewitz, Carl P. G. *On War.* Edited by Michael E. Howard. Translated by Peter Paret. Princeton, NJ: Princeton University Press, 1989.

Vorster, Johannes N. "Androgyny and Early Christianity." *Religion & Theology* 15, nos. 1–2 (2008): 97–132.

Vuolanto, Ville. "Family and Asceticism: Continuity Strategies in the Late Roman World." PhD diss., University of Tampere, Finland, 2008.

———. "Selling a Freeborn Child: Rhetoric and Social Realities in the Late Roman World." *Ancient Society* 33 (2003): 169–207.

Walsh, Efthalia M. "Overcoming Gender: Virgins, Widows, and Barren Women in the Writings of St. John Chrysostom." PhD diss., Catholic University of America, 1994.

Walters, Jonathan. "Invading the Roman Body: Manliness and Impenetrability in Roman Thought." In *Roman Sexualities,* edited by Marilyn B. Skinner and Judith P. Hallet, 29–46. Princeton, NJ: Princeton University Press, 1997.

Watson, Alan. *Roman Slave Law.* Baltimore: Johns Hopkins University Press, 1987.

Wickham, Chris. *Framing the Early Middle Ages: Europe and the Mediterranean, 400–800.* New York: Oxford University Press, 2005.

———. "The Other Transition: From the Ancient World to Feudalism." *Past & Present* 103, no. 1 (1984): 3–36.

Wiedemann, Thomas E. J. "The Regularity of Manumission at Rome." *Classical Quarterly* 35, no. 1 (1985): 162–75.

Wilken, Robert L. "Free Choice and the Divine Will in Greek Christian Commentaries on Paul." In *Paul and the Legacies of Paul,* edited by William S. Babcock, 123–40. Dallas: Southern Methodist University Press, 1990.

———. *John Chrysostom and the Jews: Rhetoric and Reality in the Late 4th Century.* Eugene, OR: Wipf & Stock, 2004.

Williams, Craig A. *Roman Homosexuality.* New York: Oxford University Press, 2009.

Wilson, Roger J. A. "Vivere in Villa: Rural Residences of the Roman Rich in Italy." *Journal of Roman Archaeology* 21 (2008): 479–88.

Winkler, John J. *The Constraints of Desire: The Anthropology of Sex and Gender in Ancient Greece.* New York: Routledge, 1990.

Winter, Sara C. "Paul's Letter to Philemon." *New Testament Studies* 33 (1987): 1–15.

Wise, Susan. "Childbirth Votives and Rituals in Ancient Greece." PhD diss., University of Cincinnati, 2007.

Wittig, Monique. "The Point of View: Universal or Particular." *Feminist Issues* 3 (1983): 63–69.

Yonge, Charles Duke, trans. *The Works of Philo: Complete and Unabridged.* Peabody, MA: Hendrickson, 1993.

Ziadé, Raphaëlle. *Les martyrs Maccabées: De l'histoire juive au culte chrétien; Les homélies de Grégoire de Nazianze et de Jean Chrysostome.* Supplements to Vigiliae Christianae 80. Leiden: Brill, 2007.

INDEX OF ANCIENT TERMS

sathros (σαθρός), 77
schēma (σχῆμα), 114–16, 118, 161
semnotēs (σεμνότης), 118, 235, 243, 247
semnotētos (σεμνότητος), 235
skeuos (σκεῦος), 115
sōma (σῶμα), 27, 242, 284
sōmatemporos (σωματέμπορος), 14
sōphronizō (σωφρονίζω), 206, 232
sōphrosynē (σωφροσύνη), 118, 147, 149, 155, 159,
172, 175, 183, 192, 206, 222, 226, 235–36, 268,
273, 276
spaō (σπάω), 257
sperma (σπέρμα), 50
spoudē (σπουδή), 105, 273
stenochōria (στενοχωρία), 192
stoicheia (στοιχεία), 47
syndouloi (σύνδουλοι), 56
synētheia (συνηθεία), 178
syngeneia (συγγένεια), 138
syzeugnymi (συζεύγνυμι), 237
syzygia (συζυγία), 100

tetrapous (τετράπους), 171
thaumazō (θαυμάζω), 69
therapainis (θεραπαινίς), 240
Thessalida (Θεσσαλίδα), 213
thlibō (θλίβω), 257
threptos (θρεπτός), 154
thryptō (θρύπτω), 112
thymos (θυμός), 209
titthē (τίτθη), 128
trophos (τροφός), 128
typhos (τῦφος), 118

zeugnymi (ζεύγνυμι), 237

LATIN

adulescens, 148
adulterium, 222–24, 231, 239
aliud genus spadonum, 257
alumnus, 154

bulla, 132–33, 142, 149–50

castratus, 256
censor, 198, 200
cinaedus, 224
collegium, 92
coloni, 86–87, 89
contubernia, 237

crimen, 235
cursus honorum, 148

dies lustricus, 132
dies sanguinis, 258
digna condicio, 222
dignitas, 235, 241
diligens dominus, 196
disciplina, 146–47, 151
domina, 92, 196
dominium, 223
dominus, 84, 89, 196
domus, 20, 93

erro, 188–89
eunuchus, 256

familia, 12, 19–21, 82, 92, 94, 97, 126, 132, 164,
187, 274
femina, 224
filiafamilias, 140, 144, 192, 245
filiusfamilias, 43, 103, 118, 145, 149, 151, 158, 168, 192
flagellator, 214
flagellum, 214
fugitivus, 184, 187–89

gallus, 258, 260, 265

habitus, 114, 161
historia, 187

infamia, 235
insignia, 132, 142
instrumentum vocale, 13, 33
instrumentum, instrumenti, 13, 33, 240
ius naturale, 13

libera servitus, 69
Liberalia, 150, 155
libertas, 241
luxuria, 121

magister, 144
Magna Mater, 257, 265
mango, 14
manumissio in ecclesia, 22, 166–67
manumissio inter amicos, 22
materfamilias, 241–42, 244
matrona, 220, 241
moecha, 224
moechia, 233
moechus, 233

mollitia, 172
mulier, 172

natura spadones, 257
nutrix, 128

obsequium, 23–24, 69
obstetrix, 128
ordo Dei, 55
ordo naturalis, 55
oricularii servi, 201
otium, 86, 88

paedagogium, 144–45
paedagogus, 141, 151
palam, 240
paterfamilias, 13, 46, 49, 63, 82, 84, 90–92, 94, 97,
    99, 124–26, 164, 177, 183, 202, 216, 237, 256, 274
patria potestas, 97, 106, 110, 123–24, 126, 147, 152
patrimonium, 13
peculium, 17, 21–22, 90
plagiarius, 14
poena, 215
professor, 144
prostitute, 239
pudicitia, 175, 222–23, 241
puella, 224
puer, 102

repraesentatio, 114
res mancipi, 12–13

semen, 37, 50, 52
severitas, 105
spado, 256–57
stuprum, 222–24, 226, 231, 239

thlibiae thlasiae, 257
toga, 143, 156, 240, 245
toga praetexta, 142, 150
toga virilis, 144, 148, 150, 155
tribas, 224

valetudinarium, 144
venaliciarius, 14
venalium greges, 13
verna, 14, 16, 18, 82
vilicus, 32–33, 59, 196, 201, 209, 257, 265
vir, 172, 223
virago, 224
virgo, 241
virtus, 172, 197
vis, 172
vita militaris, 146, 152
vita rustica, 35, 88–89

COPTIC

schmschal (ϢⲘϢⲀⲖ), 154
sayon (ϬⲀⲨⲞⲚ), 154

Dio Chrysostom, 24–25, 37n154, 172n7
Dionysus, 251
discipline, 6, 9, 42–43, 84, 103, 152, 180, 192,
    198, 216–19, 273, 275, 278; of children, 103,
    127, 135–36, 139, 146–49, 151–52, 154–55,
    158; Foucault on, 84, 195, 198; Manichaean,
    264–65; of slaves, 60, 84, 112–13, 171, 176, 180,
    182, 184, 191, 198, 203, 206, 209, 211, 216–19,
    273, 275; and surveillance, 184, 112–13, 198,
    218; and virtue, 145–55, 184, 191–92, 195–96,
    216–18
discourse, 34–35, 39–44, 55, 70, 75–76, 118, 121,
    134, 282; Christian, 24–25, 34, 45, 48–49, 51,
    62, 69, 100n68, 139, 221, 226n23; of fertility,
    88; of love, 61, 73, 141; of masculinity, 29, 43,
    63, 121, 125, 129, 135, 190; of mastery, 38, 190;
    of naturalization; 26, 29, 54; of nursing, 140;
    of oikonomia, 29, 34, 38, 125; pathologizing,
    75; of philosophization, 183; popular, 55; of
    prostitution, 246; punishment as, 217; sexual,
    225, 262, 261–67; of slavery, 2–7, 10–12, 34,
    41–45, 48, 75, 110, 129, 135, 138, 141, 153, 207,
    271–72, 278; of spiritual castration, 262, 269;
    of the suffering slave, 207; of virginity, 225;
    virtue as, 43, 63, 190; of war, 30, 283. See also
    doulologization
disgrace, 17, 67, 73, 75–76, 79, 96, 104, 112–13,
    116–19, 140, 148, 157, 159, 179, 187, 193, 197, 211,
    237, 247–49, 256, 266, 273, 276; passing from
    slave to master, 17, 179–81, 218, 239, 247–49,
    252; and punishment, 211–19; sexual, 147,
    222–26, 232, 234–39, 241–49, 252–56, 266,
    274; of slavery, 17, 20, 75–76, 112–13, 140, 142,
    159–60, 167, 180–81, 184, 211–12, 214; of vain-
    glory, 43, 116–21, 161. See also honor
dishonor. See disgrace
dominicide, 60, 74, 161, 218, 221
doulogenia, doulogenic, 51, 100, 103, 282
doulologization, doulology, 2–7, 40–44, 47, 51, 61,
    68–69, 74–75, 86, 107, 123, 126, 134, 160, 239,
    247, 264, 271–73, 278–79, 282
doulomorphism, 3, 74, 119–20, 177, 258, 262,
    282
dress. See clothing
drunkenness, 96, 104, 129, 179, 216, 248–49,
    251–52, 256, 269, 276–77. See also wine

education, 4, 6, 9, 42–43, 64, 103, 128, 135, 158,
    171, 218; of boys, 43, 103, 141–44; of girls, 103;
    in monastery, 154, 165–68; by slaves, 128, 135,
    158–59, 218, 275; of slaves, 13, 64, 103, 134, 145,
    163–68, 171, 181, 276. See also pedagogy

Elagabalus, 257
emotions. See passions
endurance, 125, 175, 194n105, 207–8. See also
    suffering
envy, 74, 117, 122, 131, 133. See also jealousy
Epictetus, 38
Epicurean, Epicurus, 34, 198. See also Philode-
    mus
equality, 19, 37, 53n13, 63–64, 66, 69, 97–102, 123,
    206, 234, 236, 253, 273, 278
eschatology, 23, 42, 51, 59–64, 165, 208
ethnicity, 63, 115
Eudoxia, 93, 246
eunuch, 43, 48, 80, 115–16, 128, 194, 221–22, 229,
    256–70, 272, 277. See also castration
Eustathians, 11, 67–68, 111
Eutropius, 194, 256
evil eye, 131, 33
examination of slaves, scrutiny, 15–16, 196,
    199–200, 227. See also surveillance

fairness, just/unjust treatment of slaves, 61, 67,
    161–62, 166, 172, 178, 204–8, 211, 218–19, 273
fasting, 68, 93, 96, 155, 160
Favorinus, 129, 140
fear, 15, 34, 59–60, 97, 99–102, 132, 134–35, 138–39,
    146–47, 152, 190–91, 195, 201, 251; of God/
    Christ, 60, 134, 177, 182, 190–91, 197, 199; of
    hell, 60, 99, 134; of manumission, 22; of the
    master, 9, 17, 50, 59, 99–102, 178–79, 190–91,
    199, 203–6; of the pedagogue, 143, 146–47,
    149, 158; of punishment, 60, 99, 134–35,
    139, 146–49, 185, 190–91, 195, 203–6, 214; as
    respect, 50, 97–100, 102, 177, 181; and the
    teaching of virtue, 134–35, 146–49, 190–91,
    195, 203–6, 214. See also respect
feminization, effeminate, 76, 79, 122, 136, 142–43,
    156–57, 161, 174, 245, 253, 255–56, 266–67, 273
fertility, 33, 88, 153, 251–52, 258, 260, 268, 277
fornication, 99, 147, 149, 179, 192, 231, 234,
    237–38, 243, 247n127, 248, 256, 276
Foucault, Michel, 3, 4, 41, 92, 174, 221, 282, 284;
    on the care of the self, 120; on discipline,
    punishment, 195, 215n218, 218; on govern-
    mentality, biopolitics, 83–84, 92; on hetero-
    topias, 89; on masculinity, 174; on sexuality,
    221; on the soul, 36
freedom, 12, 17, 22–23, 40, 45, 49–50, 52, 54,
    65–66, 68–71, 74–75, 80–81, 89, 104, 117, 120,
    152, 182, 185, 190, 199, 223, 241, 254, 264, 273,
    278–79, 282; in Augustine, 15n51; as carceral
    mechanism, 19, 40, 49, 70, 73–75, 272, 278;

Jews, Judaism, 26, 38–40, 45n2, 48, 62n46, 63,
71n84, 95, 137, 155–57, 259–60, 263–66
John the Baptist, 255
Joseph, son of Jacob, 40, 71, 103
Julian, 253, 257
Justinian, 166, 264

kidnapper. *See* slavery: trader
kinship, 18–21, 38, 101–2, 138, 278, 281; anti-, 20,
281; as carceral mechanism, 18–20, 278
kyriarchization, kyriarchy, 3, 17–18, 21, 23–24, 42,
58, 77, 100, 124–28, 135, 139–43, 156, 158–59,
161, 163–64, 168–69, 171, 175–80, 183–85,
189–90, 193, 195, 198–200, 203–4, 208, 216–19,
221, 256, 268–69, 273, 275–76, 278, 283
kyriophorism, 16–17, 283

Lactantius, 172, 203n155, 258n180
law, 12–15, 47, 54, 150, 155–59, 185–86, 197, 220,
231–38, 248–51, 257, 263–64, 284
laziness, 31, 34, 136, 196, 198, 209, 214
Leo I, 253
Libanius, 31, 72, 86, 142n75, 143, 146, 165,
204n159, 233
literacy, 18, 113, 144–45, 165, 168
liturgy, 90, 93
liver, 259, 261
lust, 39, 71, 76, 80, 146, 148–49, 151, 157, 159–60,
162, 221, 225, 228, 234, 242–44, 247, 258–62,
267, 282; same-sex, 150, 235, 260–61
luxury, decadence, 61, 106, 115, 118–21, 127, 136,
140–42, 158, 160, 229, 245, 255, 261, 270, 273,
277

magic, sorcery, 131, 213, 249–53, 256, 269, 277. *See
also* superstition; Thessalian
Magna Mater, cult of, 257, 260, 265
Manichaeism, 259, 264–65
manumission, 21–23, 83, 112–14, 182, 278; as
carceral mechanism, 21–22, 31, 278; fear of, 22,
31, 171; *in ecclesia,* 22; *inter amicos,* 22; mass,
22, 62, 109, 112, 114; by testament, 22, 114
Marcionites, 67–68
Marcus Aurelius, 35, 39
marketplace, 109, 117, 119, 146, 191–92, 244, 254
marriage, 43, 84, 95, 98–100, 127, 131, 144, 149,
151–52, 220–25, 230–38, 251, 254–56, 262,
265, 274, 276; and Manichaeism, 265; as
slavery, 98–100, 274; of slaves, 22, 171, 184,
234, 237–38, 262, 268, 278; spiritual, 79,
266–67
Martial, 200

masculinity, masculinization, 29, 35, 41, 64, 88,
110, 118, 122, 125, 129, 135–37, 139, 146, 152,
158–61, 167, 173–76, 180, 205, 208, 223–24, 235,
243, 266–69, 273–75; ambiguity of, 221, 257,
266–69; and biological sex, 172–73, 257; and
chastity/modesty, 152–53, 174; Christian, 110,
118, 124–26, 152–53, 156, 161, 167, 174, 194, 208,
223–24, 257, 262, 267–69, 273; and clothing/
adornment, 118, 142, 245; crisis of, 42, 86, 88,
124, 140–41, 151, 174, 273; formation of, 29, 43,
64, 84–85, 104, 110, 125, 128–29, 143, 146–49,
158–61, 164, 168, 174, 216–18, 273, 275, 281,
283; hegemonic and subordinated, 74–75,
174–75, 208; and moderation, 173–76, 205,
243; and the passions, 35, 134, 152–53, 223; and
penetration, 174, 223–24, 235; and regimen,
160; Roman, 36, 86, 88, 124–26, 140–41, 143,
146, 151–53, 158, 161, 164, 174, 217–18, 223–24,
262, 273; of slaves, 64, 167, 217–18, 273; and
virtue, 43, 63, 125, 135–36, 147, 149, 152–53, 171,
173–76, 194, 212, 217–18, 256, 273, 281, 283; of
women, 64, 118, 173–74, 211, 217–18, 274. *See
also* aretagogy; virtue
master, 1n2, 11–12, 16, 47, 50, 53, 58, 66–68, 83,
100, 106, 112, 161, 163–64, 166–69, 171, 176–82,
185–86, 191, 194–97, 204, 208, 214–15, 224,
231–37–38, 261, 273–75, 283; absentee, 32–33,
51, 59, 87, 158, 198; caring for slaves, 9, 78,
88, 102, 141, 178, 206, 209; death of, 22, 60,
74, 161, 218, 221; devil as, 58, 240; equal to
slave, 19, 37–39, 59, 62, 69, 73, 102; fear of,
9, 17, 50, 59, 99–102, 178–79, 190–91, 199,
203–6; formation of, 3, 104, 108, 158, 168;
God/Christ as, 29, 46, 50, 56, 69, 96, 191,
199–201, 208, 273; just/fair/virtuous, 71–72,
100–102, 127, 161, 168, 178–82, 190, 193, 195,
226, 274; murder of, 60, 74, 161, 218, 221;
natural, 27, 28n114; neglecting slaves, 9n21,
55, 140, 179–80, 182, 276; non-Christian, 208,
275; passions as, 71–74; relationship with
slaves, 6, 10, 50, 68, 100–102, 111, 165, 177–78;
represented by slave, 17, 146–47, 182; seduced
by slave, 229, 231–32; slave as, 92, 97, 183, 218;
slave having many, 49, 58, 71–72, 78–79; as
slave of slaves, 71–72, 92, 103, 119–20; slave
spying on, 201–4; sold as slave, 15; strict, 143,
161, 171, 179, 191; unjust/wicked, 60, 71–72,
78–79, 162, 180, 185, 193, 208, 226. *See also*
kyriarchization; mistress; slave
medical, medicalization, 75–77, 113, 128, 131, 137,
144, 160, 173, 226, 242, 260, 283
Melania the Younger, 22, 109, 166

www.ingramcontent.com/pod-product-compliance
Lightning Source LLC
Chambersburg PA
CBHW020455270326
41926CB00008B/614